THE GREEN
KNIGHT EXPEDITION

Also by Richard Leviton

Seven Steps to Better Vision

Weddings by Design: A Guide to Non-Traditional Ceremonies

The Imagination of Pentecost: Rudolf Steiner and Contemporary Spirituality

Brain Builders! A Lifelong Guide to Sharper Thinking, Better Memory, and an Age-Proof Mind

Looking for Arthur. A Once and Future Travelogue

Physician: Medicine and the Unsuspected Battle for Human Freedom

The Healthy Living Space: 70 Practical Ways to Detoxify the Body and Home

What's Beyond That Star: A Chronicle of Geomythic Adventure

The Galaxy on Earth: A Traveler's Guide to the Planet's Visionary Geography

The Emerald Modem: A User's Guide to the Earth's Interactive Energy Body

Signs on the Earth: Deciphering the Message of Virgin Mary Apparitions, UFO Encounters, and Crop Circles

Encyclopedia of Earth Myths. An Insider's A-Z Guide to Mythic People, Places, Objects, and Events Central to the Earth's Visionary Geography

The Gods in Their Cities. Geomantic Locales of the Ray Masters and Great White Brotherhood, and How to Interact with Them

Fraser's Angel

Geomythic Earth. Readings and Field Notes in Planet Geomancy

Stars on the Earth. Domes and Stargates, and How to Interact with Them

The Geomantic Year. A Calendar of Earth-Focused Festivals that Align the Planet with the Galaxy

Healthy Gaians. How Healing Our Body, Mind, Spirit, and Culture Helps Heal the Planet

Welcome to Your Designer Planet! A Brief Account of the Cosmogony on Earth

Santa Fe Light. Touring the Visionary Geography of Santa Fe, New Mexico

Walking in Albion. Adventures in the Christed Initiation in the Buddha Body

Hierophantic Landscapes. Lighting Up Chalice Well, Lake Tahoe, Yosemite, the Rondanes, and Oaxaca

My Pal, Blaise. Notes on a 60-Billion-Year Friendship

The Blaise Conjunction. Selections from the Geomantic Journals, 1983-2004

The Mertowney Mountain Interviews. Merlin and the Secret of the Mer-Line

Theosophon 2033. A Visionary Recital about the World Event and Its Aftermath

THE GREEN KNIGHT EXPEDITION

DEATH, THE AFTERLIFE, AND BIG CHANGES IN THE UNDERWORLD

RICHARD LEVITON

A Primer on Earth's Geomantic Reality, No. 14

 iUniverse®

THE GREEN KNIGHT EXPEDITION
DEATH, THE AFTERLIFE, AND BIG CHANGES IN THE UNDERWORLD

iUniverse books may be ordered through booksellers or by contacting:

iUniverse
1663 Liberty Drive
Bloomington, IN 47403
www.iuniverse.com
1-800-Authors (1-800-288-4677)

Because of the dynamic nature of the Internet, any web addresses or links contained in this book may have changed since publication and may no longer be valid. The views expressed in this work are solely those of the author and do not necessarily reflect the views of the publisher, and the publisher hereby disclaims any responsibility for them.

Any people depicted in stock imagery provided by Thinkstock are models, and such images are being used for illustrative purposes only. Certain stock imagery © Thinkstock.

ISBN: 978-1-5320-0275-5 (sc)
ISBN: 978-1-5320-0276-2 (e)

Print information available on the last page.

iUniverse rev. date: 07/14/2016

For Judith A. Lewis and Silver Boy

Foreword

It's that Blaise again. I thought this as I sat in my study composing my thoughts to introduce this admittedly unusual, perhaps very strange, account. The Blaise I refer to is a certain human with interests in angels and geomancy who induced me 20 years ago to literally run out the front door of my house and life and marriage into an uncertain but decidedly mystical future and all sorts of unexpected eye-opening experiences, all of which led to the current adventure.

I used to be a college professor, a Ph.D.-tenured professor of comparative mythology at Dartmouth College in Hanover, New Hampshire. I used to be normal and well-adjusted enough to take this position and myself seriously to pass as a plausible, sober-minded grown-up responsible for the education of students and exhibiting the mental pleasures of scholarship. Or something like that. Then my whole world was turned inside out.

I was stood on my head, spun around, and told to start seeing the world reversed in a magic mirror while my instructor cracked jokes like a *shlemiel* doing stand-up before the great White Head of the Ineffable Mystery in an arcane temple of the Ancient of Days. Can you imagine telling jokes to a rapt audience of one, or is it an infinity? If the jokes work, the applause would be awesome, going on forever, a comic's dream.

Readers of *My Pal, Blaise* will remember me from the twilight days of my social adjustment. I was tasked with editing an unruly series of handwritten notebooks purportedly composed by a man, then 69, calling himself only Blaise, who claimed to have lived out in the high New Mexican desert somewhere near Chaco Canyon, putting his life in order, escaping the clutches of the secret government, and preparing to—are you ready for something very unlikely?—depart the planet for the Pleiades, which he claimed was his original home. I edited his notebooks, prepared them for publication, annotated where needed, and, without realizing it, was deeply, immedicably, and urgently infected with his antic version of an angelic apocalypse and a celestial rebooting of the Earth.

Like any scholar possessed with a requisite measure of sobriety and detachment, I resisted the blandishments of his angelic view of the planet and humanity, its history, prospects, and near future (which included, this Blaise asserted, the imminent bodily incarnation of an angelic order into human form), and held all his outré claims, his metaphysical assumptions, his alleged mystical experiences, encounters, contacts, colleagues, safely, I thought, at arm's length. That was an illusion, I will tell you. It was not at arm's length. I had swallowed it whole and didn't even know it until it grabbed me from inside, shook me, and pushed me out the front door to meet this Blaise mystery at the end of the lane.

Much of what happened to me, what kinds of adventures I found myself in, have been reported in *The Theosophon*, another strange book (they are all strange, no argument there) written by my own editor, Edward Burbage (who edited this book: more, who *accepted* for publication this book—you'll see), based on several years of visionary recitals by this Blaise, then more than 90 years old and inhabiting a body of dubious provenance, meaning nobody was sure if it was biologically real or a mere simulacrum of Light tarted up to look like him.

In that scenario, Blaise sat down in Edward's living-room and every Saturday debriefed the astonished editor on what he'd been up to for the last 20 years since he left the planet for the Pleiades via first a wormhole then a stargate. It turns out a fair bit of his time had actually been spent back on the Earth, though it remained vague to Edward in what kind of (or whose) body Blaise did all this.

Blaise took me in hand and organized my Mystery initiation which included, and I can say this, having released all fantasies of tenure reinstatement at Dartmouth, trips to the Pleiades, in fact, back and forth in a regular commuting schedule and all across the planet to meet a variety of other happy-crazy mystics and fools of God, all in preparation for an enormous multiple planet event, a kind of celestial song-fest in a specially constructed "temple" that was 1,000 light-years tall and presented by choirs of higher celestial spirits, masters, angels, and aliens and called the "Theosophon" and which took place now exactly 13 years ago today. I certainly have not been the same since that event, and I doubt the planet has felt normal

either. That of course was the intention of the event. Honestly, I haven't been certifiably "normal" since I first met Blaise.

Further evidences of bizarrerie were compounded via my marriage. Yes, I was married for a long time to an accomplished pianist called Philomena. First she was bereft when I ran out the door; then she edited a second monstrosity by this feral Blaise and it spun her head around so much before she knew it she had ascended into a body of Light and completely transfigured her physical form and has subsequently been living in the higher spheres as an ascended teacher.

This Blaise is assuredly a home-wrecker and marriage-destroyer, God bless the blighter, and please don't send us any more of your notebooks. They are like slow-motion hand grenades. We have had enough metaphysical explosions already! I still see Philomena now and then, though the material circumstances of our encounters (and marriage) have changed. She figures prominently in the report that I offer in this book.

In fact, for a while our home outside Hanover was probably known as the House of the Vanishing Professors. A disturbing anomaly. First I vanished. I knew where I was certainly, but Philomena did not. She could only surmise. I was with Blaise and his pals, the Blaises, better known as the Ofanim, a pack of rowdy, mystical, joke-cracking, epiphany-showering angels of a high order. I wasn't able to let Philomena know what had happened to me. She was left alone for years, though not entirely alone because Blaise arranged to send her nine gigantic boxes of typed journals and asked her to prepare them for publication.

He was a sly one. He didn't care about the publication. It was all about the transmission her exposure to those pages would surely deliver. Another head sent spinning. Philomena started to moult and Scriabin now took a backseat.

She finished her editing and annotation, spiced with journal entries of her own gradual mental transfiguration, and it was published as *The Blaise Conjunction*.

Before she knew it, she had rushed off to Somerset, hiked a hill, and ascended in a blaze of Light. Working with those journal pages had been her preparation, she later realized. They activated something old in her. Now she was vanished. Technically, she turned her body into Light, but for the ordinary, materialist-minded authorities she disappeared without a trace. She's probably still listed as a missing person, presumed dead, by the Somerset police. I'm pretty sure they would not credit my reports of having travelled with her since her disappearance and that technically she died, but she is terribly alive. So now I am back from my vanishing act, and Philomena is definitively gone. Judging by past events, I can expect to vanish again in the not distant future. So long, house. Blaise always has something up his sleeves, even when he wears a teeshirt.

When he had set our heads to spinning, he next worked on Edward. He was a Boston editor in his thirties. First Merlin got to him, whisking him off on an odyssey to discover the magus's true résumé across many cultures and times. Edward survived that and remained at least putatively sane and adjusted. He surprised himself by writing a long book about Merlin's disclosures called *The Mertowney Mountain Interviews*. I say surprised because as an editor he had not thought of himself as a writer. Well, he is now. He stuck his head out of the editor's cabin on that book, and even if nobody believed his claims or even credited their possibility, I hear they enjoyed reading his report.

Then Blaise showed up for the second act, and for three years told his Theosophon story which (more strangeness) Edward had apparently participated in seven years earlier and was only now remembering. This led to a book which has sold well. Apparently, readers didn't mind the account's high weirdness, or maybe they liked hearing more tales of the Blaises, or maybe they kept their misgivings quiet or maybe they mistook it for science fiction or fantasy, or maybe their heads are still spinning and they don't know up or down.

That's the strange, delightful outcome of all this metaphysical madness. Edward is now editor of a promising line of occult, visionary non-fiction titles mostly orbiting around the trouble-maker and prime exacerbator of normality, Blaise, and his angelic exacerbators, who shook it all up in his head decades earlier. This current book is the latest in that series. I am in good (if crazed) company now. We are a small gentleman's club of our own consensus reality along radical new lines, and we are accepting new memberships from a few qualified applicants. If you feel inclined to join our cadre of Outsiders, put this book under your pillow and sleep on it for a week. You'll already have joined. The vapors will seep upwards through your pillow and rearrange your brain.

If my discipline were anthropology, my colleagues would shake their heads when considering me, saying I had gone native, that I went *troppo*, through the looking-glass, down the rabbit-hole, joined the tribe I was researching. I had been studying, with requisite scholarly detachment and agnostic disbelief, the rituals and images and deities of world mythologies, never thinking any of it real. Until. Yes, until I realized it all was real, realer than ordinary reality by far.

The numinous jumped out of that rabbit-hole, grabbed me by the lapels, shook and yanked until my head spun around 25 times, then showed me the lay of the land. I assure you that is a landscape not ordinarily seen, yet its reality is arresting. I speak as one who has walked this visionary landscape, as a modern-day burnable Gnostic, a man crazed with empiricism, ordering a brand new world on the basis of an off-the-road gnosis that just won't stop. I could almost understand the Inquisition now: maybe those boys ordered the definitive burning of heretics as the only way to stop their own heads from spinning off. Stay around this blissful Blaise madness long enough and your world will spin.

The present book reports a journey of three months with eight people. They were all people, in a human sense, though their existential status varied. One was already dead, so he, technically, was a spirit living in the Other Side. That is young Tommy, suicided, forgiven, now working hard for the good guys. One was Merlin. What can we say about Merlin? He was probably a human once. Now he was a master of Light operating at recondite levels above me. One was Blaise. I still can't make up my mind about him. He's a kind of quasi-human. Then there was Edward (human), Pipaluk (human, though a very old one), Matthew (human, fortyish), myself, 67, at the time of the expedition, and Philomena, post-human, post-wife, now occupying a lovely form of Light. Our expedition started on November 1, 2043, and finished on February 2, 2044. We made a brief coda reprisal of our expeditionary activities on February 2, 2045.

The expeditionary roster is straightforward and mostly believable. What will challenge the reader's belief system, I suspect, is where we went, and how. We went into the Underworld, looked around, and made some big changes.

Yes, it sounds preposterous, but we were actually invited to do this. By whom? Higher-ups. Such as Yama, the Lord of Death, Hades, King of the Underworld, or the Green Knight, the Celtic mythic picture of the same guy. The Tibetans call the part of the Underworld where the dead go when they drop their bodies the *Bardo* and the Egyptians call it the *Duat*. It has in fact many names. It is an in-between place, a troubling, quirky, protean realm made of Light and human fantasy, which unfortunately too often becomes dark dreaded illusions. The place and its protocols had not been updated for eons, possibly never had. It was time for an overhaul, the Green Knight told us, and we were there to do that.

Death is inevitable, but it doesn't have to be so Godawful confusing. That was our brief. Come up with recommendations to streamline, clarify, edit, abridge, and expedite the procedures. People are not understanding their death experiences, the Green Knight said. He almost looked forlorn when he said this. People don't get what death is. The place is a cognitive mess as a result. It needs an overhaul. The dead are sleeping through what should be moments of illumination and refreshing clarity, when their life's outline comes clear. Instead, for most it's a nightmare funhouse scripted by their unconscious. Or as James Joyce might have said, it's a funferal for nobody but the spooks.

The old protocol guides, from the Egyptian, Mayan, and Tibetan cultures, no longer service the way contemporary human minds are put together. Nobody recognizes any of the gods referenced in those procedural texts. The spirits just look weird, scary, idiotic, inimical, nasty, threatening, horrible, or whatever, and the dead behold imps and ghouls instead of figures of Light, and so people fail to comprehend the self-revelation their appearance is meant to convey to them. The Death realm, the *Bardo*, is meant to be a nonstop disclosure of actual reality, but now for many it is a nonstop nightmare, an irritation, an inconvenience, or they manage to sleep through it altogether and incarnate again as soon as possible.

If America were a shamanic culture, all this would be easier to explain. One in our expedition was in fact a shaman: Pipaluk, a traditional *angakkuq* from northwestern Greenland. She made an appearance in Edward Burbage's

Theosophon account, having been enlisted by Blaise to play an important role. If the whole U.S. were Greenland, full of indigenous people, like Pipaluk's village, all this would make sense immediately and be welcomed as a wonderful story. Shamanism doesn't have a big footprint in American culture, or even one at all, and what impact it does have tends to impress only the psychic dilettantes. It would be easier to present this as a filmscript idea. *Anything* goes in that world.

I'll just have to step forward and say it, tell you *how* we did it. Somehow we all stepped out of our physical bodies and for three months conducted our business in this *Bardo* in bodies of Light, then we returned to our physical bodies and normal life and breathing resumed. Compounding the eldritch nature of all this was the fact that during the three months of the expedition, our bodies, our putative daytime selves, were conducting business elsewhere in the physical world, oblivious to what our other half, the astral form, I suppose we should call it, was up to. As you will see in this chronicle, it was up to a lot.

Maybe I should say each of us was going about the world as our own *Doppelgänger*. If you have ever read anything by Carlos Castaneda, that kind of shenanigans is normative, though, unfortunately, most people think Castaneda made it all up, especially the part about the huge butterflies and crazy witches.

We strolled through the Underworld like inspectors with clipboards, auditing the success of all its protocols, assessing the progress or failure of souls to make it through the cognitive obstacle course and either reincarnate or take off for a fun-trip in one of the higher educational heavenly realms. Sometimes it seemed that all eight of us were Virgil guiding Dante through the levels of Hell. Dante, I suppose, in this analogy was any soul in the karma-divestment process.

That's what the death protocols are about: processing the momentum and accruals of your karma, the expenditures on your free-will credit card account while alive. Karma is quite neutral; think of it as a balance sheet, showing debits and credits. It has no implicit moral judgement; just necessities to balance things. All this would seem audacious and presumptuous had we not been invited to make this tour of assessment by the Lord of Death himself, the Green Knight. It just isn't working as well as it used to; I was hoping you'd all suggest changes. Well, we did, so all I can say, with requisite jocularity, is next time you're dead, expect big changes in how they do things around here in the upgraded *Bardo*.

In defense of the sobriety of my former profession and academic position, my knowledge of comparative mythology was quite practical on the journey. Much of what I had read about, places, deities, temples, devices, spectral lands, came in handy because on an exigent level we were meeting it all in the flesh. I still have my Ph.D.; they haven't taken it away from me yet, though they might wish they could if they read this book. But the mental discipline it took to earn that doctorate served me well on this most ontologically feral of expeditions. Just because you're now an official Fool of God with a spinning top for a head doesn't mean your hard-earned mental habits and knowledge aren't still needed.

These gods of death, these tutelary spirits of the Underworld, the Underworld gateways, guardians, passageways, passwords, even mantras, were all real. It was like the Hobbits seeing Mordor and its chief bad guy, Sauron, in person, and they sit around having their sixth meal of the day and tenth pipe of the Shire's best, gob-smacked that all of these rumored awful things were in fact quite true. They sat there, huddled together, contemplating the shock of the real.

Prior to that this invidious place and its world-conqueror manqué were rumors, held at a safe distance because nobody could verify their reality at first hand. Until Frodo and Sam found themselves on the slope of Mount Doom with that stupid ring in hand and Sauron, real though in a body of fire, very close by. I use this example to invoke the shock of discovering the undeniable reality of this. It actually wasn't the least bit scary or intimidating, although the Druj, better known as the Antichrist, was a tricky one, always trying to get her hands into it. She was far smarter and more devious than Sauron and a good deal better looking. Every good story needs an antagonist, and the Druj was ours, but the adversarial nature was more on the order of a well-strategized game of chess. I am happy to announce, per this analogy, that Checkmate! was ours at the end.

Technically, you can't checkmate a Queen, for the Druj is a She (way worse than Rider Haggart's She, incidentally: maybe her prototype), and it wasn't really a definitive routing of the cross-dressing monarch of the *Bardo* because I'm sure there will be another match in the future, and maybe the competition will persist forever, as long as there are humans to fool. It's the Great Game. The Druj is a Persian name for the Adversary, Antichrist, Chief of Lies. She is a *good* liar, utterly accomplished at befuddling and beguiling cognition.

But the word "checkmate" is Persian, from *shāh māt*, meaning "the king is helpless" or the "king is dead," or at least destroyed and broken or in check. The word "mate" in Farsi means a person who is frozen, open-mouthed, staring, confused, and unresponsive, really laid out properly, comatose and finished. We can only wish. I would be overstating our results if I let the reader believe we had decked the Druj once and for all and that she was as mate suggests, staring blankly in the confusion of her total rout by the Green Knight expedition. She'll be back

one day, just like Gandalf said Sauron would return. In fact, we never took her off the playing field of the Underworld; we just improved the human handicap to potentially recognize her sleights-of-hand, ruined a few of her favorite, always successful tricks, showed how the magic illusion worked.

Yes, it's all Blaise's fault, and the Blaises too, and I can't thank him enough, or them. I never would have conceived such things were possible, at least for me. That kind of wanton disregard for the proprieties of sleep-walking while alive that they consistently demonstrate, ruthlessly shaking people, or a few at least, startlingly awake until they open their eyes, look around, and see reality, and exclaim—I can make the case that the world could use more of this.

That's Blaise's brief, both of them, to break the icons, smash the pedestals of the haughty gods in their grand celestial palace, betting against humans to ever wake up because, petulant unceasingly, they disbelieve humans deserve the privilege, and surely the Old Man was off his meds that day when He did it, gave humans the full run of the psychic store, all the powers and levels of consciousness which had been *theirs* exclusively until this ill-bred moment. It probably doesn't help matters that many cultures keep scary pictures hanging between the living and the dead like spectral banners, discouraging inquiry.

I suppose there were worse ways to be inducted into the Underworld than to have your head chopped off with a giant axe by the Green Knight. Breton folklore speaks of the *Ankou*, a spectral iconic figure representing death, your death, who pulls up at your front door driving a death-wagon with a creaking axle and piled high with corpses as if it is a spectral autumn harvest. The *Ankou* represents the spirit of the last person to die in your village and appears as a tall, haggard man with a wide hat, long white hair, and a revolving head that sees everything (an image with obvious comic potential if it weren't so bizarre).

Or would you prefer the Irish *Dullahan*, a figure who clutches his own head under his arm (it can be female too), a head with large eyes and a face-widening smile. The *Dullahan* rides a black horse or sits in a carriage pulled by black horses and stops at the house of somebody about to die and calls their name and they die. In contrast the Greeks had a genteel death-messenger, a youth called Thanatos. Or sometimes he'd appear as a bearded winged man, shown with his brother, Hypnos, the god of sleep. Death and sleep as twins. Thanatos is just and gentle and he guides you, dead, to the ferryman Charon.

If you are Jewish, expect gallstones. The Angel of Death, Azrael or Azriel ("One Whom God Helps"), has twelve wings and many eyes. Or he has four faces and 4,000 wings, and his whole body consists of eyes and tongues, one for each human soul ever living on the Earth. He appears before you, moments before your demise, often as an old man, a cruel snatcher of souls, with a drawn upraised sword on whose tip clings a drop of gall. The dying person opens his mouth and the drop of bile falls into it, causes death, and turns his body putrid and yellow. He has experienced the taste of death and exits his body by his mouth or throat. That's unfortunate: you arrive in the *Bardo* having just had your final episode of gall bladder dysfunction and jaundice and you didn't take the elevator all the way to the top floor and leave by the crown. Did the drop of gall signify the bitterness of bodily life or the galling necessity to one day die from it?

Maybe not just the Jews associated death with poisoning by the death spirit. The Lithuanian *Giltine* was an old ugly woman with a long blue nose and a deadly poisonous tongue usually portrayed as dangling menacingly out of her mouth. Her name meant stinging and

yellow, suggesting gall and jaundice again. She collects the poison from graveyards then licks the dying with a layer of it which is on her tongue: they die, like the Jews, tasting the gall of life or death. If you prefer the comic-book version, there is Europe's Grim Reaper, a male human skeleton in a black robe and hood, wielding a scythe, offering you his patented Death Touch by which he carries you off, in most cases without any negotiation.

Merlin was with us, as you might be wondering why that Celtic sage was part of our expedition (its organizer, in fact), because he wrote the original texts. He was Anubis, supervisor to the Egyptian Weighing of the Heart ritual in the *Duat*, and he was Padmasambhava, the Tibetan sage who wrote the occult text *Bardo Thödol*, or "Liberation by Hearing on the After-Death Plane," more popularly known since it was published in 1927 as *The Tibetan Book of the Dead*. Prior to that, it had been a secret handwritten manuscript in Tibetan seclusion.

He assured us he wouldn't mind, would not be put out in the least, no feathers ruffled, if we amended, right in front of him, his venerable text with our modern-day corrections and upgrades. If the Polynesians had gotten off the beach and written down their death protocols, he would have been credited with their whole playbook too because as the demi-god and culture hero Maui he journeyed into the Underworld of the great Goddess of the Night, Hine, in whose inestimable chthonic folds lay all the death mysteries and its landscape.

For all anyone knows, Merlin may have written the famous medieval text, *Sir Gawain and the Green Knight*, which provides the rich Celtic portrait of the Lord of Death as a hulking jovial guy dressed all in green, his horse's raiment green too, carrying a huge axe. It's for chopping heads off, starting with his own. He demonstrated that insouciantly one day at

King Arthur's Camalate before the astonished and, to be honest, cowed Grail Knights, all except doughty Gawain. Most people today don't regard *Gawain* as a funerary or afterlife handbook, and nobody likes the axe, while the Tibetan text traditionally was read aloud by a monk sitting beside the body of the deceased, hoping he'd hear the recited instructions on how to survive the *Bardo* and avoid those awful "womb-doors."

As for the *Egyptian Book of the Dead*, the "Coming Forth By Day," it was written in hieroglyphs, sometimes on temple walls, so you'd better memorize all those details before you died if you expected to make any sense of the *Duat* and make it to the paradisal, tony neighborhoods of the Field of Reeds. Wallis Budge may have done a spectacular job translating the hieroglyphs and preparing the written text, but as a Victorian he would have no doubt been nonplussed, his pudgy face ablush, with the prospect of the authentic Anubis joining the expedition, stepping out of the funerary texts into real life and explaining things.

Our expedition assembled in the desert hills outside Santa Fe, New Mexico, at the end of November, and we finished up there too, three months later, our feet standing in snow that of course wasn't there when we departed. I make this otherwise obvious remark because the time differential between being in the *Bardo* and occupying a human body running on solar clock time is confusing. When we returned to our bodies and restarted our body-based cognitive processes, it seemed as if we had only moments before stepped out of them and passed through the massive Underworld gates presented before us up in those spare hills.

Our *Bardo* experience, so protracted and time-spacious while we were logging it, now seemed evanescent, transient and ephemeral as a dream. It assuredly was not a dream, not even one of those validated lucid dreams you hear about, and I have done the best I possibly could recording its many details. It also seemed like two versions of ourselves were squirming to fit into one body, and we both had radically different tales to tell, and we both wanted to go first.

I write this Foreword aflush with the enthusiasm of the spiritual world heating me up from within. The classical Greeks called this *enthusiasmos*, "having the god within you," feeling bright and aflame, burning with the divine fire. No, I'm not saying I was possessed by an Underworld deity and rendered ecstatic. That is hardly my temperament, and no psychic boundaries were violated.

It was rather the sense, the knowledge, that we had touched something real, numinous, and that *numen* rubbed off, entered our systems like a vapor of the pure gods. It was probably due in part to such prolonged proximity to the Blaise angels. Their quality is contagious, a blend of focus, fondness, and amusement, plus all the wings. I certainly won't discount the numinous potential of Merlin, the Green Knight, or any of the other spiritual beings, such as the five *Dhyani* Buddhas, we met there. We could have wholesaled all that *numen*.

My text itself, I trust, will strike the reader as reasoned and sober in tone, though that won't do much to increase its credibility. That's Blaise's fault.

—Frederick Graham Atkinson, Ph.D.
Hanover, New Hampshire,
September 29, 2046

1

I held the Golden Bough in my hand, not sure what to do with it. I knew what it meant, what, classically, it was used for. I just didn't see how that pertained to me, former Dartmouth college professor turned metaphysical rogue.

No, I didn't think of myself as a rogue, but I was sure my former colleagues would. I had committed an act they would never condone or understand. I had made contact with authentic reality, with an area they held at arm's distance. I had crossed a line they considered inviolable. I had gone native. Of course, who cares? I still hadn't returned to my normal human life, and it's been years now. I had mistaken myself for Gawain and chopped off the head of the Green Knight; now it was his turn to chop mine.

The branch felt light but it hummed with electricity, making my hands buzz. It was more like a wand, or a combination of a wand and a golden apple. The Golden Bough is not at all what people think. It does not particularly resemble a branch from a tree. I admit, I never would have believed this had I learned it 17 years ago when I ran out the door of my house, marriage, profession, belief system, maybe sanity, chasing after—well, it's Blaise of course. Blaise was at the root of all this roguery. He's the reason I'm holding the Golden Bough, unsure of what my next move is. Open up the Underworld, I suppose.

This is what I've learned about it: The Golden Bough is shaped liquid gold Light from a living gold reserve managed by the Pleiadians at a total of 47 installations around the Earth. Possession of this implement certifies your worthiness to enter the Underworld, so the Pleiadians told me, and that certification is based on your demonstrated wisdom, and that, as I learned, is based squarely on your initiation proficiency. It is projected from the crown chakra, itself also golden, comprised of a thousand flaming golden-fire petals. The crown chakra is where you "stand" when you hold the Golden Bough. Naturally, a part of me cannot believe I am reciting facts of this nature. It is, or I should say, used to be, so unlike me to talk to casually about arcane matters.

The Golden Bough, you could say, is a Hyperborean pass-key opening all doors. Yes, I freely, still a little shamefacedly, admit to my staid Dartmouth colleagues, I, Frederick, who once walked among you and all the footnotes and citations of our dry, safe profession, am now and have been for 17 years, as of the time of this expedition, a full-fledged heresiarch. I have gleefully plummeted over the deep end, and the deep end fell in after me too. We're still plummeting.

Since I've unreservedly gone off this legendary deep end, let me add two more statements in support of that as I get started on this chronicle. First, you don't wave the Golden Bough at the Underworld door-keepers or gently shake the bough and its leaves like you're a Celtic emissary with a musical silver branch and dangling Golden Apples. You expand it into a Light pillar ten feet tall and enter it like a columnar building made of golden Light.

The Golden Bough becomes a radiant protective shield and door-opener, and you walk through the Underworld and past its guardians with impunity. It is a bit like a bird-watcher's blind or a stealth-veiled surveillance platform. You can watch without being noticed, or you can observe and be part of what you see. You can mingle, converse, study conditions, or, as we did, make changes, and not have to worry about inadvertently, prematurely, or inconveniently dying.

Second, the Underworld is not inside the Earth or underneath the surface. It is above. Above the head, specifically, the crown chakra. It is "under" only from the viewpoint of the Supreme Being, the world under Him, but it's above us. That's why the Tibetans always tell people who are dying to remember to exit their body through the top of their head, meaning their crown chakra, because that's where you'll find the *Cinvat* Bridge, the Bridge of the Decider, the bridge that gets you *up*—vibrationally up, as in raised—into the Underworld. Yes, exit from the crown and you greatly increase your chances of making that bridge. We didn't need to worry about that. We had the Golden Bough for our pass-key. It was like a Manhattan dweller's E-Z Pass for the George Washington Bridge.

The "we" I allude to was a curious collection of eight people. That's not correct. I'm not sure it's accurate to call several of them "people" any more. Among the certifiably alive people were myself; my book editor, Edward Burbage; the Canadian Matthew Orniston who had helped out at Avebury during the Theosophon ten years ago meditating with 11 other people at the stone circle; and Pipaluk Qasigiannguit, the elderly shaman from Greenland. Elderly is an understatement: at the time of our expedition, she was aged 110.

I will note, irrepressible scholar that I still am, that although the Welsh poem called *The Spoils of Annwn*, which to a degree framed our journey, giving it mythic cachet, is decidedly vague about the expedition count, making it seem it was Arthur and six others who returned, I can state with certainty it was Arthur plus seven, at least on the outbound journey. Actually, only five of us returned, or four, if you don't count Merlin who was never "here" in any finite, enduring, bodily sense. As our expedition neatly matched the mythic picture, I suspect Merlin arranged that. The symmetry of the two expeditions is mentally pleasing.

Among the questionable members of our expedition was Tommy Hevringer, technically dead of insulin shock close to 20 years ago. If he were alive he'd be almost 39, but being dead, I suppose the clock stops so he still looks 19. There was Blaise, the desert-dwelling human who allegedly left the Earth for the Pleiades for 20 years and should be, at the time of our expedition, 93 years old. He doesn't look it, and I don't think it's his diet or regular exercise regimen. I must mention Merlin, the legendary magus of Camalate and recently Edward's mentor. I will deal with his ontological status later, that of being a Ray Master; actually, he is a step above that, Master of the Silver Light which precedes the Rays. I'm sure he is the moving force behind this whole strange outing of ours.

Last on the list is the most troubling and hard to account for: my deceased wife, Philomena Wilcox. I shouldn't say "deceased;" she did not "die" in any conventional sense. She turned her body to Light and ascended. In fact in one flamboyant gesture worthy of a diva she transcended the whole dying business forever. She was done with it, would never have to do it again. This triumph was part of the Theosophon, a planetary event jointly detailed by Edward and Blaise in their recently published chronicle (June 2044) called *Theosophon 2033.* (From the time standpoint of our expedition, it would not be published for another eight months, but from the standpoint of writing this chronicle, that was now two years ago.) Since her acension, Philomena could manifest the semblance of a human body whenever she required a seemingly material presence, like for our Green Knight expedition. If you didn't know better, you'd take it as a real body.

I was once a classical scholar teaching at Dartmouth College, so the academic habit dies hard which is why I will not refrain from pointing out that our expedition, as I like to call it, bears irresistible similarities to a number of earlier mythically recounted journeys into the Land of the Dead, or Underworld.

I am thinking right now specifically of *The Spoils of Annwn,* or *Preiddeu Annwfn,* an old Welsh poem about King Arthur and six others journeying in his magical glass boat or crystal ship (interpretations vary) called *Prydwen* into the Celtic Underworld called *Annwn,* a word from Old Welsh usually translated to mean "Very Deep," but it was also called Mound Fortress, Four-Peaked Fortress, and Glass Fortress. Arthur set out with a lot more than six companions, but only six came back with him. The poet says he started with three boatloads of warriors, three "fullnesses" of *Prydwen.* They had been in search of a number of spoils, including a cauldron kept in the castle of *Caer Sidi* ("Spinning Castle") and which belonged to Arawn, the Hades-like chief of the spectral realm of *Annwn.*

So we were those seven who went and returned with Arthur into *Annwn* and our expedition. Our fullness of *Prydwen* totaled eight. At the time I didn't know which one of us was the Arthur figure, though I do now, and we didn't journey into *Annwn* to nick precious objects but to make changes to the place. All its spoils are still there. Anyway, those particular objects cannot be removed from *Annwn;* they comprise it, and that's the only place where they can ever be.

I remember the scholarly discussions, even disputes, we (my colleagues in the department at Dartmouth) used to entertain regarding the details of this poem from the *Book of Taliesin,* all the tiny matters, the academic minutiae we strove with passion and contentiousness to clarify and to provide justified, unchallengeable interpretations. It all looks so different now after you have actually *been* to the places mentioned, seen the objects and spirits referred to. When you have visited the place you understand all its components directly. There isn't anything to dispute or reinterpret other than to get the spelling right.

What were the spoils they brought back from *Annwn?* The poem is vague on this— the poem is vagueness itself—but they seem to include Arawn's magical cauldron rimmed in pearls and warmed by the breath of nine maidens; a famous prisoner named Gweir who had been kept in the spinning Four-Peaked Fortress; a flashing sword belonging to Lleawch and which had been inserted into the cauldron's open space; and a brindled ox wearing a collar of 140 chain links.

I said all eight of us returned. That is not true. Only Edward, Pipaluk, and I did. We three are, as best I can tell, still living and materially embodied. Merlin ascended into his Light body ages ago and lives on his Mertowney Mountain, a side-slope of the great Mount Meru. Tommy is currently "dead" and without a physical human body, nor has he decided if and when he will reincarnate. My Philomena has completed her human journey, no longer requiring a material body. Again, she is not "dead" in the usual sense, but she is never coming back here, at least not in the old solidly incarnate mode as before. Matthew—well, he was alive and in a human male body when we started, but....As for Blaise, that vexing mystery, I never could tell whether he was still in a physical human body or if it was merely a convincing simulation, or if he had reverted permanently to his earlier Pleiadian embodiment form. As for whether he came back or not, he seemed to, at least briefly, yet he seems unfixed as to residence and permanently peripatetic. He comes and goes from the Earth and other places as he wishes.

We left at sunset on October 31. That's called *Samhain* in the old Celtic yearly calendar, and the date was significant. It lasts a full 24 hours, and Celtic lore says this is the liminal time the portals to the Underworld are open, when all the *sidhe* or Hollow Hills in the ancient geomythic landscape are flung open.

The Gaelic word essentially mean's "summer's end," the conclusion of the harvest season, and the beginning of the "darker half" of the year, the shortening of the days into winter. It was celebrated with great purifying bonfires throughout Ireland, Wales, Scotland, and parts of England (such as Cornwall) for many centuries. The Catholic Church grabbed this Celtic holy day and renamed it All Saint's Day and, naturally, depaganized it, then later, the Americans conflated it into a vaudeville cartoon commercial blow-out called Halloween.

Our expedition would last about three months, culminating on February 2, another Celtic "turning" day called *Imbolc* but better known as Candlemas. The Catholic Church appropriated that "pagan" holy day and retasked it to their own dogma, downsizing the majesty of the event to a modest lit-candle processional. That is a time of the fattening of the Light, and, once, of domestic livestock with new life, the seed of spring, and it is attributed to the Irish goddess Brigit ("Exalted One"). A member of the Tuatha de Danann, Ireland's old gods, Brigit presided over this day, encouraging the Light (human awareness) to "fatten." Later, the Catholic Church made her behave and turned her into a pious saint.

Samhain, as we learned from our meetings with Colm Flanagan at Magh Slécht in preparation for the Theosophon ten years ago, is associated with the putative dark Irish god, Crom Cruach, portal master. From the initiates' side of this holy day, it's not that the Fairy Folk, the People of the *Sidhe*, stroll into our world; we are invited to enter theirs during this liminal 24-hour open-house moment in the year. You enter the Underworld through the swinging door of *Samhain*, then, three months later, as it was for us, exit the place through the *Imbolc* door. In between is a three-month *Bardo*, truly the "in-between" place, as the Tibetan sages put it. I called it a "swinging" door. Perhaps that is inaccurate. A certain amount of concentration is required to open it and pass through it; in fact, for best results, you need the Golden Bough, and I happened to have it.

I should make one thing clear at the outset. We sailed in Arthur's ship. That of course is a metaphor, all of it, because we didn't sail and it wasn't a ship. On a literal basis, *Prydwen*, the ship's name, means "handsome" in Old Welsh, but by reputation, *Prydwen* evokes the image of a glass or crystal ship. A few years ago I would have regarded what I am about to say as fantastic and not to be credited with even a semblance of sobriety or rationality. Clearly, a ship made of crystal is impractical and probably impossible, at least in this world. So what does it mean? The ship is a conveyance in consciousness, a concentration of attention that is crystalline in its sharpness, capable of movement, and the sea it travels across is not physical water, but Light, the great astral sea of Light.

It was Edward, principally, who helped me understand this odd idea. He said he had been introduced to the whole business by Merlin as part of his training. *Prydwen*, he told me at the beginning, is a name for the inner heart chakra. The crystalline quality comes in by way of its geometry. It consists of, it looks like, an eight-sided figure made of eight equilateral triangles, two groups of four each forming a four-sided pyramid, one facing up, the other down. They appear to be made of transparent crystal. It's called an octahedron, and when it is turned on or activated, it spins rapidly on its axis. It creates a spinning blur of Light, and that is its means of motion, you inside it. It can be expanded to any size; every human being has one. The Norse seers called it *Sleipnir*, an eight-legged celestial horse belonging to Odin, their chief god, and he rode it often.

The crystalline quality comes from the fact that it appears to be a pure concentration of Light, as sharp and as perfectly defined as a polished crystal. So the trick is to get yourself, your awareness, that is, inside this eight-sided figure. To climb into *Prydwen* is to move your consciousness into this recondite chakra. Every human has a copy of this, so you could say it accommodates any number of passengers. Seven humans in their own crystal *Prydwen* can all travel together. If seven people each occupy their own *Prydwen*, functionally, holographically, they are all in the same *Prydwen* commanded by Arthur, as the Welsh poem says.

In case you're thinking this *Prydwen* is a kind of glass spaceship made of two oppositely facing pyramids that you simply climb into, you're mistaken. You have to change your position in consciousness, find a certain place inside you, then you may enter this ship of crystal that, surprisingly, can expand to any size. Here is something else about *Prydwen* you possibly may not have known. When you "sail" in this crystalline ship, it is surrounded by many bright angels.

These are the enigmatic though seemingly ubiquitous high angels Blaise is always talking about and whom he calls the Ofanim, the Holy Wheels. You looked out from inside the *Prydwen* and you seemed to be enveloped by angels. It was like a terrific fluttering of diamond white-fire wings in all directions. Yet they also gave you the impression of stillness, perfectly poised motionlessness, as if they existed in a space and time outside of all spacetime and any need for it.

As for the chakra part, I don't want to get into this deeply here. The chakras are subtle energy centers, likened to revolving wheels of Light with differing numbers of spokes, that have a lot to do with how we experience our consciousness. The heart chakra, as it's known popularly and which is correlated with the cardio-vascular region of the chest, has three parts, namely, an outer, inner, and secret part. *Prydwen* pertains to the inner part which yogis call the *Ananda-kanda*, which means "Place or Abode of Bliss and Delight." This crystal ship, this spinning octahedron, this happy abode, recurs often in our story.

Let me dispel another possible misinterpretation. The poem conveys the clear impression that all of Arthur's men were crammed into the one ship, a large crowd going forth, only seven returning. It wasn't like that. We each had our own *Prydwen*. We set out with a fleet of eight *Prydwens*, except, and here is the spatial paradox that I know will challenge the ordinary mind fixated on the conventions of space and time that normally define our frame of reality, we were all inside the same one *Prydwen*. The eight individual ones all "collapsed" or "coalesced" into one. Neither of those verbs does the situation justice, but the practical or functional result was we were all inside the same shared space but we had to first attain this space on our own; then the eight individual versions reverted to the one space. In this upside-down world, eight are the same as one.

Why was Arthur, yes, the reputed King Arthur, famous in Celtic myth, in charge of this expedition, and why was *Prydwen* said to be his ship? I wondered about that at the start of our journey. It seemed a matter of familiarity and jurisdiction. In a sense, Arthur was in charge of this area, this *Caer Sidi*; he knew the way there, the protocols for entrance, how to safely pass through its tricky labyrinthine landscape. You could say it was his job, his responsibility, to do this. He *knows* this special place, this rapidly turning octahedron packed with Light.

I seem to be called upon to offer a lot of qualifications at the outset. Our "Arthur" was not the singular one, not the original high god around whom all the myths and *numen* constellated; rather, he was Arthur's representative, his understudy, his emissary. The original is the Solar Logos, the chief of all the gods of the Great White Brotherhood. Arthur is a functional place in consciousness. His role is generic and hierarchical; he completes a Round Table of Ray Masters. These Masters and their 14 Rays are implicit in the geometry of the octahedron itself, in the armature of *Prydwen*, and as Arthur leads them *Prydwen* is his ship.

Don't worry. I too was confronted with a lot of obscure terminology at first. The Great White Brotherhood is like the United Nations at the galactic level, though they get along better and accomplish more. They occupy forms of Light which to people like you and me will suggest a sunlike quality, that they are suns. The Solar Logos is their boss, the chief of all the suns or Ascended Masters. That is someone who has converted his physical body to Light, like my wife did. That's the qualification for being a full-fledged member of this Brotherhood. The Ray Masters are like divisional chiefs within this Brotherhood; they administer streams of color, themes, and consciousness called the 14 Rays. King Arthur is a name some cultures use to denote the boss of this conclave. All of this, and this part I found hard to believe at first, is based in Ursa Major, the constellation of the Great Bear, better known to us as the seven-star Big Dipper.

This Arthur representative among us had been trained in some of the protocols of consciousness over which the genuine King Arthur as Solar Logos is the unassailable master. I don't mean to impute anything fraudulent to this representation; that is how it works, King Arthur overlights human simulators of his qualities. You live the myth of King Arthur, occupy his rightful place in the projection. It's a map for positions and actions in consciousness. I know it's confusing, because at the same time I will state without any reservations that the Merlin who travelled with us was the genuine article. Magus, shapeshifter, prophet, psychopomp, and, suitable for our job, necromancer, as real as Light.

There we were, the eight of us, lined up in our octahedrons before the gates of the Underworld. The eight double pyramids were spinning rapidly, emitting an almost blinding effulgence of Light. At the risk of confusing the reader, let me say our octahedrons were each about ten feet tall, pleasantly commodious; you can make it any size you need. I saw faint traces of the human occupants of these Light conveyances, and these figures seemed stationary. From a certain perspective these spinning octahedrons looked like turning car wheels, yet, oddly, there was no evidence of a "car," just these rapidly spinning wheels.

If you happened to be a rigid literalist you'd also note you saw nothing resembling a ship either, but as I said the "sea" *Prydwen* breasts is not of water but Light. The scene was like eight sports cars racing their motors in neutral, yet the sound was not a physical one, not due to "motors" of any kind, but from the humming of the Light. Even to call it humming is imprecise: it was Light and it was sound. The Buddhists call this spinning octahedron the Buddha Body, place of the astonishing transfiguration of a human body into a figure entirely of Light.

I eventually formed the impression we were waiting for something. Pipaluk nudged me, although I suppose it must have been with her thoughts. "Present the Golden Bough," she said telepathically. I was after all holding it.

I presented the Golden Bough. I expanded it into a golden Light pillar big enough for all eight of us and our spinning octahedrons now to be inside it. The Underworld gates started to open. Before us I saw a concave crystal basin about three miles wide and upon this basin were the entrance gates carved upon a cube of Light. I soon realized the gates were the sides of this cube, and upon the crystal basin sat a celestial city as big as a sports stadium. I caught a few glimpses of its interior past the gates. The *Bardo* is in there, I thought with trepidation.

We were about to step into the In-Between realm and leave the material world behind. Physically, we were somewhere in northcentral New Mexico, less then ten miles from Santa Fe. Blaise, who once lived here, had informed us of this Underworld entrance and suggested for various logistical reasons it would serve our needs, and so as soon as we arrived in town we drove out here and hiked to this hill and placed ourselves where we now stood, before the gates.

Theoretically, we had 1,746 entrances to choose from. That's how many were awarded the planet in its original geomantic allocation of Celestial Cities. Yes, what we call the Underworld is actually a celestial domain like a city. Some of these Underworld entrances are famous from myth, such as Avernus near Cumae, near Naples, Italy; that's where Aeneas entered the Underworld, accompanied by Deiphobe, Cumae's Sibyl at that time, and Avernus is where he acquired his Golden Bough, the special key that opens the Underworld door.

In Virgil's *Aeneid*, the hero Aeneas secures the Golden Bough from a physical tree growing near the cave of the Cumaean Sibyl. Two doves guided him to the site, and when he tore off a limb, another immediately grew in its place (a good sign, meaning others in the future could replicate this act, like us, and get a bough). He has to present the Golden Bough to Charon, ferryman on the River Acheron, then later to Proserpina (or, for the Greeks, Persephone), Queen of the Underworld, consort to its king, Hades. The people who run Hades (also its place name), or the *Bardo*, are very particular about who gets to visit; normally, the rules of entry require you to present proof of your decease. If you're dead, you get free entry; if you are among the living, expect red tape. Possession of a Golden Bough enables the bearer to circumvent that red tape.

Among other entrances there was Troezen, a sea-perched southern spur of the Peloponnesus of Greece, not far south from Mycenae and Tiryns. Herakles exited the Underworld there carrying triumphantly the three-headed Cerberus as proof of the success of his 12th Labor. Mythic narratives say he entered elsewhere, at Taenarum (or Tainaron) at Cape Matapan, located at the southernmost tip of the Peloponnesus and of all mainland Greece. Those protocols of entrance and exit did not seem operative; these gates were swinging doors. You could enter and exit whichever ones you wished, even the same gate for both. We were dealing with 1,746 identical doorways into the same Underworld hologram. We could have entered the Underworld through any and arrived at the same place.

Pipaluk, I realized with delight and a shudder, was our Deiphobe. In Virgil's *Aeneid*, Deiphobe is the Sibyl of Cumae, the famous oracular center in the hills above Naples. She was 700 years old and operated out of the Temple of Apollo and the Cumaean caves where she dispensed oracles, guidance from the gods, and, for Aeneas, who proposed to enter the Underworld to meet with the "shade" of his father, she gave him precise instructions on the correct protocols of Netherworld entry. She was the designated prophetess or *sibylla* for the Apollonian oracle center of Cumae. Her long life was a gift from Apollo.

Aeneas must collect a Golden Bough from a special tree that grew near her cave on the edge of Lake Avernus, a site comprising a lake and a large volcanic crater and whose name meant "without birds." It carried the classical reputation as an entry point for the Underworld or Hades. Aeneas would present it to the Queen of the Underworld, Persephone, to secure admission. Aphrodite, Aeneas's Olympian mother, sends two celestial doves to guide him to the tree; then, when Aeneas meets Charon, the Underworld ferryman for the River Acheron, and Deiphobe shows him the requisite Golden Bough, he grants them access to his boat and takes them across. I guess we cut a few corners on the protocol because I got my Golden Bough from Kubera during my tour of his Celestial City of Lanka. I gather that means Avernus is not the sole source of the Golden Bough.

That was during my high madness and mystical adventure tour with Blaise as preparation for the Theosophon. He had dropped me off at Kubera's place where the Old *Lokapala* and Directional Guardian gave me a proper tour of the facilities and gave me a keepsake (the Golden Bough) for later use. Hindu myth tells us eight Celestial Cities are arrayed on the slopes of Mount Meru, an ultimate mountain of Light at the center of the cosmos. Each city has its specialities in consciousness and superintends a cosmic direction. Kubera's place is all about treasures, divine objects made from consciousness. I kept the Bough safe for a number of years until I learned what its use would be, as a gate key. No, I knew what its use was; I didn't know why I was given a Golden Bough.

If we were following classical Greek Mystery protocol, we should have first travelled to Eleusis

and taken initiation in the Eleusinian Mysteries that would have instructed us in how to enter the Underworld while still alive. That's what Herakles did in preparation for his entering the Underworld at Taenarum. I suppose we cut a corner on that one because, for one, we had Herakles with us, in his true guise as Merlin, Lord of the Silver Robe of the Underworld Queen, and for another, we had the Golden Bough, which opened the Underworld gates. Third, and this is something Blaise explained to me, we already had the practical initiation results of that Eleusinian revelation in the form of our spinning octahedrons. To achieve this we had to contact that arcane part of ourselves, the undying soul and immortal Higher Self, that is revealed to the Eleusinian initiate.

On a practical level, the attentive reader no doubt will wonder how we pulled this off, this seeming paradox or impossibility, namely, how do you enter a spiritual or psychic realm in your physical body? You don't. You match it.

Blaise told me we shifted most of our awareness into our Double or astral body. Ostensibly, we met at Santa Fe for a conference, at least those of us in putative physical forms. Philomena and Tommy joined us when we had suited up. Merlin took the guise that Edward used on the cover of the book about his adventures, the stubbly taxi driver with a woolen toke pulled over his head. Occasionally, I was aware of myself and the others in our physical bodies going about the activities of a conference, mostly unaware of what else they were doing. Blaise says that happens a lot; your Double often leads a separate life, and usually you never get a memorandum recounting the minutes of your other life. Our astral Double was suitably resonant with the *Bardo* so that we could pass through the Underworld gate in a vibrationally congruent body. We doubled up.

Then the Green Knight appeared and he chopped off our heads at once. To tell you the truth, I wasn't that surprised. I had read the book. I was prepared. The anonymous medieval poet of *Sir Gawain and the Green Knight* had described this otherworldly fellow as awesome, the handsomest of horsemen, half a giant in form, his size outstripping that of all men. He was grim, fierce, and all green. His skin, his raiment, everything about him, the poet said, glittered in green. The axe he held, the death-wielder, was formidable, huge and monstrous, made of green-hammered gold, and its cutting edge was acutely keen and razor sharp. Our necks tasted its sharp bite, as the poet might have said, waxing prolix.

"That's Yama," whispered Merlin. "Mind your manners, lads. He can be a bit touchy at times." It seemed like advice given too late. Our severed heads were lined up like Halloween pumpkins in a neat row before the feet of the Green Knight (Yama). I hoped he had it not in his mind to practice his football field goal kick. The Mayans used to offer grim portraits of that infernal soccer game. The situation looked grim, decapitation and all that, but frankly it didn't feel bad. It had an oddly clarifying effect on my awareness. I felt more in focus, my attention sharpened. I felt more attuned with this strange new environment we had precipitately entered. We knock on the death door: next thing, we're decapitated.

You might think that with our heads lopped off we would be viewing the world a bit forlornly from our vantage point on the ground. It wasn't like that. I felt as if my awareness had risen and elongated and was a pillar of bright fire. That my severed cranium had enlarged itself to become a full body of Light. Don't ask me how that's possible or what its mechanics might be. I don't know. But as I looked from left to right at the cut-off heads of my fellow travelers, they too were now upright as towering pillars of flaming Light, as big as the Knight.

In the poem, the gruesome Knight, as green as summer grass, and his horse was green

too, his mane and tail plaited in green tassels anyway, showed up suddenly, roaringly, it seemed, at King Arthur's hall, like a phantom from Fairyland, the poet said. The time was Yuletide, meaning the winter solstice, and he demanded "good sport." He offered to have one doughty Knight chop off his head with his huge axe, then within the year for that fellow to journey to the Green Knight's Green Chapel and submit his own brainpan for decapitation. Naturally, everyone resisted the idea and scrambled to find ways to master invisibility on the spot or considered significant last-moment career changes.

Everyone except Gawain, who stepped forward and agreed to the reckless challenge. Gawain lopped off the bearded head, that face full of goading and provocation, and the Green Knight collected his own head in his hand and smiled, unperturbed. He mounted his horse and rode off, gripping the severed head by its long hair. "Insouciantly, I would have thought," you might have heard Gawain say to himself, wondering what it all meant and from what strange country he hailed and starting to say fond farewells to his own cranium.

"What's with the axe job on the head?" asked Tommy.

Merlin fielded this one. He was amused with Tommy's directness. "Consciousness is centered in the head, especially when the sixth and seventh chakras are in an activated, illuminated condition. The Green Knight severs the head to mean consciousness is now focused in those two centers free of the confusing input and distractions of the body and the lower five chakras, and to state this is how you are best advised to conduct yourself in the Underworld.

"Even more to the point, the severed head reminds you the best way to enter the Underworld, and really the only way that guarantees cognitive certainty, is through the head, and, within the topography of the head, its top or crown. In this story example, he has Gawain chop off his head to demonstrate how you concentrate your attention in your crown chakra. It's to preview the recommended mode of action for when you enter the *Bardo*. It's a psychic act; your physical head remains intact, securely fastened to your body, but your consciousness rises upwards, into the head, and, in fact, beyond it, above it."

"I'd like to point out another aspect to this head-chopping part," said Blaise. "Severing the head is the same as deploying the Golden Bough. The Golden Bough is a gold staff of Light generated from the crown chakra that then encompasses the human form so you enter the Green Chapel encased in it. Do you see how that is identical to decapitation? You enter *as* a golden head.

"You have your head cut off and you enter as the head, meaning all your awareness is centered in your crown chakra. Or you deploy the Golden Bough from your crown center to encase your body in a golden Light pillar and enter the Green Chapel as the crown-generated golden staff. It's the head either way. The equation is simple: to chop off the head is to enter while in the crown. All of your awareness is gathered up in your crown chakra and you enter that way.

"The folklore version of this, in the *Gawain* poem, puts it all in literal terms only. The Green Chapel is an awareness zone; only consciousness, free of the body, can move about and comprehend this realm. You enter it in the decapitated state. Your consciousness is severed and thus free from your body's physical life. Don't be fooled by the seeming modestness of a chapel. The Green Chapel is much larger on the inside; it is merely a portal to an entire green realm.

"Once the outer gates of the Underworld open, Yama or the Green Knight checks to see if your head is cut off, if you hold it with your hand as he showed you. You may also see this figure as Hades, accompanied by the Queen of the Underworld, Persephone. Yama, too, has a feminine counterpart, his twin sister called Yami or Yamuna. He checks to see that you are in your crown chakra, in the Golden Bough, before you pass the gates. The reason is simple: you would not otherwise be able to see anything inside the Underworld. It would confound and disorient you, and it would likely be dangerous to your mental well-being. That's because the discovery you make is the Underworld lies *above* the head."

Our Green Knight was not riding away, saucily or not. He still stood there in front of us, as big as a mountain covered in greenery. That was true to story. True to the myth, he was standing in front of the Green Chapel. The *Gawain* poet says this was a hillock topped with a stone barrow beside a stream in a ravine. This barrow had an opening at both ends, suggesting it was rectangular in shape, and it was hollow inside; the top of it was overgrown with grass. Gawain regarded it as a "chapel of mischance" and the "hideous oratory" of a fiend and the "most evil holy place" he ever entered. I suspect there is some medieval Catholic editing in this image, adjustment of the picture towards the negative. The Green Chapel was your basic Celtic Hollow Hill, the physical features of the mound and stonework acting as a liminal doorway into the psychic zone of it.

We had before us our own local version of the Green Chapel. It offered no evidence of a barrow, but it was a hillock in a shallow ravine amidst the stubbly dry hills between Santa Fe and Pecos. None of this, I learned from Blaise, our resident geomantic topographer, was necessary for the placement of an Underworld entrance, because as he explained originally all the Earth's Light temples were arrayed when the planet's surface was flat and physical correspondences between the current shape of the landscape and this original imprint were not to be expected. Still, it was at least intriguing to find the coincidence between our entrance and one attributed to the Green Chapel.

There are two points to make about this Green Chapel: first, it's far bigger on the inside; and second, it's the little door that opens into a great inner chamber. City is more like it. It is a huge psychic realm. So what does this place look like from the outside? Like the Roman Coliseum done in green, perhaps six stories high, circular, its sheer and sheeny sides flanked by numerous dark green pillars, but without the arching columns and copious arcades. Let me note this one is many times larger than the Roman Coliseum, which was an ellipse that measured 615 feet long, 510 feet wide, and 157 feet high. But the general shape of the Coliseum is sufficiently close to use it as a way to describe the Green Chapel. As for its name, you could say the Chapel is the place where the occult meaning of green is revealed and where you in fact turn all to green as an initiation result.

My deployment of the Golden Bough not only opened the gates of the Underworld, but revealed Yama, in his Green Knight guise and in his more formidable Hindu and Buddhist appearance, as the fierce Lord of Death. No, we were not in danger of dying, but we might, I realized, get a bit spooked.

Classically, Yama is depicted as a roaring, fiery, *green*-skinned god of the death realm, encased in an aura of searing flames, accompanied by his flaming helpers. He carries an enormous mace (a long club with knobs and flanges at the tip, used functionally like a sledge-hammer to bludgeon people) and a noose to secure the fresh arrivals of the dead. He is the Judge of the Dead and chief of this realm and for good reason because, as the Hindu texts state, he "found out the way to the home which cannot be taken away." He knows the route to home. That suggests a permanent, pre-incarnational paradisal realm, that the *Bardo*, Hades, the Green Chapel, lead to a desirable, permanent spiritual "home."

Yama dwells in the Lower Worlds in his Celestial City called *Yama-pura*, the City of Yama. It is one of the eight divine cities on the slopes of Mount Meru. He rides a black buffalo and carries a rope lasso to collect the freshly dead soul by the neck. In *Yamaloka* (the directional realm of Yama), he resides in his palace, *Kālichī*, where he sits upon his throne of judgement called *Vichāra-bhū*, assisted by his recorder and councilor, Chitragupta, and two other attendants; they have the complete karmic dossier on every collected or lassoed ("reaped") soul.

When necessary, his messengers, the *Yama-dūtas*, collect the souls of the newly dead and bring them before him, while a porter named Vaidhyata watches the door to his throne-room. Two dogs, named Shabala and Shyama, guard the gates to his city; they have four eyes each and flaring nostrils; they also act as his messengers to the dead when needed.

Souls have to swim the Vaitarana River, full of pus, bones, and flesh, to reach *Yama-pura*. If they cannot swim it, they remain in purgatory, not reborn. I suspect that refers to the necessities and unpleasantness of dropping the material body. Apparently, it's only the Greeks who offer the complimentary valet boat service. The city has four gates and seven arches, and contains two rivers, Pushpodaka, "River of Flowers," and Vaivasati, "Roaring River." Yama has two ministers, Chandra, which means "Anger," and Mahachanda, "Terror," and Yama is accompanied by both demons of disease and wise counselors. Souls meet Yama unaccompanied (no lawyers allowed for this meeting) while Chitragupta reads out the karmic charge sheet on them, detailing the "offenses," and he does this with the studied neutrality of a tax-auditor reciting your status.

Yama is a *Lokapala*, the Guardian of a Direction, in this case, the celestial South. He is *Dharmaraja*, Lord of Death; you often see his frightening head looming over a large wheel, the *Bhavachakra*, representing the Six Worlds of *samsara* and illusion, our world and reality as we take it. Those worlds represent the life of embodied or, I should say, embedded, stuck consciousness, everything we have to surrender at death and everything we resist. That's humbling: from Yama's viewpoint, our dear and familiar human life on Earth is one big illusion.

There are six zones of potential experience and 12 mental conditions that flavor your experience. It's a map of the post-life processing zone we must enter when dead. It's an operatic overture reviewing the main themes you'll encounter inside. The *Bhavachakra*, also called the Wheel of Cyclic Existence, or, simply, the Wheel of Life, is a teaching device in Buddhism, showing people where they get lost in the material world, represented by the wheel and its many divisions. Let me mention that Yama's wrathful guise is an act, a pose, a salutary goad. He is pretending to as scary as hell for a benevolent purpose, to help you wake up.

Buddhists regard him as a Wrathful Deity, which means he is scary on purpose, like a high-level, ultra-sophisticated, upscale gargoyle, *Bardo* muscle. He wears a crown of five skulls; he sports a big third eye; he wears a tiger skin; and he has four arms. He scowls; he glares. He looks wrathful, and he's good at it; he tries to terrify us mightily so we will take the death process seriously. All of this is to show us the impermanence of everything we thought had durability.

I don't mean we are disallowed from finding any humor in it, but that we should accord it our due attention because it is the transition zone out of embodied consciousness and, potentially, a step up into a more wakeful state. Above the wheel is the Moon, not our local Moon, satellite of the Earth, but Moon in the esoteric sense, indicating a state of exalted consciousness. The Moon here means liberation from *samsara* and illusion, because it lies beyond life and the *Bardo*. Naturally, at this early stage in our expedition, I had no idea how central this Moon as a destination for liberated consciousness would prove to be.

Yama's wrathfulness says consciousness, lucidity, is a terrific force. It is as sharp as a sword, as riveting as an ocean of fire. He looms fiercely, menacingly, over the bewildering *Bhavachakra*, the labyrinth of human reality, to show that consciousness is senior to all obscurations and befuddlements in this wheel. He shows that awakened, empowered awareness is the master of the Wheel of Life, that liberated consciousness, awareness represented by only the head, is the key.

You don't get that nuance with the Green Knight. The Celts portrayed him more as an anomalous friendly giant with a big axe and a somewhat warped sense of amusement and entertainment. The Buddhist picture gives you more of the naked truth of Yama; he gets in your face as he cleaves your head. When you think about it, Yama's scariness is helpful, a gift. It says, look, this is the fierceness you wield to extricate yourself from the confusing bonds of life. Here is the warrior's posture necessary to get free of all consciousness entanglements. Yama's fierceness is a door swung open for us to achieve our original condition. Yama says, in effect, *Be like this* if you want to totally wake up in freedom. He is the state that cuts away all obscuring, confusing points of illusion and darkness.

"There is a reason why you only see Yama's head and feet, and the rest of his celestial form is covered by the Wheel of Life or *Bhavachakra*," said Blaise. "It's because the Underworld is inside him. You enter his form to get there. But note his head: as if decapitated like the Green Knight's, it looms above this wheel.

"It's making the same point as the Green Knight: negotiate this realm through the head, meaning deploy awakened consciousness in the two highest body chakras, the head chakras. Find your autonomy over the Wheel of Life by moving your awareness up into the head centers; survey the *Bhavachakra* landscape from there, from above it, with fierce mastery and insight. Yama is a name, one among many, for the first mortal who died. He was the first to find his way out of the bewildering Wheel of Life into the pure Upper World. As a result, he became appointed the Lord of the Departed, chief of this realm. He knows the route, the traps, the deceptions, the sure ways through this labyrinthine realm. You travel through the Wheel of Life, the *Bardo*, to reach his wide-awake head. Then you too, only seemingly dead, are the immortal master of this realm. You are senior to all the conditions and perturbations of subtle and material life.

"Even so, when we transit this Underworld, journey through his body, penetrate his consciousness, which we will do soon, it will seem to be a separate world and that he is its gatekeeper. But it's inside him. He is the consciousness condition, the role model and the mystagogue, for this perilous passage. You lose a lot of that high consciousness nuance in the Green Knight picture, don't you think. The axe mostly has to represent the needed fierceness, death as the separator. The Green Knight seems sly, like he's holding back something, chuckling to himself at the chumps he's found at Camalate, how they never suspect the trick he has prepared for them, never read the fine print of his deal. Your experience of Yama, in contrast, is like getting a football kicked right into your face, smack, ouch, wake-up now, and he's still glaring at you like a coach."

"Blaise is right," said Merlin. "You have to copy Yama's fierceness and take it with you when you enter his realm. It keeps you clear. He superintends the realm which means, practically, his vantage point is the one you want to emulate. He understands it all; he is its master. It's like he says to you: Be like this if you want to make sense of the Underworld. This is the fierceness of discerning consciousness you need to navigate this realm. You must ruthlessly cut through all illusory forms and misperceptions, these interlocking realms of *samsara* I show you in this Wheel of Life display. The image is reversed: the *Gawain* story has him carrying his severed head in his hand, but the truth is the severed, liberated head carries the cut-off body. Freed awareness shows the body, phenomenal life in matter, consciousness stuck in it, how to find its way."

"In other words, it's time for us to put on our game face," said Blaise.

It seemed to happen all at once. I don't remember willing it, but I must have. I found myself mimicking the fierce ruthlessness of fire-girt Yama. I now had more arms and they held implements including his trademark twisted white rod or *danda* topped with a tiny leering human skull; those twists also looked like six spinal vertebrae one atop the next. My body felt dynamic. It had assumed an athletic, muscular, almost impossible posture, dispelling illusions. I realized with alarm that it was my consciousness that had taken this body form. My focused awareness was expressing itself in this metaphor of Yama's warrior body. Uncharacteristically, I felt widely, copiously, furiously aware—of everything. I felt my head was looking in all directions at once even though it wasn't moving.

I felt the heat all around me. I felt it searing out of my red-garbed form. It was not anger, but an unbending insistence on a condition, namely, the true state of reality. In one of my four hands I held a mirror reflecting the karma of humans; in another, I gripped a *pāśa* or noose, for extricating souls from deceased bodies, as if Yama were some kind of spectral midwife, yanking breeched souls out of moribund corpses. My eyes glared red; they felt red, like when your eyes get irritated by shampoo. I felt myself scowling with considerable force and conviction, though I knew it was an act. I was a poseur just like Yama.

After all, a gargoyle or *Dharmapala* has to come across as convincingly ferocious, somewhat like, I thought then, a military drill sergeant. You have to set the right example. It felt like reality itself was on fire, outraged, burning up in an Armageddon of Yama's flames of enlightenment around me. I looked at my companions. The same was happening to them. We were all Yama, and liking it.

I have to say the effect of this was to marvelously clear my head. I felt like a sword of Light had just invincibly scourged my mind of all obscurations. I also found I had been shifted to another place. I gathered I was now inside this place. I saw thousands of egg-shaped processing spaces with a single human inside each. It looked like a private movie-watching chamber. Images flickered on the curving walls around each person. It seemed like both a continuous narrative presented in visual terms and myriads of individual images from within that.

I realized my fellow expedition members had passed through the Green Knight and were observing this curious phenomenon as well. At first I wasn't sure what I was seeing, but as I noted the constant appearance of the particular individual in these moving images I understood they were watching their own life records. They were watching the home movie of their life just finished, starring them. They seemed encased in soap bubbles on whose surface played the full movie. This is what people meant when they said their life suddenly flashed before them. Here they pulled up an easy chair and watched the film.

This was consistent with the mythic record which says Yama is a *Dharmapala* or wrathful god who judges the dead and presides over the *Narakas*, which is usually translated as "hells" or "purgatories" and the cycle of rebirth. It was as if they were students at a film school and he was the master filmmaker assessing their apprentice efforts to produce a decent movie. He checked dialogue, editing, narrative drive, the quality of the acting, the dramatic peaks. He pointed out blindspots, muffed interactions, incomplete explanations, failed opportunities, epiphanies achieved but overlooked. Yama is the critic's critic.

That is too literal and too compressed to yield a correct understanding. These people in their own movie chambers were reviewing the record of their immediate past life. It was what death chronicles call the life review, reeling off the "movie" inscribed in your own personal *Akashic* Records of the etheric body. It is hellish if your life was full of pain and misery; it is purgatorial because you will not advance, either into post-death tutorials or your next incarnation, until you complete the life review, so for a while you are in this in-between place.

After the etheric body, you review the records of the astral body, and from what I hear, they can be strange, disturbing, and weird. If the etheric body movie is a comedy of manners, the astral body flick is a horror show, a real chiller for grown-ups, full of twists you never saw coming. You see evidence of actions you don't remember taking, yet you clearly did. The etheric film clips are the daytime you; the astral body cinema is the *noir*, nighttime you. Yama doesn't judge you. He watches neutrally, though with acute discernment, as you review the footage and judge yourself. You're the judge. He watches you judging yourself, astonished, dismayed, delighted; you are the judge of the dead, of yourself. He just lends you some of his penetrating discernment and wide-awake fiery gaze.

My first impression was that these people were watching their own "home" movies in the privacy of wrap-around viewing chambers. That wasn't correct. I realized these chambers were in fact the encircling auric energy fields. The images reeling off their etheric bodies were being displayed on the inside "walls" or energy membranes of these silken-thin envelopes of Light. I also figured out it was much larger inside these auric chambers than it looked from the outside, and that the interior size was adjustable based on a person's intent.

Before me was a plain with thousands, maybe millions, of these auric movie theaters. People die, then they may take as long as they wish to review the life. Some do a rush job and are done in days; others stretch it out into years. There is a "pause" button where you can halt the movie and take a break, or you can slow the speed of the film and watch it in slow-motion to catch the nuances.

Confusingly, this etheric body life-review takes place during the 84 hours traditionally assigned as the wake for the newly deceased. The understanding is that after this time the etheric body dissolves and with it the copious life movie. Then you bury the physical body because the etheric body is finished with it. The confusing part is even so you can spend as long as you like reviewing the footage, because the time flow is radically different in the *Bardo* than in life. It's 84 hours on the outside, but inside, in the *Bardo*, it may seem like a year or more.

Numerous attendants stroll about the plain ready to help out, counsel, or explain as needed. I saw numerous viewers calling on these superintendents for help, but in the way that if you rented what used to be called a home entertainment center, the equipment providers would dispatch technicians to monitor it for you. You'd ask, in a moment of confusion, advice on which button to push next or how to do a rewind. In an odd way, everyone was having a near-death experience in slow-motion.

The irony spun my head around a few times: they were dead and they were seeing their life revealed before them, and this was *supposed* to happen *here*. Each was accompanied by an angelic figure who stood by companionably (I presumed that was the individual's Higher Self or Guardian Angel) and by what I would have to call a theater attendant, an Underworld counselor and explainer.

I had the impression this attendant was an emissary of the Green Knight and was on hand to answer questions, clarify matters, and encourage further viewing. It is not the most straightforward of activities, I realized, to review your just finished life with riveting lucidity and full disclosure of all details. We are so used to blurring the edges, conveniently forgetting the unpleasant bits, editing them out. This is your unexpurgated, unedited autobiography, absolutely factual. Full lucidity can have a scourging effect on consciousness and really wake it up. This was a cram-course in self-knowledge, and for most people reverting to their soul essence, it was not something they were accustomed to.

"Is it different with each gate you enter?" This was Matthew asking.

"No, though I wondered about that at first," said Tommy. He should know; he actually had died about 20 years ago and gone through all this. "It turns out all the gates lead to the same place, to right here, to the life-processing zone. The cartography here is not spatial, but pertains to zones and stages in consciousness. You first enter this zone because it's the first mandatory stage in the dropping of your body and life consciousness. The function is the place. You sit in a movie theater made by your Higher Self wrapping itself around you, the images projected on its great angelic form, its wings like the movie screen. The *Bardo* is like a great house with 1,746 doors. They all lead into the same house.

"I did notice that some doors or Underworld entrances were decorated differently, according to culture and belief and psychic picture reports of earlier initiates. It's like people put up their own pictures and images of what they thought the Underworld was, or how they saw it, based on reports of psychics who went in. Underneath all these projections, though, the Underworld gates are the same, 1,746 identical, generic, and thus neutral copies of the same design. Some are scary, like awful, red gaping mouths full of teeth and deep gullets, and others are more heavenly looking, angels girting the doors like fresh flowers."

"So you went through this when you got here, right?" Edward asked.

"Sure. Everybody does. It's required. But you can put the movie on pause whenever you want and go off and do other things. I did that all the time. You can take as long as you want to review the film clips. I took rather a long time." Tommy grinned. He might be dead, but he was still a cocky teenager as needed. "I went back and forth between doing the review, which was boring at times, I mean I'd already seen this movie, and researching the Theosophon and working out improvements to the plan, as you know, which was way more fun." He looked at Blaise as he said this, and Blaise nodded, approvingly, with a grin.

"It reminds me of a studious night at the college library, like a Wednesday, too far from the weekends, everyone pouring over their books, preparing for papers, exams, or oral presentations, cramming their brains," said Edward. "It has that concentration atmosphere of a study hall. Do you notice how we can walk among these thousands of auric bubbles and their life-movie projections and remain unobserved? I wonder if we're invisible to them. Do you see those spooling vapor trails that lead

from their bubbles back to the physical Earth? They resemble tunnels made of smoke, and they're filled with images."

"Those are traces of the manner of their dying," explained Merlin. "You will find the full range of experience from unconscious to fully conscious, from unexpected and unprepared to carefully planned and accounted for in advance. Not too many, unfortunately, exit from their crown chakras, so they often arrive here disoriented, confused, and bewildered and require a fair bit of counseling.

"Mostly there is a period of sleep after their exiting from their physical forms. It eases the transition, though sudden deaths may jettison souls here wide-awake. That can be disturbing and calls for extra attention from the death attendants. When they're ready, they begin their review. Often it feels like you have just returned home from a long trip, and you remember yourself where you live. They often scratch their heads and wonder how they could have forgotten. They realize how poor their daytime memory was, as they see everything was recorded. It's like you turn on the video camera at birth and it runs until your death, and during its time of operation you forget its existence, until now. Then you are duly amazed at the wealth of detail, every last life moment, it recorded."

"It's that damn River Lethe," said Blaise. "I keep telling the Old Man He ought to revisit the necessity of that enforced oblivion. It's a real nuisance."

"Spoken with your trademark heat, Old Grail Knight," responded Merlin. "You may be surprised, possibly delighted, to learn He has agreed to change it."

Change the River Lethe, or the requirement to drink fully of it? That sounded promising. You would have to redo the entire Greek mythic system.

Lethe was one of five alleged Underworld rivers and was known as *Ameles Potamos*, River of Unmindfulness. The word also denotes oblivion, forgetfulness, and concealment. Lethe flows through the Underworld and souls are required to drink of it before re-entering the incarnate world. The thinking was that full knowledge and recall of one's previous existences and of the nature of the Underworld would undermine one's confidence and prove overwhelming. It would suborn the possibility of making free-will choices while freshly alive. You would arrive in the incarnate world pre-loaded with too much knowledge. Take a sip of Lethe water and you arrive in the physical world your mind wiped clean. We all start out in the physical world in a condition of complete amnesia.

Yes, amnesiac, you're open to possibilities, everything is freshness and discovery, but you are burdened with a failure to remember anything about life before incarnation. It's like waking up from a concussion; your mind is blurred. I can see why Blaise gets cranky about this condition; it can hamper your effectiveness on the job. It's like a perpetually recurrent Groundhog Day; you can't remember your progress or mistakes from the last round and you have to redo everything. Every new life is like a repeat of the same day. You never get off the wheel. You cannot remember your context or understand why you are here.

Not everyone of course is on the job like Blaise is. Maybe the amnesia part doesn't bother them like it does him. Most people seem content with their consciousness being devoid of any memory of its true context. In fact, I often have the impression people prefer it this way, not knowing their soul's history.

We saw groups of people walking through this river, dowsing themselves in it or cupping their palms to hold some of its pure water. Entering the river you could see all their spiritual knowledge, their soul's résumé, forming an auric picture field around them, but upon stepping

out of the river at the other side, it was gone. There was only empty sparkling space around them. Lethe is not a river in the way we think about them in the physical world. I mentioned water but that is a metaphor. It is a river of Light or fire, an energy current, a certain frequency of consciousness. In the strictest sense Lethe is a mechanism that selectively dims consciousness, scrubbing memory, putting a veil over it.

When I say their memory was "gone" that is not quite accurate. It is veiled, concealed from them, put behind a kind of stealth-veil that deflects all inquiring Light of consciousness trying to find out who they have been and done. The memory remains intact, but it is for most people inaccessible for their lifetime. It's like the way police say a juvenile's criminal record is sealed. You cannot examine it. It is not irretrievably inaccessible, but it takes a lot of effort to get to it. You need a court order unsealing the records, here, that's an epiphany. There are so many people in the world walking the planet with their memories concealed from them, all this vital soul information packed behind a thick veil. You could say they each carry a miniature River Lethe, for this water, this vibration, eclipses the soul memories and in a functional sense forms the veil. Souls leave the Underworld with the River Lethe imprinted in their auric field.

Merlin gestured for me, Edward, Matthew, and Pipaluk to stand in the river. Of the group, we were the only four still officially, unequivocally alive and in bodies. Tommy would be again, eventually, when he felt like it; Blaise, well, who knows about him? As for Merlin, any guise he assumed was for illustration purposes only. We stood in the current of Light. It had the effect of brightening the auric reflectivity around us. We already weren't remembering our soul's history, although since we were in our Light bodies, the proximity of that history was almost palpable. If I sat down and tuned into it, I would probably retrieve a lot. Merlin indicated we should fully immerse ourselves in the river then get out.

When we stood up again outside the river, I felt a great Light surrounding me. I felt like I was in a movie theater that consisted of perhaps a hundred theaters. All the movies were running and I could watch any I wished, slow it down, zoom in on details, even walk around in it like an expandable living hologram of my past. For that's what this was. It was the undoing of the concealment, the forgetfulness: the dilution of the River Lethe.

"Not fully," Merlin commented. "That would be too much at first. But 50%. We thought we'd try that out, see how people handle that amount. It is still considerable. You can see how your recall, your access to this great river of truth, or *aletheia*, unconcealment, can be modulated as to speed and perceivable detail. You may thank Blaise for this change. He suggested it when I first broached the topic of an Underworld expedition and asked for his recommendations. He said, Do something about Old Man Lethe and its baleful effects on soul memory. He'd had quite enough, he said, of working around its restrictive effect on memory."

I sensed a great array of living images behind me, then surrounding me. It was as if I had stepped into a sea of personal history, me along with hundreds of others, our life stories detailed fully down to the minutest detail, all accessible. It felt like a great sun had risen in my auric bubble. The Light was strong, but it was not threatening nor did it feel in any way inimical. It felt friendly, domestic. I admit that is an odd word for the circumstances. I mean it felt the way when you come home and enter your study or livingroom or the room you spend the most amount of time in (not counting your bedroom): it feels familiar and welcoming. You know all the furniture, its placement, the stacks of books, papers, and magazines, where the lights are, the cushions, the blanket for when it grows cold.

In the present case, a lot of this "furniture" I hadn't seen in a long time. It was as if a great warehouse of furniture was now being unconcealed in a sweeping gesture of *aletheia*, as the Greeks would have it. I speak in metaphors. I felt the breath of hundreds of past lives over my skin. It was palpable memory. It was like seeing a hundred people each occupying a node on the circumference of a circle. One was a scholar, a monk, a scribe; others were illiterate, or book burners, or scholar-punishers; still others were spreaders of false information, while others probed for the truth, like early forms of private detectives. I saw a few being tempted by the Faustian bargain, a few succumbing, a few recovering.

I saw doctors who used the truth of the body, emotions, mind, or soul to heal, and I saw ill-advised occult practitioners who used this knowledge to hurt people. I saw myself in previous lives reading aloud from great tomes, bibles, writing in them, decorating their margins with colorful illustrations. I saw other versions of myself studying in libraries, deciphering Greek, Hebrew, and Latin texts, making notes, reflecting on the implications of newly worked out etymologies. Male and female, young, middle-aged, and elderly: all were here.

I recognized colleagues, some from today, some I knew at Dartmouth. I saw Edward, Matthew, Philomena, and Blaise in some of his human permutations. More importantly, I understood some of the overarching themes of all these lives. I had a strong passion to understand the styles and structures of initiation. I wanted to see how esoteric Mystery knowledge was transmitted and absorbed. The bulk of these many lives had been devoted to studying nuances of that idea. The display was like a kaleidoscope of permutations on this single great theme. Each life added to the complexity and richness of the interpretation.

I understood how all this knowledge, this grand panorama of some of my past lives, those organized around this core theme of initiation research, would have radically broadened my self-understanding and professional approach at Dartmouth, how it would have eased the doubt, skepticism, and scholarly restraint that characterized my tenure as a professor of comparative mythology. Had I known all this, I could have gone so much further, progressed with so much more confidence and the requisite assurance that I was on the right track. I saw that had I known all this I never would have bothered being a professor. I would have run out the front door of my house and life long before Blaise came.

At least I hadn't followed my father's advice and become a corporate lawyer. Somehow I had seen and heeded a tiny spark of Light guiding me to mythology. I realized that Blaise in his clever cultivation of me, sending me his infernal desert notebooks, his whisking me out of my house and life, his tutoring and travel mentoring in the years leading up to the Theosophon, had acted from this knowledge. His tactics with me must have been based on knowing me this way, having the dossier on my lives and preferences and passions all laid out before him like the engineering schematics for an evolving soul. He's a sly one.

I looked at Edward and Matthew. They similarly had enlarged auras filled with living pictures of their many past lives. It looked like they were the Titan Atlas bearing the Earth on their shoulders, although it was not a burden, not an overwhelming weight, but rather a world of images as light as a globular feather.

It resembled a pair of wings, outstretched in such a way as to make an iridescent arc around the back of their body, wings of scintillating fish scales, like arms raised so the fists rested on the head, forming a kind of triangle, and all of this space glinting like fish scales, each reflecting a life image and all its details, ready to instantly unconceal itself the moment you directed your attention towards it. Edward and Matthew seemed to be expanding, like dry plants taking on water. Pipaluk seemed to already have an expanded *aletheian* aura; apparently, she had managed to expand the bubble of past-life truth around her during her long life.

"Self-knowledge affects everything about one, as you see," Merlin said. "But with enhanced self-knowledge comes greater responsibility. You can't make excuses any more for your failures, inattentions, or wayward distractions. You are too well-informed now to cite ignorance or lack of having the full picture. Now you know what you have to do, what you have agreed already to do, what in fact you have planned from a long time ago to do, and you know why as well.

"There is no defensible wiggle-room when you possess the full picture of your intentions. Only one thing to do and that is to get on with it starting right now. Incidentally, that information about your previous lives has always been on your back in something called the past-life aura. But it has been under concealment. Now we remove 50 percent of the River Lethe veil upon it so it may be unconcealed to you. That much new self-knowledge can change the world, can change you. Normally, you would have potential access to this aura when you are 'dead' and processing your immediately concluded life; now you may access it while alive. That will keep many people wide-awake and on their toes."

I turned to Philomena. I did not see a past-life aura on her back. She looked like Philomena, though an exceedingly vibrant, younger version of her. "It's all gone," she said. "Burned up and turned into Light, all urgency released. I remembered them all and integrated their essence into my new body of Light. I am, in this Light form, the total and completed momentum of all my past lives."

I looked at Blaise. His looked like a series of concentric circles forming haloes around his upper torso; each was filled with well-ordered, brightly lit images. A great deal of information was thereby presented, but it too lacked any urgency. "Less perturbations this way," he said. "It's the only way to go, pal. I organized it like my personal library. I know where every life-book is now."

Tommy's past-life aura looked like a creative person's cluttered studio. It looked like an artist or writer busy at work, opening file drawers, posting up outlines on the wall, drawing out numerous books from the shelves, studying reports. He was working with his past lives, extracting meaning and detailed explanations from them, extrapolating new directions, having all of it on hand.

"I'm drawing on all those lives that bear on my present interests and activities," he said. He still had the vitality and aplomb of a teenager, though you could see the old soul and its earned wisdom shining through his adolescent insouciance. At least four copies of Tommy dressed in robes of Light and only resembling him in basic terms seemed to be hustling about his auric field getting things like accomplished reference librarians in the old British Museum stacks.

"Tommy's example highlights the new dispensation, the new lessening of limitations exacted by the big bad old river, Lethe," said Merlin with jollity. "You two," he added, indicating myself and Edward but, strangely, not Matthew, "will be able to draw upon past-life archives as they are germane to your current pursuits or as they may illuminate current conditions and possibilities. These lives and their contents will step forward and gain prominence in your daytime awareness as you need them. This enhanced recall will become

fairly automatic. You, Pipaluk, have already been doing this for some time; it will be even easier now. Those extra versions of Tommy you saw are his still extant four higher bodies, ever subtler versions of himself simulated in Light, now helping him."

I wondered why Merlin had excluded Matthew from this explanation. His past-life aura was churning, roiling like a storm. Its images were girt in flames. This was way past perturbations; major changes were underway in his space. It looked like a city on fire, burning up. The flames, which were a diamond-white tinged with scarlet, were not consuming his images in any normal sense; they seemed to be transforming them. Dark charcoal smoke seeped out of these pictures and they grew brighter until they flamed with this diamond white fire enveloped in the scarlet.

These images were continuously popping out of the deeper layers of his aura like toast. His auric space was decompressing, ejecting many pictures. He looked like Kansas in June, storm clouds massing, Oklahoma in tornado season. I had the impression Matthew did not understand what was happening to him. He turned to me and commented wryly, "Bloody busy place today, isn't it."

I felt myself lightening. Some of that quite bearable lightness of being was due, I am certain, to the fact I was conducting business in my Double or astral body. From the accounts I had read of this experience, it is a fluid, fleet, mobile body, capable of all manner of surprising feats, adroitness, speed, creativity. But more was at play in this lightening than my presence in this Light form. It was the unconcealment process; awareness of my deep past itself was a lightening. Think of it: not knowing, ignorance, being in the dark about oneself and one's true motives, intentions, and the accurate history of one's soul over time, is a heavy weight. We're burdened under this unrelieved weight, being in the dark. This darkness was lifting, the weight was dissolving, and I felt terrifically light.

"Conditions are changing in the nature of the planet itself to support this," Merlin said, evidently aware of the direction of my thoughts. "Changes have been underway now for almost 60 years to the basic energetic fabric of Earth and human reality that will enable most people to be compatible with this unconcealment. Without these global changes its impact would be unbearable.

"The planet's Light body, its geometric pattern of Light, what we call its Light grid, that structures human reality is upgrading to match this level of psychic insight that comes with this dissolving of half the veil of Lethe. A person's own natural psychic ability will be sparked to match and help process the revelation of this panorama of past lives. Less ignorant of the history of their soul and less oblivious of the true condition of their consciousness, people will start relating to Earth reality in better ways, more in accord with the truth."

The term "Light grid" was one that Merlin and Blaise would bandy back and forth a lot. I got introduced to it in my Theosophon travels with Blaise. It refers to the totality of all the Earth's sacred sites and geomantic nodes, and all their subtle temples of Light within these points. All of this comprises a grid, and this grid made of its distribution array has a geometric pattern, though a complex one, and it has an overall vibrational quality, a frequency signature, a sound, a Light quality, an intended, even engineered, effect on consciousness and all the aspects of the planet's biological and psychological life. It is Earth's master Light patterning. It affects and conditions everything in physical reality.

Merlin turned to Blaise, encouraging him to add a few comments. "The original Light grid design and its energy settings made this unconcealment difficult. You had to work

against a significant psychic gradient to dissolve some of the Lethe veil from your past-life aura, that image of folded-up wings on the shoulders. The new Light grid's design parameters are set at the psychic level of the sixth chakra, a place of power and perception. Despite a person's disbelief, prejudice, skepticism, or any other kind of long-held resistance, it will be easier.

"The sixth chakra is the ideal, the preferred, place from which to view these contents. People will find themselves, despite their habits, eagerly pursuing this process. After all, everyone has the same basic equipment, the same psychic chakras. These changes to the planet's Light grid free up their access to them. At this rate, I mean even your mother will start showing signs of being psychic."

I asked Blaise how long ago those changes to the Light grid were made.

He made as if to look at his watch. He wasn't wearing one. "58 years ago."

"We've learned to be patient with Earth conditions," Merlin commented. "First we introduced the major changes to the geometric configuration of the Light determining all aspects of Earth reality. That was June 1985. Then we waited for it to settle in. Now we lessen the hold of Lethe on the incarnate's memory of past lives. In about another 50 years these two alterations will be anchored into human reality. You will have a basically psychic planet and a humanity without much of the Lethe veil. Yes, I know, Frederick"—Merlin evidently was reading my thoughts—"we plan ahead. We take the long view, take the necessary steps, then wait, usually a long time, centuries, often. It is an organic process, so we have to let human consciousness match the upgrades at its own rate though with just an edge and push to it from us to keep it moving."

The lessening of the grip of the River Lethe on a person's soul memory would not affect those disincarnate people processing their lives here. They had full access to all the veiled contents; that was required for them to complete the life review and processing, basically their own self-administered Judgement Day. Some might complain they had too much access, the details were overwhelming. But Merlin let us have a glimpse of how this would work in living people. Since this change was only now, in November 2043, being introduced, he moved us forward 30 years to observe how it played out in living people. It was as if we stepped into Earth's timeline from our timeless astral world location at a node precisely marked November 1, 2073, and started watching Earth reality there.

I was of course intensely curious as to the mechanism of this download. You can't force people to be more self-aware, to know more about themselves. Yet the planet needed people to achieve both conditions, because the planet itself, as Merlin and Blaise indicated, has been changed and it was now in a position to facilitate this enhanced self-knowledge and soul memory. For humans to be congruent with the changed planetary conditions, they had to do this, yet they could not be coerced to do it. That sounded like a conundrum.

"It may seem like a quandary, but it isn't," Merlin said. "We organized this access to past-life memory as like an IV-drip adjusted by each 'patient.' You can get a little at a time, or big revelatory chunks of recall. You decide the rate."

I watched a number of people access their past-life auras. One person allowed the information to trickle in steadily, mingling with the daytime contents of consciousness in such a way as to not disturb his mental stability. It was like a very slowly turned dimmer switch for awareness; he kept inching the dial forward by tiny increments until he became used to remembering the lives and details of what would have otherwise seemed foreign, as if of other people. He allowed the strange information

to enter his mental stream as if he had issued a permit to himself to operate intuitively. He framed the input as the product of intuition, and at times he felt he was experiencing telepathy and image transfer. Anyway, this was how he made this daring process in consciousness feel safe.

Another person would sit down periodically, as if to meditate, and go off researching a question, wanting to find the extended causal chain in her soul's long life that led to a current situation. She would access the relevant files in her own records room and allow a rich stream of images and information to flow in. She was the investigating detective and her past-life aura was the mystery and the place where she would eventually nab the "culprit," the committer of the deed or the generator of the thought or emotion that had led to the "crime" in question. She knew, for she had done this many times by now, that the causal chain that explained current conditions was long and complex, stretching far back in time. She had a great appetite for this level of information, and she "digested" it ably.

This kind of reciprocal interaction with her past-life records tutored her in recognizing the quality of information she needed to explain a current situation. She consulted these records frequently, seeking clues to current injuries or pathologies, dominant emotional tones, or repetitive mental states or thoughts. Invariably, she found levels of antecedents from previous lives that led to these. She studied the long causal train in which the same issue was played out, extrapolated, and eventually resolved, in many cases by her in the present life.

The time-frame was compressed, or, rather, she saw its full extent over the many lives, and through this she could understand the necessity, the unavoidable forward momentum, of a strong emotion, leading to an injury then a pathology then a compromised physical or emotional condition, faulty or provisional self-definitions drawn from these bodily facts, and finally the resolution of the pain. The totality of this past-life information was displayed in a complicated geometric pattern, like a grid of Light in the fourth dimension. Her attention or the specific focus of her inquiry brought certain sections forward. It reminded me of a time I daringly (I'm not a technology-minded guy) looked at the engineering schematics for a television, panicked, and ran out of the room. Perhaps I exaggerate, but the life plans she was studying were complex like that.

The biggest, sheerest fact she derived from these reviews was that reality made sense. Life events were not accidents, but purposeful, dramas and missions scripted in advance in service of self-awareness and karmic resolution. Reality, not only her individual life, but everything around her, the life of the planet and its billions of humans, was now rational, sensible, full of purpose. This was reassuring, and it led to her having more confidence in making creative changes. She was screenwriter, producer, director, leading actor, and the audience for this.

I saw lots of people acting this way. Earth reality would be changing forever now, not through sudden, radical shifts and upheavals as people used to assume, but slowly, organically, sustainably, the way plants grow given their ideal conditions. Equipped with more knowledge, facts about themselves and their deep back-story, people would approach their life differently. If I were to compare the average psyche to the New Mexico high desert, the best way to introduce water, or, in this case, consciousness and knowledge of one's history, is through slow-drip irrigation. You don't flood the dry land because it will just run off and create other problems and not be absorbed; you give it water by the drop.

Knowing their goals now, they could approach their life with a tactical view. I saw

that because the woman I was watching had this enhanced level of self-knowledge; she was more aware, better briefed on the mechanics and necessities of the dying process. She was in a position to perform much of the after-death processing while still alive. She could see how "she" had done this, laboriously, painfully, in previous "deaths." She could deal with much of this required life-experience processing while alive. It almost seemed routine, like preparing your tax return. Instead of waiting until she was "dead" and being confronted with an enormous backlog of required processing, she could start digesting her experiences daily. This too would add to her self-knowledge. It would certainly take the sting out of the *Bardo* and reduce the paperwork.

"This is a great idea," exclaimed Tommy. "I wish it had been in place when I got here. A lot of the life-review was drudgery, like being a security analyst and having to review a stack of boring surveillance tapes. I won't even talk about the nastiness of the astral body review. Talk about delinquency. I had no idea I had been up to some of the stuff I saw revealed in my astral body review, though, I admit, some of it looked like fun. Flying, shapeshifting, jumping time dimensions and time periods—okay, yes, I admit, that was fun.

"But the thing is it seems pointless, lacking in traction, to become fully acquainted with your carryings-on after you've left the action body behind. It's almost theoretical and abstract because you can't do anything about it on the spot. This new plan of debriefing yourself of your life actions while alive is a great improvement. It will streamline the whole business, make it interesting. You can make changes, course adjustments, in the place where it matters."

"Well said, Tommy," commented Blaise. "It may also help us exit the phylogeny with greater ease and efficiency. I'm always looking for the way out.'

"What do you mean, Blaise?" Tommy asked. "The way out of what?"

"Just because you're dead doesn't guarantee you passage out of the wheel of human life, also known as the phylogeny. You're still stuck in the funhouse, like a spaceship that can't make it past the Earth's gravitational field and remains stuck in the planet's atmosphere, deep space, the galaxy, still lying far afield. You die and you watch the news-clips, process the movies of your life, but you're still here, liable to be sucked back in for another round. You're still in one of the Six Worlds in Yama's *Bhavachakra*; you're still running around in a *samsara* riot.

"I'm talking about making a clean get-away from the human phylogeny, everything to do with being human. Getting out of the *Bhavachakra*, into Yama's warrior head, his viewpoint, which is outside the system and thus senior to it. That's the different wheel, a much bigger one. We plan to make changes to that."

Merlin was nodding his head. "We're going to sort out the *Dhyanis*."

2

Merlin was referring to the *Dhyani* Buddhas, the five Meditation Buddhas said to be emanations of the Buddha himself. These are known as Wisdom Buddhas, each occupying a cardinal direction within the Diamond Realm or *Dharmakaya*, the domain of truth and pure reality. They were made famous in the *Tibetan Book of the Dead*, if famous is the right word to use about something so arcane. When you're newly dead, you meet with each of them, one per day, and usually you have no idea who they are, what they represent, or what's going on.

That's part of the problem here. Most people fail their *Dhyani* Buddha exams. In case you're not a Buddhist, as I wasn't either, Buddha means "the Awakened One," the one fully awake to the full condition of reality at all levels. The Buddha is not a Buddhist, but an enlightened spirit, fully awake. He is not a promulgator of dogma, a salesman for a belief system. He's an empiricist. The *Dhyanis* each embody a nuance within that full spectrum of absolute awareness.

"Nobody has made any changes to the procedure since Yama went through," said Merlin. "And he never died anyway. It was just a story we laid out. Myth credits Yama as being the first Man to die. He didn't. He superintends the death process and its after-life protocols. Let's say he simulated his death, making himself into a massive Light temple for these stages and revelations. He thought through all the stages,

visualized them in detail, acutely imagined them.

"That's why you see him looking down over the *Bhavachakra* which he holds before him, from chin to ankles, like a richly decorated shield. It is his body. Extricating consciousness from the body is easy. The difficulty, or at least the challenge, is to free that consciousness from the cognitive assumptions of that *body* as it has lived on this *planet*. We are dealing with two specifics here. The framework of those assumptions, or habits, is what we refer to as the phylogeny.

"The goal of the human, whether alive or in the *Bardo*, is to extricate oneself from the Wheel of Life and its Six Worlds that Yama holds as the *Bhavachakra*, and to rise up into his head space, to emulate his *Dharma*-warrior's ferocity of attention. He looks fierce and raging because that is the quality of the liberated mind in the face of worlds of illusion, *samsara*, and the sticky, elusive, deceptive nature of reality, that is, everything inside the Wheel of Life he holds. Look at the wheel; you'll see it's divided into six sections: each is a World. World doesn't mean a planet, but a zone of existence and a quality of consciousness.

"The whole thing is like a net or a web, carefully woven, many-layered. You hardly notice it when you're alive and walking about the Earth, yet you are thoroughly embedded in it. It informs all your actions, guides your assumptions. It is a Light grid that stamps the generic essence of Human on an incarnating soul. That stamp influences everything, body, mind, thought, emotions, life. It is the infrastructure that makes it possible to construe yourself as a separate identity, as possessing a selfhood, a distinguishable individuality, a persona. The tricky bit is, on the one hand, you need this infrastructure of selfhood for the great safari of incarnation, but, on the other hand, it soon becomes an impediment, something which, eventually, you want to free yourself from.

"When you die, you are confronted with its reality in a stark, naked, unmediated manner. Unfortunately, most people are poorly prepared for this and fail to understand what confronts them, and they succumb to old habits and quickly reincarnate again. They re-enter the 'womb-door,' as I put it in the *Bardo Thödol*. They hop back on the *Bhavachakra* merry-go-round because it's the ride they know. The wideness and wildness of the *Bardo* is the ride they don't know."

"Given all that, when you were Padmasambhava teaching in Tibet, why did you write this handbook for the after-death experience?" asked Edward.

"To show them the Exit. Incarnation and disincarnation are bewildering. It seemed only fair to give them a leg up on how to do the moves correctly to get free of the place. I say 'place,' but the *Bardo* is a condition of consciousness. That is the real infrastructure you need to extricate yourself from; its qualities comprise the template printed on consciousness as it enters the womb-door. The *Bardo* is the Light grid that structures your experience inside the phylogeny.

"I know, it's not the usual way of looking at this, but you could say the *Bardo* is the etheric body imprint that informs and structures the physical incarnate body. The *Bardo Thödol* is a reliable map for getting out of this place: *Bardo*, for after-death plane, and *Thödol*, for liberation by hearing. It was read to the dead soul, with the understanding they'd hear it, like reading or talking to a coma patient, and it would orient them to their current, if strange, condition. The *Bardo* is the place of divestment, but that means it is a place of revelation because the details of the divestment also explain the intricacies of taking human form. The *Bardo* shows you what you are made of, both individually and generically."

The official story of the composition of this text is that in the 8th century A.D. Padmasambhava composed it, his principal student and colleague Yeshe Tsogyal wrote it down, then buried it per his instructions in the Gampo hills of central Tibet. Later, in the 14th century, the *terton*, or wisdom-text discoverer, Karma Lingpa, found the buried text and revealed it to the Tibetan world for the liberation of its monks. It was as if Padmasambhava buried the text in a time capsule, set the timer for its appropriate discovery 600 years in the future, and went away; eventually, the time was ripe to find it. Karma Lingpa, appointed in advance to be the *terton*, found it, then released it to Tibet where it enriched Buddhist practice. Much later, the rest of the world got it, principally starting in 1927 when W.Y Evans-Wentz published a scholarly English translation of it.

Bardo is the liminal zone between life and death, which is why it is often translated from the Tibetan as "intermediate state" or "in-between condition." It may loosely be correlated with the Christian notion of Purgatory in the sense that Purgatory is neither Heaven nor Hell, but an in-between place awaiting results. *Thödol* (or sometimes *thosgrol*) is equivalent in meaning to the Sanskrit *bodhi*, which means awakening, understanding, and enlightenment, and with *nirvana*, the blowing out, extinction of illusion. It is the goal of all Buddhist meditation.

The text strives to instruct the newly dead soul in how to attain *liberation* (*thosgrol*) from this bewildering *intermediate* or in-between state (*Bardo*) by hearing somebody alive read the instructions out loud over their inert body. It's like having a voice-over narrating and explaining your afterdeath experiences, or like touring an art gallery with a tape-recording explaining all the art pieces. The goal of the *Bardo* is to wake up, definitively, to your human condition, to perceive the mechanics of its operations and illusions and to get free of it. Buddhists see the *Bardo* as the optimal condition for consciousness to extricate itself from this. They probably also figured the newly dead person would be too bewildered to remember any of the instructions in the text and would need a quick refresher.

"That's right," Merlin said, as if annotating my scholarly thoughts. "The goal is to create a Bodhisattva, a post-human awakened being of total truth and manifesting the highest level of *sattva*, meaning truth, purity, Light, and *Dharma*. That speaks to the purpose of our expedition with the Green Knight, by the way. We want to make Earth's Albion a Bodhisattva, an enlightened Truth-Being, to empower him with such a force of awakened consciousness that he will be propelled into lucid self-awareness. We'd like Albion to emulate Yama's glare. It will say to the galaxy: Look! Earth's human collective, fiercely, ragingly awake."

Albion is another one of those big words in the geomantic lexicon. It's a way of pointing to a personification of the collective essence and lived, biographical consciousness of all humans over time on the Earth and taking the form of a colossus of Light, designed to include cosmic elements, overlaid upon the Earth at many levels of scale. C. G. Jung spoke of the collective unconscious of humanity; this is humanity's collective consciousness at all levels possible. Every human is a living, if small, copy of Albion, and Albion is our large copy.

"Actions in the *Bardo* will get transferred to Albion's planetary body," Merlin continued. "This will take some time, a century at least. But the example will be contagious. Since all humans are little Albions, walking and living in the great Light form of Earth's Albion, the changes will be reciprocal. Albion's emerging Bodhisattva condition will be transferred to living humans, like the way morning dew falls so subtly upon your skin as you walk, and every gesture of Bodhisattva quality emitted by humans will reciprocally fuel Albion's further awakening. The plan for Earth is for its Albions to wake up and be self-aware."

"You see, Edward, it's from the same people who brought you the Theosophon," said Blaise. He never loses that cheeky, smart-ass side to him.

"Now I see the point of the Green Knight appearing at Arthur's court," said Matthew. "It was Yama offering a tour of instruction in the *Bardo* to one prepared Grail Knight but on behalf of the fraternity of Grail Knights. The Green Knight offered to introduce Gawain, as it turned out, the only one to volunteer, to a thorough review of the after-death protocols and psychic landscape. The entire mechanism of the *Bardo* and the after-death protocols is a Light temple, a landscape of Light, a structured terrain for consciousness, just like on the Earth.

"The Green Chapel is the gateway into that world of fresh revelation about death. People need to be acquainted with this while alive; geomancers must maintain the links between the alive and *Bardo* conditions of consciousness. Now the Green Knight brings us back, Gawain plus seven others per the mythic *Annwn* model, because, as you said, Merlin, it is time to make big changes in the Underworld and that is the main purpose of our Green Knight expedition."

"Correct," Merlin replied. "It's part of a series of revelations permitted to Earth humanity now as part of the Apocalypse, the revelation of the original revelation. Think of it as disclosure by increments. The Theosophon was one; this expedition is another. Earth reality has become a slow-motion book of revelation.

"Edward, you will remember, I trust, what I told you about my time as Maui when I journeyed into the body of *Hine-nui-te-po*, the Great Mother of the Underworld and Great Woman of the Night. Hers was the cosmogonic form-generating body, source of all embodiments, and I had crawled into that vast cavernous space with the intent of securing immortality for humans, and failed. That was the way the Polynesians saw Maui's adventure, but what I actually was doing was showing humans the Exit and the correct protocols to make that exit. I was acting as psychopomp and mystagogue for human souls entering the *Bardo*. I show souls around the inside of the Great Mother's body, because I know Her.

"The Underworld is the complex form of the Great Woman of Night. It is the extrapolation of all Her manifested forms and their various levels of consciousness. All of it is a Light temple, and my role is to guide consciousness through it back to Her because where She resides is the place of unity, the domain of consciousness before it differentiated into all these forms and conditions, these gates. She resides outside the Wheel of Life. She resides in the Moon, as you see it depicted above Yama's wheel. That's the Silver Light realm.

"I guide you, anybody, all humans at death, if they wish, through this bewildering *Bardo* labyrinth of forms and manifestations, back through all the gates and guardians, to their creator. That's where the Silver Light comes from; it is Her Light, and I am Her emissary. In a sense I don't do anything, or have to either. My role or placement in the hierarchy of consciousness is itself the guide, like a light. My position is hierophantic, showing the Holy Light. That's what Maui was doing 'inside' the

Great Mother. Turning on the lights! The Great Mother is Isis, Demeter, Hine, the Moon, and all the names people in the world have assigned the Mother of all forms and of the original unified consciousness.

"I help you achieve the view of this landscape, to see it as a Light temple. I provide the map. I annotate the map as we walk through it. I am its docent. To appreciate Yama's *Bhavachakra* wheel or *Hine-nui-te-po*'s body as a template. The whole Underworld is a sacred site, a numinous node in a landscape of Light. That's our expedition with the Green Knight: to see all of it and make changes.

"I don't want you to form the impression the Underworld is a formidable temple of Light with challenges outside your own framework of experience. I will let you in on a secret. The Underworld is also you, everything below the crown. Stand there and look down: that's the human Underworld, body and chakras. That's why you should exit the body through the crown chakra at death. Then you are Yama, glaring over the *Bhavachakra* physical body you just left. That's the form of the human Underworld; the *Bardo* is just a larger version of it.

"You want to be the ferocious Yama, wide-awake above the *Bhavachakra* which he holds like a shield. You want to be like Yama surveying the Underworld from above. You climb up out of the Underworld to the gateway to the Upper World, which, confusingly, has been called the Underworld, which people think means below. It is below in the sense that the Underworld means your body and self, from the top of the head to the feet—that's below, that's under—but the world's Underworld lies *above* this body and self, accessed through the crown chakra, and then you keep going *up* to the Upper World."

"You can see all this in the Tarot image of the Hanged Man," said Blaise. "A man hangs upside down from the Tree of Life, his head just short of the ground. Some people say this man is a picture of Odin, the Norse high god and world creator. Sure, why not, but the more important point is that it says the crown chakra was created last; the root chakra, closest to the tree, was first. But this becomes our road map and set of expedition instructions. You start at the crown chakra, the last extruded energy center of this cosmogonic form, its perfection, and then you turn around and enter the Underworld inside this man.

"You might as well call the Hanged Man our pal, Yama: you enter through his head and climb up through his Underworld form, his *Bhavachakra*, to reach the circumference from which his form hangs. That is the Exit from the phylogeny. Take the image of Yama and the *Bhavachakra* and flip it. Put it next to a picture of the Tarot's Hanged Man card. They are equivalent disclosures. The Hanged Man's upside-down body is the same as the wheel of the Six Worlds. Yama looming above the wheel is the same as the illuminated head of the Hanged Man. It is consciousness lucidly taking stock of its actual condition. And both are the same as the Green Knight cavalierly carrying his own talking head. Yama, his head under the *Bhavachakra*, is the front door *up* into the Underworld. You go through his head, his wide-awake awareness *up* into the *Bhavachakra*."

"You pass through his body, all the messy internal organs of the *Bhavachakra*, the *Bardo*, and exit through his feet," said Tommy, gleefully. "Don't think the feet aren't sexy. Yama stands in the Moon, so you pass up through his body and exit all of it through his feet and enter the Moon realm of Silver Light. That gives new meaning to the saying, 'boots on the ground.' The Moon is the ground of Being, and Yama's karmically washed-clean feet are standing right on it. It's funnier than that. You don't pass through Yama's glowering head. You travel in it, as it, through the bewildering *Bardo*. It is a conveyance, a tour

bus. Then you, in Yama's head, with his fierce awareness, exit the *Bardo* for the feet."

"Well put. From this place of lucid cognition you retrace your cosmogonic steps back to the origin. That's why the journey through the Underworld begins at the crown, and that's why the Tibetans remind the dying to extract their consciousness through their heads as they enter the *Bardo*. Enter the Underworld through the crown. Otherwise, through any lower chakra, you'll enter the Underworld already inside it and be immediately disoriented. Exit through the crown then you can view the Underworld from outside it first, then enter it reasonably oriented. Paradoxically, your destination is a place above the crown. The realm of Great Hine of the Night is a step above and beyond the crown. It contains the whole world and Man but in a state before either was differentiated into chakras, which is to say, it's a hierarchy of energy and consciousness states.

"This means, if you think about it, the Hanged Man is actually an oroboric man, his feet touching his head: his place of origin and destination are the same. This is why I always encouraged people at the Blue Room institute to cultivate their crown chakras, to gain full use of this marvelous research tool because it is essential for making a successful, fact-finding journey through the Underworld."

At this point, I will admit, these explanations seemed beyond my understanding. Merlin realized this, and said, "Don't worry. This will become clear as our expedition proceeds. Maps make more sense after the journey. Let me show you what Blaise meant by exiting the body through the crown chakra at death, and what happens when you do not. Look over there, if you will."

Merlin directed our attention to what resembled a large gate topped by an arch. At first I almost laughed when I saw it because it looked cartoonish and I figured I was not seeing it clearly. Humans in vaporous form were bouncing off the sides of the gate like kicked soccer balls missing the net of the goal. Only a few were making it through the entrance. These souls proceeded directly to designated processing areas, like we had already seen, people in their auric chambers watching the movies of their lives, first the etheric then the astral clips. The ones who didn't looked like astronauts who had been outside their spaceships trying to fix a damaged part but had been knocked off into space, their tethers ripped away. They were drifting and tumbling in a scary free-fall.

It should not surprise the reader if I confess at first I did not understand what I was watching. Then Merlin directed us to follow a few souls from the beginning. I realized by "beginning" Merlin meant the moment of their dying. There were many to chose from. People seemed to be dying by the truckloads. I saw a woman die of a miscarriage followed by massive hemorrhaging. At first she had been outside her body; her female human form was huddled above her head. When the baby was delivered dead and her uterus started bleeding copiously she rushed back into her body down to the level of her second chakra.

Then her body died and she was stuck in her second chakra, the energy and consciousness center that corresponded with her uterus and its heavy bleeding. She exited her body through this low-lying chakra, as if ejected out of her lower abdomen, and then I saw the problem with this style of exit. In the same manner in which a newborn baby is covered with placental residue, so was her exiting soul enveloped with the unprocessed emotional contents, images, spirits, and other energy configurations of her second chakra. She took this confusing residue with her into the *Bardo* and it influenced everything she saw.

She saw the *Bardo* through this emotional placenta of undigested experience, and as a result she saw the *Bardo* poorly, inaccurately, and it was largely a product, a shadow projection, of these unprocessed emotional contents, and a scary one. She entered the after-death state bewildered, frightened, in pain and sorrow. She didn't know where she was, what had happened to her, or where her baby was. Her second chakra and its priorities framed her viewing.

My attention was next drawn to a hospital bed. A man about 75 lay in it. He looked very ill, deathly pale. I understood he was dying of liver cancer. He was angry about his fate, and of course just as his liver was riddled with cancer so was his third chakra, his fire, will, and lower ego center, possessed by anger. All the misdirected fire that had taken the form of anger was exploding in him. A lifetime of anger now surrounded him like a wildfire consuming a forest. He was angry that he was dying, and he was angry at everything that had angered him. His thwarted will was the fire, and it was burning up his liver like dry firewood.

It was like watching an explosion in slow-motion. I saw him propelled out of his body through his solar plexus region like a cannonball. His face was glaring. He entered the after-death state in a condition of unresolved rage and resentment, and his fire was burning through all the issues, crimes, offenses, hurts, and lists of unforgiven trespassers his third chakra had meticulously maintained for decades. His soul exited his body through his third chakra wrapped in the unyielding warrant list of the 100 most wanted villains. He wanted justice. He wanted vengeance, retribution, payback. It is understating things to say his view of the *Bardo* was seriously beclouded. He could not see past his own anger and all the "causes" and justifications for it. He bounced off the gate like a poorly kicked ball and went tumbling into the dark, cursing it.

These examples were chastening. Next I saw a woman in meditation. She looked about

50, not an age at which you would expect to find yourself dying. But she was. It looked like an immune disorder that was affecting all her body. Her hair had turned grey and looked a bit scraggly and her face was drawn, but in her eyes burned a determination to stay awake, focused, to die on her own terms. The bulk of her attention was focused in her forehead, in the sixth chakra. Her body grew fainter, less distinct as the life-force seeped irreversibly out of it.

I saw her collecting every molecule of her awareness from her chakras, starting at the root. It was as if she were an usher encouraging dawdling members of the theater audience, the show over, to get up, head for the exits, and leave the building. Wisps and swirls of her consciousness were rising as if on a psychic elevator. She repeated the procedure at each chakra, moving it upwards through her body to reach the place of *Bardo* embarkation at the crown chakra.

She extracted a great quantity of psychic vapor from her heart chakra, then when she arrived at her sixth chakra, ostensibly the command seat of this operation, she gathered herself up and a great cloud of vapor rose to the crown. The six chakras below the crown looked withered and desiccated like autumn leaves in November, dried up and awaiting burial by the first snowfall. The physical body's chakras were finished for this lifetime. They had done their work. This vapor cloud rose above her head like a well-formed sphere and went steadily upward, like a spaceship powerfully exiting the Earth's gravity field. It went straight through the gate like a perfectly kicked soccer ball. She got a goal.

I watched what happened to these three souls once they got here. The first two, the woman hemorrhaging and the man livid in anger, had to be constrained and cajoled the way you would comfort and reassure a child woken suddenly by a nightmare at 2 a.m. These two souls would eventually be settled to sleep for a while; when they eventually woke up they would be better able to handle their new circumstances though they would still be wrapped up in their own contents.

The meditating woman went straight to sleep, like you would take a luxurious afternoon's nap, all worldly cares abandoned. The next step for all three was a trip to the movie theater, but I knew without a doubt the meditating woman would watch the film clips with more equanimity and would probably derive more meaning and insight from them, like a seasoned film critic who knew how movies were put together, or ought to be, than the other two who would likely spend their time carping and complaining about the lousy film.

Next I saw an old man lying in a bed surrounded by his family. He must be a grandfather, I thought, judging by the range in age of those attending him. Their love for him and their imminent sorrow at his passing were evident. His Higher Self stood behind him as tall as the two-story house his bedroom lay in. He inhaled sharply, then sighed, closed his eyes, and his vaporous soul started to seep out of his chest in strands and rivulets. Immediately, the outstretched hands of all his family members clutched at him, first trying to force this vapor back into his chest then holding "him" in his vaporous form as with sticky tentacles. This was their love for him refusing to let him go, and it created logistical problems. It was like a halt called to a jet pulling back from the boarding gate.

His Higher Self was ready to escort him to the initial *Bardo* processing area, but the elongated hands of Light from the bereaved family members were holding him back, keeping him Earthbound even though his physical body was no longer viable. The grandfather was torn between two incompatible obligations, not to desert his family who loved him and to undergo the requisite death protocols and potentially advance on his soul's path of evolution. He was trying to slip away and finish dying and remain in the bedroom at the same time.

Images of his family members and pictures from their individual emotional lives now girt his vaporous form all round like a pictorial atmosphere. It was confusing to him, and their emotions, coupled with the sticky elongated hands, kept him stuck. Even when he eventually freed himself, his post-death review would require him to winnow through the cloying atmosphere of their pain pictures and separate them from his own. His own were now complicated by bearing the emotional weight of the ones deposited in his space by his family.

"Merlin," Edward asked, "I was wondering if this expedition was a second chance on your part to restructure the death world and its requirements more favorably to humans. I'm thinking of how the Polynesians said Maui entered the dangerous body of Great Hine of the Night with the intention of upgrading the death experience. The Maori said a man who had just died would find himself creeping through the dark womb of the Sleeping Mother of Death, but Maui saw this as degrading to human dignity and often without good result.

"The Polynesian sentiment seems to say the after-death experience should be quick and streamlined, and life should be renewed as quickly, imitating the manner in which the Moon grows from new to full in a matter of only a few weeks, cyclically renewed every month. Or death should be like the Sun: it sets in the evening, rises in the morning, and you can depend on this cycle. Why shouldn't death be like this, a speedy renewal of life, whether it's in another living body or in a higher plane? The Polynesians said this motivated Maui.

"You helped me understand that possibly one aspect of the death protocols that diminished human dignity was human ignorance of the rules. Most people get here unacquainted with the procedures, the landscape, the guardians, with essentially no idea of what to do or what is expected of them. You find yourself creeping through this huge, dark body of an unknown goddess populated with strange or frightening spirits and incomprehensible obligations.

"As Maui, you were accompanied by your brothers in the form of birds, and they journeyed with you in your quest to wrest the secret of immortality from the great goddess of the Night. You wanted to find it; you knew it was inside her. You wanted to rip it out and bestow it triumphantly upon humans. Unfortunately, according to the Maori story, your mission failed. A bird tipped off the goddess and you barely escaped from her body with your life intact."

Merlin was chuckling. "You're right. Didn't look so good on my résumé. The story sounds like I was trying to get people through the red-tape of after-death processing faster so they could return to the brightness of the sunlit world. But it wasn't that. The indignity was how souls are quickly caught by the Wheel of Life and precipitately spun back into the human world, still ignorant of conditions. The real Sun brightness was not of the physical human world, but of the celestial realms, the place where the souls came from. The immortality Maui sought was permanent release from this wheel, to not have to continuously reincarnate like the endless Moon cycles, to get souls back to that eternal Sun. Here of course Moon means the Earth's satellite that does have monthly cycles.

"Maui was trying to show humans the way out of this treadmill of life, death, and rebirth. The indignity was that of humans getting continuously sucked back into the gravity field of human incarnation from their lacking the necessary facts. I wanted to help people navigate the death-realm intelligently, equipped with facts. Here is the landscape, the guardians, here are the rules. Here's what you have to do to not die, to have immortality, which means here is how to get off the Wheel of Life and not have to compulsively reincarnate again. Or as you put it, Blaise, here's how to escape that vexed human phylogeny."

"The simplest interpretation of that story is that Maui, our Merlin, is the pre-eminent guide through the Underworld," said Blaise. "He knows the terrain thoroughly. He is the *Bardo* hierophant, whether you call him Maui or Anubis. He has sympathy for the human plight, for human ignorance. He has the cure. He willingly guides souls through this tricky domain. He would like to facilitate their immortality. So, Merlin, are you going to tell us now your revision plans?"

"Surely you can't expect everyone to read the *Tibetan Book of the Dead* before they get here," said Matthew. He was obviously teasing Merlin a little. "That's the deluxe *Bardo* packaged tour, the premier, enhanced travel itinerary."

"Yes, it's time, and I will tell you what the upgrade plans are. We are instructing Charon to act more like a mystagogue than merely a ferryman. We know him as Charon of the Bridge. He will offer souls a tutorial before crossing.

"You won't understand this mechanism until I clarify some of the topography of this place, and to do that, I will have to mix a few different descriptions together because they all provide clues but not the full picture. Let's start with Charon. He is the ferryman who transports the newly dead across the River Acheron, which means sorrow and woe, what most people feel when they die. Though Charon is usually associated with the River Styx, or Hate; that is a late alteration. His river is the Acheron. This was correctly stated up until Virgil.

"He wrote that the newly dead were ferried by Charon across the Acheron into the Underworld and that the Acheron was one of the five rivers in Erebus, which meant 'deep darkness and shadow'. Everybody now thinks

it is the River Styx. That river and the Cocytus were said to spring from the Acheron, the principal river in Tartarus, and the Phlegethon emptied into the Acheron as well.

"The Greeks, by the way, used the names Hades, Erebus, and Tartarus interchangeably to point to the Underworld, though they also gave these regions some functional differences. Tartarus had five rivers. This river—you know it is not really a river, right, that it is a current of Light?—divides the human mortal world from the after-death realm, the Underworld. It's a firm boundary, an energy gradient one does not normally cross, or want to, until the time of dying.

"The classical tradition says the name Charon means 'of keen gaze.' It evokes an image of a fierce ferryman whose eyes are fiery, flashing, or feverish. His ardent, passionate gaze suggests either the anger of death or the sharpness and lucidity of his view of the Underworld. The Greeks hinted that Charon was the glowering Yama in disguise. Either way, people were afraid of him. They were expected to pay him for their passage which is why those friends of the deceased who survived his passing put a coin in the dead person's mouth.

"Was it to pay for their passage or to placate the intimidating Charon? This coin was called Charon's *obol*. Originally, it was made of copper, bronze, or iron, but the Athenians used silver as the metal. That is a clue, don't you think, to the soul's final destination. The *obol* was to pay passage for the soul's trip to the Moon, the Silver realm. Charon was depicted as rough, unkempt, an Athenian seaman wearing reddish-brown tattered clothing; his right hand holds his ferryman's long staff, his left is extended to help the newly dead to climb aboard his ferry. Later, Charon became viewed as a mean-spirited, even demonic, figure.

"Let's add another element. The Greeks described a ferry *across* the river, but the Persians told of a bridge *over* the water. It was the *Cinvat* Bridge, the Bridge of the Decider or Requiter or Separator. The Bridge of Judgement, the bean-shaped bridge, the sifting bridge. It had lots of names. It was a perilous bridge; if your soul was contaminated, it would appear narrow, hard to traverse; if your soul was pure, the bridge would seem broad, expansive, easy to cross.

"All souls at death must cross this bridge, just as the Greeks said they had to hop on board the cranky, ill-mannered Charon's ferry. Cross the bridge or take the ferry: they are interchangeable images. Three divinities guard the approach to the bridge, which is to say, they accompany the newly dead to it. These were Sraosha, which means Obedience; Mithra, or Covenant; and Rashnu, which means Justice. Charon is a partial, distorted picture of the Angel Sraosha. Yes, Charon or Sraosha is a high level, even exalted, celestial spirit, truly angelic. He knows the way across the river; he knows how to get you across the bridge.

"Sraosha's name also denotes Observance and the Voice of Conscience. He is the teacher of the *Daena*, a name indicating the soul in its variable state of purity or corruption. The important point is that Sraosha was one of the six *Amesha Spenta*s, or Bounteous Immortals, created by the thought of Ahura-Mazda, their name for God. Sraosha is the only one of the three Angels (the 'birds' or 'brothers' who accompanied Maui) who walks with the soul across the bridge; therefore, this *Amesha Spenta* is the designated mystagogue for the dead. The Persians never said he was cranky or rude; that was the Greeks' amendment.

"Sraosha, according to the *Avesta*, is mighty, the incarnate word of reason and truth. He is holy, the first in all of the Creation to adore Ahura-Mazda, the great god; he is the Lord of Ritual and humanity's perpetual protector and, note this, his mentor, Ahura-Mazda or Ohrmazd, "Mighty Lord of Wisdom," is the top god of Zoroastrianism, seen as the Supreme Being and sometimes as the Christ, the epitome of the pure Sun. Now that's a right and proper ferryman.

"Humanity lives constantly under Sraosha's guardianship, and his vigil is never interrupted by sleep as he guards humanity against the *Druj*, the Spirit of Lies. He always returns victorious in his battles against evil and the adversaries of wrath. His epithet is *Darshi.dru*, meaning 'of the strong Ahuric mace.' So he's the guy on the boat, the guy on the bridge—either way: he's your mystagogue."

"You're saying the ferryman's boat is the same as Sraosha's bridge?" I said with enthusiasm. I was reveling in the connections Merlin was making for us.

"Yes. They are equivalent or interchangeable images. Both get you over the water, which is the vibrational gradient or 'river' between the two worlds. You could say it's the treacherous no-man's land between the crown, based in the body, and the eighth chakra, which lies outside the body and above it. The bridge or ferry represent the passageway from the crown to the eighth chakra."

"And Sraosha is a more accurate, more richly nuanced, picture of the ferryman Charon whom the Greeks painted as too dark, nasty, and grim?"

"Correct again. Nobody would expect Charon to explain the niceties of the Underworld to the newly dead. The Greeks made you feel lucky if he didn't bite your head off if you even looked at him wrong or if your coin was dented. Sraosha is there, at the bridge, to explain the Underworld to the soul. The trouble was only the initiates, those already prepared in the Mysteries, could understand the explanation. It was like the long, unabridged version of the Eleusinian Mysteries. The realities of this strange world overwhelmed the unprepared mind; all most people could discern was that Sraosha was bright, a great angel of terrific Light and understanding but speaking a foreign language, standing at the transition point between what was familiar and what was terrifyingly unfamiliar.

"The *Tibetan Book of the Dead*, as it's called in English, says that after the requisite 84 hours of wake-time, consciousness is gathered up from the chakras. The soul is presented with the ground luminosity or clear light, the *Rigpa*, of one's essential nature. This is a pure revelation of the true state of consciousness. It is the clear light of Mind, of Buddha-Nature, of the basic ground of reality.

"If you get it, understand what it is, the precious gift of insight given you, you can get off the Wheel of Life right then. Very few manage this; it is too formidable. This is the soul getting a view of the naked Sraosha, which means the Angel of Obedience revealed in its essential truth, all its energy conditions revealed. You skip the explanations and go straight to *satori*. They are implicit in you now. But the disclosure is so blinding, so sudden, and for most, so utterly unexpected, it confounds them, and cannot be assimilated. It's like you look at Charon right in his craggy, cranky face and, shocked, you fall off the boat.

"It is a terrifically bright Light, a blinding flash of Light, followed by confusion. We had intended this as the cue-card for the discerning soul to get with the program. We have since come to the conclusion it is too steep a gradient; it is wasted on most. That's why we are going to adjust Charon's role.

"He will still accompany the soul to the bridge, but rather than flashing the incomprehensible Light of naked reality that mostly confounds and bewilders people, he will reduce its intensity and speed by 50 per cent and he will present a hologram of the complete death world, its rules, procedures, and opportunities. It will be a map of the Underworld, its processes, mechanisms, and guardians. The newly dead will view this topographical presentation at his own rate, and he will not finish crossing the bridge until he is certain he has a clear picture of it. He can dial up the intensity of this Clear Light as he wishes during this tutorial. You can balance *Rigpa* revelation with absorption of rules."

Padmasambhava, or Merlin, in his *Bardo Thödol* text called the first stage of entering the *Bardo* the *Chikkai Bardo*. Here, immediately at death, you are presented with the "fundamental Clear Light." Charon turns to you full-on, but maybe the impression is of a mouthful of all his teeth suddenly shining at you. This used to always spook Agatha Christie; she was always commenting in her books on the scariness of people when they reveal all their teeth, like when they smile. She found that quietly horrific. Maybe Charon has too many white teeth, and it's the teeth that scare the daylights out of the freshly deceased souls.

If you recognize the truth of this revelation of Clear Light, you will achieve the Unborn *Dharmakaya*, the Truth body of reality, the Tibetans say. This means you win Buddhahood or enlightenment and can skip the rest of the *Bardo* passage, including the teeth. You will have achieved spiritual emancipation; all *samsaric* bonds of illusion are broken at once and you are awakened into Reality.

In terms of what Merlin had just told us that means staring Charon in the face and getting what he was about, or, more friendly, accepting the fullness of Sraosha's metaphysical tutorial. Either way, you skip the boat or bridge phase, avoid the cataclysm of falling off the boat into the churning river, get the *Rigpa*.

In the setting face-to-face with the Clear Light you recognize Charon or Sraosha. It's just different ways of describing the same introductory experience, the overture. You die, then immediately you meet Charon the ferryman or Sraosha, the counselor of the soul represented as the *Daena* or beautiful maiden. You are in the boat or on the bridge; it's the same place, as I understand Merlin.

"Yes, the same place," said Blaise, picking up on my thoughts, "and the *Cinvat* Bridge begins at the crown chakra and arcs *upwards* to the eighth chakra. That is the realm of the Great Mother, Isis of the Silver Light, the great form factory, the place where all the Light temples are made. Qabalists call it *Binah*. The after-death process begins just beyond the crown chakra when you get on the bridge or into the boat. The *Bardo* passage is mostly your time on the bridge. The long night of the soul on the Bridge of the Decider. That's your *Bardo* trip. This is where you balance your accounts, and where most of the confusion enters into the picture. The goal is to reach the eighth chakra, the Underworld proper, which will appear as a coliseum or circular sports stadium many miles wide."

"What about the business of the dogs?" I asked. "The Underworld entrance is always associated with dogs in myth. Hades had his Cerberus with three heads, and Yama had two insatiable dogs with four eyes and wide nostrils. They wandered everywhere in the vicinity of the Underworld entrance. Why?"

"That's a reference to Canis Major, the constellation of the Greater Dog," said Blaise. "It's a mythic picture about the crown chakra. That is the location of Shiva's flaming hoop, the *tiruvasi*, before which he dances on his four legs. Hindu psychics attributed Shiva to the star Sirius at the throat of the Dog and called Shiva the Hound of Heaven. In practical terms, Shiva is the Dog of myth. The two or three dogs associated with him denote Sirius and its two companion stars, which astronomers have reported. The hologram of that sits on your head. It's droll. Everyone has a dog or three perched on top of their head. That's Sirius.

"The flaming hoop is the gateway into or out of the Underworld. It is the crown chakra, and the rippling, dancing flames are the crown petals lit in gold flame. The *tiruvasi* is the fiery surface of the severed head the Green Knight holds. You pass *up* through this hoop and pass the dogs to enter your personal Underworld, your body and its seven chakras from head to base of the spine.

"You pass upward from the crown through this hoop and enter the greater, original Underworld. The flaming hoop is the transition zone from crown chakra to upwards. Shiva dancing before the flaming hoop is you with your clairvoyant consciousness raised to stand on top of the crown chakra, amidst its thousand flaming petals. You must pass through this space guarded by the dogs, or Shiva, which, as I said, is a picture of your crown chakra, where the expedition starts. The dogs are place-markers, showing you where to start from, but the dog also hints at Anubis, the jackal-headed *Duat* guide. The dog will guide you through the Underworld, faithfully escort you from your body. You meet Anubis just past the flaming hoop and he guides you through the labyrinthine experience of the *Bardo* and up to the Moon, the realm of Isis.

"The image hints at galactic structure too, for the star Sirius and the Canis Major constellation dance at the transition zone, the *tiruvasi,* between universal space and the Milky Way Galaxy, the Underworld at the level of a galaxy. The galactic body and your human body—do you see: they are both Underworlds. You'll find Shiva, Sirius, the dog, Hound of Heaven, dancing and barking at this site, whether it's the top of your human head or the crown chakra of the galaxy.

"The yogis say Shiva is a swinging door between the manifest and unmanifest, between the five manifest stages or styles of consciousness, called the *skandahs*, and the Absolute Light and the unconditioned state of being. That would be *Rigpa*, the Clear Light, or Buddha Nature. You pass *through* Shiva. The dogs may appear fierce or challenge you because your attachment to this manifest, conditioned state of consciousness is strong, usually unquestioned."

"Our intention is to have this meeting on the boat or bridge be the inverse of the River Lethe veil of concealment the soul undergoes upon incarnating," said Merlin. "In the old system of protocols, you are born knowing nothing about your previous spiritual state, and you die being just as uninformed about the world you have entered and what is required of you. Now Charon or Sraosha will offer each newly dead soul a full tutorial, in slow motion and with as much repetition or explanation or reiteration of essential points as that soul requires. We want everyone entering the Underworld to be briefed on conditions here. The appalling degree of ignorance that has characterized the death process to date has introduced too much entropy and degeneration into the Underworld."

"Merlin is entirely right," said Philomena. "It is asking too much of newly dead souls to comprehend the Clear Light of the *Chikkai Bardo*. It strikes nearly everyone dumb, like being struck by lightning or waking up from a concussion. The Greek image of Charon is an inhospitable, churlish one; you're not going to expect a metaphysical tutorial on the *Bardo* from that uncouthly presented figure. The *Bardo* is like being presented with an enormous credit card bill for expenses you mostly did not know you had accrued and getting it while concussed and hallucinating. And receiving this news under the blinding brightness of police interrogation lights. You could say it is the shocking disclosure of the credit card itself. It's as if you just spent an amnesiac two weeks frolicking in Las Vegas. You charged all sorts of expenses to your credit card and you remember

none of it. You even forgot you had a credit account, a running tab at the bar for drinks.

"Unconditioned consciousness is Light, the truth of yourself when you strip off the persona. No wonder most people get sucked back onto the wheel again. They completely lack the necessary frame of reference to understand this place. They have gone to sleep while alive, so they arrive here similarly somnolent. It's easier, it feels safer, to continue sleeping; waking up is like the explosive end of the world. Most people, understandably, shy away from that."

"That's right," Merlin responded. "From now on everyone gets Charon's tutorial on the boat or Sraosha's seminar on the bridge before they go further. He will regulate the disclosure of the Clear Light like a dimmer switch, calibrating the brightness exactly to the comprehension level of each soul. Starting today, the newly dead will be presented with a detailed diagram and site map of the Underworld. Sraosha will explain every aspect of it, gates, guardians, tests. The mechanism of karma and the protocols of recompense and balance. Putting on a persona to hide the Light and divesting yourself of that mask to reveal the Light. Sraosha will help each soul remember their original briefing with the Supreme Being which took place before their first incarnation into the human phylogeny.

"They will remember their agreements and resolutions. They will remember they asked to be allowed into the incarnational merry-go-round, that they vowed to achieve liberation one day and to bring the fruits of that illumination back to the Creator. Probably the biggest revelation Sraosha will help them have is to realize they are an alive, evolving unit of consciousness, and that this aliveness straddles both the *Bardo* and the living phenomenal world. Here you are, you are alive, and aliveness means you are conscious, and what is this condition called consciousness upon which you are standing right now? Your consciousness is born with you in a human body and it comes back with you in the *Bardo* when you drop that body. It is the place of continuity in you.

"That's why most people fear death, because they fear life even more. The fear realizing the tremendous responsibility it is to be little breathing holograms of the Supreme Being, seemingly set off on their own to achieve an arcane purpose against great odds. Fear of death is identical with the shock of realizing you are alive which means you are aware—you are consciousness. It's not so much a matter of pulling out the rug from underneath you, but realizing you are standing on this rug, and this rug is woven of consciousness, of the Clear Light.

"People tend to shut down that perception, then they forget they are alive points of awareness, and then everything else that is darkening and obscuring follows. They arrive here on the bridge in a state of spiritual blindness and ignorance. I use ignorance in the Buddhist sense, that of being oblivious to the true conditions of reality and the requirements of consciousness: uninformed.

"So we will change this factor by 50 per cent. Sraosha will be 50 per cent less dazzling and provide 50 per cent more explanation of terms and conditions. We want to preserve some of the shock value of this disclosure because it can be liberating and a useful catalyst to proceed further and wake up even more richly. But we don't want to shock you so much you pass out, as if lightning-struck.

"Souls will be told, and Sraosha will make sure each one understands this fully, that they are entering a landscape in which *interior* conditions of their own consciousness will be presented *outwardly* as if they comprised a world itself. Charon, instead of glowering at you with an air of petulance and disapproval, will explain the mechanics of the *Bardo* to you like the best of private tutors. Your tendencies

and obscurations, your quirks and shadows, will be dramatized outside you as if they have separate, sometimes threatening, existence, and the challenge for you as the soul is to recognize all this is yourself, to not resist it, and to see through it, to recognize its essential voidness, and thus become free of it.

"It is a performance piece with bells and whistles and demons and angels. The special effects are stupendous, the CGI parts awesome, Charon will say. The raw material is your karma, the accrual over time of the results of your deeds in body and mind, thought and emotion. The Christians would call this 'sin' but that is too simplistic a term and does not accommodate the multi-lifetime balance sheet. Here is a picture of what you have made of reality, your assumptions and fears, Charon will say to you as he rows the boat. He'll be on his best behavior.

"It's surprising, but a great many people do not realize they are dead, that they have just exited their bodies and have entered the after-death realm. In our original approach, Liberation through Hearing, we had a monk or teacher read the *Bardo Thödol* text to the newly dead, sitting in proximity to the inert body. This person would 'vividly impress' upon the transiting soul the stages and mechanics of the after-death process and the symptoms of being in the *Bardo*.

"This might have worked with well-prepared monks who had spent their lives fine-tuning their 'consciousness principle,' as we called it then, but we found for the bulk of people who had no preparation in this field that they failed to hear us. They couldn't and they didn't hear us. They were too confused and frightened. Reading the *Bardo Thödol* aloud to them would be as comprehensible as reciting *Finnegans Wake* to somebody who was a cheap drunk after downing eight beers. Most likely they were already laid out on the floor, nearly comatose."

"Or it's like a movie director calling out instructions to an actor who was deaf, blind, recently concussed, in shock, and hypoglycemic, staggering about the stage, knocking over all the props and mumbling to himself," added Blaise.

"And I hear the voidness is a bitch," said Matthew, a smirk on his face.

This got Merlin laughing. "Well said. Matthew is referring to the moment when the Clear Light is revealed and complete spiritual liberation is possible. You experience a universal voidness. This emptiness can seem disastrous to consciousness used to occupying a field of objects and references and a self. Suddenly that is gone. Voidness is worse than death, it seems. It is hard for the soul to realize this voidness is actually the dawning of pure Buddha Nature.

"Your consciousness, your intellect, your Mind, everything that has constituted for you your separate selfhood, is dissolved instantly, leaving only this voidness. You are so accustomed to having your consciousness filled with objects, constantly processing the outer and inner world. Now there is nothing.

"Your consciousness is now devoid of all limitations and obscurations that arise from the contact of the primordial pure consciousness with matter. You don't know yourself without those obscurations. You desperately want them back even though they were the cause of a lifetime of suffering and ignorance. For most people even if we got through to them that this was a good thing, the goal of the process, this dawning of the pure original radiance of Reality and Truth, they would look at us with horror or disbelief, unable to dispel the impression that this bizarre, unprecedented vacuity was positively the worst thing possible, and the sooner it was finished and they could leave the better."

"I didn't mind the voidness, but to tell the truth I didn't get it," said Tommy. "I didn't understand what it meant, or where I was. It's the sudden change of context that throws you off. I didn't mind being dead. I did it on purpose. But this being dead wasn't what I expected. I was no longer there. It's like standing on a rug and it gets pulled out from under you. Then the floor is yanked, then the house, then your body, your thoughts, feelings, everything. You don't know where you stand any more. In fact, you are not a 'you' any more, at least not in a way you'd recognize. Awareness still is, but it has no brand name.

"It's the suddenness of the change that threw me, and the fact that everything was reversed or turned inside out. I was no longer facing a world of details, and I was no longer a person of details, a teenager disliking his diabetes Type I condition, disaffected with high school and his so-called peer group. The empty quiet behind all that was now in the forefront. It was everything. God, I would have killed for an obscuration. Anything to fill up this void.

"This was massively disorienting. I wasn't prepared for it. After a while, I adjusted to things. I began to realize, possibly it was a remembering, that this is the original condition of consciousness, when we were first created by God. We are so used to the carnival show of physical life that memory of this vanishes. You've been watching TV all day long and somebody turns it off, takes it away. Then when the carnival spectacle dissolves, we are completely disoriented. That is the genuine disorientation, entering the illusory world. Coming back here is the orientation. We just get it all backwards. Here, the intellect or knowing mind is suddenly empty, void, with no compulsion or desire or in fact the means to know the world or register itself as a fact in reality. The slate is wiped clean.

"You'll have to get Sraosha to tell the newly dead this is their original condition and not some clever dick's idea of a horror show to entertain the freshly dead. You know what else? I rather like not having to confront the world any more, to keep up this dichotomy of me versus the world, me against the rest of reality. In this state, you don't keep up the adversarial nature of me versus everything. In this condition of pure consciousness, *Rigpa*, there is only Reality, a unified field of empty awareness. It is not aware of any*thing* because no thing is separate from *Rigpa*. All of reality is this unified, singular field of awareness.

"They explained *Rigpa* to me after I settled down. Knowledge of the ground of being, original wakefulness, primordial purity, the unity of awareness and emptiness, clarity and emptiness, a nondualistic state, no grasping at objects by a subject. No subject. Just one reality. What a cool trip that is. I said I liked it so much send me a dozen *Rigpa*s. Get me a teeshirt that says 'I'm nondualistic!'"

"Yes, a cool trip, but one that many people sleep through," said Merlin. "The meeting with Charon in the boat or the encounter with Sraosha on the bridge happens very quickly. Often when a person dies they go directly into a sleep state and remain there for a time until they are ready to wake up in this new realm where the first order of business is to review the etheric and astral body tapes. They may glimpse the brightness of Charon, feel the impingement of the Clear Light of Pure Radiance, then quickly fall asleep and then forget it later. What we're doing now is slowing down that encounter moment or stretching it out; either way, the intent is to give the newly dead person a better chance to see it, then, once they've seen it, they can have Charon's full tutorial on conditions.

"But here is the important part. If the soul gets this phase, understands what the revelation of Charon is, realizes the disclosure of *Rigpa* or Clear Light is the statement of the true condition of their existence, it makes everything else easier. Cuts through enormous amounts of red tape, circumvents protocols, potentially obviates the obligation of reviewing the life records as the soul comprehends them in a flash and dissolves them in a salvific fire of recognition.

"Well, one can only hope. We always have high expectations going into this. People need to know the *Bardo* has a short form, an express lane. At the least, they should be able to process their life records with greater clarity. Let's watch a few new arrivals and see how these changed conditions play out."

We observed a boy of about 16 come through. He died from leukemia. He knew he was passing over and had been preparing himself for it for weeks. He surrendered his body and extracted himself, his awareness, from its perishing form. We watched the vapor seep then gather itself outside his body at his head. As soon as it was clear of his head, the boy saw Charon the Ferryman. For a moment he saw him in the traditional somber guise of boatman with pike. I realized though the classical Greeks never forgot about Charon, they did lose track of his meaning, and for the Greeks Charon was merely a grim ferryman.

Apparently, they no longer saw past this rustic guise to his role as Sraosha, nor did they see through Sraosha's angelic form the dawning Clear Light of *Rigpa*. It seemed obvious to me the problem was basically this dawning was too intense and happened too fast, and before souls could understand what it was, it was over, and they were shuttled off to the next round of afterlife processing. Souls didn't seem to have enough time to take advantage of this great opportunity. It was too quick, too scary, too confusing, too ungraspable.

We watched this boy's encounter with Charon with great interest. It was like a movie slowed down to a snail's pace. Everything happened slowly. As soon as he registered the presence of Charon, presented as the standard picture, Charon's form started to change. It grew in illumination as if a sun rose inside.

Charon's image morphed into the more celestial and angelic guise of Sraosha.

The boy's Higher Self formed a protective auric bubble out of his outstretched wings around him and counseled him to be calm, not to worry, and to watch. Sraosha took the boy back to that time long ago when he had his first audience with the Supreme Being before undertaking his inaugural human incarnation. Blaise had told me some years ago that the *Zohar* says every soul has this briefing, though few remember it. But remembering, and Blaise said he'd remembered his briefing, it seemed the key to Sraosha's new strategy.

"When you forget your starting point, you usually cannot make sense of everything that happened after that," said Merlin. "That's the big problem. It's like retracing your steps to find out how you got here. You suddenly wake up and find yourself in a strange place. How did I ever come to be standing here? So Sraosha is taking this boy back to his point of origination, to his first briefing. That will give him a context, a justification, an explanation for all that follows."

Then Sraosha showed the boy the Tree of the Knowledge of Good and Evil, and the two celestial spirits, Lucifer and Sophia, who maintain this august tree. It was richly hung in fruit on both sides. I knew that was a metaphor, but the intent was to remind the boy that his selections from this tree represented his deployment of the gift of free will and it provided the reason for the life review. One must observe, digest, and make recompense for the effects of these choices. The fruit, the apple on the limbs, Blaise had told me, represented self-awareness of one's separate individuality, one's being-bodies, or "nakedness" in a fundamental sense, in the context of the free-will choice of good or evil actions.

Next the boy was shown the planning room where with his Higher Self he charted his life in

meticulous detail, people he would meet and when, debts to pay and collect, old doors to close for good, new ones to open and explore for the first time. Then he watched as his form was constructed—all seven bodies. He watched as the galaxy and celestial world seemed to be compressed inside these seven concentric spheres of Light, that each was filled with a specific quality of consciousness, like an atmosphere, each with its own chemical composition. These seven bodies resembled a human, at least the physical body, and this human was encased in six spheres of Light. All of these swelled, grew bright, flashed in a supernova explosion without noise, then vanished.

"All of this is you," said Sraosha, "both the form and the emptiness, the bodies and the Clear Light. This is what you have been striving to experience. Eventually, you will master this experience while inhabiting all seven bodies. The form and the voidness are both part of you, part of your truth. You will review the events of your most recent life, both known and unknown to you, daytime and dreamtime, and see this interaction of form and emptiness."

Sraosha revealed the layout of the Underworld for the boy. The life review stations, the *Cinvat* Bridge, the entry into the various zones of the place, what were traditionally called Heaven, Purgatory, and Hell, but which I knew were wildly inaccurate, too literal and too mechanistic to take seriously as presented, the gateways, the guardians, the testers, the *Dhyani* Buddhas, the *Pitrs* or divine Fathers, the whole layout of *Yamapuri*, Yama's Celestial City, and the goal of this topography, the precious silver realm of the Great Mother, the revelation of Demeter, the great form-maker, goal of the Eleusinian Mysteries. He saw all this.

Next Sraosha explained the purpose of each zone of this topography in detail. He explained the sequence by which the boy would transit these various zones, and he explained the overall intent and desired goal of this transit until all was clear. Gradually, the boy realized that his recent life had been a kind of short-term field trip designed to test out a few variables, assess conditions, and gather facts that could be weighed against the more permanent conditions in the Underworld. He began to appreciate that his incarnate life had been, if he were honest with himself, stranger, weirder, and more puzzling than anything here.

This reversal of perspective was what Sraosha was waiting for. It wasn't that Sraosha wanted the boy to regard his recently concluded physical life as bizarre, only that, when framed against the longevity of his Underworld condition, it was experimental, tentative, not a definitive condition or location, only provisional. Now that he was anchored in his truer, older reality he could process it all better. He had returned to his starting point, where he was before he departed on the sojourn, the odyssey, the riotous safari of incarnation, and mistook that for his normal, safe ground of being. He was oriented again.

"That is Sraosha instructing the *Daena*, or soul, as the Persians put it," said Merlin. "But we have upgraded the quality of the tutorial. We have asked Sraosha and his helpers to spend as long as required for every soul until they get it, can state calmly and clearly they are fully briefed on the program, that they have seen the layout of the place and know what's expected. Do you think we should have a multiple-choice quiz at this point to test retention? All the key figures are introduced, their names and functions given, even tips on how to see through their metaphorical guises to their essential conditions. The individual nature of the gates is explained, what each represents, how they comprise the full human. The cosmological human phylogeny is laid out plainly for the soul.

"We have instructed Sraosha to offer the full disclosure of the landscape. The whole merry-go-round of the human phylogeny, and how to get off it so that the soul can get back to the place that represents his original condition before entering form. This may be just a quick visit, a refresher of original conditions, or for some it may be a permanent return, or at least the offer of a long-term residency. If we were Egyptians and I was Anubis again, I would say this is the Temple of Isis and her sister, Nephthys, the place where all forms are created, and therefore, the place where consciousness exists without requiring a form. As we'll see, all the business with gates and guardians and tests pertains to the passage through the infrastructure of the human form, the phylogenetic temple. We're still at the beginning of this expedition, at the stage of the bridge crossing.

"As I mentioned earlier, the accrued confusion of millions of souls entering the Underworld unprepared, bewildered, and frightened has had a deleterious feedback effect on the physical world, creating a contaminated reciprocal loop that in turn has introduced entropy and degradation of the spiritual landscape. A real mess, in other words. Anubis has been complaining about working conditions. It's hard to weigh the heart of the deceased in conditions like this. Too many winds, and people rushing about in a comatose state. I guess that means they are zombies. Asleep yet in crazed motion. Originally, we thought the afterlife passage should be an initiation, and in initiation you tell the candidate nothing. They have to discern what's happening. That just hasn't worked out. The gradient is too steep, the cognitive demand too formidable. Most people fail to get what is happening and are simply miserable."

We watched as Sraosha repeated his disclosure to the boy. He did it slowly, and he watched the boy intently to be certain he was following every step and to look for changes in his auric field to indicate he had comprehended.

We watched as he tentatively explored the landscape of the Underworld. He met his *Daena* on the *Cinvat* Bridge, understood what her condition meant (the *Daena* is either a beautiful or an ugly maiden, depending on the weight of one's unprocessed karmic and shadow areas of consciousness, said the Persian sages), met with the Judges of the Dead or what the Egyptians called the 42 Assessors of Ma'at, looked through all the gates, studied the nature of the guardians, and passed through this realm into the Land of the Silver Light, for that is what it looked like from here, a realm of brilliant silver illumination, fires, and angels. In this silvery realm, the boy no longer had a recognizable form, yet he was aware.

I need to clarify this unusual term from Persian mysticism. *Daena* is a way the soul represents itself to the newly dead consciousness finding its way in the Underworld. The name means "she who sees" and in simplified terms she represents the moral conscience. She stands on the *Cinvat* Bridge and greets the deceased. How she appears is variable and depends on the weight of your good versus bad deeds. She will appear either beautiful (of "unsurpassed beauty") and chaste or hideous and deformed; either guise is the face of the accumulation of one's good or bad deeds, whether we have draped our pure form with darkness. She sees you in your true moral condition, and like a chameleon, she mirrors this.

She supervises the assessing and weighing of the soul's qualities before the bridge. The Persians suggest she is the celestial I, the Heavenly Twin, more like one's eternally pure Higher Self than the karmically adulterated astral body, but in the logistics of the soul's passage through the *Bardo* she acts as if she is both, as if her body presents the record of the consequences of your life deeds.

The *Avesta* says she acts like a psychopomp, conducting souls from the bridge to their proper destination. The width of the bridge and the ease of passage depends on the weighing outcome. The bridge is as wide as the soul was good. If the weight of their life deeds is "good" they go to the House of Song, a paradisal realm; if badness and evil predominate, they go to the House of Lies, not a nice place, one not recommended, gets bad ratings—it's a hellish realm.

The demon Vizarsh, and sometimes a few others, waits for the soul under the bridge. Vizarsh will drag the unrepentant to the *Druj-demana*, or House of Lies, operated by *Angra Mainyu*, Ahriman, Lord of Lies, the Destructive Spirit, and enemy of Ahura-Mazda. The Druj, in short. She is a feminine personification of the Antichrist, devious, clever, nasty, relentless. We would meet her soon and she would form an essential, tricky part of our *Bardo* expedition, in equal measures confounding and illuminating our trip, even entertaining us. The name *Angra Mainyu* is Zoroastrian and suggests a destructive mind, malign mentality, and inhibitive spirit, a celestial entity completely opposed to humans. We would know her by her nickname, Druj, the way American gangsters had nicknames.

The Persian picture of the *Daena* is instructive but seems too absolutist and literal. It reminded me of two statements made by Rudolf Steiner. He spoke of the Lesser Guardian of the Threshold; it is a spirit we must encounter and deal with if we seek to enter the spiritual worlds regularly, safely, and without confusion. Its hideous form comprises the totality of our unresolved karma and shadow content. We have to pass through it (i.e., purify it) to enter the spiritual world. He also said if we were to meet our own astral body in a dream, we would most likely fail to recognize it as part of ourselves but regard it as foreign, an inimical, hideous, bizarre, or generally frightening nighttime apparition.

These two points address the relative or variable presenting condition of the *Daena* for that is another word for the unprocessed astral body, rough and raw. To use another term, we might say the *Daena* is the guise of our karma body, and for most of us, she is likely to be closer to the ugly than beautiful presentation. Our time on the *Cinvat* Bridge or in the life-records processing chambers is our coming to terms with the state of ourselves as presented by our own *Daena*. You can see how many people will fail to comprehend who she is. The *Daena* is perhaps the personification of the outcome of the Weighing of the Heart ritual, as described in Egyptian thanatology, a composite portrait of this. The relative valence of the *Daena*, her beauty or ugliness, is an index of results.

Our karma body, or our rough and raw astral body, will seem utterly bizarre to us, like somebody else's infernal notion of a demon, like the Persian Vizarsh perhaps. Vizarsh, it turns out, has five buddies, all just as nasty: these are Astvihat, the demon of death; the evil Vay; the demon Frehzisht; the demon Vizisht; and Wrath, the demon of active ill-will equipped with a sharp and bloody spear. None of these, Merlin assures me, despite their seeming ferocity and unremitting ill-will, are inherently separate from ourselves, outside us. Each is a manifestation of a quality of mind or a concatenation of karmic deeds, and our job, the task of anyone newly dead, is to recognize them as mind-generated, and to "slay" them by recognizing their inherent emptiness and self-generation.

That is implicit in the definition of *Daena*, which means conscience, discernment, and insight, to see, view, contemplate, and ponder with clarity—to see oneself. The *Daena* stands there and says, *Look* what you have done to me, made of me. It is not said in the spirit of judgement or resentment; it is factual and quantitative. Like an accountant's balance sheet in preparation for settling your taxes due; then you go into the details in the etheric and astral

body life-review process. You see the steps by which you venerated or slimed the *Daena*. To continue the analogy, that is you reviewing the box of receipts for purchases.

The Theosophical tradition has another way of describing this residue. It has a different nuance than Steiner's use of the term. The phrase "Dweller on the Threshold" is used to denote what H.P. Blavatsky called "certain maleficent astral Doubles of defunct persons" that haunt the deceased person as they enter the *Bardo*. These dwellers are remnants of old selves, ghosts of dead men the soul has been in the past, like cast-off personality clothes, and they embody karmic consequences and unresolved issues and inconclusive results. The soul must recognize and overcome these haunting parts of oneself from the past. This Dweller, or the haunting composite mob of dwellers, can contaminate the *Daena*.

The *Daena* is the personification of the condition of one's ideal body, one's inner self, of the momentum and summation of all one's life deeds measured against the purity of original conscience. There is the suggestion that the *Daena* possesses all the innate spiritual wisdom and knowledge a soul was endowed with and which derives from Ahura-Mazda, the soul's creator.

The *Daena* is an "eschatological figure," said Zoroaster, previewing and prefiguring the *Bardo* journey and the developmental schedule our soul must fulfill. She descends from "High Hara," *Hara Berezaiti*, the High Watchpost, also called Mount Alborz and akin to the Buddhist celestial cosmic mountain, Meru; she takes the soul of the just, whose life deeds are pure, across *Cinvat* Bridge and to the ramparts of the invisible *yazatas*, the pure angels in the highest Heavens.

So we watched as the boy went through his Sraosha disclosure a few times. Each time he seemed to retain more of the portrayal of the landscape, until finally he was able to merge into the effulgent form of the Angel Sraosha and experience the bright lucid emptiness of Clear Mind, the truth of his being. I saw him step outside of everything that had ever defined him, his thoughts, feelings, experiences, all his bodies, his deeds, his perceptions, his consciousness. "Yes, it is that," said Sraosha. The boy nodded, after he had regained his form.

This kid would not get tossed off the bridge to be devoured by the demons, as the Persian image precipitately presented one of the outcomes. Not only are the demons merely mind-generated, created out of our shadow and karma, but they are not demons at all, not in an ultimate ontological sense. They are the picture labels we put upon the array of unprocessed life experiences and feelings, energized negatively by our resistance and compounded by escalating fear. I realized it's the same mechanism operating in bad dreams or nightmares.

We are desperately fleeing something terrible, horrific, fraught with jeopardy. No rescue is in sight; the phones don't work; our voice itself doesn't work. The way out is to stop in your tracks and realize the monster is a projection from yourself. Correct recognition will disarm the monster. It is something you haven't wanted to see or acknowledge; you relegated it to the shadows where it grew in fierceness and scariness. As you resisted it so it grew. Acknowledge it and it will diminish in ferocity and you will likely see it in its true form, as a cast-off part of yourself. Then you'll get the salutary revelation your unconscious has prepared for you. The monster is probably a hidden ally.

"You realize by now, I trust," said Merlin, "that there is no bridge or boat. You cross the dimensional gradient, the river, by a boat or a bridge. They are equivalent metaphors of conveyance. They are physical-world images to indicate a process. That dimensional

crossing entails a hard, cold look at yourself naked, meaning stripped of self-deceptions, prevarications, or distractions, as you are. That process is your life review, and it is a bigger deal than you may realize. There is no bridge or boat, but you stepping naked into this in-between realm precipitates the release of your etheric and astral body contents for your review.

"Nor are there Judges of the Dead, as the classical accounts suggest, only neutral supervisors and counselors on hand to explain or advise. You are the judge. You are systematically extricating yourself from everything that defined you as a human, the seven chakras and the five elemental bases of Nature. You get to see both in their limited, subjective, human-nuanced aspects and in their universal, transcendent qualities. You assess the moral valency of all your deeds.

"This is where the *Dhyani* Buddhas come into play. They reveal the purest aspects of the five elements, as conditions of consciousness. Sraosha reveals this personal projected landscape to the transiting soul so one can traverse it, ideally, possessing this Clear Mind quality as a spotlight. It does make things go easier. I said the life review is bigger than you think. It is everything you take for granted while physically alive, all the ways you structure or distort or construe your world now laid out before you, seemingly *outside* you as a *separate* landscape. The Clear Light is meant to illuminate the inherent voidness or insubstantiality of it. You see it but you realize it is a concatenation of mind-generated empty forms. Without the Clear Light activated, it may appear as a horrific phantasmagoria.

"All the fears, doubts, hatreds, worries, grievances, and miseries you lived with, stuffed inside the shirt of your various being-bodies hoping you'd forget them, are now projected *outside* you like a three-dimensional movie, your new reality, as if some inimical agency came up with this to scare you mightily. If you are not discerning, you will conclude that is being *done to you* as a torture. Sadly, or funnily, most souls react to this as if it's somebody else's crazy movie, and they start frantically searching for the Exit to get out of this bizarre theater."

"That's the thing you realize when you're dead," said Tommy. "You see what a gigantic structure you've gotten yourself into and have taken for granted your whole life, to the extent you don't see it or suspect it, but you live inside it. It's like standing outside yourself and contemplating your body's appearance."

"Yes, and this gigantic structure is your personal life Light grid," said Blaise. "You have spent your life constructing and decorating a Light temple."

Merlin indicated it was time for us to test out this new Sraosha setting. It seemed like we were back at the front gates of the Underworld coliseum, just after it had opened, and we had stepped forward and perceived the effulgent form of Sraosha. His form expanded radically, grew as brilliant, as blinding, as a sun, and through this burgeoning Light I saw a landscape. It was structured and complex, and my first impression, a bit silly, I admit, was of an amusement park. I saw parts of me flying off, being shed, flayed, stripped free, dissolved, dried up.

It was as if I had been made of a million picture postcards, and these were flying off me as if drawn into the vertical suction of some great wind all about me. I caught a few of the images: these were gestures, faces, grimaces, smiles, expressions, the great circus act by which we convey our emotional take on the reality around us. Likes and dislikes, as the Buddhists put it, and they add, rightly, as I was now seeing starkly demonstrated before me, these have no inherent self-nature. I had just stepped into the land where all form is emptiness, and my task was to not get seduced into seeing this emptiness

as genuine forms. In other words, taking all this at face value, as literal, and running off pell-mell.

I saw images fly off of the five elements as they had informed my life and body. Each element—fire, air, earth, water—had its own emotional entourage and portfolio of pictures. Moments of anger, grief, fear, betrayal, expansiveness, willed action, power were scraped off my "skin" as if somebody were applying sandpaper. Then I saw the elements in their naked condition, as fire and water, for example, and knew these were formations of consciousness, the basic expressions of the *skandahs*, the five essential bundles or "aggregates" by which consciousness creates a perceivable world. I was now disassembling that world.

I had misconstrued and personalized fire as anger, water as feelings, air as thought. I had forced these generic qualities of "matter" into a subjective formulation. On the other hand, so had everybody else who ever entered a human body. But I was starting to understand why Buddhists depreciated the innate value of this. This was the human-made subjective world of sensations. All humans over the vast life of humanity on Earth had converted the *skandahs* into subjective filters and built up a false world around them, false meaning inherently empty yet taken routinely as substantive—the arch human illusion.

I saw that each of the *skandahs* each had an exalted celestial spirit supervising it. These must be the *Dhyani* Buddhas Merlin had referred to. These sublime Buddha-like spirits had their own magnificent Light temples, and these were anchored to specific locations on the Earth. One of them looked like the Acropolis in Athens; another evoked Mount Kailash in Tibet. I saw two wheels or interaction zones before me. One pertained to the wealth of pictures that was being extricated from me. This seemed to be a personal processing zone, a display (or debris) field perhaps for the results of the life-records review.

Surrounding this was a larger zone, a wheel, and here I saw the *Dhyani* Buddhas. Beyond both wheels I saw another set of gates, and I glimpsed a number of realms beyond these gates. These must be the Heavens, Hells, and Purgatories commonly alluded to in classical accounts of the afterlife landscape, though I knew by now I should expect these to be metaphors, not literal zones, if by that I meant physically discrete areas. They were conditions for processing the compacted contents of consciousness as accrued by a personality in a body.

I was aware that Sraosha was explaining each new landscape aspect as it appeared before me. He did this so subtly it seemed part of my own cognition. But yes, I can report I found the terrain greatly clarified for me. I understood, at least provisionally, what I was seeing, what was expected of me, where to go. I understood, and it was more like an immediate intuitive knowing rather than the result of studying, memorizing, or acquired learning, how it all related to me, that it was a mind-generated projection of the personal and transpersonal structures in which I had lived and slept while alive as a human being, and I use the word "slept" with irony, for it was more like a prolonged unconsciousness.

I saw a new figure. He seemed to be a reference librarian. He was holding a large open book, pointing to some pages, even to certain lines on these pages. He looked at me, and I knew that book pertained to me: it was about me.

"The Hindu sages called him Chitragupta," said Merlin. "They called him the Recorder, and the record comprises the deeds of your most recent life. His name gives it all away. It means 'rich in secrets' and 'hidden picture.' You. The dossier, known and unknown to you, conscious and subliminal, of your life.

"Brahma conceived Chitragupta in his mind (*chitra*) in a condition of secrecy (*gupta*), meaning, in practical terms, don't ever think you can hoodwink the Old Man. Chitragupta works behind the scenes and records everything, but the secrecy nuance suggests a certain confidentiality to his records review. He reviews your record, your life performance evaluation, and it's a private matter. It only concerns you and Chitragupta; he will keep the secrets of your failures. Sadly, though it has its amusing aspects, these are secrets kept from you by you. These are crucial facts about yourself so secret even you don't know about them.

"He reads out the account of your life, the summation of the tendencies to good or evil deeds, from the register called *Agra-sandhani*, and, so the sages say, he then passes judgement as to the disposition of the defendant, you, where you go, whether you proceed to the heavenly abodes of the *Pitrs* or Fathers, or the 21 Hells from which you gravitate toward another human incarnation. This is the traditional description, but it's too literal a picture, though essentially accurate.

"Chitragupta does review your record, but this is the distillation of everything you have already studied in your life-records review of the deeds registered in your etheric and astral body. He doesn't tell you anything you don't already know, and, frankly, *you* choose your next move. It's just that to a large degree you are bound by the necessities of the register. You could say he is much like a high school guidance counselor offering recommendations that, in his view, best match your abilities with a vocation. With scores, test results, and grades like this, he says neutrally, you're likely to get into these colleges, but it would be a stretch and I believe unlikely to expect to get into these other ones."

Blaise interrupted Merlin's explanation to make a joke. "The whole place is a large version of the Sorting Hat ritual at Hogwarts in the

Harry Potter stories. The Hat decides which House you are best suited to join. It sorts you."

We looked at Blaise for a moment and couldn't help grinning. Merlin resumed. "Hindu lore says Yama sometimes got confused over the details of a 'defendant' and assigned him to the wrong zone. Then Brahma assigned Chitragupta to be his first assistant and scribe. He is his chief-of-staff. He knows all the names, the full records; he holds the complete files for each soul. He is fully briefed on all the particulars of each case and can prompt Yama as needed.

"The register he holds is also known as the *Akashic* Records, the universal record of everything that has ever happened. The original CCTV surveillance. The book is your chapter within those vast records, your personal Book of Life. Yama is *Dharmaraja*, King of Laws or *Dharma*; like a court judge, he is bound to administer the laws of karma, retribution, and rebirth according to the Book. He goes strictly by the Book, and sometimes he throws the Book at you. He has to administer your correct placement to the 84 *lakh yonis* or life-forms in the three worlds. That comes to 8,400,000 different life-forms, a fair bit of detail. You can see why he needs Chitragupta to handle all the files and keep them in order."

I felt like my awareness kept expanding, like a balloon being inflated. I became aware of ever more detail in this burgeoning landscape of Light. I saw the structures and temples and zones, the attendants, the obligatory sequence. I saw the necessity of it all. I understood why it had to be this way. I saw myself as if completely disassembled, cut up into pieces like the shamans say of initiation, but I also saw the transpersonal and transcendent aspects of the *Bardo* set-up.

My head felt like it was spinning. I thought of Santa Claus and the ditty recited to children: "He knows when you've been bad or good, so be good for goodness sake." Chitragupta had that level of thorough, intimate knowledge of our lives. Nothing was overlooked or discounted; everything was seen, recorded. I remember reading Rudolf Steiner commenting that the spiritual world was always observing humans, that the sensitive person might register this as a sense of always being regarded by disembodied, attentive, but benevolent eyes.

I felt my awareness was as wide as the world. It was so sharp and clarified it was humming, emitting some steady sound, as if you heard monks chanting from far away in a steady drone. The stronger this sensation grew the less I felt myself. I can't say I felt to be any one or even any thing now, but it was fine with me. It was refreshing to feel this way, even liberating, if I dare use that exalted word. I was going through all the required protocols and stages of afterlife processing, and I was watching it all as if from above and around it, like a spiritual panopticon, and there was a third perspective, more like a non-perspective, where I seemed to wink out, aware of nothing specific, yet "I" was not asleep. It's hard to explain: there was awareness of everything, but no "I."

I was ready to get started, and I surveyed the field like an obstacle course. The Egyptians called this afterlife landscape *Amenti* or the *Duat*. *Amenti* means "the hidden land," but scholars are unsure of the origin of the word *Duat*. Both connote the same realm the Greeks called Hades, which means both place and supervisor, where the name means "The Unseen One" and hints of great fires. In the original allocation of the elements, the Greeks assigned fire, the unseen spirit Underworld of the dead, to Hades. Zeus got the air, and Poseidon the water.

I saw the route, appreciated the cognitive hurdles I had to surmount, and I was set. Committed. Everything was clear. And I wasn't even dead. Which means this was all theoretical, an advance review, a simulation, as I already knew, but I think for a few moments I forgot. We were testing out Sraosha's review upgrade. I wasn't about to reincarnate—I couldn't: wouldn't it be akin to existential bigamy?—but I would eventually return to my same life, whatever form that took, but it would still be in the context of being tied to a human body.

I started to see how this disclosure by Sraosha, what it taught me about the structures of consciousness, the human subjective infiltration of those conditions, and how it generated a kind of solipsistic world about each of us, would inform my life. I would use it as a lodestar, a compass, to complete this current life. The revelations would not be wasted; they would instruct my use of my remaining life. I would do many things differently; I would complain less, comprehend more. I would treat my everyday life as a component of the *Bardo*.

Even better, and probably this was a practical advantage in terms of the evident amount of paperwork you have to handle when you're dead, I would start processing the contents of my chakras and elements while I was still alive so I would not be presented with such a burden when I was dead. I remember reading that Steiner advised this; he said if we started processing our consciousness while alive, going through the stages of disclosure and initiation we can count on in the afterlife, it will streamline our transit experience there. It gives the term "mindfulness meditation" a richer meaning and wider scope, and it would act like an anchor, a grounding cord, for my consciousness in the body.

Here is the most essential fact I took away from Sraosha's disclosure. I will remember this as the context of my life, as the larger framework of my selfhood, and that in some senses I am already here, processing my life, that I am still here. I will remember that the reality of this afterlife disclosure zone explains my life, puts it in perspective, informs all my actions, frames all gestures in awareness.

"That would certainly make for more interesting tea times," said Philomena. "Both of us enjoying this, shall we say, enlarged perspective, knowing that with every move we will be excruciatingly conscious of the karmic implications and of the necessity, should the action go wrong, of yet more paperwork and processing once we get back here in the *Bardo* processing zone. Just think of the karmic complications if I passed you the lemon wrongly at tea."

I appreciated the irony of Philomena's remark. You lift the teapot to pour and you wonder if you're creating more *Bardo* work for yourself if your thoughts go sideways. Philomena would never be home again for tea, and judging by how my life has been going since 2026 when I ran out the front door and missed my first of many teas, maybe I wouldn't either. We'd always have the tea we'd had. But I would constantly scrutinize every proposed action: can I do this without it costing me more paperwork in the *Bardo*; can I do it cleanly, get away scot-free? How fitting is that word, *scotfreo*, from the Old English, meaning "exempt from royal tax" or *scot*, without consequences or penalties—more *Bardo* processing.

"It's like a certain metaphysical exercise to build mindfulness that my pal, Blaise, the other Blaise, told me about," said Blaise. "At the end of the day, before going to sleep, you review the events of your day in reverse, like rewinding a tape. You see them in reverse order, all the way back to when you woke up. What happens after a while is you find yourself during the daytime, when you are accruing new events to review later, reviewing them right as they happen.

"You say to yourself, I will be reviewing this action tonight. You end up imparting a sharper concentration on the daytime events as they happen, and that I believe is a prime purpose of the exercise, to get you to pay more attention to what you are doing in the daytime, to act with heightened awareness. On the other hand, you can find yourself up half the night reviewing the day's tapes."

I saw what Blaise meant. The daytime review will be more lucid, except it will last the rest of my life and not just one day. I will be reviewing my lifetime events as they happen to shorten the afterlife records review. It's not about saving time. It's about sharpening my attention and insight. It is likely that after a while this will tend to knit the two realms of experience together; afterwards, life and afterlife will not seem so irrevocably separate, such different realms, and you will likely be more aware of whether your actions create karma or not. More karma means more processing, and less karma means you get done faster. The way you don't create more karma, as I understand it from the Buddhists, is to perform your daily actions recognizing the inherent emptiness of phenomena.

"This review is a major slap in the face, and a valuable one, I'd say," Blaise said. "Think about it: here you are forced to recognize the reality of your own consciousness. It is a matrix in which you have been embedded all your life and probably taken for granted, never looking at it on its own terms, as a Light grid.

"The biases of the world train your attention outward to perceive objects, to assemble a world, and to construe yourself as its perceiver and often its opponent. Now it gradually dawns on you, and it can be horrifying to many who are unprepared for the reality disclosure this entails, that everything you see is a projection from this matrix of consciousness; there is no real outside anymore. Even worse, or better, if you regard this as a chance to do some quality meditation (free of any knee pain, let me add), is the absence of any distractions. There are none. You have to focus. You have to acknowledge this vast field."

"Where does the Weighing of the Heart by Anubis fit in?" asked Edward.

"Right here," said Merlin. "See, I brought my portable weighing scales."

For a moment I was certain Merlin would pull out a set of miniature balance scales from a great bulging overcoat with copious inner pockets like Harpo Marx was fond of doing. Maybe he thought of it, but he refrained.

"You have, I suspect, surmised that this ceremony from the Egyptian funerary texts is equivalent to the life-records review and the time on the bridge?" Merlin waited for Edward to nod in agreement. "The keynote from the Egyptian picture is my involvement, that I, as Anubis, Merlin, or the more abstract *Mer-Line*, am implicit in this afterlife stage as mystagogue for the soul."

Anubis is portrayed as a human with the head of a black desert jackal. He performed the "Opening of the Mouth" ceremony with mummies and the "Weighing of the Heart" ritual with the newly dead. He placed the heart of the deceased, believed to contain the person's spiritual essence called the *Ba* (depicted as a human-headed bird that hovers above the deceased physical body), on a scale balanced with a single ostrich feather that represented the purity of Ma'at. Egyptians believed the *Ba* resided in the human heart during life, so to weigh the heart, to assess the *Ba*, is to evaluate its moral condition after a life. To say "heart" is to indicate the heart as a place-marker for the inner *Ba*. The *Ba* is another version of the *Daena*, the face of the soul's moral valency.

In a sense, it's like telling the *Daena* to hop up on the scales so Anubis can weigh her. If she weighs more than Ma'at's feather, that is the same as appearing ugly. In effect, the ugly, corrupted *Daena* was now in the guise of the *Ammit*. That was the name for the Egyptian picture of the karmically-tarnished human soul appearing externally as a frightening, threatening, and in fact dangerous spirit.

Ma'at is depicted as wearing this single Feather of Truth in her headband. Upright, it stands more than a foot tall, rising off the crown of her head. She was the goddess of absolute truth and justice, the unvarying standard for conduct and all protocols of consciousness as established at the Creation. She is the implicit regulator and standard of first reference for cosmic harmony; she is implicit in the heart-weighing ceremony taking place in the Hall of Ma'at (Truth) under her auspices. If your heart weighed less than the feather, you were okay; if not, you were screwed regarding any hopes of a happy or even paradisal afterlife experience. This ritual strikes me as another version of meeting your *Daena* on the *Cinvat* Bridge: beautiful maiden, your soul is pure; hag, and it's a sorry loser.

The Egyptians used the term *ma'at* to denote this abstract quality without personification. The Greeks knew her as Themis, the Titan of "divine law" and "of good counsel." Themis was the personification of *tithemi*, which meant "that which is put in place," which was immutable cosmic law as ordained by Zeus. The Persians called her *Asha-Vahista*, the *Amesha-Spenta* of "truth, rightness."

In the three cases, you had the abstract essence, *ma'at, asha*, or *tithemi*, and its personification as a deity. Usually, Osiris, the high god, and Thoth (the Greek Hermes) are present as witnesses as the soul's qualities are weighed against this perfectly pure standard. There is nothing arbitrary or capricious about this judgement; it is impartial and absolute, based on factual Creation laws of the cosmos implicit in its design, like a manufacturer's recommended usage guide.

You could just as well substitute an engineering schematic for the Light grid that specifies cosmic reality as personify this

knowledge as the Goddess Ma'at. Here's how reality was made, and here is the best way to operate it. Failure to heed these guidelines may result in injuries or unwanted "side-effects" to the operator. That connotes the quality of *ma'at* as the irrefutable reference point for this crucial *Bardo* ceremony. To call this a moral code enforced by a high deity with a strong will is too simplistic; *ma'at* is like a design setting, a frequency parameter, exact engineering schematics for operating the reality machine. *Ma'at* is like a perfectly executed mandala; disregard for the rules of reality is like crashing through the walls of the mandala, introducing disorder and chaos.

But how should I have behaved, protests the soul, dismayed at the stark presentation of his shortcomings. *Like this*, says Ma'at, or her male counterpart, Tehuti-Thoth, or his Greek counterpart, Hermes, formulator of the Hermetic axioms which describe seven fundamental laws about the workings of energy, including the famous one, "As above, so below," which is a geomantic field axiom, a design specific for Earth-Heaven relations, and the moral code's basis.

Tragically, the heart-weighing procedure may be the only time the soul learns of these immutable laws of reality. It's not like people are handed a manufacturer's recommended use of reality booklet when they incarnate or a pamphlet outlining the club's rules of behavior or get a complimentary full-color photo of Ma'at's immutable feather, or even a button imprint. The metaphysics of cosmic design are not taught in schools, and in fact are hardly ever alluded to, thanks to Darwinian myopia, and at best were once only the provenance of esoteric academies and in recent centuries have been at best rumors or hints.

In classical times, Themis imparted these laws of rightness and obedience to the divine codes through her primary oracle center at

Delphi, but compared to the population of Greece, only a few got to Delphi and most heard only rumors of these divinations and probably never not a coherent explication of their meanings. Obedience, even rightness, have squirmy connotations for people today. Let's say Themis put forward the optimum operational specificities of the machine of reality, and suggested if we, the users, wanted the optimal results, follow them. Her "obedience" meant her ineluctable *alignment* with true reality. Themis was obedient to the actual conditions of truth, Light, and reality design.

Yet here the inquiring, suffering, confused soul gets to examine these laws of *ma'at*, even as they are wielded to exact assessment of his own failure to follow them. What, the soul protests, you're saying there are rules to incarnation? The soul realizes that the puritanical word "morality" is the façade for the engineering specifics of reality's Light grid, the neutral design mechanism for consciousness. Still, I felt how salutary would be the impact of the discovery of this fact: reality and consciousness have operating rules set down at the beginning. How often do people complain that reality, their lives, what happens to them, seem random and chance-driven, products of chaos and accidents, that there are no fixed rules governing reality, it's all colliding billiards balls. Here is the definitive refutation of that erroneous assumption; here's the factual proof.

Surely that is an initiation experience that should impart a terrific reorientation. You get into the *Bardo*, get your heart weighed, and discover, to your dismay or astonishment, there actually are rules regarding the use of reality, and you are screwed because you never knew this and lived in reckless disregard. The moral codes of religions barely touched on these actualities. So the heart-weighing ritual has the potential of re-anchoring the soul in the normative briefing first imparted to him by the Supreme Being

prior to the soul's first incarnation. That was the first explanation of the rules of reality; Ma'at's touchstone is the second. If souls had been able to keep that feather it could have acted like a perpetual reminder. On the other hand, somewhere inside us there must be an imprint of it. It's as if she says, ever so politely but firmly, don't you remember what the Supreme Being told you in your meeting? No? Unfortunate.

I understand now that the revelatory encounter with Sraosha on the *Cinvat* Bridge is a stretched-out moment. It is the prolonged experience of the feather. The Egyptians say the balance scales have your heart on one tray and a feather from Ma'at on the other. That feather represents the reference point. Blaise and Merlin helped me see that the Weighing of the Heart, the encounter on the bridge, and the boat ride with Charon are the same moment. If your heart, your *Ba*, weighs more than Ma'at's feather, you are *Bardo*-screwed. You will have to scrub clean the impurities in your *Ba*, the little black stains that weigh it down, and that means entering the frightful crazy spectacle of your karma suddenly dancing a horror-show burlesque before your astonished eyes. On the other hand, I exaggerate, just as the ancients did: you're not screwed exactly, but you have work to get through, papers to process, accounts to balance, karma to fix.

It is a massive download for consciousness, but it seems to entail a disclosure of the original rules for reality, the full briefing package on *ma'at*, the divine laws. Themis reminds you of the ordinances for behavior and consciousness that put you in accord again with cosmic reality and its protocols and design principles. It's as if you have the oracle all to yourself, and this is a cosmic version of Delphi and she is imparting the ordinances of reality to you.

You think, maybe I should have made that trip to Delphi to get some guidance, and, since Delphi has been closed for centuries, it means maybe I should have inquired about this business of metaphysics, seen about getting some answers, asked a few intelligent questions about the genuine nature of reality instead of living recklessly in oblivion of the fact reality actually had immutable rules, or, if you are a different sort of person, maybe I shouldn't have put all my trust in some old religious dogma and its limited model of reality.

You see in an instant where you come up short in contrast with these pure laws. It's as if you have a speeded-up life-review session on both your etheric and astral body records; you see the "body" of unprocessed karmic illusions, your own personal "beast" of the unconscious revealed shockingly before you, the hideous *Ammit*, and you get the summary of your meeting with the *Dhyani* Buddhas and what this discloses about the universal nature of human cognition.

You could say in this moment with the feather your entire afterlife journey flashes before you, reversing what people almost dying say about their current life flashing before them. You get a detailed, instantaneous view of the full *Amenti* terrain. You comprehend the human phylogeny expressed as a landscape; you see it laid out as a mandala of Light and the route you must take through this labyrinth. After the Sraosha illumination, you set forth, go through these stages and processes, complete the cognitive challenges, do it all thoroughly, and start to understand, at last, the authentic conditions consciousness finds itself in.

Blaise helped me understand that even to construe this moment of the Weighing of the Heart on the scale against the lightness of Ma'at's feather is only an analogy. It is not literal, nor is it a judgement handed down from outside you. Rather, it is a moment rich with the possibility of you, the soul newly entered into the afterlife, to assess on your own the quality and problems of your condition. You are your own auditor, your own judge, jury, and appeals court. (It's funny but I realized in this analogy you don't need a lawyer as you don't have to defend yourself.) For this moment is not about exacting the correct degree of "punishment," but for *you* to see *your* condition, to see it revealed all at once, to measure the balance of your life's deeds against the norm of Ma'at. Rather than thinking in terms of punishment, we have moments of remorse, clear seeing of our deeds, their effects, the shadowy factors that compelled us to them.

Once again, Themis will be instructing humans in the laws of the divine world, and with this new commission to Sraosha she will spend as much time as needed on each new soul who comes before her. Delphi is open again, here in the afterlife, and Themis is freely dispensing divinations and oracles to all everyday.

"This revelation slams right into you," said Blaise. "Suddenly, you are obsessed with certain questions, such as: I am conscious, but why am I conscious? What is consciousness? What is this 'I' that is conscious? You feel gripped, possessed by these questions; you feel shocked you have no answer. You feel chastened the questions never arose in you when you were alive. What kind of infernal brickbrain was I walking around asleep all those years I lived?"

The outcome is momentous and will determine the soul's future experience in the afterlife, Blaise explained. If your heart or *Ba* is judged worthy and pure, your *Daena* beautiful, you proceed to the heavenly realms in the Egyptian afterlife, but if it comes up short, your *Daena* ugly, you're in trouble. Expect to be tossed into the mouth of the devouring *Ammit*. She's nasty. This is a female demon, a hybrid death-monster whose head and jaws come from a crocodile, whose torso is from a lion, and whose hindquarters are as massive as a hippopotamus. The Egyptians left us this vivid picture of the chief *Duat* demon.

The *Ammit* is the "Eater of Hearts, "Great of Death," and "Devourer of *Amenti*." The Egyptians make the *Ammit* sound like the disaster you'll meet at the end of the world, and you hope you don't. Thoth impartially records the verdict, while Anubis, like a security guard, protects the *Ba* from the hungry, ruthless *Ammit* until the weighing result is confirmed. If the judgement goes against you, expect to be tasty lunchmeat for the hungry *Ammit*, all teeth.

"They painted a dramatic, compelling picture, don't you think?" Merlin commented. "If you get tossed to the *Ammit*, it's the same as being thrown off the *Cinvat* Bridge. It is a way of saying the momentum of your dark deeds will own you and direct your afterlife experience. It means they will claim seniority over you. The shadow side of your consciousness, the negative accrual of your life deeds, will consume you, overwhelm, master you, eat you *like* a hungry beast.

"There is no independent monster of *Amenti* called the *Ammit*. You bring your own. Everyone has an *Ammit*, though some are fiercer than others. It's another way of pointing to the Lesser Guardian of the Threshold or the Shadow. The tricky part, though, is recognizing that the frightful, monstrous apparition before you with wide-open mouth and sharp teeth is a portrait of *your* dark side. It seeks to devour your daytime consciousness, to make it part of its own infernal flesh. Your shadow-side seeks to own you, direct all your actions and thoughts. It's the same mechanism by which consciousness generates a monster that chases you through the dreamland because you have resisted the disclosure it offers. You can appreciate how many souls could miss that subtlety of discernment and regard the *Ammit* as a barely restrained awful demon of untold inimical intent."

"I see now that I was stripping off the skin and bones of my own *Ammit* during the final years when I was preparing myself for my ascension," said Philomena. "Naturally, I didn't understand that at the time, but it was intense."

"The *Ammit* doesn't become apparent to you until you've done the winnowing process," said Tommy. "I watched as it grew before me. As I reviewed my life events, both conscious and in my astral body, I saw the dark materials start to form and flesh out my personal *Ammit*. Before it was implicit in me but not as personified as it was by the time I was done watching the clips. I think the *Ammit* of suicides can be fiercer than for people who die naturally. To kill yourself means you have given in to the persuasions of your own dark side. The result of the Weighing of the Heart ritual is to see your *Ammit* before you. Yikes! You have spent a lifetime feeding it, now here it is full-grown, hideous, awful, glaring at you hideously with criminal intent. You are its next big crime."

"Our challenge is to get people to recognize the *Ammit* is of their own making," Merlin said. "So many fail to discern this and have a terrible time in the afterlife. They run perpetually from monsters and have no peace. They don't recognize the *Ammit* as home-grown, as their own. You could say all the nasty demonic spirits the *Bardo Thödol* delineates were born from the one *Ammit*, as if the *Ammit* split itself into a hundred forms in the *Bardo*. They do not realize they are feeding the *Ammit* in every dark moment of life. Anyone have a suggestion?"

"Show them how they have created it layer by layer over time," said Pipaluk, "like a brush continuously going over the same stretched canvas. This is often part of the shaman's training, and certainly what an *angakkuq* often discovers in her Underworld explorations to find the reason for a sickness. You see you have spent a lifetime creating and shaping this illness that will kill you."

"Christianity and most other religions have made the soul lazy," said Matthew. "Our cognitive muscles have grown slack. Nobody is encouraged to squarely face off and recognize the Tree of the Knowledge of Good *and Evil* in its fullness; the Evil part gets excised and never dealt with. It becomes a Shadow, and then when you die this Shadow swells up, attacks, and bites your ass.

"The multiple lifetimes perspective is excised from the Christian's spiritual model, and this further distances people from understanding *they* have built up their own dark register over large stretches of time and are not the victims of fate, an angry God, hostile subsidiary deities, or other anonymous, inimical agencies. Instead, they are grossly misinformed and deliberately disempowered. They are dangerously exposed, vulnerable, unaware of what they have set in motion. They are like children, still expecting to be protected by ever-watchful parents. They are told to beware of the one bad Satan, but are left altogether vulnerable to the hundred little Satan-adversaries they have created.

"Worse, Christianity falsely counsels people that their sins are already forgiven, exonerated, by the sacrifice of Jesus Christ on the Cross. This is not the case. It's not even close to being true, and again it throws people off what they should do. The consequences of their dark deeds have not been expunged though they may receive sympathy for their ignorance. It's not debt excusal.

"You still have the karma, the debts that need paying off. They get here utterly unprepared and wrongly advised. They have a child's simplistic notion of the tally sheet: I am either completely good, no worries, or I know I am so bad I'm damned before I get here. Most are some of both. No, their sins are not in the least forgiven; they are still debts with momentum and they still have to rectify the consequences of their deeds, and there is this dreadful monster called the *Ammit* ready to devour them entirely that suddenly jumps up out of nowhere, and nobody

ever told them about this awful creation of their own, and here it is.

"There's more. Most people pass through their life with no metaphysical model. Neither religion nor culture provide one. Religion's model is a cartoon for children. It equips the mind with nothing of value or traction. It instills only obedience, diligence, submission, set in an unrealistic materialist model. You get no inkling your consciousness has any power, any efficacy against the great forces of the world, against the arch-enemy, Satan. You must pray for benign intercession, like a medieval vassal prostrating before the feudal master. Nor do people comprehend the true nature of the physical world, what it means, and, more importantly, how it got here, how it is the inverse of the spiritual world. What was outside us in the spiritual world is now inside here, inside our bodies.

"As they don't understand the physical world, when it reverses again and everything interior becomes projected outside to form the spiritual environment, they are struck dumb with incomprehension. They don't understand what has happened. They have no context for the experience and it bewilders and confounds them. All they have is the useless, unreal, dead-end briefing they got from religion. Then you get here, the *Ammit* jumps you and takes huge bites out of your spiritual ass and you wonder where this creature from Hell came from.

"You struggle to understand *Bardo* phenomena from the familiar but now departed physical world mental framework, and fail badly. You're left with great uncertainty. This is the handiwork of *Isfet*, the opposite of Ma'at. This was both the quality and personification of chaos, evil, violence, and doing injustice. *Isfet* works behind the scenes, behind the props of reality, utterly confounding you."

"An antipapist after my own heart, or, should I say, *Ba*," commented Blaise. "*Ammit* or *Ba*? I wonder which weighs more? Merlin, got your scales?"

"There never were any scales," Merlin replied. "Sorry about that, another metaphor. Same with the jackal's head. Simply to make the point. No real dog. But, as I wrote in the *Bardo Thödol*, when the soul fails to hold on to the Clear Light of Reality when it dawns, things move to the next *Bardo* phase when the karmic illusions start to appear as exterior agencies, spirits, and living pictures.

"This is another way of saying you perceive the *Ammit* leering on the other side of the weighing table. The *Ammit* is the laminated body of your karmic illusions. They are real, and thus not illusory, in that you must resolve them; but they are illusions resulting from life deeds in the physical world committed in ignorance. They have no traction when held up against the Clear Light of Reality; they dissolve into clouds of vapor that soon vanish in the force of the Clear Light. It's like standing right next to the Exit, but frantic about how to get out of the place. The tragicomedy of the *Bardo*, of embodied life itself, is you don't realize your means of safety, escape, rescue, salvation, are immediately at hand, in you, and, were you to call out stridently, demanding to see the manager, you would behold yourself, possibly grinning, stepping briskly out of the manager's office."

"There is no real judging of the dead, is there, Merlin," said Edward.

"No, not in the human world juridical sense. It is more of a sorting out of tendencies into two aggregates. The dark deeds start to flesh out the *Ammit*. By the time you're done with your life review the results have already determined the vibrational tier to which you will be directed. It is a matter of resonance. There is no need for judgement, if you mean by that the determination of a case by a presiding magistrate or perhaps before a jury of your peers, the pure *Daena*s of your previous lives. Your karmic balance is neutral, quantitative test results.

"The relative weight of your deeds, the summing up of your actions, your *Ba* versus your *Ammit* weighed against the absolute scale of Ma'at, hold up a mirror to your soul. This is you after all these deeds. You have to go there. You would not fit in anywhere else. Your vibration would be incompatible with it. The astral afterlife world is a vastly striated domain, comprised of myriads of frequency shelves for each quality of consciousness. Your deeds pre-choose this."

"I have a suggestion for how people can recognize their *Ammit* is self-made," said Edward. "Give them a little Silver Light, like a lamp or wand. From what I learned with you in our visits to the domain of the Silver Mother or Isis, that is the place of unity, before the soul's consciousness is split into the 49 parts, and the Silver Light is the means by which we realize and reacquire this unity.

"So if we give the newly dead soul some Silver Light, it will enable them to discern their *Ammit* from the viewpoint of the place of unity to which they are headed. They will study their *Ammit* from a place where it doesn't and never will exist. They can heal the 'sins' of their soul from a higher level than its field of action. This should give them enough perspective and neutrality to see it clearly. I'm sure it would do that for me. It would likely keep them from panicking."

"Would you like to show us how this would work, Edward?" Merlin said.

Edward walked over to a man who was reviewing his life records. His *Ammit* stood by, massive, intimidating, scary, warty, excoriated with pustules. It was a real horror show. You could see how edgy the man felt in its presence. It was starting to dawn on him he must be dead, but he did not understand this malevolent spirit looming before him, how it got here or what it intended to do.

As he sorted through his life records, the *Ammit* kept enlarging. It was a bit like balancing your checkbook after having neglected it for a long time, like years. You realize you have been hovering over if not visiting regularly a negative balance, and you realize you should have monitored expenditures more carefully starting a long time ago because things now have gotten shockingly out of hand. You couldn't help but feel sorry for the guy because his *Ammit* grew quickly and dramatically with the addition of new slabs and chunks and wedges of darkness, while his *Ba*, valiant, heroic, Light-filled, and miniscule, grew by only the tiniest of increments, as if the best he could manage were grains of sand, one at a time. The man grew ever more dismayed as the balance sheet emerged.

Yet he did this winnowing and separation like an accountant doing somebody else's books. He was aloof from the reality; he hadn't owned it yet though he recognized the imminence of danger it posed. It was like a man feverishly bailing water out of a rowboat while it kept streaming in through a big hole in the floor. He wasn't sure if he could bail faster than it was filling up. His expression was one of valiant desperation, a certainty that he was doomed.

Then Edward stood behind him and created a silver column of Light. He made it from a silver staff he held upright, its base touching the ground. He expanded this staff into a column of Light about 20 feet wide so the man and his *Ammit* were contained within it. The man immediately calmed down and relaxed. Even though he no longer had a physical body, it was if he released all the tension he had been holding in his shoulders. They seemed to slump. His attention brightened and the acuity of his focus on the life review strengthened, like he had switched from standing on a cliff's edge to soaking in a hot tub.

His *Ammit* was now revealed to be a palimpsest of hundreds of individual layers. These layers were packed with images, sounds, voices, gestures, actions. Each had the vividness and color and drama of a movie. You could hear shouts, imprecations, curses, vows, denunciations, cries, lamentations, supplications, and these laminations of sounds had added flesh to the *Ammit*, a layer at a time.

The man was able to review and examine in detail, even in leisure, each layer. He watched the movie of that layer, saw how the events portrayed generated the layer. He saw himself as the principal actor, which surprised him. It shouldn't have, since it was obvious to us that it was a self-generated palimpsest, but as Matthew had pointed out, regrettably most people had lost track of the mechanics of the generation of the *Ammit* out of their karmic illusions. So this was a revelation to the reviewing soul, which was the point.

He was watching these layered generations with the neutrality of an observer, yet he knew with certainty he was the principal actor and the karmic illusions were his. It had the studied calmness of an accomplished athlete reviewing tapes of his last performance on the basketball court with his coach, seeing all his game mistakes, listening as his coach explained he would have played better if he had done that, gone for a three-pointer instead of a lay-up.

The *Ammit*, while it continued to burgeon in size, diminished in its scariness. It was still ugly, even hideous, but it was not inimical, foreign, or threatening. It was more like the way you'd react if you found a mess on your kitchen floor, say a shelf had broken and tumbled out all its contents. No big deal. I detected a faint maternal presence within this silver column, as if the inside surface of that pillar was the wraparound face of the Great Mother. She wasn't excusing the man from his responsibility, but encouraging him to fulfill it and infusing him with a gentle sympathetic regard of maternal affection and a quality of lucid consciousness anchored in a reality beyond all karmic illusions.

Under the influence of the Silver Light, which imparted neutrality and lucidity in the context of a warm maternal notice, the man watched in slow-motion as every dark or critical aspect that flared up in his awareness contributed to a layer of the *Ammit*. Moments, hours, or days when he had obsessed on a particular issue, seeking retribution, revenge, or validation, and "fed" this spirit-form. Moments of callous disregard for the feelings of others, of betrayal, false assurance, lying, deception, hiding, veiling, subterfuge, petty thievery, resentment, simulated homicide, gossip-mongering, and even *Schadenfreude*, made the "flesh" of this grim personification of his unconscious.

You are the farmer enriching this personification of prime karmic livestock every moment of your embodied life, guaranteeing you'll have a proper monster on your hands when you arrive in the *Bardo* and wonder what it's all about here. You are the farmer fattening this beast for the eschatological feast, only the one thing you don't know is *you*, not the fattened beast, are the luncheon meat. I say "you;" the sad fact is each of us is that lamentable fattening farmer.

Let me not understate matters: this is a subject that will cause most people to squirm. To settle face-to-face with all the nasty, dark, unevolved, rejected, disavowed aspects of yourself, the burn notice issued to your shadow side that it can no longer operate as a rogue covert agent, the deeds, thoughts, emotions, the harsh words, the cold disregard of other people, the attitudes and convictions you pushed off to the subliminal side of your awareness, the slow-motion rape and homicide of your lovely *Daena*—it is all here, disclosed indisputably in full reality in all its ugliness, and it's all yours, and you've been busted. As cops like to say, this

is your rap sheet, the history of all your deeds against the law.

What was most important to him, the part that I saw he most genuinely understood, was the *mechanics* of the construction of his own *Ammit*. He saw how he had made it, "grown" it at home, through his own life as a feeling, hurting human. Lack of that perspective no doubt defeats many at this revelatory moment. There is the *Ammit* suddenly before you and you cannot comprehend how it relates to you. You feel you have been senselessly thrown into a horror movie with no escape or rescue likely, and you utterly cannot understand why.

This man was now getting past that considerable roadblock. He understood it. He was understanding that you are not mercilessly thrown to the *Ammit* (or tossed off the *Cinvat* Bridge) by the cold-hearted Judges of the Dead. The meaning of that grim mythic picture is that a soul runs the risk of being overwhelmed by the dark gravity of his own *Ammit*. Its feralness has suction, but the key discovery you make is that *you* created this vortex in the first place. It consumes you. You lose your autonomy to your own shadow. Every displaced dark emotion, like anger, resentment, jealousy, the desire for revenge, punishment, self-justification, and all the others, creates the matter of this "beast." Then your own displaced emotions strive to draw you back into themselves and have you for breakfast, lunch, and dinner, every day hence.

Your non-recognition of the origin and creation mechanics of this fearsome spirit and your subsequent resistance to its presence and your wish to flee at any cost from it makes you liable to lose your seniority and detachment and to fall into its world, to live under its influence. Your resistance activates its gravity pull, then it becomes even harder to recognize the *Ammit* as yourself. Now here comes the Silver Light, and its maternal lucidity and compassion give you a needed detachment and cognitive distance. You still have to process the karmic illusions that compound the *Ammit*'s form, but you do so knowing it is a mind-generated demon, created by yourself. You start reclaiming your power.

While I was impressed with the results of this Silver Light upgrade, I was wondering how Merlin planned to make it a permanent feature of the afterlife.

"I'll show you," Merlin said, reading my thoughts. "Edward, if you would step away from the fellow and retract your silver staff please." He did so. Then Merlin extruded a line of Silver Light from a glowing orb several feet above the man's head and directed it into the man's head. It was as if Merlin had flipped on a light switch in this orb above the man's head and it projected a straight beam of Silver Light down into the man's "head" to his sixth chakra. The man registered the presence of the Silver Light (he was already used to it) and expanded it easily to form a pillar of this illuminating color all round him and continued his *Ammit* review under the influence of this self-generated Light. It was like he had created a new office space in the form of a column all done in silver to finish his work.

"With the cooperation of the Great Mother who works through this higher consciousness center, or eighth chakra, as you would call it, above the head, we have opened up a channel between this center and the crown chakra of the human. You could say we have modified the original design slightly to do this. Everyone has this chakra and everyone's eighth chakra has the Silver Light in it, and everyone has the potential to open up a channel between the head and this.

"We have improved the odds that they *will* do it, and do it without difficulty. We have modified the eighth chakra so that the Silver Light can be exported in the form of a little silver wand, yes, a magic wand in terms of what it accomplishes, and from this wand a column of Silver Light will be automatically projected into the awareness of the *Ammit*-reviewing soul, like making the reading lights in a library brighter.

"We cannot force this upon people, so the activation trigger for this will be the moment when the soul recoils at the appearance of the *Ammit* and wishes for understanding as to its nature. Even if the 'wish' takes the form of 'Bloody hell, what on Earth is this monstrosity before me?' That will still activate the wand. The desire to know, to comprehend, the minute separation that implies between viewer and subject, opens up the possibility of the Silver Light perspective. Only the merest gesture of consciousness towards that illumination will kindle it. Then this silver column of Light will form between the crown and the eighth chakra, and then their complete Light form will be inside this silver column, like a man standing in a beam of Silver Light made of the grace of the Great Mother."

"I'm sure the Great Architect Visvakarman insisted on this upgrade, all of it, right?" This was Blaise speaking. "We cannot upgrade the planet's Light grid to a psychic sixth chakra frequency and not make comparable changes to the Underworld, which is the labyrinth by which you extricate yourself from that Light grid. The two realms, the door in and the door out, must be compatible."

Merlin nodded and gestured for me to look around. Everywhere I saw pillars of Silver Light encasing humans reviewing their *Ammit*s. It was like being in a large library at night; everybody was studious under their bright study lamps. I'd often seen this at Dartmouth, especially around exam time. The change Blaise referred to and which Merlin had demonstrated was now already a fact, and the Underworld had changed before our eyes. There seemed to be less shouting, fewer cries of dismay, imprecations and coarse whispers of fear.

Souls would now contemplate their *Ammit*s with the clarifying aid of a silver pillar. It would appear the second they acknowledged they wanted help. These three, the Lethe reduction, the Sraosha elucidation, and the descending silver wand, were the first among many changes we would witness in our tour.

3

There came a fierce roaring all around us, like a terrific wind or tornado. It sounded and felt like an event in the physical world, but it couldn't be. I couldn't tell if this roaring sensation was inside or all around me. It seemed like it was both. I started to look for the agency behind this massive disturbance.

I sensed a presence, though I couldn't yet form an image of it. I could say it seemed huge, but any reference to apparent physical size is misleading. It's more accurate to say its impact was huge. It was a formidable presence of consciousness. Everything, the world around me, was bathed in a blue Light. It seemed as if all perceivable reality, whatever mass there was in the *Bardo*, had melted into this all-encompassing rich blue Light, as if the world had been submerged in a blue ocean that drowned all of reality, like the ultimate Flood.

This blue Light was so radiant, so dazzling, I could barely see it at all. It seemed to shoot forth directly out of the heart of reality, whatever that might be. I made the gesture of shielding my eyes, but that made no difference. The blue Light seared through all of me, through all of the Light body I was occupying.

The tornado-like roaring was coming from this blue Light. At first it seemed to be everywhere, and I could not distinguish its origin point. The Light at first made me feel edgy, as I was uncertain as to its source or intent, but when I felt it, listened to its roaring, swam in this bizarre ocean of blue Light, I realized I need not be alarmed or worried about its presence. Somehow I knew it was benign, possibly exalted, though I couldn't have explained why I thought that. I felt that my awareness itself, the means by which I was observing this blue Light and noting my reactions to it, was being sucked fully out of me by a vacuum.

If consciousness is a muscle, mine was going slack, losing tone and mass. It was like being inexorably sucked into the event horizon of a black hole, at least the way I had imagined it and scientists had attempted to model the event. The point of Light that I was and that was being dragged into the ultimate gravity well was my consciousness, my awareness of all that was presently happening to me. *That* was being definitively whisked out of me into the Light. I had the fleeting impression before "I" vanished that everything in the *Duat*, the afterlife landscape, my expedition companions, was similarly sucked into this Light.

I seemed to flash in and out of having consciousness, of perceiving a world. First I would have the impression I was on the threshold of a spiritual figure possibly the size of the world's biggest mountain; then that vanished as did any sense of myself having a perception or awareness of anything: lights out. I fluctuated back and forth like a yo-yo between these two opposed positions. When I could see something, when I was at the fullest extension of the unrolled yo-yo, I saw a celestial figure, like a Buddha, seated on a lion throne.

This Buddhalike figure, blazingly white, held an equally blazing white wheel with eight spokes in his hand in a manner that suggested it was a special *mudra*, a symbolic gesture, an iconic picture, that attested to his level of consciousness. When the yo-yo was retracted, it seemed I vanished into the heart of this figure. When the yo-yo of my awareness again rolled out, I had the quick impression that this figure had four heads, each facing a cardinal direction, that his vision was panoramic, boundless, maybe infinite, that he had cognitive dominion over all aggregates of matter, all aspects of the material world, the cosmos, in fact, the original *Ge* or Gaia, meaning cosmic Earth, matter's matrix, the original, first, primordial matter, so subtle it was more like ether than mass.

This dominion had the quality of unsurpassed wisdom and great understanding, as if this Buddha-figure possessed the razor-sharp clarity of the original Creation, that it was the epitome of the incorruptible truth that was the hallmark of all reality. I had the impression that all these aggregates of matter not only collapsed into this primordial vacuum, but they originated from here as well, in this yo-yo manner. Here is the crux of the matter: these matter aggregates all required consciousness focused on them to exist. I made them exist by bearing my consciousness upon them; they would cease to exist when it was withdrawn.

That is what this immense celestial figure is all about: deploying consciousness. When consciousness is withdrawn from its outer focus, these aggregates cease to exist as separate, exteriorly-placed realities; they are part of the consciousness deployed by this figure, now part of its own infrastructure. They are no longer perceivable, are no longer being perceived, no longer being.

I was certain of my conclusions, though I won't deny the uncanniness of them. If one extended this logic further, it spelled the end of the world, of reality. Nothing would exist, at least separately, on its own, the way we think of humans. Everything was also starkly transparent now, see-through, empty. It was as if all the aggregates of matter that could exist were now rendered empty. No, they weren't changed; they were always, already inherently empty.

Everything that had been separate, that had seemed separate, was now part of this universal illuminated body yet possessed of a great emptiness. This voidness shone through their outer form, mere outlines now, with a terrific brightness, a brightness that blazed and burned and seared in ultimate clarity. It was as if the attention of this Buddha figure illuminated everything from within with a lucidly wide-awake fiery quality of complete emptiness. It was bizarre. I felt my astral body's head spinning in quick loops.

"It only seems bizarre because to you it is so unexpected," said Merlin. "But don't worry. It seems bizarre to nearly everyone first encountering it, though you have penetrated further than most into the mystery of this apparition. You are witnessing the cognitive activity of the *Dhyani* Buddha called Vairocana, the first of the Peaceful Deities, who appears on the *Bardo*'s day one.

"Many, confronted with this illustrious spectacle, experience fear and terror. They fail to understand what they are being shown, and the momentum, habits, and predisposition of their own karma, little flakes off the skin of their own *Ammit*, persuade them to regard Vairocana as a hostile, inimical spirit best avoided. You cannot avoid Vairocana, or any of the other four *Dhyani* Buddhas. They are part of the structure of reality, of cognition, of how you put together a perceivable world, and now, in the *Bardo* transit, these mechanisms are being taken apart. Nobody ever said it's pleasant, but it's necessary, unavoidable, and instructive. It's what our friend Blaise, the human one, calls the *skandah* grid."

Merlin turned to Blaise and waited for him to explain the *skandah* grid. "This is the second phase of the *Bardo* passage. The first is subjective, personal. You review your life records from the etheric and astral body registers, and you encounter your *Ammit*, and, if you're wise and a little bit gutsy, you own that. Now in the second phase you move into a more transpersonal aspect of yourself. If the personality is a brand name, then the *skandah* grid is something generic. It is a structure and mechanism for consciousness to construe an outer world in a context of illusory or transient separateness, as a separate self perceiving a world.

"This grid has five components: name and form; feelings and sensations; will; perceptions; and consciousness itself, the presumed wielder of these first four. All of these create and maintain a perceivable world seemingly outside oneself. Your encounter with the five *Dhyani* Buddhas ruthlessly erases that illusion. Each *Dhyani* Buddha exemplifies the exalted, transcendental condition of one *skandah*, illuminates it, renders it transparent and empty, with original Buddha Nature, or, if you like, with that brilliance of Light Sraosha provided. Each *skandah* or cognitive condition is converted to wisdom, to enlightenment consciousness; each of these Buddhas expresses that wisdom, models it for you.

"Sure, it's scary as hell to most people because they don't understand what it means, but for the few, either indigenously wise or well-briefed beforehand, it is the way out of here, off the Wheel of Life, through the labyrinth to the center. Each of these *Dhyani* Buddhas, you could say, flashes a big neon 'Exit' sign. Here's the door, pass through here, and you are out

of here, gone and finished. Copy my example. Here's how you convert a limitation into Light.

"It's what the Buddhists chant—hell, it's what I used to chant when I was young and had no idea what it meant but it came with the *koans* and sore knees—*Gate, gate, paragate, parasamgate, bodhi, svaha.* Gone, gone beyond, gone even beyond that, and goddam, isn't that Light something, it's about time, well done, and we are so out of here. That's a rough translation from the Sanskrit, adapted for an American audience and presented in the vernacular, of course. This big fellow, Vairocana, is on the other side of all that *gone beyond* business."

"It makes you realize you probably have a poor notion of what consciousness is," commented Edward. "We so take it for granted while alive."

"I'll say," replied Blaise. "The Zen Buddhists have a saying, 'The dog chases the bone.' I find it very helpful. The dog is sensory-based consciousness, running the *skandah* grid with all five cylinders firing constantly. It runs after all sensory data and experience, a sound, a voice, a feeling, an image of something seen, a thought, an opinion, a mental construct, a grievance, a person, anything. It goes there. It sprints towards that sensory data object, and grabs it with its teeth like a dog snatching up a bone for itself. Then it brings the bone, the sensory data, back to its den or some private place to gnaw on it obsessively.

"That's what consciousness does: it chases after every last sensory datum possible. Did you ever observe this? Say you are sitting quietly. Then you hear a truck. It's backing up, making that obnoxious beeping sound to alert people to its presence. Your awareness rushes out to where that sound is and snatches it up. It returns it like a dog carrying a bone between its teeth back to this still vast wall of silence that seems like the anchor point of the world. The beeping sound goes into this and before you know it your mind has interpreted and catalogued it.

"When you erase the *skandah* of consciousness, enter the illuminated Buddha state of Vairocana, you follow that sensory data into the great wall of silence and pull the door shut behind you, or pull the hole down over you as you go down. You follow the sensory data back to the *place* where it is registered as proof of external reality, and you go past that. Down the rabbit-hole, then you pull the hole in after you. No sense data, no you sensing it. It's *gate, gate,* pal."

Blaise looked at me. He was having a hard time keeping a straight face. "Did you see the Densely-Packed Ones in there, in the wheel, by any chance?"

I was outside this Buddha figure now and able to see it in some detail. Vairocana held the *Dharma* Wheel like an upright shield resting on his lap. It was blazing white, and inside this whiteness was an even brighter, more fiercely blazing white sun, and inside this I saw what looked like a myriad of identical figures packed in tightly—*densely*—like hundreds of sardines in a tin. They resembled seeds, or somehow I had the impression that was their function.

"Remind you of anyone?" Blaise inquired. His eyes were twinkling. This guy—if he ever is at loose ends for his next life, he would make a great trickster.

Suddenly these densely-packed "seeds," if that's what they were, rose up. They weren't seeds. They were angels, angelic forms, as if made of purest crystal. I saw thousands of them, probably millions, rising up at the center of this blazing white sun, itself at the center of the *Dharma* Wheel and that at Vairocana's heart, forming an upward curving mandala of Light, a fierce diamond white fire, like a million crystalline hands made of this fire or a million angelic forms made of it. I understood why Blaise's eyes were twinkling, like he was

waiting for me to get the joke. I got it. It was a magnificent punchline. It was his Blaise angels: Ofanim.

Later, I understood how that was relevant to Vairocana and what he does. It's implied in the meaning of his name. Vairocana means "in shapes making visible." He is the manifester of forms and phenomena, the spreading forth of the seeds of all things in existence, everything that consciousness could apprehend. Vairocana has dominion over all these phenomena; he is victorious over them, meaning he is not fooled by their appearances, taken in by their semblances. He sees straight through them to the Great Void or *sunyata*, as the Buddhists call it.

He seeing straight through them is why he's called the Great Illuminator, the Radiating One. Pure, nondualistic consciousness illuminates all aggregates of matter, all semblances pretending or construing themselves to be separate units. His Light is the wisdom of one who possesses, *who is*, absolute reality and truth. That's why Vairocana is positioned at the center of the mandala of the five *Dhyani* Buddhas. It's also because he represents the element of ether, space, or *Akasha*, which precedes and thus organizes or "births" those of fire, earth, water, and air. His dominion through consciousness sets the standard for them. The Ofanim, the myriads of Blaises in their angelic forms, provide the cognitive force, the movement, the wheels for the Wheel of Vairocana, to perceive this clearly. The Ofanim, the Holy Wheels, turn the wheels to make pure cognition possible.

They are the seeds of transcendent consciousness force that underly all matter. The Tibetans call them *Og-Min*, which means "no down" or "no fall," which seems odd or incomprehensible at first. It means they never lose their dominion. They never succumb to the lures and blandishments of separate consciousness, which nearly all humans do routinely, easily, and constantly, construing an outer world. They never incarnate their awareness into separate forms, though they will illuminate reality through these separate forms, like us. They are field agents for the Great Illuminator, the Radiating One, Vairocana, but even he is a field agent for the Buddha, the Awakened One of the *Dharmakaya*.

It's hard to avoid all the Buddhist jargon because it well describes this. The five *Dhyani* Buddhas are differentiated emanations of the one Buddha, which means, starkly, of the awakened state, five essential gestures and qualities. Other names for them are the five Wisdom *Tathagatas* ("ones who have thus gone or come") or the five *Jinas* ("conquerors, victors"). They are correlated with colors, elements, directions, symbolic objects, specific wisdom qualities, their own Pure Lands or paradisal Buddha Fields, and complementary consorts; their array forms a mandala exemplifying the original design of consciousness.

"When the *skandah* of consciousness is raised to Buddhahood you get Vairocana," said Merlin. "Being dead gives you the opportunity to realize this, but you don't have to be dead to get the insight. You can do it while alive. In fact, we recommend it. We even have a dedicated Vairocana temple for you to visit."

By the time Merlin had finished saying this, we were already there. It was as if this temple, as he described it, lay vibrationally sideways to our location and all we had to do was shift our attention, look over to the left, and we were there. Yes, we were inside a temple, one larger than any structure I had ever seen or imagined. The golden walls rose upwards for hundreds of feet; the place was suffused with the same rich blue Light that surrounded Vairocana, and it seemed even the air was blue, as if misted with blue paint. I saw lions everywhere. Not actual ones of course, but representations of lions on the walls as bas-reliefs, and I would estimate at least one hundred of them forming a base for his throne, and when I studied this otherworldly pride of lions they seemed to comprise a single lion that was the foundation for Vairocana's seat. These lions were of gold fire.

Vairocana sat on his throne and appeared as he had in the *Bardo* a moment before, except now I saw effulgent rays streaming out of his head in all directions. I tried not to laugh. My first impression was that he had been quilled in the head by a monstrous celestial porcupine, but I think that was a nervous laugh I was suppressing. He hadn't been quilled. If anything, he was the prickly porcupine and these rays were adamant, invincible lines of Light and connection, and I was the curious prying dog about to get a snoutful of his Light quills.

For a moment I saw Vairocana and his temple from the outside. It seemed to be in the same place as a significant mountain, though many times larger. Vairocana sat on his throne upon the surface of the Earth at this mountain like a transcendental Buddha King, exuding complete dominion and authority. But it was the kind of dominion I could live with because it was not about political power or control over people; it was about dominion over all limitations of consciousness. He was a role model, an exemplifier, showing us how to do it. Here is how you convert the consciousness *skandah* into enlightenment, he said.

I saw that the streaming rays from his head flowed out to join the head rays of four more figures similar to him, similar in size and majesty, though differing in appearance, costumery, symbolic gestures, and ritual objects. They formed a grid around the planet and this grid was connected upwards to an even more celestial figure. That must be the Buddha himself, if "himself" is even applicable here, being the epitome of voidness and the emptiness of all notions of selfhood. The Buddha and his five principal emanations, the

Dhyani Buddhas, the Meditation Lords, the masters of contemplation, each representing the transcendental aspect of a *skandah*, formed a pattern of enlightenment around the Earth. Who would have suspected this? A Light grid made of six Buddhas?

Anticipating my next thought, Merlin started to answer it. "The mountain is called *Ol Doinyo Lengai*, a still active stratovolcano near Arusha, Tanzania. The mountain is holy to the Maasai who regard it as the residence of *Egai-Khambegeu*, their principal deity, the one responsible for creating them in the Golden Age.

"It is the site of many pilgrimages. They also call this deity *Enkai* or *Engai*, and they say when she is displeased she signals her wrath with volcanic eruptions. *Mogongo jo Mugwe*, this 'Mountain of God,' is only 10,459 feet high, but it has unique geological features for a volcano, the physical and chemical qualities and characteristics of its lava staining its surface black as seen in the sunlight. This feature, coupled with the way the peak rises right out of the flat landscape, imparts a spectral and powerful dimension to this holy mountain."

Vairocana wore this mountain like a skirt, meaning his size far exceeded the girth and height of this volcano. I could see why the Maasai would attribute such exalted attributions to their *Engai*, noting this deity could not be seen by mortal eyes. That probably meant that first one had to be clairvoyant, and second, one had to be clairvoyant from a *strong* crown chakra which we had achieved, possibly by way of assisted handicap, from our Golden Bough which, as I understand it, puts our field of consciousness inside the crown chakra. I assumed the Maasai were referring to Vairocana when they saw *Egai-Khambegeu*.

Though I could see Vairocana as a figure, the *Dharmachakra* or wheel he held at his midsection like a shield was paramount. It grew

larger, a blazing white sun. The blazing sun burned at the center of this wheel and was as fierce as a furnace. Our group stood attentively in observance of Vairocana's furnace. We were waiting for something to happen. We all knew something would happen.

Then it did. It felt like the irresistible suction coming off a white hole. This may not be accurate according to astrophysics but this is how it seemed. We were being drawn as if by magnetic pull into this blazing white furnace which widened radically the closer we came to its mouth. I felt my consciousness, the framework by which I was observing this and noting my reactions to it, was both enlarging and being stripped away from me. If my consciousness was like an open mouth, the wider I opened it, the more I lost it. As you can see, it was not an experience easy to describe, and it didn't seem like it was going to hurt much.

The phenomena had some curious features. I felt I was already inside the white furnace watching myself being pulled inexorably into its huge white maw. I watched as I was stripped of flesh, as if all the molecules and atoms comprising my "body," though certainly this was not my physical form I was observing, were being flayed off and were streaming towards me like a million rivulets, like a million grinning, blushing Frederick faces saying, Hey, don't blame me for this.

This "body," I gradually realized, was the mechanism of my consciousness. It was the force of awareness that I had personalized, rendered hostage to my subjectivity and self-reference, so taking this for granted I no longer noticed it. It was the body, the framework, the Light grid, the *skandah*, by which I deployed consciousness to construe an exterior world confronting an interior world. Consciousness seemed like a great open mouth consuming reality like water. Or it was the canvas on which reality was painted?

It seemed passive, but I knew it was the epitome of activity. It was the cognitive mechanism that habitually performed that delusive miracle of registering a world, registering anything, that was rapidly streaming off me, out of me, and flowing into this indomitable furnace. The habitual bedrock of my awareness was roaring out—remember my earlier reference to the sensation of a tornado? It felt like that.

I wasn't injured or harmed in any way. I can honestly say I was not frightened, though I was certainly surprised by the force of this divestment. It was like becoming suddenly wide-awake, as awake as you could possibly be, but without yourself as the one who could say I am awake. It was naked wakefulness. Like reality had just chugged a five-shot espresso. There was nothing to see, nothing to be aware of, nothing the wakefulness wanted. It did not need to grab at a world and possess it by seeing it. That compulsion was gone. It was like somebody asked you if you wanted a glass of water and you said, no, thank you, I just had one. My stomach is already full of water. Or maybe it was because you no longer had a stomach. Or had become an ocean.

I did not need to be aware of anything particular. I already had a surfeit of awareness. No, that's not it. I was awareness. Awareness was. Forget the I part. Everything that I could have cognized, seen, thought about, was inside me. No, it *was* me. Once you've had that drink of water, you don't have to think about water anymore. The water is part of you. The world was part of me now, not that "I" was here and the world was there. We had done a merger. It was one world.

As you can see, it gets a little vexed trying to talk about this afterwards.

"I hope you will appreciate," Merlin said, "that the Earth is equipped with this and other *Dhyani* Buddha meditation temples for the benefit of humanity. Nobody can be forced to access this quality of consciousness, but it has been provided for humanity by the planet's designers as an aid for awakening in those who wish to take advantage of it. It does subtly flavor the planet's atmosphere. Our hope was that some people might seek to experience the *Dhyani* Buddhas and their *skandah* revelations while still alive to be better prepared for the *Bardo*. Their revelations illuminate both poles of human experience, alive and *Bardo*."

The experience confounded my sense of normal spatial distinctions. Were we in the *Bardo* in the afterlife terrain of the Green Knight's world or were we out in the planet's Light grid amidst its visionary temples? It's a fallacious question. There is no distinction as to terrain. It is all what the Buddhists call the middle realm, the *Sambhogakaya*, the delight and bliss body of the Buddha, the Enjoyment or Participation-Together Body, the subtle body of limitless form and innumerable Light forms, his intermediate realm full of visions and spectacles of Light, from Avalon to the Underworld, where emptiness has *lots* of bright forms.

That's what the Tibetans said of Vairocana and his Densely-Packed Realm of the Og-Min, our Blaises, inside his heart: it's packed densely into the *Sambhogakaya*. The *Bardo*, the Underworld, this crazy place of karma processing, is like a small colony, a picture outpost, in this vast spectacle of the Buddha's subtle enjoyment body of limitless form. I half expected Vairocana to inquire if we are enjoying ourselves yet, like a gracious, bubbly host of a cocktail party.

I confess I did feel some sympathy for those encountering this fantastic apparition of truth, reality, and the maw of nondualistic consciousness that was Vairocana without the benevolent supervision and elbow-guiding of Merlin. I had no trouble conceiving it would be a tremendous ordeal for recently disembodied consciousness already struggling to come to terms with this troubling new landscape known as the *Bardo*. I could see how many people would regard being sucked into this roaring white furnace of emptiness as what death is, annihilation, the utter end and ruination of themselves. They would not regard it as a major stepping stone on the journey to their liberation.

To make sense of Vairocana, to applaud his disclosure of the *sunyata* or emptiness of the aggregate of consciousness, was probably expecting too much of most people. God knows what I would have made of that awful spectacle had I really been dead and not simulating it and not among friends on this commissioned expedition and not with Merlin, premier Underworld docent.

I could easily picture most people running for the Exit door, in this case, for the way back into incarnation. Better the Mystery you're used to sleeping through than the Mystery revealed naked and unmediated before your very eyes, especially when you don't even have physical eyes any more and you are not used to chakras. That is what most people in fact do, according to the *Bardo Thödol*. They get spooked, deeply alarmed, jump quite out of themselves when presented with the roaring furnace-like illuminating sun of Vairocana on day one. Anything but this, they protest; show me the door back into another body, *please*. Whom do I have to bribe, and how much, to get through a womb-door?

I said "most people," but I did not mean to imply nobody got the secret. I saw ample evidence here that lots of people got the Mystery and were waking up. Innumerable Bodhisattvas surrounded Vairocana; they all looked Buddha-like. Their forms emanated Light in all directions; their heads blazed in Light. Around them were many souls, not all human by any means, meditating, or so it looked. They were

concentrating their attention. They moved in and out of the roaring white furnace in a manner that struck me as similar to testing the water temperature at the beach on a day when it is perhaps too cool for swimming.

These "meditators" moved their forms, which I surmised meant their focused awareness, into the raging white maw and their forms instantly vanished. Then, after some time had elapsed, and this was variable for each meditator, they re-appeared and reconfigured themselves, though each time it was a little fainter. It reminded me of watching swimmers at the ocean, your own children perhaps, and they submerge and swim underwater, and you begin to wonder when they are planning to resurface or are they, God no, drowning? Then they pop up out of the water like breaching porpoises and grin at you.

"Are all these people dead," I asked Merlin, "trying to wake up and get into Vairocana and, as it were, permanently swim underwater?"

"No, it's a mixture of conditions," Merlin replied. "Some are quite alive, meditating in monasteries, ashrams, mosques, and some are walking on a beach. Others, as you surmised, are dead, their physical and etheric bodies dropped. They are spending a long day one coming to terms with the Vairocana revelation. The *Bardo Thödol* makes it seem that the time period is constrained, that everything pertaining to Vairocana happens in the first day. That day can last as long as you need it, a hundred Earth years if that's what you require.

"Think of 'day' as meaning something more akin to a vibrational condition, to a landscape of consciousness, a terrain of awareness. Day is like a *Sefira* in Qabala; it is a zone of reality. Day One is Vairocana consciousness. Stay as long as you need. It's the way the Egyptians meant it, when they called their funerary text the 'Book of Coming Forth by Day.' They understood 'day' meant a condition of awareness. Day, to the Egyptians, was much like *Rigpa* or Clear Light to the Tibetans. The goal of the *Duat* or *Bardo* experience is to come into this *day*light condition, to convert your nighttime-focused awareness, the condition of incarnate ignorance and sleep, into the true Day Light of wide-awakeness."

"Based on what I am seeing, I would say some people are working on mastering their Vairocana revelation while they're still alive. Is this right?"

"Indeed they are," said Merlin. "It is the ideal approach. Don't leave it all until the last minute when it becomes, potentially, too formidable for most. The prospect of dissolving their function of consciousness into its primordial constituent, an undifferentiated field of blue Light, overwhelms most people. It creates a tricky problem for us. We cannot force anyone to become conscious. Yet it is imperative that one day, at some point, people realize the layout and intention of consciousness, of separate existence. Study the engineering plans. Realize the better they understand the design diagrams and the operating instructions the quicker they can become masters of the mechanism itself."

"Tell me about it," said Tommy. "When I got here I couldn't believe how many people had spent their lives oblivious to the set-up, which, to me seemed so obvious it was incomprehensible that people couldn't see it. Nobody wants to. They find ingenious ways to keep themselves mesmerized by the surface allurements of being alive and walking around in bodies, to keep themselves asleep to the Mystery in which they move and breathe which is, as I would put it: How do you account for the fact there is a you who has consciousness right now?

"It stares them in the face for 70 or 80 years, they ignore it, die, get here, and are crazed, confused, frightened, bewildered, angry, defiant, or supplicatory. I knew when I got here it would be a challenge, a bit uphill at times, but

the gains would be worth it. The perspective would justify it, like climbing a mountain. It's all about the view, isn't it, seeing the vast stretch of landscape and its features. The *Bardo* is the answer to this vital question that everybody should be asking. It was like I finally got to examine the stage props behind all the magic tricks, to see how they appeared to slice the body in half without ever slicing it in half."

"I started to realize the scope and grandeur of consciousness from my time with the Thunderbirds," said Matthew. "You know, those Blaises you guys are always on about. They tutored me at James Bay in Ontario in their Thunderbird guise and through that I started to see how large a landscape is consciousness. The Indians I was acquainted with already knew this. They smiled when I told them my discoveries. They said the Great Bird does that.

"In the years leading up to the Theosophon, now ten years ago, I dilated my perception of the field of consciousness under the Thunderbirds' influence. That is fitting, don't you think, since one of the commissions of the Ofanim, as our human Blaise is always reminding us, is to remove the obstacles to consciousness. If you remove all the impediments, what remains is naked consciousness, and that is an excellent preparation for the Vairocana disclosure."

"My grandmother taught me it was like flying into the Sun as a bird," said Pipaluk. "The heat and fire of the Sun strip you of all your feathers then your skin then your bones then all that makes you this courageous bird is gone. Yet you keep flying. It seems like flying, but it also feels like you're expanding. You become as big as the Sun, the same as its fire and heat and its terrific force, and then that is stripped away too. Neither the Sun nor yourself as a bird remain, yet there is this still, steady, loud drone. It remains. You and the Sun are now this. We were taught not to fear this but to welcome it as the source of our powers."

"Our commission is to make the Vairocana disclosure more palatable to arriving human consciousness," said Merlin. "Anyone have any suggestions?"

"We could offer prizes and discounts," said Blaise. "That usually works."

Everyone turned to Blaise, either in disbelief or merriment. He had that effect on people. I had travelled with him enough now to know that for sure.

Merlin answered with a straight face. "Could you elaborate on that?"

"Knock a few lives off what they owe as a reward for good discernment. I'm sure you could fix that with the Lords of Karma. You know everyone. As for prizes, how about their Book of Life autographed by the Ancient of Days? I'm sure our pals, Blaise, could talk the Old Man into doing a little book-signing."

At this point, Philomena stepped forward and made herself more visible. She had been fluctuating between a seeable and a mostly invisible presence. It reminded me of when her attention would wander slightly at the tea-table, and she would pull herself back as if with a finger-snap saying she had been reviewing some complicated right-hand fingering from a Rachmaninov piece.

"As you know, seven of us ascended, as you call it, at the Theosophon," she began, speaking to the group. "Also at that time and in the years after, members of the Great White Brotherhood started meeting in greater numbers with selected humans, reviewing their life-plans and helping them see more. In the last ten years a great number of humans have followed our example. I have the impression the leaders have stepped things up and need a lot of helpers. The Theosophon did quicken many people, opened up their psychic faculties. Now they need, and now they are receptive to, directed instruction from us. The leaders, or whatever I should call those responsible for this in the Brotherhood, have asked me and the others to take a role in this instruction of willing people.

"The trick is to see through the illusion, to see how your mind generates realities around you. It's not just here, but back in the living, physical world too. Some of the people I've worked with were, in many ways, like myself, and I acted in a role that was similar to how you, Blaise, and your angelic pals visited me in your Rotunda of Light over the course of a few years getting me ready. Your visits were, and this was to do with me and my receptivity and its blocks, on the edge of my daytime awareness, and often just past the liminal threshold.

"But now we can work more closely and lucidly with the living in their daytime world. We have to be careful and sensitive with our initial approach, but once they have accepted the plausibility of our presence, we can make progress. When they're ready, I show them what the *Bardo* will be like, because its nature and mechanics are a stripped-clean version of how living Earth reality works. They are not very different in their mechanisms, only in speed. The *Bardo* is a faster version of physical reality; material reality is slow-motion *Bardo*. In both, the mind projects its realities. The tutorial will help them navigate both worlds.

"Naturally, the inclination is to import one's familiar surroundings when you get here. You walk about amidst your home, your friends, your possessions. It's like unpacking your suitcase when you arrive at a hotel room, putting your clothes in the drawers, laying out your favorite things on tables and dressers. It helps to reduce the shock of the transition which, no one will disagree, is big. A friend of mine who had played harpsichord in a Boston Baroque music group died and came here. He came reluctantly. He was only 71 and thought he still had many more years. He loved his Bach and Vivaldi and Scarlatti. It was like me and my

Scriabin and Rachmaninov. I recognized the symptoms in him.

"As soon as he arrived, he resumed playing the harpsichord. He pictured himself still with his group, though when he considered it, their reactions seemed a little slow and staged, like clever mannikins. He regarded being dead as nothing more momentous than being hospitalized. It wouldn't stop his practicing and performing. He would continue to live for his Baroque music and perfect his fingering technique on the harpsichord. Death was irrelevant to that.

"At one level, he knew something was wrong, had changed. He knew he had passed over, as they say, left his body for good for parts unknown—to himself. But at another level of himself, he wanted to keep up the façade of livingness, that nothing fundamental had changed, that his music flourished. I sat with him as he projected a concert hall with an audience of 700, his chamber music group, himself at the harpsichord, in the middle of the Bach 'Suite for Violin and Harpsichord'. He was rippling with the music, loving its precise sound. He knew the audience was listening raptly. The music was everything.

"Then I opened a door for him or pulled back the curtains. The reality he thought he was ecstatically embedded in grew faint. The images weakened, the sounds diminished, and soon they were mere outlines of themselves, then gone. He suddenly realized he had been reviewing his life records, one concert in particular. He was not, in actual, bodily terms, there at all, certainly not now. He saw that he was projecting that experience, animating it, then entering it, and convincing himself that it was his reality of this moment, what he was doing. He looked dismayed and intrigued as he found himself retracting himself from it.

"Next I showed him that even the impression of his reviewing his life tapes was illusory, that in fact he was in the staggering effulgent field of Sraosha. He was on the boat, on the bridge, getting the full disclosure and preview of the terrain. He watched as all his projections withdrew back into himself as if drawn by some pervasive magnetic field or like newspapers swirling down a whirlpool. He was aware of this process, and he was aware of his own awareness of it. He had become conscious of being conscious; his consciousness turned back on itself and dropped everything it had been grasping except its own self-awareness.

"He turned to me, his whole being asking a question. Am I? 'Yes,' I said.

"By the time he reached the Vairocana challenge, he practically ran into the furnace. You see, it does make a big difference if sensitive souls are briefed in advance. They can drop a lot of their resistance, which comes from fear and lack of knowledge of their context and its intention, and progress smoothly through the system. I've seen this repeated many times. It's even more impressive when you do it with somebody still alive, drop the veils while they are still embedded in the heaviness and plausibility of physical reality. Show them it's all a magic show and they are the magician projecting the phantasmagoric images.

"A part of a person remembers, a very old aspect of their consciousness is quickened by this. 'I remember,' it says, and the reference is to the time before they ever entered incarnation, before they signed up for the phylogeny, as you put it, Blaise. That long dark vacuity of forgetting is dissolved and they remember it brightly. They come to their senses: Here I am again. I remember it."

"It's like they say with sudden realization, 'Man, what a dream I was just having!' just like when you wake up from a monumental nighttime dream," said Blaise. "You marvel at how gullible you were, how you took it all in as real. Then you marvel at how you managed not to be aware that you were dreaming it."

"You see the problem we're dealing with, how to step up the pace of disclosure without forcing people to become more aware before they're ready," said Merlin. "The balance point between those two imperatives is exacting. But as a whole human consciousness, its resting state, its normative assumptions, must be upgraded to match the big changes happening to the planet's Light grid. That in turn tends to make it easier to approach people individually and encourage them to take a few steps forward in their understanding of reality.

"The Light grid improvements, facilitating a sixth chakra frame of reference, tend to make it easier for embodied human awareness to expand its framework. Almost against their own disbelief, people will start being more naturally psychic as these Light grid upgrades are anchored into permanent Earth reality. They will gradually see more of actual reality, see what's behind the curtain of the physical world, and it will gradually seem not such a big deal. So when they arrive here, they will already have some habits of psychic sight."

Merlin stopped talking. He waited attentively, patiently, for us to speak. I remembered he had asked us to come up with practical suggestions for changes.

"The numbers are too big," said Philomena. "In the last ten years I have been able to counsel people at the rate of about 10 per day. That's 36,500 souls, and that's by duplicating myself so there are 10 Philomenas on the job. The other six ascenders from the Theosophon have done about the same. So that's 219,000 people who enter the *Bardo* better prepared than otherwise. Yes, certainly many others in the Brotherhood are performing the same mission. But we calculate people are dying at the rate of 105 per minute, constantly. That's 42,300,000 a year, and the number is probably higher with

each year as people decide they don't want to upgrade themselves to match the changes in the Light grid. You can see we cannot keep up with this influx. We are tutoring only a few souls."

"So many people are arriving here unprepared for the cognitive challenges, and the results of their ill-preparedness are affecting the Earth," said Merlin. "It is a kind of bleed-through effect. Keep in mind, the Underworld, *this* Underworld, is a large Light temple or landscape of Light in proximity to Earth. Not only proximity but relevance. It is the specific human phylogenetic *Bardo*.

"It has conditions and requirements specifically adjusted to Earth-human conditions. The failure of so many newly dead souls to navigate this terrain correctly creates a backlog of fear, unconsciousness, and dark emotions which starts to seep into Earth reality. That sets up a negative reciprocal loop in which unawakened Earth conditions feed back into the Underworld, and unawakened Underworld experiences flow back into Earth reality as a subliminal influence. Well, that's the wrong kind of reciprocity. We need a flow of comprehension."

Merlin gestured for us to follow him. At first I thought we were walking to a new location, but we were there instantly. We never walked. We just went. I saw before us the queerest sight I can ever remember seeing. Picture a soap bubble the size of a city. The bubble is transparent, flexible, but serves as a solid, impermeable membrane. Inside it, pressing up against it, is a horde of humans. They seem to be mostly faces, the heads and necks, sometimes raised arms. They are all pressing against the bubble membrane to see through it, to call out, to beseech, to wail, to complain, and some try to squirm their way through it.

Nobody looks happy. Not even close. Their faces speak of misery, anguish, pain. It is not a physical pain of course but one that suggests alienation, a great sense of disorientation, bereavement, of being irreversibly lost, forgotten. You take in this spectacle and you'd think, they all feel like they're locked out. Or they are in prison, in the exercise yard, peering through the fierce, resistant fences at the outside world, their former world, the bright living world, the world of bodies that are breathing and feeling. They are utterly, grievously, unable to get there, to go past the fences, and they kick against these fences.

Nobody is content with their condition. They all want to escape it. They see the bright world of living humans on the other side of the membrane and feel desperate; they try to claw their way through the membrane, to push against it with enough collective force to burst it, to have their ceaseless wails of discontent be heard. They look like they are in Hell, like they feel their condition is hellish.

I began to see Merlin's point. A cloud of black, grey, and brown splotches continuously emanated from this horde of malcontented dead humans and it continuously flowed into the lit human world, like anomalous storm clouds. They were storm clouds of distorted, frustrated desire, the desire to live again, to reclaim, to grab, hold in their hands, wrap themselves around, human bodily life, as if it represented their original, correct position, and death the aberration of it. The air was thick with their clamoring presence, as if they crowded against the membrane between the worlds seeking for a way through, a way back, into life. I began to appreciate the scale of the project to reverse this faulty perspective.

These protestors were not physically visible to the people walking around on the Earth, but it was obvious they were a steady psychic influence, a baleful dark energy field that kept wafting in petulant waves through human subliminal awareness. The more sensitive among the living humans registered it as a coolness, like a sudden chill in the air, or sometimes as a shout, or the cries of an angry crowd, or maybe they felt they had come in contact with something ghostly and most unpleasant. Most people did not wakefully notice this menacing energy cloud, but it affected them in ways and places under their own consciousness radar, making them feel unaccountably grumpy, critical, fearful, defensive, paranoid, or generally edgy, like standing on the brink of a precipice.

Unfortunately, it also subliminally fueled a sense of nonspecific or generic desire, of unfulfilled passions, free-ranging acquisitiveness, almost to the point of frantic desperation, like shoppers queuing for a fabulous store sale, and this in turn darkened their self-awareness and diminished the chance they would wake up in the present moment because it yanked their attention entirely outwards. The dead protesting souls were not recognizing the true condition of their consciousness, not acknowledging their authentic location in the landscape of reality, and, under their influence, nor were many of the susceptible living. It was a self-reinforcing blindness, waves of obscuration reciprocating between them. I wondered how many times in my life was I influenced from this source?

For some it fueled moments of despair, depression, pessimism, or atheistic displeasure. They felt their lives were pointless, without direction, serving no known goal. Death, the inevitable dead-end, awaited them like a 150-foot high brick wall. The dead, pressing against the membrane between the worlds, perceived such thoughts as these and grew even more despondent, seeing Hell everywhere now. It was horrible to be dead, and just as horrific to be alive and without purpose. God did not fare well in the general assessment. He was a no-good torturing shit of a deity for having created this unending Hell condition. Or worse, any God that would have created this infernal realm is no God of mine. Or even worse: There is no

God, and this Hell realm is the proof of that absence. I could have spent an hour collecting quotes like these from disgruntled souls.

The litany continued along these despairing, vituperative lines, and you couldn't blame these pained souls for these conclusions, yet you knew they were wrong. The sad part was these souls probably did not understand that they had created these Hell conditions themselves, from a lifetime of spewing darkness. It reminded me of the character of Mrs. Dudgeon, a rigid Puritan mother in 1777 New Hampshire in Bernard Shaw's play, *The Devil's Disciple*. Before she dies of heart disease in act two, she is a whirlwind of spewing negativity, casting aspersions, vile, spite, criticism, hate, dismissal, intolerance in all directions. She's a moralistic slasher, and nobody is good enough for her harsh Christian standards. I cringed as I watched this years ago, knowing this woman would have a miserable afterlife as all the products of her spewed darkness would form a dark grid, a storm front around her, and she would suffer and not know why.

I was shocked then dismayed to see the dark conclusions these lost souls came to. They were astray and stuck in heavy, dark places within themselves, and the longer they stayed there, growing these infernal plants of despair and gloom, the more these "plants" started befouling the living human world with darkness. Many of the Earth's Light temples looked like English hills veiled in thick fog. Others were enveloped in obsidian clouds through which silvery-white jags of lightning kept striking in a chaotic, seemingly random, uncontrolled way.

Some of the constellations of negativity looked like distorted geometric grids that were delivering winds, storms, lightning, and thunder to the physical world. In physical life, you walk across a hillside and you wonder why you suddenly feel like snarling. Why has my mood shifted so suddenly, you query. You have

just passed through one of these individually projected Hell grids and have inhaled its noxious vapors and they have briefly stained your mind dark.

"This is the *Loka* of the Hell realm, one of the Six Worlds around Earth," said Merlin. "It's part of the Wheel of Life or *Bhavachakra* that Yama holds. The Six Worlds are contingent realms of human experience; people experience them while alive and may gravitate towards one when they die. Some are divine, others hellish. The two you are seeing are the lowest and most miserable of all.

"The Hell realm is where, as you can see, souls are in torment, suffering, miserable. Behind them you'll notice another large group, though not as tormented looking. They look dissatisfied, disgruntled, peevish, unsated, like they've been cheated of something, shortchanged; they haven't had enough to eat or experience. The Buddhists call them the *Pretas*, Hungry Ghosts.

"They want back into the game. They don't like where they are, their new condition, and they want to live again, as soon as possible, and with improved conditions. They want to storm the gates. They are envious of what you, the living, have. They want to take it from you. You don't deserve to have all this livingness. They do. They want it all back now. They will keep clawing for it, reaching out, all in futility. This is the realm of unsatisfied desires. The Hell realm is of pain and purgatory.

"This has always been the case with the afterlife realms of the Earth, but in recent decades, or perhaps centuries, the problem has intensified. These two *Lokas* have filled with far more souls than before. We now have a considerable population of stuck, lost, miserable souls crowding the Underworld membrane. There is no possibility of the membrane failing, but the problem is rather one of incompletion. All these souls are not finishing their required

Bardo processing. That incompletion exerts a stagnating effect, a stifling, quagmire atmosphere, and that seeps into Earth reality and contaminates all natural cheerfulness.

"Think of it like a postal strike. No mail is delivered for weeks. It has piled up. You can barely move through the aisles of the post office for these great piles. All the communication represented by this undelivered mail is starting to stagnate. Each one of these unfortunate souls is like a one-person postal strike with the burden of unprocessed life records from their etheric and astral body upon them. It's like carrying around an angry black bear on your back, its claws at your face. You are not yourself, not on your game, not in a game-ready state of awareness. Everyone is wary of everyone else, or ignoring them or oblivious of their existence. If this were the physical world, you'd worry about a riot erupting. You'd call in extra officials to handle the crowd control. It's volatile."

"Traditionally, religions and many metaphysical models impute the hellish conditions to a state of punishment and reprisal *done* to the dead souls," said Matthew. "But I don't see punishment agents amidst this teeming mass."

"No, there are none," Merlin responded. "There is no punishment imposed from outside. The souls do it to themselves. They go about wrapped up in a cloud of self-generated crankiness. It feels like a bed or nails or a hairshirt. They have forgotten they created it themselves, extruded it like a black ink. They spent their lives creating this grid of misery around them; now it greets them. It is where their consciousness has been living all this time, both creating and fighting it. Now they react as if they have been maliciously attacked, victims of incessant inhuman torture and despicable conditions, but it is all self-generated.

"They have entirely lost track of themselves, of their own consciousness as a creative source, and fail to see that they are generating these inky black gloomy vapors, these grids of attacking demons, all around them. This in turn further sours their mood, deepens the hole they've dug themselves. They fight, they flee, they complain, or wail, moan, shout, demand, plead. It is a dark chorus.

"They are now far from the self-empowering revelation of the *Dhyani* Buddhas. They are three large steps away from their disclosure now. Their realization that their conditions are mind-generated is eclipsed; the powers of consciousness to generate any kind of reality is veiled; and the emptiness of this *skandah* and its transcendent universally wide-awake condition will not even dawn on them. They are stuck, unable to climb out of the hole they have dug for themselves."

Again Merlin paused, waiting for us to speak. The problem seemed bad.

Then a giant swell of diamond crystalline Light like the fire of a million hands rose up in an enlarging wave under this domain of the stuck and cranky ones. It was as if the ocean had welled up into a half-sphere, like a cup, then a chalice, enveloping the Hell and Hungry Ghost realms and their tormented souls. It was like the Sun coming out from behind the clouds after a rainstorm. This Light seemed like the striking of a million exquisitely sharp swords that cut through the self-generated darkness of these souls and gave them a moment of something else, the possibility of a way out of this hellish realm.

The abundance of diamond-fire hands seemed to be individual cells in one great hand, and this hand was lifting up this Hell realm like it was a precious bubble. It was like shaking a drunk or somebody in a trance and they suddenly wake up. Or they had been sleepwalking or walking about under the effects of concussion. In a flash they come back to themselves, get re-anchored in what they used to be. They had been wandering about in shock, out of their bodies, out of themselves, delirious, hallucinatory, none of their cognitive processes working correctly. These diamond-fire hands were like finger-snaps exploding all around the deluded lost souls and saying to them, "Do you remember now?"

These flashing, Light-filled hands collectively seemed to emit a roar. It was a sound somewhat like ocean surf crashing on a beach at high tide, but it was also a sound that spoke of a steady, unrelenting, even ruthless, insistence.

Blaise found this amusing. He was shaking his head and grinning. "It's Blaise. The Lion mount under Vairocana. It's the Ofanim in their lion guise, ruthlessly removing all the obstacles to consciousness comprehending Vairocana and the revelation of the transcendental emptiness condition of consciousness. They support the reality of Vairocana *like* a pride of roaring lions. Their fiery fierceness clears the way for limited, sensory-bound consciousness to raise itself up to Vairocana's disclosure of unlimited, sensory-free, unbound consciousness. They are Vairocana's throne which means you pass *through them* to reach Vairocana, which means they assist consciousness in *attaining* that high state. It's uncanny how these guys always position themselves at the center of the action."

For a moment I saw these millions of diamond hands transformed into lions made of a blazing diamond-white fire. I nearly jumped back. What a sight.

"Yama has asked the Ofanim to intensify their Light emissions, and to broadcast their lions' roar aspect more frequently by a factor of about 50 percent," Merlin said. "As you saw this has the potential effect of jarring more souls awake, like throwing cold water on their faces so they can snap back to themselves and start to remember their condition and take responsibility for it.

"Sometimes a shock to the system is curative, just what a soul needs to sober up. The Ofanim Light suddenly illuminates the dark fetid cave in which these souls stand. They had understood that they were underground in self-made dungeons. The other *Dhyani* Buddhas will be stepping up their Light emissions also. Vairocana isn't even the *Dhyani* assigned to the Hell and Purgatory realms, but any kind of upgrade in the Buddha radiance around here has a salutary effect.

"It will still be their choice whether they start assimilating the angelic input or not, whether they take action based on now seeing their condition. If they choose to match the angelic infusion, the lions' roars, they will be assisted. The Ofanim will work closely with each soul, allowing them to regulate the infusion like a water tap. As they want more shock stimulation, they can have it.

"The Brotherhood will allocate more members to act as tutors and several angelic orders will also step forward to act as mentors and guides for the newly woken. These two realms are a great weight, a burden of negativity on the world, and they constitute such a dense ball of darkness that it is in danger of rolling off the emerging crystalline surface of the planet's new Light grid, ejected into space. I speak by way of metaphorical pictures of course, but energetically it's like this."

The scene reminded me of what you see after an earthquake or a major flood, disaster-relief workers everywhere, helping people, cleaning things up. Life in the Hell and Hungry Ghost realms could easily be likened to a disaster that is continuously unfolding and worsening and shows no sign of abatement.

People assume they will be punished in Hell by a displeased God for their actions. It's not like that at all. That is the cruel or simply mistaken notion of Christianity. The souls here are entirely self-punishing. They are self-flagellating. If anything, God suffers with the souls in the Hell and Hungry Ghost realm, hoping they will exert their volition to try to get free, then He can help them. The Supreme Being can't act against His own endowment of free will for souls. They have to freely will themselves free of this quagmire, just as they willfully made it.

They have created grids of such unrelieved nastiness, evil, pain, or darkness around them that when they get to the *Bardo* it's still with them, projected like a cage around their darkened immaterial forms, and its nastiness is unmediated. It's the kind of unwanted lucidity that renders all details in a horrible brilliance. The irony is there is no need for God to punish these souls. It's superfluous. It would be like trying to drown somebody when they are already drowning. These souls already have their just punishment well in hand.

"Here's a little more on Blaise's role," said the human Blaise. "We know Blaise is the mount for the Christ. You see that in the Hindu icon of Garuda, the magnificent celestial bird, with the golden body of a strong man, a white face, red wings, eagle's beak, and a brilliant crown on his head, flying Vishnu and Sri through the heavenly realms. Those are names for the masculine and feminine aspects of the Christ Light. We know too from Hindu myths that Rama, Krishna, and the Buddha are equal emanations or *avatars* of Vishnu, the composite name in Hindu belief for the Christ.

"So why shouldn't Blaise be a mount for all five *Dhyani* Buddhas? For three of them it's obvious as the mounts or *vahanas* are described as Garuda, an elephant, and a horse, all well known Ofanim metaphorical presentations. So now we see them in a lion form, a strong, mighty animal, its roar expressing the force of Vairocana's enlightenment disclosure to the soul. The fifth is a peacock.

"I saw the five *Dhyani* Buddhas, including the one currently under study by us, Vairocana, arranged in a circle. Each sat on its mount or throne, which was Blaise in one of five guises. From the center of the circle, though it was as wide as the circle itself, rose the throne-mount for the Buddha, the consummation of the five. Each of the *Dhyani* Buddhas is an emanation or partial face of the Buddha. Each represents the transcendental aspect of one of the five *skandahs*. The Buddha embodies the transcendental aspect of the five *skandahs*, all converted to wisdom.

"The Buddha, at first seen as a human-celestial figure seated on his throne, towered above the five *Dhyani* Buddhas, and as I looked at them, I saw in truth they were part of him; each was a reflection cast by this singular personification of wakefulness. The Buddha is the perfection of the enlightenment of the *skandah* grid, the five cognitive states raised to a transcendent state of self-illumination and Light. Our goal is to get to the other side of this *skandah* grid and dissolve our selfhood in the Buddha Mind or Christ Light. Here is the Buddha having *consumed* the grid. The Buddha Mind has utterly dissolved the *skandah* grid.

"The Buddha's form now appeared as a slender upward-rising pearl-colored flame of several layers. This flame was bright but it was also transparent. You could see it yet you could see completely through it; that was its emptiness. Underneath the Buddha and the *Dhyani* Buddhas was a tray or carpet or broad flat dish made of millions of identical diamond facets. This was Blaise as the *Nimitta* acting as the throne-mount for the Buddha and his five emanations. It's typical of Blaise that in the midst of presenting this august spectacle they inspired a joke picture too. I couldn't help noticing the way this diamond dish looked like the fabled flying carpet such as King Solomon was known to have.

"Yet the joke collapsed into another revelation because I realized this meant we *go through* the Ofanim, through their *Nimitta* expression, to *reach* these Buddhas. They are a layer of purified consciousness that purges us of all obstacles to consciousness attaining the state of Buddha, the Awakened One. And if, in our august nondualistic condition, we require transportation, Blaise has provided for this in the form of the diamond-studded flying carpet. No matter what they do, there's always a joke waiting like a bubble inside it all."

"Did you see all those long brown strands like fishing lines extending from the fingers of the souls in the hellish realm out into the physical world?" asked Matthew. "They connected with living people. They were sticky like cobwebs. Most of the living people seemed unaware of these attachments, but I noticed these dirty brown strands tended to redirect their thoughts at times. The dead people were reluctant to be dead, separate from their bodies, left on their own in this inexplicable place full of the torments of great awareness and reality.

"They were so used to living in their bodies, defining themselves by their bodies. Consciousness was no more momentous than the fact they breathed or yawned. They parted with their bodies reluctantly, without preparation or understanding. Once here, the heaviness of their consciousness caused them to sink to the bottom of the afterlife barrel, and they strive to reconnect with the living, with anyone. Strangers will do. Anyone that will accept their lifeline. Such discontented dead people are known as Earthbound souls among living humans, and generally they are a problem. They attach themselves to you like leeches. That is, if you're not careful or vigilant. The connections lower the vibration of the physical world, like offloading cargo from a large ship into a tiny rowboat."

"Did you see, Matthew, how when the Ofanim started to pulse their *Nimitta* Light through this ocean-ball of diamond hands around the Hell realm it started to loosen and unplug all these brown cords," said Blaise. "It disconnected them from the senders, the dispirited, ill-adjusted souls, and the cords shriveled up. They had been only half-aware of their actions, too immersed in their desperation. Now they became lucid about what they had done, and the *Nimitta* Light started to birth the possibility in their consciousness of seeing that it was a wrong move, pointless and futile, and that they should take stock of themselves. It's like when you shake someone who is delirious or in shock and they come to and say, 'I didn't know I was doing that, or what came over me.'"

"I saw that when I got here too," said Tommy. "You'd think if you were dead you'd know it, but many people arriving here don't, or they resist the truth. They don't have a body any more, but they still have the habits of the body. The way the body moves their awareness through space, its functions and pleasures, its modes of acting and feeling. It is a familiar interface between them and the world. Now they suddenly have to drop this trusted servant, this faithful retainer, and it's difficult. They keep remembering this body—it's a whole-body version of the phantom limb symptom. Here your body in full has been severed from you yet you have these waves of seemingly real, even palpable, reminders."

"If you're alive and you have the phantom limb sensation, in the area of a severed limb, it's your etheric body's arm or leg you're registering," said Blaise. "It's a reality. But it is not physical and palpable like the physical limb had been, but it is the same shape and occupies the same space in your body. But here, when you are certifiably dead, no arguments or refutations tendered, you don't have an etheric body any longer. That's the first thing to go after you drop the physical form. So you are remembering the mental construct of housing your consciousness in a human form. You remember the outline of it, and the habit of using it to negotiate your way through space and time as a unit of consciousness.

"It's a bitch, but you have to drop that habit. It has no standing here and it will interfere with what you have to do, pull you back into the world of karmic illusions and the clamoring for repeated incarnations, and you'll never get out. The tragicomic aspect of this is originally you had to learn how to inhabit a human body, how to work the muscles, run the emotions grid, perceive a world. That was the weird part, forsaking your spirit form for a mortal human body. Except you have forgotten that and regard dropping the body as a disaster."

"The Ofanim are providing an additional service to help those among the dead who wish to climb out of the gravity well of misunderstanding they find themselves in after the Ofanim have wrapped this realm in their angelic Light," said Merlin. "Have a look."

I saw the Blaises take this underlying Nimitta carpet of diamonds and make a smaller copy of it and fold it over individual souls as they exited this dark area. Each soul, if he wished it, got a Nimitta cloak of diamonds, each identical facet emitting a brilliant white blazing fire. Any who wanted this would have one, instantly; it was clear to me it had to be done on the basis of free will.

This cloak then started acting like an individualized mystagogue, an Underworld docent, explaining conditions, helping disembodied consciousness gain clarity. It was like an individualized *Dhyani* Buddha throne-mount wrapped around the consciousness field of each soul as a talking diamond cloak. We each got a cloak too, but the set-up was different. Ours went over the Golden Bough pillar of golden Light we each stood in, so it seemed the pillar wore the cloak. That would be odd in physical terms, but here it sharpened our clarity. If this were intelligence we were trying to sharpen, it would be like having your IQ

jump 50 points, maybe 100, all at once, and seamlessly, effortlessly, wonderfully.

The dead souls who got a Nimitta cloak would still have to do the work of divestment, sloughing off all residues of their physical body and disavowing its habits, but the cloak would keep their awareness sharp and focused at each stage. It would be like having a portable *Dhyani* Buddha mount. The Nimitta cloak would be their foundation, support, even throne, through which their consciousness would move, fortified with the atmosphere of sheer clarity, on its way to the Buddha, the condition of being an Awakened One, or at least to waking up to the reality of their changed conditions here and making it through the otherwise vexing, bewildering labyrinth of the *Bardo* to a Light-filled place.

How far they proceeded was variable, up to them, a matter of their will and determination. Some would reject the cloak, fling it on the ground in disdain, cursing the interference, and resume being miserable. Many would reincarnate no doubt, but possibly with greater awareness of the set-up. Some might achieve a "scholarship" to more exalted neighborhoods in the *Bardo*.

Over time, the *Nimitta* cloak would facilitate continuous progress in comprehending the consciousness *skandah*. It would depend on the free-will wish of each soul. Realistically, you could take as much time as you liked doing each test. It's like first you attend a meeting, then you take home some documents summarizing or elaborating the meeting's subject area to study at your own rate. Others might, unfortunately, lapse, falter, fall down, give up, fuck it, go no further this time.

"It's okay, you know," said Philomena. "They have still improved the conditions for their next circuit through the Underworld fun park. You fall down a few times, get up, try again; eventually, you get past the turnstile to the Exit."

4

Finding the Exit was not our concern at the moment. We were going further in. I wasn't dead, but I was getting the sense of what it entails. I had experienced my consciousness being extracted from myself and put into play in a much larger field. I realized the illusion it is to label it "my" consciousness, and I think that is the point, in part at least, of the Vairocana revelation. I had an image of consciousness as an elastic substance, drawn in individual threads out of Vairocana into each of us, like stretching gum or a rubber band. At death, or a moment of revelation while you're alive, it suddenly snaps back to its source.

It had only been on loan to you, like an elongated helping hand that reached out to you and is now retracted because "you" do not need it any more because the individuality you falsely labeled "you" is now dissolving into its basic parts. All of this might strike you as grim and a matter for despair, but I assure you it was empowering. It was a disclosure of the truth of our making. It's like somebody handed you a fishnet and asked you to hold it for a while; after a time we are so used to holding it we come to believe it is a genuine part of us. You can't understand why you have to relinquish it; it's a part of your body.

Once you understand the mechanics of this place and the necessity of the experiences you are put through, it is easier (it was for me) to accept the process. You are extricating yourself from a complex Light grid of conditions and specificities of consciousness through which you passed to incarnate but which, regrettably, you have completely forgotten about thanks to that River Lethe. You are now being re-introduced to the indigenous infrastructure of consciousness that defines a human at a generic level, at a level deeper than your self occupies.

It is an indispensable aid for human incarnation and an impediment to consciousness and the soul when you are trying to extricate yourself from all that. I think of it as like trying to leave a particular country which requires you to present certain authenticated emigration papers you received upon entry. You must present these arcane official papers plus your passport (your self) to exit.

You so take this infrastructure for granted you don't notice it while you are alive. That is not surprising. The emphasis in human incarnation, at least in our time, is entirely outer directed. Everything in culture, including most religions (except Buddhism perhaps), colludes to pull your attention outside you. It becomes unlikely you will reverse that and head into the interior searching for this invisible but pervasive infrastructure of the five *skandahs*. The seductions of the external world, the blandishments to perceive its trinkets and allurements, are strong. The whole world, it can seem, conspires to pull you out of yourself.

It's the same with the body, which, though unarguably more visible, we similarly come to take entirely for granted, forgetting that we were awarded both, the body and the cognitive infrastructure, as necessary tools for our incarnation. Our Judeo-Christian culture does not prepare us for that discernment. We don't think of our life as an incarnation, certainly not as a *serial* incarnation, but as a unique, one-time, and essentially bizarre, torturous, or unexplained advent. All these factors progressively pull us away from attaining the right viewpoint. Souls get here with no mental framework for the *Bardo*.

Taking the past-life or multiple-life framework out of Christianity was probably the nastiest thing it ever perpetrated on humans. It disempowers consciousness, lulls it into a false reality of absolutist standards, and woefully ill-equips the disincarnating soul to cope with the *Bardo* demands. I feel sympathy for souls only indoctrinated in Christianity and its laminations of deliberate ignorance and rigid intolerance. What a shocker this place will seem to them. Nothing they have been taught will correspond to anything they see in the *Bardo*.

The problem seems clear and well delineated as we make this expedition. You die, you come back here, and stand in a cloud of amnesia about it all. Who are these bewildering and gigantic celestial spirits with frightening colors and ill-defined intent and why am I being exposed to them and what am I expected to do? It unrolls as a decidedly unpleasant, even nightmarish, situation for many who arrive here devoid of preparation or any conceptual framework or context.

I see why Merlin and his associates have decided to restructure the death protocols. They aren't working. Too many souls arrive obtuse to the true conditions of reality; they suffer, they don't understand the Light, and collectively this failure to comprehend the terrific possibilities for liberation here in the *Bardo* feeds back dolefully to darken and further confuse the living world. The ignorance of actual conditions keeps recirculating like contaminated water.

For the first 50 years of my life I was exactly like that, cut from that cloth. I may have studied these topics and taught some of them in my comfortable sinecure at Dartmouth College, but they had no traction on my life or awareness. They were facts, or maybe not even that—opinions, anecdotes, unsubstantiated reports that I held safely at arm's length, like specimens for a microscope exam. They didn't change me; they didn't even touch me, though they titillated my mind. Then in 2026 all that changed when the Earth (in me) shook. That was when the manuscript that became *My Pal, Blaise* exploded on my desk as, I see now, a smart-alecky challenge from Blaise himself to start changing. I changed.

Had I died then, rather than run out my front door into the angelic excesses and discoveries offered by Blaise and his angelic pals, I would have entered the *Bardo* with my consciousness as leaden and brick-filled as nearly everyone else does. Still living, I would have sat at our familiar tea table in mid-afternoon, enjoying our uxorial ritual of tea and discussion, making a comment about Eliade or listening to Philomena wax enthusiastic about a Scriabin nuance, and I would have never realized I was "wearing" a *skandah* grid with five components enabling me to project this semblance of rationality and coherence. I would not have suspected the vast cresting wave of Buddha Mind behind it, the apocalyptic illumination poised to instantly reorder my phenomenal world by paradoxically taking the phenomena and the observer entirely out of the picture.

If Philomena had started discoursing on the necessity (and advantages) of converting my limited selfhood-defined cognitive aggregate of consciousness to an enlightenment condition of universal nondualistic consciousness I would have stared at her in noncomprehension, wondering what had gotten into her. If she had broached the subject of Vedantist nondualistic empty awareness or perhaps hinted at Dzogchen's epistemologically rigorous descriptions of *Rigpa*, I would have spilled my tea, spluttered, and quickly changed the subject, or run.

Now, ironically, we both, in differing degrees, understand what this fact means. She because she ascended (that still astounds me) into Dzogchen's state of primordial perfection, me because I'm on this expedition into the Underworld investigating the conditions of the Dead realm, one that, I am certain, will continue to stagger my sense of normalcy for years, but through which we hope to instill some of that primordial perfection into this troubled, murky realm. Yet, when I think about it, when I look at the matter dispassionately and see it in its nakedness (as mythology uses that term), I realize this: How else could it be? *How else* could "I" be here, be an individual "I," without this dual framework?

Suddenly, I felt I couldn't see any more. I was blinded by a blazing white Light. It was a wall of unremitting brightness. Gradually, within this effulgence I made out the outline of another Buddha figure, this one appearing blue-black. This figure held a five-pronged *dorje* or what the Hindus call a *vajra* (suggestive of Indra's thunderbolt, Thor's hammer, a lama's scepter, and a king's sword in terms of implied potency) and sat on an elephant throne, like he was astride a massive stationary elephant—actually, it looked like two elephants.

This *Dhyani* Buddha of an intensely rich deep blue was framed against what the *Bardo Thödol* (Merlin, in fact) described as bright, dazzling, radiant, transparent white Light. With the fingertips of his right hand, this figure was touching the ground, as if to say, the Earth is my witness, even though the physical planet was nowhere in sight. Nothing physical was present here, but I realized, after some reflection, that the Earth in this gesture also meant every form, solid and shaped, named and catalogued, accounted for, in its place.

That is the word for the *skandah* or sensory data quality called *rupa*, or "name and form." It's the habit of mind to assign forms and names to all perceived objects, to individualize units of energy into describable shapes and to assign them names. To convert amorphous, protean energy fields into plausible visual metaphors, seeable, nameable, discrete forms. The naming is very subtle: it isn't just assigning catalogue tags to each item, it is seeing individualized units in the first place, participating in the apparent fragmentation of one universal mass of Light into discretely seeable, separate units, known to us as names and forms.

I had the impression this Buddha was holding a great mirror in which all the form-objects of the world, everything that could be seen, named, filed, and catalogued as separate data of perception, were being reflected. Nothing stuck to the mirror. It reflected everything. He held this mirror at the level of his heart or mid-chest, and all the possible, conceivable forms of individualized reality everywhere, not just Earth reality but throughout existence, were effortlessly bouncing off the mirror's surface like Light rays. He was unaffected by all of it.

I felt a nudge in my mind to approach this second *Dhyani* Buddha from the perspective of the first one, Vairocana, and what I had learned from him. I went back into that white blazing furnace at the center of the revolving white wheel Vairocana had been holding and dissolved into the sheer emptiness. I popped out of that nothingness for a second to position myself at this new figure's great mirror then became empty again. I had the impression of a vast number of objects clamoring at the mirror's edge for my attention, my validation of their separate existence, and being turned back like water dribbling on glass.

Nothing stuck. Everything was sent back, and these myriads of objects demanding my attention were sent back as if X-rayed and rendered transparent. I understood the gesture of his fingers touching the ground. All of solid matter is my witness, it seemed to say, to my recognition of the inherent emptiness of all created things, that awakened consciousness does not cling to any name or form. His Earth-touching gesture also said this is the fundamental bedrock of existence; it is all of one piece, one universal, undifferentiated mass. This is the only reality. All separate names and forms revert to this place of unified origin and rejoin it.

My fellow expedition members seemed to have drifted away for a few moments, pursuing separate interests. I was fascinated by what I saw with Philomena. She had assumed the shape of a fierce male warrior on a horse. But it was a different kind of fierceness than you would normally attribute to a warrior. This figure was possessed with the fierceness of complete truth and total reality.

He was what Buddhists would call a *Dharma* warrior. He was a large man, Asian in facial appearance, possibly Mongolian or Tibetan, and his skin or clothing was mostly red. He wielded a *vajra* in his right hand, his left held a banner streaming off a slender long spear. His head was a mass of flames and his auric field was ablaze for many feet above his cranium. Even the horse looked fierce, as if made of fire. It was white, large and powerful, like an Ur-stallion. The apparition Philomena was generating was encased in a large hoop of fire, and accompanied in many directions by a retinue of high-level celestial *Dharma* warriors (I counted seven, each horse-mounted). All of this was blooming in color and urgency in the air, as if suddenly emerging and expanding rapidly out of Heaven and storming invincibly down to a worldly landscape in need of it.

But the face of this figure—it was adamantly focused yet clearly blissful. It was as if this warrior was attacking an inimical agency and serenely meditating. The apparition made no sound yet emitted a roar like a thousand diamond swords slashing through the resistant ethers in all directions at once. I mean the effect of seeing this, the impact of this on everything around it, suggested a sound like a thousand striking swords or a raging furnace, like from a sun. It was a paradox: stillness and action, contemplation and sword-slashing, silence and roaring. Was it doing something, or was it not doing something? I couldn't tell.

The image kept enlarging too, as if swelling from the inside with more Light. I had the impression of slashing swords and *vajras* emitting diamond-bladed Light, yet the image of the *Dharma* warrior, his retinue and the horses, seemed inexplicably motionless. All the figures were lucidly, unquestionably wide-awake, yet all was stationary, not moving, the way you see Buddhist meditators. Yet the fierceness, the bright, clarifying sharpness of this image, was unassailable. I realized it wasn't a physical image that was delivering the impact; I was witnessing a mental state personified, acted out, a quality of consciousness. It didn't have to move in any physical or spatial sense; its self-definition itself was that imputed movement, that combination of bliss and fierceness did it all.

Then all this dissolved and it was Philomena again before me, or at least an outline in Light of what she used to look like. It shimmered. It was radiant. She looked Buddha-like. I asked her why she was generating this image.

"I'm practicing whole-form *mudras*, emulating some of the major mandalas and their celestial figures by embodying their conditions," she replied. "They become living mandalas, grids of Light and influence, demonstrations of power and purpose, and, even better, they help to sharpen the cloudy psychic atmosphere around here. That clarity helps people do their afterlife processing.

"It has the effect of turning on a high-wattage light bulb in a somewhat dim room. I go around the *Bardo* doing this, like a human celestial mandala, a pulsar. It flashes this picture and body of clarity every few moments to sharpen things up. It's like ringing a bell in a meditation hall. It rivets attention. It pulls people out of the heavy places, the gravity wells they have sunk into while here, and it gives them a moment of lucidity and perspective; it brightens their mood. I've been doing this a lot since I turned my physical form into a Light body. They put you to use over here; no ascension is unexploited. You don't get to sit around—and just drink tea while discussing Scriabin or a theory by Eliade."

"What was the horse—I mean, what was its significance?" I asked.

"Didn't you recognize it?" she replied. "It was our friends, the Blaises. They take that guise to indicate their support, their ability to provide movement, for this living mandala of power, focus, and enlightenment. They like horses."

"Hey Frederick, what do you think of this one?" called out a voice. I looked in its direction and saw a mandala of Light in patterns of circles and squares flashing before me, as large as a building. The central figure was Buddha-like, perhaps a Bodhisattva, but certainly a figure of high spiritual attainment, sitting at the center of a labyrinthine web of spheres and squares. There were gates at the four cardinal directions in all the layers of this image. Other celestial figures with bright auras of flame flanked this central figure. The whole apparition resembled a Light temple as if unmoored from any fixed location; it shimmered and waved in the "air" around it like a painted sheet. I studied the face of the central figure. Something about it looked familiar to me.

I opened my mouth to exclaim but he beat me to it. "That's right. It's me." It was Tommy Hevringer. "I do this often. It's a kind of exercise, like a martial arts move. It trains my awareness, and they tell me it improves the atmosphere. I create the image in my mind, though it's projected outside me, as everything is over here, then I occupy the central figure, then gradually everything in the image. I hold the image steady for as long as I can manage and feel kind of empty. I understand that is part of what animates it, to simulate this emptiness. The whole thing is like a great painted eye that sees everything around it. If I could have done cool stuff like this when I was alive, I might have reconsidered killing myself and stuck around school to impress my so-called friends with it."

Merlin smiled slightly when he heard Tommy confess this. "Here, when you think something, when you generate a mental image, it appears outside you. That is how much of the world works here. Everything is outside you, except that outside is a projection of your inside. It's a subjective, projective reality. Your interior states form your outer environment. You walk inside yourself.

"That is why the *Bardo* is so bewildering to people unprepared for its inversion of reality. All of your mental contents, your projections, all the previously unglimpsed shadow content, are conveyed to you as an exterior world. The challenge is to recognize this. How did I put it in that book—you are greeted by the abundance of your karmically-driven illusions creating a seeming world."

"Merlin, who is this large Buddha-like figure I was watching just now?" I had been studying the advent of this new *Dhyani* Buddha with the great mirror when Philomena appeared sporting her magnificent Gesar of Ling apparition. I hadn't flashed on that identity at the time; her appearance so surprised me. But yes, now I recognized the great Solar Logos representation from Buddhist lands, King Arthur dressed in Buddhist garb, given a *Dharma* warrior cast, as it should be. That was at least something I could recognize from my academic studies.

"It is Aksobhya," said Merlin. "He is the *Dhyani* Buddha of the East. He is known as the 'Unagitated One,' 'the Immovable One,' and he also appears as *Vajra-Sattva*, 'the Divine Heroic-Minded' or 'the Indestructible-Minded,' and also as *Vajra-Dhara*, which means 'the Indestructible or Steadfast Holder.' The great mirror he holds is the key to understanding him. He embodies mirror-knowledge, which means discerning the real from the unreal and illusory. He holds, through the mirror, all forms, all *rupa*, all the names for corporeality, and reflects them without being the least bit tarnished, affected, or stuck in them.

"His consciousness remains steadfast, immobile, never grasping at the fleeting forms. He never validates the myriads of names and forms the way humans in bodies do. Their apparent separateness dissolves and vanishes in the bright voidness. They are not acknowledged; the mirror reflects them back as having no existence. The mirror is the action of Aksobhya's emptiness state, and that is meant to show you, the embodied, the named and formed, how to convert *rupa* into enlightenment. Then this *skandah* has no effect on your condition.

"He remains untouched by all forms, merely reflecting them back in enlightenment, in a blaze of radiant white Light. He is the 'Wisdom of the Great Mirror' which you'll see as this great white Light, pure and colorless, that shines from his heart like a wisdom-reflecting mirror. As always, we deal with metaphors here, such as the mirror, to make the key point. It contrasts with the dull, smoke-colored light behind him. You want to avoid that light if you can.

"Aksobhya holds the five-pronged *vajra* or *dorje*, the diamond thunderbolt, similar in function and intent to the Western image of a Light sword, to emphasize this quality. The fierce lucid sharpness of the *vajra* cuts through all illusion like so many shells and reveals the inherent emptiness of all individual forms inside. The diamond aspect suggests indestructibility, the thunderbolt denotes irresistible force, and both exemplify the power of awakened consciousness to mirror back all forms asserting their separateness.

"The *Dhyani* Aksobhya is the image of the perfected conversion of this *skandah* to wisdom. Each *skandah* is a web that traps awareness, and each *Dhyani* Buddha shows you the conversion of that liability into enlightenment and complete freedom. Name and form transformed into a mirror's reflectivity. Nothing sticks. No name or form confounds the emptiness of this Buddha."

The mirror was busy reflecting everything in existence. I saw innumerable objects, people, places, all individual objects that had perceivable form, streaming back from that mirror as if turned back at a national boundary. I started to understand how as living humans we maintain extensive file cabinets. Everything we see, think about, picture, imagine, or interact with, gets labeled. Everything has a name, a shape that can be remembered, quickly recalled. We decode this fantastic Light field of reality into individual objects. Then we compel these otherwise amorphous energies to remain in these forms, or let's say, we compel ourselves to keep construing them as separate forms. We build up worlds of names and forms, and thereby assign to them a separate reality.

We invest reality with belief in their existence and build up a world that way. Now Aksobhya was sending all that filing and labelling back into my face, showing me with *vajra*-like indestructible force that none of it is real or existent. He was emptying out all the file folders and throwing down the file cabinet too.

All forms are empty, reflected back to their creator, me, without any clinging. It doesn't mean these myriads of forms and names are without value for they constitute the palpable world the Supreme Being generated on our behalf. But it means they have no permanent existential standing; they are illusions of matter. They have short-term, provisional, transient reality, for illustration purposes. It's like teaching summer school. You know you have these students only for two months, then they return home to their own schools. Only the Great Void is like an unstoppable searchlight of tremendous wattage. I realized how used I was to anchoring myself, my individuality, in space through reference to this myriad of labeled individual objects and forms all around me, and again, I emphasize, it was not just the catalogue of *rupa*s, but the mechanism, the habit, the routine, of naming forms itself. That is the *skandah* in its nakedness.

Now that familiar anchorage was removed, revealed to be empty, without truth. The *vajra* cut through all this semblance of forms with names. They were empty. What did that leave me with? How could I define myself if all reality and its myriad of discrete forms vanished? Oh shit, you mean none of this is real?

I understood how newly dead people could be besides themselves, mentally undone, and unappeasedly distraught when presented with such a shocking fact. This welter of names and forms is ungraspable, like clutching at water. Water has no inherent form, only the temporary form of its container. The fact that it is true, names and forms are empty, that to touch this is to make contact with genuine reality, to see through the great magic act of perceivable reality, would not assuage the sudden wave-rush of fear and confusion this entails. I was getting only a simulation; I had the master mystagogue

Merlin to explain things to me whenever my understanding grew dim and confused.

Then I felt a flush of panic because Merlin had disappeared. Well, not quite. I saw him streaming back with all the other effluvia of name and form from the mirror. I knew I was suddenly in trouble, big trouble. I might as well be dead. Merlin himself was but a name and form and the Great Mirror of Voidness just sent him back, another reject from the Absolute Reality validation machine of Aksobhya. It got worse. I saw myself streaming back from the Great Mirror. I, too, my sense of I-ness, was rejected at the border as being ontologically invalid. When the reflected image of myself reached the supposedly real version of myself, both disappeared. I guess that means I disappeared; at least my form did.

Yet uncannily I was still aware. There was an unbroken continuity in my awareness, though I noted that awareness had been radically sharpened, clarified, and, oddly, simplified. It was broader and stronger but it perceived nothing. My lifelong habit of construing names and forms had been defeated. I wasn't perceiving any of them, no matter how much I tried. Then I realized that was okay. I didn't mind being stripped of all conceivable *rupas*. It felt all right.

In many respects it was a relief, like I had put down a great burden I'd been carrying, like a pack-horse so used to the crushing weight it had borne all these years it had forgotten what it was like to have nothing weighing down its back. Or like I had been carrying a heavy box crammed with picture cue-cards identifying everything in Earth and human reality I was likely to encounter. The box's contents spilled out before me, thousands of names for all reality's forms.

I held a five-pronged *vajra* in my hand. It seemed as sharp as a sword. I held a great mirror at my chest and it was busy reflecting back everything. My form, if I could even call it that, seemed a shade of blue-black, yet a transparent, radiant whiteness enveloped me. I sat on two elephants. Except it seemed like a lot more, dozens, hundreds perhaps, facing every possible degree of direction. They were elephants rampant, their fierceness defeating, trampling all illusions of form. My attention seemed focused everywhere at once. It wasn't bad, actually, and I suddenly understood Tommy's delight in occupying that shimmering flaglike mandala of the meditating Buddha he had shown me.

I had no thoughts. I didn't see anything after I initially registered these few details. I felt wide-awake, probably more so than I had ever felt after many espressos, yet I was not aware of anything in particular. I was not perceiving forms and objects. They seemed too inconsequential for my attention or too little, too fleeting: too gone. They were effervescent, transient phenomena on the mind's surface. I did not need to keep track of them, make records, or issue responses to them. It was like sitting quietly on a mountaintop in a strong wind, and then the mountain and wind and the sense of myself meditating: all gone.

The wind had no bearing on my concentration, and even that seemed effortless. I didn't have to do anything. I was not doing anything. Who? There was nothing to do. I didn't have a face but I felt myself smiling. The invisible air felt full of joy. It's like when you're happy as a child: you don't know why and you don't care why. In fact the "why" question never occurs to you. This seems a natural state to you. Later, Merlin told me Aksobhya is Lord of the Eastern Pure Land or Buddha realm *Abhirati*, which means "Joyous." It means the "World of Wonderful Bliss" and "Pre-Eminently Happy." It is a desirable paradisal Buddha-Field, part of the *Sambhogakaya*. I could live with that. Starting now.

That's where souls dwell who emulate Aksobhya's mirror-like wisdom regarding name and form. It's a community of like-minded souls who converted the *skandah* of *rupa* into the primordial perfection of awakened consciousness. It's a tony retirement home, I thought whimsically, for those who have retired their habitual allegiance, their enslavement, to this *skandah*. Goodbye name and form!

All the objects of my life, what had filled my visual field and seemed normal, habitual, domestic, were flying off the mirror back at me, empty. I saw trees, the trees in my former backyard in New Hampshire, the rose bushes, the fences, the pastures beyond, the mountains beyond that; the tea table, the cups and saucers and plates, the stacked magazines, the books half-read and overturned on the table, the daily ritual and its nuances; I saw the faculty room at Dartmouth College, the chairs, the side-tables, the faces of my colleagues, the books, papers, reports, and monographs that constituted our cloistered world.

I saw Philomena, professor, wife, female, human, and her scattered relatives, and mine too, and I saw the essence of men and women, the male and female body, all the differences in anatomy and temperament I once took so seriously as a bedrock condition of life—I saw all the objects that had formed my world of name and form and possessing substance and seeming solidity and perdurance come back at me like blown leaves in a November wind from the Great Mirror. All the trees were stripped bare of leaves; they stood there naked.

The forms were transient, mere containers, wrappers, presentation formats, but their truth was voidness. They came back at me transparent, empty, without permanent, enduring form. Their separate name and form were illusory, untrue, momentary gestures of the Light, like a proliferation of *mudras* in Light. As if the Buddha were generating these many shapes, with each saying, "like this, like this," as if explaining the nature of reality, of the

Buddha Mind in action. I had given them their name and form. I had individualized them into units of perceivable mass from out of a great undifferentiated field of Light. It was my habit of naming—it was the *human* habit, a generic one, a *skandah* habit. It was the predisposition of the *skandah* grid to construe reality as named forms.

If this had happened during normal life, when I was embedded in the unconscious, unconsidered assumptions of daily embodied life, I might have reasonably concluded I was losing my mind to have such thoroughly entropic perceptions. Things were falling apart all around me; all of reality was being sucked up into some kind of ultimate vacuum cleaner with enormous suction. Someone had pulled the pin on a hand grenade at the heart of material reality.

But this wasn't normal life, if by that you mean asleep at the wheel as usual. This was true life, life as it really is, when you are awake and unplugged from a body. It was revelatory, the full disclosure of how things genuinely are, blissfully empty. It was, oddly, relaxing, a relief, and even reassuring to see this. I didn't have to keep assembling a plausible object-filled reality all around me. I didn't have to keep clinging to these objects as if they were each a life-preserver flung at a drowning man at sea flailing his arms in the rising waves. I settled into the delight of *Abhirati* without a care in the world, with nothing, like a former bad habit, I had to keep insisting had separate, independent, material existence.

I was, after all, losing my mind, and loving every minute of it. In this full disclosure, I understood how the "mind" is comprised of the five *skandahs* and how they construct a plausible world and maintain its illusory existence. You realize you've been living in a false epistemology. Nothing is true along the lines you construed it; you have it all ass-backwards, pal. To

lose your mind is to dissolve the grid of the *skandahs*, the habits of sensory perception. It is to gain true knowledge, to re-establish your correct epistemological footing. Seeing reality through the kaleidoscope of the five *skandahs* is functionally necessary but epistemologically fraudulent, like living permanently inside a magical trick. You need it to be a plausible, functioning human, yet it is innately unreal and illusory.

It happens whether you like it or not over here in the *Bardo*. It isn't even something you can accurately say "happens." It is already there, inside you, an innate part, a primordial feature of yourself, there from long before you ever became a you. The you is a persona lamination you painted over this fact. What makes it an experience of joy rather than fright is knowing the context, that this is the revelation of the mechanics of consciousness fit over every human like a geometric grid, a programming field, a generic aspect of the human design. More than that, you can't help it. *Abhirati* is a smoking-hot place of bliss and delight, and once you get a taste of it, you'll want to book long-term accommodations.

What is fit over us can be lifted off, and that happens to everyone in the *Bardo*. The trick is not to resist it; not to flee from this disclosure for the nearest womb-door, as the Tibetan text puts it in so antique a manner. Don't regard another incarnation as the only way out of this nightmare; you just go deeper into it. To call it a nightmare is a subjective labeling though many will chose this.

It's probably a lot like an addiction or food allergy. It feels better to have another drink or another bite of the allergenic substance and resume the chronic allergic reaction than to withdraw from the addictive substance and experience the craving full on. When you're in the *Bardo*, don't ask for another hair from the dog that bit you. Realize that incarnation is a habit; it has allergenic tendencies for the soul. Ever seeking the womb-door is an addictive behavior. Yes, not the observations on life you'd expect from a (formerly) staid Dartmouth professor.

Suddenly, the other members of the expedition were with me again. Maybe they had been here all along as I was usefully engaged by *Vajra-Sattva*. Even though Aksobhya, this *Dhyani* Buddha of inestimable importance, was himself, from my viewpoint, a product of name and form, a *skandah* construct, he loomed gigantically and impressively before us, much like a treeless mountain.

So did a cone-shaped mountain behind him. It looked like a crystalline ice cone shaped into four facets, as if each shaved side faced a cardinal direction. The peak seemed to stand isolated in a barren, bleak, wide-open, high-altitude landscape. The peak, snow-covered, was flanked by smaller mountains and massive ridges and valleys. Even on a physical level it was bright; whatever spiritual features it possessed, evidently they were so strong as to "bleed" into the physical world and surround the rock mass with a strong numinous charge.

"Kailash," said Merlin. "Northwestern Tibet, 800 miles from Lhasa. Holy."

That was an understatement. I knew about Mount Kailash, though I had not initially recognized it. It is the premier sacred mountain of Tibet, referenced in the early Bon shamanism, Jainism, and figuring importantly in the later Buddhism when it converted Tibetans to this new version of the *Dharma*. The Tibetans called the mountain *Kang Rinpoche*, "Precious Jewel of the Snows;" it's the focus of many pilgrimages and, once here, of repeated circumambulations. Each circling of the peak, which stands at 21,778 feet, takes a minimum of 15 hours. *Kailasa*, Sanskrit for "crystal," probably references its Light emanations. Circumambulating pilgrims spend a minimum of 15 hours immersed in that crystalline emanation of *Kailasa*; some do their circling by way of prostrations, assuring that they soak up even more of the peak's exalted spiritual atmosphere.

How far was Mount Kailash from where we stood in the *Bardo*? It was both a fascinating and useless question because it seemed we had to only make one step towards the peak and we were there, not just at the mountain, but inside it, in one of the Light temples that co-occupied the same space as it on the Earth. I surmised this was Aksobhya's temple on the Earth. It was massive, its ceiling domed, all of it done in gold, however illusory all this might prove to be.

I was girting myself for another momentous disclosure of fundamental emptiness. Identical images of Aksobhya beamed down at me, onto my crown chakra and its floriated landscape of golden petals, from all directions inside this temple. I saw an imprint of Aksobhya's blissful, detached countenance settle on each petal of my crown chakra and on those of my expedition companions.

The *Dhyani* Buddha sat on his double-elephant throne. He held the five-pronged *vajra* in his right hand, and his other supported the great mirror at his chest level. I saw innumerable Blaise angels inside those elephant forms. I was about to laugh, and I knew the human Blaise would be chuckling at this disclosure of yet another insinuation of his pals, the Ofanim, into the heart of things, but my attention was drawn away by the mirror. It seemed as big as Kailash. It was reflecting everything; images of everything in Creation, the mountain, its physical and Light aspects, us, everything that was a separate element of physical and even spiritual existence, was streaming back from it.

This streaming was backlit by a pure white Light, like sunlight on fresh snow. The myriads of objects and forms the great wisdom-mirror reflected back were still individualized, yet they appeared empty and were part of a single big thing. Aksobhya looked unaffected by all this activity, completely neutral and blissful. I realized the mirror itself is an illusion, or, more generously put, a high-level metaphor. Aksobhya holds no mirror at his heart. He has no heart either. He's not even there. I was getting the hang of the set-up. He was a place-marker for a condition in consciousness, even if technically you couldn't give it a name.

Aksobhya, this one-fifth differentiation of the Awakened One, or Buddha, is the *process* in consciousness whereby all names and forms are mirrored back to us, their innate voidness in bliss revealed. Aksobhya himself is a product of name and form, and so is the mirror. So am I. So is the *Bardo*. I saw the utility of the metaphor; it put a name and form on an ineffable process. I didn't feel shortchanged that Aksobhya was not truly there as an articulated Buddha. He was there, a *condition* of pure consciousness, but without any name or form, and if you gave it a name, you and the name and the naming mechanism would be turned back at the border, your passport not stamped and no entry visa granted.

I appreciated how unsettling this might seem to a newly dead person trying to get his bearings in this strange place called the *Bardo*. Everything is so protean here. Which would be worse: to see this proliferation of broken-apart things streaming back at you like lost friends or to be told it is all illusory, fake, essential voidness—where would that leave you? The revealed emptiness might feel more frightful than the assault of all these forms galloping towards you.

But all the objects streaming back at me were not non-existent. It's more subtle than that. It's another episode in the "form is emptiness, emptiness is form" drama. They exist, surely, though transiently, but the nature of their existence is innately empty and void, metaphors comprised of Light for the mind to enrich a world, but my job as a *Bardo* meditator, dead or alive or in-between, is to not cling to any of them, to not reach out and grab them and claim absolute, fixed reality for them, to not download my identity or self into their fleeting forms, their relative names. Those are short-term forms and forgettable names.

Aksobhya's enlightened consciousness held the universe of name and form in his compassionate hands. His palms cupped myriads of separate units of existence, each with a name and form, yet his bliss, nonclinging, and awakened state unified them, like a mother gathering her many children about her in a gesture of family unity. As the embodiment of the mirror of the Great Void, Aksobhya acknowledged and reflected these myriads of objects of the world without holding on to any. He didn't need to. They couldn't be held on to anyway. They were like pretty soap bubbles, inherently empty, lacking permanent existence, but with alluring, catchy images painted on their surface. All these forms are inherently empty, yet emptiness must assume these forms.

I discovered Matthew had been standing at my side waiting politely for me to finish my reflections and open my eyes to see him. "I think the point here is we can—we should—copy Aksobhya's gesture with the mirror. We emulate him as much as possible, make ourselves copies of him, and use the mirror. There is no mirror, of course, as you know, but the mirror indicates a function. Send the name and form of all units of consciousness back to themselves. It's like being at a party and the butler comes around with the drinks tray or a delicious-looking platter of canapés and you say, 'No, thanks,' and he takes them away. You've already eaten, or you have no hunger, or the food means nothing to you.

"Most people would naturally want the drinks and canapés, and the idea of sending them back would either seem pointless, or, more acutely, frightening. You send them back with your compliments, meaning, in the Light of your voidness, bliss, and terrific awakened Buddha Light. You will nonplus the waiter! People want, they *expect*, the myriads of objects named by sensory data. They anchor themselves in daytime reality with reference to that naming.

"To take this process, this habit, away from them would be ungrounding and scary. It would feel like removing all the solid ground from underneath them. To suddenly see these great crowds of objects streaming back at them, no longer habitually validated by consensus reality as having genuine existence, would be unsettling and disorienting. *Where* am I without these names and forms? *Who* am I without them? Questions like these would probably arise, and there would be no immediate answer because the experience would be so novel."

"I know, it's a real bitch, turning away that drinks and canapés platter," said Tommy. "When I got here, I saw so many people desperately reaching for it. They would do anything to reconstitute the details of the physical life they had just lost. They immediately created a semblance of what they had formerly lived within and surrounded themselves with all its names and forms as a safety net. They immediately instituted all their domestic habits cultivated while alive. They felt less or no inclination to send the objects back when they're alive. It's a habit.

"To most people this would seem an incomprehensible, even absurd, proposition. Short of giving the entire human race a near-death experience, it's hard to see how we can get them to see any of this while they're alive enjoying the party. Yet they need to because otherwise they arrive here confused and frightened by it. The sudden, revealed emptiness of all supposedly substantial forms is awful, the worst kind of nightmare, inexplicable and undigestible."

"And the next thing they do is run screaming for the nearest womb-door," said Matthew, though he said this with amusement. "Let me out of this nightmare town, as Dashiell Hammett might have termed it. People keep coming out of houses shooting their guns off and people fall down dead. Anything but this. It is too unbearably shocking to have all the familiar sense objects of the world—*my* world—revealed to be frauds, empty shells, with no surface you can cling to any more and no existence guaranteed beyond the passing moment, to see all these names and forms lying dead in the streets, shot like gangsters."

"You have both laid out the problem well and clearly," said Merlin. "Any ideas for improvements? I have my pen in hand, if I might name three forms."

"You could give everyone a complimentary serving of bliss and bright emptiness in which they see it's safe, even pleasurable, to put down all the balls they've been juggling so desperately." It was Blaise who said this. He continued, but now he sounded slightly more serious or at least less whimsical than usual.

"The thing they realize here is how embedded they have been in the humanness of their perceptions while they were alive. They so take that condition for granted and do not see it until they arrive in the *Bardo* and watch it get stripped from them. It's the second of two layers and two assumptions. The first is their own selfhood, the operation and products of the *skandahs* filtered through their sense of self, what they take themselves to be. The second layer is their humanness.

"These are factors bearing on their body and its survival, its status, both short-term, such as hunger or warmth, and long-term, such as illness and eventual mortality. Other factors include objects in the world of interest, utility, or necessity for a human life, the actions of other people and our assessment of them, a diffused sense of empathy that enables us to feel others around us and, perhaps on good days, to feel compassion for their condition and prospects and to accept the fact, based on our observations, that most are not very self-aware, that we, each of us individually, are not very self-aware on the average. Their humanness means they believe they have a right to come home for tea, to settle comfortably into a domestic routine and put aside issues of philosophy, and our compassion recognizes that because we like coming home for tea as well. Taking tea, we might say, Frederick, is the epitome of what we have to let go of. No tea!

"You'll probably appreciate this observation, Frederick, as odd as it might seem. It's the right, the expectation, to be at home, at the tea table, drinking a cup of Darjeeling, in a place of safety and familiarity, comfortable in a domestic nest. The trouble is this gesture is a summation of being embedded in one's humanness. No, I don't mean there's anything wrong with it or objectionable. Even acts of high aesthetics, the tea ceremony at its most refined, are still *skandah*-driven, another deployment of the *skandahs* that has to be divested in the *Bardo*.

"That is painful and shocking to most souls arriving here. It seems worse than dying in the first place because this is a more conscious loss of their essence as they have come to understand it. It's too upsetting to see how relative it is, how provisional a definition of consciousness it is. They see, unless they find ways to render themselves unconscious or functionally nonperceptive here, that it is but one in a list of possible self and phylogeny constructs of the *skandahs*.

"It's like thinking that being an American is the only nationality one could take on and now you discover you could have been French, Italian, Czech, or Russian. You get here and you have this assumptive layer stripped from you ruthlessly and you are suddenly naked, without tea, without the humanness *skandah* filter. So who are you? If you are not defined by your human name and form, who are you? Have you fallen into an irreversible amnesia, finally waking up from one in which you were so entrenched you never suspected any of this?"

"So you're suggesting living people should get a little foretaste of that?" said Merlin. "How would we do that without forcing anybody to wake up?"

"Stories that make them yearn for a brighter place," said Pipaluk. "That's how we teach young shamans, those preparing to enter this path of Light and responsibility. We share stories of places of wonder and power they might visit. We tell them stories of shamans who shapeshift into all the animals and birds, see what it's like to have these different forms, how these feel and see the world. They understand that being in a human form is only one among many form possibilities, that all forms see the world differently, according to their nature.

"We watch as it awakens something in them, like twigs catching fire. Grand trees of Light filled with souls that look like brightly plumed birds. Chalices filled with jewels or gold coins that represent retrieved wisdom and celestial insight. Stories that tell of great and difficult journeys to god-filled lands of delight and magic, journeys that are necessary, important, that help the world and secure safety for people, that challenge and put the heroes into great peril and demands for personal sacrifice, even of life, until they triumph in the end.

"All these stories are true. They are the deeds of the old shamans, from long ago. The truth of these stories ignites something in the listeners; they start to burn. They want to go to these places, make the journeys, find the exciting treasures. They start to change; by the time they have made the journey they are changed. They understand more of the world, how it is made and works, what it needs. They have a deeper sense of their role, their responsibilities, of their awareness. They feel they have woken up from a long sleep full of dull dreams.

"They have travelled with animals and spirits, angels and very aware ancestors. They see the world has a goal and a purpose, that it is straining towards a fulfillment. The shaman travels in the spirit world to help souls, often to rescue souls. Sometimes the shaman has to find something that is lost or broken in that world. Then she comes back to her body and the world of breathing people and makes her reports. This is where the stories come from, from this enduring world of Light and truth. You know this. We do it this way."

I saw where Pipaluk was going with her suggestion. Infiltrate more pictures and stories of this bright world of purpose and gods and trees of Light into the living human world, into culture, art, literature, movies. Get the *skandahs* to focus on this for a while. J. R. R. Tolkien was certainly a marvel of scholarship and imagination, but I suspect the timing of his introduction of the Middle-earth mythos was carefully planned by reality directors outside the human world. Maybe it was an early insinuation of this drive to present pictures to the world.

They must have calculated that the eventual impact of this kind of mythos seeding would be beneficial for world evolution by showing these myth doors. Great wafts of *numen* flow through his mythos, exciting yearnings for memory. There would have to be an upgrade in the metaphysical quality of these stories and reports; none of the spurious glamours that have passed for esoterica, propagated by low-level astral spirits intent on keeping humans in a trance. These new stories would have to feel so real your ears tingled just from hearing them; they'd have to be so genuine you'd feel the psychic wanderlust ignite in you, and you might just dash out the front door, like I did (and like Bilbo did).

So we let more of the true nature of the *Sambhogakaya* seep through into the human world. We are all like Hobbits only minimally aware of the rest of the world. We broaden our knowledge base and expand our experiential horizons. Show them some marvels of the greater world that surrounds their physical realm and help them feel the spiritual charge of these vistas, the *numen* of the golden peaks. Let them suspect that these stories are not merely metaphors, but actualities, pictures of realities they might experience directly, genuine glimpses of higher worlds. Through these stories, rumors, reports, and direct experiences, these views of holy peaks and genuine activities of the gods, people will experience levels and qualities of consciousness other and beyond the human, and—this is crucial—it will *feel* wonderful. They'll know it is good.

What does it feel like to be an immortal of Valhalla, an angel of the Light world, a *deva* of a lake or valley responsible for all units of consciousness in her realm? People will start to get a taste of other conditions of consciousness and find it interesting, intriguing, and even desirable, as if it is a lost patrimony of theirs. When they get here and find their humanness starts to dissolve, it won't upset them because they'll see it is an aid, a necessary step, to achieving their goal, to get to that place, that landscape, that feeling-consciousness, they saw.

The input of positive images suggesting wholesome, even exalted, states of awareness will be a necessary and valuable antidote to decades of negative imagery, bleak, grim evidences of powerlessness against ruthless enemies. People will never be tempted to loosen their humanness when presented with this continuous onslaught of antihuman behavior and disaster scenarios. They will only grip it tighter and harder as the last refuge of an honorable person.

It's true that since 2020 there has been an improvement in cultural images, a gradual lifting of consensus reality out of a dark foreboding of future catastrophes. But this could certainly benefit by a significant upgrade, a bigger push from here. The Ofanim, incarnating in 2020, gave the human world a spiritual anchor; now we need to see our world with better, more accurate, more uplifting pictures. This—do you see this, I hear myself saying, as if in class again—is what reality actually is like, without the nonsense, without the confusing, misdirecting, opiated illusions draped all over it by deviant spirits.

Merlin was nodding. He had followed my thoughts. "That should work. We can direct some of our Ascended Masters and Adepts who deal with seeding human culture with art, beauty, and inspiration to step up their transmissions and seed more alluring ideas and pictures into human consciousness. We'll give them examples of seeing beyond the human, of experiencing other levels and qualities, even nuances, of consciousness, in angels, *devas*, animals, and aliens. When they arrive here, it will not be as unsettling a proposition to let go their humanness because they would already have tasted the alternatives. We can also encourage the now incarnate Blaises who are walking amongst the humans to amplify their inspirations, to plant and nurture more empowering suggestions."

"I *like* it," said Matthew, with enthusiasm. "At first it looks like deception and dissimulation, but it isn't. This is seeding them with the truth, and that is irresistibly alluring because it is bedrock as far as reality goes. Who can resist? As before, I see that a large part of the problem is inadequate preparation while alive. People fail to develop a concept of this place and its mechanics or requirements. This creates a disparity for consciousness; it is not trained for the transition and considers it inimical. The truth is there is continuity of awareness.

"Ideally, human consciousness will experience itself with one foot in the living world, one foot here in the *Bardo*. Then it's just a matter of shifting one's balance. You incarnate, you shift both feet to over there; die, both feet into the Underworld. Get off the Wheel of Life altogether, say goodbye to Yama, then you have no feet anywhere. Remember your context, the change is not so scary. Then when you encounter this *Dhyani* Buddha, Aksobhya, who personifies the perfection of this awareness of nonclinging to human-flavored names and forms, you will have a better chance of comprehending the revelation offered to you."

"If that doesn't work, we can hand out yellow sticky notes with reminders on them," said Blaise. "In the spirit of how they used to give the dead person a few coins to pay off Charon for the boat ride. The sticky notes will remind them of who they're seeing, like a mini-playbook. The big guy with the mirror, that's Aksobhya. The overweight Buddha with the white wheel is called Vairocana. And watch out for the guy in black. He wants to spin your head around and have you headed backwards. He's trouble. He's dark. He's bad. Against it all."

5

We all turned toward Blaise in surprise. What bad guy was he talking about? This was new information for us—well, not for Merlin. He nodded.

"His identity is hidden behind several veils," Merlin said. "The Egyptian equivalent for the Green Knight and Yama is Osiris. He too is green-skinned and the Lord of Death, though he also has some qualities usually attributed to the Supreme Being which somewhat confuses the picture. He is opposed by Set.

"Set is presented as the evil figure, the brother of Osiris, who dismembers the body of Osiris into 14 parts, puts them in a casket, and dumps it in the Nile. This is traditionally misunderstood. Set is not the bad guy. Set is Ursa Major. The hieroglyphs clearly indicate this, and Wallis Budge makes a note about that. The story of the body of Osiris being cut into 14 pieces is a way of pointing to the origin in him as the egg of white Light of the 14 Rays that work through Ursa Major, or Set. This is not a bad thing. Set as the bad guy hides the real bad guy.

"You find a more accurate picture of the real enemy in *Avestan* cosmogony. There this enemy of the truth and Light is named. It's not a guy. It is a she. Her name is the Druj."

I knew that name. As a scholar of comparative mythology, how could I not? Merlin was right about the gender. The Druj is an *Avestan* feminine noun. No, I don't think this is another example of patriarchal blame-shifting but a true picture of a fundamental dichotomy or schism in the Creation. *Asha*, or *Aša*, means the correct order of law, truth, and Light. It is like the Sanskrit *Dharma*.

As a word that denotes Light and fire, it is a masculine-nuanced term, because fire is a *yang*, solar, hot quality, like the *pingala nadi*, and designated masculine. The opposite of that is necessarily feminine, as the Druj is associated with night. Druj is the lie, falsehood, deceit, error, illusion, the blackening, the dark *yin*, pollution, decay. The Druj is associated with the shadows of the night, in both senses, that of the absence of daytime sunlight (sunset to dawn) and the subliminal, subconscious areas of the psyche, the dark matter of consciousness. These are examples of the *yin* side of the polarity, dark, moist, decomposing. Still, a *yin-yang* polarity sells the true story short: it is a deeper opposition at play.

The *Avesta* says humans can *choose* which they prefer, *Asha* or Druj. The polarity is like the Egyptian one of Ma'at versus *Isfet*. The Druj is a personification of the condition of *Isfet*, if you'll permit this blending of cultural images. The *Avesta* states "the Karapan [dark-oriented priests] preferred Druj to *Aša*." The Druj *betrays* the contract of *Asha*, the law of reality laid down by the high gods, in *Avestan* myth ultimately by Ahura-Mazda, the chief deity.

The Druj has a cosmic residence called *Drūjō demāna*, "the House of Lies," and it is described as a Hell realm, offering a long life in darkness, foul food, and much woe. The House of Song, of the Good Mind, the Best of Existences, is *Asha*'s cosmic residence. You would think everyone would prefer this as a holiday estate, but the Druj is crafty and her sales pitch, clever, devious, and insidious, converts a lot of people. The Karapan bought it. Took a long lease. I am not exaggerating to say people flock in great numbers to her popular resort.

Unlike *Asha*, the Druj was not created by Ahura-Mazda. The inference is that the Druj and all the evil divinities with her were created by humans over time, gradually extruded as a metaphysically feral form from the collective consciousness. Eventually, humans and their *Fravasis*, a term suggesting what Judeo-Christian culture calls the Guardian Angel or Higher Self, must definitively defeat the Druj and renovate the world, re-anchor it in *Asha* in a grand eschatological gesture. This is still in our future and is akin to the Jewish *Tikkun-olam*, the regeneration of the world and restoration to its original order.

Later, Zoroastrianism renamed the Druj *Angra Mainyu*, or Ahriman. This is the Angry Spirit, the Stinking Spirit, the prime agent of chaos and destruction, the perpetual enemy of humans. *Angra Mainyu*, Zoroaster taught, is the destructive, malign, angry mind or spirit, the evil thought, the evil mind, diametrically opposed to Ahura-Mazda and the Light. Rudolf Steiner adopted Zoroaster's formulation and characterized Ahriman as the spirit that condenses spirit into material forms, as the spirit of literalism, contraction, blood identities, mechanism, genetics, materialism, and the death of the spirit in humans. He said Ahriman propagates the ultimate lie that the vastness of spirit can be compressed into mere materialistic forms and thus encompasses no revelation beyond matter.

"The Druj is the collective version of the personal *Ammit*," said Blaise, "and she has done a masterful job of mucking up and confusing the *Bardo*."

"Shall we pay the old girl a visit?" suggested Merlin. "She's not far away."

The rest of us looked at one another in surprise and some dismay. We hadn't expected this. I hadn't even expected the bad guy angle. Merlin grinned.

We were there before we could resist or raise any objections. We stood before her house. I knew I was walking in the land of metaphors to see a house. My mind filled with fearful images, of female demons far worse than Rider Haggard's infamous She. Of haglike, skull-encrusted variants on the Hindu Kali. I felt like Beowulf about to meet Grendel's mother, an even fiercer opponent than her progeny whom he had just killed. We were about to meet Kali's wild mother, and if we were not terribly careful, on guard always, she would likely—

I felt someone shaking me. It was Blaise. "Frederick, it's okay. Calm down. Relax. The old girl isn't like that. She isn't so bad. Treacherous, deceitful, and sly as hell, even tarty on occasion, but she has some fine moves. You may appreciate them from a technical viewpoint. She's far more intelligent than just a monster."

We stood before a citadel, a fortress in shiny obsidian black. She stood there, at the front gates, as if to welcome us. She wasn't hideous, warty, or scary. She looked like the sister of the *Daena*, like an attractive, smiling 15-year old girl. Maybe I caught a gleam of treachery behind her eyes, some lurking mischief. I was tempted to look behind her to see if the monster was loitering there. Blaise must have sensed my imminent movement and put a restraining palm on my shoulder. Where's the scary, baleful stuff, I wondered. She didn't look like the big sister of the *Ammit*, the *Ammit* of all humanity over time. How could this be?

I suppose her eyes gave it away. They were those of an older woman, calculating, tactical, someone who had seen everything and was pretending to not be jaded or cynical about likely outcomes. They were the eyes of duplicity. Still, I understood Blaise's remarks. There was something intriguing about her. I couldn't say I disliked her, but she made me edgy. She didn't even look scary. Even my Dartmouth colleagues probably could have told me, shaking their heads, that the devil who seems pleasant and appealing and not scary is the most competent, dangerous of devils and around whom we should be most vigilant.

"Having fun with the Buddhas I see," the Druj said. "They can be a handful. I could give you a few tips on how to handle them. They're mostly bark. They never bite. They're too empty to have any teeth." She laughed at her joke. "My point is you don't have to waste your precious time in the *Bardo* on them. Nor do you have to go running and squealing to the nearest womb-door like most of the humans who arrive here. They never get their bearings and look for an easy exit out of this place. It can be challenging. I'll give you that for nothing."

I heard growling like that of a dog behind me. I turned to see it was Philomena. For a second she looked like a dog, its tail up, its snout in a snarl. Dogs are like that. They often sense something inimical long before people do. I felt Philomena was trying to warn me of something, but I didn't see any danger. In retrospect I see that was her point, that I, blinded by the Druj, didn't see it.

The door to her citadel was wide open and she was gesturing like a gracious hostess for us to enter. I did. Inside the walls were hung in paintings. The place was more of an art gallery or museum than a deity's cosmic residence. The room had the height equivalent of at least three stories but without floors. Paintings hung on all the walls starting at about four feet from the floor; the space below them was occupied by bookshelves groaning with enticing volumes.

No, it couldn't be, I thought. Was that Rachmaninov I heard in the background? I felt like I had walked into a room designed specifically for me, which of course it was. That was Philomena's point. But I didn't realize that until much later. Instead, I was fast on the way towards being entranced with this scholar's den. I was going the way of the Karapan and didn't know it. The others in the group seemed to have gone somewhere else. I didn't see them.

The room seemed suddenly full of people, like at a faculty cocktail party. People were milling about, holding drinks, talking, laughing, gesturing, smiling. I had the uncanny feeling they were all talking about me, or looking my way, as if, permit me my fantasies, I had just published a national bestseller and I was here by celebrity suffrage to regale an admiring public with my literary presence.

Everyone had something to say to me. I heard a hundred whispered voices in my ears. I saw mouths moving and words flowing out of them and entering my mind. I heard my name repeated in tones of appreciation and even sycophancy. These people were passing on messages, sharing gossip, telling me many secrets. It was like I was in Hollywood and I was getting the backstory on everyone, and this included more than people. Heavenly spirits, angels, Masters, were exposed. Even frauds, lies, and deceptions discovered about the Supreme Being Himself. This murmuring of whispers and comments was disclosing the universal con. Nothing is as it seems; reality is riddled with falsehoods; here is the naked truth. Better start from scratch, Frederick; you have been misinformed.

I started examining the paintings. At first glance they looked like portraits, the kind of family pictures of fustian ancestors you see in the country estates. Then I saw they were more than that, and this wasn't England with its old houses and crusty ancestors lingering balefully on the dry-rotting walls. They were scenes of dramatic settings with many people, objects, and places, more like stills from an action movie. As soon as I looked at one, I was inside it.

I saw a man at a desk. He was writing down words a spirit was speaking. The spirit looked like a human at first, though he was larger, taller, not human at all, but alien, I gradually realized. It was as if this spirit were making a report or revealing a formula and the man at the desk was taking notes on the revelation. I didn't hear his words exactly, but I caught the essence of what he was saying. His alien thoughts were translated into the man's own language.

"Forget the angels. They are pansies, weak, obedient, dutiful, never deviating. They don't know as much as they make out, and most of what they do know is useless. It will never open the doors you need opened. It only opens closet doors. The Masters won't tell you anything. They are too proud, too vain, too stuck on their rituals and ceremonies and images of hierarchy, precedence, and command. The spiritual tutors expect you to follow too many protocols. They are prisses. They expect you to train for decades before they let you have a shot at things. Forget them. Their so-called rules and laws are easily bendable.

"I can show you innumerable ways around them. It's far easier than people realize to circumvent their authority. You do not need all that training and preparation to get through the gates. A man of your stature should not have to trivialize his time with such pedantries. You may go straight through to the genuine article. You are slated for considerable accomplishments. They're more facile than you think. You and your work are very important to the world. You should realize that, and people around you must start acknowledging that now."

I felt a firm hand grab my shoulder and yank me out of that painting. I was standing outside the obsidian citadel again. It had been Blaise's hand on me. I had been about to nod my head in agreement with the tutoring spirit's words. They had gotten through to me. I was persuaded. I was about to buy the product. Blaise looked at me, his head tilted slightly. His eyes were fierce, a slight smile bloomed on his face, but he looked at me like I almost walked off a cliff's edge.

"Got to you, did she?" he said. "The cocktail party, the spirit-tutor. She's good. That was just one painting out of thousands, maybe millions, she has. Each is a tactical variation on the same sales pitch. She knew just the right one for you. You were about to walk off the cliff and think you were crossing another *Cinvat*."

Then I saw what he meant. The man at the desk in the painting was me. I had gone from examining the image to being the leading character in the picture. I hadn't noticed the transition. But Blaise had, and he had yanked me out in time. Then it hit me. That tutor had been praising me for being a man of high stature, and I had nearly bought the compliment. I had no stature. Twenty years ago when I was a professor I wasn't even chairman of the department, just one Ph.D. among many. My stature rating, I should think, was modest, not important, and Dartmouth would flourish quite nicely without enjoying my "august" presence.

Since then I have been in a strange kind of intermediate state, off and on with Blaise. Not even always on the planet. That carried no stature. I wasn't even sure what I was any more. Alive, probably. Dead, unlikely. A human occupying a position others could admire and attribute stature to? No. Not worth any sycophancy. An under-appreciated human susceptible to artful flattery and inflation? Yes. She knew where to hook me. That lure had allure, and I bit at it.

I was back with the group again. Edward was shaking his head, worriedly. "She got to me too, though in a different way. She is quite clever. I didn't see it coming nor did I get it while I was immersed, or stuck, in it. I saw a man in a long silver cloak with a ritualistic headpiece in silver as well. He held a staff which emitted a silvery light. Many people stood around him, waiting for orders. He seemed a combination of commander and archpriest. Heavenly spirits hovered in the air waiting for him to speak. I saw Merlin among these. These spirits had an air of sycophancy fueled by fear and uncertainty. The figure was me. As soon as I realized this, I was yanked into the picture and became the man.

"I saw that I was standing at the altar in a large cathedral. It reminded me of Chartres. The cathedral was packed, people everywhere, hushed, waiting. I raised my staff and everyone bowed, then kneeled. There was not a sound. Angels were layered in tiers around the interior of the cathedral up to the ceiling. I felt serious, earnest, a little petulant, impatient, irritated with the slowness of things. I had plans. I had been shown images. I had worked out tactics for this. I felt flushed with purpose and justification. I was entitled to do this. I *knew* that.

"I felt swelled with pride and valor. I had a commission straight from the top. The Supreme Being Himself had asked me to please undertake this assignment. I always thought I had something big planned for my life, more than being a mid-level editor for a large publishing company. That job was small potatoes, trivial. I had been chosen to edit that line of Blaise books because I was in the know. I had special knowledge, unique training, unprecedented contacts in the spirit world. Spiritual beings, angels, Masters, even Merlin, needed me, an intelligent human with my feet on the ground, to accomplish their missions.

"They were feckless without me, inconsequential. They needed me. They were virtually powerless without bodies of mass and substance. They all yearned to be human, to have a chance at being real masters of the physical. I understood I was specially blessed and gifted to be in this privileged position.

"When I was at this crest of pride and vanity I heard a woman's little chuckle. I flushed red, irate that someone was not taking me seriously. It was she, the Druj. She wasn't taking me seriously. Why should she? She's the one who wound me up to this ridiculous pitch. I de-inflated at once, chastened. I was back at my starting point, watching the scene from the outside. The man in the silver cloak was gone, the cloak itself a diminutive heap of rags on the ground. I was disgusted with myself, at how easily she had conned me, puffed me up."

"Don't beat yourself up over this, Edward," said Blaise. "She got to me too. She always fits the lie to the psyche. It was in the last months out in the desert in 2019, the time period covered by the journals you published. I was alone and in hiding, reviewing my life. I felt empty, useless, like I had failed. Frankly, despite my enthusiasm and discoveries, not many people cared about Blaise. Few had been impressed with their metaphorical fluency of form. Few had taken up their challenge to be the Blazing Star they were, to own that Star.

"I figured I must have been the wrong person to represent them. I'm not a salesman. America is all about products, whether they are objects, ideas, or even people. If it doesn't sell, it's a lousy product. All Americans know that. It was oppressing me. If I had failed in my mission, then maybe Blaise didn't amount to much either. Maybe that was why I had failed; the product itself was insufficient. I hated thinking that, because Blaise had meant so much to me my whole life.

"I think even the coyotes kept their distance from me. This gloom was contagious and they didn't need any other reasons to yip at three in the morning. I felt these conclusions were like a leaden wall that was pushing me into the ground. It was flattening me, pushing out all the reserve optimism I once had. It felt like a cosmic coffee press and soon I would be squeezed dry and pointless. I felt like I was being buried under a massive rockslide, hammered into the Earth.

"I couldn't muster the energy to picture the Rotunda of Light anymore. I was finished. Amusement was a vague memory. I couldn't muster even a chuckle. Nobody cared, nobody would remember, humanity was indifferent. I had a vague impression of a female figure, bigger than a person, more like a cosmic spirit of feminine valence, leaning over me asking, 'Is he dead yet?' Something flared in me, the last shred of dry kindling, and I shouted, suddenly roused back to myself and my true self, 'Up yours, bitch!' She disappeared."

"For a long time I did not see her at all," said Pipaluk. "I saw a forest of blackened trees. They had been burned, covered in tar and black slime, and seemed to be rotting and falling apart at the same time. This was our shaman's forest, where we often went for wisdom, cures, understanding, even lost souls. It looked ruined. Where would we go for healing after this? It was dispiriting to see. The central tree in this special grove was clearly diseased, corrupted, dying. This was our spirit forest, a special place in the world of Light you call astral.

"A nasty spirit seemed to have taken over this tree and it was dark and scowling. I saw many of my colleagues sitting at the base of these trees, forlorn, depressed. They sat as if at a wake for loved ones who had died horribly of a wasting disease, something terrible like rotting skin. They had stopped acting, stopped flying, stopped seeking for answers and cures and understandings from here. They had given up. They wouldn't even talk to me, or look me straight in the eyes. They acted as if they had forgotten who I was, and worse, did not care.

"It felt like my village had burned down, all its houses, including mine, destroyed, and all the occupants either burned or driven out into the wilds. But I detected something, a foreign presence, or an extra attention standing behind me. It was trying to remain invisible, undetected, but perhaps not trying that hard. I saw mostly a face. It was that of a female demon. It was a *torngarsuk*. That is a special demon in Greenland, a supernatural being who looks like a male bear or sometimes a one-armed man. This *torngarsuk* is powerful but can be an ally. Normally, only the *angakkuq* can see this dark spirit; it is tricky and mischievous. It might go left, it might go right; you could never be sure; its form could change.

"This *torngarsuk* image had something strange about it, something wrong, untrue. It felt female, though in an ugly, haglike way, and not its normal strong masculine way. I began to suspect I was being deceived. This demon felt deceptive, malevolent, full of tricks, and I knew I would not like any of them. I felt she hated humans and was pleased to do so, liked hurting and deceiving us. I immediately went to my circle of power, a private place of concentration and spiritual essence I maintained in a secret place in the landscape near my home.

"This is my place of truth and deep anchorage. I sat there until I became clear. Yes, this is not a real *torngarsuk*; it is a female demon pretending to be this male spirit. Then I realized the rotting forest, the dying trees, the despondent shamans I saw were also untrue, deceptive images put before me by this untrue *torngarsuk*. I flashed my right hand forcefully from left to right in a banishment gesture. The untrue *torngarsuk* disappeared; so did the dying forest and grieving shamans. I was back here, as if I had never left and no time had passed.

"Everything I had seen and done had been untrue, a false image she had painted. It could have led me to despair, to sit down with those shamans who had quit. I am of an age when I could leave anytime, when I could choose to drop the body. Then my village would be without any assistance; the land would be alone too. Nobody had been assigned yet to take my place. If I departed without this replacement, my village would be another node taken over by the darkness. This was like putting black coins in a dark pot; when it was full you could buy the Earth with these coins of misery, despair, and abandonment. She would buy the Earth this way. She has always been intent on buying the Earth."

I noticed Matthew was shivering, as if out of fright and a sudden chill. I surmised he had just had an encounter with the Druj as well, and it had shaken him. He was stomping his feet as if they had been almost frost-bitten, and he was turning around in tight circles. He was trying to get back into himself, to anchor.

He looked up, shook his head a few times to dispel confusion and vapors. "Yes, me too. Man, was I seduced. I never saw that coming. It was so subtle. I was with the Thunderbirds again by James Bay in Quebec. A dozen had settled around this end of the lake, their backs to the water, their faces toward me. They looked fiercer than usual. Everything about them seemed sharper, tougher; they reminded me of myself after I made the mistake one morning of reading the newspaper and got well briefed on the cruelties and stupidities of the world. I should have picked up on this shift in nuance; this aggressive stance was not typical of them. They seemed, in an unspecified way, out for revenge and payback, as if they were going to correct the wrongs of the world this morning.

"I admit, I had a long list of social grievances, of desired retributions. I suppose any intelligent person even half-aware of what governments do has one. I had a personal list of those who had affronted, insulted, or injured me as well. Suddenly, both these lists seemed to be at the top of the day's agenda. We were out for blood. The Thunderbirds were finished with people ruining the world. They would not tolerate their abuses any longer. They would put them down. I'm dismayed I wasn't surprised by this new aggressive, almost pugilistic, attitude. I should have been, and that I wasn't should have been a clue for me. This was unlike myself or the Thunderbirds. This is not how you fix the world.

"I rode on the back of the chief of the Thunderbirds. He was screaming, or however you would describe a Bird of Heaven calling out to the world to heed. We stormed out of the skies down over the land. It was Washington, D.C. These Thunderbirds must have been ten times the size of the U.S. Capitol building. They swooped and grabbed people with their talons. They slashed buildings. Threw them down with people inside. They crashed into the Capitol, the White House, and other government buildings, knocking them over, smashing them.

"They were ruthless. Nobody was exempt. They would all be made to pay now. There was no point in trashing the Canadian seat of government; they took their cue from the Americans. This was the true source of all the world's evil, and this is where the debt to humanity and the Earth would be collected for all time. I was delirious with the Thunderbird's rage and destructive power. Kill them all!

"I felt as if my mother were riding with us, like this Thunderbird were a horse and she rode on the same saddle right behind me, holding my waist. Her long black hair streamed in the wind, Her fingernails were long and sharp. She was screaming. I felt like I had a crazed Valkyrie, a Harpy, a vengeful Fury on my back out to avenge all the enemies of the world, of Nature, of Mother Earth. We had become avenging

Erinyes, just the way the Greeks described them. We would punish and destroy all those who had harmed the Earth Mother. This was matricidal vengeance at a global level. This was the justified apocalypse.

"You can see I had no rein on myself or my emotions. I had lost myself in this fury of retribution and punishment. We would renovate the world *today* by destroying all the enemies of the Creation. Not a single one would survive this purge. It was happening. We were leveling the scales, getting payback at last.

"'We come as Love from Above,' said a single voice, very faint, behind me. I was back at the lake. A single Thunderbird stood before me, wrapped in a cloak of dazzling diamonds and surrounded by a towering lilac flame as tall as the sky. It regarded me with a look of neutrality, compassion, and concern. It reminded me of how my dog used to look at me when I would suddenly get angry at something and throw a book or start vituperating out loud. 'What's wrong with master?' the dog's look would convey. Indeed, what is?

"Suddenly, the storm stopped. The tornado of revenge halted, grew still. I came back to myself. I had never left the lake. I had never been riding with Thunderbirds transformed into demented, homicidal Valkyries. It had not been my mother riding with me. This insight burst open the whole illusion. The Druj. It had been she. God, was I taken in. What a masterful con she draped over me and set fire to, enjoying the conflagration in my consciousness and the terrible distortions to reality I committed on its behalf, making the Thunderbirds into crusading zealots out to avenge all the worlds' wrongs without any mercy. None of this was true, but it had been possible. Its seeds had lain dormant in me. The Druj simulated their sprouting and blossoming. She almost sold me the fruits."

These stories were sobering, yet they gave me a vivid picture of the Druj. I saw her as an enormously bloated demonic female figure, her skin comprised of thousands of layers, like scales with living images on them. I realized that had we succumbed to her seductive visions today and lost ourselves in them these would have been added to the myriads of dark images encrusting her skin. That is what her skin was made of, where it came from. Humans empowering dark pictures. Giving up, despairing. Getting enraged with justified vengeance. Buying the illusion, the lie, that she fostered in a near infinite number of ways. *We*, humans over time, had grown this monstrosity. We fed and nurtured her. Engorged with human consciousness, she turned on us and devoured all of us. Her body was like a vast scrapbook of autographed action pictures, a myriad of human endorsements for every defilement of goodness and Light she ever had.

Merlin was shaking his head, glad we were at last getting the message. "She's some girl, that Druj," he said. "Very clever, and usually up to no good."

"The Druj is a combination of femme fatale, trickster, and sociopath," said Blaise, as if underlining every word. "The motto for us is watch you back, pal."

Merlin acknowlegded the comment, grew silent and concentrated within himself. Then he spoke. "This expedition is an installment in the *Frasokereti*."

We looked at him with incredulity and incomprehension. "The old man is reverting to his John of Patmos high-prophecy vein," said Edward, looking at us.

He looked at us with clarity and some merriment, as if he had not just uttered a statement none of us understood. "The renovation of the world. It's an old word from the *Avesta*, the early sacred documents of Iran. It refers to an eventual time when the world is finally, definitively, renovated, restored to its original pristine condition. All the evil in the world is overcome and destroyed. *Isfet* vanquished. The Druj in rout. Gayomart, the Primal Man, alive again. All of the Earth creation is put back into alignment with the true and the good, known to the Persians as Ahura-Mazda and the world's design quality of *Asha*. The renovation of the world means the redemption of truth, its reality restored.

"It is the correctness, the truthfulness of reality, the realness of true reality, the orderliness of the original plan. The Druj will be thrown down. The *Saoshyant* or angelic world redeemer, what others call the Maitreya Buddha or the *Mashiach*, will resurrect all the dead. The mountains will melt, releasing all their metals, and the land will flow with rivers of molten metal. All humans will have to wade this river. Those in alignment with *Asha* will see these rivers as made of soft warm flowing milk; those not in alignment will perish in the inexorable streams of metal. The metals are the chakras of fragmented vision melted down.

"This river of molten metals—it's like the River Acheron without the boat. This will purge the world of the Druj and all her dark minions. You know, it's a vision of apocalypse after my own heart. It has some nice touches I could have usefully put into my Patmos vision, but I guess one shouldn't hog all the glory, let some other prophets have a go at describing the coming world renovation."

Now, much later, I can reflect on Merlin's portentous announcement and get the words straight, which is always a good foundation for approaching big concepts. *Frasokereti* connotes a future but inevitable (guaranteed, you might say) eschatological purification of the world, a transfiguration, renewal, a definitive refurbishment, a making fresh and perfect, as the word at its core suggests. This renovation will be facilitated, spearheaded, perhaps catalyzed and certainly completed and validated, by the *Saoshyant*, the "future helper," the "bringer of benefit." This is a divine redemptive figure appointed by Ahura-Mazda.

The river of molten metals, certainly a powerful image, refers to the chakras. The human Blaise alerted me to this correlation a few years ago in our travels. Individual metals are associated, through astrology, yoga, and Anthroposophy, with the prime cognitive centers along the spine, the chakras. Classically, they were listed as mercury, tin, lead, silver, gold, copper, and iron. They represent a series of seven different "eyes" or cognitive zones, and that represents a fallen condition, a diminishment from single vision to multiple. The metals of the different chakras will be melted when single vision is called for. Another name for single vision is cyclopean, the round eye of unitive seeing. All the chakra-metals melted to form a molten river is the arising of single vision.

This is a salutary act, though it sounds unsettling. The Persians viewed the rising up of the world's mountains as evidence of a primary aberration in *Asha*. In its original design, the Earth was round but its surface perfectly flat. In their model of the Earth, the global orogeny leading to mountains was a consequence of primordial disturbances in the rightful order, the killing of Gayomart, the primal cosmogonic Human, and of Gavaevodata, the primal Ox; overall, it constitutes a worldwide upset. The dead Gayomart's body became the metals. Of course, the way myths work "dead" probably meant Gayomart was "anchored" in or near the physical world, or at least in the lower planes of cosmic Earth. From a celestial viewpoint, he had fallen, diminished, died to his spiritual purity.

Melting the metals of mountains and chakras reverses an unnatural condition. Merlin said our expedition was only an installment in this world renovation; again, it was the human Blaise who told me (though he got it from the angelic Blaises) that all this wouldn't happen until about 3,000 A.D. That would be the time of the prophecied Battle of Shambhala, famous in Buddhism. That's when the *Mashiach*, the World Redeemer, would arrive on the Earth. Still, even an installment in a great project like this was not a trivial undertaking.

Merlin gathered us around him. "You have had a brief look around the House of Lies. Seen a few dramas of personal interest. The Druj casts her pall over the human world, the living Earth world of sunlight and the Underworld that pertains to the human passage through the *Bardo*. She confounds it all with lies. Her presence is like a shadow, sometimes mocking, sometimes menacing, or sometimes leering. She is protean. Her guise and tactics depend on the nature of the soul in passing. She is terrifically adaptive and creative. She is a pervasive influence here, and it is not to the good. It never was, but it has grown worse over the millennia. She troubles, confounds everyone's passage, and that is largely why we have launched this expedition to reform the afterlife protocols."

"Blaise said that the Druj is the collective version of the personal *Ammit*," said Edward. "That suggests she is home-grown, generated from out of humanity's shadow and unconscious over time. Is that the correct picture?"

"Yes. Humans have created and fleshed out the Druj over time. As you saw, every time a person succumbs to her influence, it adds an image scale to her bloated body. If each of you who was tested by the Druj had given in to her persuasive pictures, which were based on seeds in your own psyche, you would have thereby added to her massive size. That in turn makes her more competent at confounding the unprepared dead as they pass through this already tricky place. She recirculates her human-endorsed pictures, the autographs, into the living human world as proof and validation of the various lies she propagates. Given the implications of the upgrade underway of the

Earth's Light grid to a sixth chakra frequency, it is imperative we reduce the scope of her influence."

"So the Druj is grown out of the human over time," said Edward. "It is what philosophers would call a secondary creation or a sub-creation, surely not as real as the deities created by the Supreme Being. The *Ammit* is not truly real."

"Correct. I like your subtlety of interpretation. Yes, not as real. The Druj was given birth, or the possibility of birth and a kind of half-life, with the introduction of physical death to a humanity already granted access to the Tree of the Knowledge of Good and Evil. When you can choose, you can be deceived. Deception is the cost of free will. Free will requires discernment and lucidity. When you are allowed to deviate from *Asha*, from the justice, order, and rightness of the Creation, spirits will rise up to challenge and test you and suborn your alignment. The Supreme Being allows that. In many respects it is unavoidable.

"The Druj, or what Christians call the Antichrist and Muslims *Masih ad-Dajjal*, was born when the first human, and I mean literally the first in line, the first to die, and who died after a lifetime of free-will access to that dualistic, very troubling tree, entered the Underworld burdened with the unresolved, pained consequences or black seeds of his life choices, what you could call sin or karma. Yes, on the one hand, that was the birthing of his *Ammit* in the *Bardo*, yet each *Ammit* became a seed for this larger version, the Druj. It took life from the *Ammits*. In a sense, the individual *Ammits* had to start paying tribute, a fee, to the Druj, the way imperial Rome used to exact tributes, an early form of taxation, from their subjugated colonies. Humans have kept growing the Druj ever since.

"People expect the Antichrist to appear as a terrifically scary monster. Only those very dense and hard to persuade of this reality require that degree of personification. The Druj adapts her form to suit the expectations of the viewer. You will agree, I think, that she is far more dangerous when she is devious and sly, manipulating your perceptions and interpretations through her slim look. In truth, she may be enormously bloated, but she doesn't have to look that way. The best way for a devil to sell you something is to clothe herself as the purest angel.

"It is very exacting, if you think about it. Every choice of 'evil' from the Tree is a validation of the Antichrist. Evil is what opposes the Christ or Buddha, the authentic Light of awakened, nondualistic, empty awareness: Christ Light. This Light arises in freedom; it could not be any other way, or else souls would not be humans with free will but angels with no free will but created already perfect. Every act, gesture, imprecation, even thought, that supports that which is opposed to the Christ Light or that which blocks or distorts it for a living soul, contributes to the Druj because the Druj is the personification of that opposition. Don't discount the power of thought in this strengthening of the Druj's hegemony over the human soul. A thought is a mobilization of the *skandah* grid to make a modulation in reality; all five *skandahs* are deployed as a tactical unit.

"Then, once the Druj got started, became viable, spirits inimical to the project of human freedom of consciousness got involved and started supporting the Druj. It is like the way influential people support political candidates for office. The Druj spawned more spirits like herself. The Zoroastrians called these secondary spirits the Followers of Falsehood, or *dreguuatąm*; they were *daēuuas*, false gods or chimeras without any real existence, but they proliferated quickly. But don't be fooled into complacency; they still have a believable false existence. What I mean is they can still kick your ass good and proper if you're inattentive.

"Over the epochs, the Druj's influence in the *Bardo* has been tidal. There have been peaks of her interference and troughs of our successful resistance to her. A bit like a troublesome skin rash you just can't shake off, you could say. She keeps coming back. One time in late Lemuria, when there already was a fair degree of entropy and spiritual deterioration in the outer physical world, she laid down a sticky net over the entry aspects of the Underworld, such as the bridge, the boat, and the Weighing of the Heart, where a soul can get stuck or lost.

"This net was at one level a mechanism of passive interference, an atmosphere, like a low-pressure front that keeps the sky cloudy, gloomy, and humid. The moment a newly dead soul experienced a moment of doubt, confusion, despair, anger, or any nuance of negativity, bemoaning his horrible fate, you might say, that would activate the overarching black web and it would send down a sticky tendril to hook into the soul. One dark thought breeds many more, and soon the unprepared, unwary soul would be covered in sticky threads, and these enhanced the baleful atmosphere of gloom and despair. She was exceedingly careful to design this so as to not contravene human free will. That would have got the Supreme Being on her case instantly; she orchestrated it so the net only dropped in response to a subtle movement towards it by the soul.

"Then the Followers of Falsehood would appear and like an infernal chorus intone litanies of darkness and anguish, intensifying the soul's doubts and fears. The soul was likely to take their dark choruses for the truth, mistake them for angels and emissaries of Ahura-Mazda and conclude God was an angry, cruel God incapable of mercy or redemption, or far worse, unwilling to intercede to help suffering humans or even to commiserate with them. All this was false, but many souls believed it anyway. They couldn't see the truth.

"The goal of course was to get the soul to fail the afterlife initiation challenge, to cringe in fear in the face of the *Dhyani* Buddhas as if they were the worst of demons, and rush for the nearest womb-door for rebirth and to reincarnate never having gained any lucidity here. Then he would re-enter the human physical world with a consciousness of obscuration. This would add to the thickness and spiritual density of the human world and make it less likely humans on dying would enter the *Bardo* well-prepared. It was an insidious tactic; it worked extremely well. She ended up having millions of beclouded souls working for her on both sides of the divide, the alive world and the *Bardo*. Each beclouded soul added a lamination of obscuration to the Druj's world of lies."

"Merlin, you said such endarkened souls would fail the afterlife initiation challenge," said Matthew. "What does that mean? What are you referring to?"

"You could think of the *Bardo* journey as like the journey of Odysseus from Troy to Ithaca. There is a route and a destination, a homecoming. Yama's Celestial City has some routine but necessary processing zones, involving the life review, the Weighing of the Heart, assessing one's *Ammit*, crossing the bridge; it has some paradisal areas for those who complete the processing and wish to stay; and it has a goal, the equivalent of Odysseus's Ithaca and his Penelope. The 'Penelope' you get here is a reunion with the Great Mother, Isis or Hine, She of the many names and myriads of forms, She who generates all these forms. If I may adapt a famous saying of Rider Haggard, it is She Who Must Be Obeyed because, really, why wouldn't you want to since She is the source of your life?

"If you will permit me to relapse into my Anubis format and language, then let's say the newly dead soul is the emulator of green-skinned Osiris, the pharoah of the land of Upper and Lower Egypt. That is the soul in a state of power, self-awareness, and awakening consciousness. He journeys to Isis, his Throne, as her hieroglyph indicates. He travels from the realm of the physically embodied, out through the crown chakra, over the bridge that links the crown chakra with the Underworld (as you know, it is better called the Upperworld), and journeys through this realm of tests and challenges, including the *Dhyani* Buddhas, the Wrathful Deities, the 42 Assessors of the *Duat*, the regal domain of the 72 *Pitrs* or awakened Fathers of the different peoples among humanity, until he passes through the 49 Gates and enters the realm of the great Silver Mother. That is the basic map of the intended *Bardo* journey for the disembodied soul.

"There he is rejoined in original wholeness and unity as he was before he ever passed through those Gates and had his consciousness fractured into 49 parts. By the time he reaches the Great Mother, he has shaken himself free of all bindings. Those bindings are the mechanics, processes, protocols, and grids of the human phylogeny, all the rules, regulations, red tape, and paperwork involved in being a human, and of extricating oneself from that particular definition. Can you see how it is a definition of the wholeness of consciousness?

"To be a human requires you to take on more than a human body. You must take on the human cognitive apparatus, its assumptions, habits, history, prejudices. This is the *skandah* grid adjusted to the human phylogeny. You voluntarily have your cyclopean wholeness of consciousness sliced up into 49 chakras, 49 eyes, the 49 Gates into the human world, both bewildering and astonishing, as no one will dispute, and exceedingly tricky and nastily subtle. To have all these eyes is an aberration like the rising up of the mountains upon an originally ordained flat surface Earth because it means the original wholeness of cyclopean perception has been sundered and you are fragmented.

"The moment arrived when we had to act. The Druj had too much power. Too many souls were succumbing to her dark influence and losing their way. From a certain viewpoint, this was fascinating, instructive, and even comical. The Druj has no genuine ontological existence, nor do the Followers of Falsehood. They do not have the Creator's imprimatur. They are false creations, simulacra.

"Yet they have a kind of psychological and anthropological relative existence. Humanity has spawned the Druj and her followers, and now humans cringe when they draw near. They are afraid of their own shadow, their own dream images. The trouble is humans kept energizing the Druj, enhancing her seeming reality. We had to stop that, or at least diminish its worrisome momentum.

"It took a lot of drawn swords. We used silver blades that blazed with a fierce Silver Light and flashed insinuations of the Great Mother through them. We surrounded the Druj one 'day,' not that time is reckoned in solar units here. We made a peaked tent of our blades over her. There were 200 of us, a lot of blades. Our intent was not to harm the Druj; that would not improve conditions. We intended to blaze off laminations of darkness from her aura, and we would do that sheerly through the spiritual force of our poised blades of Silver Light. It was like how a mother commands obedience from her children by a look.

"The Druj has an incontestable right to exist. Humans in free will created her. They shaped her body and fleshed out her form from their choices with the Tree. She is a human thoughtform generated over time that has gained autonomy and now harasses its creator, inchoate human consciousness. The Supreme Being, indirectly, allowed her to continue to exist; she served the useful purpose of testing humans to develop discernment, even if most of them failed.

"Still, we had no permission, no authorization from the Creator, to destroy the Druj. We still don't. We never will. We can only periodically prune back her growth within human reality. We can only help humans realize who she is and choose to free themselves from her sticky threads of lie, error, and deception. We can show them the truth, *Asha*, and hope they discern the falsehood of the Druj. We can occasionally level the playing field and fix the net (think tennis) or repaint the boundaries of the court so the great game of consciousness may proceed. This time our brief is to align the playing field with the changed Light grid and that grants us extra latitude in reducing the influence of the Druj."

Merlin paused to make sure we were all listening closely. "There is something else we are permitted to do this time. We may generate a *tulpa*."

Naturally, none of us knew what this word meant, but coming from Merlin we knew it would be interesting and important. Then he explained it.

"In Tibet we call a magical emanation or illusion a *tulpa*. It is an illusory form constructed by the mind in concentration. It is considered a psychic power. A *tulpa* is a conjured thoughtform, often in the guise of a formed spirit. It is a mind-created apparition, yet one capable of acting in the psychic world. The Buddha is said to have multiplied his emanation body, his *Nirmanakaya*, into countless other forms simultaneously sufficient to fill the sky with semblances.

"These generated forms are called *nirmanas* or *nirmitas* in Sanskrit, *sprul-pa* and thus *tulpa* when the Tibetan is translated into English. The Druj is a *tulpa*, but it was created from the unwholesome, ill-attended, subliminal or subconscious part of human consciousness. The

Druj *tulpa* was generated from the shadows of human awareness. You could say it is the product of a psychic power or *siddhi* wrongly used, or deployed inattentively. Humans have created a burgeoning demonic thoughtform over time distractedly using this power of mind. Now we will generate a truth-filled *tulpa* of Light from the wholesome, wide-awake, daytime-conscious part of awareness during the time we are here in the *Bardo*.

"The durability and even potential independent sentience of a *tulpa* depends on the strength of concentration of its generator. The Druj is a very effective *tulpa*. It was generated by the enormous repetitive concentration by billions of humans over time. While the creative attention of each individual person is minimal, when you multiply this small amount of focusing power by billions it becomes strong. We few will have to counter that through our *tulpa*-generation to create a worthy match with the Druj. Our *Asha-tulpa*, if you'll indulge me this hybrid term, will have to emulate the clarity of Ahura-Mazda. We shall have to mind-birth this thoughtform in far less time than humans had to construct their fantastic phantom the Druj which now harasses the *Bardo*."

Our attention turned to Matthew. He looked like a samurai. He appeared to be holding a great sword at a diagonal about to slice it down onto something. His body showed poise and balance, the perfect mastery of *qi* and center of gravity you'd expect from a master swordsman like a samurai. His eyes were focused, his face cast an expression of fierceness wrapped in a focused scowl.

I said he "appeared" to be doing this because I knew at once this was a simulation. This was a thought he had projected around himself, but it had been sufficiently strong to assume a semblance of reality, that is, for others to see it that way. I couldn't see his opponent but based on where we were and our recent discussion topic, I assumed it was the Druj getting exactly what she deserved.

"What's up, Matthew?" asked Tommy. He was grinning. He liked the image Matthew was projecting. "You're looking very buff there, pal."

"I'm not sure, actually," Matthew responded. "I suddenly found myself in this position. Just before that I felt a few layers of myself slide off as if they had been unnecessary layers of clothing. My body divested itself of them. It was strange. All this seemed to happen independent of me. I felt lighter, as if stripped of 'flesh' or self-definitions I no longer needed. I was stripped of my unreality. That's the only way I can put it. Then I found myself holding this sword. The oddest part of it was I knew this was not a fighting posture, even though it looks like one. The sword does not have to strike to purge. Its blade is the invincible sharpness of truth. Motionless, it clarifies everything around it.

"It felt like being inside a hollow sculpted action figure. In myself I felt entirely empty. I saw the movement, the gesture of sword and body posture and attention, but at the same time I was removed from that. It was empty and quiet, and I felt my awareness itself was growing steadily thinner and more vague. Yet it was not like falling asleep but like waking up, sheerly, definitively, suddenly."

Merlin was nodding, but he didn't say anything. Whatever he knew or foresaw at this time, he wasn't going to tell us. Well, we'd find out soon enough.

6

I saw a big guy in dazzling yellow Light holding a jewel and sitting atop a magnificent horse. I reached for my sunglasses then remembered where I was.

It was a horse and it was a throne at the same time, depending, I supposed, on whether the figure wished to be mobile or stationary. He was flanked by six dazzling orbs of Light; inside each was the semblance of a female celestial deity. The yellow was so bright, so unexpected, so thorough and unarguable in its reality, that I felt a little edgy in its presence. Forming a weak penumbra around this appearance of figure and Light was a paler, dull, bluish-yellow Light which oddly seemed more attractive, suggesting comfort and respite, like an easy route up a steep mountain or hinting at a kind of welcoming sanctuary, than the intimidating brilliance of the yellow and its fierce bearer.

"Watch out for that dull blue-yellow Light," said Tommy. "It's a trap. A womb-door exit back into the incarnate human world. I almost got lured into it. All these *Dhyanis* have that side-door behind them. It's not their fault. But there is a dull light of varying colors accompanying each of the *Dhyani* Buddhas. It offers wavering consciousness the option to leave, to jump back into a body. These dull colors make a good sales pitch; they can be persuasive, but it's trading one perplexity for another one that you think, mistakenly, is more familiar. These big Buddhas are like alarm clocks ringing right next to your ear. You are tempted to turn it off, flip over, and sleep another hour—defer it all, take on another life."

"Before you know it you're back here choosing between the same sets of lights," said Blaise. "It's a kind of incarnational recidivism. The relapse rate is high. Old ways are persuasive. The womb-doors are painted with alluring colors. The *Dhyani* Buddhas see a lot of familiar faces. 'So, you're back. What will it be this time?' More of the same, usually. 'I'll take the dull blue-yellow light, thanks. I'll take the color I know. At least I know what to expect. Here, I have no idea.'"

"Consciousness is lost in both realms, without any sure footing," said Philomena. "It does not understand its true nature or condition, so it suffers. It is embedded, although I could just as well say stuck, in a state of obscuration. Nothing is clear; all realities and perceptions are relative, and largely deceptive. Consciousness struggles within a thick, obscuring cloud or is paved over in tar."

I turned my attention back to the newest *Dhyani* Buddha to appear. A bright yellow Light streamed out of his heart center like the midday sun. This figure sat in a full lotus meditation position. His right hand rested on his right knee with the palm open and facing outwards, as if in the gesture of giving gifts. His left hand held a bright jewel of blazing yellow-gold. His entire body blazed in yellow Light, yet it seemed also he was wearing ornate yellow robes. His face radiated an expression of love and compassion, sympathy for all created beings. It was the compassionate look you'd expect from a perfect mother, like Mother Earth, with sympathy and concern for all living beings, seeing them all as equal.

My attention was drawn to the bright jewel this figure held in his left hand. It glowed. It beckoned. It expanded. Soon it was all I could see. I entered it. I felt like I was inside the essence of all matter, of everything solid, made of earth. I mean the element of earth, not the planet. I was in the original idea of matter, primordial matter, the realm of feeling, the way something solid resists the sensation of the other elements against its "skin," such as light, air, fire, water. That is what an "I" is, I realized, the nature of selfhood, a resistance to the Light, yet it is a formed, solid resistance in the same way that a chalice resists the Light; but it also may hold the Light, which is why it has a hollow receptive interior. I marveled at this paradox of resistance and acceptance and felt the double tug.

Then I saw the central *Dhyani* Buddha and the six enlightened beings around him as another expression of this paradox, but of the paradox resolved. They were like a chalice yet they were transparent, offered no resistance to anything. All feeling sensation the chalice, or selfhood, or any expression of earth might emit was converted into this enlightenment immediately, and any localized sense of self, whether it was of matter or a human selfhood, was similarly converted to universal compassion, like a Light beam of infinite width.

I understood what the jewel the *Dhyani* Buddha was holding meant. It connoted this widescale enlightenment, this conversion of selfhood into compassion, of the feeling of individual units of earth into a universal benevolent regard for all. The tendency, the in-built habit, of consciousness to say "I feel

this or that" is now upgraded into a universal sympathy for all created beings, for all aspects of earth. This was one of the *skandahs* Merlin had been talking about. The way feeling, the resistance of earth or solidity to its environment, reinforces the notion of separate selfhood—this was now rendered transparent, ablaze in Light.

The experience answered a question that had been forming in my mind. It was odd because though I had not yet voiced the question, I heard Merlin answering it in my mind, or my notional sense of separate mentality, if you'll indulge my attempt at apprentice Buddhism. My question was this: The Tibetans, and the Asian Buddhists in general, have a distinct visual *style* of representing celestial and spiritual beings, but what if you come from a Western culture, or at any rate, a non-Buddhist culture, should you expect to see these exalted spirits in that same stylized manner? Isn't it a relative way of seeing?

This was Merlin's telepathic answer delivered to my illusory sense of resisting separate selfness otherwise known (so falsely!) as Frederick Graham Atkinson: "To a degree it is a relative, culturally-conditioned style of seeing, but in many respects it is an accurate portrait of how these celestial figures look to humans. It is not so much conditioned by a culture, but more by the human psyche itself.

"These enlightened figures, left to themselves, have no form, nor do they need one, but when rendered into some manner of name and form, they are figures of great Light, their forms and implements and appearance, even the objects they hold, are symbolic of sublime states of transparent, empty, wide-awake awareness, and in this manner they are instructive to conditioned consciousness. Think of this as plausible metaphorical personifications of enlightened states. Plus we helped shape the image to make it more accessible to wakeful humans who wanted a credible picture of the enlightened condition.

"Each of these *Dhyani* Buddhas reflects the natural brightness of your own pure awareness, your ground condition, your inherent foundational state. You could say this *Dhyani* Buddha was pulled out of yourself, out of your original essence, you and all other humans. It is an innate transpersonal quality.

"The brilliant yellow Light of this *Dhyani* Buddha is the awakened wisdom of the equality of all created beings, and all elements of earth that register a feeling of selfhood. At the same time, this glorious personification acts as a *hook* for attentive consciousness to draw it into this true, clarified state of reality. The Light-rays of this *Dhyani* Buddha are poised and waiting to hook you into the awakened reality amidst the bewildering labyrinth and false paths of the *Bardo*."

I was back with the rest of the group and now Merlin was speaking out loud to us. "This figure is called Ratnasambhava. His name means 'Jewel-Born' or 'the Origin of Jewels.' These jewels are the Three Jewels of Buddhism known as the Buddha, or state of enlightenment and full awakening; the teachings or *Dharma*; and the collegiality of fellow practitioners called the *Sangha*. His essential nature is one of giving. You see his right hand opened up to offer gifts? In his other hand lies the *cintamani* jewel indicating the earth element and its *skandah* of feeling raised up into its purest form as a beautiful gold-yellow jewel.

"All feelings and sensations are equal in Ratnasambhava's enlightenment. That means no feeling or sensation warrants more attention or less than any other, and none is more indicative of individual selfhood, of earth formed into beings, than any other, and therefore, and this is the key part, all are equally empty which means equally transparent and radiant with the Light of absolute reality, which is none other than

Buddha Nature, or, if you like, the Christ Light. The correct state of the element of earth, of the habit of sensation and feeling, is this dazzling yellow Light, to be raised into it, converted back to its true nature."

Merlin was laughing. "The hope of the designers of the *Bardo* was that the Light-ray hook of Ratnasambhava would be compelling enough to keep the journeying soul on the path out of the labyrinth and away from the dull blue light of the human realm. That was wishful thinking, let me tell you. It hardly ever succeeds. Most souls find the yellow Light too overwhelming, too scary, too undefined and without explanation or context, so they default to the blue light. We are not allowed to call out to them, 'No, the blue light is a trick. Don't go to it. It's the karmic product of your habits and lifelong ignorance. Stick with the yellow. It's your only ticket out of here, we assure you.' No, we must be silent."

I saw why Merlin was laughing. Long lines of souls were approaching the fantastic apparition of dazzling yellow Light and deviating off to the right. That was where the dull, pallid blue light of the human realm flickered at them. When I say human realm I mean Human World, one of the Six Worlds in the Wheel of Life. Ratnasambhava is correlated with that World. But the blue light was like a lurid neon sign advertising a desirable rest stop on a night's highway journey. It offered rest, comfort, hot food, human companionship, and ease. Your intention had been to drive through the night to reach the city of your plans, but this invitation to pull off the highway, rest and relax, was too alluring to resist.

You're hooked, though it's the wrong hook, from Ratnasambhava's viewpoint. You never reach your city. You never leave the restaurant, at least not from the front door. You'll exit the rear door and soon find yourself back in human form. That's why Merlin was laughing, though it was not in derision, more amusement tinged with sympathy. "They never get the magic trick. They always fall for it. They're always conned into watching the wrong hand."

"Nice horses, don't you think," commented Blaise. "Well-chiselled heads." He was indicating the horse throne-mount underneath Ratnasambhava. I wasn't sure if I was seeing one horse or one hundred. My vision seemed to blur. I did perceive that they only resembled horses, that they were grand visual metaphors. Within or perhaps in the same place as the well-chiselled heads Blaise had praised I saw Blaise angels. Many of them, packed inside their Rotunda. It was like horses with the heads of Ofanim, and I knew those were metaphors too. Appearing as one horse, the mount faced in all directions at once; seen as one hundred horses it also covered all the directions from this one stationary place.

I felt like I was mounted on one hundred horses galloping in all directions at once. This galloping I experienced as a brisk, bright run into increasing clarity. With every forward stride of each horse reality clarified radically for me. It was as if the horses (the Ofanim, as I didn't forget for a moment) transported me further into the searing, crystalline sharpness of cognition of their essence. As you can see, all conventional notions of space and movement were defeated here.

With each stride closer to the goal, the destination, the Ofanim grounded me more firmly and definitively in this fundamental point in consciousness, which, as I saw it, went through stages of simplification from horses to Rotunda of Light to diamond geode to single Blazing Star to riveting wide-awake awareness, shining lucidity at the core of reality, tinged with wisdom and amusement. Fleetness of insight, the swiftness of consciousness to reach discernment, the virility of the gallop, the fierceness of intention—I knew these

were among the qualities the horse metaphor invoked. But it was funny too.

There is nowhere to go, no place to race swiftly to, even though this horse runs fast. Nowhere to run to, but there is something to gallop away from. Ratnasambhava's fleet of horses will gallop your consciousness away from the alluring, lurid, and dangerous pale blue light of the beckoning human realm. They will transport you swiftly and decisively away from the habitually tempting womb-doors, the shutes that slide you sleekly back into your next incarnational body. I say they gallop you away from the womb-doors, but their actions are meant to move you *towards* the truth, the recognition of the enlightenment-essence of the *skandah* of feeling and sensation of earth as exemplified by Ratnasambhava. The womb-doors, left behind, grow faint.

Before I continue let me offer a few words to explain this Rotunda of Light that has been mentioned often in this narrative. It is a meeting place the Ofanim conceived for humans, a kind of half-way location. It looks like an upscale outdoor gazebo, though architecturally it is more formal, more like a rotunda, if you can imagine a rotunda serving as a gazebo for open-air meetings. It has six diamond-crystal pillars, a round table made of glass, and upon it a massive, semi-flattened diamond geode, the Ofanim's expandable crystal cave. The Rotunda itself, it should be obvious, is a construct in Light, accessed through your focused consciousness. It is entirely real, just not physically manifest.

You step inside this Rotunda and the Ofanim start stepping out of the pillars and before you know it you have a host of Ofanim surrounding you, all saying *Hello!* On occasion, the Ofanim can close up the Rotunda, and it looks as if the six pillars expand to merge with their neighbors and the Rotunda becomes a transportation device for your consciousness, moving you to whatever location you or the

Ofanim desire. You are instantly there. Blaise assures me this is very practical on geomantic missions when either you don't feel like climbing a big mountain or property restrictions or other logistical problems preclude your physically going to the site. No matter. The Rotunda will transport you there.

If you saw it from the outside it would appear as a terrifically bright Blazing Star. The Blazing Star, incidentally, is how the Ofanim appear when they are super-compressed into an essence manifestation, and every human has a copy of this Blazing Star in their auric shell. You may also penetrate further into the Ofanim's realm while you're in the Rotunda by moving your awareness into that flattened diamond geode which, you realize, now inside it, is suddenly the size of a sports stadium, or even larger, with about 40 million seats, all filled.

It's important to remember that while encountering the five *Dhyani* Buddhas you are still on the *Cinvat* Bridge, still in Charon's boat, and you are not safely *over there* yet. You are still in transition, in this protracted orientation. You are still in the process of divesting yourself of the snares and grids of habituated human consciousness, of *skandah*-lock, freeing yourself from the coils of the phylogenetic labyrinth that for so long you took to be absolutely, forever real. The horses gallop you decisively into Ratnasambhava's enlightenment which illuminates the inherent emptiness and transcendent nature of all feeling and sensation and raises the element of earth into its true condition of transparency.

The horses—the Blaise angels—clarify awareness, remove obstacles from it, trample all cognitive impediments like male elephants slightly pissed off. They run us into this place of safety (safe because it is true without reservation) where we have unfastened the second of five strong bonds, the *skandahs*, that secure us. They clarify and strengthen consciousness to free itself

from these *skandah* bonds. The throne-mount, the Ofanim guise, enhances our cognitive strength and clarity to see through the wiles and confusions of the *skandah* to its wisdom condition. We deploy the particularly nuanced Ofanim cognitive strength, here represented by the virility and muscular might of the horse, to discern the *skandah's* voidness.

I sympathized with people experiencing this. I suspect the majority find it alarming, even terrifying, to have these familiar infrastructure grids stripped away. It would be like, I imagine, being alive and having your body dismembered with you still in it. But for those intrepid of spirit and well-briefed on what to expect and the reasons why this dismemberment of the *skandah* grid is a good thing, this would be a moment of liberation, long desired and welcomed.

At last, I may get a leg up on this all-encompassing confinement I've been locked within all these years, get some perspective from the mountain top, see reality without the cognitive compulsion of the infernal generic *skandah* grid. It's like going to Disneyland and seeing exactly what everyone else sees, the rides, the crowds, the amusements, the refreshments—exactly as everyone else. The *skandah* grid delivers humans a packaged tour version of material reality. This grid is like a pair of 3D sunglasses you put on when you hit the funland of life. If you didn't wear them, you'd see nothing; wearing them you misperceive all of it.

I imagine it would help the process if people still incarnate could get little tastes of this liberation, brief moments of sudden, delightful transcendence of the grids, when you're lifted out of the gravity well of these binds on perception and raised up into the higher view, the one divested of the *skandahs*, the bright view. Would I have liked it if the Blaise angels suddenly lifted me out of the uxorial domesticity of afternoon tea with Philomena into the lucid emptiness of the *skandah* of sensation and feeling and everything correlated with the earth element into this mountain view of universal awakened emptiness? I tend to doubt it.

Without prior preparation and conditioning, it might have seemed a psychosis. Is that tragic or funny? Strangely, it seems both. You get introduced to true reality and you think you're going crazy. You get stripped of all falsehood in the *Bardo* and you think it the God-awfullest nightmare ever conceived by horror writers. That's why I fully empathize with souls in the *Bardo* confronted with this. If you don't understand the context of this shocking disclosure, it seems frightening beyond belief and, regrettably, it probably won't deliver the intended enlightenment but push a soul further into resistance to the *Bardo* experience. Which means people are almost guaranteed by the design of this place to fail the initiation by the *Dhyani* Buddhas of the enlightenment state of the *skandahs*.

Where we found ourselves next did not strike me as a horror show. I quite liked it, as a matter of fact. I recognized the place at once. Mount Rainier, which lies 54 miles to the southeast of Seattle. This is a prominent volcanic peak, at an elevation of 14,411 feet, whose original name for Native Americans was Tacoma. It is the home of Dokibahl, the "Changer of All Things," a prime creator-deity who resides at this peak, entitling it to be called "Mountain That Was God."

Mount Rainier, prosaically "named" by white people after an American admiral as if the existing name Tacoma was of no consequence, is also the home of Tatoosh, the Thunderbird. He shakes the mountain mass with thunder and lightning; other dwellers here are related spiritual beings called *tomanowos*, dreaded supernatural spirits engaged in magical activities and who might when riled become wrathful and produce avalanches or volcanic eruptions. You have to watch out for these guys. I knew from my travels with the human Blaise that Tatoosh was a Blaise angel, and it seemed likely the correlated *tomanowos* were the prolific Ofanim as well, multiplying their forms and making trouble for all the sleepers. They do like their majestic big bird guises and use them often.

I saw the same image of dozens of Blaise horses galloping off in all the directions, this time from the mountain. Yes, Mount Rainier was galloping too. The Ofanim horses were rapidly bringing this mass of rock and Light into that same lucidity that I experienced as the core of reality, the Blazing Star. In a sense, the horses were transporting Mount Rainier away from the mundane stuck world into the realm of searing wide-awake Light and awakened consciousness.

The mountain became a nodal point, a vortex, for nearby Seattle and Tacoma for this surprising, radical quality of consciousness, for those people who wished to take advantage of the live demonstration. I saw Tatoosh the Thunderbird as the towering majestic upright bird-form of the Ofanim, like the Persian Simorgh, yet I knew this Tatoosh was also all the horses under the throne of Ratnasambhava. Dokibahl, it seemed likely, was the Indians' perception of this *Dhyani* Buddha. Tatoosh gallops your awareness into the *Dhyani* Buddha reality.

What was I galloping toward? We (myself on the horses) seemed to be moving rapidly yet not moving at all. I saw that we were penetrating that *cintamani* stone Ratnasambhava held alluringly in his left hand. We were galloping into the heart of matter, into the lucid transcendent state of earth. Everything made of earth and capable of sensation and feeling, from inchoate automatic responses to the heightened nuanced sensitivities of Marcel Proust, was experiencing the raised state of this *skandah*, its conversion into Light. Its resistance, expressed through sensation and feeling in reaction to earth, was transformed into Light, into the enlightenment condition of bright voidness.

Everything was feeling compassion for everything. It sounds silly to say it. We (I guess I still mean the horses and myself, though since the horses were the Ofanim they already had this enlightened state and I was the one catching up on things) were receiving Ratnasambhava's gesture of giving the Three Jewels, the *Triratna* of Buddha, *Dharma*, and *Sangha*, and we were Ratnasambhava himself giving the Three Jewels to all conscious beings. This presentation ceremony was solipsism at a high level. We were giving it to ourselves. It was funny, yes, but more so it was profound. If we were giving it to ourselves, it meant we already had it, and that meant this sublime sculptural gesture was the enlightenment condition of the *skandah* of sensation transformed into wisdom devoid of self. At that point, you didn't need to *see* any of this any longer because you *were* it now.

"Well, if we could get everyone to visit Mount Rainier we'd have the problem solved," said a voice in the distance. As I tuned in I recognized Blaise. "Plus we may have to start handing out free horses so they get that same ride."

I took his point even as I enjoyed his irony. The presence of a Ratnasambhava Light temple at the already geomantically charged Mount Rainier was a boon to humanity, though, as Blaise implied, probably few took advantage of this or perhaps even knew of its existence. It's true, if more people could come here and experience even a little of the initiation impact of this *Dhyani* Buddha it would greatly aid their *Bardo* passage. Briefing always helps.

Similarly, if more people could experience the Ofanim and understand what their presence means, what the Blazing Star is and where it is in them, have the ride on the hundred

angelic horses streaming into crystalline clarity, this would greatly facilitate their Underworld journey. They'd die, get here, and remember they'd already experienced this, and relax. They could say to themselves, "Hey, it's just like at Rainier." Then I laughed. I saw the problem.

Basically, we were saying, Blaise and myself, if people were more on the initiation track while alive, astute meditators, clairvoyant practitioners, and well-briefed in the metaphysics of the afterlife, their *Bardo* journeys would be easier. But they are not, and they are not likely to be, not the majority of people. They simply aren't focused on these matters while alive; if anything, they don't want to be, don't want reminders of their mortality and the fraught afterlife journey.

I can't blame them. I was no poster boy for diligent pre-*Bardo* initiation romps. I resisted the metaphysical insinuation along with the best of them. No thanks. I was attracted to the bright surfaces and seductive allurements of the exterior world like everyone else: it seemed the whole point of being alive, to enjoy it. I took the magic show to be reality itself, and never turned around to find the projector sending out this beam of light that formed this bright world.

Most people, I have to admit, spend their life staying unconscious of all this. It's true, the lack of mental preparation while alive makes the Underworld experience harder, scarier, and more bewildering, but most people accept that as the cost of doing business, that is, of a human incarnation. They'd rather sleep. I can't blame them. I was like that before Blaise whisked me out of my house. So were my colleagues at Dartmouth, and the whole college professor fraternity.

Heaven help us if it were revealed that our subject matter was actually real, that all these stories and objects and deities from myth were factually existent, *real*. If everything you read about in Eliade is actually the picture playbook for a psychic reality as real today as it was at the beginning of humanity…. If people could only have the *Bardo* journey while they're still alive, what they have to go through when they are officially dead would be so much easier. There it is. Ridiculous, poignant, tragic, and so unlikely, yet so desirable, so recommended. You would, pretty much, have to revolutionize the entire world of humanity to bring that about. I could foresee massive resistance to that.

"Okay, you have all seen the landscape and the props. Any suggestions?" It was Merlin speaking and he wanted us to propose ways to upgrade this area. As before, we had to figure out ways whereby more humans would "get it," understand the Ratnasambhava disclosure and assimilate its exalted message.

"The way to increase awareness among living humans of the transcendent, enlightened aspect of the element of earth and the *skandah* of feeling and sensation," said Matthew, with noticeable earnestness, "is to make matter brighter. To get more Light into earth and have it radiate outwards. Living people take matter for granted; often, they don't even realize it comprises their world. I was like that for many years until I started living at James Bay."

"People over here, like me, for example," said Tommy, "can brighten up the earth element from right here, in Ratnasambhava's temple, from where he is in the *Bardo* and where he appears on the Earth at Mount Rainier. It could work. People would likely start appreciating matter, everything solid, earthy, seeing it as if for the first time, freshly, wondering at its wonderful emitted Light. It's like the way after an accident or a shock reality looks terrifically brighter, sharper, and you feel, many people report this, as if seeing it for the first time. You are startled, maybe enraptured, by the new *realness* of matter. I'm saying we need to make physical Earth reality more like a Pure Land where the Light streams, gallops, if you like,

out of all material forms into the eyes of the people in bodies.

"I could round up several dozen buddies over here, and they could round up the same, until we had hundreds. Then we could meet regularly, in Earth time, I guess that would be about once weekly, and broadcast the reality Ratnasambhava holds. We could ride those Blaise horses into the heart of earth, then hold our concentration in there steady and empty, as it turns out. We would be the Ratnasambhava reality, the conversion of sensation and feeling to universal compassion and nonspecific benevolent regard, and broadcast this. I suppose our being concentrated in this state would be the broadcasting itself. People would start noticing matter and experience stirrings of compassion for it. Basic fellow sympathy for other living material forms, for the Light in matter."

Sympathy for matter. Compassion for the Light incarnated in matter. I hadn't thought of that before, but it made sense. All matter, everything physical, is slowed down, incarnated Light, which means consciousness. Compassion for matter, for all the forms it takes, is the understanding that Light has voluntarily diminished itself, stepped on the brakes, to inhabit a gravity shell as our world.

But it's all Light waiting for our recognition of that to free it from its material form. That recognition also frees us because then we'll realize we live in a world of Light and the forms of matter are only temporary containers for the Light. We have always lived in a Pure Land, a Buddha-Field. We just had to strip the material covering off the apparent forms which means from our eyes. The Pure Land quality of matter has always been existent behind the façade of physical form, even in this darkest of ages, the *Kali-Yuga*, only just now ended.

"Good picture," Merlin said. "The changes to the Earth's Light grid, underway since 1985 and intensifying as we move further into the

21st century, will coordinate this upgrade to the earth element on the incarnational side. All the physical elements, all aspects of the Earth's physicality, are generated and maintained by this geometry of Light around the planet, so it necessarily will translate a heightened quality to everything solid and material. It will impart an enhanced psychic aspect to physical matter, as if you can see through it, as if it holds revelations like ripe apples for you to pluck. The planet Earth is on its gradual way to reclaiming its former status as a Pure Land, a Buddha-Field, in which Light comprises 75 percent of matter, and matter pulsates, bathes in it.

"A reasonably sensitive person will examine anything solid, a leaf, a stone, water, and be astonished at the amount of Light that streams out of this. That astonishment, that sudden new respect for the mystery of matter, will potentially open their eyes further to a condition of self-awareness. The Light will reflect back at them as a force of consciousness and they will take stock of themselves. They too are material forms suffused with Light and emanating it.

"In a moment of lucidity they might perceive the awake consciousness in all expressions of earth, that this consciousness possesses universal regard, individual feeling and sensation upgraded to a universal quality, and that this lucid awareness is illuminated with the truth of emptiness. It may strike them oddly at first, that something so full of Light is also so empty, but for an increasing number of people it will be possible for them to understand this emptiness is actually the fullness of the awakened state, of Buddha Nature, and when they contemplate the Light within a stone it may kindle a recognition that they too have this Light within them, they are a Light-infused form of matter. The Light streaming out of matter will instruct the incarnate human to recognize the same condition as the truth of his physical and spiritual form, that it's Light."

"Then we will have both poles of this reality anchored, one over here by Tommy and his colleagues, the other by sensitive alive humans holding matter," said Matthew. He paused for a moment as another thought arose in his mind. "I have it. The link, or umbilicus, if you prefer: the Blaises, the horses. They can keep the two poles of this upgrade linked and energized. They can gallop back and forth between the *Bardo* and the physical human world, keep it all bright."

"I think I could persuade the Boys to put that on their appointment calendar," said Blaise, drawing it out for full effect. "They have Mondays free."

"Often you only have to look at something familiar, like a stone or a bird, from a slightly different angle than usual and a door opens and you are filled with wonder," said Pipaluk. "My teacher showed me that early in my training. The shaman needs to break habits of perception, to see things freshly, as they are. She would have me sit in the landscape, alone for hours, staring at objects, twigs, a handful of snow, rocks, feathers, until I felt I did not recognize it. Then a door would open and I could pass through it into an unfamiliar wide-awake world. I felt the strangeness, the otherness, the presence of this now unfamiliar object, and it made me wonder where it came from, who made it, and why. These were all useful doors to have open before me. They led to much insight."

"The same happens with words," said Edward. "Often when I'm editing, or when I was writing the Merlin book, a word would catch me at an odd angle, and I would no longer recognize it. It would widen, open up, and Light came out of it. It became a Light temple, a House of God, if you will, a holy word, full of Light. Well, you're going to be a very slow editor if that happens with every word you encounter, but I took the point. Everything in matter, including words, is a potential House of Light, a *Bayt-AL*, as the Qabalists put it, a Light temple, that is capable of illuminating the mind, opening it up to reality. If you learn this principle while you're alive, it won't be unfamiliar over here, and you have a much improved chance of *passing* Ratnasambhava's initiation."

We were ready to move when we discovered Matthew was now missing. It had seemed like only moments ago he had made his statement, but you can't tell about time over here. It could have been yesterday as much as it was five seconds ago. Nobody had seen him disappear, for he did seem to have vanished. Merlin was saying nothing. He knew of course where Matthew had gone. Then Matthew was back with us, looking bedraggled, confused, yet clearly elated. Merlin nodded, and we waited for Matthew to explain what had happened.

"I don't quite know what happened," he said. "I lost track of myself. I know I was possessed by a strong, unwavering desire to enter the revelation of Ratnasambhava, to experience that conversion of feeling and sensation and the element of earth to Light and the enlightened state as fully as possible. I jumped on a Blaise horse and galloped into the interior of that mystical stone. I felt myself being stripped, flayed almost, of the skin of my personality and awareness. It felt like being inside a washing machine, as I might imagine it.

"I felt tumbled and jostled, as if I was being taken apart by the force of the washer. The Blaises kept my attention focused; it was sword-sharp, invincible, lightning-quick. This washing machine was like a tornado, some kind of centripedal vortex. I was swirling down it, yet wide awake, still aware of everything. A moment came when I felt I had one thousand heads, all Blaise angel heads, and I saw in all directions at once. Everything I was seeing I was also part of—I was it and myself regarding it. Then I lost track of myself, of everything. Blacked out.

I don't know what happened. Then I arrived back here."

"You entered the enlightenment state of Ratnasambhava," said Merlin. "You entered the nondualistic lucidity of wide-awake Light and emptiness. You disappeared. You, meaning your selfhood and all notions of name and form and substance. Only awareness remained, and that was invisible. Then you reformed and arrived back here among us, noticeably reduced in weight, a full stone lighter." Merlin was chuckling. "My, wherever did that excess body fat go to?"

I noticed Philomena was observing Matthew with an odd but curious and intent expression. So he asked, "What is it, Philomena? Do you see something?"

She didn't answer at first, then she said, "It's nothing. Just reminded me."

"The trouble with emptiness," said Blaise, interrupting my musings on Philomena's odd remark, "is that people usually interpret it to mean reality is useless and matter is a fraud. Emptiness means there is nothing there and that sucks and they've been shortchanged. Emptiness means matter is worthless, without any inherent value. God has cheated them out of genuine substance. It's a magic show, mere devilry. They think it means they've been swindled. That the seeming hardness of things is a con and they have been duped big time, that all of physical reality is invalidated, and the apparent durability and primacy of matter are irrelevant, and therefore, and this is the part that hurts, they are fraudulent creations too, lacking innate worth or value, transient on the best of days, and without point. Worse, it tells them life, existence, has no purpose.

"But that's not the truth at all. Not even close. The inherent emptiness of everything is a revelation of the truth of reality; it is factual, not an invalidation. Because the truth is it's reciprocal, circular, form is emptiness, emptiness is form. The Supreme Being didn't create a false reality to hoodwink our cognitive trust.

"No, the Old Man generated a reality that has a surface physical plausibility but which at its core is consciousness without name and form, but terrifically awake, and that wakefulness is a state of enlightenment, of universal nonspecific awareness. It is not separate from anything; it encompasses everything. That's not a fraud. That's an impressive feat, to engineer a reality that has this quality. The *Dhyani* Buddha conversion of *skandahs* to enlightenment is not an invalidation of reality. It's a confirmation of higher possibilities. It reveals the innate possibility of transcendence which is the expression of the original true state of the *skandahs*, their illuminated condition as the guises of *Rigpa*.

"This enlightenment quality, this Buddha Nature, shines through the *skandah* grid. It illuminates the five *skandahs*, renders them radiant with enlightenment. The Supreme Being, pleased with Himself, with His cleverness, sits back and waits for us to get it, to sit up and exclaim, 'That's smoking hot, Old Boy, well done!' He does like a compliment now and then on His ingenuity."

Blaise paused, then a mischievous look blossomed on his face. "We should hand out complimentary tee-shirts that say 'I'm *Really* Happy To Be Empty!' Then with everybody walking around the place sporting this message, people might change their minds and run towards emptiness like it's Christmas."

We all turned to look at Blaise. Being dead, or among the dead, or in proximity to the dead in this *Bardo* realm, seemed to have gotten to his head. I didn't remember him being this flippant during our years of preparing for the Theosophon. He seemed almost giddy, which you wouldn't expect in somebody 93 years old. On the other hand, he hadn't spent much time in his human body in the last 20 years which throws off the body-age accounting and maybe the Pleiadian reality had gotten to him too, leavened him, and there is the Blaise influence too, unmediated by physicality so the human Blaise gets it straight from the bottle and the angelic Blaises, as we all knew, were all merriment. The human Blaise used to liken his pals, the Blaises, to the Marx Brothers, to perhaps 40 million copies of Harpo with voice-over commentary and jokes by Groucho.

He must have been following my thoughts because Blaise said, "No, it's not that. It's proximity to the Exit doors that has got me a little bubbly inside."

Now Edward picked up the thread of this problem. "Most people prefer the solid illusion of the daylight world. They expect reality to be solid, material. When I walk down Boylston Street on the way for a morning espresso, I am like this. I am like the other hundreds of people moving along this bright street full of shops, displays, signs, traffic meters, cars, the full, delirious illusion of the physical. I expect my quadruple shot espresso to deliver a caffeine rush like a fresh slap on the brain. I expect it to be hot, dark, and strong. My body wants it.

"Most people find the illusion more familiar than anything else. They expect reality to continue being like this forever and they're content (or maybe it's resignation) to live without an explanation, to die without understanding the set-up or to settle for a convenient fable, to get as much fun as they can while here. It's true, the explanation is a shocker. But isn't it worse not knowing?"

I knew what Edward meant. I pictured myself with Philomena at our table having afternoon tea, books and magazines piled around us. I could see the trees and pasture around the house, hills and mountains in the distance, lots of leaves. I luxuriated in the uniform greenness of summer, the birdsongs, the breezes.

I could thumb the fat pages of a new biography of Edith Wharton, admiring the excellent binding and paper quality of this university press edition, enjoy the writing style. I could pour another cup of tea and pass the tray of biscuits to Philomena, but what if, in the midst of this comfort and alluring familiarity and the habitual gestures of an immured domesticity, it all started to go vertical, to get sucked into an invisible centripedal black hole like water swirling down a drain and the inexorable brilliance and lucidity of the Ofanim's diamond Rotunda that was producing this inward suction of reality into nothingness, exchanging it for an invisible but unarguably lucid sharpening of consciousness freed of sense data, rose into the forefront in our nice tearoom?

The fact that it is true, a revelation of the actual nature of reality, would not guarantee I would like this rude disclosure. Surely, I would be discomfited. Or at least until I got used to it. "Philomena, dear, don't forget, form is emptiness and emptiness form, and this tea is both real and unreal, here and not here."

I'm not sure how many people would initially welcome this disclosure, understand it. I suspect they'd revert to the I'm-going-crazy or dissociating interpretation and seek immediate medication or professional psychiatric help. It's the naked truth of reality you tell them; no bloody way: I'm losing it, reality is *not* like this. Or if it is I want an immediate refund. A restoration of normality. The trouble is when they're dead, over here, processing the *Bardo*, they'll say the same thing, offer the same resistant disavowal: reality can't possibly be like this. I am so gone from this idiot place. They think these thoughts but they go nowhere.

"It's like a Golem protesting that it is not made of mud by way of a rabbi's Qabalistic invocations," said Blaise. "You can't budge a created being's position."

Philomena was spinning rapidly, terrifically fast, in fact. It took me by surprise. It was not her body that was rotating, but two transparent four-sided pyramids of Light, their bases touching, their tips pointing in opposite directions, one up, the other down, the whole thing spinning straight on its vertical axis. The Light was nearly blinding, yet it felt ecstatic, desirable, like something I'd like to enter. It emanated a feeling of delight, happiness, ease; it hinted of bliss. Afterwards, I realized the reason I said "hinted" was more to do with me than it. Bliss and ecstasy, which is the feeling of the Christ Light, is powerful; it can uproot the self perhaps before it is ready to be pulled out of the dark ground, so I allowed myself, then, just a sampler, dabbling my toes in the water to test it.

I had always had a general, outsider's impression of Christ and Christ Light, until Blaise explained the nuance that the Ofanim had shared with him. I had always casually assumed Christ stood for love and forgiveness, but certainly not voidness. That sounded harsh and not very inviting. The Christ Light, Blaise said, is a nondualistic condition of consciousness; it includes everything. It is not a matter of "*I* love *you*," because that is dualism, two things. Nondualism means one. It is the condition of *Ananda*, bliss, and its designated reservoir in the human is the *Ananda-kanda* chakra, the inner heart chakra, the place of bliss and delight.

It may feel to you, from the outside, like a terrific wave, even a cascade, of love and forgiveness, that you are truly, fully *seen* and *accepted* in your conflicted totality, but the love and forgiveness are aspects of this unified field which the yogis call *Sat Cit Ananda*, the foundational vibration of the Supreme Being and consisting of Being, Consciousness, and Bliss. The wave of love comes through the *Sat* quality, the essential initial goodness and goodwill by which the Creator began Creation; the Christ as a field of Light and consciousness emits—*is*—all three aspects. The Christ is the "personification" of Being, Consciousness, Bliss.

To a degree, Blaise told me, the Christ demonstrates the outward focusing of this nondualistic field of consciousness, the Buddha the inward. The voidness, the emptiness of the nondualistic condition, is really a total fullness. It is devoid of self, of any notion of a perceiver, and it includes everything there is. This Christ Light, Blaise also told me, is the power we draw on to render the *skandahs* void in our perception; it reveals their fundamental state of bright emptiness.

The area around her spinning form seemed invincibly purged of every molecule of darkness, dissension, confusion, and resistance, of all feeling and sensation, and this cleansing effect was spreading. I felt brightened within, smiling for no reason, and without control. I saw the same effect showing up in most of my companions, not Merlin, though. He was already there. He was always there where Philomena's spinning was now taking us. Tommy looked different. He seemed older, lighter, more see-through. He had died just short of adulthood, but now he looked like a wise older man, like an Elder, even a sage, someone who had seen much, understood a great deal, and knew the big picture.

Her form was expanding. We were inside it. Philomena said nothing. She wasn't there in any normal, individualized sense of herself. She seemed to have diffused her awareness throughout this spinning form, dissolved into it like mist. The atmosphere was riveting, sharp and crystalline, without a trace of thought. Awareness continued, but we were disassembled into the Ofanim's crusher or what Matthew had called Blaise's washing-machine vortex.

The strange part of this was that it felt wonderful, absolutely desirable and irresistible. Who would not want this fullness, this state of relaxation of mental stress and self-posturing,

where all questions were answered because questions never arose? The brightness was not different than this crystalline lucidity of awareness. It was like entering the ocean, registering the delight of the skin as the salt water enveloped it, then losing all sense of your self and body.

I don't know what happened after that. It's like the camera had no film. My mind was utterly empty, like somebody had erased the recording tapes. There was no camera, nobody to wield it, and nobody to watch the movie. I couldn't remember what we had been talking about, what we had been trying to work out a solution for. It was gone. Either we had succeeded or it didn't matter.

"Why did you do that?" I asked Philomena. She had stopped spinning.

"I didn't do anything. There is no why. That is what I am now. Philomena as a discrete individual is illusory, an assemblance for convenience, a transient place-marker to direct your attention. I'm sorry, dear. I'm just not her anymore."

I think it was at this point I realized with certainty Philomena was gone. The Philomena I knew, had loved and lived with for years, was no longer here. She remembered our history together, of that I had no doubt, but it no longer defined her, clothed her consciousness with meaning and purpose and warmth. Her individual self had been "converted" to enlightenment, to a rapidly spinning octahedron filled with Buddha Nature and Christ Light and total wakefulness.

Yet, and this was the strange part, I could still talk to her and she could still reply. She was part of our Green Knight expedition—when she was here with us. It was a paradox. She was Philomena, and she wasn't. She was here, and she wasn't. She could put on a semblance of a limited nature, yet she was limitless. She had form, but this form was emptiness. I knew

Merlin could understand this, but he'd never been married to Philomena.

She and Merlin had something in common. They were both free of the *Bardo*. When Philomena "ascended" and turned her form into Light, she became free of the *Bardo*, of the merry-go-round labyrinth of sequential incarnations. Her ascension completed her *Bardo* requirements, even before she entered it divested of her body. She did the *Bardo* while she was still alive, living at home in fact. Technically, she did not die. She converted her physical body to Light. She had gone on ahead. She had gone beyond, the Buddhists say. Certainly gone beyond me. She was the role model, the example-setter, of what every human expedition through the Underworld was destined to achieve, however many lives it took.

She appeared again, but this time she looked completely different. Regal. Robed. It was an exquisite robe of orange-gold and crystalline purity and sharpness. It went from her throat down to her feet. Her head was radiant, translucent. It emitted Light and I knew the robe was Light and only a "robe" by metaphor. The top of her head seemed crowned, not by an actual imposed crown, but out of itself, as if her crown chakra, that field of one thousand petals, had been ignited. It seemed fractal. Each burning petal seemed to envelop another crown of a thousand burning petals all in that same orange-gold Light.

She gestured for us to follow her. We were instantly somewhere else. We were in an area that reminded me of a busy airport terminal, especially the waiting area for a large, long flight where you'd have hundreds of people. Here there were thousands. They gave me the impression of being new arrivals with the kind of surprise, confusion, and uncertainty you'd likely see with immigrants. They looked like they had just this moment been transported here, and they were not sure what this "here" was and what they

were expected to do. I surmised these were newly deceased people who had not started their life review yet. It was for them like the first day of school or summer camp.

They hadn't yet boarded Charon's boat or stepped on to Daena's *Cinvat* Bridge. I saw that there were hundreds more of these arrival zones. They looked like tree leaves floriated from the same branch, maybe a thousand copies of the same pattern, occupying slightly different frequency and compatibility zones to accommodate the differences in soul vibration of the new arrivals. In one respect, these copies were identical; they were in the same place with the same function; yet in another sense, possibly a crucial one, they were nuanced.

Upon dying you would gravitate towards the arrival zone precisely suited to the composite vibration, soul frequency, and metaphysical attainments you had. Your vibration pre-selected your arrival zone. A physicist might explain that these thousand arrival zones were phase-shifted from one to the next, all occupying the same space but not the same frequency. For a moment, I saw this from above. It resembled a fractalized four-leaf clover. Within the overall clover shape were a thousand smaller four-leaf clovers, each contiguous with its neighbor, almost touching, but vibrationally out of phase with more inside them.

Philomena drew my attention away from these musings about fractals and phase-shifted patterns to attend to what she was doing. She would be a docent for these new arrivals, most of whom looked skittish, worried, scared. She went through a series of shape transformations, like laying down a deck of cards. First she appeared as Philomena, a human female about 60, dressed in academic conservative style, hair in a bun, some earrings, and a necklace—my wife at tea! She spoke to them the way an expert tour guide would rally and organize her tourists as they first step off the bus at the tour's first stop, it turns out, the *Bardo*.

She exuded warmth and confidence as she explained where they had arrived. I understood she was using the semblance of her former Philomena guise as an anchor point of familiarity for these newly dead and arrived souls. It made her seem she was one of them, just better informed and better acquainted. What I saw next caused me to catch my breath, not that I was breathing since I was here in my Light form. I saw a thousand copies of this. A thousand identical Philomena's explaining arrival conditions to the visitors. It was as if—it must be—she had made a thousand copies of herself, or split her attention into one thousand classrooms, delivering a welcome address in each.

I admired her slyness. She always had a knack for it. Slowly, without drawing extra attention to the change, she started to transform into the robed and regal ascended guise. She let the attention fall first on the lovely robe, as if it were a fashion statement, the newest sensation from a tony designer. Then she allowed her crown chakra to appear in its true form, with lights and beams and auras radiating out from it for hundreds of yards. Then she made her body and the orange-gold robe translucent, then transparent, emitting much Light.

When her audience had been attending to that for a few moments (or maybe it was hours), she let it dissolve and the spinning octahedron with golden Grail chalice inside appeared, and she stood there like a human pulsar, rapidly rotating, spinning out Light. Then she expanded this field of Light to include her audience. They got to experience firsthand this marvelous effulgence of bliss and emptiness. All the time she was explaining the process to them, extolling its benefits, emphasizing that all this was possible and available to them, should they wish it, that they were witnessing certain irrefutable facts about reality.

She left out the bits about confronting the spectacle of the five *Dhyani* Buddhas and the challenge to recognize the enlightened state of each *skandah* and the trickiness of not getting seduced and sucked back through the womb-doors at least until they've had sufficient time to evaluate their options. To disclose all this would be too much at this preliminary stage; better to interest them in bliss first, then that would fortify them for the more challenging parts later.

"There were seven us who took the Light body at the Theosophon," Philomena said. She was speaking to me, more or less in her tea-time form. "We were assigned this task, to welcome and anchor the new arrivals and to acquaint them with some of the features, challenges, and possibilities of the *Bardo*. Seven of us, each making a thousand copies of ourselves, can accomplish a fair amount, reach a lot of people. Certainly more than I ever had at my Scriabin recitals. We can spread ourselves out over more copies for arrivals than for the soul tutorials. This way we increase the likelihood that newly arriving souls will have a better understanding of the procedures here, and already we have seen evidence that more souls make it through the *Dhyani* Buddha challenges with understanding."

"You've been doing this all the time you've been travelling with us, yes?"

Philomena smiled. It was a little Buddha smile. Very charming. Very awake. "Yes. We can do more than one thing at the same time over here. It's very efficient. Time-saving too, not that there is any time in the *Bardo*. It is all now." My wife, the *Bardo* Adept. She has gone way past Scriabin's *Mysterium*. Scriabin himself would be first in line for a private tutorial from Philomena on this topic.

"Is each copy a complete you, even in the Light body form?" I asked.

"Not exactly," Philomena replied. "It is more like an animated simulation, an autonomous hologram in which we deposit a portion of our full awareness. But it is sufficient for providing the needed orientation for souls in the *Bardo*. For the more detailed arrival counselings, we make fewer copies of ourselves so we can stay concentrated in our essence and not be spread too thinly."

"Do you get an inkling of what we're doing here?" It was Blaise. He looked like a man who had just spent several hours contemplating a complex problem and was now elated with the satisfactory results of his study. "We're heading upriver, in reverse, against the current, through the form-making process into the Upperworld that led to *you* with all the form-trimmings. We are journeying up-current back to the Form-Maker, the Great Mother, Mrs. God, Isis, the source of the current and all it shapes, back to the place before any form.

"It's better than the *Odyssey*. He had Pallas Athena, lovely with her silver-grey eyes, always watching his back, but we have a cloak of Blaises. Hundreds of them with us at every step. Who could resist that entourage? The Underworld is the infrastructure of the form-making process. It's a body shop. We travel upriver through the *Duat* jungle. We're taking ourselves apart along the way, stripping away the *skandahs*, everything that made us. We are unstrapping, unscrewing the human phylogenetic grid from our consciousness, taking it off.

"If we have courage and discernment and don't freak out and run to the nearest womb-door and exit into another incarnate life of disorganized unconsciousness, we stand a good chance of making it back to the starting point, to the place where we started, before our form was cast, before consciousness was proliferated into 49 eyes, all seeing differently. We return to the place of original wholeness. Raise your nonexistent hand if you're in favor of that.

"The Underworld is the equivalent of Odysseus's Mediterrranean Mystery temple, the landscape from Troy to Ithaka, his travel route. We travel from the Troy of the phenomenal world to the Ithaka of our unified home. Yama's Underworld is the human structure of consciousness and form-generation laid out as an instructive psychic landscape. It's meant to be educational. It's Yama's Wheel of Life that he holds at his chest, glaring over its top to encourage us to maintain steadfast bravery and clear-seeing in our journey. That's the Underworld, the map of the human psyche, that Yama holds.

"With each step, we should be saying to ourselves, 'See, remember, you took this on, this *skandah*, this predisposition to deploy consciousness into perception or feeling. You took it on because you needed it to complete your human form, to be able to assemble and cognize a physical world, but it is not ultimately who you are, but more like clothing chosen to suit the long journey.'

"Do you see the problem? We take the journey and forget we put on these clothes. We think they are intrinsically part of ourselves, permanent features. They aren't. Then it's the shock of the year to have to divest ourselves of these familiar parts. You get here and get progressively stripped naked of illusions, all these veils. You think you're being horribly robbed of what belongs to you. They don't. The *skandah* grid was loaned to you as basic operating hardware for consciousness. *Skandahs*, body, world, created reality, all are on loan to you. It's like you get a job, like Edward at a publishers, and they give you a computer to use. Leave the job, the computer stays in the office. It wasn't yours to take. The only thing that is 'you' is the history of the negotiation of *skandahs* with world."

When Blaise wasn't making jokes and being a general smartass, he spoke with passion and ardor. These subjects mattered to him deeply, that was clear. He was like a detective who was always on the job, constantly pursuing the case, hard-boiled enough to generally suspect the suspect was lying, and he usually was. Probing reality (the victim) to find out what the perpetrator (God) had done. He never let the prime suspect out of his sight, always knew He was holding back. We know who did the crime, he says; we don't know what He did. Blaise would be monumentally bored if reality were properly explained already.

He had more to say. He was engaged with his topic. "When we're alive, walking around in bodies with sneakers, hairstyles, and demanding coffee everywhere we go, the tendency, the seduction, is to blend in with the herd, to find ontological safety, even self-definition, in our mingling with other humans. We complement that with our favorite distractions, and leaven it with the vituperations of our lower self and its views, positions, and denunciations. There is little to provoke us into questioning our position or to challenge our approach.

"You get over here and all that's gone. No herd. No distractions. Just nakedness. You are a single separated unit of consciousness and guess what, pal, you are responsible for it. It has been entrusted to you; it's the sole basis of your youness. Even worse, *way* goddam worse, is the fact you've never seen yourself naked. As you said, Edward, it's a shocker. The bigger shock is that it is not only the condition you're stuck with in the *Bardo*; it is in fact the *true* condition of your reality while alive, stomping around the place demanding your coffee. You are just as responsible for your consciousness there as over here, but you have more options for hiding, obscuration, procrastination, and general oblivion there, in embodied human life. The rug is very commodious for sweeping things under it.

"Here you are forced to confront the fundamental question: What am I? But while incarnate, you can slip around it, often for a whole lifetime, though it will nag at the fringes of your daytime awareness as a slightly unsettled feeling, an edginess. The trick, the recommendation, is to raise the question while you're alive, and start taking stock of this unit of consciousness (the complete God-universe, it turns out) and appreciate it as the bedrock of your awareness in all its nuances wherever you find yourself so when you get here you'll recognize it."

7

The next bedrock we had to appreciate was at least one hundred feet tall. I was sufficiently acquainted with this place now to know it was another *Dhyani*.

His Light was so bright I could barely see anything else than an effulgent red. Even his form seemed to blend in with this blazing scarlet brilliance. I was able to see he was mounted on a peacock in whose upraised tail flared thousands of eyes. The figure held a white lotus; it rested serenely on his two cupped hands as he sat in a full-lotus meditative posture. If he were a Zen student, he was answering his *koans*. He looked like nothing would hinder his perception of true reality. Like the other *Dhyani* Buddhas he was surrounded by six enlightened spirits, and he seemed to be embraced by a celestial feminine figure, maybe his consort, or, as I was starting to understand, "himself" as his feminine alternative. Deities (like archangels) manifest both valences of their essence, a masculine and feminine aspect, as a way of conveying the totality of their presence and activity.

In the background of this mighty figure was a dull red light. It was far weaker in brilliance, as if diluted, than the terrific, dazzling, almost intimidating, crimson flames around the *Dhyani* Buddha, yet it was easier on the "eyes," or psychic perception, and appealing, promising to not overwhelm perception. As soon as I granted myself this distinction, I started seeing shadowy figures in it. I thought I heard the sound of grumbling, as if a crowd of humans were complaining, walking around throwing aspersions, criticizing, shouting, wailing. It sounded like a dissatisfied, restless, cranky crowd of disembodied humans.

I had the impression these former human spirits were filled with unappeasable desires, that they wanted everything, desired the world, and could have nothing. They were wandering about, restless, driven by their desires, as if lost in a trance. They were exhibiting complete immersion in *samsara*, the realm of illusory life. It seemed like a stadium full of figures all like the Greek Tantalus. He was forever within reach of food and drink and forever denied access to them. These figures seemed similarly eternally hungry, incapable of any satiation. They were like Christmas shoppers lured out of their houses to queue in front of a chain box store at 4 a.m. for astounding bargains and finding it closed. Except inside were hundreds of customers milling about the well-lit corridors packed with consumer goods. To call those on the outside disgruntled would understate their degree of frustration. They were tantalized and denied.

This was an aggregate of dissatisfied, eternally acquisitive, hungry ghost-men. Considering this was the Underworld, the terrain of the afterlife, they seemed stuck; they hadn't reincarnated to satisfy those desires, or moved up higher where other interests could supplant those unappeasable yearnings for earthly life. And they were resentful that other shoppers were being admitted into the store via other entrances, but those remained closed to them and without explanation. Others were getting what they wanted, but this crowd was not.

I don't know how this happened, but I found myself mingling among them. It seems as I watched them, pondered their condition, that drew me there. I began to appreciate their position, see merit in their complaints, justification in their demands. Why should humans remain tantalized by insatiable desires just because they were dead or without viable human bodies? It was unfair. I started to feel restive; a critical edge rose up in me like an iceberg. Before I knew it, I was voicing complaints, old hurts, frustrated desires from long ago, as if I had kept a carefully detailed list in a file folder and had brought it out. I realized I had never gotten what I wanted, had always been short-changed. I became vividly aware of all the times when I hadn't—then I caught myself up. I think I blushed.

I was grumbling out of association, or resonance, with a flock of chronic grumblers. I hadn't meant to complain. I had not even been feeling restive. It started the second I got drawn into this field of complainers, into this crabby world. As I realized this I started to snap out of the grumbling mode. I didn't feel hungry. But I appreciated what an emotionally sticky and persuasive realm this was, how easily you could get enmired in this carping sludge and start to copy it.

Yes, the dull red light was easier on the perception. It challenged you much less. But the visual dullness was matched by a cognitive torpor, a mental sloth and sluggishness. The light in this realm was dull because consciousness was dull. It lacked lucidity; it was incapable of clear perceptions, discernment, clear seeing.

Philomena would have termed it: "A colony of bloody whingers." She'd be right. It was like a million souls crowding the membrane separating the subtle from the physical world, complaining they weren't getting their due and their whining, grousing voices passed through the membrane and some among the living, the sensitive, possibly the disgruntled living, heard their grievances.

Her imagined characterization helped me understand where I had been. It was one of the Six Worlds described in Buddhism and as presented in the *Bhavachakra*. It was an easy guess to say it was the realm of the Hungry Ghosts, the *Pretas*, the desire realm, the *loka* of what one translated source provocatively called "tantalized ghosts." From Tantalus, as I had surmised earlier, eternally unsatisfied, incapable of satiation at even the most minimal level. Complainers.

It was one of the six basic cognitive worlds human consciousness can be trapped in. Buddhists say we transit these Six Worlds during an average day, as transient states of identity and styles of perception; but in the *Bardo*, they are actual zones, pull-outs from the *Dhyani* Buddha expressway. If you fall for the blandishments of the duller light associated with this *Dhyani* Buddha you drive into a World. I have described how I was lured, sucked into it, like into a black hole. The dull lights around each of these *Dhyani* Buddhas are lures for the unwary. If you went for the dull lights rather than the brilliance of the *Dhyani* Buddha Light, you were in trouble. You'd be among the ever-crotchety ones.

This gave me a vista, a clear perception, I might say, of the *Bardo* layout. You had each *Dhyani* Buddha representing the conversion to enlightenment of a *skandah*, a facet of human consciousness and its mechanisms. You had in a sense "behind" each *Dhyani* Buddha the realm or *loka* of the failure to convert that, or the business-as-usual, daytime-sunlight world expression of that aggregate of consciousness, and maybe almost its inverse, or at least its corrupted form. Each of these dull lights acted like a lurid neon billboard outside Las Vegas seeking to draw customers in off the road to the blandishments and deceptions of Sin City.

The dull light signifies, and promises, dullness of consciousness once there. Before you know it, you're in resonance with its frequency and nearing a womb-door. The allure of another life starts its gravity-well draw on your shaken psyche. It promises a safe harbor because at least it is a familiar port; you've used it before. You might, though, get stuck in one of these *lokas*, whether it is a dark, nasty one like the Hell or Hungry Ghost realms, or one full of apparent Light, happiness, bliss, delight, or the promise of paradise like the *Deva* or Heaven *loka*.

In the rather puritan Buddhist rigor of categorization, even the gods get stuck. If you succumb to the lures of one of the Six Worlds, you don't get off the Wheel. If you're a Buddhist, you know that's bad; if you're not, you'll find out one day. You may be so stuck you don't even incarnate because you don't know you're dead. You think you are just inexplicably locked out of the funhouse from some perversion of justice that will soon be righted. Dead? No way. Not me.

Each *Dhyani* Buddha is a *skandah* pivot, a place of choosing, and the newly dead soul is tested five times. Can you discern the set-up here, the test purposes? If you choose the *Dhyani* Buddha, that is, understand what this personification represents, don't falter in its strong Light, and make the correct discernment, then you get to experience what reality feels like when this *skandah* is converted to enlightenment, raised to its highest, most exalted, and yes, most empty level.

If you choose the alluring duller light behind the *Dhyani* Buddha, then you will experience the reversion of this *skandah* to ignorance, possibly to a darker state. The whole thing is like a five-leafed clover with a front and a back aspect to it. It's a choice between mastery and subjugation, a grid of Light or darkness. It's ironic because when alive, in the bustle of life, we never take the *skandahs* for agents of darkness. We use them constantly and never give them a thought. But when you choose the *Dhyani* Buddha of a *skandah*, then you might see this darkness function of the *skandah*. It's an eye-opener, I assure you. Each of the *skandahs*, neutral mechanisms in themselves, is a swinging gate. It's what we, when dead, make of them that makes all the difference to our outcome, but that is just as true for we, the living, and how we perceive and manage the *skandahs*.

The *Tibetan Book of the Dead* makes the sequence sound like clockwork. On the Fourth Day, you will encounter this *Dhyani* Buddha now before us. You get the impression everything is on a tight schedule. That is not the case. You will spend as much time, as many solar-reckoned days dealing with any one of the *Dhyani* Buddhas as required; the pace is determined by your cognitive fluidity. I don't think anybody is in a rush, on a tight schedule with other appointments they must meet. You are here at each stage of this fivefold *skandah* pivot for as long as it takes you to choose. Nobody will complain if it takes you 49 years.

"That's correct," said Merlin. "It's similar to how the Bible says God created the world in six days. Ridiculous if you take it literally. There 'days' refer to *Sefirot*, the cascading spheres of Light, energy, and consciousness. It is not a time reference, but a map of the hierarchical descent of God's consciousness through six fundamental conditions of higher reality. Days here in the *Bardo* also refer to conditions of consciousness and reality, to cognitive terrains. You may spend absolutely as long as you wish in each 'day' in the *Bardo*, until you get it.

"The big fellow before you, Frederick, is Amitabha, the *Dhyani* Buddha of immeasurable, infinite Light and life, of unending splendor. The meaning comes from *amita*, which means infinite, without bound, and *abha*, Light or splendor. That infinity of Light and life, its immortality, is signified by the white lotus he holds in meditation. The *skandah* he converts for your edification is perception, intellectual discrimination, distinguishing by recognition, seeing the world and its images. He converts this into discriminative wisdom, clear, intuitive vision.

"The element correlated with perception is fire, and you see the peacock with its myriad of clear-seeing eyes is his throne-mount. Those eyes, I'm sure you realize, belong to our pals, the Ofanim, said to be the many-eyed ones. Amitabha sees all of reality as a luminous paradise, as a diverse world of Light. The Ofanim, as their throne-mount, help you master the *skandah* of perception, as they flood each of these innumerable eyes with Being, Consciousness, and Bliss."

At this point I marveled at the plan, the engineering behind all this. You have five primary categories or mechanisms for deploying consciousness to see, interpret, and interact with a world, for making conscious humans viable on Earth. You have the perfected expression of these mechanisms, the *skandahs*, represented by the five *Dhyani* Buddhas, and you have the cumulative effect of the failure to convert these mechanisms to Light represented by the Six Worlds. A *Dhyani* Buddha stands before each sense door, each *loka*, as a place-holder. These figures personify the perfected condition of each cognitive mechanism.

The *lokas* are not inherently bad, or even good. They are the consequences of our style of using the *skandahs*, of what we create when we do not convert them. From the standpoint of enlightenment, they are all delays, traps, artful

distractions. Some, nobody will argue, are baleful, like the realms of Hungry Ghosts and Hell. Others are alluring, such as the Heaven realm of the *Devas*; the Human *loka* splits the differences among the other five, including the Animal realm which does not have a *Dhyani* Buddha standing before it as a guardian.

It is the realm of fear, the Buddhists say. On any given day we spend some time in this animalistic fear realm, possessed to a degree by the limited framework of animals, subliminally afraid of lurking or inevitable predators, but also participating in some of the animal kingdom's finer aspects too. Rudolf Steiner said the animal kingdom was extruded from the evolving Human form, so the animals are "family," in a sense, just one we grew out of long ago.

Amitabha's fall-back realm is the Hungry Ghosts, that of dulled, darkened perception animated by unsatiated dreary but nagging desire and resentment; it is the grim atmosphere of unsatisfied desires, of the tantalized ones. If we fail to convert perception to enlightenment, we may be lured into this gnarly realm. It may seem more appealing than the rigorous empty enlightenment of Amitabha.

The Hungry Ghosts see everything through the distorted, dirtied filter of their own unfulfilled desires. The world, all of reality, is food, and they are hungry. They want some of it, all of it, but they're getting nothing. None of it.

This realm is fueled by passion and its failure to find satisfaction. The *Pretas* clutch at live humans, as if trying to reach through an invisible boundary to take what they have, to take it right out of their hands, if possible. They want what they see; they are peevish, petulant, aggravated they can't have it. Their perceptions fuel their dissatisfaction. Their perceptions are a fallen *skandah*, a polluted and corrupted *skandah*, and it leads to their undoing. They perpetually misperceive the phenomenal world and from this draw the wrong conclusions.

They narrow the focus of their perceptions to a small, self-obsessed framework. In contrast Amitabha shows you how to expand your perception to perceive an infinity of unending, undying, and undifferentiated Light, Light everywhere. The fire element, associated with perception, in its ideal condition devours the sacrificial offering of Soma, the consciousness substance of the world, like Agni burning up the world in a perpetual ritual of the flaming hearth. The *Pretas* just don't like anything they see; they corrupt their own perceptions.

I suppose the *loka* of the Hungry Ghosts is marginally better than the Hell realm. Observing its conditions helps me better understand the Hell realm and how it works, and I blush to realize how often I have visited that realm during my alive time. If you stay there too long while you're alive, indulge in futile complaints all the time, when you're at last dead, you'll naturally gravitate towards the *Preta*-world and regard it as familiar, known, like a homecoming.

Aksobhya stands before the Hell realm. It is the world of pain and purgatory, fueled by hatred. The *skandah* we need to convert to avoid tumbling into the infernal realm behind him is name and form, *rupa*, run through unilluminated selfhood and in the context of the water element. In the Hell realm the purgatorial, pained souls spend their time hating all names and forms. They have named and formed their own forms of suffering, and are completely stuck in them. They have created grids of bitterness and revulsion for the world, and now these grids encase them like miniature prison bars wrapped around them.

I can see how we could create a self-torturing condition of consciousness if we couldn't get past the interpretation of all names and forms in the context of our singleness. The Hell realm was not created by God as a human punishment zone. Humans have created it, and, regrettably, maintain and add to it every day.

It's the product of this *skandah* which has become toxic, turned in on itself, cannibalistic, self-devouring, demented and obsessive, lacking all outside perspective or Light, even though Aksobhya stands nearby demonstrating the conversion of the *skandah* to enlightenment. It is a circumscribed vibrational zone in which a billion souls are caged in their own Hells, flagellate themselves, stagger around in solipsistic torturous circles, suffering self-inflicted torments, cursing every molecule of matter, everything named and formed, we, the living.

All the doors are sealed. Outside help, no matter how compassionate, can't get through, and these souls remain obdurate, miserable in their self-imprisonment. It can't get through because they're blockading all the entrances. They're so miserable they don't even bother to blame God, Who, after all, is innocent of this situation. He cannot lift them out of the Hell *loka* unless they ask. The Hungry Ghosts are similarly unappeasable, forever desiring what they lack, and the Supreme Being, or Amitabha, can show them the way to appreciate perceptions and the fire element converted to enlightenment but only if they ask. It has to be that way, because they created their *Preta* condition out of free will.

"You know what it is?" It was Tommy, speaking with ardency. "Here it is all explicit, laid out before us, unmistakably, out in the open, all exteriorized. Here are the choices, the enlightened version or the darkened dumb-ass version. When we're alive, it is implicit, subtle, recessed; and we easily and often miss it. When I got here, I saw how often I had failed to see the choice. I visited the Hell realms a lot as a teenager. I was disaffected, alienated, felt too different from my age-peers, not to mention the diabetes which threatened my life every day. I would say, almost every day, my life is hellish; high school is hellish; adolescence is hellish; being alive in hellish. I voted myself right into the Hell realm this way.

"I drew conclusions. I created interpretive pictures, and I lived in them, surrounded myself in them like a sphere decorated in images, but all of them pessimistic. I wasn't depressed when I let the insulin shock take me out, more like fed-up, but I have to confess I wasn't immediately drawn to the Heaven *loka* when I got here. My predispositions, my emotional habits, drew me to Hell's nasty cliff edge. I understood I had done it all myself; I had propelled myself to this exact place. There was nobody I could blame for this, not my friends or parents. It was me. I had created this slow-motion suicide, I realized in shock.

"Here was the map of the negative emotional states I had lived within now displayed around me as a virtual environment, peopled and nuanced all by me. Later, they told me that this perception itself was what got me out of Hell. I realized finally there was nobody to blame except myself, so I stopped blaming myself. What was I going to do? I'd already killed myself. You can't do it again.

"Now I get that everything we see in the *Bardo* is a radiant expression of the Godhead within the human soul, that God packed everything into us, and here we unpack it and construe it as an outside world, even though it isn't. All the *Dhyani* Buddhas, the Lights, the attending deities, are parts of that soul-package, but we won't see any of it, and certainly we won't understand it, until we get through our own secondary or sub-creation, what we packed in around ourselves in a kind of infernal, insipidly stupid and ill-advised imitation of God.

"I brought my Hell realm with me and unpacked it in an available *Bardo* space. This was my version of the *Chönyid* phase of the *Bardo*, the confused dream-state in which my karmic illusions rose up and sought to delude and entangle me and I ran the risk of becoming estranged from the liberating truth the *Bardo* offered."

Tommy may have died as a teenager, but he was speaking as an old soul. Now Edward spoke. "The Heaven realm can be just as alluring and seductive. It is the world of enjoyment. I fell for that one, almost before I realized what was happening. It's funny, but this bliss realm of the gods is fueled by ignorance, a fundamental lack of knowledge about reality. Here the Light is the opiate, and from one perspective the Heaven or *Deva* realm is like a dreamy opium den. It's a more refined way of remaining stuck on the Wheel of Life, addicted to bliss.

"I was looking past Vairocana at the drab white light behind him. By itself I doubt it would seem dull. It is only in contrast with his dazzling brilliance that this background light pales. I was feeling nervous in the presence of his searing blue Light; it seemed to leave me no room to stand other than to enter it and I wasn't sure I wanted to do that. It seemed queer and embarrassing to be afraid of a bright blue Light but I was. It was consciousness converted to wisdom. The paler white Light behind him felt welcoming, not intimidating but warm. The place emitted an atmosphere of happiness, spiritual ease, and certain bliss.

"I walked towards that *loka*. When I entered it, what I saw struck me as a delightful combination of imagined images of Mount Olympus and Avalon. I saw *devas*, celestial spirits, strolling, lounging, reclining, talking, or laughing. I saw figures in bodies of great Light luxuriating under gorgeous apple trees upon which hung golden apples with silver leaves. I saw whole orchards of this.

"I saw other gods and deities assembled at sumptuous banquet tables with goblets of silver and chalices of gold having the grandest lunch you could imagine. They were seated within spacious banquet halls with soaring domed ceilings and many stained-glass windows. This reminded me at once of the Irish accounts of the *sidhe*, the fabulous residences of the Tuatha de Danann accessed through the Hollow Hills. The Irish bards painted an opulent picture of those accommodations, with music, laughter, and tinkling golden apples abounding. Whatever they were drinking, it must have been on the order of Soma.

"I was welcomed to one of the tables. It was like being invited into the most exclusive billionaire's club and treated like an equal. Such a fantasy. Everything, the food and drink, the goblets and platters, the servers, the guests, were of the highest order, absolutely at the top of the opulence and quality scale. The tone of the place was one of happiness, ease, relaxation, and surging bliss. No worries, no agitations or anxieties, no competition or one-upmanship—none of the discomfiting human-flavored emanations you'd expect at a human table.

"I felt I could stay there forever, that I must have arrived, graduated to an exalted level from, I don't know, my accomplishments with Merlin perhaps? I didn't know what precisely had earned me this seat at the gods' table, but I'd take it. I wanted to sign up for a slow-motion bender that would last forever.

"I have no idea how much time passed. Five minutes or five days. These people were always happy. They had no obligations, They feasted and laughed. To be aware, merely to be conscious, was to be in bliss. The fundamental quality of consciousness was bliss and delight. I didn't appreciate the subtle distinction, the dualistic trap, of consciousness feeling blissful and bliss itself. To be around bliss, like in a cloud, was dualistic; to be bliss was nondualistic, and the *Deva* realm seemed to hover at the boundary between these two nuances.

"If they were humans, I would have guessed they were all living off trust funds or stock investment portfolios that were paying rich, regular dividends and bonuses. Old Money, the kind that never ran out. Or perhaps they had worked hard for 20 years, made a terrific success of their business affairs, got knighted, celebrated in court, and retired early to enjoy many decades in ease. But that meant they were using up their own resources; eventually, their capital would diminish and they might have to withdraw from this paradisal condition. They had not converted the *skandah* of consciousness to wisdom. They were deluded, to the extent they equated this *devic* condition of bliss with that state.

"I knew I was working with an analogy, but it flashed in me what if their capital were good karma, the boons accrued from previous good, meritorious deeds? They were spending these accruals lavishly, prodigiously, in this god realm. I had thought all these *devas* were bright and luminous, that their bodies gave off a lovely brilliance, as if they were comprised of Light itself. Maybe their brilliance was like that of light bulbs; eventually, they wear out and grow dim.

"Then I had an odd but riveting insight: their radiant god-bodies illuminated the room, but they did not seem to illuminate the *devas* inwardly. They lighted up the room, but I realized this did not guarantee they themselves were enlightened. Inside them I detected a kind of dullness of Light, as if the brilliance of their outward lights did not penetrate fully to their interior. I contrasted this with what I had seen with Vairocana, the blue Light searing out from his heart center. This Light radiated from the core of this *Dhyani* Buddha like a sun in a galaxy. With the assembled *devas*, by contrast, their lights were mostly on the outside and they failed to penetrate all the way to their own cores.

"I wouldn't say at this point I felt I had been conned. Nobody had lied to me. But I felt that I had drawn incorrect conclusions, had been mistakenly lured into this god realm thinking it was a Buddha-Field or Pure Land. It wasn't. These *devas* were brilliant and well-illuminated, but they were incomplete. They were on a long lunch-break; they hadn't finished their journey of consciousness. Their consciousness was flushed with delight and bliss, but it was still relative, dualistic, centered on their individual selfhood as *devas*. They had not yet converted the *skandah* of consciousness into enlightenment which, nondualistic, was a selfless awareness of all the world—all the world was this awareness.

"They were still at the level of the blissful state of the privileged and the entitled. I guess all the charm of the *sidhe* evaporated with that insight, and I left. I left the music and the golden goblets and silver service and bubbling laughter behind. It was sobering, but I saw clearly that there are no viable shortcuts to waking up. If I stayed in this *deva* realm I would remain asleep thinking I woke. My consciousness would be tainted with opium fumes, unconverted to wisdom."

"I found myself pulled toward the Human realm. That was in the dull blue light behind Ratnasambhava." It was Pipaluk speaking. "This is the world of pride and action. I saw all the people there and felt sorry for them. Many were suffering, struggling, in difficulty. I saw the people in my village and the nearby towns and villages of Greenland. They needed their *angakkuq*. No, I wasn't the only one, but I saw I could help them. I understood their conditions, how their minds and feelings worked, and I knew the land where their bodies dwelled, where the points of power, Light, and focus are, and how to make them bright.

"I knew all the names and forms of Greenland, my home for many lives. It was the old familiarity and pathos of this realm that drew me—that snared me. I could easily by-pass the enlightenment of Ratnasambhava for these names and forms. They needed me. There were so many, each with her own grievances, each with his desires, all with their seeds of selfhood still dimly lit. All these feelings and sensations were piled up as if in great mounds, unresolved and calling for action. The Human realm is the domain of feelings related to the element of earth, about how physicality feels, and how it cannot feel past itself.

"I saw the patterns of connections that linked people, though they didn't see them. They were like nets with pictures stuck on them, images of previous lives together, deeds completed and others left in tatters or only at the level of hopes. I saw the spectrum of feelings birthed as illnesses and accidents and manners of disease and death upon their backs like carrion birds, cruel, ruthless, and, sadly, entirely self-generated, their own, and their many feelings about them. I thought I could walk among them and help them, that it would be good.

"I realized I was about to enter this human realm of suffering and possibility out of habit. I was drawn to it like a familiar home I've lived in often. I started moving towards it without even thinking. It was like a compulsion. Then a ray of the impossibly brilliant heart light of Ratnasambhava got me in the face. It was as if the *Dhyani* Buddha said my name in the glow of this radiant yellow Light. That is the color of the enlightenment of feelings emitted by this Buddha. Pipaluk is the name for my form, but Ratnasambhava made it seem transparent.

"He showed me the enlightenment beyond these feelings and sensations compounded of the element of earth in resistance to the Light, that it was a door, and what was through that door was more valuable and enduring than the door. He showed me that all feelings, all humans in their bodies and genders, in the sensing world of earth, could possess and radiate this wisdom Light, this Light of true, correct reality, this condition of full awakening that made all the world's sensations like it. Empty and transparent on the one hand, but also completely brilliant with Light. Ratnasambhava shone through these earth-type feelings.

"I saw that I had been discriminating among the types of feelings and sensations, trying to heal the ones that seemed painful. This was a mistake. I saw Ratnasambhava in the gesture of giving and embodying the wisdom of equality. All examples of this *skandah* are equal, because they are equally empty, which means not without value but illuminated by the clear enlightenment of emptiness. I pulled myself back from the tidal pull of this *loka*.

"Ratnasambhava was giving them all equal attention by recognizing their voidness. He gave them back to the propagators, filling the feelings with Light. He shone this brilliant yellow Light on everything like a sunrise. Feelings became wisdom, sensations were converted to enlightenment." Pipaluk shook her head but with a little smile, then said: "I must be careful. I will turn into a Buddhist staying around you people. This is not how I usually talk, but still I understand these new concepts. Ratnasambhava must have inspired me to talk this way.

"I walked away from that world of dull blue light and its strong pull on my soul. I slapped my head. That had been a powerful dream working on me from there. I saw that it was an illusion, a dream made of imaginings, and these included my own notion of being a big helper among them. That was my dream state talking. I would not normally have understood this and taken the human realm as my duty, but when I held it up against the *Dhyani* Buddha I realized how it paled in comparison. It was incomplete. It would never complete me."

Pipaluk paused. She seemed to be remembering something. "As I felt myself being drawn towards the human realm, I heard a voice, as if behind me. 'You are needed there,

don't you know. You have accomplished much, you are an advanced soul, and those sufferers need someone of your advancement.' It was sly and almost persuasive, but I caught an unwholesome tone in the voice. I felt it was serving me up a lie wrapped in bright ribbons of compliments. You know, I think I may be old enough finally to not fall for that kind of seduction."

Edward looked up and seemed to catch his breath. "I just remembered something similar happened to me. I was surveying the delights of the *sidhe* world, especially those golden goblets and silver chalices. The element of ether, *akasha*, generous wide-open space and the *skandah* of consciousness, like a party—how gorgeously delightful, to live like the gods, happy, fulfilled. I was entranced because here was the real-life version of what I had read in the Irish stories. Here it was, spread out like Christmas before me, and I was invited in. I was in the *sidhe*, being feasted, toasted, enjoying all the delights of the *devas*. But here's the part I didn't tell you the first time because I had forgotten it myself:

"A voice said, 'With all you accomplished with Merlin, you alone among many who failed, surely you can see you deserve a place at that fine table, that in fact, you may expect to be toasted and praised before the company, as another champion. You are entitled to it, surely you see that. Blessed by those on high.'

"I almost fell for it, bought the flattery outright, but something in the word 'deserve' held me back. Maybe it was my editor's ear for the nuances behind words. That word didn't sound right. It didn't fit the occasion. Merlin would never have used it. The corollary words of 'blessed' and 'entitled' also did not sit right with me. I honestly did not see reality that way, though I had met many writers who did. I realized something else. I did not see Vairocana among the *deva* party-goers. If you fail the test of the consciousness *skandah*, you may slip into the *Deva loka*. I was still in the Wheel, reveling in *samsara*: its spiritual loftiness was still a trap. I was still in the *Bhavachakra*'s atmosphere, just high up."

"You were both tempted and challenged by the Druj," said Merlin. "She is clever. She found just the right crack in your spiritual preparedness to attempt to widen and tease it open to become a doorway through which she'd push you. Often it only takes a word to hook you: 'needed' for Pipaluk, 'deserved' for Edward. They were well chosen because they carried special nuances for you. Do you understand now how you prepare your susceptibility to a *loka* while alive? That you might spend more emotional time in such a realm while you are alive than you realize, predisposing you to be lured or seduced into that realm here.

"Don't think the Druj is not operative during your incarnational time either. She is. For her, there is no meaningful boundary between incarnation and *Bardo*. She sees them as equal, even equivalent, opportunities to mislead human souls. She knows, though most alive humans do not, that people are creating their preferred *lokas* every day, dwelling in them throughout the 24 hours of each day, and deciding which one best suits their emotional temperament. When they get to the *Bardo*, they have already been in the *lokas*, usually one in particular."

This was a sobering realization as I saw how it had worked in my life. The days I worried about the cash flow I needed to complete needed repairs and renovations to the upstairs bedrooms and how the payment deadline was fast approaching and the funds were not: here I was visiting the animal world of fear. The fear of predators or not getting enough or any food, the naked death fear. Or when I became peevish, even resentful, my mind going off on rants and rages at the accolades I saw my peers being awarded and how none of that came

to me. Welcome to the Hungry Ghost realm, Frederick, where everyone is tantalized. The fun times with the human Blaise and the mystical moments with the angelic Blaises and the entire Theosophon, both preparation and aftermath, was the *Deva* realm. Who wouldn't like that, but it still kept me fast on Yama's Wheel of Life.

Yes, we visit the Six Worlds regularly, favoring one of them eventually, but what struck me next was that the only difference regarding this between being an alive human in a body and a human soul in the *Bardo* minus a body was that in the *Bardo* you get the qualities of each world naked, stark, unadulterated, right in the face, whereas in the human world you can distract yourself easily enough so you get only fleeting glimpses, then the next thing comes. You are equally there in the Six Worlds, but you don't usually know it. Here you may find yourself enmeshed in a *loka* but not comprehend its nature or the reason. In both cases, add to this the Druj's artful, Machiavellian whispers and deceptions. That can act like glue or a magnetic field or as unmediated gravity, pulling you.

"I don't think I was accosted by the Druj, but I felt like I was blinded," said Matthew. "I was observing the *Dhyani* Buddha Amitabha and his radiant red Light, and noting the pallid, dullish red light of the Hungry Ghost realm behind that fringed his form like a faulty spotlight. I saw the area where the other *Dhyani* Buddhas were positioned, and I had a general clear picture of the architectural layout of this zone of the *Bardo*. I saw all of you guys. Then everything seemed to brighten, almost blindingly, and all the images before me started to grow transparent and hollow, as if all the life-force had drained out of them and they were mere shells of their original forms, clothes empty of people.

"It struck me that I might be going blind, that my eyes were failing me, but then of course I remembered that it wasn't my physical eyes that were seeing all this. All the pictures of *Bardo* reality before me, all the products of my perceptions, were now rendered in a bright red Light, see-through yet substantive. Here is the strange but wonderful part: the Light seemed to go on forever. It had endless depth and height and volume—definitely boundless.

"This Light without limitation or cessation also seemed to have an eternal quality to it, as if it had been here forever and would continue on forever into the future. All the perceptions that had filled my visual field a moment before were now the merest outlines, like transparent postcards barely discernible in this Light field. All of this, even how I felt, had the quality of a paradise, a wisdom-realm, in which everything I saw, everything I could see, that could be seen by anyone, possessed this effulgence of bliss and paradise, had returned to its original condition of perfection, as if, I suppose, this is how God sees all of it.

"All possible images were rendered in their paradisal condition, as perfect, as Light. It was the *skandah* of perception raised to its ultimate enlightenment level. Perception converted to discriminative wisdom. It was like seeing and not seeing at the same time, but it was not being blind. It was perception made transparent, hyper-lucid, as every perception reverted to Light.

"Then I heard a voice, no more than a whisper, like a woman's soft voice, 'The Thunderbirds are impressed and convey their congratulations on your skill.' That was all. Normally, a compliment feels warm and welcoming; this one had a peculiar chill to it. It seemed off, wrongly placed, and it put me on edge. The words 'impressed' and 'congratulations' had a false brightness to them."

"That was discerning on your part, Matthew," said Merlin. "It was the Druj you heard. She played off your time with the Thunderbirds at James Bay, that you knew you had contacted a high-level order of spiritual beings, the Ofanim, and that this accomplishment reflected on your cognitive merit. She found a seed of spiritual pride in you and sought to fertilize and nurture it. You must be vigilant when we visit our last *Dhyani* Buddha. She will try this again."

"Come, I want to show you guys something," said Blaise. As soon as I turned to face him we were already there, inside another massive Light temple. I knew now that each of these five *Dhyani* Buddhas had an Earth installation, or possibly more than one, in the form of a Light temple of considerable size situated with respect to a geomantically prepared landscape site. This one, I presumed, pertained to Amitabha, but its location was hard to ascertain. The landscape looked austere, cold, and barren, like the Russian steppe perhaps if it had been relocated to the arctic north. In other words, I wasn't sure where we were. It felt remote, devoid of people, in the far north of everything. I liked it.

"I discovered this some years ago," Blaise said with the proud enthusiasm of a new homeowner showing off his facilities for the first time to friends. "The Ray Master Lao Tzu was introducing me to the *Dhyani* Buddhas and showing me their Earth Light temples and the kinds of experiences you could expect at these. When we arrived at Amitabha's I looked out the window in surprise. I know, no windows, but let's say when I surveyed this arctic terrain from the position of the Light temple, I was surprised, delighted to see the Blue Room across the way.

"That's right: I was looking at the original Pleiadian Blue Room installation, a pale blue, semi-visible, extraterrestrial four-leafed clover structure on the land. I had been there many times before but I never knew where it was in terms of Earth topography. Only that it was in Siberia. Now I knew where: it lay close to the Laptev Sea in the far north of Siberia, and I saw it out the window.

"I believe you are all well briefed on the Blue Room by now. It was the original and primary Earth Light grid geomantic design and implementation center. Everything geomantic was coordinated from here. All the maps and diagrams, the specifications, the numbers, the *information*, were kept here. This was the prime engineering field office for the complete planet Earth Light grid. It still is, though a copy was made at the Theosophon in 2033 and placed in Idaho. But what I wanted to show you is what you can see through Amitabha's temple."

Blaise gestured for us to stand close to the throne-mount of Amitabha. A formidable impression of this *Dhyani* Buddha appeared to occupy it. I qualify my description because by now I was realizing the relativity of my perceptions of these august figures of enlightened consciousness. Whatever form this *Dhyani* Buddha might have, it was probably only an exalted, projected Light impression. I realized that technically, these Buddhas, their consciousness, extended as far in all directions as the size of the universe. That thought, that perception, I admit, made me feel dizzy, so I tabled it for now so my head would stop spinning.

Whatever this figure's precise ontological status and actual size might be, we stood with his towering presence behind us, like a spotlight as its radiant red Light illuminated our minds. Blaise pointed to the Blue Room close by on the flat barren land. I felt the *Dhyani* Buddha's enlightenment radically brightening my mind, like the brightest Light imaginable expanding and sharpening my powers of perception. My perceptions felt like they were on fire, my thousands of eyes blazing in this radiant red Light, and emitting flames of discriminating wisdom. Well, the Blue Room is all about making Light grids, so with Amitabha on hand our potential perceptions of these Light grids would be greatly enhanced. Light grids "made"

at the Blue Room under his influence would "burn" up the world, inflame human perception everywhere with the fires of awakened perception.

The Blue Room installation itself is not strictly a three-dimensional structure. I guessed that as a minimum it occupied fourth-dimensional space but possibly fluctuated between that and 3D and 5D, although that might have been my own perceptual apparatus struggling to hold down a fixed, steady image of it. But now I was clearly seeing it in a 4D mode. It seemed to have replicated itself and was displayed in a circle of perhaps one hundred contiguous copies of itself. Images flashed like movie stills in the space of each copy; the images were much larger than the facilities and they appeared to be records of past activities.

I was watching a pictorial history of the work—the *adventures*, I was tempted to say—of the Blue Room over a terrifically long stretch of time, billions of years. No, I wasn't exaggerating. The Earth, geologists assure us, is 4.5 billion years old and the Blue Room arrived as soon as the ground solidified, maybe even before, and the Earth is a recent design project for this itinerant Blue Room initiative. Many design projects had preceded it. I was seeing evidences of that.

Blaise had sketched some of the history of this vast project and it spanned a great stretch of time and galactic space. It had been in operation for a long time. He said he had to date retrieved in memory only a small amount of the full history of this effort. These movie stills were flashing highlights of its illustrious history. I saw hundreds of planets being designed, their Light grids implemented and adjusted to match the sentient life-forms seeded on those physical planets.

I had impressions of the paradisal possibilities intended for each Light design, its highest achievable point in consciousness, where awakened awareness converted physicality into lucidity and cosmic consciousness, like a dimmer switch turned to its full illumination setting, the room, or planet, flooded with glorious Light. I saw one after another of these planets and their geomantic engineering specifics. There were so many images displayed now they eclipsed the Blue Room itself. It was as if we had opened a reference volume in the *Akashic* Records Library and it was displaying all its information, its pages leaping into an animated live presentation of all relevant activities over time.

All these images, all my perceptions, I realized, were illuminated by Amitabha. They were pure images, immaculate ideas, paradisal conceptions, regardless of their outcome. It wasn't even images I was seeing anymore. These were pristine conditions of consciousness, each one lit brilliantly from within by Amitabha. They were Light grids for temples, planets, and phylogenies. Here is a simplistic way of putting it: you have an image of something, say a Light grid design for a desired state of awareness, a teleology for a consciousness quality, and you present it to God. The Supreme Being examines it with interest, and the Light of His attention is so incalculable that it renders the image you gave Him entirely in radiant Light, and that lighting up of the grid is to give it first breath.

You have to speak about activities like this in analogies. The image now is transparent to the Light of a million watts of illumination. You can still see the essential outlines of its shape, but it is now a vector for effulgence. Your perceptions come back to you like this, as embodiments of enlightenment; it changes your notion of what a perception is, which is Amitabha's whole point. It's even more singular than that: the images and your consciousness are one.

Blaise was nodding his head with quiet enthusiasm. "You see?" he said. We saw. It was, no argument, a marvel. Blaise seemed validated, quite pleased. He had shown us all something

important to himself and important to the Earth.

"If only it could be like this for everyone in the *Bardo*," said Merlin. He was baiting us. His voice had that tone. He wanted us to suggest improvements. We were back in the *Bardo* labyrinth next to the image or presence of Amitabha. Merlin swept his arm out in front of him, indicating the landscape before us. We saw innumerable souls struggling with their perceptions. They saw scary things and recoiled from their perceptions. Just as the flash cards of historical events appeared luminously exalted before us around the Blue Room, here they had the opposite valence, a negative coloring. They were perceptions of fear and anxiety.

"To see any spirit, whether it's an exalted *Dhyani* Buddha or a fuckbrain demon with fangs, is a perception," said Blaise. "It requires the *skandah* to shape a wave pattern of Light into a perceivable image, and often we shape perceptions into appearances that then scare us, sometimes right out of our minds. The Hungry Ghosts are mostly tantalized by their own *mis*perceptions."

Before us, people did not realize the *Bardo* was stripping off their own image banks and revealing these perceptions to them, like a display of flaked-off dry skin or like a plumber showing you the corrosion in your pipes. They thought they were seeing legitimate revelations of the nightmarish quality of the landscape they had blundered into or had been involuntarily abducted to. They were squirming, recoiling, looking for the nearest Exit doors to get away from it.

Nor did they see the Druj standing behind each of them, inflating their fears. She could manifest as many copies of herself as the task required; she was prolific. She was the consummate saleswoman; she never missed a trick to make a sale. At the other end of the sales counter was Amitabha, demonstrating the clarity of discriminative wisdom, all perceptions converted to their enlightened state. The Druj wanted the sales; Amitabha was radiantly neutral to our choices. He was like the model coolly exhibiting the clothing fashion out on the runway. Compassion radiated off his shape for all life-forms, but he did not intervene. He was the product, the end-result: perception and fire elevated to full awakening.

I watched one woman. She shuddered as her perceptions glared back at her. Her fears and hurts were personified as ogres and monsters before her. Then some Blaises formed the Nimitta Cloak of diamonds around her and it all changed. She relaxed, smiled, her mind brightened and clarified, and she sighed.

She realized all these horrific, inimical, and bizarre images were coming from her. They were only as real as she energized them to be; they were just cast-offs. Her perception *skandah* was operating in over-drive as a thoughtform factory, spewing out new scary perceptions at a dizzying and perversely prolific rate, then she was recoiling in fright or envy, trepidation or resentment, before them, as if her consciousness had been cruelly, invaded by barbarian hordes.

I realized that the Nimitta Cloak is a portable throne-mount for the *Dhyani* Buddhas, any or all of them. It is the Ofanim, the Blaises, congealed into a foundation that could empower human consciousness to rise through the *skandah* and into the enlightenment state of the representative *Dhyani* Buddha. It is a force of consciousness that can remove all obstacles to clear-seeing and freedom.

Instead of seeing them customarily as outside her, inimically surrounding her in all directions, threatening to avalanche her mind with a surfeit of images, now she saw them correctly, as inside her, innate, her own brightened awareness encompassing them, as if they were no more than niggling thoughts she could dismiss. During this moment of

revelation, the Druj was not permitted any influence. The Blaises removed the Cloak and allowed the woman to contrast the two experiences of perception. It was her choice; it had to be. They waited.

As soon as the Blaises withdrew their clarifying Light, the woman faltered. It may seem as if the Ofanim deliver the power of consciousness on a silver tray, but you, the person, must pick it up and amplify it through use. This woman was doubting she could do that; it was as if her legs were asleep. The Druj gave her the impression her legs were wobbly, she couldn't support herself, hold her body upright anymore, the ground underneath her uncertain, as if an earthquake were underway and fracture zones were appearing. This was a way of dramatizing the way her self-assurance was now wobbling. She knew what she had seen, but she was starting to feel she could not sustain the rigor of that Nimitta Cloak clarity on her own, that maybe it was a godly hallucination sent to momentarily cheer her up but one not destined to last in her own awareness.

Her pain images started calling to her like lost children. They became persuasive. You know, I really was horribly shortchanged by that perfidious bastard, John, you could hear her start to think. The fright images moved closer to her, like semi-wild dogs offered a treat and willing to consider the human a new friend. And that time Elizabeth, my so-called friend, promised she would take care of the children and….

We were saddened to watch as this woman's Blaise-inspired seniority slipped away from her. Her fright images rushed back to her like forgiven children. They formed their own cloak about her consciousness and started whispering. They reminded her of the painful realities she had endured, the betrayals, the indifferences, the attacks, the unfair judgements, the nastinesses of people, the glimpses of demonic enhancement she had sometimes perceived in people, that as they spoke or acted demonic spirits lurked behind, pumping them up. This was *how* she *saw* the world, and her erroneous perceptions encloaked her.

These images were like fluttering translucent posters all around her, with voices shouting in them, fists raised, faces streaked in tears, bodies ravaged with scars. She was no longer recognizing their inherent emptiness and unreality, and certainly not regarding them as her own self-generated projections, that she in fact had drafted all these images. She was looking at the perceptions and taking them as immutable brick walls. She was seeing the world *through* them; they were mediating, filtering, directing, *creating* her perceptions. The liberating transparency the Blaises had inspired was now lost. She was sinking back into the dismaying quagmire of her own karmic illusions, and Amitabha's illumination of paradisal possibilities in perceptions seemed beyond her reach. There was still too much unfinished business, too many desires she had to fulfill.

She was by-passing Amitabha and entering the realm of the tantalized ghosts, those souls still desperately hungry for sensory experience, still carrying the frustrations of the world as they saw it like back-packs on their burdened shoulders, still seeing the world through their own contrived, distorted perceptions. The fire burned them up, burned their eyes; it did not illuminate their seeing. She'd probably take the first womb-door out of here, but it seemed likely that when incarnate again, she'd book a lot of time in the *Preta* realm.

"This is a tough one," Merlin commented. "Many get stuck here. Letting go of one's perceptions is harder than seeing the emptiness of name and form or sensations and feelings. People believe their perceptions define reality, that they are reality, that if they are seeing

it, then it must be real. They are not used to hallucinations or thoughtform generation. It is hard to shift that presumption about perceptual reality over to the truth that these perceptions are self-drawn and self-projected to flesh out a personalized world and are innately illusory."

Philomena spoke. "The element associated with perceptions and Amitabha is fire. Maybe we can take advantage of that. It wasn't enough for the Blaises to sharpen the woman's cognition to see through the perceptions. She lost that clarity as soon as they withdrew. Let's set the cloak of perceptions on fire. Make it look like a thousand pictures are burning up all at once around her. The shock of the mutability of these perceptions, which she had presumed to be solid, permanent, and unassailable, to see them yielding to destructive flames, might jar her loose from her death-grip on them as if they represented the last perceivable stronghold of her sanity and her familiar life in physical reality.

"It will give her a moment in which her consciousness and self-awareness feel separate from her perceptions. She can see she is still there, alive, aware, but apart from this cloak of images and that she can endure without them. That momentary wedge can be crucial. It can be clarifying. New ground to stand on.

"She might realize the relativity of these perceptions. They can arise and they can desist. They have no permanent existence. They are burning up. It is still a free-will response, but we will have sharpened the truth aspect of these perceptions, amplified the true state of affairs, thereby freeing up her attention. We simply turn the dimmer switch on cognitive truth up a few degrees. Reality itself, the sheer truth of its actual conditions, then makes its own case to her."

"Then the Blaise Boys can step up and do their lucidity of cognition thing, and we've just upped the odds the soul will get it and shake loose the images." It was the human Blaise of course, jocular but on point. The two steps could work. The recently deceased were still left to make a free-will choice, but they would be equipped with having received a heightened level of clarity about conditions. Like a shopper who has well researched a product they were proposing to buy, they can now make an informed choice. They might still succumb to the familiar burden of their self-generated images, but probably more might be liberated.

Merlin nodded. "Yes, this upgrade may improve the statistics. Many will still fail the test and collapse under the weight of their perceptions, but more will get past this to the transparency and emptiness phase than before. I think the Green Knight and the Lords of Karma will likely approve this tactic. It will set the Druj back a few notches. She'll have to think long and hard to come up with new ways to screw up human consciousness at this stage in the *Bardo*."

Suddenly everything around us, Amitabha and his peacock throne, my expedition companions, Merlin, my own form, all were subsumed in flames. I could not see anything. I was blinded. Everything I had been noting in this area of the *Bardo* was gone, burned up, even the ashes were gone. There was nothing.

"Maybe not so long, Enchanter," chuckled a raspy woman's voice. It was the Druj, and she was addressing Merlin in one of his old Celtic magus names.

I suppose there was a joke in this. Everything we were taking for granted in the Amitabha zone of the *Bardo*, including the *Dhyani* Buddha, were but perceptions, and the impermanence of these could be demonstrated by the agency of fire. Perception is fire, devouring reality to yield seeable images, forcing the inchoateness of unformed reality to reveal forms, as if coercing reality to disclose its occulted forms and truths to us, to show itself clearly, so, oddly, the Druj was actually making a useful philosophical point for us. Even the august *Dhyani* Buddha Amitabha, he of infinite Light and life, was a still a perception, even if a collegial one, co-generated by Amitabha and ourselves, and subject to dissolution in the ruthless fire of transparency of the awakened Mind.

8

Before we even realized what we were seeing, Matthew was in trouble.

I couldn't believe what I was seeing. He was quarreling with a group of people. Shouting, waving his arms, making fists, his legs spread like a pugilist. The scene was enveloped in a dull green light, a kind of moldy vaporous haze. It seemed to be inspiring this atmosphere of warfare, quarreling, and struggle.

His antagonists appeared to be humans, though clearly dead ones, *Bardo* people. But another circle of much larger spirits watched the conflict as it escalated. As I studied this group I realized they were far larger than I had first thought. They each stood perhaps one hundred feet tall, possibly much more; it was hard to be sure. They looked like warriors; they were armored, held various types of weapons, and their faces emitted glares, scowls, frowns, and snarls—a nasty lot.

I doubted this at first, but I saw lightning flashes around them and heard rolls of thunder. Forceful wind currents streamed out of their chests, like a storm at crest. How many comprised this group? Maybe 100. Their numbers kept increasing, but what was a consistent impression was that they were jostling one another, pushing, shoving, squaring up their shoulders in resistance, grunting, showing signs of preparations for a fight. They seemed full of conflict energy.

But back to Matthew. It was like seeing an unexpected side to the fellow. He had up to now seemed earnest, reserved, well-controlled, and introspective. But now it was as if a hidden Matthew had emerged, a contentious, irritable sort. Matthew had a wild look on his face; it was a face of outrage, one that rails against injustice, against being shortchanged, cheated, given less than his due. It was a look of covetousness, a kind of general jealousy, not sexual but universal. It was the face of insecurity, fear, concern, anxiety, about the anticipated or accomplished loss of status or value, that something important had been taken, that someone else, like that big guy over there, had far more than his fair share. It was, pardon the cultural cliché, the dull green wincing face of envy and jealousy.

The big guys seemed to be dividing into two camps. They were throwing small jags of lightning at one another, their voices thundering, their arms raised. They were like mid-level creative gods at the beginning of Creation, fighting over turf and glory; each group wanted the full share of both, nothing for the other. It was like watching two gangs of Sumo wrestlers with *Qi-gong* powers. They swelled horribly with the will to prevail, and winds raged out of them.

Yet there was something fraudulent about this display of masculine powers. Something seemed staged. I had the impression they were acting out parts, that the quarreling and intimidating postures were for show, scripted. I had that impression because I saw (I don't know how, but I saw it clearly) full chalices of golden Light in their chests, and this Light was beautiful and holy and precious. It belied their pugilistic stance; they were Bodhisattvas pretending to be fighters. It was a reality show choreographed to suggest contentiousness, yet all these guys, these fighting actors, had hearts full of the ichor of enlightenment.

The problem was it didn't seem that Matthew saw through their charade. He appeared to be taking it seriously, the rowdiness of the humans and the gods. He also seemed oblivious to the rest of his Green Knight expedition companions. I stood behind him though at a safe distance, or so I estimated, for more insight. I saw that the human irritants were each draped in body-length posters with images drawn from Matthew's life. I knew that because I saw Matthew in them. It was a picture history of his grievances, his life's catalog of cheats and swindles.

Many of these had somebody other than Matthew as the prime recipient of the shortchanging, but something about these other figures told me it was Matthew. Previous versions of him, I should say so, in other words, images from past lives. The faces, bodies, genders, were different, but the complaint was the same. This long layered history of jealousy, covetousness, and grievance had erupted at once and like a rash was spreading over the people surrounding him. That was a key factor here: he was projecting his hurts onto these souls, the winds of his thwarted will, the raging airs of his contravened volition, then preparing to punch and lay them out in recompense for their bad behavior.

I saw the Druj standing in the background. Was she smirking? It seemed so. She had deftly maneuvered Matthew into a place of spiritual weakness where he lost his psychic autonomy to his own emerging unconscious; now it ran him. Matthew seemed covered in pictures too,

but one on his chest was throbbing. Probably this was the pain picture the Druj pushed on, amplified to get him going. It was winter, and he was meditating by himself at the shore of James Bay. The Thunderbirds had drawn near and made a half-circle of mighty celestial birds before him. Lightning and thunder streamed out of them like breath.

Matthew saw how those powerful emanations shaped the ethers. They were like crystalline sword strokes clarifying and activating the psychic air. He wanted to be able to do that. He wanted those powers. He wanted to be able to move the air like that, make it surge according to his will. He wanted his will to shape the air into raging currents, storms that quelled all opposition, volition that never accepted "no" as an answer. He wanted no opposition to his desires. Why didn't he have this? He should have this power. He would have this, he declared.

I saw his emotional train of thought. I saw the derailment, the calamitous train-wreck coming up as the logical result of such feelings. The *skandah* of will and volition and the air element were undoing him. Matthew felt he had been cheated. I'm not sure what he based that on. He was not created as an Ofanim and given their powers after all, so where was the cheat? I saw images around his head from his earlier life in business: his colleagues and associates from the stock market and investment world who had been able to manipulate prices, maneuver themselves to be in the right position, edge out competitors, basically, lie, cheat, and steal, like you'd expect in business. The big successes through devious means by his associates got to him.

You could see how it churned him up, made him feel second-rate, left behind. He wanted those powers. He wanted to be able to create desirable realities. The world of business, he realized, was trivial, not worth his attention, not the proper place for the deployment of these creative, world-generating powers. He sought a bigger playing field. How about reorganizing society itself, the physical world—that's too limited: how about human consciousness itself?

I saw that the Druj had highlighted this particular picture, breathed on it until it caught fire and enflamed Matthew's emotions and lit his unconscious. Without thinking, he was drawn to that dull green light, the moldy green haze. He never saw the *Dhyani* Buddha it backlit, that massive figure of radiant green Light. He had gravitated to the *Bardo* default position for this *Dhyani* Buddha, into the dullish green light, without even making a choice based on seeing both poles of this dichotomy, for we were now in the domain of the fifth *skandah*, that of will and volition and the element of air, and the awakened, Light-emitting personification of the conversion of that aggregate into enlightened wisdom.

His name was Amoghasiddhi, "Infallible Power." This *Dhyani* Buddha shows you how to change ego-bound, karma-generating action, the will to action, and the churning winds of will it creates, the tendency for struggle and competition, to strive to be better than everyone, to compete with reality itself, into karma-free, selfless activity, how to act without desire to produce good accomplishments that carry no karma and do not bind one to the Wheel of Life. Selfless actions generate no karma; you wield volition from an emptiness state, and while it produces results, you remain free of all traces and accruals of karma.

Matthew looked like he had lost himself. He was flailing about. He was about to punch one of the big guys, take on the lurking horde of fighting gods. That would be foolish and probably disastrous. Suddenly, Amoghasiddhi lifted his right hand to shoulder height, the palm facing outward, all the fingers upright and joined. It looked like the hand making a "stop"

sign yet its calmness somehow assured one of safety, fearlessness, and divine, benevolent protection, the dispelling of fear, even the fear of evil and ignorance, protecting against that.

His gesture expressed fearlessness against all psychic poisons and mind delusions, and his ritual implement, the double thunderbolt, called the *visvavajra*, reinforces this idea. It was as if the *Dharma* itself raised its hand, signifying sanctuary from all fears, from all compulsion to quarrel, strive, and compete, and to further enhance this gesture, the *Dhyani* was mounted on a throne of Garudas. That was the angelic Blaises in their sublime bird form flying the highest gods.

As soon as Amoghasiddhi made this gesture (it's called the *Abhaya mudra*) Matthew froze. He stopped all his physical movements; even his emotions seemed on hold. He collected himself like waking up suddenly from a trance. You could see self-awareness dawn then blossom on his features; he smiled. He took stock of himself, his frozen gestures, where he was, and of the *Dhyani* Buddha. He shook his head as if to dispel the awesome unconsciousness that had so recently possessed him and directed, willed his actions, almost disastrously.

This was typical of Amoghasiddhi. A story goes around Buddhist circles that once Devadatta, an envious cousin of his, tried to murder the Buddha by getting a rampaging elephant to charge into the Buddha's path and trample him. Amoghasiddhi stopped this by making the *Abhaya mudra*, calming the enraged beast, imparting an atmosphere of assurance and safety and thus defeating envy. The enraged elephant was a personification of Devadatta's activated envy.

That seems a fair description of what this simple hand gesture did for Matthew. No offense to the Blaises, who, as we all know by now, like elephants as a preferred metaphorical form (their elephants have six tusks), but the

Abhaya mudra quelled the mad elephant in Matthew. Merlin explained all this to us later. The important fact about the *skandahs*, in this case the *skandah* of will and volition, is that if you are not careful you can default to the negative, karma-generating aspect of this tendency of consciousness. Will and volition degenerate into impulses, and prime among these are envy, jealousy, covetousness, and fear. When these inspire and lead to action, you are in big trouble, karmically. You're entering the realm of the unbearable miseries of quarrelling and warfare; these are the chief raw passions of the denizens of this realm, a very contentious lot.

The more time you spend there, whether in your alive daytime life or dead in the *Bardo*, you gravitate towards the *loka* of the *Asuras*. These are the antigods or Titans whose main characteristic is conflict fueled by great power and force. That is how they are described from the outside, by those who don't understand their actions. Opposed to the enlightened gods, the *Suras*, the *Asuras* ("against the gods") are demonic spirits of struggle, conflict, and strife, perpetually straining against one another and the order of Creation and competing constantly with the *Suras* for power and dominance in the world.

These spirits are significantly misrepresented in general discussions, and even in translations of the Puranas, in which the *Asuras* largely figure, they are called Demons. They aren't. There is nothing demonic about them. The correct term from Sanskrit is Daityas, indicating the progeny of the Earth goddess Diti ("Brilliance"). Daitya means the variously differentiated and personified aspects of universal force and will, made into myriads of powerful warrior-gods for the purposes of executing the details and mechanics of the Creation. They are more like a host of burly, loud-talking, brawny construction workers, blue-collar gods.

They are antigods only in the sense that the gods, the Ascended Masters of the Hierarchy called the Great White Brotherhood and to an extent the angelic orders, have to constantly balance out and harmonize their strong, potentially overwhelming forces to preserve consciousness and the galaxy from them. It's more a matter of weights and measures neutrally applied to this polarity. The antigods pull, the gods push, and the galaxy, consciousness, created forms, stay relatively balanced, or at least not torn apart by wildly tidal forces of the *Asuras*. You have the construction workers and you have the foremen and site bosses. They work together as they build, maintain, then repair, the order of Creation.

Amoghasiddhi represents the perfection of action that creates no karma, or perfect deeds that leave no trace, enlightened volition conducted from a place of lucid emptiness and transparency. The *Abhaya mudra* of fearlessness says to us this is how you convert actions driven by envy, fear, covetousness, and jealousy, the *skandah* of volition and will run amok into ill-advised impulses, into perfectly transparent selfless deeds that benefit everyone and will cost you no new karma.

It's like saying, Look, you have to act, so here's how to do it without it costing you anything. You can move energy, ideas, people, without accruing any karma. To use any of the *skandahs*, to assign names and forms, to feel, perceive, and even to maintain consciousness as a passive resting state is to exert your will. You can generate fresh karma merely by perceiving something or registering a sensation. You start to feel you cannot move at all without creating more karma.

His *visvavajra*, or double *vajra*, which looks like a four-leafed clover with a *vajra* "head" at each quarter-mark and is as powerful as the Western image of Zeus's thunderbolt or Thor's hammer, means this clarity and purity of action is extended into the four cardinal directions, meaning throughout all of reality. He extends his double thunderbolt of karma-free willed action in the four directions. Amoghasiddhi may act in any direction without obstacle or any attachment. Acting *without* attachment to the result is key here; attachment means karma. It means you got seduced by the *skandah* grid again, the will aggregate got you. Amoghasiddhi shows you how to act without trembling the *skandah* grid at all.

"I get it!" shouted Matthew. He was enthused with Merlin's explanation (which I have just related, though put into my own words). As he said this, sheets of images started streaming out of him like a fan blowing a deck of cards in all directions. Hundreds of images that seemed etched on large silken posters or curtains blew out of Matthew's body and dissolved in the air. When it was finished, he looked lighter; he certainly looked calmer and more himself. He looked more like himself than he ever had. I know, that is an odd thing to say. But it seemed that more of Matthew's true nature had been revealed, that these many decks of "playing cards," each card with its portrait of an offense tattooed on it, had obscured this true essence and greatly distorted it. Now he was free of this, and he looked purged of envy.

Merlin explained that the Druj had deftly prodded Matthew's picture deck of pain images sufficient to enflame Matthew and get his envy roiling. The unconsciousness is always (and so easily) open to manipulation and triggers. It's always looking for a fight or some drama or something worthy of histrionics. If you were a grifter or pickpocket, you'd say it is an easy mark, a simple touch. This carries a double message. The unconscious is so easily riled up, but the genuine easy mark is the daytime consciousness, so easily directed this way from the shadows and murky areas, from where all the invisible bystanders call out, making lewd

suggestions, urging fights, stirring trouble, placing bets you'll do it.

Matthew carried this susceptibility to the *Asura-loka* within him in these images. You could say he specialized in this *loka*. He knew it well. In many respects he dwelled there in his daytime psyche and employed its manners. When he was here in the *Bardo*, those daytime protective layers of consciousness were stripped clean from him and he was exposed, naked, and vulnerable. In the daytime world he could always get distracted and wander off to another *loka*. But here it was his natural gravity well, and it pulled him in and held him. The familiar gravity field of the *Asura-loka* started yanking him and he didn't see the *Dhyani* Buddha Amoghasiddhi—that's hard to believe given how big he appears.

"I am embarrassed that I was so taken in by my own envy pictures," Matthew said, "but, putting that aside, it was so educational to see how this works. Once chastened like this I won't forget it. I can assure you of that. I get the set-up. It has three aspects. First, you have a *skandah*, one of the mechanics of cognition. Second, you have the realm in which this *skandah* has degenerated into something negative. That's one of the Six Worlds or *lokas*. Third, you have the *Dhyani* Buddha who represents the radiance of enlightenment that has converted that *skandah* of will to lucid transparency and awakening. This *loka* is a big test.

"If you screw up, get confused, lose your way, or succumb to your own karmic tendencies, then you by-pass the *Dhyani* Buddha as I did and head for the *loka*. There you are likely to further lose your bearings and look for a womb-door. Then it's all over. You get back on the incarnational merry-go-round on a new ride. You defer waking up until the next time you come through the *Bardo*. The trouble is each time you screw up it makes it harder to be lucid when you come back here because you've created this karmic habit of failing. It's like trying to quit smoking. The hardest thing is starting. I'll start tomorrow. Just one more drag today, then I'll be ready. If you're not careful, you never start quitting.

"Here's the set-up as far as I've figured it out. We started with Vairocana. The *skandah* was consciousness, the element ether or *akasha*. The emotional default zone was anger and hatred in which consciousness gets distorted to become a weapon. Consciousness gets bound up with a self-identity, and even the gods may see things from their own self-interest; when they differ, there's the anger. The *loka* you could get lured into is the Heaven World, the realm of the *devas*, a high-level spiritual pleasure world, potentially of great self-indulgence.

"The *Dhyani* Buddha Vairocana represents sovereignty of consciousness over all its modifications, liberation from all conditionings of consciousness. Granted, as far as alluring illusory worlds go, the Heaven realm is a lot better than others, but it is still a trap, a sinkhole that pulls you down out of the possibility of freedom. He emits the radiant blue Light, but the *Deva* World emits a dull white light. His mount is the lion, the fierce roarer, showing the strength of self-mastery, showing the power of consciousness over all disturbances of clarity.

"That is the first day in the *Bardo Thödol*, meaning the first cognitive zone. Day two you meet Aksobhya and deal with the *skandah* of name and form and the element of water. Here the danger area is ignorance and delusion, of granting absolute individuality to these myriads of differently appearing names and forms, to see them as all irreversibly separate. The *loka* you run the risk of getting sucked into is Hell. You are aided by the throne-mount of the elephant, the Ofanim in their obstacle-removing, invincible, charging male elephant form.

"Well, nobody is happy in that place, whether it's the hot or cold section of Hell.

Representing the alternative, the enlightened choice, is Aksobhya who personifies the individuality of name and form converted to a universal one body in which you see all forms as empty and exponents of the Great Void. He is the mirror-like wisdom that touches the Earth of all names and forms and reflects back their conversion to enlightenment consciousness, lucid emptiness. His mount is the elephant, Ganesh, the Ofanim as invincible consciousness powers, and he emits the radiant white Light contrasted with Hell's dull smoke-color.

"On day three you get Ratnasambhava and the *skandah* of sensation, feeling, and touch, how you respond to and interpret all incoming sense data from the earth element. This is the cognitive function where we decide we like this and don't like that. Ratnasambhava shows what this looks like when raised to universal compassion. The liability is to get lured into the *skandah* default realm of desire and pride; the *loka* is the Human World, where people have raised this *skandah* to a fine art. His mount is the horse, the Ofanim again, expressing the fleetness, virility, strength, might, and speed with which enlightened consciousness gallops through this *skandah* world, hardly touching the ground of its allurements, not settling for likes or dislikes, knowing they are all equal, equally empty, and equally possessed of enlightenment consciousness.

"Then on day four it's the *skandah* of perception, the element of fire, the *Dhyani* Buddha Amitabha, and the *loka* of the Hungry Ghosts, the tantalized ones. The default area is malignity where the fire of frustrated, unsatisfied perception leads to bad behavior, misanthropy, and you're liable to end up with the walking disgruntled, the tantalized ghosts, dead but still awfully hungry. Amitabha demonstrates the wisdom of discrimination as he sits atop his peacock mount, its myriad eyes in the tail feathers emphasizing clarified perceptions, and his radiant red Light advertising the merits of enlightening fire and perception. The proliferation of 'eyes' on the peacock's tail feathers means you see things from a multitude of angles and perspectives. Your perceptions are from all sides. You do not get locked into a single angle of viewing; you see things all at once.

"The fifth day and its fun and games I have deftly and fully demonstrated for you. I came into this zone of the *Bardo* loaded for bear with my envy pictures. I was the easiest touch for the Druj. She just needed to nudge me and I was off. I was oblivious to the *Dhyani* Buddha, the portrait of my own salvation, and got embroiled in the acting out of these pictures of envy, fear, covetousness, jealousy, accrued over time, stored up in stacks and heaps until this moment when they could be activated as one bad truckload of karmic illusions and propensities. The *Asura* realm is the *loka* of hot air, stirred-up, roiling air currents, misdirected will.

"I was about to buy a time-share in the *Asura-loka*, set myself up as a new *Daitya*, and defer my enlightenment and liberation from the old *Bardo* to God-knows when. Action tainted by karma, volition stained by envy—it's a ticket for *Bardo* jail-time and that's where my karma was leading me. Amoghasiddhi's lovely hand *mudra* of fearlessness and protection woke me up, shook me out of the trance of my karmic illusions, compelling as they had seemed. He showed me selfless action, karma-free deeds, volition rendered transparent, converted to Light, and when I got that, my liberation from this *skandah* finally began.

"You know what else? I saw how powerful is volition. It is a clamp or harness strapped onto consciousness. It grips it fiercely and adamantly. Even when you were letting go of the *skandahs*, erasing the *skandah* grid, dissolving yourself into emptiness, the bliss of voidness, there it is, asserting itself in that very act of letting go. You

realize your will is saying implicitly *I am doing this*. You have to erase the *skandah* grid and enter the Buddha Mind without asserting your will: you have to do it through non-doing. It's vexing to try to put into words. The minute *you* try to *do* it, you are caught tight in the volition *skandah*. Your will forces your consciousness to attend to the process of divesting itself.

"The thing you need to remember at all times is that in the *Bardo* you're naked. You don't have the protective layer of daytime unconsciousness laid over your karmic accruals. They can flare up but you can always go back to sleep again. Here you don't have that protective layer. Your skin is raw and exposed. The true nature of the game, the test, is more starkly revealed. It's shocking. You see the driving power of your karmic illusions, your fallacious conclusions. You see how little autonomy you have exercised over them while you were alive.

"Now all these debts, these tendencies, come calling. The bills are due: you pay. You either buy another installment of appalling ignorance and delusion or you sign up for a nice rendition of your mind's innate radiance as the *Dhyani* Buddha. You realize, Man, was I ever suckered into believing such nonsense."

Merlin was laughing. "I must put that line in my next edition of the text."

Now that we had seen the downside of this *skandah* demonstrated—performed, I am tempted to say—we could turn our attention to its perfection. Amoghasiddhi sat before us in wakeful meditative posture, all radiant green. His green, which seemed to include his skin, robes, head, everything, was dazzling. You needed sunglasses to be around him. Think of June sunlight blazing on a rich field of early summer grass framed by trees and multiply this by a million.

His throne-mount is Garuda, the Ofanim in one of their regal bird forms, but as Merlin explained, sometimes the Tibetan sages interpreted this more generically as a "Bird-Man" which represents the winged human, the human in transition from *skandah*-bound to being able to fly their consciousness without making karma. That's why the element of air is associated with this stage: the Bird-Man soars through it, unimpeded by karmic tendencies to act out of self-interest or envy. Action moves, will is directed, volition is deployed *like* flowing air but none of it leaves any trace, just as wind is invisible other than through its effects on matter; the deeds are all perfect, the quality of mind entirely radiant. You move through the air, your will like wind, traceless you make no karma.

"I'm beginning to understand the *Bardo* process better now," said Matthew. "Here are a few more notes on what I experienced with *Asura-loka*. My body seemed shingled with numerous long, stretched-rectangle sheets of images. These went from my chin to my knees; they were translucent, with some Light coming through the pictures; and all of these picture-shingles were in layers. It was like taking a ream of laser-printer paper and piling the sheets all over you.

"As for the images, they were biographical, drawn from my life mainly, though some I did not recognize or remember, so they may have been earlier lives of mine. What was consistent is that among all of them was an emotional charge; these were each drama photographs, memories of heightened moments. The themes of many of these images involved pain, wounding, and the frustration of envy, jealousy, covetousness, fear—what drove me to the *Asuras* and inclined me to match their mental state of struggle and warfare.

"You enter a *Dhyani* Buddha station, which is a way of dividing up this part of the *Bardo* into five domains, and the figure shines a bright Light on you. With Amoghasiddhi, it is a terrifically fierce and brilliant green Light. You squirm. You probably resist it, even recoil from its impact. It burns through you. This Light beaming in upon you penetrates all the pictures you have in yourself. You may divest yourself of these emotional memories or you may succumb to them. It is a perilous poised moment. You either let go of them or act from them.

"Meanwhile, the *Dhyani* Buddha is showing you your own innate radiance of Mind. This is the nondualistic, unconditioned quality of consciousness when the particular *skandah* in question, here will, volition, and impulses, is converted into enlightenment, when your actions are empty of desire or selfhood and move as effortlessly as air, as wind through a valley.

"At the same time, the dull green light surrounding Amoghasiddhi may start to seem persuasive, welcoming, like a safe harbor for a storm-tossed ship. Your own emotional pictures, strapped like a shield on your astral body, may start to tingle and grow warm; they may seem like they're talking to you, whispering suggestions, urging action, such as retribution, vindication, conflict, and if you do not start releasing them, which you do, it seems, by recognizing their inherent emptiness, their illusory nature, seeing them as karmic illusions, conclusions drawn from life experience but filtered through an unpure *skandah*, then they will grab you by the shoulders and stiff-walk you right into *Asura-loka*.

"With each *Dhyani* Buddha station, you have a bright and a dull light. One corresponds to the radiance of the *Dhyani* Buddha, the other to the default *loka*. You have the white radiance of Aksobhya contrasting with the smoke-colored light of the Hell realm; Ratnasambhava's yellow brilliance against the dull blue light of the Human *loka*; Amitabha's red radiance framed against the dull yellow hue of the Hungry Ghost realm; Amoghasiddhi's green effusions counteracting the dull green light of the *Asura* world; and Vairocana's deep blue against the *Devas'* dull white. The brilliant Light in the foreground may seem formidable, even threatening, but it is the only true sanctuary; the dull light behind it may feel safer, easier, welcoming, but it is a guaranteed karmic trap and a dead-end.

"Each of the five *Dhyani* Buddhas represents the conversion to enlightenment of the particular *skandah* and the refuge from falling into a *loka*. But more than that, they each represent the transcendent, awakened presence of the Buddha in that *skandah* realm, the Buddha radiating enlightenment through name and form, will, consciousness, feelings, and perceptions. Amoghasiddhi, for example, is the Buddha, the condition of the Awakened One, the enlightened state, radiating through the *skandah* of will and volition and the air element.

"It's as if the Buddha had five heads, one peering luminously into each *skandah* world. Five awakened heads offering you permanent escape from the Wheel of Life. They blaze with Light, and it is the Light of completely lucid wide-awakeness. Yes, you probably feel you desperately need sunglasses to deal with these big guys, but the reason they are called Wisdom Buddhas is they represent the wise choice. The wisdom of converting a sense organ, a *skandah*, to Light.

"Once I realized how this works, I immediately went back to stand before Amoghasiddhi. I basically said to the big guy, Let me try this thing again, okay? He gave no response which I took to be agreement with my request, and I stood in his green Light again. I saw the layers of pictures on my body start to tremble. It occurred to me the maybe this is the fifth initiation is because it's the hardest. Letting go of self-directed willed actions is hard, saved for the fifth day in the *Bardo*, because it may be the epitome of your selfhood, of your free right to act.

"I felt the heat-waves of the emotions they contained rise up to warm my body. It was a prickly, rough feeling, like sandpaper scratched across smooth skin. It felt like being in the same room *again* with the world's biggest whinger and non-stop *kvetcher*. This guy is always grumbling, carping about injustices, threatening to get revenge on all the miscreants who ever looked at him the wrong way or, worse, ignored him, promising he will engage all offenders in conflict and contention whenever possible because he's right and the world is wrong and he's sick and tired of always being relegated to second place. Enough!

"Amoghasiddhi's green Light helped me see through these pictures. Yes, they had relative reality; they were snapshots of my personalized travails; they were karmic residues created by my life experiences and stored in my body. But from the point of view of wide-awake, lucid, nondualistic consciousness, they were trivialities not worth keeping my attention on any longer. I let them go. They instantly streamed out of my body, like printer-paper blown by a wind.

"As they blew off my form, they started to dissolve in a slow-motion atomization. They looked like they were made of millions of individual consciousness atoms that had been organized in a pointillist rendition to create the picture, and that picture was held together by the particular emotion. The consciousness atoms were now free of the obligation to cohere this picture and flew into me. I had invested percentages of my available consciousness in these emotion images. Now I was getting all that back, like calling back hundreds of bad investments and now suddenly I was rich in consciousness, fortified in it.

"The degree to which this divestment made me feel instantly lighter is staggering. It was like being on a crash weight-loss regimen, and one that worked. I felt unburdened of such a heavy weight, this load of old whinging pictures. They would never be satisfied; they would generate more of the same. I would always be carrying around this emotional rubbish if I hadn't acted on it.

"You can easily lose yourself in these pictures. You can enter into them and see all of reality from their distorted, subjective filters. You enact policies on this basis. You keep throwing your will around, instilling conflict, radiating it like heat waves. Patterns of behavior, routine responses, emotional stances. You're lost in them. It's terribly exacting. Even to say, to assert with ardor, I *will* gain enlightenment, I will convert this *skandah* to wisdom, will subdue my will, this creates karma. It is not clean. You are still deploying your will to produce a willed effect. It is not a selfless act. You must do this without yourself involved.

"When I saw through them, the pictures dissolved. It's not a matter of disavowing the emotional truths of the pictures, of suppressing their reality, of pretending they don't exist. No. You see through them with compassion and discernment. Yes, they are images of suffering, but the reality of Buddha Mind far surpasses that. You see that they were interpretations of reality based on seeing events through impure *skandahs*, karmically tainted cognitive equipment, that the conclusions you drew have only a relative merit, not an absolute one.

"I started to see how acting on these images would be like punishing the wind for blowing my hat to the side, chasing after it with raised fists and imprecations, like Arabs chasing the *ghibli* ill-wind with their raised daggers. You realize in that lucid moment you have the choice, to enter the pictures or not. Your prime act of will is to not act. To take all selfhood out of volition.

"If you refrain from identifying with them, you gain great psychic traction. If you enter them, you get wrapped up in their emotional atmosphere, and with that, all the voices and commentators and complainers inside them, jabbering on critically and constantly about the state of affairs and the lamentable condition of the host and sponsor, like a hundred yammering radio stations, like nonstop talk radio.

"I understood too why the Tibetans depicted the *Dhyani* Buddhas as accompanied by female consorts, high-level enlightened female Buddha figures. It's part of the balanced polarity theme in the descriptions of *Bardo* conditions, such as with the bright and dull lights I just mentioned. You get the masculine and feminine aspects of the enlightened states, somewhat paradoxical because how could enlightenment be distinguished as to gender, yet it is, and usefully.

"You get representations of God in His masculine guise and Her feminine personification through these *Dhyanis* and their goddess consorts, giving you a double advantage to attain liberation from the *skandah* grid. You have White Tara, Locana, Pandara, Mamaki, and Green Tara offering you help. These are the Buddhist names for the female consorts of the *Dhyani* Buddhas.

"Take Locana. She is the consort to Aksobhya, and Tibetan sages describe her as pale blue in color, "the One with the Eye" or the "Clear-Visioned One." She stands for pure awareness, direct seeing of reality, as it is, without adornment. Her left hand in the *dhyana* (meditation) *mudra* holds a *vajra*-bell in her lap, and her right hand expresses the *Bhumisparsa mudra* (Earth-touching or Earth-witnessing hand gesture, the palm and fingers touching the ground) and holds a five-pointed *vajra*, a thunderbolt. This is key to the consort business: Locana is the *prajna* of Aksobyha.

"That means she embodies the wisdom, insight, intuitive apprehension, and discriminating knowledge of that enlightened state. It's like the *Dhyani* Buddha exemplifies the enlightened state of the *skandah*, and the consort *delivers* that quality to you with a sharp *prajna* sword. She is the action-figure expression of this wisdom. She *demonstrates* it; the *Dhyani* Buddha *is* it. *Prajna* means direct insight into the true nature of reality, recognizing its impermanence, suffering, non-self, and emptiness conditions. It sees through all illusions and veils, all the glamours. It cuts through these deceptions like a honed sword. To add to the richness, each *Dhyani* and consort oversee a Pure Land paradise, including *Akanistha, Sukhavati, Shrimat, Prakuta,* and Aksobhya's *Abhirati.* It's like if you make the wise choice, you get all the riches of enlightened awareness at once."

Matthew was right. He looked much lighter in form, more full of Light. It still looked like him, but it was as if a smoky mist had obscured his bright eyes. Now that was blown away and you could see him clearly, his face and eyes were perky, wide-awake, full of available attention, interest, and strength. He did in some manner look like he had dropped 30 pounds of unneeded weight and he had gained a formidable wisdom transmission, seemingly straight from Buddha.

I saw some of Amoghasiddhi in him, as if he were emulating that great figure, which I realized is the point. Each of these Buddha figures personifies an innate radiance of consciousness every human *already* has and which can become manifest once the *skandah* has been purged of karmic taints and converted to enlightenment. Amoghasiddhi and the other *Dhyani* Buddhas are innate parts of human consciousness only seemingly appearing outside oneself as celestial figures. I was starting to see how everything in this part of the *Bardo* was a projection from the inner contents and infrastructure of human consciousness and what a person has done with this "equipment" over time, that is, in their many lifetimes. While alive, it's all inside us, roiling and clamoring for attention; when dead and we've dropped a few bodies, it's displayed *outside* us as a world.

I also realized that no doubt this did not appeal to all *Bardo* travelers. This approach, converting the *skandahs* to enlightenment, is perhaps akin to Virginia Woolf's remark about George Eliot's *Middlemarch,* published in 1874, that it was one of the few English novels "written for grown-up people." She helps the reader share the lives of the townspeople with sympathy, without satire or condescension. Getting off the Wheel of Life perhaps appeals only to grown-ups, but the sense in which I mean that is not snobbish in any way. I mean people who are tired of the six-ring circus of life, old souls, I suppose we should call them. They have sympathy for those stuck on the wheel. They have seen all the magic tricks. Adults of God, grown-ups of the incarnational cycle, they want out.

They are beyond enchantment, fooling, or foolery and want the naked truth. They have suffered much, gained self-insight, are ready to retire from the playing field of *samsara* and move on to a metaphysically lucid reality. Realistically considered, the *Tibetan Book of the Dead* is perhaps only for grown-ups, and Merlin writing as Padmasambhava is the George Eliot of the *Bardo.* But with the significant Light grid upgrade, maybe lots more souls will be grown-ups in the near future, preferring the elevation of awareness to a sixth chakra psychic level in which they may enjoy the sights of true reality behind the façade. Still, I am sympathetic to those who find this difficult or don't desire it, because I know there are days when I live, when I *want* to live, securely in Middlemarch.

I must count myself among those rushing to achieve grown-up status, and I think this got propelled when Blaise showed up in my life and opened the door. All I can say as a rapidly promoted candidate for grownuphood is I'm beginning to see the advantages. I rather like this expanded view of reality it's offered me. Woolf attributed this grown-up quality to George Eliot's authorial stance because she gave the reader a chance to empathize with the sufferings and difficulties of ordinary English people in a middling midlands town circa 1830 and the strivings for advancement of a man and woman to rise above this mediocrity framed against the staid provincialism of the majority of the town's residents.

You could say the same of the *Bardo*. Most souls are struggling to survive its bizarre rigors of psychological and ontological divestment, and a few are flourishing. The grown-ups part, I propose, is letting people operate at their own level knowing that eventually they will progress and match the new Light settings and conceive a desire to liberate themselves from this incarnation compulsion. As *Bardo* "grown-ups," we let them go at their own rate; we don't evangelize urgency. Meanwhile, we'll help those in the *Bardo* who allow us to.

There is another nuance to this grown-ups business. I didn't appreciate it at the time, when I was embroiled in the firsthand lucidities of the *Bardo*. For many people, this will be the first time they acknowledge their consciousness as a force and that it follows their lead. Reality and events in consciousness don't *happen* to them; they are *generated*, manufactured, created the way a short-order cook fries on the grill whatever the customer asks for: you're customer and cook.

How often I found myself, before this expedition, before the years of traveling with Blaise, suddenly the recipient of an emotion, as if it had snuck up on me. Or surprised at some turn of events, an acknowledgement by a colleague or a spurning, a desirable development or an unfavorable outcome, and how often I concluded it was fate or destiny that had scripted these results. I never thought it was myself, or that, had I started earlier, I might have persuaded reality to act more in accordance with what I had in mind. What did I have in mind anyway? The *Bardo* is a nonstop tutorial on what *you* have in mind. It's all acted out before you like a *commedia dell'arte* skit, or is it a Punch and Judy show? Either way, as Blaise would say, you choreographed the whole funny show, pal.

Philomena was regarding Matthew carefully. He did look much lighter, as I said, but now I realized the weight aspect was only an analogy. He had dropped a great deal of psychological and emotional content, like layers of fat. He looked like he had been scoured of impurities from the inside, as if thousands of dark grainy particles, like black sand, had been flushed out of his insides, and the dim, oily, dirty puddles and noxious rivulets in which these black sand particles had been embedded had been purged and washed out of his system.

I surmised that these details of Matthew's internal landscape represented old hardened feelings, outmoded self-images, and emotional tendencies and habits. It was like a fetid, moldy, dank basement in an old house situated in a wet, humid landscape, like England, that hadn't been cleaned out for a century.

"You know what's happening, don't you, Matthew," said Philomena.

"Yes, I'm starting to understand the process," he replied. "It's okay."

That was all that was said on this subject at the time. It was obscure to me.

What wasn't obscure was where we now were. The Acropolis in Athens. In the same place as the magnificent ruin of the Parthenon stood a Light temple many times its size. It seemed to be set at ground level and rose up through the rocky prominence and into the sky some distance. It was Amoghasiddhi's outpost in the human world via the Earth's geomantic terrain. The *Dhyani* Buddha sat on his throne-mount of the Bird-Man figure, our pals, the Blaises. They winked at us. Amoghasiddhi was broadcasting his fearlessness *mudra* in all directions, and he sat there in consummate stillness, emptiness, and bliss.

He was flanked by hundreds of *Asuras*. I hadn't expected that. They were representing the population of *Asura-loka*, a legitimate, necessary domain among the Six Worlds, the domain of world-builders and force-wielders. They looked composed and well-behaved; it seemed unlikely they'd start throwing things.

I shouldn't have been surprised. The Puranas frequently described the death of a Demon, or Daitya, in battle with the gods. Their heart centers would be filled with a glorious pure elixir of god-blood called ichor. They died enlightened. That's why I never trusted the translation of Daitya as Demon; it didn't fit. These spirits seemed as exalted as the gods, just as self-aware of their own God-nature. They all had their own names and were regarded by the gods as divine in nature. To call them contentious, quarrelsome, always in conflict and initiating warfare, is too simplistic; their profile requires more subtlety and nuance to be accurate. Their job is to juggle and administer lightning bolts.

They build worlds and wield universal forces and powers without attachment to the powers or the results. They are Amoghasiddhi's field agents. They act but not out of their will; nor is it Amoghasiddhi's will. They are technicians acting out the intentions and volition of the Supreme Being. Does the Supreme Being act out of self-interest? The question is both fascinating and absurd. The Supreme Being's "self" interest is the entire Creation, the universe which is all inside Him and He encloses all of it. His deeds are perfectly selfless, yet they are all done on behalf of his own enormous self-interest, the Creation.

Action is the culmination of the organization and momentum of the first four *skandahs*. They generate the compulsion to *do something*, to deploy will. We get ourselves into serious trouble and complications with this *skandah* of volition. That's probably why the dead get to Amoghasiddhi last. His is the hardest topic.

The karmic illusions compounded from the first four *skandahs* now seek action. We are accustomed to this syllogism, taking action to redress grievances, to exact revenge, to balance the accounts, to initiate new projects that serve ourselves. It's insidious: action out of self-interest validates our selfhood that is deploying the *skandah* of will to produce a desired effect. Say *Hello!* to karma.

Now Amoghasiddhi confronts us with the emptiness of all volition; that's why he is called the All-Accomplishing Wisdom. Here is how to take any action cleanly. Here is the wisdom that takes the self and the karmic illusions out of volition. Watch, here is action without the self embedded in its outcome. Here is deployment of the will without any taint or debt accruing to its deployer.

It's a sharp slap in the face to see this. We take action out of self-interest and this gets us further stuck in the sticky web; soon more action is required to adjust the consequences of the previous action. Everybody knows this; we take it for granted: every day we create more karma. It's like you drop a pitcher of water on the kitchen floor. You start cleaning it up, mopping the water, carefully picking up the glass fragments. But you bump into a rickety table and it falls over and the flower vase and picture frames on it crash. Now you have more work. You get irritable and start banging things around. More things break, more messes require cleaning-up. The phone rings; it's a solicitation. You tell them to fuck off. Now you've passed your anger to somebody, generating karma. It's a cascade. You're in the kitchen a long time because you keep compounding the original problem with new ones. Unless you get hold of yourself and stop.

"I've worked out one detail, at least," said Edward. "Why these *Dhyani* Buddhas have Earth Light temples. They each direct a paradisal realm. Amitabha, for example, is in charge of or presides over *Sukhavati*, the Western Pure Land, also called the Red Western Realm of Happiness. Aksobhya you'll find directing *Abhirati*, the Eastern Land of Exceeding Great Delight, also called Pre-Eminently Happy. Amoghasiddhi administers the Northern Realm of Heaped-up Good or Perfected Deeds; Ratnasambhava is at the Southern Realm Endowed with Glory; Vairocana looks after the Central Realm of the Densely-Packed, the Og-Min Brotherhood, better known to us as the angelic Blaises.

"Here's the connection: Each of their Earth-based Light temples is a simulation, or a hologram perhaps, of the paradisal realm which is their actual anchor point, their consciousness condition, in higher reality. Potentially, when we visit one of the Earth-centered copies, we can transfer up to the original. The Earth Light temple is like a travel brochure, a film clip, of the Pure Land realm."

Merlin looked at us. It was time for us to make suggestions, I realized. How can we change things here to help people realize the karma-generating nature of their will so that they can let go of it or at least realize the compulsion?

"I have a suggestion," said Blaise. "It will require moving some furniture. The Elohim have this feature out in the Earth's geomantic landscape that's like TV. They can watch the multiple permutations of cause and effect, action and consequence, in the past and the future, even in overlapping dimensions. You know the massive stone ruins that archeologists call cyclopean in construction? Stones of unbelievable size and weight, perfectly chiseled and fit into walls? Places like Mycenae, Jerusalem's Wailing Wall, Sacsaywayman at Cuzco, Peru.

"There are many more, 6,300 in all originally, though most are physically gone now. The consciousness technology they use is still largely beyond our comprehension, but on a practical level, I do understand that this enables them to study multiple outcomes. That's what the transiting dead need when they reach the volition platform with Amoghasiddhi, to appreciate the cascade of potential or likely effects from their actions, to see this cascade played out over time and many lifetimes, but to see it before they commit it to reality by acting. They can study the results of an Elohim permutations calculator before acting.

"Matthew was immediately sucked into the clamor of the *Asura-loka* realm by his own pictures and tendencies towards action based on envy. He was like dry straw when he got here, easily ignited. He didn't see the consequences of it. Let's set up a viewing station, like a movie theater, in which the soul can see multiple permutations of the will to act and how it can play out in a hundred variations. Include in this list of variations the outcome based on selfless action. At least the soul can see it; if he wants to reject it or fails to value it, it's his choice. It would be like an architect presenting 100 different models for the proposed house; the client, you, the person in the *Bardo*, can select the most desirable one.

"The Elohim could help with the construction. They could create this feature here. Obviously, you won't need the cumberstone stones, just a Light version of them. You step into this permutation theater and watch all the differently nuanced outcomes. I want to pulverize this idiot for ruining my chances at promotion. You watch the holographic demonstrations of each different way of pulverizing. You see how it plays out, what it leads to, what the charge for karmic damages comes to and whether you want to pay it (accrue it).

"Our hope is that, having viewed all this, the soul will reconsider self-interested action. Some more observant souls might be intrigued with the outcome scenario that results from will deployed free of self-interest. When you *see* those results, it will be harder not to be persuaded of its merits. At any rate, this set-up could potentially produce a pause in the *Asura*-like action, a moment outside of the flow of time and space that enables the soul to reconsider action.

"You get to observe all the different play-out scenarios and the new karma generated from each and what that in turn leads to. It's a theater of branching, multiplying realities, a graphic, even visceral, demonstration of the law of consequences, of the continuous karmic cascade resulting from self-actions. Physicists talk of new universes being constantly set up to allow the playing out of every different choice. Here is what follows when I pulverize this guy twice. When I shout and curse at him at the same time. When I refrain and sulk instead. When I steam up my resentment and spend all my time imagining him fully pulverized. When I complain all the time to friends that he did me an injustice.

"Each of these, physicists suggest, will generate a universe to contain its play-out. They call this the quantum model of many worlds, parallel universes, or branching realities. Reality, based on our choices, constantly branches out into worlds with alternate histories. It makes for a fractalized cosmos. The Elohim take that principle of cascading reality and put it all in a little stone box: their theater of branching, permutating realities. You watch your own script play out. The advantage here is that it is only simulated; it does not change any realities. You haven't further floriated the universe with additional branching realities.

"There will be no compulsion in this of course. The soul is free to disregard everything he's seen in the theater and take 'normal' self-focussed action that generates more karma. He'll just be here longer than he has to be. It seems likely, though, that a certain growing percentage of souls will find the experience chastening and salutary, like a pail of cold water thrown over a hot head. They might feel suddenly restored to their senses, if you'll pardon the oxymoron. The whole point is to render all the senses, or *skandahs*, empty. Then souls might understand that the outcome scenario from selfless action looks the best. If they do, they will better appreciate Amoghasiddhi's presentation and find more interest within to emulate that demonstration of perfect deeds."

Blaise looked like he had more to say. "Hey, Merlin. Any chance we could get a commission on all these clever ideas we have for upgrading the *Bardo*? You know, like some favorable commutation of our life sentence? Some days cut off?"

We looked at him with disbelief then of course we started laughing. It was just the sort of crazy, off-tilter but practical question Blaise was likely to ask.

At this moment the angelic Blaises swooped down like a flock of swallows. "We sentence you to life with us, without parole or mercy. Here's a sledgehammer. Start smashing diamonds, Blaise. Show us some ruthlessness."

It was a strange request. The human Blaise started smashing the diamonds in the angelic Blaise's diamond Rotunda of Light. He went at it vigorously. Sparks flew everywhere yet no diamonds were smashed or broken up. The airspace around us with filled with glittering diamonds. Inside each of these diamond fragments was a Blaise angel, beaming fiercely, ruthlessly. It had become a galaxy of diamond stars forming a globe around our group. The air around us grew staggeringly clear and sharp, as if reality itself had been brightened. My mind felt like a sharp sword facing 360 directions at once, poised, lucid. I felt there was nothing I could not understand, see, penetrate, or comprehend. I felt I had become a diamond fragment, a ruthless spark of Blaise.

I should have realized Blaise had more than spectacle and entertainment at play. These guys always have multiple cards up their angelic sleeves. They were raising us up to what looked like a platform, or perhaps it was a throne. We seemed to be rising through a pentagon pattern with the five *Dhyani* Buddhas. Each occupied a vertex in this five-sided figure that overlaid the planet. This pentagon of five *Dhyani* Buddhas formed a throne-mount for a larger figure.

This figure looked much like the *Dhyani* Buddhas but was somehow more complete, as if it represented the fulfillment of the five which were parts of him. I say "him" thereby imputing a gender distinction to this celestial figure. That is always a cognitively risky venture, as I learned from my travels with the human Blaise. Yet there was a distinct masculine aspect to this figure. Perhaps it was the sense of command and authority in its powers of concentration and attention.

He seemed to sit above the Earth on this platform of the five *Dhyani* Buddhas like another version of Brahma with his five heads, and in some striking manner he held all the Light threads of the planet's grid. It wasn't that he was doing anything to this Light grid pattern he held in his hands. It was the force of his awakened attention, his enlightenment, that was the factor. You could say he embodied the planet's innate Clear Mind and Buddha Nature. The five *Dhyani* Buddhas were separate yet each was a part of this one Buddha. He seemed to represent the bright culmination of their five levels of enlightenment. He was the emptiness of the *skandah* grid; they were the voidness of each *skandah*.

At this point I was starting to understand the mechanics of this revelation. It was beginning to resemble a grand Mystery play as ever new actors came forth. The five *Dhyani* Buddhas represent innate radiances of the awakened mind. Granted, that is not your ordinary mind and its conditions, but the mind, or consciousness, in a state of diamond-sharp clarity, crystal clear and wide awake. We were seeing an outer display of fundamental truths about ourselves.

Each *Dhyani* Buddha personified the perfection of each element and *skandah*. Our goal, the goal of the newly dead, was to recognize that, then own it as ours. Here before me is the perfection of volition, raised to the level of a perfect deed. All five *Dhyanis* represent aspects of the complete, singular Buddha, the Awakened One, who I now saw seated on a throne made of the five *Dhyanis*. That one Buddha also signifies something innate in humans called our Buddha Nature. That's the primordial, original diamond purity of mind, *Rigpa*.

Buddhists are always going on about its importance, how we must attain this. They had various ways to describe it, but it was all one Mind. I tried to imagine Buddha Mind coming to Middlemarch, what people would do. It's a predicament, because our personality in the present lifetime is a transient expression, yet it feels familiar, domestic, comfortably provincial, while Buddha Nature is a permanent truth about ourselves, the only truth in fact, but it can seem intimidating, overwhelming, unbelievable, and worth running away from.

Now this Mystery play spectacle expanded and took on new actors. First I saw the five *Dhyani* Buddhas occupying their directions in a pentagon. Each was emitting its fundamental color in great brilliance. I know it should be a square with a Buddha at each corner and one in the center (because the five are given cardinal directions in the implicit mandala of their array), but I saw it as a pentagon, with the five Buddhas each at a vertex of this figure.

The Buddha's throne-mount was situated on top of this pentagon as if the second story of a building or a Hindu sacred temple called a *stupa* or a Tibetan *chorten* in which the architectural layers each represent fundamental conditions of consciousness.

Without crowding or crushing the five *Dhyani* Buddhas on the "first floor," the Buddha's manifestation extent seemed completely superimposed over them. Now it was not so much the Buddha with five heads as the Buddha with five Buddhas inside him forming a pentagon of enlightenment. It was perhaps slightly dimensionally different than the *Dhyani* Buddha layer because the two layers, more clearly seen, occupied the same space yet it still seemed correct to say the *Dhyani* Buddha layer was inside the primary Buddha layer. The Buddha's throne-mount was the pentagon formed of the five *Dhyani* Buddhas. His mount was the enlightenment condition, the wisdom conversion of the five *skandahs*.

Many new deities started appearing in the pentagonal space. They stood before gates, as if they were the gatekeepers. I counted 42 celestial spirits. This number caught my attention as a scholar. The Egyptian funerary texts say at a certain point the newly deceased meets the 42 Judges or Assessors of *Amenti* in the *Duat*. They stand in attendance with Osiris who acts as the high judge, and many scholars, including Wallis Budge, suggest the specificity of the number corresponds with the number of administrative districts, or *nomes*, in ancient Egypt, which in classical times was 22 for Upper Egypt in the South and 20 for Lower Egypt and the Delta in the North.

The Tibetans say the number 42 refers to projections of energy features in the psychic center of the heart chakra. Each figure is a deity of the heart center allocated across the *Bardo's* first six days. The numbers fit nicely: six days, six chakras, seven deities per day or chakra: 42. If, as geomancy teaches, a national landscape, energetically, is akin to a giant figure in Light, then you can justify the inclusion of 42 administrative *nomes*, or landscape chakras, in this figure of Light.

The Egyptians call these 42 deities the hidden Ma'ati gods who feed upon Ma'at during their lives. That means they each exemplify the truth of Ma'at. The *Duat*-wandering soul makes 42 Negative Confessions to these Assessors of Ma'at, the minor deities of righteous conduct, attesting that they did not perform various unsanctioned deeds such as theft, murder, slander, lying, fornication, misrepresentation, shady dealings in grain exchanges, cursing, or stealing the *Khenef*-cakes from the Blessed.

Clearly some of these punishable infractions will have to be updated. They are too idiosyncratic for modern understand, or relevance. If you are a secular American and you show up before these stern judges and have to prove you have not stolen the *Hefnu*-cakes of a youth you'll have a problem. I never saw any *Hefnu*-cakes, Your Honor, and I swear I don't know that young fellow. Possibly the confessions represent typical ways in Egypt where one might have defiled an aspect of the chakras through ill-advised, morally corrupt actions.

The Tibetans see it differently. Each of these 42 personifies an aspect of consciousness correlated with the chakras and psychic centers. You get the impression they see these deities as manifestations and personifications of them. Each chakra has seven expressions or nuances, each being one of these deities. The *Bardo Thödol* doesn't talk in terms of apologizing for anything or making confessions or attestations of one's moral virtue; rather, it emphasizes cognitive and epistemological clarity and precision of perception, recognizing these 42 are outer-projected expressions of innate qualities of one's own consciousness.

The Egyptian version makes you feel like a suspect in a criminal trial, that you have to convince 42 stern judges of your innocence. The Tibetan version pushes you towards a neutral, rigorous, clear identification with the judges themselves. The Egyptian picture evokes somebody from 17th century colonial Massachusetts appearing before a board of icy Puritan judges, while the Tibetan description feels more like an eye exam where you have to show you can read the smallest print on the eye chart before they'll let you go out and drive a car.

The 42 deities were arrayed equally distant from one another in a circle within the pentagon of the *Dhyani* Buddhas. Each stood before a gate, or, as the Egyptians called them, a Pylon (from *Sebkhet*), representing in architectural terms a formal entrance (twin adjacent towers) to a physical temple, but here a psychic entrance to a consciousness domain. These are the Pylons of the House of Osiris (they number 10, 14, 16, or 21), and each of the Doorkeepers is named; the first Pylon doorkeeper or warder is Neruit, the second is Mes-Ptah. Other deities at the door have a lion's head, cow's head, a ram's, the head of a hippopotamus. If the *Duat* were a gangster movie, you'd be tempted to call these guys the muscle.

In other words, it is a well-documented topographical landscape which to a modern sensibility will combine story elements from Kafka and Lovecraft. It's like you get a briefing packet on each Pylon master, name, history, preference, the whole thing flavored with a surrealistic tinge of horror and weirdness. An administrative male or female deity sat on a mat before each Pylon, and you had to act like you knew the person if you expected to get past the front door. At the First Pylon, the deity is a vulture-headed goddess, holding a whisk, wearing a disc on her head, her back to a wall of spears. The *Egyptian Book of the Dead* is the playbook listing all the actors in your eldritch drama: it is an ensemble cast.

It's important to bear in mind that there is no single canonical Egyptian text. What we call the *Egyptian Book of the Dead* comprises several funerary texts including the Pyramid and Coffin texts, as they are inelegantly called in English. A large portion of these texts consists of spells and magic invocations for negotiating the *Duat*, and much of the text was originally written in hieroglyphs on tomb walls and sarcophagi and not neatly inscribed on papyrus rolls.

As for the name, the usual translation of the Egyptian text name, *rw mw prt m hrw*, is "Book of Coming Forth by Day" or "Book of Emerging Forth into the Light." The implication is that Day and Light are synonymous and both point to a realm of undying Light and spiritual illumination, the "Day-Light" of the immortal soul. The goal of being dead in the *Duat* is to emerge and come forth into Light, to step out of the carapace of darkness and ignorance that characterizes "normal" asleep human life and enter the field of illumination. It is basically the same as the Tibetan idea, to attain liberation through hearing. Liberation in the *Bardo* is the coming forth into the Day and Light of the *Duat*, but I get the impression the Egyptians were expected to memorize the funerary texts, including the spells, deity roster, and guidelines on how much to bribe them all. It was better to be a Tibetan; you could expect your pals to read you the playlist.

Confusing the picture is the fact the Egyptians said there were only 21 Pylons, or 28 if you include the gates of the Seven *Arits*, which are also door guardians. The Egyptian texts plot your route past these 28 and then into the Hall of Ma'at for the Weighing of the Heart ritual with the 42 Assessors of the Dead observing. But in Merlin's psychopompic route this time, we've already done that: we started with it. Further complicating the picture, at least for me, is that the Tibetans call these 42 the Peaceful Deities; they appear on day six. On day seven come the 10 Knowledge-Holding Deities (five pairs of primary male deity and female Divine Mother consort) flanked by innumerable *Dakinis*. These are female celestial wisdom spirits, called Sky-Dancers, exemplifying the infinite movements, the dance of the nondualistic Clear Mind, the sky of the Buddha.

I guess we have to allow for some screwiness in the timing of these appearances, to expect things to be fluid and changeable. This time incongruency is possibly due to the knots in our own karmic body coming untied out of linear order. The Tibetans strongly emphasize that everything you see in the *Bardo*, the heavenly and demonic deities, is a projection of your own mental contents as driven by karma. They are "hallucinatory karmic thought-forms" that comprised one's mortal personality now displayed as a living Mystery tableau before you.

If you're hallucinating, don't expect a linear unfolding of events, one after the next. It will be more fourth-dimensional, a time tableau presented as around you. What happened tomorrow may precede what you experienced two weeks ago. Be grateful your analytical brain, as you know, it, didn't survive your death because if it did it would be spinning itself into apoplexy figuring this stuff out.

Even the crowds of secondary deities correspond to human thoughts, feelings, desires, and impulses. They are the personifications of these emotional drives, ranging from sub-human to superhuman in quality and nuance, and they are conditioned, shaped, or even distorted, by the momentum of our karma, what we have made of them, how we fleshed them repeatedly in successive lives. They take shape according to how we have nurtured the thoughtform seeds lying within human consciousness, a kind of generic human psychic DNA. They are visual metaphors sketched according to the shape and flavor of karma. This means the Tibetans and Egyptians have left us their conditioned pictures as a guide to the possible appearances and forms these amorphous deities can take.

I was seeing most of this. It was a big crowd of additional celestial figures. I felt sorry for the average dead person. How would anyone make sense of this? The Egyptians say each *Arit* gate had three figures, a Watcher, a Keeper, and a Herald, and some didn't look like humans. You have to know their names and a spell or incantation to get past them. That's 21 different figures just for the Seven *Arits*. You'd have to be a well-seasoned occultist to know all these passwords. You'd have to figure out how to scribble their names in indelible ink on your palms and probably feet before you got here or you'd never keep them straight.

It sounded like early travel tales where you'd have to know who to bribe and how much to pay them to get through the security checks at the border crossings. Being a dead Egyptian sounds nightmarish: you are confronted by no end of scary unfamiliar spirits, you don't know their names, and they all need bribes. Somehow if you were a dead Egyptian, you had to remember all the names of these officials and a special formula for each *Arit* to prove your bona fides or your soul was toast and would never make it to the Field of Reeds.

Here's an example of what you'd be up against as a dead Egyptian: The Third *Arit* is guarded by three deities, one with a jackal's head, another with a dog's head, the third with a serpent for a head. The Doorkeeper is called *Unemhau-auentpehui*; the Watcher is *Seresher*; the Herald is known as *Āa*. You had to know all this. The *Arits* were understood to be mansions, halls, forts, strongholds, or gates, forming a chain across the *Duat* within the Kingdom of Osiris. You had to memorize this map or you'd be lost in the first five minutes. Boundaries within the land of Osiris demarcated the different districts, and at each you had to pass through an *Arit*-fortress supervised by three gods. These guardians were armed at this one too: expect to meet a whisk and two knives. And remember, their heads will look bizarre, so don't be alarmed.

I can't imagine the average dead person knowing all this. People would get stuck. I can imagine some souls getting irritated, saying "Fuck this nonsense," and looking for a quick way out. It seemed clear to me that the Egyptians held this crowd of deities at arm's length; they did not, like the Tibetans, emphasize the gods as outer projections of internal consciousness states or as personifications of the radiances of the Mind. They made it sound like a long line of crotchety, volatile border officials all needing bribes and respect from us, the stupid dead. As Rudolf Steiner might have said, the Egyptian soul was still living in the consciousness field of the gods whom they saw as outside them. That meant they had to supplicate, petition, bribe, or beg for their good favors.

But in the nondualistic absolutism of the *Bardo Thödol* why should I have to bribe anyone? Everyone, every spirit I encounter, is a projection of my own mental contents. This great field of the gods, ultimately, is inside me. So forget about knowing their names: they all have my name. Keep your money in your pockets; your own projections don't need it. You don't have to petition anybody.

The Tibetan text says at this stage of your *Bardo* journey, after the *Dhyani* Buddha phase, you're confronted with 110 deities. The 42 Peaceful Deities, associated with the heart chakra; the 10 Knowledge-Holder deities correlated with the throat center; and the 58 Wrathful Deities connected with the brain center, which must mean the sixth chakra, the center of psychic perception. If the Egyptians had enumerated this roster, they would have presented these gods as standing outside the

human and possibly indifferent, maybe inimical, to our well-being. The Tibetan picture seems like an epistemological upgrade. Thanks to Merlin, writing as Padmasambhava, humans are now told, correctly, these 110 *Bardo* deities are all necessary, indigenous components of their own chakras. They appear externally, but they are projected from out of your own anatomy.

You can cut down the numbers a bit by realizing the Wrathful Deities are just the inverse of the 52 Peaceful Deities (the Knowledge-Holders are peaceful too). They are the Peaceful Deities in an excited, agitated, or wrathful condition, and that is produced by the location. The heart is peaceful, the brain center is not. Buddhists are always referring to our "monkey-mind," always chattering, never restful. So the intimidating size of the crowd under the Buddha throne diminishes a bit. I will pass over the small but vexing matter that somehow another six Wrathful Deities snuck in unannounced to the noisy monkey-mind cocktail party of our awful karma, and I can concur that the brain can be a rowdy place, full of critics, worriers, and complainers, though so can the heart.

The Tibetan version (thank-you, Merlin) is streamlined and simplified. You don't need to know all the names of this horde of celestial figures or their retainers; you don't need to supplicate them, offer bribes, petitions, apologies, defenses. You don't even have to recite any stupid formulas, having committed dozens of them to memory before you lose your physical brain upon death. You just have to remember that basically everything you see is a hallucination scripted by your karma. Who cares what the names of these illusory figures are?

You could name them after figures from a Walt Disney cartoon if you like. It's definitely easier, much less paperwork, to die as a Tibetan than an Egyptian. I suppose, to continue the logic, it's best to die as an American. Then you enter the *Bardo* knowing nothing, no map, no deity roster, no clue as to correct protocol.

The best way to sail through this dizzying hallucinatory dream world is to be like a yogic adept, meditating in emptiness, knowing everything parading before you, clamoring for your attention or provoking your fright, this entire panorama of self-projected thoughtforms, is innately unreal. It is merely a pageant of gross and unarguable nonreality, the trite fodder of generic dreams. Another B-grade movie made by a hack director and crammed with clichés. The only supplication you need to make is to petition yourself to please wake up *now*.

The human Blaise now made a comment that seemed to follow up on this. "You get into the *Bardo* and they say, 'Strip! Get naked.' It's abrupt, even rude. You take off your clothes; they get hung up on a clothesline before you, and you don't recognize a thing. Not a single shirt. You don't recognize your own clothes that you've worn your whole life. Can you see the joke? These are the images, notions, interpretations, and karmic illusions you have clothed yourself with during your recent sojourn as a human. Now they're displayed vividly before you yet you cower in fright and tremble in confusion in noncomprehension. Now, with the appearance of this next level of glorious karmic illusions, you find unbelievably you have 50 times *more* clothes than you ever remember owning."

"Ah, Blaise? Merlin?" It was Edward speaking. He sounded frightened. "We've got some trouble. A bit of incoming here." He gestured to all around us.

We were standing in the center of a mandala filled with scary spirits. They all seemed encased in auras of flame; they had multiple heads and arms. A lot of blood was involved, to put it nicely. They seemed to be swilling it like beer. They all seemed in a bad mood, cranky, irritable, nasty—in a word, wrathful. All of them, more than 50 at my first estimate, were glaring at us menacingly. They vaguely reminded me of the Peaceful Deities; it was as if those benign spirits had suddenly flushed demonic, like the way a person changes when their Shadow gets activated and you see the other darker, feral, and even infernal side to them.

I kept reminding myself that all apparitional appearances in the *Bardo* landscape are unreal and powerless, parts of myself projected outwards, even "old acquaintances," as one commentator on the *Bardo Thödol* quaintly put it.

I felt fear, terror, and awe in rising waves and quantities, yet I felt one-pointed in my attention. The sudden appearance of more than 50 Wrathful Deities can do that to you. I wasn't even dead but I definitely wanted to get out of this place in a hurry. I looked around at my expedition mates. Edward and Matthew looked upset, a little bewildered. Pipaluk seemed calm, undisturbed. Tommy seemed to recognize the spectacle, having already encountered it. Blaise was pondering the apparition, like someone studying a magic trick for the mechanics of deception.

I heard laughter. Laughter! It was Merlin. "They put on a great show."

9

Suddenly, I got Merlin's point, why he was laughing. These guys were a bit histrionic when you think about it. Over the top, special effects by the truckload. It reminded me of hearing a pack of coyotes yipping and howling at 4 a.m. in the New Mexico desert. On the one hand, you appreciate their wildness, their solemnity, the dignity and nonhuman intent of their pre-dawn feral calling; but on the other, to a human, it sounds overdone, like humans hamming it up. What gave it away for me in the midst of this fearsome, spectacular display of scary spirits with undiscernible intent were the horned eagles they stood upon.

Blaise got it too. He was chuckling, shaking his head. "They always find a way into the center of the action. They just can't resist it. You see the Blaises?"

He was referring to the horned eagles. They were copies of Garuda, the majestic bird-form the Ofanim took to please and inform the Hindu psychics. This massive three-headed, nine-eyed, six-armed scary Wrathful Deity standing before us, flaming like he had a raging furnace inside his body, was standing on a dais supported by these horned eagles, or Garudas. From what I had learned to date about the Ofanim if you see them acting as a throne-mount for the world's most frightening spirit, it can't be as bad as it looks. In fact, forget how it looks.

It took me a while to get the point of the blood. It's not the kind of sight most people, including myself, will immediately take to. This big fellow was swilling it, like a blue-collar worker in his pub after a hard day in construction will down a pint of ale, slam the tankard down on the bar and call for another. What is the point of the blood? *Samsara*, phenomenal, passionate existence. Blood as in life-force, the carrier of personal and molecular identity, of your living life.

Think D. H. Lawrence and his musings about passion, blood-force, and the meaning of the color red. "Man all scarlet was his bodily godly self," he wrote. Blood is our desire to live, to experience, to fulfill our desires, to be passionate, inflamed with the world's longest list of quenchable desires for sensory experience. It's our selfness expressed as physical blood with its DNA print. It's to be on the prowl with the five *skandahs* heated and ready, all hormones engaged, hot-blooded, a fire in the blood, a blood-rush to the face, one's blood boiling. When I got what blood meant, that it was a metaphor, then this guy's get-up wasn't scary. I just pretended he was chanelling D.H. Lawrence on redness. Lawrence was ranting somewhere out in the *Bardo* wilds.

The Tibetans call wrathful-appearing deities *Herukas*. They guard the *Dharma*, like upscale gargoyles, so there must be a nuance of *Dharma* at work here. This *Heruka* had three heads, one red, one white, the third one brown. His body emitted radiant flames in all directions. All nine of his eyes were wide open offering a terrifying gaze. His eyebrows sizzled and quivered like lightning. His teeth were fearsome, more like a predatory animal's dental work than human. He emitted whistling sounds; he was droning some kind of repeated utterance.

His heads were unpleasant to behold, featuring human skulls like bizarre jewelry. Black snakes slithered around his torso like a garland. In his three right hands he held a wheel, sword, and battle-axe; in his left hands he held a bell, skull-bowl, and ploughshare. His feminine consort clung to him like a knapsack. From all the hair pores of both spirits appeared a flaming *dorje* (the Hindu *vajra*). All of this rested on the platform supported by the Garudas, as I mentioned, and this fact alone gave it away. I let my shoulders relax. I breathed easier as I saw it. I knew by this time the Blaises might be ruthless, but they were always nice, putting my best interests (anyone's) foremost to wake up searingly right now. As long as you considered that "nice" you had nothing to worry about from them.

"The whole get-up is an emanation from your brain and intellect," said Merlin. "An embodiment, a personification, of an aspect of the brain's psychic center, one of the 58 Wrathful Deities, which are the conversion of the Peaceful Deities, what they look like on a bad hair day. I wrote it all down in the text, but I appreciate the fact that for most people seeing this is a bit much to take in.

"In the *Bardo* you get the full package of projections distorted by karma: you get the epiphanously sublime *Dhyani* Buddhas and the God-awful scary *Herukas*. *You*, the dead person, are in charge of all special effects. It is entirely your doing. You get the good guys through the heart, the wrathful ones from the brain. You need to think of yourself as the film editor critically reviewing the daily footage."

"In short, keep telling yourself all this scary shit comes out of you," said Blaise.

"You're making it up." He seemed to enjoy the irony of his remark. "You see, Frederick, the trick is to find the copyright mark on the ankle of the *Heruka*. This image copyright Frederick Graham Atkinson, Ph.D. in *Herukas*. Recognition equals liberation. You say, this scary fellow is a projection of my mind. Who's afraid of their own shadow? Only a fool. *You* tarted up the *Heruka*. If you get what you're seeing, it all stops. You only need see the one *Heruka*. If you don't get it, he calls in all his brothers and you get *Herukas* stomping your pathetic ass for the next week, or longer, until such time as you understand the deception.

"Then, if you still don't get it, these boys whistle for all their household pets to come. You get another series of monsters, this time with animal and bird heads, all of whom are evincing appropriate scary features like protruding eyes, drooling fangs, huge physical size, the usual shock effects. It's like a cheap Hollywood horror film full of all the cliché tricks and monsters. You get a brown lion, red tiger, black fox, white vulture, red bird, blue wolf, black crow, blue crow. They appear suddenly from the different directions bearing their favorite instruments of cognitive torture, such as a skull bowl, sword, *dorje*, knives, and various shredded and dismembered human corpses to add to the horror impact.

"These animals, called *Htamenmas*, step out of the eight regions of your brain. Plus these animal horrors are accompanied by the eight *Kerimas* of the Abodes or eight directions, the four cardinals plus the in-between directions. These, if you are a traditional Buddhist in Tibet or India, will resemble female cemetery deities; they're each a different color, such as yellow, red, black, and green, and they demonstrate actions and hold objects, such as intestines or severed heads, like it's Halloween and they're on a proper demented bender. If you're from elsewhere, as we all are, God knows how you'll dress them up.

"The point seems to be to present a kind of *Noh* drama of the catabolic death processes of the body. The thing is these fright-girls are actually *Dakinis*, Buddha wisdom emanations, in fact, only play-acting the part of demons, Furies, and Harpies, so you can be reassured there is wisdom to their antic madness."

"When I first went through all this and I saw them, I thought, 'Bloody, hell, what an awful thing to do to the human body,'" said Tommy. "Then I thought: so what? I don't have a human body any more; my actual form is a mouldering corpse in the ground somewhere in Oregon. I am watching this from a Lightbody stance. Then I relaxed and was able to understand what these dismemberment deities meant. They were showing the deconstructing process of the human body, of my former body, the forces that build it, run it, and take it apart, all of that and their processes personified as these so-called scary spirits. It was like visiting a chop shop, where a team of mechanics take your car apart, down to the last screw and hubcap, all the parts that used to comprise your car displayed nakedly on the garage floor as the mechanics grin crazily at you.

"I appreciated the cleverness of the display. It was entertaining. Yes, on a physical level my former body was decomposing; but more importantly, I realized, my identification of my consciousness, my point of view, my stance in awareness, all of that, were no longer fastened to this specific human body or any body, and *that* identification was being ruthlessly taken apart by these *Kerima Dakinis*. When I got that, I saw that the whole spectacle was educational."

"Once you get that, then you can give the thumbs up to Pramoha," said Blaise. "She's the red-skinned *Kerima* from the West carrying the victory banner. Go girl! Nice deconstruction! Well done. It's like you're at Lord's cricket ground and you stand up with the crowd to roundly applaud a good bat by Harrow. It

doesn't matter it's your sorry ass that got the bat and is soaring through the wicket. It's how the game is played. It takes the edge off the entrails, cut-off and twisted heads, blood-drinking, and the implications of the *dorje* and skull-cup, and the fright of seeing this other *Dakini*, Candali of the yellow and white skin, walking towards you from the northwest carrying a corpse and a human heart like she's some dreadful combination of *femme fatale* and Ninja butt-kicker."

I could see we had by now a lot of cataloguing and processing to get through, starting with this eight-sided figure around us of fierce-looking *Dakinis*. It was an octagon and the four major and four minor directions were represented; a *Dakini* stood at each of these points, seeming to glare at us. It felt like a circle of neighborhood mothers and you just broke all their windows while playing baseball in the street, or perhaps a circle of your former girlfriends, all of them still having issues with you or demanding alimony or sufferance pay. I felt the heat rising on my physically non-existent neck as these correlations arose.

No matter. These were *Dakinis*, not irate Moms or old girlfriends. I took an odd comfort from the fact that these scary female deities were so well known and previously encountered that their group had a name as did the individuals. They were the *Kerimas*; all eight were named and described and had been seen before. If you were an educated Tibetan, you'd expect to see the *Kerima* girls here. If nothing else, that assured me that we were *supposed* to be seeing them; they were accounted for, on the *Bardo* payroll, and that in turn assured me their sudden appearance had a legitimate purpose and maybe we'd survive the encounter, and if we didn't, at least our survivors would know who to name in the lawsuit.

I didn't see the others in the group at this point. I surmised we were meant to experience and evaluate the *Kerimas* each on our own then regroup. Tibetan iconography maintains this exquisite balance between the terrifying and the blissful. The *Kerimas*, on the one hand, were unquestionably fearsome, their arms full of intimidating, baleful objects, their gestures insinuating bad things for the human body, but their faces—their faces were horrifying yet spoke of bliss.

The scary bits were just for show. These were upmarket gargoyles, showgirls in an odd metaphysical sense, and their musical was a pantomime of our body's death. You'd think you were watching a Lovecraft horror spectacle, then suddenly it all changes, and it's the *Folies Bergère* with dancing girls, songs, leg-throws, big smiles, the whole cabaret music hall spectacular, provided you can emulate the lucid discriminating wisdom of a Buddha PDQ and go void.

As Tommy pointed out, if you are dead and you have dropped your physical and etheric body, baleful shows of body dismemberment should not bother you. They carry no practical implications because your body is already gone from you. It's like watching a violent scene in a movie: it's shocking to your body, but you know it's not you, but somebody else, in fact, it's nobody because it's all fake anyway, you can watch it neutrally. Seeing the violence here, only your residual body-image and your identification with it as the seat and face of your formerly localized identity may be perturbed, but I saw now the point of this show was to get us to drop that lingering notion of being contained by it. In fact, the violence was meant to portray our resistance to accepting this basic fact.

The spectacle was the dramatization of a psychological fact, a mental process: you, letting go of your former body-image and the belief it defined your essence. The *Dakinis*, each in a state of bliss, fully possessed by that lucid emptiness

everyone keeps going on about around me, this Buddha-Nature of Clear Mind, act out the dismemberment of that identification of consciousness with the body, to be not a clown face-painted in karmic illusion but a sage in *Rigpa* with no face.

They take it apart before us, entrails, heart, blood, head, the whole karmic illusion. Form is emptiness, they say implicitly, and your form is a pile of parts. That means—now I was beginning to get their realization—you are more than this, or, more precisely, you are not this. The body and its human aggregates is an illusion you put on for the purposes of (regrettably) generating karma, or, more charitably, for experiencing the physical world and gaining life experience.

The *Dakinis* also demonstrate the seniority of awakened consciousness over all the visceral limitations and modifications of consciousness made by this body. It is not to dishonor the biological form, even though it can easily look like that, but to prove the primacy of lucid, empty awareness over all illusory forms we take. That means consciousness is triumphant over all limitations of name and form, such as "I am a human male called Frederick occupying this human-style body." That is the door to liberation: How can the *Bardo* be frightful when you know that? The *Dakinis* encourage you to shift your center of gravity from the residual human lingering identification to your condition before incarnation. The wrathfulness is meant to demonstrate your seniority over ignorance, how you must be ruthless regarding everything that obscures the Clear Mind in you.

The Tibetan text says this octagon of *Kerimas* emerges from the brain center. I assume that means the sixth chakra, the *Ajna*, and not literally the physical brain. That means if you're going in the other direction, through a womb-door, you must put on this octagon like a subtle tiara around your *Ajna* for life, and that during your incarnation these eight *Kerima Dakinis* are resident there. Later, after our expedition was finished and I had access to scholarly books, I discovered that esoteric yoga talks of the *karana-rupa*, the seat of the seven causal forms, a subsidiary chakra located near the *Ajna* center in the head.

These seven causal forms surround the individual self at the *Ajna* and are the origin of our subtle bodies. They are named and their functions described, yet clearly this is not ordinary knowledge; if you did not study yoga, you would unlikely ever hear of these until you got to this stage of the *Bardo* and saw them. Eight *Kerimas*, seven causal forms—perhaps the discrepancy is accounted for in that the complete system of causal forms is counted as the eighth *Kerima Dakini*.

Gaining knowledge of the *Kerima Dakinis* struck me as similar to a mechanic lifting the hood of your car and starting to explain all the engine parts to you. Unless you are a car expert, it is likely to be new, even exotic, information, possibly overwhelming at first. You need to have all these esoteric machined parts working properly for your car to run, but you never thought there was any utility in knowing what they were. Now you do. Similarly, the *Kerima Dakinis* disclose to you a formative part of your *Ajna* center, one that is necessary to generate seven subtle forms you didn't even know you had. It's like driving a car and not even knowing you are sitting in a moving car, driving it.

I found sideways corroboration of this explanation through a Gnostic text (part of the Nag Hammadi library) called the *Apocryphon of John*. It said 365 angels originally each contributed one body part, such as the liver or spleen, to the cosmic human form. An angel or power called Eteraphaope-Abron created the head and another called Meniggesstroeth generated the brain. The text also said "the powers" created the seven "souls" of the natural (embodied) human.

Goodness created the bone-soul, foreknowledge made the sinew-soul, and the other five powers generated the flesh-soul, marrow-soul, blood-soul, skin-soul, and hair-soul. Odd names, indeed, but maybe no stranger than the yogic description of the causal forms known, in translation, as the Moon, Arch Causal Vibration, and Partibility, among others. It is likely these two seemingly divergent traditions are pointing to the same fact, and maybe somebody will get around to giving these seven souls or causal forms more modern names, and maybe they can delete the *Hefnu*-cakes violation from the Egyptian rule book too.

What one tradition calls angels, another may well label *Dakinis*, but the consistency in these two descriptions is that all the body components are superintended and possibly created by personified intelligent spiritual figures. If these celestial figures originally each contributed a component of the mortal human form, then at some point you'd be likely to meet them. What better time than in the *Bardo* when this mortal form is being taken apart at your death?

That makes the *Bardo* revelation the necessary inverse of the creation of the "natural man" of the original Adam, as the Gnostics put it. Now you sequentially disassemble it, look under the hood, see all the constituent parts. Still, if you lacked the necessary esoteric knowledge about the arcana of the human form, how could you ever figure out who these female spirits were? Or the additional circle of eight figures around them with bird and animal heads?

These, I later learned, are known as the Eight *Phramenma Dakinis*. That's a translated Tibetan word, sometimes alternately written as *Htamenma* and they're sometimes called the *Ma-Mo* goddesses. They are construed as *Dakinis*, but their presentation valence seems clearly masculine. W. Y. Evans-Wentz, the pioneering Oxford University scholar who in 1927 supervised an English translation of the *Bardo Thödol*, suggested that this group was likely pre-Buddhist deities known to practitioners of the earlier Bön religion. That was the original, dominant, shamanic-style of spiritual protocols practiced in Tibet before Padmasambhava, our Merlin, showed up and told them to become Buddhists.

The *Phramenmas*, Evans-Wentz said, had totemistic qualities, human torsos but animal or bird heads, but in any case they were understood to represent a particular karmic impulse or emotional drive, presumably primitive or atavistic, one subject to appearing as a vivid hallucination at this stage of the *Bardo* journey, day 12. You could put this in your daily appointment calendar: Thursday, 10 a.m., meeting with the *Phramenma* Girls to order new body parts.

"It's like eight alternate versions of Anubis, the man with the dog's head," commented Edward. "Of course, that was Merlin, and these girls are not him."

Still, Edward's comment opened a door to understanding the *Phramenmas*. Edward understood from the beginning, thanks to Merlin's tutelage, that the jackal-headed Egyptian deity was a visual metaphor, not an ontological reality. It was an interpretive picture put over Merlin, as primary psychopomp through the *Duat*, to explain his function. He acts *like* a guide dog taking you through the confusing Underworld. Like a jackal, he knows the holes into and the paths through the "desert" of the *Duat*; he guides you straight to the tony, upscale parts of *Amenti*. Like the jackal, he knows the landscape fully.

Similarly, the Egyptians pictured the disembodied human soul, the *Ba*, as a bird. The *Ba* was a bird with a human head; it is the human form in the *Duat*, they said. Also

of the 21 *Arits*, which include the Gatekeeper, Watcher, and Herald at seven stations, all but two have animal or bird heads atop human torsos. It seemed a good idea to construe these *Phramenmas* as pictures of human qualities too. The details of their physical forms were meant as visual metaphors for specific functions of the human form, now being disassembled and displayed. If you could relax enough you'd laugh at the *Duat* as a big fun game of charades.

These fierce-looking figures occupied the eight principal directions so that we had 16 spirit-figures, basically all scary if you didn't keep yourself in check, forming two slightly overlapping octagons. They looked like siblings in an odd way, as if the *Phramenmas* were the crankier, nastier versions of the *Kerimas*, or possibly their consorts, or maybe, American-style, bad cops to their good cops.

"The trick is to not react," offered Tommy. "I realized that after standing here shaking in my non-existent shoes the first time through. I kept thinking I had to do something. Run away from them, fight them, fidget, whistle, anything. Then I realized I did not have to do anything. Non-reaction was the best action. They weren't going to do anything to me—how could they? I didn't have a body anymore, so if they got off on their body dismemberment antics, what did I care?

"If they personified cast-off parts of my generic human constitution, that's nice and so what and see you later. I realized I could watch them and not react. I didn't have to run towards them or flee from them. So I did nothing. It's true, they looked transparent, a bit on the empty side, like they were holograms or projections or something not quite substantial enough to hurt me. Now I understand that is what you're *supposed* to do, observe them neutrally."

I commented at this point that the Egyptian funerary text was always advising the dead person to do something, name the

Doorkeeper, utter an incantation, recognize a guardian, if you wanted to survive and pass forward. The Tibetans didn't bother with any of that; recognize the innate emptiness of what you're seeing, that it is all mind projections and hallucinations based on karmic illusions, and no further action is required. The Egyptian approach was thaumaturgic, a dualism based on magic, propitiation, and rituals, while the Tibetan approach was purely cognitive, epistemological, a global perception of the inherent emptiness and fundamental non-existence of everything you see.

The Egyptians construed it as the gods versus me. The Tibetans said the gods are me, and both of us participate in the illusory phenomena of apparent existence so don't take anything seriously or at face value. And don't waste your money trying to bribe the officials. It's like trying to seduce yourself with offers of chocolate. Funny, and pointless. You're a sure thing already. The Egyptian model was based on dualism, while the Tibetan was solipsistic; for them, the *Bardo* is the demonstration of the rigors of the nondualism Buddhism teaches.

"The quality of your hallucination will depend on your cultural background and cognitive biases," said Blaise, like a museum docent explaining an artist's color technique. "These spirits, the *Kerimas* and *Phramenmas*, have perhaps an essential form, though it will be tied in rigorously with their function. A person passing through here will see them according to his cultural, religious, and iconographic background compounded by his personal karmic baggage, the karmic illusions the Tibetans so love referring to, and rightly so.

"The fears, hurts, emotional wounds, unresolved problems, all of that, contribute to how you create the picture you then see. You have to remember that what you see in here is real but a visual metaphor. This particular function looks *like* this, if you prefer, or perhaps like this instead. They have a book of these. Forget what we look like, the metaphors say; discern the *function* we show.

"Our innate resistance to seeing things step out of the shadows will add to the fearsomeness of the image, just like in dreams where the more you run from a monster, the scarier the figure gets. Our fear and resistance fuel the scary bits. The key to surviving this crazy place is to *see through* all these semblances, to appreciate the fundamental nondualistic emptiness of all visual phenomena.

"Even when we're alive, we have psychic scenarios like this in our space. When we are in the grip of an obsession, an emotional focus, a fear picture, amplified by spirit-beings lurking in our aura or in the crevices of the chakras, and when a kind of sub-personality version of ourselves forms out of this, if you could see this psychically (which is what a trained clairvoyant does see in a reading), you'd realize it is virtually the same as the *Kerima* and *Phramenma* spectacle. The difference is that while alive we stand inside this hallucination, but when we're dead, minus a few hyper-reactive bodies, we see it from the outside, and, laughably, tragically, and regrettably, we do not recognize it. It seems foreign, inimical, usually frightening; we forget we've lived inside it."

"It's like seeing a photograph of yourself taken from behind you," said Tommy. "You don't recognize the back of your own head. Who is this person?"

"People don't realize they are getting a walking tour of the human form when they enter the *Bardo*," said Matthew with enthusiasm. "It's like Isaac Asimov's *Fantastic Voyage*; you're in a spaceship traveling inside the body. Everything you see here, all the fantastic, alluring, and disgusting sights, is part of yourself, organs, bones, sinews, and blood vessels, inside your consciousness. Once you get that, it's not bewildering anymore; in many respects, it is fun. The *Bardo*, properly understood, is an *anatomical* expedition inside your own form."

"It is tricky, though, because most people assume what they see outside them is real, solid, and actual, part of the permanent, credible, daytime world," said Tommy. "You get into this place and everything you see is a hallucination. That's a shocker to the system. You can no longer take what you're seeing for granted; it is most likely generated by your own mental states and emotions. That's two steps a person has to take, both new. First, you created this image. Second, it's not real, only metaphorical, and even the metaphor is an empty one. You know how when it's cold you can see your exhales. The *Bardo* is like that. You're exhaling all this imagery, like whisps of white clouds in front of you, and you get spooked by what you see, forgetting *you* are conducting the magic trick."

"What the *Bardo* is showing you," said Edward, "the disembodied soul, naked consciousness, is that even the human phylogeny, the entire generic container for all humans, is illusory, though a high-level illusion, and from the vantage point of Buddha Mind, everything about it is hallucinatory, including all the conclusions and, sadly, misinterpretations you formed while living inside it."

"They should put up big neon billboards all through the *Bardo* landscape that say, 'Don't worry. None of this is real!'" said Blaise. "That would help the tourists. I mean, the Supreme Being has high expectations of the cognitive capacity of the average dead person trying to stagger through this queer place. Does the Old Man really think people are going to get it? These days people are not trained in the dualistic thaumaturgy of ancient Egypt and their complexities of deity supplication and bribery, nor in the rigorous Advaita-Vedantist nondualism of the Tibetan approach, the absolutism of *Rigpa*, where everything is seen

as aspects of one's Clear Mind, and even all the *Bardo* is a hallucination.

"The Egyptians were genuinely alarmed at the inimical nature of the wardens of the many gates and boundary crossings in the *Duat*. Your best preparation was to enter this land equipped with mental flowcharts and diagrams of all the key players, the magical formulae, spells, and power words you'd need to survive. They pictured the *Duat* as innately hostile to disembodied human consciousness. The Tibetans said it's no more hostile than the persuasive power of your own mind and its incorrigible tendency to spin out hallucinations and karmic illusions. You didn't need any magic words of power to survive it. Just stop believing that all this shit parading before you is real. It has no reality.

"Why fight yourself or cast spells to charm or overpower your own shadow? I don't mean any disrespect to the ancient Egyptians, but you could make the case that the whole Egyptian after-death notion was a vast karmic illusion generated by their magic-based shamanic culture and dualistic notions of self and deity. They overlaid that picture and its expectations on the *Duat*. You have to placate and manage the ambivalent *Duat* deities or you are screwed.

"The Buddhists and Tibetans come along and blow up the entire shamanic fantasy world with this rigorously simple statement: it is all from your mind. The Tibetans said you don't need any magical assistance to make it through the *Bardo*. Just a Clear Mind understanding of the nondualistic nature of the place. Can you see how the Tibetan text is a major upgrade in the *Bardo* epistemology? It takes potential human understanding of this afterdeath realm to a new level.

"The Egyptians say if you don't have the power words, magical formulae, spells, amulets, and names of all the key wardens you need to supplicate, your safety in the *Duat* is not assured.

You will likely be overcome by the hostile *Duat* spirits and never make it to the House of Osiris. You may find yourself reciting any power words you've ever heard, even fragments of them, hoping they'll work. Do you see the implicit sacerdotal elitism in this model, the Underworld privileges of being educated and of the priestly or magical castes? What about the average Egyptian unversed in these arcane protocols? What about the Egyptian chumps who swept the pyramid passageways after the big-shot initiates came through and had their amazing visions? They'd have no hope.

"The Tibetans say the only threat to your safety is to be overcome by your own hostile illusions and to not recognize them as your mind's products. You don't need any power phrases to wake up from that trance, just a brisk slap on the face. You're like a dog dreaming he's chasing a rabbit, his legs twitching. There is no rabbit, no chase, and the body reactions are conditioned simulations. The dog wakes up and wonders, perhaps, where did that rabbit get to? I am sure I was gaining on it. There never was a rabbit except in the dog's imagination.

"Even for the priestly caste and those educated in the *Duat* nomenclature, the Egyptian text gives you the impression of an enormous seating plan you have to know. Titles, positions, passwords, magical spells, sequences, flow charts—it seems unlikely somebody will be able to remember all of this in a deceased state. I mean, there you are, dead, concussed, in shock, and you can't even remember your own name. Forget about the 42 Assessors and all the rest.

"Meanwhile, as we progress through the *Bardo*, I'm gaining a new definition of interiority. When you're alive, if you are at all sensitive, you will have interior thoughts and feelings, reflections on life, existence, mortality, purpose, and consciousness. You are aware of yourself as a consciousness focus. Some days you may even regard your mental contents as

excerpts from *Ulysses*. But here all that is now projected outside you. Your interiority is now your external environment. Our interior of karmic illusions, tendencies, and momentum, the infrastructure of our selfhood, is now disclosed *outside* us.

"People still run away from their karmic content even when it's outside them. When it's inside us, when we're alive, we do our best to be oblivious of it; when it's projected outside us as a bewildering environment, we don't recognize it. Even the most compassionate of celestial beings must find that slightly amusing. I mean, I know they are too polite, too discrete, too British really, to laugh when we can see them, but they probably crack up in the privacy of their clubs. Alive, you don't acknowledge it; dead, you don't recognize it; but all the time *you* are generating it, peopling your interior-exterior world with spirits, chasing after it, in fear or fascination, like puppies running after their own tails.

"What takes the place of your interiority in the *Bardo* is the Buddha Mind which, paradoxically, is a no-self condition, no interior, no exterior, no two things, only the one thing. It's nondualistic, you and the world. *That's* how you assure your safety in the *Duat*; that's how you get to the House of Osiris. *You* are the *Bardo*, and you're empty, pal, so unbelievably devoid of genuine content. The correct orientation of awareness is the key; that gives humans a much better chance than what strikes me as highly unfavorable odds in the Egyptian model.

"As for all these fierce-looking *Herukas* standing around us in circles outside those of the *Kerimas* and *Phramenmas*, they exemplify that correct orientation of awareness we need to marshal and present to the *Bardo* world. They display the ferocity of focused, awakened consciousness against its own karmic illusions. They show us how we must stand in our awareness, glaringly ruthless and aggressively vigilant against our own illusions and hallucinations. You need to become a *Heruka* and confront your own *Bardo* nonsense with it, never forgetting—it is funny—that both are innately void with no permanence.

"This is a personification of your karmic tendencies, and this, and that too. The valence, the scariness, of these animal-headed figures is based on, scripted exactly from, your own identification with those aspects of your consciousness. You don't need to know any names or spells for this: just emulate their stance. They don't say, as the Egyptians thought, bribe us or we'll destroy you, sucker. They say, look pal, if you have even half a brain, copy us, *do this*, and you'll live.

"If you're loose and unperturbed by their supposedly frightful forms, you might even regard these performing *Herukas* as a pack of histrionic drama queens. Or divine vaudeville clowns. They are Wisdom Kings, after all, evincing indivisible bliss and emptiness in a fierce visual package to benefit all sentient beings, to shock us into a sudden recognition of the power of our Clear Mind. Try to picture them as zany characters in a Mel Brooks movie about the *Bardo*."

"We can always count on you for the smart-ass perspective, Blaise," said Philomena. "Though in essence your attitude of whimsy and sarcasm is helpful. The trick is to not fear, be in awe, or terrified in any way by these *Herukas*. When you recognize them for what they are, reflections of your own intellect or consciousness in an activated power stance, that is the door of your liberation.

"Consider *Ratna-Heruka*, as the Tibetans named him. He is a yellow-skinned blood-drinking deity. He has three heads and thus three faces: one is white, one red, one yellow. He is enhaloed in flames. He has four feet, squarely and firmed placed, and six hands. In these hands he holds a gem, trident-staff, a baton, a bell, skull-bowl, another trident. His female consort, called Mother *Ratna-Krotishaurima*, wrapped around him from behind, her right hand clinging to his neck, has a red shell full of blood and she's trying to pour it like a libation into the *Heruka*'s open throat. What a sight. The other *Herukas* offer variations on this basic appearance. They all look scary, engaged in similarly gruesome acts.

"How is this a door to liberation? The *Herukas* are trying to show you consciousness is powerful. Copy this gesture, they say, but without words. Do this, they demonstrate for you. But you wrongly think the gesture indicates their hostile intent towards you. Consciousness is a fierce force, a mighty entity. It has seniority over life itself, represented by the blood. It survives life, meaning bodily death. Living people tend to be so immured in passivity regarding their consciousness. They are schooled in nonaction, in cognitive impotence. They only experience the empirical personality overlay on consciousness but never the naked reality of consciousness, which is more like a surging, titanic ocean.

"They get here and they fail to recognize all these *Herukas* are demonstrating this oceanic might of the consciousness they have lived upon all their life, thinking it more like a mere mill-pond. They never understood that consciousness is powerful. The Ofanim are always demonstrating this power in their varied guises of horse, bird, and elephant. Souls see the *Herukas*, who, at first glance, do look frightening and hell-bent, and they recoil. They see a power, but they don't realize it is *their* power; they see it as external and foreign, arrayed against their self-interest. Instead of embracing it as an innate part of themselves at a deep level, as an ally they may mobilize on their own behalf, they seek any means possible to elude its terrifying grasp, its brute disclosure, and to escape. They fail to understand this titanic ocean generates all those power shapes.

"Here is another problem compounding clear recognition of conditions. People coming into the *Bardo* generally do not realize which body they are in. Unfortunately, when they are alive, few realize they occupy a physical body within a shell of six more subtle bodies, each more celestial than the previous. A lot of people barely register the fact they occupy a physical body when alive.

"They take it so for granted that it becomes virtually invisible to them. Perhaps that is what animal consciousness is like, not being self-aware of your body. They get here and act like it is the usual physical body with its presumptions they are occupying, but it is like driving an imaginary car. The controls don't work the way they're supposed to. After the daytime and nighttime reviews, they have dropped three bodies, physical, etheric, and astral.

"Yet many people, certainly for some time, fail to understand they are not in their physical form any more so their personality is no longer supported by the elemental life of their material form. They are in a body of Light now. The only way to cope with changed conditions is to become more aware. They don't realize the rules are different when you are conducting business in your fourth body. It's a much subtler, ethereal version of your former self. People need to take their bearings in the *Bardo* within the actual consciousness container they now occupy, not the remembered remnant of three they have already dissolved."

"These fierce spirits you speak of are not foreign to the Inuit," said Pipaluk. "We know them as the brothers and sisters of Tapasuma. We are introduced to them in our training. We learn how to work with them and use their powers to help people. Tapasuma's name means 'the Indweller in the Land Above.' She is the goddess who rules over the afterlife, the land

we call *Udlormiut*, Land of Perpetual Daylight. Tapasuma's siblings do not appear as fiercely to us as these *Herukas*. But already we understand their powers are available to us, and we have been trained well and for many years to be strong within before we encounter them. When we finally meet them we are ready to handle their powers and strengths, and we make good use of these powers."

"Pipaluk makes a good point," said Merlin. He had been silent for a long time, probably just following our conversations until the moment seemed ripe. "I suggest you try emulating the *Herukas*. Copy their stance, gesture, and powers."

I did. It was strange and marvelous, completely surprising. Such power. I had never done any martial arts training, but this felt the way that must feel. My body, even though it was a Light body and not my physical form, manifested strength, power, might, and invincibility. Though these moves and postures were all new to me, at the same time they felt uncannily familiar, easy to do. Philomena (the old Philomena, when she was alive) would blush and turn her head but I felt like roaring. My whole body posture seemed to be emitting roars.

Even though I talk here about my body assuming *Heruka* postures, thus postulating a dualism between awareness and body, it was not like that. They were the same. My body was my awareness. They were seamless. My body was my consciousness and that was reconfigured into a *Heruka*. One expressed the other. I wasn't occupying a *Heruka* form; I was that form, identical with it. I felt I belonged in this landscape, this tricky *Bardo*, that I was meant to be here, that my presence here was unquestioned, sanctioned, and, most surprising, *necessary*. It had nothing to do with being dead, which I was not. It had to do with standing in a fundamental, and fundamentally correct, position in myself as a new myself.

I looked around at my expedition mates. They were similarly flexing their flaming forms, exuding power and sharpened awareness in all directions. Amidst the body flexing, flaming haloes around my form, its postures and might, I felt like I was serenely meditating, a credible simulation of the Buddha. I would not have said I felt alive, nor would I say I felt I was dead. I was existent. I was immersed in consciousness, like a sea, and this sea was shaped like a *Dharma* warrior. I appreciate the strangeness of putting it this way, but it felt like I was exactly, precisely, *right here*, in one-pointed, clear, unwavering anchorage in the present moment. It wasn't a point in time or outside of time. It was right here.

"And you didn't have to petition anyone for special formulas. No bribes. No recitations, No supplications." It was Blaise. "You'll get through the gateways as easy as a finger-snap in this manner." He was right, and I took his point. The only tool we need to flourish here is our own consciousness, and we already have it. We brought it with us. We just have to recognize it for what it is: a microcosm of the original powers of Creation, turned on. Then we become our own *Herukas*. I understood why their name suggested royal kings.

We are, and I hope this doesn't sound inflated, kings of the *Bardo*. No, we haven't received some special promotion or elitist privilege. It's the original plan for us. Consciousness, through its power of cognition and recognition, realizes it is king. *Heruka* also connotes one in whom absolute space and primordial wisdom unite. *Heruka* is sometimes translated literally as "blood drinker" which would sound gruesome until you realize it means it has seniority to the blood and thus the passions of the material body and the human personality in it, and how that blood-passion runs through the *skandah* grid employing it like slaves. Its seniority, the wisdom of emptiness

and bliss, consumes (transcends) blood. It can drink the blood, which is a kind of strong poison, and be unaffected by it.

"I drank blood," exclaimed Edward, looking at us, one by one. He looked bewildered and exhilarated. "I always thought that was a nasty item in mythic pictures. Now I understand it. In that *Heruka* posture, I was asserting the autonomy of consciousness over biology, over selfhood, over blood and its demands. Not in a cocky, arrogant manner, but simply by right of hierarchical precedence. Consciousness came first and as it predates biology it is senior to biology's demands and presumptions. Consciousness, formulated as a *Heruka*, a royal king of awareness, drains the blood out of the *skandah* grid—drinks it. No more blood redness of the passions. D. H. Lawrence would be dismayed.

"To drink the blood means consciousness devours the body and its life-force and selfhood essence. It masters it. Directs it. Commands it. *Survives* it. Takes the bite and fangs out of it. Swallows and dissolves its teeth. Absorbs it without any effect on itself. It's like the way in the Vedas Agni's fire devours the offering or sacrifice of the Soma. It burns it up. Anyway, the blood is fake. It's an illusion. It's only the idea of drinking blood. The *Heruka* is consciousness in command of itself and the circumstances of its existence. The *Heruka* drains the cup of blood, as if to say, 'See, it disappears inside my vastness. What *skandahs*?'"

"I liked the bit about having multiple heads," said Tommy. "Very practical. You can see so much more. You don't have a single, fixed view, like we have with just one head. We can see three different things, directions, angles, at once. We are not limited by space and time considerations, by spatial facts. The same with the extra legs. Enhanced mobility, and again, less of a fixed stance. It's a metaphor for expanded cognition, free of biology, space and time factors, all the usual restraints we experience as living humans. It's a great metaphor.

"I had the impression I could move in multiple directions at the same time, as if my body had multiplied itself. All those devices and objects the *Heruka* wields in its six hands are modes for moving awareness, sharpening, focusing, directing it. The *Heruka* shows us that consciousness is innately unlimited and unconditioned. It is the king of space, as the name suggests, and you fill that space with wisdom. More, the *Heruka* is that wisdom-filling space. I felt that."

I was about to ask Matthew if this was at all like his experience with the Thunderbirds at James Bay when I realized he was no longer with us. He was gone. Nobody had seen him leave, and nobody knew where he had gone to.

"Matthew has gone off to resolve some final issues," said Merlin. I noted a tone of solemnity in his voice. "The outcome is not assured, but it is important."

At this point I was wondering, given the initial extreme foreignness of this ambivalent spectacle of *Herukas*, *Kerimas*, and *Phramenmas*, deities surely unknown to most people entering the *Bardo*, how could we make it easier for these people to get their bearings when it was time for these deities to appear? Even the Peaceful Deities, emanations of the finer aspects of the heart chakra, could throw people way out of their comfort and familiarity zone and into a condition of fear, confusion, panic, uncertainty, and cognitive immobility. Again, reality was being disclosed in a ruthlessly straightforward manner. It was naked, and these newly dead souls had never seen reality naked and disclosed like this.

No longer could our daytime preoccupations and the distractions of the sunlit world and of our individual selfhood cover up these fundamental truths. Those layers were the pretty but insubstantial banners and curtains laid over this part. When you enter the *Bardo*, they are stripped away, blown off, shredded, and dissolved, and the primary reality layer they were obscuring is now revealed. All those activities and preoccupations are colored baubles on the water's surface, but below this surges the real current that makes them possible.

It is so easy, I realized, and I was not exempt from this assessment, to take the baubles for the main thing, for reality itself, pouring the tea and hanging the laundry outdoors on the swivel clothes rack, for the basic substance of reality. What a shock to our certainties to get here and find all that has vanished and the substrate that had been there, buried all the time during the tea pouring, is now paramount, that it is the main thing, and, panicked, we do not recognize it at all.

Blaise interrupted my cogitations with an exclamation. "I found Matthew. He's doing battle with the Druj, and losing badly. I think he needs our help."

Matthew had taken Merlin's suggestion to emulate the *Heruka*. He was emulating all right. He had made himself into a *Heruka* 50 feet tall. He was his own special effects department. The three heads were glaring, the four legs spread like a fighter to provide maximum stability and forward thrust, all the tridents, bells, bowls, and batons were enlarged, and it looked like he had thrown accelerant on the flames because they were raging all around his form.

The Druj was even bigger and more formidable. She was hammering Matthew. She didn't have a fixed form. She was shapeshifting through a repertoire of forms. She was a black bear; a mountain with arms; a giant with a club; a demented Thunderbird; Matthew's mother engorged to ogre size; a rabid dog. Nor was her position fixed. She was somehow all around him constantly. Even with his multiple heads and extra legs he couldn't keep up with her presences. She was like a tree with innumerable branches and vines; they were thick, snarling, and sticky, and they stuck to Matthew all over his large form. He had to keep whacking at them, but their stickiness was awful and daunting.

The Druj seemed to be scaled, and these scales flashed pictures at Matthew. I could tell they were biographically relevant, snapshots from his life, and not the happier or more enlightened moments either. Moments of pain, misery, grief. The Old Girl knew how to choose her images. She was adept at negative spin. She was broadcasting voices, like a hundred radios, each with a commercial message disparaging of Matthew, or, contrarily, seeking to inflate his vanity and pride, or to incite his wrath and unfulfilled desires for retribution. She was probing, poking, stabbing him, searching for seeds of unsated vengeance, stones of resentment, unvented spleen, anything dark, angry, nasty, combustible.

She knew how to wind him up. She had an accurate map of all his sore spots. She came at him from all directions at once, pressing on a dozen sensitive areas at the same time, knowing most would produce a reaction that would throw him off. She showed him pictures of his father and grandfather, disapproving of his choices, that he abandoned the sensible world of business for vague mystical pursuits. She showed him girls and women who had trashed him, insulted him. Pictures of boys and men who had surpassed him in physical or mental pursuits. She flashed pictures of intense disappointments, betrayals, and failures of friendships and projects that had grieved him during his life. Each she pushed with fiery fingers until she could see Matthew squirm and grimace.

Except he wasn't squirming or grimacing. He almost was, but he pulled himself back each time. Instead, with each assault from the Druj, he made his *Heruka* vigilance and indomitability stronger. He made himself more empty. He knew if you fight this, you match it and you have already lost. That's basically martial arts logistics. It was as if with each new insult thrown at him, Matthew's entire form was saying calmly but with authority, "Not this. Not this." That meant, I think, I, the being once known as Matthew, am not the sum of that.

This wasn't to deny the facts of his own biography, but to refute their seniority over how he deployed his consciousness. It was like the blood-drinking insight Edward reported. I am senior to the facts and sorrows of my biography. He was standing in the position he'd occupy when he completed the *Bardo*. He was simulating his *Bardo* conquest and thereby actually achieving that victory. They are pages from a magazine that soon I will be finished with and file on the bookshelf or, better, incinerate. His gesture declared: "Look, Druj. Behold: I drink my own blood, this blood of misery, grief, and shame. There is none for you. I consume it all. I convert it to emptiness and bliss. Not a trace of blood remains."

Every time Matthew remained neutral to the forceful presentation of something the Druj expected him to react to it fell like a broken shingle before him. Quite a pile of these biography shingles was building up in front of him. He seemed to be shedding essential aspects of his personality, which, considering where we were, was not a bad idea. The *Bardo* is all about dropping your old self. There were moments in this "battle" in which the Druj seemed like a *Dakini*. Was she acting as a wrathful wisdom-spirit encouraging Matthew to divest, or was she, as we had originally been introduced to her, a no-good lying *Bardo* bitch?

Pardon the rough characterization, but the Druj's ambivalence was excruciatingly intense. It was like watching a professional tennis tournament, the ball kept getting served back over the net, and all you could do was keep moving your head, back and forth, following the zooming ball. She's helpful, she's inimical; she's a wisdom-teacher, she's an exacerbator. Devil or *Dakini*? There were no net-balls, no resolution to this dichotomy. She was one, the other, both.

"Most likely, her guise as an ecstatic *Dakini* is part of her lie package," said Blaise. He had been studying the Druj intently. "I would assume everything she presents, all her guises, have lie energy wrapped up in them as a prime motive."

That makes the Druj even more complex. Now she's a fake *Dakini*. Man!

Blaise must have been anticipating the Druj's next round of appearances. She draped herself in copies of Matthew at all ages of his life, even the ones that haven't happened yet, as an elderly man. The Druj was a totem pole of full-length Matthews, one for each age of his life, dozens of them, and now Matthew was fighting himself, or resisting himself, or not resisting, but in any case, it was himself who now confronted him and he had to maintain the same obdurate nonreactive neutrality to all these nuances, the suffering, complaining, crying, the anger, rage, sadness, disappointment, yearning, all his different faces.

It was a double deception. They were not him in the sense that he had to disidentify himself with his own biography and personality, and they were not him because it was the Druj's magic trick, tarting herself up in these illusory self guises. He had to convert his emotional reactivity to this picture gallery of biographical images into a full-body *Heruka* fierceness of insight.

As if she were merely testing out consumer response to a proposed product, the Druj now changed all this and displayed *Dakinis*, *Herukas*, and angels in front of Matthew, including the Ofanim in their Garuda and Ganesh forms. She was like a garish Christmas tree, and all these high-level spirits were its bright twinkling lights, except they were all turning away from Matthew. You got the impression the heavenly hosts had all suddenly abandoned Matthew, that he had said or done something irretrievably wrong or injudicious and they could not forgive him for that lapse, or, maybe simpler, he had failed a basic test or disappointed them and they could do nothing more for him until he evolved more, and maybe that would take a hundred lives, so forget it, see you later, pal.

It reminded me of a poem written by the Greek poet Constantine Cavafy of Alexandria in 1911 about the god who forsakes Anthony. The empire was over; all fortunes failed; all hopes revealed to be illusions; the city and the deity now abandon Anthony to his mere humanness. It was sad, poignant, frightening in a fundamental sense, the kind of outcome that if you are in collegial attunement with the spiritual world and its players, you dread ever happening. It seems inconceivable that it could, yet if it does, you will be inconsolable for who could recover from this rejection. The Druj was playing this Cavafy celestial abandonment card, seeing if it killed Matthew or at least threw him off stance.

Matthew almost bought the illusion when he saw his dear Thunderbirds turning their backs on him and images of his shamanic cohorts from James Bay walking away from him, dismissing him with hand gestures. It was cold, brutal. It was also a lie. Matthew caught himself just in time and flushed himself neutral.

The Druj was inventive, and she didn't give up easily. Her new approach was to present scary creatures and scenes to Matthew. She covered herself in enormous snakes, lizards, and spiders and towered before Matthew with this. I felt shivers along my spine, which shows you how potentially upsetting and alarming this sight was since I didn't even have my physical spine with me. She showed these creatures, herded by demonic figures, taking over his former home.

She showed them attacking his parents, siblings, and childhood friends.

She created fire elementals, big burning balls of furious flame, burning his house. All his books burned up, his favorite reading chair, the paintings on his walls. His stock certificates, banking records, transaction cards, all incinerated. This new approach failed. Matthew was not bothered. He had left all that already for James Bay; he had already reduced his former life to ashes, so it had no appeal, and the threatened loss and destruction of it was an accomplished fact.

Now she came at him with images of indifference. Scenes that argued nobody cared in the least what he did, whether he survived the *Bardo*, that he went up to James Bay to find himself, met the Thunderbirds, played a role in the Theosophon. He saw all his friends, and their friends, everyone who could possibly have heard of him, even by secondhand rumor, at the beach, lounging in the sun, having picnics, barbecues, cocktail parties, oblivious of him, flagrantly indifferent to his activities and their import. They were enjoying their earnings and privileges from being on the winning side. They didn't care what happened to him, and anyway, who is this Matthew fellow you're on about?

I could see she was starting to get to Matthew. He had sensitive spots on this topic. I saw the emotional logic of her tactic: indifference is the true opposite of love. He registered indifference as a source of pain; it often put him in despair. It was worse than hatred; if you're hated, you still matter to someone, just negatively. But indifference—you could die and they wouldn't care at all. But he had also come to realize his despair and his reaction to indifference were a lie; the minute he touched on this sensitivity, like hot sand, the Druj would jump on him and pound him into the burning grains. But this time she could not do it. He converted into emptiness, wisdom, and bliss, every flicker of a

possibility of reacting to indifference. A *Heruka*, he devoured this indifference like empty air.

The Druj tried one more tactic. She mimicked Matthew behind a steadfast Buddha. She burned up this form, She laughed at him, mocked him. When his form was incinerated, there was nothing but ashes. No soul, no spiritual essence that survived the demise of his incarnational form or his meditation body. She was trying to convince him that without his body he was nothing, and he was a fool to believe his soul would survive his physical demise. It would not. See?

She showed him an image of God as an old man walking away, shrugging his shoulders, raising up his empty hands in that stylized gesture of resignation. She showed all of us walking away from Matthew; even worse, shouting at him, criticizing, denouncing him, accusing him of treachery, betrayal, and perfidy. Even worse (or better, tactically), she showed him his business peers dismissing his interest in spirituality and meditation as useless, wasteful, futile, and stupid, that he was chasing an illusion, trying to hold water in his hands while running.

"She tried all this before and failed magnificently," said Blaise, "when as Mara she tempted the Buddha as he sat under the bodhi tree at Bodh Gaya. She threw everything at him, all the tricks in the book, and then the book itself. She paraded her beautiful, alluring daughters before Gautama, like at a brothel. Tempted? Surely, dear Gautama, one of these women must please you. Failed miserably. She couldn't get the Buddha to budge in his steadfast concentration."

None of it budged Matthew from his set position, which he now amplified with a massive upright sword of Light. It was a *big* sword, easily 50 feet high. First it seemed he was holding this sword, like a valiant, imperturbable knight. Then he seemed to be inside the sword, that it was a column of sharply focused Light that faced all directions at once with its adamant crystalline cutting edge. The inside of this sword roared with a blazing white Light, like a lit furnace. It was a force of consciousness, the sheer lucid power of being completely awake.

The Druj ran pell-mell into this sword. It seemed to slice her into a hundred identical pieces, like the way a delicatessen cheese cutter slices cheese. A hundred identical Drujs stormed Matthew's sword. She wasn't dead; she wasn't really cut into slices either. It only appeared that way. It just gave her more angles of attack; now she had one hundred and they raged at Matthew. Then she added to her forces by manifesting one hundred seething *Herukas*. They ran at Matthew from all sides, furious, intent on his dismemberment. Pictures, images, devices, grids, spirits, leaped outwards from inside Matthew. At first it seemed they were a reserve army now released for the final onslaught, that Matthew had mobilized everything in his arsenal to aid his last-ditch defense.

Then I realized it wasn't that, but psychological content of Matthew dying off. He was freely surrendering more pages from his book of life, his biography. He wasn't fighting the Druj, calling in all his markers from ally spirits. He was rendering himself transparent, one skin cell at a time, to use an analogy. These "skin cells" fell like dried autumn leaves at his feet and dissolved into air. He was purging himself of life and personality content, reducing his target area. Soon there would be nothing left of Matthew for the Druj to assail. He'd be gone.

It was funny, ironic. The Druj had tried to disarm Matthew's certainty by stimulating his susceptibility to indifference. Now he was demonstrating he was the master of indifference. He didn't care that he was losing his biographical self. He was indifferent to this radical divestment of everything that was

himself. He watched it the way you might watch the wind blow dry leaves off a tree.

The Druj would increasingly have less material to work with, and soon there would be only the sword, and that sword would be in her face, and it would cut. It was the sword of *Prajna-paramita*, the focus of bliss and emptiness. I emphasize that Matthew was not actively fighting the Druj; he was holding his own ground, purging himself. The sword wasn't fighting the Druj either. It was a sword of truth, of the correctness and actuality of reality, and that was a cutting blade. He held the sword and it cut the lies, though he never moved the sword. Invincibly and without effort it cut through all bodies of lies and the Druj. If she wasn't careful, it might convert her to bliss and emptiness, ending her long career as the Queen of Darkness, the tempter-adversary of the House of Lies.

Then it was over. They both disappeared as if in a whirlwind. All was still.

"We have the matter of practical recommendations to help people get through this phase of the *Bardo*," said Merlin. He was determined not to comment on what had just happened. He was acting as if it had not happened.

For some reason I had not noticed that a certain change had come over us. I had been raptly following Matthew's engagement with the Druj. Each of us was encased in a brilliant golden pillar surrounded with diamonds like cupped palms. These were the diamond facets in the Ofanim's Rotunda of Light, what we had been calling the Nimitta Cloak. Each of us was thoroughly surrounded by these handlike diamond facets and inside each one, or maybe it's more accurate to say that each one was this, an Ofanim angel was grinning at us.

I have abandoned any expectation that the Ofanim will appear to us with any semblance of solemn angelic spirituality or mystical ecstasy.

That is clearly not their style. That would be akin to expecting the human Blaise to play the straight man in a comedy routine. I guess when you are at their level in the angelic hierarchy, the second angelic order ever created, older than all the rest, there is no need to put on airs or pretense. You clown around all you want. You spin out the delightful image of 40 million grinning ski-slope-nosed Bob Hopes.

Still, it felt wonderful, like wearing the warmest coat imaginable in a fierce snowstorm. The levity and warmth were delightful, but I understood this served an additional purpose. We had been supporting Matthew in his duel. The six of us, inside the golden pillar and the Nimitta Cloak, had been exuding a forcefield of clarity, focus, fondness, amusement, and absolute truth for him. It fortified him in his own rising resolve to not give in to any of the Druj's manifold lies.

The problem remained. How do you get people new to the *Bardo* to regard the sudden dawning of 110 frightful flaming *Herukas* as a good thing? To welcome this alarming presence as a revelation of the powers of consciousness? As something they should embrace, should *want* to? That it was an inner portrait of the condition of their consciousness, the substrate of their personality. Picture you're seeing a generic cosmic form of the human. Out of his heart storm 42 Peaceful Deities; from his throat, another ten; and from his head roil 58 more. All of them enhaloed in flames, with multiple heads and legs, and lots of devices. And then some wiseass tells you this is yourself: lovely, do you like the picture?

Add to this the fact you have never in your life seen anything like this at all. Not in person, God forbid, and not in books, and if you saw anything like this in a movie, it would have been in the context of scaring the pants off you. So when would the average American encounter a *Heruka*? It's not a Buddhist country,

and the population percentage of Buddhists in the U.S. is still quite slim. The Baby Boomers made inroads on this number for a time, but the last time I checked it was only a few million, a tiny per cent of the population. Anyway, it's only in Tibetan Buddhism you get the rich "hallucinations" like this. In Zen they hit you with a stick if you see anything; in other modes, it's about piety and mindfulness, and you don't want a mind full of *Herukas*.

"I think the trick is to get a person to recognize their mind has spun out a plausible metaphorical form representing a certain power of consciousness," said Edward. "Like a cinematic superhero perhaps. America has been populated with those images for years, the protean superhero with all the *siddhi* powers engaged. The superhero with his powers activated is a comic book version of a *Heruka*. Americans can relate to this. Think of yourself, your consciousness, as the invincible superhero, and the evil bad guys you're fighting as your own karmic ignorance. It's just a small shift in emphasis and identification. It might work.

"True, people are not used to doing that, recognizing generic impersonal aspects of themselves such as their own consciousness, and most people are probably not familiar enough with how metaphors are created, especially visual ones, to appreciate the subtlety and power of this process of the mind. Psychologists talk about projections, how we impose our own pictures or notions on other people, but this goes further. It's more generic. These 'projections' personify objective and generic functions of human consciousness, ones that are true for all people. People tend to not understand metaphors. They see only a poster on a brick wall. They don't go through the poster and wall to the truth they represent. They don't see through the metaphors but take them literally."

"You know, it gets worse when you turn the page of the *Bardo Thödol* and see what's coming next," said Blaise. "You get the Four Female Doorkeepers, and these horror-girls have heads of a tiger, sow, lion, and serpent. Each has her own color and animal head and emerges from one of the cardinal directions. Then you get another Las Vegas chorus line of 28 goddesses, also with animal, insect, or reptilian heads, and various frightful carry-on implements.

"How about this one: from the West, you better expect the Greenish-Black Vulture-Headed Eater-Goddess with a baton accompanied by the Red Horse-Headed Delight Goddess holding a dismembered human torso. Also appearing with these awful goddesses are more female figures with heads of a yellow dog, white eagle, red hoopoe, and green stag, with urns, arrows, *dorjes*, and clubs. Merlin, you must have had a grand time coming up with these crazy images.

"The queer thing is you don't have to do anything about any of this. In effect, you get the best results if you ignore them. Give them a glance, then move on. Nice special effects, boys; I couldn't have done better myself, which of course belies the basic fact that you created all these thoughtforms out of your own consciousness. Think Halloween, and you just opened the door to see your own children dressed up as ghouls, vampires, and hideous Underworld spirits. Who's afraid of them, for you dressed them in these costumes yourself. Give them a treat, compliment them on their scary outfits, and gently wave them away.

"The text says if you sink into fear and trembling, you're done for, but if you can remain steady and say, 'Nice job, horror-girls and fright-boys, but I have to get back to my emptiness meditations,' then it's a straight shot through the rest of the *Bardo*. We have to keep in mind that this is the Tibetan picture, and some of the imagery will be adjusted when translated into an American psyche. I suspect the American psyche might lean towards superheroes gone demented.

"Just as we realized the Egyptians were seeing their own style of imaging and projecting their notions of petition, bribery, and supplication with magical power formulas to survive the encounter with the unyielding gods, so were the Tibetans putting their relativistic, culture-specific, *Buddhist* pictures on the afterlife, their propensity to elaborate the complete family trees of all deities, the mandalas of their complex connections, and all details of their appearance, like a fashion review television show discussing the gowns and suits the celebrities wore at the Oscars. The products of these images are not necessarily relevant for all humans. I mean, really, Merlin, do you expect a newly dead American from Elizabeth, New Jersey, to see (and understand) the Dark-Brown Yak-Headed *Rakshasa* Goddess with *dorje* and skull coming out of the East? Very unlikely.

"There's too much. Too many actors. Too many new dance numbers to watch. It fatigues consciousness, but maybe that is the point: to get wandering human consciousness to say, 'Enough of this bizarre diversity; it's all bright illusions.' It's like that scene in the Marx Brothers' movie where about a hundred people are crammed into a tiny room on board an ocean-liner; then they all tumble out into the corridor in a big pile of bodies. That's your *Bardo Thödol*. You're more likely to get an edgy version of Margaret Dumont in baritone drag.

"The text says, don't surrender to awe and terror. Regard all these as your own thoughtforms. Your mind is a carnival and today is Mardi Gras. Your progression through the *Bardo* is a Fat Tuesday parade of flamboyant, debauched horrors. Masks, music, trumpet blasts, gaudy colors, purples, golds, blues, huge leering puppets and surreal effigies, shrieks, revelry, drums, cymbals, songs, misrule, comedic demonism—Mardi Gras as a farcical version of the *Bardo*, or an accurate one? Basically, the Tibetan text's advice is glance once, then ignore, even when some of the tarts swell up to 18 times a human's height and others are the size of Mount Meru, grinning and drooling. It's all histrionics and over the top.

"But in my younger days, when I pretended to be a Zen student, we called these *makyo*. We were taught to be wary of them. A ghost or devil's cave, an objective-world devil, Mara-made illusion, a *makyo* is a mind-spawned delusion that results when you cling to an experience or turn an image or situation into a conceptual residence or nest. The meditation monitor would whack you with the Zen paddle to shock you out of that illusory ghost cave. We need *Bardo* monitors with Zen paddles! The *Bardo* is an astral Broadway packed with neon-lit *makyo*.

"Wait. I have another idea, possibly the best, an absolute corker, I'm sure. We need a *Reader's Digest* version of the *Bardo*, stripped lean and abridged for those newly dead souls who don't want the complexity and vast *dramatis personae* of the complete *Bardo* to deal with, who do not want, cannot handle, have no interest in, the full disclosure of the human phylogeny. Theirs would be the shopper's express lane: with ten items or less go straight to a womb-door."

Blaise was funny and wry as usual, but I could see he was a bit burdened with the complexity of detail and the abundance (or excess) of *Bardo* players. We all were; Blaise just acted out our bewilderment. There is too much going on. Why should the afterlife experience be so complicated and over-populated? And what was the point of having it be so arcane and convoluted, so "peopled" with strange, unrecognized spirits with animal heads and *dorjes* so the average person would completely fail to make any sense of it and wander lost until rebirth?

It was at this point we were starting to realize the Tibetan picture was not definitive. It was richly, even exuberantly, detailed with iconographic imagery relevant to the rigors and perceptual diversity of the Tibetan consciousness, but maybe it was not an absolutely objective, generic map of the *Bardo* landscape. Maybe, like Hollywood producers, we had to think in terms of a modern remake. All cultures do not perceive angels, celestial spirits with big wings; some, like the Buddhist and Hindu countries, see Bodhisattvas with body-sized tiered haloes. The *Bardo* images are relative and adjustable, mutable according to your culture. Perhaps the Tibetan renditions of *Herukas* are just an illustrator's suggestions.

"Maybe it's simpler than a matter of divergent cultural images," said Edward. "The essential facts a person needs to hear when they get here are: first, everything you see is an aspect of yourself projected outward and you are walking in a self-projected landscape with the same mental mechanism as dream creation which you have done every night while you lived; and second, it comes from a level of the human below your personality and sunlit daytime self, from a generic substrate of you as a human then influenced, shaped, or distorted by your karma. Specifically, *how* these multiple deities appear to you is of secondary importance. Christians might see horned, leering demons instead of wrathful deities. That's the imagery they were surrounded with during their alive time.

"These multiple deities appear because they must appear. They are as necessary to the full disclosure of the *Bardo* as is finding 206 bones inside the human body. The bones, the whole skeletal system, are inside each of us whether we like it or not, even if we are aware of it or not, or seek to discover it or not. They are *facts*. They express, they dramatize, function and structure: this is how you're made, they declare to the astonished human witness. We bet you didn't know that. If the *Herukas* would just smirk, everyone would immediately relax."

I noted later that of this stage of the *Bardo* experience, called the *Chönyid*, which is the second of three stages, the Tibetan text states all the shapes the disembodied soul witnesses are emanations of *Dharma-Raja*, the Lord of Death, even though, at the same time, they are all manifestations of one's own mind.

I guess it's a matter of sharing the authorship credit, the *Bardo* as co-written by Yama and you. You'll get *Dharma-Raja*, your co-writer, in three sizes: ridiculously vast in size, equaling the Heavens; hugely vast, the size of Mount Meru, which is no small peak, some 80,000 miles tall; and the 'smallest' size, still pretty damn vast, which is 18 times the size of the average human, 100 feet tall. Plus you get gnashing teeth, glassy eyes, big gaping belly, and the formidable fellow stands there in all three sizes with his karmic record-board, a document listing all *your* karmic offenses, opportunities, tendencies, and, shortfalls, and he says menacingly, nastily, challengingly: What are you going to do about it, pal?

Then the text gives some good if super-arcane advice: don't worry about all this. The multiple terrifying forms of the Lord of Death are merely casting emanations from your own mind or consciousness and are not made of any matter than can hurt you and do not exist in reality. (Who are you kidding: they certainly exist in whatever psychotic reality you call *all this*.) Any fear or terror you experience is self-generated. These forms are void and empty, as are you. Voidness cannot injure voidness. If they are void, why bother seeing them? (Maybe so, but if they're void, why can't they be invisible too? That's much easier on the nerves. Who do I see today about making this change?)

"That's exactly what I asked when I got here," said Tommy. "Then I figured out the whole thing is a test. One big raucous test with special effects. They're trying to see if they can get you, get you to react, to fall for the act. No, my images didn't look like the descriptions in the Tibetan book. But many of them looked demonic, more like psychotic dancing gargoyles. They all looked powerful. I thought I was watching an animation of an illustrated anatomy book. I know that sounds strange, but I mean these *Bardo* spirits were acting out the processes of my former body, like digestion, circulation, breathing, perception. This is what this physiological or mental function looks like as a pure process."

"They are going to appear," said Merlin. "They are part of the landscape. They are aspects, body details, you might say, of *Dharma-Raja*, the Truth-King. He is also our Green Knight, as the Celts saw him, and Yima, for the Persians, and Yama, as the Hindus called him. The first human to die and make it through. Yama is green-skinned, rides a black buffalo, and conducts the newly dead to the Home of Heroes and the realm of the ancestors, called *Pitrs*, the Holy Fathers. This is an important category of *Bardo* spirits we haven't investigated yet.

"The *Pitrs* are the divine first fathers of each of the peoples, the ethnos-soul groups, the 72 divisions of the soul of Adam. They are called heroes because they successfully made it through the *Bardo* and now dwell happily in *Pitr-Loka*, their own zone within Yama's heavenly city, *Yama-Loka*. They copied Yama's example, so you have, for example, the first Armenian to make it through the death process, the first Frenchman, the first Irish, and on through the full list."

We were inside a circular hall with a high domed ceiling and whose circumference was lined with dozens of golden thrones. I counted 72. On each sat a regal crowned human figure, though these humans were much larger than ordinary life; they radiated Light everywhere like a gesture of benevolence. Individually, they seemed similar, like a large family of brothers and sisters, but their distinction was expressed in the design, colors, and details of their robes.

Merlin pointed out a few of these Holy Fathers. "There is Hayk, the *Pitr* from Armenia, originally known as Hayastan. Hayk was their patriarch, a descendant of Noah, and he first established Armenia in the vicinity of Mount Ararat. Over there is Hu-Gadarn, *Pitr* for Wales, the chieftain whom myth says led his people, the *Cymry*, from the island of Hav to the land known as Wales. There is Ugyek, the *Pitr* of Hungary or *Magyar Kiralyság*, father of Almos, the first High Grand Prince of the Magyars and of the House of Arpad.

"See Abraham, *Avrohon Ovinu*, 'Abraham, Our Father,' patriarch of the Jews. There is Deucalion, with his wife-consort, Pyrrha, who after the Flood repopulated Greece, the Land of the Hellenes, from Mount Parnassus which overlooks Delphi. Nearby is Lech, the first ruler of the Lechites in a country called Lechia, or Poland; he founded Lechia at a settlement now called Gniezno, meaning 'eagle nest', because he found a magnificent white eagle on top of an oak tree guarding its nest. He established his stronghold and cult center there at the eagle nest and adopted the white eagle as the emblem of his people."

"When he was narrating the Theosophon events, Blaise said Krakus was the ethnos-holder for Poland," said Edward. "Now you're saying it was Lech."

"In a sense both are," replied Merlin. "Krakus is the founder of Krak Town, or Kraków, the original capital of Poland. He earned that title by activating the resident dragon, *Smok Wawelski*. That dragon is the national dragon of Poland, situated at and guarding the national umbilicus of Poland. The name Krak probably derives from *krakula*, which means 'judge's staff,' or from *krak*, which means 'oak tree' and suggests genealogy and lineages, and both suggest ancestry, origin, and the one who presides, father-like, over all that.

"Except Krak is more like the *Chakravarta* for Poland, the original culture hero who used the *Sudarsana* discus to prepare the geomantic landscape for its people, like Bharata of Great Bharata, or ancient India. The white eagle is an expression of Poland's egregore, the way that ethnos chose to personify its essence. Our Polish soul is like a white eagle, the Lechians said. In this respect, the supposedly human figure Lech may be interchangeable with the egregore personification of the white eagle; both represent the Lechian-Polish essence."

We greeted Lech, or Krak, seated regally on his golden throne. On his robe were emblems of the white eagle, and he sat upright holding a judge's staff. I realized the *Pitr* of a people, or ethnos, would have originally passed through the *Bardo* and experienced a divestment of personality and subconscious content specific to the way, in this case, the Polish soul was constituted, its characteristic nuances, how it clothes itself and the world, the way it construes the spiritual world and its players, the names and qualities it assigns to it—the Polish mythos. The experience of Hayk for the Armenians would have been specific for the Armenian soul, its symbols, character, land, personality, and gender formations.

"Each of these *Pitrs* represents the perfection of an ethnos and a standard for the journey and divestment experience of the *Bardo* for people of that ethnos," said Merlin. "The first one through sets the tone for all who follow. Just as Abraham was buried at the Cave of Machpelah in the old city of Hebron in Israel, thereby providing an access point for those intrepid adventurers wishing to enter the *Bardo* through this side-door rather than through an Underworld portal, each *Pitr* has a place of prime anchorage and access in their landscape.

"Each *Pitr* emulates the original example of Yama journeying through the *Bardo*. Yama did it for all humanity, for the human phylogeny, then the *Pitrs* do it for the individual ethnos-holders or soul-groups, like Lech for the Lechians or Poles. Then they remain here in this hall, on call for consultations from their people. They may guide souls on the *Pitryana*, the Path of the *Pitrs*, the route through the *Bardo* which leads to the Moon, which in mythic code means the Hall of Isis, the Great Mother of the Silver Light, the goal of the *Bardo* journey. Moon means Place of the Great Silver Mother when used in initiation code. It is not the physical satellite of the Earth, but a prime condition of unitive consciousness."

While the *Pitr* or primary Father occupied a throne in the circle of *Pitrs* inside the hall, I saw that behind each throne there opened up a duplicate of this hall with more regal figures on thrones. These must be subsidiary *Pitrs* for a given country as the Vedas and Hindu texts inform us there are two classes of *Pitrs*. The primary group are the progenitors, the begetters, the first expressions of the ethnos, thus the noble ancestors of a given people; these are called the *Devah pitarah*, or divine *Pitrs*. Then there are the *Manusyah pitarah*, who are deceased humans who have made significant spiritual advancements, who also are worthy to represent the perfection of the specific ethnos or people.

I walked into the hall of the Lechians that opened behind Lech's throne.

10

It was in the Lechian hall that we found the answer for how to help people at this stage of the *Bardo* recognize the innate "voidness" of those *Herukas*.

It was as if all of Poland and its history was displayed before us in concentric tiers. You had the divine *Pitrs* representing the perfection of permanent, essential aspects of the Polish soul character as designed by God, then ranks of humans who had mastered nuances of these character aspects and stood up for them here. If you were Polish you had a standing invitation to visit this Lechian hall. Frankly, it was a welcome break from that onslaught of ambivalent *Herukas*. That was a parade that went on too long, with too many ornate, complex floats to see—floats that shout and threaten you with swords.

"You could think of all this as a massive Group Soul conclave," said Blaise. "They are joined by affiliation with the vibrational character of the Polish soul. When people are alive, they tend to think of this in terms of nationalism and patriotism, of fidelity to their country of birth and residence, but it's different here. In *Pitr-loka* you get the nationalism veneer stripped away like old paint and get down to the essential quality, in this case, of being Polish.

"The Polish ethnos is one among the 72, and these are all in service of the one Adam. Think of Adam as a name for the original human design, the phylogeny picture. Then this one unified figure is given 72 variations, each an ethnos. To complete the Adam, you have to complete the 72 nuances; you perfect the *Polish*. It's a condition in Human or Adamic consciousness. As are the French or Jewish or Hungarian, and the rest on the list of Group Souls. If you're Polish, you come here and have revealed to you those epiphanous, pivotal moments in your life when something genuinely Polish vibrates in your essence, seizes your body, emotions, mind, and shakes it. When the *Polish* in you awakens.

"Here's an example. Agnes von Kurowsky was an American Red Cross nurse, age 26, from Virginia, newly arrived in Italy in 1918 to nurse wounded soldiers from the First World War. She was destined to be Ernest Hemingway's nurse when he arrived incapacitated at her hospital. An Italian crowd was applauding an American major, giving him medals, calling out praise for the U.S. She said, 'It is certainly warranted to make one prouder than ever of being American.' You see: there it is, the welling up of the ethnos soul in a person. She felt proud to be a member of an abstraction, this American ethnos Soul Group. Its transpersonal reality swelled up in her; she felt the ethnos-spirit behind herself.

"When a quality or gesture rises up from this ethnos substrate and dawns in you, then you are anchored in the consciousness of your ancestors, your progenitors. You are with the national *Pitr*—Uncle Sam, I suppose, in her case. It's as if you grew longer legs and instead of standing on the current surface of the Earth, you sink your legs down several levels and anchor them in the *Pitr*.

"Ultimately, you have to divest yourself of this ancestor layer, as it too possesses innate voidness, but for a time your contact with it can be educational. You have the possibility of standing with Krakus and Lech and all your Polish ancestors across time at the umbilicus of Poland, which is at Wawel Hill in Kraków, the primary anchor point for the Polish soul on the Earth's surface.

"It's not out of pride or national vanity or any other such personalized feelings that might grip you were you still alive and Polish. This is more neutral: it's energetic. It's about anchoring a specific vibration, the Polish, for the benefit of the planet, and for contributing to the awakening of the Polish soul as a living Light imprint. Your psyche and the national landscape conjoin in this ethnos."

This living Light imprint, as Blaise called it, was like an animated museum at full throttle. Nothing dead and dry about it. The place was full of *Polska* life. All the imagery, costumes, dances, songs, folklore beliefs and characters, the mythic heroes, the devils and angels of Polish custom, the artists like Chopin and Górecki whose music expressed the Polish soul, the works of the writers, poets, historians, polemicists, and essayists of Poland, were all alive around us. The colors, foods, the way men and women dressed, the fears of vampires, devils, witches, the flaming castles, the dragon of Wawel Hill—the myriad ways in which the different nuances of the Polish soul got expressed in animated imagery were displayed livingly like a Polish-flavored rendition of Disneyland.

It showed the way the Poles saw the world, how they interpreted its energies and rendered these as visual metaphors and god-forms. It was if the Polish soul, personified as a person,

said, "Let me tell you about myself," and ten thousand creative voices sprang into work and expression telling us that. The same happened with the other ethnos-holders. These uprising voices included cameo appearances by national poets, artists, and musicians, creative people like Henrik Ibsen of Norway and Sándor Petöfi of Hungary, among many others, souls whose artistic creations expressed and validated their national ethnos, whose works spoke for the soul of their country, gave it tone and character, entitling them to be called national poets or artists as if they channeled the *Pitr*.

Blaise said we have to let go of our identification with the national essence, but I remembered a few lines from Virginia Woolf's *Mrs. Dalloway*. A female character named Lady Bruton, a wealthy aristocratic Londoner in the 1920s, was so identified with England, this "dear, dear land," that it was in her blood, wrote Woolf, so intensely that one could not imagine when she died she would roam any part of the Earth (presumably the astral-plane version) or be parted from any land where the Union Jack was not still flying. "To be not English even among the dead—no, no! Impossible!" It was not hard, I thought, to picture the difficulties, maybe agonies, she would undergo at the stage when she had to free herself from the *Pitr* identification, told to drop her identification with Grand Britannia and regain her essential voidness. She would likely stay stuck.

I asked Merlin if this was an official stop in the *Bardo* journey. I did not remember any reference to it or hint of the Hall of the *Pitrs* in the *Bardo Thödol*.

"It is to a degree optional, depending on a person's interests," said Merlin. "You're right: the Tibetan text doesn't mention it but the Egyptian funerary protocols allude to it in a sideways manner. There you have reference to the 42 Assessors of *Amenti*, who are presented as observers of the Weighing of the Heart ritual.

They are present not to judge but to assure fairness in the ritual. The Egyptians say the number 42 pertains to the number of *nomes* or administrative districts in Upper and Lower Egypt, and there is your connection.

"That is a reference to a functional and therefore geomantic aspect of the national landscape, and that brings in the national chakra template of 81 centers, the dragon, and the country's umbilicus and egregore—the archives of its soul. That is the geomantic manifestation of the Egyptian ethnos or national soul. All humans born in Egypt, Egyptians, participate in that soul template. Let's say the Egyptians maintained their national ethnos comprised 42 landscape nodes. When that is in the picture then you have the Hall of the *Pitrs* and First Fathers.

"The soul in the *Bardo* comes here and starts divesting itself of its national soul, where its contents cling to its Light body, and some of that content will be painful, national miseries, guilt, grievances, and obsessions, and that in turn helps the national soul on the outside through its egregore out in the geomantic terrain, to purge itself to some degree of these same difficult contents. It helps. In the *Bardo* your ethnos identification has no relevance or traction. You let it go. It is just another layer of conditioning and illusion overlaid upon your awareness.

"In Blaise's example of Agnes von Kurowsky, she will have to shed her American patriotism once she reaches this stage because it is ultimately an illusory layer. What wells up in her with the hortatory face of Uncle Sam must be dropped. She will have to see the voidness of that swelling with pride. It is not her. It has to do with agreements a soul makes to have its character shaped and influenced by the egregore and group agreements of a nation, an ethnos. It is only a relative level of self definition, and it is one that has to be let go of here.

"You cannot realistically drop these agreements while you are alive. You would be an outcast among your own countryfolk and they might in some manner turn on you. It's like you, Edward, Frederick, and Tommy—you can't take the *American* out of you while you're alive, no matter what other country you might live in. But when you're dead and in the *Bardo*, then you can drop the *American* from your soul. It is a karmic illusion too, though at a more sophisticated level than others. It's like a layer of clothing glued to your form, and so much taken for granted while you live you barely notice it or ever see it from the outside.

"On the one hand, the Earth is held together by this fraternity of Group Souls anchored through an ethnos and umbilicus in national landscapes. But this level of transpersonal identity can also become restrictive and rigid, halting the expansion of self-identity at the national level and keeping it from being global. A global sense of human identity, what you might call a Gaian self, is needed today, especially with the major Light grid changes underway. A merely national identity, where you say, proudly, I am an American, like Agnes von Kurowsky, or I will forever be English, like Woolf's Lady Bruton, is now too limiting.

"The Light grid changes make it imperative that people now say 'I am a Gaian.' For that to happen, the domain of the *Pitrs* must be purged and karmic illusions dropped. It's similar to landscape *devas* that work a much trafficked landscape, such as national parks. Periodically, they need to be spray-cleaned of all the human content that gets spewed and dumped upon them by unconscious people. It's like thick, semi-congealed tar with hundreds of postcards embedded in it coating their angelic form. The postcards are emotionally-charged images that stream off the people walking by. It makes the *deva* irritable, unable to work effectively.

Its ability to transmit the higher Light to the landscape is impaired."

Merlin looked at Edward, Tommy, and myself, and said, "Shall we try it?"

We nodded agreement. I couldn't see any reason not to even if I had no idea what would be asked of me. I had gotten the hang of divestment by now.

"We have some interesting problems regarding which *Pitr* Hall we use. You three are American and have soul agreements with the American ethnos, except the American ethnos is a new creation, compounded of all the others. So for Tommy, you'll need to first visit the American then the Danish *Pitr* Hall, for your name *Hevringer*, and thus your ancestry, has Danish and Norse roots. Edward *Burbage* and Frederick *Atkinson*, both clearly old, long-established English names, will need to visit the English *Pitr* Hall and do some divesting on behalf of Grand Britannia, England's feminine egregore, and John Bull, the jolly, stout, boorish personification of the English character. You stand on American ground now, but that ground, unless you were an indigenous native, is shallow, newly formed, and for you rests on the larger tectonic plate of the British soul."

I entered the Hall of the American *Pitr*. I understood at once what Merlin meant. It was a confusing spectacle, at least at first until I could differentiate the layers. The American landscape was first inhabited by what we now call Native Americans, the original indigenous inhabitants. Their egregore was the golden eagle, and their First Father was what I would call a chief with many names. Its umbilicus and national dragon were in northeastern Pennsylvania. Overlaid on this was a gallimaufry of ethnos qualities from all the other nations of the world.

Impressions of all the First Fathers of these nations were present in this hall, and they were struggling to generate a new, coherent composite of these parts. The egregore was

still the golden eagle, chief among predatory birds, but other more recent cultural icons were seeking purchase on the "skin" of this eagle, like Uncle Sam and Paul Bunyan, colorful posters half-stuck on to the feathered surface of the mighty eagle, their bearded or giant faces looming out.

I will not say my experience in the American *Pitr* Hall was fun. It was chastening, sobering. The visual impression was one of overlaying tapestries, outermost the American, innermost that of the original indigenous peoples. In either case, though, the qualities of the egregore were constant. The eagle is a predatory bird who flies high above the landscape searching for eatable prey. There is a masterly aggressive presumption in its behavior as king of the birds. I felt I was a wall that had been papered over with many layers of placards.

The outer layers had images suggestive of imperialist presumption, manifest destiny, divine right, bullying, war, conflict, aggression, world domination, rampant material acquisitiveness, perpetual war as the national presumption as unquestioned as the deity itself. I felt those assumptions within me, though it felt like a foreign implant, something ancestral, in a sense, genetic, that we deserved this, the world we surveyed from on high was ours for the taking, we were entitled to it, the world needed us to lead and save it from itself. I felt the residues of the wars America had fought (mostly started), a few justified and most without justification, and the vast number of deaths produced by these acts of aggression. From the slow-motion genocide of Native Americans through Korea, Vietnam, Iraq, Afghanistan, Syria, all the others—this bird was a predator.

I saw where the eagle had discerned opportunities, saw clearly, and when it had been deceived because shapes afoot in the landscape seen from high up can be misinterpreted: you mistake rocks for rabbits. I felt where this eagle was anchored in me, as if to an imprinted metallic plate; white threads from my soul clutched this plate, wrapped around it like tendrils seeking life-force, and conducted to my awareness an unquestioned sense of the rightness of its deeds.

This was shocking to me. My body shivered when I realized the grim implications. At this level of soul agreements between myself and the American ethnos I was complicit and in collusion with its national identity and its actions. At this subliminal level of agreements, I believed with certainty in its rightness. If you threatened me, I would immediately bomb you, declare war against you. If I protested a current war or international policy, I was inciting a civil war within my own psyche, both laughable and tragic, as its outcome would please nobody.

I said my soul seemed "wired" into a metallic plate. That was an imprecise impression. It was not a metal exactly, but something hard, cold, and obdurate, metallic in essence, and there was "printing" on it, the inscription of the American soul agreements. When you incarnate into a nation, you make agreements with its egregore; it's like joining a club or fraternity where you have to abide by its regulations. You agree to be resonant with the definitions and boundaries of its national ethnos. You derive your identity and meaning from it. It establishes your body's right to inhabit this particular geomantic landscape and, potentially, to use its Light temple template to be connected to the cosmos.

I was reaching for this imprinted metallic plate when Merlin stopped me. "Not until you're dead. This must remain in place until your time arrives. With Tommy, it is different. He is no longer bound by his American agreements."

My attention shifted to Tommy. He was unraveling the metallic plate, taking out the white tendrils extruded from his soul into this imprinted disk. It was like undoing a ball of string or straightening out a tangled rope.

Pieces of paper with writing on them flew out of these coils and tendrils and dissolved in the air as if burned by an invisible flame. They were agreements without life and thus no longer binding. He looked gleeful. "I'm no longer an American! I took the American out of me, finally. I am America-free Tommy Hevringer."

Layers of pictures fell off Tommy like autumn leaves falling from trees or tattoos sliding off him as flakes of dead skin. Images that had subliminally shaped a layer of his identity were chipping off. It was as if a miniature version of everything in the American *Pitr* Hall was collapsing off Tommy, like heat tiles from a rocket as it entered the high atmosphere. Thin translucent posters of Uncle Sam, Paul Bunyan, the eagle itself, lay at his feet. Jingoism, boosterism, Babbitry, blind patriotism, Puritanism, materialism, consumerism, indulgence, secrecy, surveillance, celebrity adoration, generosity, equal opportunities, entrepreneurial permission and validation, rampant *un*self-consciousness: the whole U.S. culture was sliding off him as if its glue had utterly dissolved.

"Lovely," Tommy exclaimed. "That is definitely a load off my shoulders, and everywhere else on my phantom anatomy. Should I succumb to the allures of a womb-door again, I will try a different country. I will explore a new ethnos. Why not. I am no longer bound to repeat my incarnations as an American. Now let's go kick out the Danes from my soul while I'm in a proper divesting mood."

I saw the effect on the figures in the hall of the American *Pitr* from this. It would be unrealistic to expect these secondary *Pitrs* to drop their American pictures. They need them to keep broadcasting the American soul quality to Americans. But as if these many layers of American identity expressed as pictures were a robe around the First Father and his associates in the American hall, this robe was now more loosely fitted around the figure. You could see an airspace between the figure and the picture content, a place of emptiness and separation.

The potential effect on embodied Americans would be the possibility, if individuals chose to take it up and enlarge it within their own awareness, that, yes, they are Americans by birth and soul agreements, but no, they are not absolutely Americans, only relatively, and, for that matter, only for a while. That airspace between *Pitr* and picture robe would allow people to see they are more than that identification, and when they entered the *Bardo* it would be easier to drop those agreements and pictures from their Light form, like Tommy did. Nationalism, patriotism, and holidays, like our Fourth of July, a strong glue to secure the connection between soul and ethnos-identification layer. There is a reciprocal sharing of images too, as alive Americans send back their lived images of Americanness and the *Pitrs* broadcast their generic assigned images.

With the loosening of this glue, that would further widen the airspace in the American *Pitr* with its content, and it would continue to build over time through this reciprocal interaction. The national robe would hang loosely upon the soul. Changes in the *Bardo* would feed back into the living world, and cognitive progress there among informed, sensitive, alive humans would help out here. People would be more likely to say, yes, I am an American, but I am a Gaian too. I laughed. Tough times ahead for politicians expecting docile citizens manipulated subconsciously every time you show them the Uncle Sam face card.

Tommy went off to the Hall of the Danish *Pitr* to drop more content. The rest of us, Edward, myself, Pipaluk, and Blaise, shrugged our shoulders. We can't do anything about this now on account we were still alive and bound by these ethnos agreements, but at least we understood how to drop this content when the

time arrived and why it was a good idea. Even so, this layer felt looser on me now that I saw the kind of identity grid it imposed over my awareness.

The way Tommy divested himself of all this American identity content reminded me, in an odd way perhaps, of how a hazardous materials team would subject a person contaminated with some toxic substance to a rigorous fire-hose spray-down on his naked body to cleanse the skin of all traces of the substance. I don't mean the American content, or that of any ethnos, is toxic. Just about every country has shown the world its gnarly shadow side and taken drooling bites out of the world. My image refers to the thoroughness of this HazMat cleansing, leaving you naked (without a body to define you) and purified of toxins. When we caught up with Matthew, we'd have to fill him in on the procedures.

Merlin led us to another hall. "This is the human form hall," he said. "To get clear in the *Bardo* you have to drop the human form, the phylogenetic mold. It is another layer of identity, another consciousness-shaping Light grid, imposed on you before incarnation as a human, and it tends to cover up a lot of Light."

I was unfamiliar with what Merlin was talking about, but Blaise wasn't.

"That's right out of Castaneda," he said with enthusiasm. "Another bit of old Castanedan weirdness finally cleared up. He talked about losing the human form. Don Juan said it was part of the training of the Toltec initiate to do that. He said that to a Toltec seer, or what we'd call a competent psychic, the human looks like a luminous egg. That is like an external cocoon, a luminous shell, but inside it you'll see a core of pale yellow concentric circles, like constricting hoops. That layer of hoops needs to go, and the way you do that is to lose the human form.

"Then the pure original Light, unconditioned by the human form and which lies inside that barrel-like layer of constricting hoops, can be released, and you may revert to the primordial state of awareness you had before you became human. Castaneda was never one for the subtleties of Buddhist metaphysics, but I suspect his primordial state of original luminosity is the Tibetan's Clear Mind."

This hall was constructed differently than the Hall of the *Pitrs*. It was a single large oval space, perhaps hundreds of feet tall and wide—it was hard to tell. I find that space and size over here are fluid and mutable and tend to respond to our expectations, shrinking down or enlarging radically as we expect. This oval hall was occupied by a single figure, a generic, non-gendered human form. It was nobody specific, not a man or a woman, of no discernible time period. Anthropologists would be confounded if they carbon-dated its skull. It would register zero on the timescale, the once-and-future empty human form.

This figure was probably what Qabalists conceive of as the Adam Qadmon, God's idea of perfect existence expressed here as a human form, as Original Man, First Man. This figure's form had 81 circles of Light within it, corresponding to the chakras. It was encased in seven concentric shells of Light; these would be Castaneda's yellow concentric hoops of Light, corresponding to the seven auric layers. There were six echoes of this pattern, lying either behind the figure in the forefront or surrounding it like ever more subtle shells of a faint human form. These correspond to the six additional Light bodies beyond the physical. That gave us 567 concentric circles, if you counted the spherical chakras in all these bodies.

If you added the seven auric layers for each body that gave you 49 more circles, putting the total at 616. Too bad it wasn't 613. That is the number of Jewish commandments or *Mitzvot*, 365 negative actions to avoid and 248 positive actions to take, and corresponding to 248 limbs and 365 tendons of the archetypal human form. It's not clear if the Qabalists mean this in a literal, anatomical sense, in which case it would seem to be medically inaccurate, but as a metaphor for the full complement of the original human form, it is a useful, evocative picture, and maybe it is another legitimate way of modelling the generic human form. It's likely that to reconstitute this *Adam Qadmon* means to drop the human form. You drop it because it is completed, raised back into its original Light and perfected.

The Qabalist model expresses an eschatology. Take the good actions, avoid the negative ones, and you help raise all the fallen sparks of Light into an awakened condition and reconstitute the original body of Man to its perfected Light state. The human phylogenetic form can be both an infrastructure of enlightenment and a rigid prison for consciousness, locking it into a finite, conditioned state. It's like a larger, more comprehensive national ethnos grid. You put it on like a suit, a wrap-around Light grid imposing its reality upon you. What we had before us was an intermediate state, the human phylogenetic mold standing between incarnated humans and the desirable goal of Perfected Man.

I saw before me what must be the original blueprint for the human. The generic mold, with all the bells and whistles and knobs on, as P. G. Wodehouse would say. But I doubt he ever saw anything like this. I certainly had not. All the chakras and layers of the aura were in pristine, untainted condition, karma-free. The figure was equipped with consciousness but it had not settled into selfhood. It was like seeing the robe of the American ethnos, the American *Pitr* imprint, but at a higher, more sophisticated, or perhaps rarefied level. Still, it was like a robe.

It was a conditioning, defining layer you put on over naked primordial consciousness.

It might be, as the Qabalists say, God's idea of perfect existence expressed as a human, but if we were Pleiadians that form would look different to match us. That means somewhere in the *Bardo* there must be a Hall of the Phylogenies where you would see the *Pitrs* of the different phylogenies God had created. Our Human phylogeny would be only one among many other forms.

As long as we were on the Earth, only the human phylogeny would be relevant to us. But I suppose if you wanted to leave incarnate existence for good, you would need to divest yourself of those many phylogenetic identity robes before you did. Otherwise, those non-Earth identities would be a heavy weight on your pure awareness, pulling you down to matter again like a gravity well.

Again, Tommy was the only one in our expedition team who could test out this next level of divestment. Philomena had already done it years ago. The rest of us would have to wait. This gives anthropocentrism a new meaning. How can you realize how *human*-filtered all your cognition and interpretations are until you have the chance to drop that identifying layer and step free of it?

That's just at the generic, pure level of the form. When you step into the human phylogeny, you get a subliminal download of the human life experiences of the billions of souls who have done the human form incarnation before. It automatically, if subliminally, aligns you with Earth's Albion and all he knows. It's like a foggy, dreamlike atmosphere of cries and whispers, explanations and exhortations. We hardly ever notice it, but it gives us a baseline sympathy for our fellow humans. But here in the hall of the human phylogeny it was explicit, hearable, seeable, and we were going to watch Tommy as he stepped out of this confining grid of the human form like throwing off an old tattered bathrobe.

At first the human phylogenetic figure looked like an upright human, filled with spheres of Light and framed by multiple, subtler copies of himself. Then it became spherical, like a vast round globe packed with circles of Light. There was a suggestion of forefront and background, but it was mostly, in a spatial sense, holographic, all in the foreground, one globe seen through another.

I remember C.G. Jung quoting a medieval philosopher who said the soul is round, that on the spiritual level the human figure is a *rotundum*, a sphere. Whatever the shape, this figure is a template to code human consciousness. It is a programming grid, a set of master instructions, go-codes for human incarnation. The soul, wishing to enter the human incarnational stream (or circus), passes through this template; the soul, its body dead and now in the *Bardo* and seeking to liberate itself from the stickiness of the human experience, must exit this form.

I glanced at Tommy and laughed. He was encased in a deep-sea diving suit. This must be how he fits inside the Light template of the human form. Bulbous helmet, thick, padded torso covering, and fat arms inside thick gloves. He was ready to descend into the murky depths of being a human on Earth. Now the trick was to help him get out of this heavy, cumbersome equipment. A large transparent vase appeared before him, about the same height as Tommy. It was filled with rolled-up scrolls, probably several hundreds of them. They started unrolling and revealing their written contents to him. They were his contracts and agreements, the paperwork of a major business deal, it seemed. Tommy was reviewing each one, nodding his head, making a check on the form.

I looked to Merlin for explanation. "These are the agreements 'Tommy' as a soul prior to human incarnation made with the human form to enter humanity. Think of this as an entry visa with many pages of stipulations and requirements. The agreements explain how the human form works, its range of activities, the expectations for behavior the human form imposes on the recipient of this gift. You sign all these agreements the way you would notate a complex warranty on a complicated and expensive piece of equipment. You know where you stand.

"Here's the inventory on possible feeling states, how the emotions work, their range, limitations, and liabilities, and the frequency modulations to adjust them. Here's how the chakras interact with them and the exalted cognitive states and visionary inputs they are capable of generating; here's the operating handbook on the internal organs, the body systems, the bones, breathing, and digestion. Here's a detailed operator's description on how the soul interacts with the body. Here is the topographic map showing you the correlations between the human form and solar, galactic, and cosmic levels of organization. Don't ever say you never got a handbook on how to run this human form. I know everybody does, but the fact is they did receive a user's handbook. They just forgot."

As Tommy examined each document, it highlighted a functional or anatomical aspect in the human-form figure in which he now appeared to be embedded. When he finished with one document, he nodded and tossed it back into the vase. The tossed document looked more translucent after he did that, as if it had lost some binding force or life animation. It looked moribund, dried-up.

The vase was now filled and the word "Finished" appeared across it, written in fire. The letters of the word enlarged and encircled the vase and started to burn it. Soon the vase and all its paper documents were aflame in a big whoosh of fire. Then there was nothing, just a few floating specks of ash and a bit of grey smoke. The human-form figure that encased

Tommy started to unsnap itself; clasps came undone, screws popped out, clips and fasteners undid themselves. Tommy tumbled out, but he only looked like Tommy for a moment.

He was a ball of luminous Light. He did not look like Tommy or like a human. It was a radiant sphere of hyper-awareness, seeing everywhere without manifest eyes, yet you felt it was studded with eyes and they were all looking around. It was "Tommy" before he ever became a human, before he ever entered the form. Not just before he became a teenager with Type I diabetes living in Oregon, but as a soul surveying possible planets and life-forms to see where he'd go next.

I noted that just before Tommy was ejected from the human form it swelled up enormously with Light and seemed to burn vigorously around all its spheres. It was as if in the last moments before his divestment, his awareness expanded to occupy the complete form so he could leave it in full cognition of its nature. It's like when you move out of a house you've lived in for many years, you revisit all the empty rooms, pat the door joists perhaps, listen to your feet pad across the bare floors, recall what happened in each of the rooms, then you step outside, close the door for good, and drive away to your new house.

Then Tommy was back with us again in what looked like his familiar form. He was laughing, like a kid would laugh who had just had a terrific roller-coaster ride at a fun park. "That was intense," he said. "Don't be fooled by this form I'm wearing. I just put on a replica of my former human form to be polite. I can be anything I want now. I can enter any incarnational stream that I fancy. My possibilities feel greatly expanded at this moment. Maybe I'll stay a ball of Light and not plunge into anything for a while. But I'll keep myself seeable for you guys for the purpose of our expedition and any jokes you might wish to make."

It looked like Tommy, though his form seemed a bit translucent. It reminded me of seeing somebody after a two-week yoga and fasting retreat. It was still the same person essentially, but he looked shockingly more healthy. The rest of us were not allowed to step out of the human form container yet, but I could feel its grip on my consciousness start to loosen, that it bound me a bit less. I say the rest of us, but as I looked around I saw Pipaluk and Philomena were gone. I hadn't seen them depart, nor had they told us where they were going. Then I heard Philomena speaking in my mind: "Matthew's human form is under attack. We are here with him helping him resist these attacks by Druj agents." Then she added an odd comment: "These Druj agents look like Harpies."

The scholar in me pulled out the appropriate reference books in my mind. The name Harpy means "snatcher," and Harpies were said to be ugly, winged bird-women (bird bodies but human female heads and upper torsos) who were angels or at least agents of punishment and torture on behalf of the Erinyes or Furies, the Greek female revenge spirits who punish perpetrators of matricide, most famous among their list of "most wanted" being the Atreidian bad-boy, Orestes. According to the official press releases from Greek mythology, the Harpies are vicious, cruel, violent, ruthless, and all-around unmerciful spirits.

They wreck feasts, spoil or steal the human food, and carry off the "evil-doers" to some nasty place in Tartarus, which is the *Bardo* on a bad day, beset with cranky *Herukas* who aren't pretending to be angry. Some scholars say the Harpies originally were destructive wind-spirits. There are either two or three Harpies, all sisters. Hesiod named Aello ("storm swift") and Ocypete ("fleet wing"), then Virgil added a third, Celaeno ("the dark"), and Homer alluded to yet another called Podarge ("fleet foot"). Allegedly, the ill-mannered, vengeful sisters lived in a cave in the Strophades Islands, west of Olympia in the Ionian Sea; occasionally, they prophecy dire fates for humans, but mostly they are infamous for wrecking the lavish lunch-spread of the Argonauts. The Harpies sound like a girl-band of wrathful *Herukas* gone rogue and misanthropic.

Matthew was encased and being attacked by dozens of these Harpies. It was like a swarm of large, vicious mosquitoes biting him from all directions, pecking at every last impurity, every black spot, they could find in his space. They were like hungry blackbirds jabbing the soil for seeds and grubs to eat. The Harpies were pulling out from Matthew's body what looked like images, photographs perhaps, colored pictures attached to pieces of flannel in him.

Each of these images emitted a sound, and some sounded like cries, screams, protests, imprecations, sobs, as if each was a self-contained drama from his life. Matthew seemed to be bleeding where these pictures were jabbed out of him, but it couldn't be blood in a literal sense since this was not his physical body. I realized what I had at first taken for dark blood was more like a toxic black oil. Each picture had been embedded in a pool of this fetid liquid, congealed into a colloid almost like a horrid flannel, now oozing out, and probably indicating old, unresolved, dark emotions. Matthew's karmic body was the lunch-feast for these carrion-feeding Harpies. They were gorging themselves.

I had expected to find Philomena and Pipaluk fighting off the Harpies, but they weren't. They were standing completely still, each holding a sword of Light. These swords were as big as pillars, and the two women held them upright in front of them. They did not seem to be doing anything with these swords, certainly not brandishing them, cutting with them. Yet the swords were emitting a crystalline field of Light and power all around Matthew. That Light was instantly incinerating the pictures that the Harpies pecked out of him.

The swords, though I couldn't figure out the mechanism for this, were stimulating Matthew's form to divest even more of these fetid flannel pictures. The sword-light seemed to flush the pictures to the surface of his body so the Harpies could peck them out. That meant they were *assisting* the Harpies. That conclusion startled me at first, then I reversed everything and thought that the Harpies and the two women were working together towards a benevolent goal.

The outcome, as bizarre as it initially seemed, would in the end benefit Matthew. Either the Greeks had been extremely subtle or they completely got it backwards. The Harpies were spoiling the lunch-feast of Matthew only to the degree he was trying to chronically consume the negativity embodied in these images, to "make a meal" of his own accrued negativity and misery. The Harpies were despoiling that food, pecking it off the table so Matthew could not eat it.

Matthew did not seem to be suffering, certainly not what you'd expect if any of this were taking place in the physical world on his material living body. Matthew seemed to be enjoying this, no matter how odd that sounds. I could see that on the one hand it was a disturbing, unsettling experience to have these flecks of images pecked out of his form and to continuously exude this black oil; but Matthew seemed to derive some pleasure from this and almost seemed happy it was happening and that the pecking was no more physically painful than if somebody pinched his skin here and there to squeeze out a bee stinger.

Only as this process was taking place did Matthew realize that his form was riddled, altogether perforated, by thousands of such pain-inducing stingers. The Harpies were like oxpeckers, birds that peck lice and ticks out of an elephant's skin and live in a symbiotic relationship with these huge animals. The reader should realize that I am struggling for suitable metaphors to express this.

I could see how the Tibetan sages might have described the Harpies as Wrathful Deities with bowls of blood, fanged teeth, and overall a nasty agenda, as uncouth, loutish girls, not the kind you'd consider inviting back for another lunch at the mansion. As a Harpy extracted an oil-wrapped image and as this image emitted its emotional valence, the scream or anguished sob, the Harpy held it up before Matthew to examine. I understood the intent was to show him they had extracted yet another toxic seed from his karmic space, like a dentist showing you the bad tooth he has just pulled out of your jaw. You could easily misconstrue this tableau and conclude the Harpies were wicked feminine demonic monsters torturing the crucified Matthew with no end of scary images.

You might think they are like gargoyles gone psychotic, quite demented, enjoying this horrific spectacle, gorging themselves on Matthew's form. But that would be wrong. The Harpies were actually *helping* Matthew get free of his karma. Look, here is yet another black seed of potential karmic illusion we have plucked from out of your incarnational form, they were saying. It will no longer sicken you with illusion and the sufferings of delusory selfhood. Each of these has defined and colored your selfhood, but none are true. You are free of it now.

When they said "true" I think they meant that here in the *Bardo* where you are far more naked regarding the nature of reality and your true identity as a soul, their reality is revealed to be relative and fairly trivial compared to absolute reality. Here they are a hindrance to your achieving identification with the Clear Light; you'll have to drop them anyway, at some point, so why not now with our help? The Harpies were completely accustomed to examining such fetid material. It didn't bother them in the least; it didn't affect their breathing or their attention.

I would have expected Matthew's form to have diminished a little from all this pecking and divestment of content, that he might be hunched over and weak. But instead his form was enlarging, as if filling with Light, making new flesh. I know it's not "flesh" but something substantive was being added to him. He was expanding his form from the inside, inflating with the pressure of Light. As the black flecks of painful emotional moments got extracted from him, there was more room for Light, which I suppose must mean for the truth of his soul.

I can't see anyone making a persuasive case for a disadvantage to that outcome. He was expanding, and he was becoming more translucent, even transparent in places, as if his Light form, which had resembled the rest of us with its human semblance, was becoming see-through in sections, as if made of the purest crystalline substance. Parts of his body had become like clear crystal.

The Harpies were done with their pecking. They stood back from him. Actually, they held themselves motionless in the airspace all around him, forming an oval of Harpies, their wings flexed behind them as if in the backstroke of flying. They seemed to be studying their handiwork, liking it. They didn't look demonic now; I won't go so far as to say they were beautiful, but I sensed their valence was shifting towards the angelic as their work was finished. Were they perhaps *Dakinis* with multiple personalities, like the three faces of Eve? *Dakinis* on a Saturday-morning job assignment, rough work ahead? Or was that fierceness merely their work face put on to put them in the mood?

Now they emitted a keening wail, all of them together, like an infernal chorus. The keening sound itself was a force like a sword, and this was cleaving through Mathew's form, except this cleaving, rather than injuring him or cutting him up into sections, was fortifying him, causing him to brighten considerably. The keening sword, if I may merge the two metaphorical images, was creating a vertical ribbed effect in Matthew, as if he was now made of hundreds of swords, as if his Light form was composed of these many upright sharp swords, their blades facing out, so that his form now had a carapace of hundreds of swords. But this carapace was as thin and sheer as a silken robe. It was both indomitably fierce and mighty looking, yet terrifically thin and subtle. Again, I was up against something I had never seen before, trying to describe it.

This next part was far stranger than anything that had preceded it. We were able to walk inside Matthew's sword-framed form as if it were a temple. It looked like a large open column of crystalline Light. Matthew had turned his body into a Light temple, and we were walking around inside it. It was sheer and empty, but brilliantly lit, meditative and focused.

In some odd manner Matthew seemed to be beaming at us from all the walls. His ecstatic expression, his spiritual mood of exaltation, emanated from the walls. Clearly, he had been liberated from a heavy layer of karmic impediments by the Harpies and he was now enjoying the benefits, offering them up to us. Still, it was surpassingly odd for me to observe an expedition colleague who was now a Light temple, us standing inside and admiring it.

Then Matthew started speaking to us. His voice came out of the walls. "That was a strange experience, for sure, but it had its wonderful aspects too. The Harpies pecked out of me every moment in my life when I felt black, negative, or sour, when I carried a grouch, felt irritable, petulant, despairing, pessimistic, critical, judgemental, or angry at one thing or another. Each left a residue, like an illustrated black seed that emitted a baleful tone and odor.

"In a sense I had a duplicate body inside me made of all these disgruntled life moments, and the Harpies prodded out every black cell that composed this body. I never realized how much negativity, how much spiritual darkness, I carried. A thousand, maybe ten thousand, inputs comprised this black, cranky, grouch body. The Harpies worked with unsurpassed diligence in pecking out every last picture. They were consummately neutral and focused in doing this."

I heard a whooshing sound then saw what looked like a flock of golden birds fly out all at once from Matthew's pillared body. They weren't birds. They were angels. They hovered just outside the boundary of his Light pillar the way hummingbirds remain stationary in the air before a delicious-looking flower. There were hundreds of these angel-birds, and they looked identical. Then another flock of angels flew out of Matthew; these were silver with green flecks, and they hovered stationary again, as if getting a last look at their now former residence. Then a third band of angels departed Matthew. These were purple with lilac striations. Again, there were many identical copies of these.

I turned to Blaise. He knew about angels. I was hoping he would explain.

"This is the bright side of the same divestment process the Harpies did," he said. "Matthew is dumping all the parts that comprised him, dark and light. While we are alive, walking around in bodies demanding espresso, the angel families are resident in us, in all humans, as indigenous to our form as bones. When we drop the body and enter the *Bardo*, the angels depart our form; now they are outside us. You're watching them depart Matthew, one family at a time.

"There is an aspect to the human, a functional level, that is the angelic domain. A body made of the various angelic orders, those crucial to sustaining the human. Some work through the chakras, since they are microcosms of Heaven domains; others, like the Elohim, are present as our phylogenetic god-parents, and the Blaises, as you know, are on hand as our umbilical link to everything and to fortify all the latent powers of consciousness we possess. Their presence takes the form of the Blazing Star, the pinprick of Light within us, accessed just above the navel and capable of expanding into the Rotunda of Light, their six-pillared pavilion-intermediary for us for meetings and transport."

I had seen some angels during my travels with Blaise, but here in the *Bardo* everything appeared more vivid, startlingly lucid, as clear as if you were seeing something on the first day of its creation. I suppose that's what angels are. Examples of a pure Creation that never experienced entropy, no diminution of the original force of consciousness and its absolute purity, the virtue of God. My point is the atmosphere around Matthew was now suffused with the sheer force of the purity of these angels, their form, colors, and spiritual emanations. You felt it was the first day of the Creation and God had just thought up the angels.

I'm not sure you could see these various families with such clarity on Earth. Conceive that you are a flower designer. You design a new flower, then it appears before you in sparkling, animated aliveness. Make the flowers angels. That's the sense of surprise and wonder and freshness I'm trying to suggest. Along with that you get the pure execution of the angelic family's function; in the case of the Ofanim, it is their umbilical linkage to everything. I felt fully linked. You felt the function of an angelic family was like a pattern of Light in space, a grid of Light, an alive *process* of consciousness being performed right before you.

"It's nice to finally have something fly out of you that's not a karmic illusion and a product of your fevered mental processes, don't you think, Matthew," said Blaise. "That's actually going to be real at the end of the day."

Despite his characteristic flippancy, I got his point. The angelic layer of the generic human was not a product of an individual's accrued karma. It was not illusory, at least not in that sense. It's true that one day, far in the future, the Supreme Being would inhale the entire Creation and all the angelic orders back into Himself and lay down for a nap. So the angels did not have an absolute existence. But they did not get sullied or karmically tainted during their residence inside the human form. Here's a paradox: while we are alive in our human bodies walking the Earth we could correctly say these angelic orders in us are part of us, mind-products, the way the Tibetan text describes the *Herukas*.

When we are divested of our bodies and transiting the *Bardo*, they are not of us. We do not have to recognize them as illusory manifestations of aspects of ourselves as we do with the *Herukas* and even the *Dhyani* Buddhas. You could say they were on loan to us as necessary consciousness aids for our incarnation. I was beginning to suspect some of these *Herukas* might be indigenous angels, that where Westerners saw translucent winged spirits Tibetans saw *Dharma* warriors.

"Hey Blaise, pal," replied Matthew, his voice sounding in a hundred directions. "Did I ever tell you that you too are a karmic illusion spun by my disturbed mental processes and projected outside me as a grim hallucination?"

"I get that a lot," he replied, as if walking away, his voice growing faint. "I just turn a deaf ear to all audience criticisms and carpings, like water off a duck."

We were back with the chorus line of *Herukas* and their dramatic images. I finally had a notion of a practical suggestion to offer Merlin about some changes.

The problem, as I understood it, was how to brief humans while alive that when they got to this stage of the *Bardo* they would be presented with dozens of scary, bewildering *Herukas*, all representing functions and powers of consciousness, and all they had to do to survive the encounter and not panic and precipitately rush for the nearest womb-door before they'd properly considered their options was to recognize these frightful spirits as projections of their own mental processes. There you are, newly dead, confronted by 110 monster spirit-forms, flaunting bowls of blood and swords and unfamiliar, pernicious objects at you. It's not like these poor souls have pocket editions of the *Bardo Thödol* they can reach for and like a tourist looking up a word in Armenian, get a briefing on the spirits. Nor can they write key reminder words on their palms.

The challenge at this stage is easier than with the *Dhyani* Buddhas. When you encounter each of these five formidable Buddha figures, you are expected to understand they represent the perfected, transparent, enlightened form of a *skandah*, and you are invited to copy their example and enter the emptiness. You are expected to rise to the occasion and take an active role in the process. But with the array of *Herukas*, you don't have to do anything; just don't panic and run. Hold steady; recognize the 110 scary spirits are personifications of processes that comprise *your* human form; they will not *do* anything to you other than show you, through visual metaphors, the true nature of this human component.

What could they do anyway? You don't have a body that can be ripped apart. You are in a form of Light, so the most they can do is scare you witless, if you allow that, their sudden apparitional arising before you being the prime factor in that fright. If you regard them as over-wrought, exaggerated, puffed-up, histrionic *Bardo* buffoons, like an editor examining hyperbolic prose, you will disarm through amusement your mind's penchant to demonize them. If you feel yourself getting stuck in some issue or emotion, emulate the *Heruka* and do a number on yourself. Run about the place jumping and shouting at yourself.

"If everybody read Rudolf Steiner before they died, they'd have it made," said Blaise. "He explains in meticulous detail how the human form is made. Alas, the old boy is not exactly a page-turner; never reads like Agatha Christie."

"What *do* they think their human body is, how it got here, and why?" said Edward. "They take it for granted, and studiously avoid asking the question. It leads to disturbing places in awareness and many unanswered questions. They treat it like a car; as long as it works, fine; no need to pop the hood and look at the works. Just a lot of complicated machinery we don't need to know about. We are created beings, just like an automobile is a manufactured device for moving bodies. Humans are created forms for moving consciousness, focusing attention.

"The design is generic, the human form already worked out, although our karma can adjust certain balances and symmetries in our copy of this human form. Nobody tells us that virtually the whole cosmos contributed to our generic form-making, that, as that Gnostic text tells us, 365 angels each contributed an organ or bone, and that, as Steiner explained, the angelic and archangelic worlds participate in all our life processes, that our body is an *alive* version of those cosmic processes and that when we die and walk the *Bardo* it all comes out of us.

"What is *ours* is what we *make* of this gift of consciousness with free will. What we do with it, which unfortunately generally means the karmic illusions we start piling up as we proceed through life so when we get here it's a big mess. Living people generally have no practical mental model of how they were built. So when they enter the *Bardo* and they get taken apart, one layer at a time, they have no context for understanding the necessity and naturalness of the process. Instead, it is an unmitigated, unrelieved, terrifying nightmare, a horror show. It's like, with cars, we assume they just magically, suddenly appeared fully built. Now, countering that, we get the slow-motion tour of the car-making factory and we are shown, despite our lack of interest, fully every stage of its manufacture.

"Conditions in the physical world, from education to medicine, science to religion, emphasize the purely and exclusively materialistic aspect of the human form. As Steiner would say, the world has gone immedicably Ahrimanic. The whole spiritual world has been crammed into a merely physical concept of reality, and that is treated as a composite of mechanistic and biochemical forces and actions and consciousness is only a marginally relevant epiphenomenon of finite brain chemical processes, lacking all potency or efficacy upon matter."

I had it. We can't force people to change their awareness. That is coercive, no matter how well-intentioned and no different than black magic. We have to change the conditions that shape their interpretations of reality or shut them down. We would go to the source, to Ahriman, *Angra Mainyu*, the Destructive Spirit, the Druj, the Chief of Lies, the chief enemy of humanity, and change the prevailing interpretive model that baleful spirit imposes on alive humans. It is destructive because it kills our spiritual understanding of the human form. It inspires a false model, a mechanistic, dead and deadening one, of machinery.

Merlin nodded his head in agreement. "Good. Now we may go to her."

At the time I didn't realize that in fact we were to confront the Antichrist. Well, again, as it turns out. I suspect most people don't realize that Ahriman, the Druj, and the Antichrist are the same spirit. Throw in Satan the Adversary as well. They are differing names for one spirit. The one that opposes, confounds clear human understanding of its own nature. The one who is the chief and perennial adversary of human cognitive freedom. Oh yes: let us not forget the clever disinformation campaign by which the Druj has convinced Western religious consciousness that Lucifer in fact is the Antichrist, Satan, and generally the pain-in-the-ass, bad-boy, evil adversary of human life. The Druj has us persecuting an innocent "man" while the genuinely guilty party goes scot-free. It is a well-executed, successful tactic that pays her enormous dividends.

I wasn't prepared for what we saw. No matter how much Rudolf Steiner you might read, you're not going to be ready to behold a spectacle of this magnitude. We were back in the zone that held the generic human form, the phylogenetic prototype for all human incarnations, the root form model. It appeared again as a complex series of lit-up spinning spheres within spheres. But now a massive black winged shape was draped over this form in a manner that I can only describe as untroubled and languorous, as if the Druj was a 1940s vamp.

If she were dressed in red, I'd say she was a look-alike for the Scarlet Woman, famous in Christian apocalyptic literature for being the awful Whore of Babylon and the Mother of Abominations, not exactly a flattering entry in one's résumé. The Druj was the ultimate *femme fatale*, the original prototype, the consummate feminine form of the adversary, the top-level compliment to the female gender. Why did the Persians portray the Druj as a female demon?

Because male consciousness at some time realized his feminine counterpart, the female pole of consciousness, was superior in force and power and antecedent as well, being a progeny of the Great Mother of all forms. The Great Mother is the generator of forms, but the Druj is the confuser of forms, and the scariest form the Druj could assume was female, like a demonic mother. The scary demonic form of the Devil is only for those who need special effects. The Druj's more effective guise was to appear humanlike, like this steamy Siren.

The Druj was draped all over the human form, but there were hundreds of copies of her, like seeing one form in a hall of mirrors. Christianity schools one in assuming the Antichrist will be the most horrific spirit you could ever imagine, but a far more scary, and effectively scary, spirit of opposition would be the Druj.

She does not look scary. She is beautiful, seductive, alluring, louche, persuasive. That, surely, is the superior approach to being a demonic adversary to humanity. To look desirable, appealing, as if you are humanity's absolute best friend, and, when appropriate, a smoking hot young female companion. That is a familiar motif in fairy tale literature, the witch, hag, crone, or demonic female spirit takes the appearance of a beautiful, desirable young female figure and bewitches all the idiot men who can't see past the charms to the evil truth. The designated human bonehead, usually a guy, falls completely for this glamour and is imperiled in the webs of deceit and general stickiness of this feral spirit, then wakes up one morning to the shocking discovery the tart is really a hag.

I laughed. For a moment the scene looked like a hundred mermaids or perhaps Sirens draped languidly over a glistening big rock by the sea's edge. As Sirens they called out alluringly to passers-by to come join them on the big rock. Was that me, or was that the artful suggestion of the Druj that I saw it this way?

Now I saw the multiple copies of the Druj draped over the human form. The Druj through her many bodies was pushing on the form, squeezing it like inexorable water pressure at depth, compacting it, densifying it, and she was sinking her hands into the human form. Her hands had become vines, like arteries, and they were infiltrating the substance of the human form, threading it through with dark conduits of her essence. These veins squeezed the form from inside. This may sound odd, but the Druj was compressing what first looked like an expanded loaf of bread, full of air pockets and stretched wheat fibers down to a dense stone, obdurate, packed, no room inside it for anything else.

With no room inside this compressed form for anything, it was dark. That was the point of the Druj's fierce compression of the human form. Keep out the Light. Suppress insights into the innate, bright, spiritual nature of this form. All the Druj copies meanwhile were smiling, like blondes selling Ford convertibles. Pretty faces, enticing gestures, effective glamours, keeping all attention on them. Reality is all and only about the surface, these glamorous faces were suggesting. Never mind where the faces come from or why the rock is so hard and impenetrable. Enjoy the glitter. The Druj had so densified this human form, made it so much like the hardest of rocks, that the spirit and Light had been driven into the tiniest cracks in the rock's dense matter and could not be seen.

Given all this, I understood why it was hard for living people to contemplate the mystery, spiritual origin, angelic role in, and purpose of their own human form. Whatever *Herukas* personifying forces and whatever organs, bones, and sinews, or 613 angel-bestowed components of the human there were, it was unlikely a person would be able to discern them amidst this compression. That was their consciousness, intended by God to dilate to the size of the universe, that had been so compressed, squeezed down to black-hole condition.

These were still immutable realities, truths about the human form, but they were, seemingly, buried under the tectonic pressure of the multiple, veining Drujs. Human consciousness had been Ahrimanized. Steiner was right. He said we were moving into the era of Ahriman when spirit was compacted into matter. But I say "seemingly" because I now saw all this was an illusion and easily penetrated. Easily, that is, if you were not encumbered and entranced by being in a physical body. Incarnation in a human body was like taking a narcotic while crouching inside a deep cavern with no elbow room. You felt the walls fiercely squeezing you from all sides as you happily hallucinated. Soon you forgot you were in a cramped body inside a dark cave as you enjoyed the exciting movie.

We understood the problem now, and saw its mechanism, but how were we to make a practical improvement in this? Merlin gestured for us to get on top of the human form, above the languorous Drujs. "The form needs more Light," he said. "Show it Christ Light. Infiltrate the density with some oxygen."

I wasn't sure what he meant at first until I saw Philomena doing it. She looked like a blur of diamond white Light and fire spinning rapidly, a blazing Light inside the suggestion of a golden chalice. Christ Light in the Grail! That was something we could do. I had learned how to do that from Blaise during the Theosophon. Each of us made our steps to enter the octahedral form of our inner heart chakras, place of the Holy Grail and the Christ Light. I still haven't gotten over the paradox of the fact you ignite this Christ Light by becoming oblivious of it, entering the complete emptiness by erasing the *skandahs*. You turn on the Christ Light by turning your self off. Not I but the Christ in me indeed.

That didn't stop me from doing it, and in moments I had disappeared myself. The five of us stood on top of the human form, amidst the many Drujs, following awareness into the empty core of awareness, while outwardly our forms blazed with the same diamond white fire I saw coming out of Philomena. It was like drilling through dense rock with irresistible, resolute diamond drills. The rock-dense human form started to expand as it took on oxygen, a metaphor for the incoming Christ Light. It was re-animating the human form.

Periodically, I reversed my attention and sneaked a look outward to see what was happening. We seemed to have "drilled" down to the core of this form, and our Light bodies had expanded to occupy more of the interior space. We were like spinning rotary drills, and the rotating, spirally-placed blades kept enlarging, and more Light streamed out of them everywhere as we kept disappearing ourselves. The more we vanished, the stronger became the Light.

The Druj did not like what we were doing. It threw her off her game. In many respects it unseated her. While she was compressing the human form, multiple earthquakes within this form were shaking the surface where she lay, and she had to grapple to maintain her foothold. She was now reacting, not leading, which meant we had the upper hand for a while in resuscitating the human form. As more Light entered the interior space of the human form, all incarnated humans had access to this upgrade in the resting state of their consciousness. They now had potential access to the riches of self-perception.

Just as we had created air pockets now filled with Light in this complex but densified form, so in each human were there now "air pockets" of free attention that they might deploy to raise vital questions whose answers would be useful. They would have sufficient "air space"

between themselves and the form they occupied to consider the nature of this form that up until now they had been practically oblivious to, so embedded in its density that they couldn't see it. Now it was possible (we could see it ourselves in the master human form) that embodied people could start seeing some of the indigenous spiritual population within their own bodies, the angels, *Herukas*, and various supportive deities of Light that comprised their form, held it together, made it function and be alive.

Fortified with the implicit bliss of the Christ Light, which might percolate into daytime awareness as only a scent of faraway happiness, like a planned vacation perhaps, they would register the presence of these indwelling deities as benign. That was the key, to recognize the benevolence and good intentions of their presence within them; that was something they could carry forward into the *Bardo* so when they were presented with the naked reality of these spirits, they would already have a context for them, however slim and provisional. Still, it could get them through the otherwise tumultuous *Bardo* recognition phase. They would also cultivate the notion that the human form was designed, that this design was benign and intelligently conceived to emphasize consciousness.

The Druj had a comeback. She always did, clever girl. Let them have their perceptions, she said. I will add a little something to that to spice things up.

I saw people recognizing the innate spiritual beings within them as necessary facts, but now these spirit presences started to swell, become bright and sparkling, even tarty. That's the best word for the change that came over them. Inflated with pride and self-importance, strutting like the world's foremost celebrities, exuding the tinsel of celebrity throughout the awareness of the watching human who swelled up too. The inflation was infectious, the self-importance contagious. Everybody was famous, stars of their own reality shows.

This attitude of hauteur and self-importance was like a narcotic on the embodied humans. Yes, I have spiritual beings inside me because I specifically deserve it. I am entitled because of my accomplishments; my self-value is incontestable. I am *so* blessed, can you just stand it? The Druj had a marvelous bicycle pump to inflate souls with illusory self-importance. You can see where this psychic intoxication was headed. Narcissistic blindness. Overly fat tires. A brick wall of deadened cognition so soft and undetectable you would not even know your head was now buried in layers of obfuscating illusion and puffery.

You had to hand it to the Druj. She was inventive. She didn't give up. Merlin showed us the image of a sword of Light, like Archangel Michael holds. Yes, the sword of *Prajna-paramita*, wide-awake, butt-kicking lucid awareness. We didn't have to attack the Druj or commit any offensive, aggressive moves. We had only to hold these swords upright before us and let the blades make the changes. The cognitive sharpness of the blades cut through the intoxicating nonsense the Druj was emitting like an overheated smoke and fog machine. It was like a slap in the face, a splash of cold water, a cup of espresso for humans. They started waking up from their delirious, delightful, totally illusory trance.

The blades cut through these obscuring vapors with their glamorous images that resembled the way a soap bubble can reflect an image, or at least a color pattern. The crystalline insistence of the swords started to clear the vaporous atmosphere. Embodied humans were restored to sobriety; the fantastic spirits were *Herukas* and angels again, and if these individual humans were not God's answer to the world challenge to be the

most fascinating and important person ever created, at least they had a sober, realistic, and appreciative sense of what they truly were. The Druj shrugged her shoulders. Until next time, she said.

11

Everywhere I looked people were flying, doing somersaults in the air. They were zooming around the sky like skylarks in bright bodies of Light.

Elsewhere I saw people walking through walls, hills, mountains of rock, as if they were made of the merest bubbles and their bodies were indomitable, capable of penetrating any seemingly hard surface. Everything solid and granite-like was as if made of vapor, and dead people by the hundreds were passing through these nonexistent barriers that offered them no resistance. Nothing impeded them, not even Mount Meru, the definitive cosmic mountain 80,000 miles high and made of a blindingly bright golden mass of Light—I saw cocksure dead people in their bodies of Light passing merrily through it forwards and backwards, showing off like by flying out of Meru upside-down.

"Did you ever have dreams of doing that?" asked Blaise. "I used to often. I'd fly over San Francisco, zoom low over the streets of my childhood hometown, or hover motionless 200 feet above a field, face down, like floating in water. The Tibetan text calls this acquiring the *Bardo* body, the desire body. Castaneda would call it a free demonstration of the delights of the Second Attention body.

"You now have the power of instantaneous relocation, unimpeded motion. The Tibetan text is droll about this emergence. It says when

you notice you are now endowed with all sense faculties, able to fly anywhere instantly, it means you're dead and a wandering resident of the *Bardo*. And don't get puffed up with self-importance that you are now an impressive prodigy of the *siddhis*.

"Any dumb-fuck at this stage in the *Bardo* naturally awakens these dormant powers. It quite takes the fun out of it, don't you think. You thought you were awesome, but now you realize it is a common thing. It's more karmic illusion too, the book says. Nothing more spectacular than being able to breathe oxygen when you're alive. Here is this radiant body that represents the natural condition of living in the Intermediate State; you have dissolved the material body coverings that keep these powers asleep and you have leapt out of the stream of sleep like a fish and you're deploying these innate powers like a pro.

"The text says don't think this means you are in *samadhi*, that you've left the Wheel. You haven't. You're just enjoying the normal fun and games of the *Sidpa Bardo*. They're right. Astral flying was cool, but I didn't feel any more enlightened hovering up there 200 feet above the ground than at any other time. I just liked the fleet mobility of it, the disarming ease of flying, though I did notice my usual fear of heights, anything above ten feet, was entirely gone."

"We should have people walking around saying to the people flying around and walking through walls, 'If you can do this cool shit, you're dead!'" It was Tommy, getting into the levity of the moment. Things did feel a bit bubbly.

It was just the four of us now, me, Tommy, Blaise, and Merlin. Pipaluk, Edward, and Philomena were gone, presumably off helping Matthew again. Merlin wasn't saying much. He had the bemused attitude of Mary Poppins taking the Banks children for a pleasant stroll through the park to meet her curious friends. I should expect to be taking high tea up at the ceiling next. Even though we felt elated, I noticed there was a dim grey, twilight pallor around us. We could not see Sun, Moon, or stars in the *Bardo*, only this dim astral light. Also the landscape was subject to frequent wind gusts that would blow the fliers off course or whip those standing off their balance and out across the landscape.

"Karma," said Blaise. "There's no escaping it. That's what the winds are. The momentum of the accrued body of desires whipping up the weak mind. It reminds me of New Mexico in March. Strong winds, can blow you off your feet. The Tibetans say here you see how weak the mind or intellect is, blown about like a piece of paper by the winds of your karma. And you see how strong your karma can be, unmediated by the body or physical world and their heaviness.

"There, alive, you barely notice the upwind that moves you towards a karmic fulfillment. You think you have freely chosen, soberly considered the merits. No. You've been picked up and rushed along by the imperative winds of your karma. E. M. Forster in *Howards End* called this the Punch and Judy aspect of life, how humans are puppets twitched into acts of love and war by an invisible showman by which he meant the subconscious self. It's your wind-maker. It was just sufficiently slow enough that you missed the actual updraft. Not so here. In the *Bardo*, it's all naked, exposed, unmediated,

out in the open. You can't miss it, especially when you find yourself zooming off over the land."

"You are in this Second Attention landscape," said Merlin, "and everything that has been occluded from your daytime attention is now open before you. Your latent powers, your astral experiences that you could never remember, the scope of your awareness down the soul's timeline and across the dimensions, are exposed, like an examination corpse for medical students. You are in the body that wishes and that grants those wishes, in the desire body. The trouble is all those desires are aflame, and all that fire generates big winds. Still, you are in the body that has been driving your life behind the scenes, which means, behind the curtain of daytime reality and the deluded sunlit-world self. You are potentially lined up for a revelation, though you could also blow it."

"The trick is to ask oneself, 'Why do I do *this*?' We hardly ever ask that," said Blaise. "Yet it would open the door to the mystery of the karmic winds."

"It's God's fault that we have karma in the first place," said Tommy.

His statement arrested my attention. I had never looked at it that way.

"You're a kid taken to a wonderful department store," Tommy continued. "It has everything in Creation on display. You can choose whatever you want. That is, you can select it, but then you'll have to go out and earn the money to come back and buy it. There's your karma, and the more you desire this thing, this bauble in the store, the stronger your karma grows, and before you know it you have a gale-force wind and you wonder why you're blown off your feet.

"Except—*except* the Supreme Being *wants* you to go off on the selfhood safari, explore the worlds of desire and insight, become something, achieve a goal, acquire knowledge, transmute it to wisdom, bring it back triumphantly to the Old Guy as proof of the wisdom of His originally granting you the privilege. He hopes that during the safari you don't totally lose track of yourself and start mistaking yourself for the Land Rover, the wild animals, or the sweltering heat."

"Still, overall, I think the Old Man has over-estimated a human's ability to make sense of this place, the *Bardo* safari," said Blaise. "Even though what you find here is more primary, more fundamental to the ontological facts of existence, it will likely seem many times more bewildering, like you're walking around with a concussion trying to put two coherent sentences together and failing. The more I see of the set-up the more I'm convinced the after-death protocols have to be rethought and retooled. They're not working. People aren't getting the set-up. The *Bardo* receives an estimated 142,466 newly deceased souls every day. How many of these people are metaphysically prepared for its shocking experiences?

"I don't mean to pass any judgement on anybody's rate of *Bardo* processing, but with some 42,300,000 new entries every year, that is, that many new dead people, and so few understanding and thereby mastering the set-up, there is a significant jam up. I will reiterate the point made earlier that the *Bardo* must pick up the pace to start matching the increased tempo of consciousness being instilled upon the Earth through the upgrade to its Light grid. The *Bardo* is becoming a drag on the speed of consciousness taking root on the planet.

"You could say the *Bardo* is operating in Victorian England standards and speeds, while the planet is in the mid-21st century with all of its rapid improvements. My point is we are now confronted with a discrepancy at an engineering level. Two different frequencies, too divergent, increasingly incompatible, the *Bardo* and the human-inhabited planet the *Bardo* serves; the Earth *Bardo* is lagging. It runs like some sluggish bureaucratic office in 19th century Russia, like you read about in Gogol, full of forms and incompetence, lost overcoats and missing noses, and meanwhile the physical world's Light grid is streaming through the 21st century, to Victorians like a science fiction marvel.

"What is the *Bardo*? We tend to think of it as a place, a landscape, but it isn't. Your body and psyche are taken apart in front of your astonished awareness. Everything is presented in picture form, as images, but it's a picture language that is foreign to you. The images are foreign, exotic, unfamiliar to you. With that many people dying every day, is the *Bardo* impossibly crowded with the new intakes? No, not at all. Consciousness takes up no discrete space at all. Each soul could take up the entire *Bardo* landscape with their wild karmic hallucinations and nobody would ever feel their elbows pushed against them.

"The *Bardo* is a *process* of divestment with an unfixed time period. You can take as long as you want or need to. The Tibetan text says it's all over in 49 days. That is unlikely. You can take 490 days or 490 years, if that's what you require. The drag problem is not with the speed of the dead souls passing through the *Bardo*; it pertains to the quality of that passage: it is largely incomplete and undigested. Too many people are not comprehending their *Bardo* initiation. That's the clogging factor. Our expedition has been tasked with undoing it.

"The *Bardo* is not so much an objective spiritual landscape as a karmically modified serial hallucination. You pass through certain scripted, generic thresholds, but *how* they seem to you is wildly variable among individuals. You have the passage on Charon's boat across the River Acheron; the meeting with your *Daena* on the *Cinvat* Bridge; the Weighing of the Heart ceremony supervised by Anubis; and the life-review of the contents of the etheric then astral body and the shedding of both— these, as best I can tell, are the same experience, same stage, the same basic, unavoidable generic threshold the newly dead must pass through. They are the protocols for getting out of and free of your recent body. Again, how long this takes is unfixed: take as long as you want.

"How these stages appear is a product of your culture, educational and psychic conditioning, and karma, all put in the context of how much inner-directed self-awareness you start off with. As we know, many people are prolifically outer-directed in their attention so it is a shocking experience to have to reel that in when you get here and realize that everything you see is actually an interior event, and that inside and outside don't mean what they once did.

"Your outside is your interior and it is a *danse macabre* choreography of your karma. Nor should we expect appearances to conform strictly to the Egyptian or Tibetan visual protocols if we come from a stubbornly atheistic, materialistic place like America. I can imagine the *Herukas* coming on as slick telemarketers—no: even better, as unctuous, self-righteous televangelists."

I'm sure Blaise had more to say on restructuring the *Bardo*, but our attention was suddenly diverted to a scene that apparently was on the Earth. Well, at least more on the physical planet than we currently could claim to be. I couldn't at first tell where this site was, but what was plain was the Druj was attacking, commandeering a geomantic outpost on the Earth's geomantic terrain, and Edward, Pipaluk, and Philomena were trying to extricate her from that site.

Edward wielded a magnificent Light sword enflamed in lilac and with what looked like a brilliant golden sun at its handle. He was like the Celtic King Arthur fighting back the Saxon invaders to defend Cornwall. Philomena was

a rapidly rotating blur of diamond white fire; and Pipaluk wore a blazing mantle of royal purple and was wielding a *vajra* that roared and flashed like a series of thunderbolts. When had they mastered these roles? They were enveloped by a sphere of Ganeshes, the Ofanim in their elephant-god guise, each 50 feet tall and not so much merry right now as fierce and adamant, keen elephants rampant, removing all obstacles, trampling the opposition like so much ineffectual brush.

At first glance it looked like a hundred black seals lounging on a glistening rock. Then I saw the reality more clearly. It was a dome cap, an etheric canopy of Light housing a Light temple, a circular columnar palace of Lights and crystals and spirits, and multiple black copies of the Druj were squeezing it into the ground. Instead of a half-sphere of celestial Light, it now looked like a squashed obsidian mass; black cords threaded through it and hideous black tentacles enwrapped it. What was most interesting is that I saw the origin of this baleful concentration of Druj's attention and psychic force was here in the *Bardo*.

I cannot be precise about spatial distance, but in general terms somewhere over there (you'll have to excuse the embarrassing imprecision of this) a gathering of like-minded souls had created a concentrated dark area, black and vaporous. My impression is they were each individually stuck or confused, full of fear, trembling, and confusion, and had assembled in this commonality to bemoan their fate. Picture a factory floor and see a huddled group of maybe ten disgruntled workers; they are complaining, fuming with the seeds of a strike.

They become a focal point for negativity and discontent and attract more people to them. It was like that here in the *Bardo*. This group was densifying, as if the individual members grew heavier, carried more gravity (despite the absence of physical matter), and their location started to become a nodal point of darkness. It started to press down on the apparent ground beneath them and the ground, as if burdened by this unsupportable weight, started to collapse downward. This black focal point which now looked like perhaps an elongated blackened incisor tooth, started to grow downwards towards and then into the physical world below. Exceedingly strange, I know. This focal point in the *Bardo* expanded itself and grew down and anchored into the human embodied world.

Then the Druj took advantage of this human-generated negative geomantic node. She settled on it, made copies of herself, amplified its darkness and negativity. The Earth now had a gravity well of black negativity created in the *Bardo*. As humans came in contact with this rock of blackness and matched the vibration, it would strengthen the original node in the *Bardo*, and both poles would expand through this perverse but logical reciprocal loop now established by the Druj. The *Bardo* would pollute the Earth node, and the darkened Earth node would draw despondent people to it and thereby strengthen it and reciprocally fortify the *Bardo* node. Both poles would keep growing stronger.

It was the demonstration of a perversion of the activation of a Light temple. More people would get stuck in the *Bardo* as they neared this black node, and that would both cloud that area of the *Bardo* and allow the karmic illusions to exert a stronger hold on disembodied consciousness, and it would darken and densify Earth conditions around this Earth node and predispose people to confusion and cognitive unconsciousness so they entered the *Bardo* befuddled. The reciprocal circulation of this activation tightened like a Chinese finger trap.

I used the unfamiliar term "dome cap." I understand from Blaise there are many thousands of these canopies of Light upon the planet's surface. They are part of the planet's original geomantic endowment, installed long ago. They raise the resting spiritual vibration of a locality bounded by their form, anywhere from one-quarter wide to nine miles across. If the Druj corrupts a dome-capped region, she gets considerable more traction in suborning cognitive freedom.

Here is a visual analogy. It was as if an incisor tooth on your upper jaw blackened then elongated and grew downward into the lower jaw, thus clamping the two palates together. Bizarre and scary, certainly, but the relevant application to what I was seeing is that it seemed this Druj-made focal point of blackness was now pulling the two realms together, at least in this specific area, so that the dark node in the *Bardo* would be in the same place as the dark node in the physical world. The Druj's goal was to generate many of these nodes. The effect would be to trap souls in the Hell realm of the *Bardo*, keep them from a sense of cognitive or spiritual power over their karma, and start to corrupt the burgeoning upgrade of Light underway on the physical Earth through its grid.

It seemed as if Edward, Pipaluk, and Philomena, in conjunction with the Ganeshes, were making some headway in loosening the hold of the Drujs on this obsidian mass of negativity until suddenly two of them were blown away, as if a terrific gust had swept them up and whisked them off in different directions. Only Philomena remained, and the Ganeshes. The Drujs' hold grew stronger.

Not only was our attention diverted to witnessing this strange scene, but I now realized we were there, with Philomena and the Ganeshes, by the black rock. "I rather expected this would happen," said Merlin, shaking his head. "Edward and Pipaluk have lost themselves to the winds of their own quickening karma. No, not for good, but it may seem to each of them that they are permanently lost. What do you say we go rescue them? I'm sure they will appreciate the gesture."

We found Edward first. He was swirling around inside a black tornado. He seemed to be about 50 feet above the ground, slashing his sword everywhere and failing to make contact with anything. He seemed desperate, out of control, like he was fighting an invisible enemy that came at him from all sides at once. I thought I caught faint glimpses of opponents in the grey swirling mass of the tornado, soldiers perhaps, maybe demons, even Harpies, and other psychotic-looking spirits and humans. I wondered if I were seeing actual spirits or grim projections of Edward's nightmare karmic illusions made into a feral army.

He slashed at these spectral images and his sword went straight through them, not affecting them, as if they were phase-shifted into a parallel but seeable reality. The more he slashed with his sword, the more these figures enlarged and the greater their apparent numbers grew. Now there were hundreds around him.

"The old boy's trying to do a Gesar of Ling *Dharma* warrior number," observed Blaise. "And failing impressively. It's altogether the wrong approach."

Clearly, Edward was making no inroads against this encroaching army. He slashed and they advanced further upon him; he kept losing ground. But then I saw something that explained the whole situation. I saw the Druj, a large black, veiled figure, much larger than this tornado and its attacking army, manipulating the tornado and the fighters like so many puppets.

She held the strings, the master puppeteer, and she was making them all dance before Edward, and she was inspiring Edward, mostly through amplifying his delusions, to construe their jerky movements as attack and fighting. This was her idea of a pleasant Saturday afternoon's puppet show to pass the long winter hours. She wasn't making it all up, though; she had Edward's karmic raw material to work with, then she tarted it up, enhanced its conflicts, made it jump.

Edward may once, in earlier lives, have battled actual warriors, but the current engagement was entirely illusory. He was sword-fighting ghost images. The trouble was, and this was what inspired Blaise's caustic remark, Edward didn't realize this. He took the battle seriously, and was fighting to save his life. Only his life wasn't in jeopardy: what was at risk was his cognitive discernment.

He acted like he was fighting to preserve the world, like a modern King Arthur defending the sanctity of Celtic England and the high goals of Camalate against every barbarian that came at them. Everything was at stake; he must not fail. He didn't realize he was battling images conjured up by the winds of *his* karma, deftly accentuated by the Druj pulling the puppet strings to make Edward twitch. He was (sorry, Edward, old pal) like a dog chasing its tail thinking it was a plump rabbit. Or somebody fiercely boxing his own shadow.

I knew what he was thinking, somehow. I don't know why I should know his thoughts, yet I did. He felt he had to defend the world, reality, the goodness of the Creation, against these harmful infidels of the darkness, Druj's agents. Yes, he knew the Druj was involved; he believed she had sent these agents against him, and he had to call on every occult trick he'd ever learned to defend himself on behalf of the viability of reality itself. He didn't realize it was all an illusion.

It seemed likely that if we did not intervene, give Edward an outside perspective, he might have to remain there, forever possibly, fighting them off. "Go empty, pal," shouted Blaise. The swirling tornado and the sounds of the battle were loud, and you had to shout over them to hear anybody speak. "Do the emptiness thing, *now.*" Edward looked up and nodded at Blaise. He did it.

At once Edward stopped slashing and striking, and settled the sword upright against his torso. He closed his eyes, withdrew into himself. The Light in him grew brighter. A golden sun appeared at his chest and expanded. He was now wearing a royal robe of gold, holding a golden staff topped with a white crown. He was inside a spinning transparent octahedron, and soon it rotated so rapidly it was a blur of diamond white fire, just like I had seen with Philomena. Edward, as far as his form was concerned, had disappeared. I couldn't see him.

As Edward settled ever deeper into his meditative, inward state, as he disappeared himself, the tornado's force of rotation diminished and stopped. The hordes of marauding warriors lost their animation, grew faint and transparent, then crumbled like somebody had stepped on a flimsy plaster figure and crushed it. The Druj dropped her puppet strings; all her puppets were gone; the play was over. Her little amusement on Edward's behalf was busted, seen through, ended. The force of Edward's nothingness concentration had incinerated all traces of it.

The on-off switch for this hallucination was inside him. Now he knew that. The Druj had been counting on his not realizing that. Where there had been a baleful, malevolent, dark tornado spinning furiously around Edward was now an expanding field of brilliant diamond white fire. It was a purifying force; it purged the psychic atmosphere around him of all defilements, which principally had taken the form for him of strong illusions that he believed were fighting him.

"That's good," said Merlin. "He's burned all that karma out of his system. He will travel much more lightly now, no longer beset by these winds from his unconscious, and he has awakened something important in him, or I

should say, further woken it up. He got started on this project when he was with me a few years ago, though I don't think he quite realized it then. It's coming alive now. He is starting to master the Arthur energy, to assume the Arthur position in his consciousness and even in a starting manner within an outer human group."

Meanwhile, my attention was now drawn to the source of some moaning. It sounded like a hundred women in various states of misery, petitioning someone for help, for intercession in their suffering. That someone was Pipaluk.

She was seated on the ground, with pots of herbs and burning bundles of scented plants, magic sticks, prayer flags, and her shaman's ceremonial robes, and she was surrounded by these one hundred women, their arms outstretched, pleading for her help. She was like the only qualified doctor at the scene of a disaster. The injured expected her to treat and heal them as soon as possible. I saw multiple copies of Pipaluk, as if she had cloned herself to produce a nursing staff. Still, she wasn't able to keep up with the demands of the suffering women. Every time she treated one woman, six more appeared demanding Pipaluk heal them. She was doing her best, falling far behind the demands, and growing tired.

The voices of these women carried an urgency, a frenzy that was like a gusting wind. These gusts nearly unseated Pipaluk repeatedly, lifting her slightly off the ground or throwing her slightly to one side. It took energy to resist them and maintain her center of gravity. These winds carried the moaning voices and sorrowful cries of the women too, and these made Pipaluk feel sad. She wanted to help them all; for some reason, she felt she *had* to help them all. It was her duty as chief shaman of her village, or perhaps for her region of Greenland. She was the only one to do this; if she didn't help them, these women would be lost, dead.

But the numbers kept growing. She would never reach the end of the numbers. It was the same escalating stalemate we had seen Edward embroiled in. Or maybe the better analogy would be black hole: the demands of the injured women were sucking Pipaluk into their darkened reality like the inexorable gravity pull of an event horizon. If she passed that horizon, we'd lose her, and she'd lose herself. She would be a Sisyphean healer, never reaching the end of the line of injured because their numbers kept growing as she healed even one. As she healed one, a dozen more appealed; perversely, she multiplied the numbers with each healing because she validated the reality presented to her, and that encouraged it, energized it, and the Druj put forth more hurt women.

The Druj was pulling the strings again. I shouldn't have been surprised. These hundred petitioning women all dangled at the end of her puppet strings. She even put the words in the mouths of these unhappy women. She was a ventriloquist working one hundred "dummies" at once, ever so adroitly. She was good at this because Pipaluk bought the spectacle completely. She didn't see through it, not yet. Our job was to pop the illusory bubble so she could see it.

Evidently, Pipaluk believed she had to, was obligated, to heal all these women. It was her mission, her mandate; the world would end if she failed this assignment. She knew she was steadily losing ground; the numbers of injured women kept growing, and their demands, the types of healing they required, kept getting more complex, involved, so that properly she needed a team of ten surgeons and about 50 nurses to perform the medical requirements, in her case, the herbal medicaments, the prayers to the tribal, elemental, and regional deities and ancestors, and journeys in search of missing soul fragments and treasures.

"These are images of all the women Pipaluk has ever healed," said Merlin. "She believes they all require healing in the present moment, but they do not. They are not here at all. Their forms are illusions created by Pipaluk's memory and spun up and animated by her karma. She feels she still owes them healing. She is expending all her life-force and consciousness power on an illusory deed. These women are not here and Pipaluk is not healing them. It's a puppet show."

Merlin stopped speaking. He was waiting for us to figure out what to do.

Blaise got it first. "Swallow them all up, Pipaluk. Absorb the suffering women into yourself. They are part of you anyway. They aren't separate."

Pipaluk managed to hear this above the maelstrom of the tornado and the keening of the women. A core of diamond white fire, like a compact crystal, started to radiate this Light from within her and grow larger. One by one, these many women started to walk into Pipaluk's form, or she sucked them in like a massive gravity field, as if she had reversed things and become the black hole.

As each woman approached Pipaluk's expanding form, she grew faint, wispy, and eventually transparent just before she dissolved into Light and was gone, now re-absorbed by Pipaluk. I knew she was understanding, finally, that these women were projections from herself; they might once have been real women with whom Pipaluk, in other lives as a female shamanic healer, had been acquainted, but not this one. Now they were illusory artifacts of an awakened karmic stream, skillfully manipulated and amplified by the indolent Druj, looking for activities, bored and restive with the slowness of human cognition, seeking diversions, anything to pass the long hours and increase her score.

There were no women demanding a healing. The tornado was gone. It was silent around Pipaluk. She looked like a whale that had just swallowed an ocean of plankton and other small fish and was properly gorged and sated. She looked like a wise woman who has discerned something of vital importance, an adept who has transmuted a big load of vexing karma and was now free of it.

Edward and Pipaluk looked chastened but strengthened from their ordeals, their shadow fights with the machinations of the Druj stirring up their own residual karmic content. I guess we'd have to expect that kind of thing. Matthew was gone again, and I started to wonder what was up with him. The minute I had the thought, I was where he was, witnessing his latest ordeal. The others were with me, as if, possibly, drawn by the latest focus of my attention.

Matthew seemed to be wrestling the largest, fattest Sumo wrestler I'd ever seen. The guy must have weighed a thousand pounds and he was crushing Matthew. I don't know how this was possible and I half-thought I was hallucinating, but the Sumo guy seemed to have a hundred identical heads. They kept extruding from his massive bulk like a fast-action film of the growth of Brussels sprouts. New heads kept popping out, glaring and snarling at Matthew.

"Poor old Matthew is getting his butt kicked something proper," observed Blaise. "What ever did he do to provoke the big guy? Must have said something a little off color. That Sumo hulk has gone right off his head. I'm seeing double."

I knew Blaise was hamming things up a bit. He liked doing that. Still, his question had merit. Why was Matthew wrestling this giant of a fellow?

"Because he hasn't yet recognized that it is himself," said Blaise.

I began to see why he said this. It seemed unlikely at first. Many of these heads, perhaps all of them, were hectoring Matthew, calling out insults, jeers, complaints, grievances; they were grousing, carping, criticizing, never happy. Anything they could complain about was a fit subject for their incessant cranky exhortations.

The black clouds of dissatisfaction were coming at Matthew from every direction. They were taunting, mocking, ridiculing, scoffing at him.

It was a party. Hisses, catcalls, jibes, and insults flew at him like rotten tomatoes. They heckled and they hissed. They were like café customers you would never please, never get it right, always screw up their lunch order because they kept changing it. He looked like he was getting pelted with mudballs all over. Some of these heads resembled what Matthew might have looked like when he was younger; I could see the various ages of his life represented in these faces. I saw what he looked like when he didn't get his way, when he was denied, refuted, rebuffed, or insulted. I saw the responses he stifled and never acted on. They were stored in him and now having their vociferous moment.

Even stranger things were happening with Matthew. He swelled with Light, then suddenly everything turned inside out and the big man with the hectoring multiple faces was inside the even larger form of Matthew. Then it inverted again and the brutish complainer with the irritable heads was outside. Then this got sucked into Matthew again but this time it disappeared, as if completely ingested. I saw no trace of the big fellow inside Matthew. Then he was back outside Matthew again, calling out caustic remarks, as if nothing had happened and it was business as usual, and they were open on Sundays too.

I had at first thought all these catcalls were directed at Matthew, as some were, but most were petitions to Matthew to get him to agree and express them outwardly. To pass them on to the misbehaving, incorrigible world with their compliments. They were filling him with insults and jibes to dump on the sick world. Except he wasn't complying, and they were heating up with his resistance. When he absorbed all these jeering heads into himself, as if in one vigorous inhalation, everything went silent. You couldn't hear them. Then they'd barrel out of him again and inflate to full disgusting size and resume their pestilential shouting. He did seem to be gaining on them though.

Each time they inverted his form to divulge them again, they seemed thinner, more transparent, as if they were losing life-force from an extreme anemia, until one time they popped out again and all I could see was just the outline of them, where they had been, substantially, but where they now were barely present. They seemed to have contracted a serious case of laryngitis too. What had been rough-edged shouts and curses were now barely heard whispers.

This was the strangest wrestling match I'd ever seen. The whole thing was like watching somebody inhale then exhale with his entire body. He would swell up and enlarge with the insistence of these hectoring heads; then he would suck it inside him in a big inhalation and the complainers would all disappear. Then, as if it were a haven in between this breathing cycle, Matthew would vanish and all the heads extruding like bulbous stalks from the Sumo wrestler would be gone too. It would all disappear in a sudden brilliant flash. Then I'd wait for its return. I wondered how long it would go on like this. It must be taxing on Matthew's attention to have to deal with this bizarre kind of attack.

I asked Merlin what was Matthew doing to make it all vanish at times?

"He enters and becomes one with the non-dualistic voidness of the Christ Light," Merlin said. "Or the Buddha Mind, if you prefer calling it that. That is the key to escape from your karma, but bear in mind, when I say 'escape' I mean transmute, resolve, master, and dissolve your karma. It is a definitive action. That is the point of Matthew's current experience, to succeed in transmuting it."

"But who or what are all these carping voices? Where do they come from? Why are they besieging him like this?"

"They come from himself," answered Merlin. "They are the voices of all the contrary aspects of his personality and psyche, all the rejected, marginalized parts. They are all the shadow side of Matthew accrued over a lifetime, the components of his total self he was unable to harmonize and integrate. In the *Bardo*, they are much more exposed and we become more aware of their influence. When people die, they leave this body of complainers behind in the physical world as a toxic focal point, as the Navaho well understood, They would close up their house for good if somebody died inside it; it was tainted."

I had a picture of Matthew's actions from the inside, as he might see them. This swarm of bothersome complaining heads and all their noise and the fact of their presence I saw Matthew sucking down the inexorable drain of voidness. I know it's odd to put it that way, but when you erase the *skandahs* and follow the seat of your attention back into itself, it is like the pulling suction of a drain. And you go down the drain with everything else, and then the drain goes down too.

That must be what the Tibetans mean by Clear Light and Clear Mind, the terrific opportunity for definitive release from the Wheel of Life you're offered as soon as you're dead, and which, unfortunately, nearly everyone dead misses out on. It's what remains after you, the water, and the drain all disappear into the void. Maybe there's a secret action Yama performs that we don't ordinarily see. He sucks the Wheel of Life into his own glowering form and dissolves it, and here was Matthew, copying that massive gesture of transcendence and seniority. Or, more acutely, Yama *is* the position in consciousness of seniority to the wheel. The successful *Bardo* journeyer, the *Bardo* graduate, takes on the form of Yama.

We were there to provide Matthew support. Several concentric circles of Ganeshes surrounded us and I felt the brilliant clear Light they were emitting. Ganesh is the remover of all obstacles to consciousness, and Matthew had a few. I felt their warmth and focus and love radiate through me like warm sunshine. I felt this brighten my own psychic space and, I suppose as well, my Light body, or whatever form it was precisely that I was presently "wearing" in the *Bardo*.

Tommy, Blaise, and myself seemed to have gotten larger somehow. I felt ten feet tall at least and even though I did not believe I actually held a tangible Light sword, my space felt like it had been converted to a swordlike focus. I felt myself (that is, myself as a sword) slice through Matthew's obfuscation like an Arctic ice-cutter. Blaise and Tommy did this too: we cut the ice.

The next time Matthew puffed out again back into astral corporeality the proliferation of complaining heads was silent. Their forms looked frozen, or maybe petrified is a more apt term. They were halted in mid-complaint, faces in a frozen snarl, arms raised, fists clenched, but all of it was stopped in mid-action. The next time Matthew popped back these halted, etched forms all exploded into millions of little pieces, and these popped and sparkled out of existence in the air. Matthew had not won the battle; he had obviated the need for a conflict at all. He had placed himself in a superior because antecedent position and erased all of it.

Matthew looked ecstatic. He was himself again, in a sense, though as I studied him he seemed much more than himself, or more himself because he had divested himself of an enormous weight of false self-definition. That infernal chorus of complaining voices had distorted his true valence, compromised his essence, but now it was gone and Matthew was far more truly himself than ever.

"Before he is done, Matthew will have to let go of even that," said Merlin.

I saw that Philomena and the Ganeshes had finished their dental work on the black incisor "tooth" the Druj had grown to link the *Bardo* and Earth reality. It was undone. The two realms, at least there, were now disconnected, though I suspected the Druj had many more ingrown dark "teeth" elsewhere in the *Bardo*.

"So here we are on the wind-swept plains of karma," said Blaise. "You can see people being buffeted about all over the place, like on a *tor* in Dartmoor in the winter. I was once at such a place and it was hard keeping one's balance. The trick for us is to come up with a way to acquaint people with the nature of this wind. Few while alive understand the concept of karma, and certainly not its mechanics, and the Judeo-Christian pseudo-metaphysical model discourages it. As you know it fosters the monolithic single lifetime model; sin, yes, karma, no. Sin is disempowering; you need Christ to forgive you. Karma is do-it-yourself forgiveness with the benefit of gaining power and traction in your awareness.

"Obviously, the easiest solution is to remove Christianity entirely from the Earth, and erase all memory of its destructive, reductionistic teachings from the mind. I keep proposing this to the Supreme Being and He keeps voting it down at once. The trouble is as a Christian you get here and *nothing* matches what you've been told. Instead, you're presented with this fourth-dimensional time-fluid tableau of the products of *all* your deeds, conscious and unconscious, over *many* lifetimes, and the contents of this shocking display write the script of your *Bardo* journey.

"Regrettably, you have no *context* for any of this, no preparation, so your *Bardo* experience is likely to be a big botch-up and a retreat into life again. You hurriedly write a life-script, set some goals, rush through the womb-door, get born, *forget everything*, and relapse into the illusory single-lifetime view. It's a Groundhog Day in which you don't know you're repeating the same day again."

"Understanding the reality and mechanisms of karma is the key to your gaining power over your condition," said Tommy. "You realize since you created it, you can change it. You are not powerless against the strong winds."

"Precisely," said Blaise, "and that is why the Druj, or Antichrist, keeps this little secret of empowerment from the multitude of incarnated humans. It would end the game, or certainly change the odds in favor of humans and not the Druj. She wants humans to believe they are powerless, that consciousness is merely an ineffectual spectator or passive, invalided observer incapable of joining the fray. That is probably her chief lie, and the Antichrist fosters it at every turn possible.

"While you're alive you live this illusory, parochial lie of limited time horizons. Then you get here and the truth is revealed to you in its stark nakedness, and it shocks the hell out of you because you never suspected anything *like this*. You feel like you've been asleep all your life, or suffering total amnesia, and now, finally, the mechanism is working properly, except you don't understand it. It's a cognitive jumble, incoherent, frightening, inimical, a ghastly panoply of images, just the weirdest, awfullest hallucination you could imagine.

"It's happening to you: *Herukas* storm out of the walls everywhere you look. And for reasons you cannot understand, they are intent on dismembering you. You think, shit, where is this smiley Christ guy who's supposed to forgive my sins and make everything right and how come I'm not in Heaven like they promised? If you do get over the fright you'll start feeling you've been conned.

"The *Bardo*, I'm sure you'll agree, is a strange place, at least at first. If you're making a delivery you can seemingly enter anywhere, as if through the walls. A delivery means if you are in fact dead and arriving here for your debrief. If you are here for a tour, as we are, you come in through the front gates, greeted by the majestic and awesome Green Knight, also known around here as Yama.

"Dead, you start getting taken apart and all the building components that once comprised your form, both mental and physical, are displayed like clothes on a drying rack, flapping in the breeze before you, and, ontological naïf that you are, you fail to recognize them, even to realize they are clothes, parts of yourself, *your* goddam clothes. Such amnesia. Everybody is concussed. You stand there, serially stripped of every piece of clothing that you once wore, becoming progressively naked, completely exposed with no layers to preserve your amnesiac condition you are so used to, and you still don't get the action.

"Meanwhile, the bodies and auric fields that clothed you are dissolving as they disgorge their contents, all your life experiences and feelings. It's like you have this massive moving truck and seven movers, and all your possessions, your couches, end-tables, reading lamps, beds, kitchenware, are inside this truck and the truck dissolves and vanishes and all your stuff is now stationary, piled up by the road. The truck moving you forward is gone.

"You don't have a house—a *body*—to put all your stuff in again. It's just a big pile. Your awareness is now greatly enhanced, because you don't have the amnesiac weight of your bodies to diminish your innate Light, *but* your understanding is commensurately weak. You see more, but you comprehend less. Your brain is inert. At least, that's the way it is at first. Nothing is familiar.

"God, this is insufferable, horrendous, you think shiveringly. Even the ground you seem to

216

be standing on, which is naked awareness, this exposed ball of Light, original consciousness, unclothed by all your familiar supports, is utterly *foreign* to you *until* you start to remember it was your starting point long ago, the one true thing about you that is permanent and free of illusions."

I was considering all that Blaise had just said when somebody else spoke up. "We already have an agent in place who could act as a tutor in the *Bardo*," said Edward. I hadn't noticed when he had rejoined us. Pipaluk was back too.

"I was thinking of the way Virgil guided Dante through the Underworld. Virgil, in historical terms, lived more than a thousand years earlier than Dante; he was clearly a spirit of the Underworld when he volunteered to guide Dante. He knew the place. The agent we have in place is the Higher Self, the Guardian Angel, as some call it, the Self or Atman, as the mystical traditions term it.

"The Tibetan text towards its conclusion finally alludes to this figure as the Good Genius and Evil Genius, as two complementary spirits who accompany the soul. The Genius is the 'simultaneously-born god,' the personification of the soul's higher or divine nature, or, for the Evil Genius, the demon of its lower or carnal nature. The Tibetans still don't give the Good or Evil Genius much play; the text says that if everything else fails and you're at a loss for who can rescue you from the frights and soul-ripping terrors of your own hallucinatory mind projections and the karmic fury spirits intent on tearing your consciousness apart, call on your Good Genius. Maybe he can help you out a little in a pinch.

"It's presented as an afterthought, and long after you've been dead in the *Bardo*. It seems like a waste of manpower. The guy is just standing around, waiting for something to do. Get him to help your ass through the *Bardo*. Some traditions, such as Judaism, say there is a Good Angel and a Bad Angel, each looking after the karmic products of your use of free will to do good or evil. Are there two Guardian Angels or one? I tend to think one, and he handles both poles of your actions, yet remains neutral and unaffected by either polarity.

"People have also called it the Silent Self, Daimon, and *Fravasi*. It is the primary spirit guide. Everyone has one. This figure is already in place, with us all the time. This angelic figure, who has been with us since the beginning, could be called into service to act like Virgil on our behalf as we, like Dante, traverse the *Bardo*. Normally, it is present, as it were, behind us, observing all our actions, rarely commenting or judging them, and rarely, it seems, intervening to help us.

"The Persians recognized this figure as the *Daena*, the Heavenly Twin or Eternal Partner. I know we've been construing the *Daena* as a personification of the state of our astral body, but the Persian mystics seemed to allow her multiple valences. The *Daena* is usually described as a young maiden and she meets you on the *Cinvat* Bridge. She has a body of pure Light; she is a person's heavenly counterpart or archetypal figure, his Perfect Nature, Sun of the Heart. She is our personal spiritual guide, our celestial 'I,' and our resurrection body, they said.

"Her purpose is to guide the disembodied soul through the Underworld and to the experience of the scales with a spirit called Abathur Muzania in the North Star. His name means either 'he who has the scales' or 'divine father of the humans.' This figure, like the Egyptian Anubis and Ma'at, makes the final assessment of a soul's quality before it can move on. The trouble with the *Daena* is that the Persian mystics endowed her with some qualities of what Steiner called the Lesser Guardian of the Threshold, a name for the unprocessed astral body or Double. This body carries your karma, and it can be a hideous sight.

"In some descriptions the *Daena* is presented as tainted by this astral pollution, and thus it is possible for you to miss the fact she is in fact the human Higher Self. Maybe she as your Higher Self wears the results of your karma like a soiled robe, for illustration purposes. See, this is what you have created. To a degree, the Higher Self is burdened with our karma because it impedes the incarnational goals he set for our current life and can be seen as a setback. As Oliver Hardy says to Stan Laurel, 'That's another fine mess you got us into.'

"The Persian mystics also at times exalt her status beyond the merely personal guide for one individual, but to a level comparable to the Western Albion. So the *Daena* seems to straddle several tiers of description and function. Maybe the *Daena* remains inviolately pure, as your neutral moral conscience, but broadcasts the moral condition of your soul like a neon picture-sign. The neon image is not the moral condition, only the picture of it, the balance sheet report."

As if Edward's suggestion had acted like a magical invocation, all of us were surrounded by our own Higher Self. It was like a large translucent angel within an even larger sphere of Light and it now seemed to envelop each of us. Angels do not have a gender yet the Higher Selves of us individually varied between masculine and feminine appearances. While my own felt somewhat familiar and suggested a history of what I suppose I should call friendship, I confess I did not recognize her in visual terms. Maybe I had never seen her during my so-called wakeful daytime hours. She seemed to be dancing, whirling about, but I realized she must be appearing in the fourth dimension which means human cognition can only discern aspects of her full presence, hence the impression of fervid dancing. She's too complex to be seen entirely all at once.

"I suggest we have the Supreme Being instruct the Higher Selves of humans to increase their level of afterlife *Bardo* interaction by 50 percent, that they set the intention to tutor the wandering soul, to explain the landscape," said Edward, like a magazine art director unveiling a new cover design.

"The Higher Self should be instructed to guide the soul through all the bewildering mechanics of the *Bardo*, to explain how everything is a karmic projection, a product of one's karma and illusion-making abilities. It can explain the winds of karma, the mechanics of all that, how to discern its truth and remain neutral and senior to it. It can advise the soul on the machinations of the Druj, what tactics she is likely to throw at them, how best to respond. I don't see any advantage to everyone coming through here so unprepared any longer.

"The soul remains free to listen or ignore, to heed or disregard the advice, but at least inadvertent ignorance of the *Bardo* landscape will no longer be an acceptable excuse for a *Bardo* disaster. Willful ignorance is another matter. Now the soul in the afterlife may be far better informed, better equipped for events. I find it strange there is so little mention of this spirit guide in the *Bardo Thödol*, and I wonder why, generally, the Higher Self remains so aloof from people."

"The Higher Self is not aloof from people, but, rather, intervenes with the lightest of hands, the merest touch of its feathers on your life," said Merlin. "They have been instructed to generally keep their distance and not make their presence known or at least not be overly conspicuous *until* such time as the embodied soul makes voluntary, free-will steps towards their own Higher Self. Then it's wide open what degree of interaction one enjoys with this spirit.

"In initiation programs, at some point the embodied human strives to first have a wakeful meeting then to unify with his own

Higher Self, ending the *apparent* separation. Together, the soul, or *urvan*, and the Higher Self, or *Fravasi*, wage the battle of good and evil in the material world, try to make some inroads against the Druj while upholding the original Creation standards embodied in *ma'at* and *Asha*. It is a marvelous sight: the Higher Self englobes the *urvan* like a round shield, and the soul, fortified with wisdom and Clear Light, dissolves the Druj's inroads into the field of human consciousness, the *Bardo*, and the Earth.

"The separation of soul and Higher Self is apparent because it is not real, but only functional for a time until the person changes their stance. The Higher Self, you may not know, is a soul's first auric field. When you as a spirit were extruded from the Supreme Being, and this is before the advent of your soul with its penchant for individuation and karma accrual, the Higher Self was assigned to you and formed the first protective sphere around you. It has been your constant companion, if a silent one, throughout the long saga (or, as some say, soap opera) of your incarnations. It knows everything you have planned to do, your capabilities, your soul tone. It can read you like a book. It holds that book in its hands. You can't put anything over on your Higher Self."

Merlin found this funny. He was chuckling, as if at his own joke. "We will have to instruct the Higher Selves to find ways to make discernible overtures to people while they are alive so the experience of the Guardian Angel will not be so foreign to them when they arrive here. A few people, here and there, manage an experience of their presiding tutelary spirit while alive, but most do not. Once the disembodied soul enters the *Bardo*, their Higher Self should introduce himself the way a waiter in a restaurant identifies himself as your waiter, tells you his name, explains the menu choices, and answers any questions you might have."

"When I got here, I found my Higher Self a bit on the aloof side, almost shy," said Tommy. "Eventually, I realized it was politeness and tact and if anybody was aloof, it was me. We, the embodied, the living, have to make the first move. It has to be done freely. We have to want to make contact. There's also a bit of a divide between the level of reality we operate on and theirs. They have never been material beings with a spoken or written word language, other than vicariously through us, so the mode of communication will be telepathic, usually pictorial with perhaps a few brief captions. That is not something most people are used to or even feel comfortable with, conversing through pictures.

"Most people distrust what comes into their head if it seems different than the usual talk-radio rubbish that passes for our thoughts, views of the world, and complaints. This Higher Self speaks in a quiet voice. You have to listen hard. Anyway, it's more a matter of pictures that he helps you interpret or decode. He's flashing you these cue cards with exotic images on them from a higher dimension, like fourth-dimensional crop circles, and you struggle to follow. In my more frustrated moments, I likened it to reading *Finnegans Wake* to a dog. You can see the dog is paying attention, ears perked, but he doesn't understand."

"This could lead to good and productive things, if people pursue it," said Blaise. "The Higher Self has knowledge of all your lives. That means all your life plans, achievements, compromises, and failures. It has the karmic balance sheet, and the absence of that sheet, of the knowledge it contains, is what makes the *Bardo* experience such a god-skewed mess and nightmare for most people.

"Think about it: the closer you get to your Higher Self, the closer you move towards that initiation experience of becoming one with your Higher Self, the more you get acquainted with your karma, even more basically, with the fact you have karma, that it has a momentum, a destiny, and often acts like a stiff wind, and that when you get here, it's likely to buffet your dead sorry ass all over the place, and if there were walls in the *Bardo*, you'd surely be bouncing off them. Karma is only part of it. That's the tally sheet on your business dealings.

"But larger than that is the complex history of your soul during 10,000 lives. Your Higher Self sees all of that at once; she knows it, understands it, even more acutely, she understands the implicit teleology which your soul, on the Higher Self's behalf, has undertaken to achieve through these 10,000 or whatever number of lives you've generated. It's funny, because your soul and Higher Self are running this conspiracy to achieve a recondite goal, however long it takes, and you are the latest field agent only briefed on the merest details and not, as spies say, read into the program. You're on a need-to-know basis, and up until now, thanks to the River Lethe and other injunctions, you didn't know much.

"But when you move into the Higher Self's realm, you start seeing the playing field, the real field of action, where reality is shaped and orchestrated. You've finally been approved for access; you've seen all the classified, code-word protected documents. You have the requisite security clearance. Now Virgil as your *Fravasi* finally can explain everything to you as the disincarnate Dante.

"You might even see how clearing the decks properly and thoroughly while you're in the *Bardo* can help not only your soul but the world struggle at large, you know, kick some Druj butt here, help reduce her influence there in the alive world, as well as forward your own incarnational program, which you now see. Show the Druj not everybody is a hopeless, unconscious pawn, yet another obedient, hypnotized customer for her salesman's big bright suitcase of lies."

"Why don't you try it," suggested Merlin, gesturing to these spheres of Light around us. He meant us to enter our Higher Self and have a look around.

It was like walking into a brilliant sphere of Light with a friendly face. I didn't see this face at first; I registered its benign presence. The image of a face, more angelic than human, gradually formed in the encircling spherical walls. I have described it as a sphere, but it had an unaccountable volume for a sphere. It seemed more like a circular hall, like the bottom of a column of Light, and in it were images of people, many people, no doubt many thousands of them, both men and women, dressed differently, and appearing at different life ages, as if these ages represented the moment of prime awakening for that person, that they peaked or were at their consummate best at that age, such as 34 or 46 or 59.

Each person (it took me a while before I realized I was seeing images of my past lives) stood in front of a tableau of images like color photographs from their own life. But these images were unlike ordinary photographs. Each seemed to represent a culmination or wave-breaking moment in their life, when an issue or emotion reached its fulfillment, a desired action was completed, or some definitive action took place, such as a death, betrayal, disappointment, or failure.

Each of these framed moments was like a chalice that held a concentrated feeling, and these feelings were like waves that kept rolling across the landscape of time. Or they were like winds that kept gusting long past the moment of their birth. Each was like a promise, an intention, a pledge, or, in many cases, a curse or vow. Some of these chaliced moments looked black, as if they held a black toxic liquor. Perversely, this fetid dark liquid would be preserved to be savored in the future. At some tactical moment we would drink our own poison.

It was visually complicated but I saw that various chaliced moments in the past were preserved for the future for fulfillment, that their momentum was carried forward and applied tactically in a particular lifetime. Such images might remain dormant for a stretch of time, a hundred, even a thousand years, until the ripe moment arrived, the fresh life with exactly the right circumstances in which that preserved chalice picture might be delivered upon reality to achieve a desired effect, payback, retribution, revenge, apology.

These delivery moments I saw were not always nasty or negative in nature. Sometimes it was a case of finally meeting somebody, marrying them, learning the violin, having children, becoming a healer, experiencing the angels or God. It was like having a bill drawer and you put little sticky notes on each invoice indicating when you will pay it and drop it in the mail. It was all planned out. Your Higher Self knows everything in your bill drawer, and reminds you of the payment dates you put on each karmic item. *You* have already decided this.

The Higher Self is the master reference librarian for the books charting all your past lives—really, I should say, all his past lives, for it is the Higher Self who creates this massive, extended family across the Earth, populates it with questing aspects of itself in pursuit of what to us may seem an arcane agenda. It's funny in a sense, because the Higher Self is the *paterfamilias* of your soul, the great Victorian patriarch of the vast family of lives it has generated over time.

The Higher Self knows every last book in the library, has read them, can recite lines from any page in any volume, and has them properly filed for easy access. His calm contemplation of the contents of any or all of these books is the prime point of *coherence* we desperately need, and, frankly, I think, passionately want. Here is the master viewpoint, the Higher Self's presence attests, that organizes this dizzying diversity of lives, projects, accomplishments, failures, and intentions carried forward into the future into a meaningful, comprehensible pattern in which purpose, intention, and your ultimate destiny are revealed.

Your Higher Self has been running this complex syllogism over your last 10,000 lives. Your Higher Self is the pre-eminent literary critic, finally explaining what the life-novel means, how it was constructed, its subtle mechanics, how it works. Or he is the philosopher (or magician perhaps) giving you a glimpse of the intended conclusion to this long series of linked, progressing propositions; or maybe it's more accurate to liken this cohering activity to an algorithm. Your Higher Self has been running a complex, evolving algorithm; you're part of it.

There are many ways to describe this cohering function of the Higher Self. The point of this display of lives is to present the complete causal chain of your life. Here is the sequence of events, the karmic syllogism, leading to the present moment and its possibility for action and fulfillment or for making new karma. You have to remember this causal chain is expressed in four dimensions, an intention that moves through time and lives, so its display is fourth-dimensional, and, like the Higher Self, hard to see all at once as we are used to only 3D sight.

The reason you want to take this action, feel this way, has antecedents. The winds propelling you forward are coming out of the far-away, long-ago past. An event that spun you around, unsettled you, enraged you, even killed you one thousand years and 12 lifetimes ago, is right beside you now fresh as sunshine, like a thought spawned seconds ago out of the demands of this moment. If there were any points I could not understand about the images or their purport, my Higher Self immediately stepped forward, in my mind anyway, to explain. She instructed me in deciphering this complex spherical 4D tableau of myself. It was like being inside a temple made of a wrap-around Light grid of my history.

It's like a loaded truck, ready for delivery, the motor running, lights on, brakes off. All you have to do is give the hand signal, nod your head, wave it on, to launch. However, it's up to you: you can refuse delivery and dissolve the loaded truck into energy and reabsorb that karmic intention as untainted life-force. You can use that energy windfall to take another step closer to your experiencing Absolute Reality and rendering yourself fully and at last awakened.

This was the general layout inside the Higher Self's sphere of images. For myself, I saw many pictures, many loaded trucks, many burdened chalices, with images from my own multi-lifetime past that explained details of my present life. I saw the history of my friendship with Philomena, our deeds, promises, plans. I saw points of intersections between myself and Edward, Blaise, Tommy, and Pipaluk, sometimes together as a group like we were now, while other times we met individually. I had been a scholar many times before, a writer, researcher, illustrated manuscript painter, librarian, chronicler, poet, all the permutations in vocation pertaining to the creative life of the mind and its modes of expression.

It was like finding a lost appointment book in which you had entered all the meetings and trips you had intended for an entire year, the agendas, contact information, meeting locales, preferred restaurants—your year's complete diary, your whole life before you bumped your head and got this insufferable amnesia. You'd been operating without it, in a fugue state, scrambling to remember bits, but mostly studying the appointment book and not understanding who any of these people were you were scheduled to meet, why you wanted to meet them.

I saw myself as if standing on the edge of a cliff watching a loved one die and depart this physical world, as if flying off the cliff and into an invisible, unknown realm, and I vowed to find out where they went, to discover the nature of the landscape, to chart its topography, profile its denizens, and file a lucid report. I vowed to fully explore that—what is the cliché?—undiscovered country, and, unlike Hamlet's pessimistic assessment, I would bloody well return from it.

I looked at Tommy, Blaise, and Edward. They were similarly within spacious columnar temples filled with concentric layers of life images, as if all this were the inside of their Higher Self's wrap-around cloak, and I saw myself in some of these images, saw us interacting in various combinations, like right now.

The key fact of this disclosure is that before I took one step forward, I knew I would do so briefed on all aspects and ramifications of the intended action. It was as if I had spent weeks, months maybe, studying the mission plans. I knew the details, the complete background and history of the affair, the player biographies, the "foreign" landscapes I intended to enter, the contingencies and fall-back scenarios if the primary plan failed or deviated from its intention. I had rehearsed my role in the play, mastered my floor marks, remembered my lines.

I would enter the field of action wide-awake and informed and minimize the karmic accrual. If possible I would execute the action cleanly and make no new karma. I would act without leaving a trace, as if I were invisible. It would be like what's said of the Christ, he comes like a thief in the night, or of the best espionage field agents, they come and go and leave no trace at all. You never see them; they blend into the crowd; they look like ordinary people. Action without traces, deeds without karma—that seems to be the ideal approach here. What a difference this could make if people entered the *Bardo* equipped with this tactic.

Here, my dead friend, is your long-lost appointment book, the full details of the meetings and people you plan to contact, what hopes or tactics you have in mind. The flow-charts, spreadsheets, projection and extrapolation scenarios, all laid out for your thorough contemplation and mastery before you take action. When you arrive here in this discoverable country, you'll know where the winds come from; you'll know how to hold your ground, stay balanced and upright, as they gust about you. You might as well welcome them since you created them. Why grumble about waves when it was you who dropped the stone in the pond.

We agreed that if the incoming soul were presented with this kind of descriptive tableau courtesy of one's Higher Self it might do the trick. It seemed likely far more *Bardo* travellers would catch on to what the winds were all about if they saw that they had generated them and that sometimes these winds carried over from karmic projects that spanned many incarnations. In the meantime, something strange was happening to Edward. He seemed taken over—I hesitate to use the word "possessed," but perhaps he was poisoned. He was flailing about, twitching, striking out at something getting at him I didn't at first see.

I thought he had been standing next to me, but now he seemed far away, out on a plain without trees and under an oppressive low-lying black cloud. Instantly, we were with him, with the Ganeshes, making a supportive circle around him. Merlin gestured for us to stand steady but not to intervene. Now I saw the reason for the defensive body movements Edward was making.

It looked like a man about his age, which was mid-forties. Outwardly, the man looked friendly, if one can actually be friendly when one is attacking somebody else. What I mean is the guy did not look primitive, bestial, overtly nasty, a ruffian. He looked a bit like Edward, possibly a cousin, or an Amherst College alumnus. What gave him away was his smile. It was not genuine. It was dissimulating. It hid things, his intentions and feelings; it distracted you from discerning his tactics. I guess you'd call him a ruthless white-collar thug.

One of these tactics startled me. A demonic head on an elongated neck sprung out of his midsection and went straight into Edward, expanded, glared inside him, irradiating Edward with noxious psychic vapors of contempt and disdain, then retracted instantly, as if on a spring release, and went back to the guy. I was sure Edward had not seen this. I asked him. He shook his head. The demonic head jerked forward again into Edward, this time releasing a black vapor that formed a geometric mesh over the front of Edward's Light form.

This is why I had suspected he had been poisoned, though I saw now it was not by any physical substance but by a psychic attitude, an atmosphere, like a spell. This black grid released a toxic psychic aura, one full of negativity, hatred, contempt, everything dark and nasty that can befoul the human temperament. It was starting to work on Edward, distorting his natural goodness. I saw his face grow grey, fretful, etched in worry lines and skin crevices. I wasn't sure if he was talking or if I was listening telepathically to his thoughts. They had become pessimistic, pugilistic, defiant, aggressive, very nasty. It didn't sound like my Green Knight expedition colleague any more, but like somebody else, like someone who had a big shock and is drinking it away, and it's the third bleary day of his lost weekend and he is in snarly shape.

The business with the suddenly flashing elongating devil's head—I had never seen anything like it. Frankly, I doubt many people have. It was so fast. When it penetrated Edward's midsection, it immediately expanded and seemed to fill the interior volume of his form completely. Then it flashed a baleful radiation inside Edward, like a spherical neon sign suddenly lighting up, but this neon also had an emission. It was outgassing an offensive psychic attitude.

The best I can say about it was that it was an emission of all-around nastiness. Nastiness as a policy, nastiness as a prevailing emotional state, nastiness as a self-definition. It turned all of Edward into a snarl. He had become a snarling figure. I believe I have mentioned already that in the *Bardo* everything is exposed and naked, so an emotional quality like nastiness will be more pronounced and direct. There are no veils of pretense or pleasant-seeming faces to hide it. It is there, like an exploded bomb. You can't cover it with fair-sounding words or excuses. Shrapnel is flying into your face from all directions.

Merlin had held his hand up to stop us from directly helping Edward. But it was permissible, I gathered, for us to stand there attentively with our own Light swords raised in an upright position paralleling our bodies and for the Ganeshes to radiate an atmosphere of focus, fondness, and amusement, the essential Blaise vibration of original consciousness, a formidable force. If nothing else our swords illuminated the playing, or, should I say, fighting, field for Edward, and I am sure our focused presence also clarified Edward's mind. For now he started to return to himself, as if he had forgotten who he was in the onslaught of that nastiness from the poison-emitting demon's head inside him.

Now that he was at least in part restored to himself, Edward raised his Light sword, a diamond bright blade rippling in lilac flame all around it. He expanded it to the size of a column and stepped inside it; the blade faced all directions at once as if it had magically duplicated itself into a hundred copies. Now

when the devil's head rudely intruded into Edward's energy field, it had to pass through the sword's sharp edge. You have to realize that here, in the *Bardo*, a sword of Light has a different action than a sword of steel in the physical world. Here it does not kill, for how can you kill a spirit anyway?

No, here it illuminates. It clarified the essential nature of this demon-headed spirit, and that nature is emptiness. The sword revealed the inherent voidness of this demon. It is an illusory thoughtform, a mind construct, a cartoon-demon formatted as a hologram, a visualization generated out of malice and projected outward in an attempt to convince the recipient, Edward, of its reality and inimical intentions. Rubbish to you, Edward's sword said. Be gone.

The next time the demon-head intruded into Edward's space, it couldn't leave. The sword focus had dissolved it into energy without form. Edward kept moving forward, following the now vanished elongated neck back to the man. Edward's column of sword edges penetrated his space like a steak knife in butter, and soon this figure, formerly so real-looking, palpable, and menacing, was no more. Its energy had dissipated into particles of Light then dispersed.

Edward grinned. He looked pleased with himself. "Bit of a bounder, don't you think?" he said. "No manners at all. Especially his ill-behaved cohort."

I didn't appreciate Edward's irony at first, though everyone else did. I had wondered at the striking facial similarity between the two figures, despite their radically opposed intentions and actions. "Do you mean they—?" I started but didn't finish my sentence as the answer rose up in me like a brilliant sunrise.

"That's right," Edward said, turning to me, again with his triumphant grin. "Another me, from a past life, with compounded interest, meaning all the negativity I, in my inestimable wisdom as a first-class reincarnating bonehead, developed, accrued, and deposited in the karmic bank of this rotter, came at me through his amplified, enhanced form, with complimentary demon's head. It's bitching weird, isn't it, and a cliché, when you are your own worst enemy. You guys helped, surrounding me like that with swords and copious Blaises. It brought me back to myself, to my senses. Then I understood what was before me and what I needed to do to handle it properly and definitively. Void the karma!

"That other I represented everything opposed to the current I, my prime enemy. And it had become a focal point, a magnetic center, drawing all resonant darkness to it, compounding its own nasty valence, making it yet more toxic. Then the Druj amplified it, made it all bigger, louder, more persuasive, harder to resist. She's always looking for opportunities to extend her influence. She wanted me to believe that this other guy was insuperable; that was her big lie to me.

"That guy, me from another life, another planet, it almost seemed, stood between me and any advancement I might have contemplated for this current life. I would always have to get past him—no, not get past: transmute and dissolve him, or else I would remain stuck, essentially in this same moment as you witnessed, with this opposition always innate and latent within me."

At first I thought it was wind I was hearing, rising up to drown out what Edward was saying, then dying down again to a quiet breeze. I looked away from Edward for a moment and saw many individual humans in their *Bardo* bodies running pell-mell across the grey twilight landscape pursued by demons. These dead souls were fleeing in all directions, possessed by panic and mounting fear. They were barely managing to keep ahead of their nightmarish pursuers who swelled up to look several times bigger than their quarries. These spirits were frightening to behold: they had horns, snarling teeth, wings on fire, glaring, feral eyes, sharp talons, and they emitted earthshaking roars and shrieks.

They looked like psychotic cannibals intent on taking huge bites out of the Light forms of the fleeing humans. They were like crazed, rabid, even demented, animals. At least at first glance they looked scary if you took their apparent reality for granted. I realized that would be a mistake. Apparency was the key that calmed down the scene. They were unreal karmic illusions generated by the individual souls running from them in fear of their lives, variations on the theme I had just seen vividly demonstrated by the two Edwards. They had personified their own karmic fears. They were desperately fleeing their own past-life selves.

These demonic figures chasing humans all over the *Bardo* landscape were emitting sounds, but there were louder sounds coming from everywhere. If you weren't careful, you might think the world was coming to a drastic end. I heard mountains crumbling down, as if collapsing into massive piles of stone all at once. I heard angry, storm-tossed, seething oceans as if possessed by innumerable tidal waves about to break and flood the land. There were fires, roaring and threatening to incinerate the world, all of reality, all souls. And winds, such fierce, unrelenting gales, as strong as the strongest hurricanes, unbelievable winds as if riding the backs of a thousand thunder rolls and strikes.

Was the world ending? I was torn between incredulity and sobriety. I sympathized with disembodied souls running in fear for their lives under the influence of such "awe-evoking" sounds, the understated expression I later found in a translation of the Tibetan text. I sympathized because lacking a correct orientation to context and mechanism, you could easily take reality as presented. It was all special effects revved up to hyperbole condition by each person. By this time I was getting the hang of the *Bardo*, that mostly what you see are artful (histrionic) projections from your previously unrecognized, unacknowledged unconscious, scripted by your karma into convincing and usually awful illusions, and with just enough verisimilitude to properly scare the shit out of you at once.

So what was the origin and true nature of these winds, fires, and waves?

"The apparent sounds of the disintegration of the four elements that have comprised your human body and underscored the corresponding chakras," said Merlin, anticipating my question. That wasn't hard; it was all over my face. "The gross physical elements are being taken apart, yielding their psychic equivalents. You see and hear them in their original forms, as great psychic forces, and yes, you are right to feel sympathy for the souls fleeing in all directions from forces they could never successfully flee from because they are actually coming out of their own disintegrating forms. It would be like being afraid of your breathing, thinking it an outside, inimical force. These sounds and appearances are representations of elemental components of the human form now coming apart."

I wanted to shout out across the twilight field that the horrified humans could relax, none of this was real, just hallucinations spun out by their karma. Unfortunately, I was fairly certain they would not hear or understand me. They were convinced of the horrific reality of these pursuing demonic forms; they seemed locked into that dichotomy of quarry and prey: it was absolute. As for the elemental cacophony, once I understood what these sounds and images were, it was educational to see the familiar four elements in their pure forms. It was as if you took the earth element out of the chakras of all embodied humans and congealed it into one animated mass and loosed it upon a psychic landscape, and then stood back and listened to the roar of massive crumbling mountains.

"They wouldn't know themselves if they didn't have an enemy to flee," observed Blaise. His remark sounded callous and cynical at first, then I saw he was right. As humans we do function under a dichotomy, me against something. It's the basic mechanism of dualistic perception, and it's the same at any level. It's the psychic habit of projection, imposing our unconscious, our undesired aspects, our unacknowledged, unrecognized shadow parts onto other people. Dualistic perception spawns the habitual personality reflex of likes and dislikes. If you like what you see, you run towards it; dislike it and you flee for your life.

Project, blame, and run. If you're a country, then it's your prime enemies. As Americans we are skilled at this, unflaggingly inventive at concocting new enemies to blame for the demise of our preferred lifestyles. Judeo-Christianity also inspired this basic schism in perception: there is us, and there is Satan, and Satan is the reason we are flawed, unhappy, suffering, and basically screwed up.

So we must hunt down all the supporters of Satan and kill them immediately. We must make *crusades* of this intention; later, the Muslims took up the notion, using the word *jihad* instead, calling the *Shaitan* enemies infidels. It's the same resistance mechanism, the same cognitive error at work. So when you get into the *Bardo* you carry over this fundamental mechanism and you start resisting, projecting, and animating demonic enemies you may flee from. Thank God, you declare: this is the fork I know—I know how to run from *them*.

"The key to surviving this place is to get into a nondualistic mind-frame," Blaise said, and again I understood his point after a moment of reflection. Things *seem* dualistic in the *Bardo*, but that perception is the product of karmic illusions. The possibility of realizing everything you see in these *Bardo* phases comes out of your own mind choreographed by your karma, which means everything you see has no fundamental separate existence. The whole *Bardo* is your mind terrain. You've just walked into a *Twilight Zone* rendition of an MRI of your entire self.

The nature of the *Bardo*, its thinness, the way emotions and mental conditions are so naked, makes it easier, potentially, for a soul to comprehend this and be free. Freedom in the *Bardo*, which also means escape from it, is not guaranteed, but it is certainly more likely when you understand this important fact of nondualism. Physical, embodied life is more a matter of intersecting multiple nondualisms; ultimately; your karma or unfulfilled desires script the interactions and in that sense everything you encounter is a mind hallucination clothed in matter, but it is harder, as everyone will agree, to discern the complex mechanism at play in that world. Here you get the mechanism more starkly. If people could get this mechanism, remember it, and carry it back to physical life, what a difference it would make. Reality would, I'm sure, make far more sense.

I pictured myself at a Dartmouth College faculty meeting. I had never enjoyed them. They had always been rife with tension and veiled competition. It's been 17 years since I was even at Dartmouth. It's probably new people now. All these Ph.Ds vying for status, advancement, recognition, honors, and kudos. This was the apparent reality, the one we all customarily took for granted as real, but now I was seeing the *Bardo* reality through this, what we would all be like, dead, wandering the *Bardo*, looking for clarity and orientation. Would these august, self-possessed, articulate, opinionated American dons be feverishly fleeing flesh-eating demons only inches away from devouring their backsides?

It was both funny and sad to contemplate. How ill-prepared, I suspected, how unbriefed, all my fellow academics were for the unclothed reality of the *Bardo*. I was no different. I would be the same except for this fabulous expedition. How much did any of us in the comfortable, well-outfitted faculty meeting room understand that we were each karmic illusions projected by the others' karma? That we each were temporary holders of projections from the others in the room? That we were fully uneducated regarding the mechanics of our consciousness?

I saw some of my fellow academicians arrive in the *Bardo*, step out of Charon's boat or climb onto the perilous Bridge of the Decider, the *Cinvat* Bridge. Honestly, even now, months after the conclusion of our expedition and my return to bodily life (though I cannot claim it is "normal" life after all I have seen), I cannot be sure whether I was imagining this or seeing the future. I saw a male faculty member, a professor of Germanic philosophy, someone I shared lunch with at times, talking about Goethe and his publishers, enter the *Bardo*.

His astral body looked like it was scalloped with a thousand thin sheaves of hammered metal on which were innumerable neon-framed images. These thin sheaves were stuck into his astral body at angles in the front as if they were too many manila folders shoved into too few available slots. They bulged. One after another, these garish, cinematic pictures flashed brilliantly as if lit by an interior spotlight. Wherever he pointed his hand an image flashed out there, projecting its contents into the field of Clear Light and thereby polluting it. Polluting it in the sense of introducing an illusory element into something meant to be clear.

Then, thinking this flashing image before him was a legitimate external reality, he reacted, usually running towards it, either to enter it or to push it away. In either case, he granted this pulsing outside image a credible reality, and he was off and running, regrettably, another red-nosed clown performer in the *Bardo*'s hallucinatory million-ring circus of people madly chasing their own tails.

As I knew the man I was watching, I was tempted to intervene and start explaining how the place worked, but something held me back, not the least of which was the fact that I too was hallucinating, or at any rate what I was seeing was unreal, meaning not strictly happening now, only potentially taking place. It wasn't my problem. The fellow never liked me offering comments or suggestions on his teaching methods or class references, priding himself on his own self-praised autodidacticism, so I doubt he would appreciate it now, even if I worked Goethe into my exegesis or gave him a few tips about the *Dhyani* Buddhas.

A pleasant lassitude was coming over me, a species of relaxation and great ease as if my consciousness had been suddenly transferred to an ocean-fronting, sun-lit beach, and my body was releasing its muscle tension into the warm sand.

That was how I felt, but where I was, where my consciousness had been relocated to, was a library, though not any library, not even the huge library of a major university or the British Museum or Library of Congress, but one bigger. Jorge Luis Borges would have liked this: it was the library of all the world. Every book ever published on the Earth was on its shelves, and I was in that library.

The reading room was spectacular. It was domed in glass, walls enpillared with crystal columns topped with golden sphinxes, comfortable reading chairs everywhere, but spaced for maximum privacy like Henry James's Reform Club around 1890, as I imagined it. Even the time felt spacious; nobody was in a rush. I sat in the kind of plush chair whose sleek fabric creaked luxuriously when you settled down into it, a chair you'd never want to leave, a chair in which you could read innumerable books, contemplate no end of delightful subjects, ponder inscrutables of existence, nap, wake up, and come to many fresh conclusions.

I saw my body back in New Hampshire somewhere. I didn't much care. It was in a mortuary, I suppose, or a funeral home, prepared for services and burial. I suppose I must have died. I didn't care. I had no interest, no desire at all to re-enter my former body. I much preferred my current situation. I saw my house, my library, my favorite books, my desk piled with papers and journals. I saw Philomena's studio, her grand piano, her books on the Russian pianists. I saw our house from the outside, saw that a few windows needed repainting, and one of the sills on the north side was starting to rot and must be replaced soon. I saw the orchard, the rolling fields, traces of snow, the mountains in the distance. I heard Philomena playing something mystical by her favorite, Scriabin. I liked it.

The present moment with me in the deliciously comfortable lounge and reading chair seemed to stretch all across the planet. It was an elongated now. I felt no desire or need to go anywhere. I could, and surely I would, read any book I wished, summoning them to my hand with a mere thought and the stretching out of my open palm to receive the volume from the shelves. I had my cup of Darjeeling tea on a side table, the lamp behind me was sufficiently bright, and Philomena had switched to playing études by Chopin, more calming to the ears. I vaguely remembered I had been part of some strange expedition some years ago but I couldn't remember with what outcome or even to what purpose.

I was enjoying a pleasant and even stimulating discussion with a colleague about Henry James's explorations into the occult and afterlife in his ghost stories, whether these were imaginative forays or based on direct, unsettling experience. In fact, Henry James had just entered the club and was taking off his top hat and greeting us. I could ask him. He just started to—

Something was shaking me, and a bright light was shining annoyingly in my face. Had somebody reoriented the reading lamp to be right in my face? Then I opened my eyes in mild shock. What happened to Henry James? It was my wife instead, Philomena, in person somehow, and she wasn't shaking me or annoyingly shining a light in my face. It was just the innate brilliance of her Light body that was providing the illumination, and that was shaking me awake. Oh right. Oh shit! I remembered my dear wife had ascended into an immortal body.

I had fallen asleep, though in an odd way, it was more like I had slid easily into a lovely, intoxicating trance. I had drifted off into a reverie and gave it full cinematic quality. I was still standing next to Edward, Blaise, Tommy, and Pipaluk, but I had drifted off, gone to sleep while standing up, or exited my Light form for some paradise, floated off in an unmoored canoe into the *Bardo*.

Merlin found this amusing. He was chuckling as if I had made a great joke. "Behold the other side of things, the *Bardo*'s penchant to produce karmic hallucinations. In this case Frederick's hallucination was benign, summoned out of a reservoir of innate goodness, positive karma, and accrued healthy merit. One can just as easily get lost in a paradisal condition here as to be beset by monsters. I counsel the deceased who wander the *Bardo* to resist the allurements of a delightful hallucination as much as they should resist surrendering to its frights. Either will detain you longer than you need in the various sticky *Bardo* realms.

"Frederick, I think you didn't realize you entered an expanded, full-life version of one of the karmic seeds you carried in your astral form, your paradisal library. Very pleasant, I am sure, but if you had stayed immersed in

it, reveling in its delights, it could have sidetracked you for a long time, and, absent being chased by horrible monsters and ill-mannered *Herukas* to refocus your attention, you might have forgotten entirely about the quest to wake up and enter the Clear Light. You did forget all about our little Green Knight expedition, I noticed. Sad."

"Well, officer, you'll have to let Frederick off with a warning this time," said Tommy, grinning. "It is easy to get mesmerized in this place. It happened to me. I had gotten past the 110 dancing, demonic *Herukas*, made some sense of the presence of the *Dhyani* Buddhas, and was thinking myself just about finished. Remember, I actually was dead—I *still am*, come to think of it—doing this for real, not simulating the whole thing like you guys, not pretending, not window shopping for *Bardo* illusions. I was making life and death decisions: such irony.

"I think it started when I suddenly remembered a little grove outside my high school. It was my favorite place at school, not that I liked school one bit. I often went there, stood, sat, even reclined, on the grass under the trees. It was relaxing, even meditative, though I can't remember having any visions or even insights. Mostly, the place calmed me, drained my agitated mind of its worries.

"Worries? You know, teenager angst, discontent, restiveness, pre-suicidal estrangement, the whole young Werther's sorrowful playbook for adolescents considering an early exit. So I was standing there again, feeling good, content, flush with self-understanding. Dozens of my fellow students were lined up in half-circles in front of me, waiting respectfully for me to begin speaking to them. Apparently, I was supposed to give a talk. I hoped I had prepared something.

"I started talking, and the scene seamlessly shifted to the auditorium, and the audience had greatly increased in its numbers, as if the entire school were there. They were listening to me. They *wanted* to hear what I had to say. That in itself was remarkable. As a disaffected student with only a half-hearted interest in anything the school had to offer, I was used to not being listened to. I was used to not even bothering to try to tell people anything. It seemed pointless. Now everyone was hearing every word I offered them, and I offered them a lot.

"I was explaining myself, explaining reality, the developmental curves and thresholds of adolescence, the populations and hierarchical structure of the spiritual worlds. God, where did I ever get all this information? It puzzled me, yet I spoke with conviction and authority, and I knew I spoke all this correctly. The teachers listened attentively, as did the principal, vice-principal, and nurses.

"I realized I had published a book and I had it with me at the podium, and now I was reading excerpts from it. They sounded good, professionally written. After my talk, I sat at a table and autographed copies. People flocked around me. They said they were so grateful a sensitive, inquiring person like myself had written about all these important questions, about the need for self-awareness, self-knowledge, and the quest to wake up amidst the alluring trances of life. I smiled, appreciating the delicious irony. I was being praised for precisely what I had previously been ignored, my sensitivity, philosophical inquiries, and for rating the investigation of the nature and mechanics of reality and consciousness as higher than peer relations, competition, and the newest electronic gadgetry.

"The flow of time was blurred because I had the impression I was ten years older than I should be if I were still in high school. I looked in a mirror. Yes, I did look older, late twenties; it was still me, but I looked more grown-up. I realized I was teaching at this school; I was writing more books; the students and faculty regarded me as a sage, as someone worth listening to, who knew a thing. Everything was the opposite of how it had been, how it had *felt*, when I was there as a student. It had reversed. I was no longer estranged: I was embedded. I was no longer the outsider, the Steppenwolf, peering disconsolately into the windows of the social world. I was Socrates, at the center of it, explaining things.

"One day I went to visit my body. Somehow the illogic of this did not strike me as worth any attention. How could I be alive if I was viewing my dead body? You know the crazy but plausible logic of dreams? It was skewed and screwy like that. I accepted its queerness. I viewed the body. My parents had buried my body rather than cremated it, so there it was, there I was, deceased. I saw my right index finger. I had always found it fascinating. I would bend it, flex it, point it, curl it up, marveling at how my brain commanded the muscles to move. I remember studying the exact design and placement of the freckles on the skin, the creases at the flexion point of the bendable bits, how the fingernail grew, how long it took for this dead thick skin to produce the white rounded tip.

"I slipped my awareness into my former body. It was like putting on a robe, once a favorite. Everything felt stiff, heavy, cold, leaden, and immobile. I could not lift my right index finger or flex its bendable bits. You know how it's hard to move your arm or leg when it's gone to sleep? My whole body felt that way. I couldn't move anything. None of the muscles responded. It felt as if my body had been turned to stone and I would need a forklift to shift its weight.

"It felt like I had slipped my attention, like a wisp of air or a little rivulet of water, into the heaviest stone you could find on the Earth. It was full of gravity. It was made of gravity. It was slowly falling into the deepest hole in the

Earth. No, its weight and heavy gravity were making that hole, finding a final resting place. It was sinking steadily into the ultimate black hole where all light, though in this case, it was matter, would be sucked into and disposed of, never heard from again. The world would be forevermore black, and so heavy. I felt myself falling, slowly but incessantly, into an ever-deepening, endless dark hole.

"It started to feel weird, decidedly unpleasant. I wondered what happened to me as the high school hero, the sage celebrity, that I had been reveling in. How could I have shifted so quickly from that delightful scenario to this death plummet? Then it struck me. It did actually feel like a slap on my face. Wait a moment. I've forgotten something important. I knew I had forgotten it, and I felt its aura of significance approach me. Then I remembered. I am dead.

"None of this is real. It is, on the one hand, a pleasant fantasy or hallucination spun out of my karmic seeds left over from my now departed life, and it is, on the other hand, an insinuation, a heat check, as they say in basketball, about my desire to return to a human body, which means, did I want to reincarnate? Go for another three-pointer from way beyond the circle? Did I want to slip my consciousness, my soul, into yet another mortal human body? Did I still have that Lawrentian redness and blood-passion for another round? Not that anybody specifically was asking, but I said out loud: I'll get back to you.

"I still haven't decided, but nobody is pressuring me about it. Nobody is working on commission to get royalties on souls they persuade to reincarnate. Once I collected myself, the whole dream illusion instantly disappeared. I felt I had lost myself in an alluring distraction, a daydream, and now I was back again.

"God, this place is tricky. If you're not completely on your toes, you're likely to be fooled, conned, or seduced by some attractive hallucination in a finger-snap. It's like crossing a desert full of booby traps, landmines, and pop-up hallucinations. It looks empty and relatively harmless, then when you relax, it starts happening. Suddenly it's no longer a blank desert, but a packed funhouse of bizarre tricks. And all this crazy crap coming out of my own demented head!"

"Nicely told, Tommy," said Blaise, "except for one small point. Somebody does work on commission and does get points for every reincarnation she secures. I'm talking about our old friend and scourge, the multifarious Druj. She benefits every time she gets a soul to reincarnate with an attitude, which means to enter the womb-door slightly bent, crooked, twisted, intent on a Druj mission. Pumped up with just the right amount and flavor of disinformation to re-enter the human stream misinformed, misdirected, out of focus. Here, take this nice lie with you; it will help you whenever you call upon it, she says covertly, directing the unconscious of the reincarnating individual."

"Those were both simulations of potential future lives," said Merlin. "Each represented, played out before you, the possibilities of achieving an unrequited desire, Tommy for peer acceptance, Frederick for all knowledge among a community of congenial scholars. For you, Frederick, it was the nurturing of a seed for future karma, since, as you know, you are not dead. It could have been activated when you finally did arrive in the *Bardo*, but now that you have advance notice of it, a preview, we might say, that is less likely.

"For Tommy, already deceased, it was the ripening and blossoming of a karmic seed. You could have remained in that living picture, entranced and delighted, for years, then taken that as a plausible life-script for your next incarnation and enacted it. First you test it out here, run the simulations, which we call, with all suitable endearments, hallucinations or creative illusions; then you enact it for real, etch it into matter and the *Akashic* Records in your next incarnation, creating karma. For Frederick, you would likely have retained this simulated seed and reviewed it when you came here legitimately in the future, maybe simulated it again briefly, and then possibly decided to enact it in a life."

12

I can't say how much time elapsed between what I just narrated and where we now found ourselves. All of us, except for Matthew, were seated in a half-circle. Before us was the Druj. She was talking to us. Actually, it was like a press conference. She was inviting us to ask questions, any questions we liked.

I was surprised that I wasn't wary or frightened of her. Technically, she is the Antichrist, and that spirit, the putative enemy of all humankind, is said to be nasty and intent on the destruction of human freedom and lucid consciousness. But it didn't feel that way. She seemed eminently interviewable, rather cordial. I caught myself fantasizing asking her afterwards for her private phone number.

Blaise seemed to pick up on my thoughts. "I know what you mean, Frederick. No, we're not afraid of the Druj, though wariness is advisable. She is the shadow side of our dear Albion, the collective consciousness of humanity, a kind of infernal counterpart of this colossus of awareness spawned in his sleep.

"She will lie to us on every occasion possible, but sometimes her lies will be so beautiful, so perfectly wrought and so eminently plausible, that we can only admire her artistry, and if we are not vigilant, we may take a few steps towards accepting these deceptions as the truth and thus be, as she wants, badly misled. She creates a counterpoint alternate reality of our human-flavored life. Still, can you appreciate the irony that we cannot yet talk lucidly to humanity's Albion, as he is still waking up into the daytime world, yet we can discourse freely with its Druj, collective shadow, adversary, obfuscator, and chief of lies.

"She does not have to appear to us as formidably ugly or frightening. She can seem laughing, easy-going, but the true face of her 'evil,' if we choose to call it that, is her indifference. She is devoid of any moral center, any conscience. She is entirely about expedience and efficiency. Think of all the ruthless, brutal people in the world who act with no empathy or sympathy for other humans. For a long while, decades, this was a common motif in movies: ruthless bad guys who killed, maimed, tortured, abused, took what they want with no conscience. I used to wonder why this was so. Then I understood it was another Druj lie. It was the lie that it didn't matter that they denied their conscience and empathy."

I cannot tell you precisely what the Druj looked like. That is because she kept shifting her appearance, the way fish scales or soap bubbles will reflect light and images. I had the impression she was continuously altering her appearance in response to what she picked up from us, what our expectations or fears were. If she were a human being you'd likely say the girl can't sit still and keeps squirming, but hers was a degree of subtlety far past that interpretation.

It reminded me of Proteus, the oracular sea-deity whom Menelaus wrestled with. That wily spirit kept altering its appearance to elude Menelaus's grasp, assuming the sequential forms of a lion, serpent, leopard, pig, water, and a tree. Of course, Proteus, as Blaise explained in his desert notebooks, was the Ofanim and their point was to demonstrate the metaphors and shapeshiftings of consciousness. I suppose the Druj was modeling the protean nature of her lies.

The Druj looked like a tall, sleek woman made of water and shaped like a birch tree. On her watery surface she projected numerous appearances, young woman, breast-feeding mother, tart, demon, witch, queen, sorceress, hag, Harpy, *Heruka, Dakini,* even the Great Mother Isis, one Fata Morgana after another, all clever, all artistically, flawlessly executed, but none lasting more than a second.

Her voice remained consistent. She pitched it as the voice of a woman about 40. It was rich, lilting, seductive, persuasive, infused with intelligence and wit. She was an irritant to Yama who sought to run the Underworld in an orderly manner. She reminded me of the way *Le Morte d'Arthur* depicted Morgan le Fay; she was King Arthur's sister but as a master of necromancy, as Malory quaintly put it, she periodically interfered with his activities and often undermined them. Sometimes she acted as his ally, but most of the time she basically got in his way.

I was studying one of Druj's recent appearances. In retrospect, I should say I was already entranced by one of them and slowly being drawn into its false allures. She reminded me of a faculty member in our department. This woman was up for chairman of the department, as I was; we were competitors for it. I was certain, and I even had some tangible proofs of this, documents, evidence, that she was manipulating the appointment on the basis of falsehoods and lies.

She had misled people with certain claims in her biography, contacts, residencies, accomplishments, even the details of some of her publications had been falsified. I had the proofs of her malfeasances, and I intended to use them because I was better qualified, more fitted, more deserving of the promotion to chairman. Aside from my incontestable accomplishments and academic merit, my researches alone, my conclusions, interpretations, the associative leaps in synthesis across diverse fields of comparative mythology, the hermeneutic sparkle of all my work, should have *already* unquestionably placed me in the chairmanship, and they will. I knew I had the backing of the majority of staff.

I was reviewing my publications, the monographs, papers, books, in my mind, impressed with them as if I were an outsider, a biographer considering them. I glowed in rosy satisfaction. Well done, indeed, Professor Frederick. Impressive! Then I wondered why the walls of the faculty room seemed to be shaking. They weren't. It was Edward nudging my shoulder. I woke up from my trance. I realized, in shock, dismay, and, I admit, disappointment, it had all been illusory. I had walked right into one of the Druj's artful little feuilletons, a clever holographic montage of simulated fantasies, hidden urges, and secret desires.

Pipaluk was speaking. "Do you ever find yourself about to—" and before she finished her question the Druj had already answered. "Yes, quite often I do."

Pipaluk went silent. She seemed to be staring out at the horizon. Her eyes were open but her attention had been taken elsewhere. The Druj had netted her. Afterwards, I asked her what had happened, where the Druj had spirited her to.

She still wore a mask of surprise on her otherwise serene face. Remember, she was (then) 111 years old; she'd seen just about everything. She seemed even a little embarrassed by the event, the way a teenage girl might blush if her parents found her out about something, like a secret date with a proscribed boyfriend.

The humble shaman from Qaanaaq told her story, but she smiled as she did so. "I did not notice the transition, but in the middle of asking the Druj my question, I was seated with a circle of female shamans out in the treeless snow landscape near my village. It is a place I went to often, though always on my own. Now I had company. Perhaps one hundred shamans from all over Greenland. I don't know how this happened, but I was their leader.

"They were expecting guidance and instructions from me, news of our next plans. I do not lead. Few shamans do, or want to. We work alone. We need solitude to concentrate. But here I was, speaking to the women. We were heading north to Nyboe Land. There is a place of power and focus I know of in that area, and I could see it from where I was with the women. I felt like I had been there, but I could not remember when that could have been. Yet I knew the place.

"First I had to prepare the women. They needed healing. Some were incomplete, missing parts of themselves that had wandered off or gotten lost. I had to retrieve those soul fragments. Some were ailing physically, and I had to mix the correct herbs and minerals and meditate on these mixtures to give them energy. Other women had troubling dreams or visions that needed my interpretations. A few were young, just starting their vocation as an *angakkuq*, and they needed reassurance; they needed to hear a few tales of the older ones.

"I was responsible for them. I had to make sure each woman was ready. This would take some time. I would probably have to work day and night. But I was supposed to do this. I was the only one who could. I was good at this. If I didn't help all these women, the plan would fail. They could not do it on their own. They needed me, and I was the only one who could help them get ready.

"Why were we assembled? My own spirit-guide council had shown me a picture. We were seated in a circle and were projecting copies of ourselves across Greenland, occupying its vital places of landscape power, what Blaise calls geomantic nodes. We were going to put certain images over all of Greenland, like projecting a tent made of an image, or many images, in Light, like what you call the Northern Lights but rearranged to make an image. You call it a Light grid.

"Our plan was to broadcast this picture message to all the Earth, to send it out from Greenland, a land most people pay no attention to and consider an ice field of little value in the North. But we would show them that Greenland was worth paying attention to. We had a mission to draw the world's attention to Greenland, to the Nyboe Land site, to impress them with the power of the native *angakkuq*. Now they would heed us. They would come to us for our knowledge."

Pipaluk was shaking her head, her eyes cast downward, almost frowning. "This is when I realized something was wrong. This is not Pipaluk thinking this. I work alone. The other shamans work alone. We meet seldom, more often in our spirit forms and not in a physical assembly like this. I do not have big plans for Greenland. I have nothing I need to show the world about the *angakkuq*. I do not try to change or even fix the world. I help people in my village. I do not feel I have been shortchanged or ignored by the world. I do not look for any of that.

"This is when I realized that what I was seeing, what I seemed to be doing, was a lie. It could not be. It was not. I was being shown a grand false image of myself. It was alluring. It had hooks on it, and I was the fish about to bite on them. I am sad that I believed it for as long as this vision of the woman shaman's circle lasted. The Druj was making me swell with self-importance. That is not like Pipaluk."

I laughed. Not at Pipaluk. No, I laughed because I got the Druj's tactics. She was interviewing each of us, probing us for our weaknesses, our seduction points, where she could insert a lie and inflate it to credible proportions to see if and for how long we gave it credence. She was testing us for our vulnerabilities. She was the journalist interviewing us, and confounding us behind the scenes.

I felt like my head was slowly spinning. I couldn't get a steady focus on the Druj. I was trying to figure out what was her fundamental form, how did she truly look? Was the scary Antichrist guise as hater of humanity the true one and this simulation of a Harpy who turns into a *Dakini* the lie, or was this fluctuating image of a female deity of multiple forms the true one and the Antichrist image the big lie? Was it a lie that she looks scary, or is the lie that she doesn't look scary? I couldn't tell. I could see that it played convincingly well either way. Maybe her truest image was subjective to me, whichever form best fooled me. That was the effective, persuasive lie the Druj concocted to hoodwink me. If you want frightening, she'll oblige; if you prefer slyly seductive, the Druj is your girl.

She would tell you any lie you desired to hear. If you wanted to hear that God is dead or never existed, she would present that "fact" to you convincingly. If you preferred hearing that God is your own personal assistant, valet, and butler, attentive to your every emotional or psychological nuance, the Druj would flesh it out and present it to you with bells, whistles, and knobs on. Perhaps you wanted to be let off the hook from the arduous cycle of purifications a newly dead person has to go through (or endure) in this bizarrely tricky *Bardo*. No

problem, she'd convince you; it's really, after all, just a mild entertainment option, an elective in an educational program which you may constantly adjust.

Or perhaps you were feeling just a little proud of yourself with the way you handled that rowdy gang of *Herukas*, the blighters. You could count on the Druj to pump up your self-importance, telling you spirituality is definitively over-rated. You should get your fine ass back into the material world where it was all happening and where, if you like, she could squeeze all these *Bardo* revelations and purification deities into a convenient little portable info-disk.

The *Bardo*, she'll tell you confidentially, is the actual lie, the biggest lie there is. It's all an entertaining illusion the Supreme Being dreamed up on a slow business day to keep Himself from boredom. Forget about it; the *Bardo* doesn't matter. God's a shameless grifter anyway. Watch your pockets! The physical world, the material realm, is the only place that has true, lasting reality, and the sooner you get yourself back there into a fresh desire body, the sooner you'll see and start reaping the benefits of that pleasure world, like picking ripe apples.

As for that business about concentrating on the innate emptiness of consciousness, that is just so much bosh and nonsense. Don't waste your time on that. There's nothing there, and I mean nothing, the old-fashioned kind of voidness, a really empty nothing kind of place, where even your awareness isn't worth cultivating and you might as well stare at the bark of a tree waiting for the tree to stretch and walk away. You'll be waiting in that useless emptiness until this Age of Brahma is finished and you'll have nothing to show for it except what an impressive bonehead you are and what a penchant you have for wasting time.

I realized these thoughts were running like a travel narrative in my mind, like the voice-over to a supposed educational program and like a kayak I had deftly inserted myself into its slipstream and was paddling along briskly with it. "Which is exactly why the Druj is known as the *Anti*christ," said Merlin, also in my thoughts, like a large rock that suddenly appears in the smooth river surface.

"She represents, she advocates, everything that is opposite and contrary to the Christ. The Christ is for truth, so she is for falsehood; the Christ speaks for the heavenly kingdom of the spirit, so she advocates the material world as primary. The Christ encourages clarity and discernment, so she pushes for hallucination. Can you see now that the biggest and perhaps the single and certainly the culminating challenge of the *Bardo* is to overcome the clever, prolific deceptions of the Druj? She lays snares and nets of misperception to entrap you everywhere, to cause you to misinterpret, avoid, ignore, or not see anything.

"The *Bardo* in this sense is a sustained cognitive test for the transiting soul, to see if this time, during this afterlife journey, you may finally take the true measure of the Druj and become at last free of her entanglements that have bound you for lives. This is the final purification in the cycle of purifications you undergo in the *Bardo*. If you see through all the machinations, the wiles and meretricious appearances, you may, if you choose, sail off to a world of Light of your choice. Or you may voluntarily reincarnate to help alive people wake up. In this way you defeat the Druj because she is intent on getting people to routinely reincarnate and never master the Wheel of Life, never achieve the primacy of consciousness, and remain subject to the heavy gravity well of physical reality.

"This, by the way, is the esoteric meaning of the Weighing of the Heart on the scales. It is a test of the soul's discernment ability to perceive the truth of reality. In effect, you weigh the Christ against the Antichrist; your capacity to discern, now that you have been through the rigorous cycle of purgatories or purifications, constitutes the scales. The Judge or Judges of the Dead, whether it's Anubis, Abathur Muzania, or any other named figure, are only your witnesses.

"Always remember that the Druj wants to deflect your discernment away from the *Bardo*, to block your attention or distract it so that you feel compelled to rush back into the phenomenal world and reincarnation because you think that is the only haven, the only safe place, and because you feel it is familiar. She is an adept saleswoman plying an addictive substance; you feel you can't live without it. Unfortunately, most people come to believe the physical world is familiar and therefore safe and a sanctuary; they presume they understand it. They do not. They have become addicted to the rush of material life, its delirious illusions. The blood, the passions, the hormones, the redness of incarnate life, confounds them.

"They are only familiar with the outer casings of life, a few of its ritualized gestures. The rest is as mysterious as the *Bardo*—in fact, *that* is the real mystery because all the *Bardo* is in truth the divestment zone, where the layers of phenomenality you thought seemed so familiar are stripped off your consciousness one by one. The Druj wants human consciousness locked up, bound in matter so it will not ascend or transmute its limitations, so it will completely fail to comprehend the meaning of the *Bardo* mystery, and at all costs, fail to resolve and end all its karma. That is the cement that keeps people embedded in the Wheel of Life. In these ways the Druj works profoundly and fundamentally against the Christ. The Christ liberates, but the Druj imprisons.

"Even though the phenomenal world is the place of potential liberation and ascension, it is also the place of profound ignorance, meaning your not knowing the true conditions of reality or the mechanisms of consciousness and its freedom. The Druj strives to keep people asleep while in matter and asleep to the true nature and possibilities of matter so that when they enter the *Bardo* they are similarly confounded and fail to discern the *Bardo*'s nature and free themselves. Then the two endarkened worlds feed off each other and human consciousness is bound and remains bound fast in this reciprocal loop of obliviousness to reality. As far as tactics go, you have to hand it to the Druj. She is quite a shrewd devil."

"You know the cliché that life is a stage and you are the actor?" It was Blaise. "That image has been tossed about a lot because it is a good one. Now maybe it's more applicable to movies. But put your attention on the dressing room. Here you put on your disguise, the make-up, face paint, wig, fake beard, prosthetics, whatever devices are needed to alter your appearance to match the writer's image of the character. Technical people help you with this. You make your performance, either before the live audience or the camera, then return.

"These same technical people help you remove all the costumery. This is the *Bardo*. Let's say you enter the dressing room with short-term amnesia. You thought the reality, your true nature, was the stage character you were playing. Now that is being deconstructed; everything that comprised that persona is being stripped off. You freak out. Feel afraid, full of panic and uncertainty. These same make-up people now seem like monsters to you and inexplicably demonic.

"You resist everything they do. You feel they are killing you in layers. It is awful. Impossibly, it would seem, yet there it is, you have completely forgotten that this dressing room is where you assembled the illusion of the stage character. It was fake, a contrivance, a deception, a lovely hallucinatory walking illusion, and it was intended to be; you were intent on pretending to be this person, yet you forgot that and took the pretend character to be yourself. You want to hold on to every lipstick smear, every false eyelash, the lovely fake hair.

"Do you see? The *Bardo* is where you take off your costume. You reverse the steps by which you assembled your illusory appearance. For an actor who remembers he is an actor, wearing a persona, the mask for the play, is natural. The Druj tries to get people to forget they are actors, to identify entirely with the character they are portraying, and to regard the dressing room as a nightmare zone to be avoided, tolerated in fear and panic, and rushed through at all costs."

"That is correct," said Merlin. "The paramount act the Druj strives at all costs to prevent any human from committing is to strip while on the stage. That means to take off your costume and make-up, divest yourself of the character, while you are on the stage, in the public eye, which means while you are human-incarnated. That act of voluntary nakedness is precisely what the Christ inspires. You strip off your costume, stand there naked, then become the audience viewing you. You see yourself at last, unclothed, a unit of bodiless consciousness. Your attention fluctuates from being yourself and being the audience seeing you. There's a third possibility: you become the stage and performance hall itself in which this spectacle of fluctuating identity of actor and audience is enacted live.

"The Christ Light or the Buddha Mind, the Clear Light of the *Bardo*, is the experience of the nakedness of consciousness while you are alive in a human form. It is the blissful experience of voidness, the emptiness of phenomenality, and the fullness of Light while you are in a human body, alive, on the Earth. You wake up the Christ Light while incarnated and the *Bardo* and the physical world collapse into a singularity; they are no longer separate, but two related venues.

"Then matter starts to rise into the Clear Light. Human consciousness is liberated. Your human life is now a living *Bardo* because you recognize all its mechanisms. You stand gloriously unclothed in the *Rigpa* spotlight, empty and loving it. You are the actor, the audience, the theater, and none of it as well. The Christ Light is the place of liberation within matter and in the *Bardo* too, while the Druj or the Antichrist is the multifarious, protean opposition to that, the place of stuckness, the oubliette of consciousness bound in gravity and darkness."

"People don't expect to still be conscious when they're dead," said Tommy. "It threw me off for a while. It's true, whatever they do expect is either hazy and vague or conditioned by religion and its incomplete understanding. But you get here and you find you are still aware, in fact, far more, acutely aware, yet you are missing the usual supports for that awareness, namely, your body and life, the outside world which we take for granted while in bodies. The four elements that so seamlessly flavor our subjective experience of the world are missing here. You now get the world unmediated by this elemental subjectivity.

"The two customary objects of our attention, the outside world and the me that is experiencing it, are also changed dramatically. The outside world seems like it's gone mental; it is falling apart, revealing strange spirits doing bizarre things. The inside world feels rather thin, even anorexic, and suffering from chronic amnesia. The identity you took for granted, the interior reference point, is now very weak. It's like remembering a few lines and facial gestures from an old movie part you once played. They are historical, not in present time.

"It is more like an old habit whose mechanisms are dissolving. It is like a memory that is fading, becoming insubstantial, like water slipping through your hands. You feel like you're being squeezed into a strange new place, probably somewhere you've never been before, or if you've touched into it, run away from it as fast as possible. That place is your naked awareness. It is the only place left for you to stand. Everything going on outside you is coming out of your own 'mind' or whatever rational memory structure you have, and everything that used to constitute your inner self is now draining out fast. You stand in this, knowing, uneasily, it's not even the old familiar you that's doing the standing.

"This was disturbing at first. Then I discovered something cool. If I relaxed into this in-between place of naked awareness, if I accepted that it was in truth the only viable place to stand, the only solid land in the *Bardo*, then I could be in both worlds at the same time. The phenomenal world and the *Bardo* world. They are not different fundamentally; both are, ultimately, illusory and transient.

"They are both organized thoughtform projections, organized by consciousness. The phenomenal world is a theater of expectations directed by karma, and the *Bardo* is an act that shows you where all the magic strings are in that world. In the phenomenal world the tricks unfold in slow-motion, glacially slow, while here they are instantaneous, many going on at once and in different dimensions. Imagine watching a tennis match in the fourth dimension: balls fly everywhere. You better hope your neck is loose and limber.

"One day I saw all the theater entrances. I counted them: 1,746 around the planet. Each was identical, a series of tall, imposing gates; each set of gates opened to this one same place, Yama's celestial city and cabaret of the *Bardo*. You could also call these theater entrances portals; they conduct you to Yama's realm. I saw all of them in a unified pattern across the Earth's surface, all these identical gates in a pattern wrapped around the Earth, and all opening into this one city.

"Imagine a spherical building with 1,746 doorways, as pockmarked in doors. I saw people passing through these gates, singly or often in groups. It reminded me of people streaming into a baseball stadium for an afternoon game.

"I saw Yama. He was massive and, oddly, spherical as well. He seemed to constitute the entire celestial city for which he was regent, and he also appeared to be the prime gate you passed through once you went through the outer ones. He ran the show, and it looked like he was the show, or it was all inside him. For a moment he looked like a combination of Oliver Hardy and a *Heruka*. I saw that famous Wheel of Life. At first it seemed to be inside him, like a ribcage. Then it seemed to spread out and overlay the extent of the celestial city; the six major divisions of that wheel filled out the bulk of this interior space. The whole thing is the *Bardo*, Yama, the wheel, the six divisions, and the 1,746 Earth doors into it.

"Sometimes, when I was still and concentrated, not fretting or trying to figure things out, I would settle into this single point of awareness. It was like a bright blazing diamond on fire with white flames. It was warm, a little tingling. It felt like floating in a mineral waters spa. The water emitted ripples of bliss. I felt I was floating, gradually immersing myself in a hot tub of happiness. I wasn't happy about anything in particular; it was the pure vibration of that. It grew stronger, like a feeling surrounding me on all sides; then I fell asleep. Or so it seemed. I lost everything, even the bliss. Eventually, I returned to myself.

"I suppose that means I woke up or separated myself from that unified bliss state. But for a moment, when I returned to myself, both worlds were in the same place. The phenomenal world I had left, the intermediate realm I was now in. They were mutually superimposed on each other, two overlapping holograms. One layer was the karmic opera known as my embodied life; the other was the aftermath of that performance played out in the dressing room. I saw them both. I weighed them both. My awareness of them was the scales.

"I wondered how much longer I cared to keep up this uncertain selfhood odyssey. I had an image of this: I was a ball of blazing white fire in the open palm of the Supreme Being. Whenever I wanted I could enter that Hand. No longer be a separate flaming ball of consciousness, but return to the Hand. Do you follow me? I mean have the Hand absorb that ball of white fire, absorb me."

"The Druj would count that as a failure," said Blaise. "She wouldn't like that outcome. One more player taken off the playing field of the Great Game."

In fact, I think the Druj was getting tired of our ruminations. She wanted some action. She wanted to get on with her next episode of that Great Game.

I had an impression of the Druj on the Earth. It came upon me suddenly. I'm not like Blaise (at least not yet) where I can fine-tune my focus and summon up distant psychic impressions of events and situations. I saw *multiple* copies of the Druj. I emphasize that word because it seemed all eight billion humans were flanked by a copy of the Druj, and for each human she had modulated her appearance and tone to suit the person's temperament, meaning susceptibilities. In an odd sense it was like the biblical picture of Satan tempting or harassing Job, while the Supreme Being sat back and awaited results. The Druj had eight billion Jobs to work with, and she was getting on with the Job temptations marvelously.

But regardless of whom she was working on, the Druj was always about lies. Whether she whispered or shouted, cajoled or coerced, she was the Chief of Lies. Someone had a penchant for a merely materialistic conception of reality, she would encourage that; if someone was despairing of their life's purpose, unable to find or achieve it, she would blow wind on that weakness so it would flare up. Agents for governments, corporations, and other large companies in the public eye, the minute they put out the slightest distortion of the truth, she'd expand it.

She could do lies soft-spoken and subtle, like a susurrus, or loud, coarse, shouting, hectoring, right up in your face, like a million obnoxious, petulant Mussolinis. Her constant emphasis was the misrepresentation of truth, the shifting of attention away from the actual state of things into an alluring lie or illusion. It was like she was creating an artificial reality compounded of eight billion lies. It was as if most people walked around with a thin membrane wrapped around their heads and which projected living images into their eyes then their brains like a holographic television in a thin sheet of computer plastic.

It was constantly adjusting to the psychological or feeling nuances of the person, emphasizing any deficits that appeared as seeds of negativity in their minds, such as powerlessness, futility, despair, anomie, isolation, or materialist desolation. Sometimes she would succeed in placing such a holographic membrane over a country's egregore, so the whole country would be blanketed in myriads of lies. The Druj would anchor this broadcasting net through a strong public figure, like a dictator. He would seem to speak for the nation, though it was more the veil over that nation he was channeling.

She would amplify the country's existing propaganda and spin machines to mold public opinion according to the preferred lies, ones best suited to prevail there. She would do the same for some of the religions, first Christianity, then Islam, twisting their spiritual teachings into politicized justifications for mass violence and cruelty.

Her work was both artful and despicable. She would squeeze all extra-materialist perceptions

of scientists out of the picture so that reality was only a super-compacted body of merely physical forces, and the actual reality of multiple nested interactive energy fields was entirely occluded. She was very competent at that project; she had scientists searching everywhere for a God particle, as if the ultimate essence of reality was a kind of ultra-quark, and at the same time ensuring God as a creative force was disavowed from the picture. Scientists earnestly search for a God particle while ruling God out as a factor or potency of any kind in their materialist model of physical reality and human life. The analogy sounds good, like Lovelock calling his model the Gaia Hypothesis then strenuously erasing any actual Gaia goddess from the planetary physiology.

I saw her hand everywhere behind the façades of modern human life. It struck me that the Druj looked nasty and virulent in these activities, even like a strong-armed gangster or military enforcer, while before us she appeared more like a wily, tricky courtesan, slippery and deceptive yet intriguing, like the Scarlet Woman tarted up for a debut performance of *La Boheme*. She even looked diminutive at times, not threatening, not ugly, not showing her dark side, the Donna Reed mother archetype for the *Bardo* nursery, everyone's sweet Mom. I realized she had modulated her valence to suit our temperaments and levels of discernment, knowing we would not fall for the Druj's scary monster version.

She was out to conquer the world, to own and restructure reality at all levels. It was an audacious, unbelievable goal: she was competing with God for ownership of reality. She was a corporate raider forcing stockholders to sell out. Even more incredible to me was the impression that God was letting this play out, as if He had made a sporting bet with Himself regarding the likely outcome. He was unperturbed, even amused, with the drollery of her pursuit. Why not, I realized. He owns the house, just like Yama is the entire Underworld. Was the Supreme Being in peril of loosing His control over His created reality? Not in the least. Yet clearly He wanted this little rebellion by the Druj to play out.

Those souls who discerned the nature of the Druj's deception would benefit enormously and enrich reality with seeds for future discernment by others. Every human who penetrated the ruses and illusions of the artful Druj strengthened reality, attested to the cognitive powers latent in every human, and proved God right in letting this insurrection run its course. The Druj will fail. I wondered if the Druj knew this. I thought she probably did, and did not care. The game was everything to her. She was steadfastly dedicated to her project.

Still, the Old Girl could pack a punch when she wanted to. She nailed us. At least for a while. We had shifted location, or else what we were seeing before us had changed. It was if we could see all of humanity, both as a mass and individually. Some people were trudging along, forlorn and despondent; others were skipping, whistling, snapping their fingers, as if they owned the world. The Druj continuously shaped herself into neon billboards and signs, flashing alluring or despairing messages; people glanced at these and registered the message. Nobody saw through her semblance; they took reality at its surface.

They lived with psychic shutters on their perception, never penetrating the illusory solid wall of the material world to see the myriad realms of energy and Light beyond. They accepted reality as given, believed the official explanations. The Druj was controlling consciousness levels like nudging a dimmer switch. The minute somebody's consciousness indicated a move in a direction, she adjusted the dial and strengthened that tendency.

Nobody ever noticed this. She owned the place. Humanity was hers. It was as easy as pie.

That was the impression she gave us. She sneered triumphantly when she saw our dismayed reaction. They are so easy to manage, don't you think? She smirked. They'll never see through this, she said to us, though it was more in the nature of a telepathic communication. She snickered. I will keep closing down, squeezing in, erecting ever more layers of lead around them. She sniggered. I will build this magnificent fortress of metal, dark, confining, and impenetrable.

It was getting to me. She was starting to convince me she had the upper hand, and always would. I felt a shiver. I saw no evidence that people, any people, even one person, were seeing through the pervasive monolithic wall of semblances and illusions the Druj had constructed around them. Upgrading the planet's Light grid had been a futile gesture; nobody was matching its frequency; nobody seemed even to be aware of it or its intention, or cared. Hardly anybody saw or even knew about this encompassing planetary Light grid. Was it real?

People would trudge through the *Bardo* with the same low level of perception as had characterized humanity for millennia. They would be shocked, panicked, and full of incomprehension about the cognitive tests the *Bardo* offered and fail them all. Our Green Knight expedition was a cheery exercise in uselessness, a waste of time, an enchantment, a group delusion we had agreed to keep propping up.

Reality started to swell up as if it were a balloon the size of the world. Things got out of proportion, became asymmetric, started to look a bit crazy. I saw a light blazing at the center of this monstrous distorted sphere and it came closer to me as if it were galloping, maybe stampeding, or possibly even flying. I heard the trumpetings of elephants then the dark twisted bubble burst apart.

It was hundreds of Blaises in their Airavata guise, like a herd of rogue elephants, the big white elephants that are the mount for Indra and the other equivalent solar heroes, storming in all directions from the center of the sphere to the periphery, and atop each white elephant with its six golden tusks and the gorgeous saddle and the other jeweled bits I saw a copy of Blaise, the human.

He was grinning, confident, cocky, and full of swagger like a rodeo champion. The traditional image of the upright jolly elephant god Ganesh kept popping through the four-legged Airavata guise. The two complementary Ofanim images kept alternating, creating a startling, invincible effect, upright jolly-god image and charging indomitable massive elephant guise, both declaring all obstacles to consciousness, all this Druj lying, would be removed.

Soon, perhaps instantly, only I could not see things moving that fast, these many rushing white elephants had broken up the dark, lead-lined glass of the Druj's illusion of futility and failure that I now realized I had been slipping into like quicksand. Those glass pieces were now atomized into a vague mist and soon that was gone without a trace. I remembered myself now. I was recalled to myself, restored to my innate optimism. I was disenchanted, the Druj's magic spell broken into a million pieces. I remembered why we were here, the legitimate purpose of the Green Knight expedition. I was dismayed and elated.

"Almost got you, didn't she," said Blaise from the high seat of Airavata.

Before I could answer I was seized with shivering. I suddenly felt cold. Impossibly cold, like I had been dumped in teeshirt and shorts in the Arctic. I felt a bit shaky in my mind. That was because an unsettling thought had arisen. It felt like the rug I presumed I had been standing on had just been decisively yanked out from under me and I was not on solid ground but suspended in the air.

How did I know the Green Knight expedition and everything that had happened so far, the views and experiences, the contacts and discoveries, was not my own *Bardo* illusion scripted by the vagaries and proclivities of my karma and thus unreal? How did I know for certain that in fact I was not dead, had been dead since the moment I thought our group stood before Yama's massive celestial gates? What if I was the star of the remake of *Jacob's Ladder*? Everything that had happened so far could be accounted for as a karmic illusion at death. People often die and don't realize it, still think they are alive. Remember the popular movie, *The Sixth Sense*? The guy didn't know he was dead. He thought he was still a psychologist talking to a kid who saw dead people. He was one of those dead people the alive sensitive boy was seeing. But he didn't know it.

What if I was dead and didn't know it, that it hadn't dawned on me yet? I had created the expedition, scripted its details and members, wrote the dialogue, choreographed our interactions with the *Dhyani* Buddhas, filmed my mental constructs, and was striding through the *Bardo* prolifically hallucinating all of it. What was unsettling was that I did not know for certain if this was true. I was suddenly challenging my assumptions, that I was alive but in my astral body, exploring the *Bardo* with colleagues with commissioned intent to reform its afterlife protocols to ensure more cognitive progress here to match changes outside in the Earth's Light grid. That's a convincing storyline, but was it true?

I had read accounts, provided by mediums and channels since the late 19th century and the Spiritualist advent, of after-death travels and discoveries. Often people did not realize they were deceased and remained Earthbound, stuck in the inertia of their accustomed habits and residences. Or if they knew they were dead, they immediately recreated these familiar environments in an astral recreation area where they could reiterate their favorite routines and customs.

It was like pulling off the freeway into a rest area and having a hundred-year picnic, having lost all interest in resuming the journey for which this is a lay-by. I remembered other well-regarded movies from the 1990s about dead people, like the one I just mentioned, the Buddhist horror film, some said, *Jacob's Ladder*, a guy is dying and doesn't know it, and we watch his initial *Bardo* forays and reconciliations, or *Ghost*, where he discovers to his chagrin that he's dead, but he seeks to interact with the world, kick cans, and protect his girlfriend. Was my concept of my present reality merely following one of those movie delusions?

More disturbing questions founded on uncertainty flared up in my mind. If I was in fact dead and all that had happened so far was a product of my own karmic illusions, then all of what "we" had proposed to upgrade in the *Bardo* had no reality and would have no impact on anything. They were fantasies of mine to palliate my circumstances. What if I were still alive but unconscious, dreaming, in a coma, or maybe somewhere in between, suffering the effects of a concussion. Then similarly everything we had proposed would have no impact on reality.

I realized, based on these unanswered queries, that I didn't know for sure where I was. Where in all of reality was I authentically, factually standing right now? I didn't know. Another unanswered question. All I was certain about was that I, my awareness, *this* awareness (I was presuming it was me or mine), was a question. That was my sole activity at present, asking questions, getting no answers. My

consciousness had been reduced to a series of unanswered queries.

To be honest, this perplexity was starting to get to me. I felt undermined. I felt I was standing on the San Andreas Fault in California and it was widening.

I heard a voice. "You're looking in the wrong place for solid ground, pal." It was the word "pal" delivered with inimitable American insouciance that made me recognize its speaker as Blaise, wise-ass, smart-ass, and rescuer of my ass. His composure, evident in his voice and nonchalant remark, felt like solid ground. He sounded like Henry Miller, making a droll remark, both vulgar and hilarious. But that wasn't what he meant. It was a sudden twinkle of Light. That was what he meant, and it was emerging out of the morass of uncertainty in which I felt enmired, like I had been sinking in slow-motion into quicksand or spiraling steadily towards the event horizon of a black hole of grim unknowing.

"Screw the clever metaphors, Frederick. Just breathe to your Blazing Star." I laughed. It felt like the first time I had laughed in ages, since I had died—wait: I hadn't died. The laugh rebooted my certainty and refocused my clarity. I was like a radar telescope knocked askew by strong weather or a satellite whose orbit had started to decay. I saw that twinkle of a Blazing Star and it sped towards me.

This is the primordial first point of incorruptible Light within us. It grew larger, brighter, more insistent, more *jovial*. How marvelous: a jovial star. I heard slogans being repeated as if by cheerleaders at a college football game. Be the Star you are. We are your Blazing Star. We roll towards you. Breathe to your Star. We come as a Blazing Star. It was like an ET broadcast from deep space identifying itself, a radio channel or television station giving its call sign. It was like Dorothy waking from her concussion and remembering her family's names, except in my case there was a Wizard of Oz and the hallucination had been my forgetting the mission and believing I had succumbed to the tornado of the Druj.

That was it. I got it now. My head was clearing. This was all a big Druj lie.

I saw I had an entirely mistaken notion of what an interview with the Druj meant. I had expected it would be like a press conference. We were the probing newspapermen, she was the politician or celebrity. We would ask her questions. It was nothing like that. She was interviewing us, probing us for our weak spots. I was wearing my solipsism inside out. I construed the world nondualistically, as the product of my projected consciousness and thus unreal, not to be credited. That solipsistic projection part was correct, except it is real: it is the world I see.

I still wasn't clear on one thing. "How did you know I wasn't dead?" I asked Blaise. It was still possible everything I heard him say and saw him do was my illusion, that this Blaise was a projection of my desire to see my friend Blaise.

"Because if you were dead then I'd be asking if I could have all your scholarly books," he replied with a mischievous smirk on his face. "And I haven't asked for that yet." He didn't look 93 years old when he said this; he looked more like sixteen. "I haven't asked because I'm not dead either."

"How do I know you're not dead? You could be a karmic hallucination."

"Because if I were then I wouldn't be asking about your books. Dead people don't need books, no matter how impressive the academic's library is. But I might just ask for your books if I was dead to keep you on your toes, unsure."

The illogic was queerly convincing. Its nonlinearity snapped me back into my right mind. It seemed like an island of solidity amidst a sea of uncertainty. So I would assume neither of us was deceased. And I would keep my books.

Merlin seemed to have been enjoying our inane exchange. "Let me distract you for a moment by showing you something you may find interesting."

We were inside a vast circular hall, more like a sports stadium many times larger than any physical ones on the Earth, possibly the size of a large city. Along its circumference were innumerable identical portals, evenly spaced apart and each framed regally by an archway. Souls were streaming into these many open gateways the way people move through a train station to their platforms; they seemed to know exactly which of the thousands of portals they wanted to enter.

"Think of this as a recreation area," said Merlin. "Souls who have made it through a fair amount of the *Bardo* processing and divestment come to this stadium which is much like a multiplex movie theater. The myriad of doors lead into specifically calibrated different frequency domains within the astral plane. You could, by way of analogy, liken this to a train station, a movie theater, or a shopping center with a tremendous diversity of alluring stores and merchandise. It is also in many respects a center for higher learning, like a large university. Each of these doors opens into a college offering a specific curriculum for a soul.

"For example, Frederick, say you wanted to study the spiritual and occult aspects of many of the mythological symbols you are familiar with as a scholar. Here you could get the inside story on these puzzling objects, understand them as energy constructs, and study their varied effects on matter and consciousness. Or you, Edward, let's say you wanted to immerse yourself in the mental processes of some of the great writers and creative spirits who acted as conduits for higher, exalted sources of information and perspectives on human reality, writers and musicians and sculptors who opened themselves up to inspiration from the high *devas* of those art forms. There is a door that would take you there.

"Pipaluk, let's say you wanted to study the great objects and tools of the shaman, a museum of practices from around the world, and experience these as living energy forms. Drums, spirit guides, animal totems, sacred power spots on the land, the origin of rituals and healing methods—there is a door taking you there. And Blaise, our resident funny-man, there is a school for stand-up comics. You could study with the great clowns of history, the comic writers, the great burlesque masters, the caricaturists, the satirists, cartoonists, the comedians who have leavened the seriousness of life, defied the gravity of glumness, and lifted spirits with humor. Even Aristophanes shows up for guest lectures sometimes."

"Aristophanes wasn't that funny, Merlin," Blaise said. "Could you arrange for me to have a sit-down with P.G. Wodehouse? Now he was funny."

"Most people will agree that when you get to this educational theater there is a marked easing up of the cognitive tension you've experienced in the *Bardo*. This is an intermediate state within the intermediate state of the *Bardo*. That means you can explore possibilities, experiment with simulations, investigate the higher, esoteric aspects of any subject that interests you, and spend as long as you wish doing it. It's like a summer vacation in between semesters. At some point you will either return to college or quit your college.

"That means some day, not that the *Bardo* has a measurable flow of time, you will either reincarnate or proceed further to the post-individuation theater of the Great Mother. Pass through the 49 gates of individuation back into original wholeness. That is a theater, or Light temple, that you may access from this one, when you are ready. When you have completed your experiences in one of these domains

accessed through a portal in this hall, then it delivers you to Her great temple. It's as if this first theater rotates to position the door you have entered precisely at an entrance into the Great Mother's domain, at one of the 49 Gates. Then you have the option of selecting a World of Light or paradise to move to. You can join the ranks of *Siddhas* or accomplished ones who live in divinity. As far as options go, it's close to the top of the list, short of returning to God.

"Anything is possible regarding your curriculum. Some return to the Earth as helping spirits and interact with human rituals or geomantic actions. Others prefer a more exotic exposure and visit other planets and study with their dominant consciousness-bearing life-forms and see reality through their eyes. Others move in and out of the Earth's timeline to study key moments in history from the inside, like war correspondents at the actual sites of conflicts.

"It works the other way too, towards the future. Some souls like to move forward, like in H.G. Wells's time machine, though astral journeying is far easier than that. The more philosophically inclined can immerse themselves in permutation studies with the Elohim and their complex spacetime contingency modules. You will have known them as the cyclopean stone emplacements across the Earth; here you may access the original forms and processes of those stone structures. Others study advanced sciences or medicines and experiment with technical innovations that one day will be introduced into Earth human culture; sometimes it is the same person studying them in the astral world who will later introduce these changes during a future Earth-human incarnation."

I stood inside what I may as well call the *Bardo* individuation theater and realized each of the thousands of gateways leads in turn to another thousand branching out from it. It was a fractal pattern: each gateway duplicated the design of the whole theater, so your choice of options multiplied dizzyingly. On the other hand, nobody could complain that their special needs were not considered. The curriculum was infinitely adjustable to all academic needs.

I was wondering if there was some form of guide to this prolific array of choices. Naturally, I expected it to take physical form, a sign or map or diagram as you would find in the physical world at a national park or historical site. Yes, there was a master map of the place but it was projected straight into my mind. All I had to do to precipitate this download was to think that I wanted it. This section of the *Bardo* was instantly responsive and the map appeared in me.

All I had to do was think about what interested me and the location of that section was revealed, the exact gateway leading into that zone indicated. I desired to study mythological symbols and objects; immediately, I was there. Not just at the gate, but through it, in what looked like a vast spherical library with books stacked on shelves in all directions and angles. Copiously, richly—God, what a library! There were other people already here, hundreds perhaps, studying, testing, making notes, discussing topics in small circles, welcoming me. It was better than anything I'd ever experienced at Dartmouth with its faculty. Its library was meager, impoverished, when contrasted with the riches of this place.

I gravitated towards a small group experimenting with swords of Light. They were doing fantastic things with these swords, pulling them out of their foreheads, through their spines, enveloping the pristine blades with orange or lilac flames, wielding them at different angles to produce discretely different effects. The Light swords emitted sounds to match their color patterns and these patterns, coupled with the sword strokes when the holders wielded them that way, created visual effects in the air around us, making shapes, moving energy.

They could cut through walls or body encasements of darkness, ignorance, obscuration, encrusted images, states of confusion, and conditions of pain. They did this with no damage or injury to the people, only to their dark auric fields. They inserted the swords into landscape sites, into prepared apertures that looked like locks and the swords were the correct keys to turn these locks, and when they inserted these Light swords, the geomantic nodes grew illuminated, and the Light temples reared up in enthused illumination.

The many names for these swords as developed in all Earth cultures that recognized these magical objects appeared in an etymology sphere. All the word meanings and origins of the varied names for swords appeared, and when these syllables carried latent magical powers these potencies were revealed. What an aid for teaching comparative mythology at the college level, yet I wondered how many students could upshift their understanding to realize the reality of these swords, that they were not artifacts from dead cultures for inert intellects but living magic implements, ways of moving consciousness to produce real effects.

This etymology sphere highlighted all the different nuances of swords and their names, and the uses and modes of creation or wielding humans had worked out for them over time, and I saw that much of this had been forgotten by living humans. I don't remember ever seeing most of this, even in Eliade. So much knowledge has been lost over time, but here it was all remembered and vital. It was a living pictorial history of swords of Light, stretching back through Sumeria to the earlier epochs of Atlantis, Lemuria, and, ultimately, Hyperborea. Anyone using a sword here in the *Bardo* would be *totally* informed about them.

A strange but wonderful feature of the *Bardo*, or at least of this zone, was that you could see a soul's plans and designs as if they were displayed inside them. No, you were not being nosy, violating their privacy; this information was displayed for public knowledge, as a grid, as unavoidable as one's skin or hair.

I saw that one fellow planned to use this knowledge, what he could remember when he was alive again, to write a series of "fantasy" novels about the use of swords in defense of a land ravaged by demonic forces and inimical spirits. This female soul I was observing would incarnate as a teacher of martial arts, emphasizing the use of swords. Another man I saw would experiment with swords of Light created by the mind to activate or clarify landscape nodes and to clean out entropic Light temples and dispel dark-grid emplacements, webs, cords, and ill-intentioned programming grids. He planned to gather a group of resonant men and women to practice "sword magic" on landscape nodes for the benefit of the planet. He'd hit the Earth world with surety. He meant business.

The success of these ambitious projects was dependent on how much of this full body of knowledge the incarnating souls would be able to retrieve, but since we had got the Green Knight to agree to a 50 percent reduction in the potency of the River Lethe's infernal oblivion effect on the soul's memory, prospects looked good for memory recall with clarity and without distortion.

In fact, I saw in each of these disincarnate human souls visualizations of their plans, as if they were either projecting into the future, thereby shaping it, the actual attainment of these project goals or, more simply, they were seeing into the future and witnessing themselves accomplishing these intended goals, and the act of their seeing it was a validation and a stamp of certitude on these outcomes, a type of mild magical pronouncement: *this* shall be the outcome.

I examined one of these swords. I must have generated it myself. It blazed in a diamond white fire; its Light was alive, searing, sharp as a diamond's edge. I saw its origins among the angels, even the mighty archangels like Michael. I saw them holding such swords as this, Michael, the Serafim, and others, and I saw the adamant, neutral fierceness of their gaze. Qualities you'd normally think contradictory. How can you be fierce and neutral? You can, and they were, and these brilliant swords of Light embodied and transmitted that blended quality.

The sword, the blade, the Light that comprised it, was a sheer cutting force, an activating power that sliced through ignorance with the energy of true reality. It wasn't even or ultimately a sword. That was merely a useful visual metaphor. It was the truth, the actuality, the nakedness of absolute reality, of the *Dharma*, that was the sword; the sword as an object was merely its mode of delivery. This truth was not a substance, nor was the sword a substantive object: it was a process. The truth of reality was a *process* working on consciousness.

It was a state of mind, a concentration of aware, lucid, fully awake consciousness. It was an immutable *condition* of reality, a hallmark signature and quality of truth. The sword slices through you, cleaves all the ignorance densifying your space, puts you in alignment with this fundamental condition, dissolves all obstacles and resistances in your psychic space to this truth, and then it disappears because once you're there you don't need the sword as a separate object. You, your awareness, your condition of reality, are the sword.

I was outside the sword library gateway again, still marveling. I hoped I could remember most of this and take it back to—well, wherever I was going next. I turned to Blaise and asked him how long I was gone in the library. He shrugged. "I couldn't say. Duration is a matter of the width of your thought."

"But a person could remain in one of these domains for as long as they desired?" I asked. It was starting to seem better, more fun, than reincarnating.

"That's my understanding, and many do, often for what we would calculate as hundreds of Earth years. They stay immersed in a subject until they feel sated with experience and information, then they move on, sometimes to incarnate or to other domains for more immersions. Time feels endless here. But, if they chose to reincarnate, they are subject again to the Druj's dark influences, or so Merlin tells me. She will look for tactics to darken their optimism about achieving specific life goals when they are alive again; she'll inspire futility.

"Say a person plans to do something with swords of Light when they are alive, based on what they learned in the domain you visited. The Druj will whisper in their ear that they won't remember, nobody will be interested, only material swords are real—she will exploit whatever angle works to instill doubt and distrust. She will emphasize the merely material aspect of the subject, in this case, swords, or, if she sees a seed of darkness in the soul, she may inspire the black use of swords. She can't coerce, but she can persuade, suggest, cajole, seduce, or plant numerous seeds that, given the right conditions, may sprout. Similarly, she may use any means possible to entangle an advanced soul seeking to free himself completely and definitively from the Wheel of Life, which, as it turns out, is exactly what's happening to our friend, Matthew, as you can see."

Matthew looked like a massive unruly bull at a rodeo, utterly resisting the efforts of the cocky cowboy to lasso and corral him. He reared and roared; he thrust his head forward, he pulled his form back. The rodeo cowboy was the Druj, and she was accosting him with hundreds of black sizzling cords. They writhed in black fire and burned his "flesh" every time they made contact. You would immediately conclude that the Druj was harassing, even torturing, him.

Philomena stood by the writhing Matthew as a blazing pillar of diamond Light. She kept reminding him of his mission, his true essence, the nature of what was happening to him, how he needed to persevere and resist the Druj's whiplashes. They were not actually whiplashes. They were statements, whispers, criticisms, insinuations, reminders, anything the Druj could use to weaken Matthew's resolve. She would open old wounds, push on unhealed hurts, kindle simmering resentments, whatever vestiges of Matthew's emotional body she could push on. Matthew was trying to purify himself, purge his psychic field of all impurities, karmic seeds, debts, credits, and potentials for more illusions, and the Druj was trying to stop that, hold it back, instill new limitations in him.

The black cords she whipped at Matthew were lies in all their variations. She was continuously, prolifically, shamelessly creative in her guiles. When she saw the desperation and futility angle didn't produce results, she took a different tack. Okay, say you want to ascend and live in a Light body. How about setting yourself up as a teacher, a leader of men and women, a spiritual guide?

"People in bodies are always looking for a new person who has all the answers. You could do that easily, even blindfolded; humans are so gullible and hungry. You could rally some around you, build up a following, get them to do your bidding. You are a prince among humans, an advanced soul with spiritual powers. You deserve adulation; you would do well with an obedient, reverent following. It would make all this travail in the *Bardo* pay off, be worthwhile. You deserve a privileged position among humans. It is your right, yours, so take it."

She says all this, pulling on the thread of pride and vanity dormant within Matthew. It's fertile ground in him, as it would be in anybody. He never got that kind of validation in the stock exchange world or from his family. Now it was his for the asking, the Druj suggested. The world owed him that. Time to collect.

"She's playing the guru card," observed Blaise. "Sometimes it works. She is subtle and clever. It is true, Matthew *could* become a guru, a spiritual guide. He has the requisite spiritual development in a generic sense. The lie the Druj puts forward is that this is his destiny, his specialty, his mandate. That he *should* do this; it is his privilege, the world wants it, is waiting for him, so he must do it.

"The Druj compounds this lie with another, that embodied humans need to be directed, told what to do, commanded, and, ultimately, taken advantage of, that they are sheep mingling mindlessly in skittish herds, in Group Soul identities, that their loyalty, obedience, reverence, and supplication are there for the taking, and Matthew, advanced soul that he is, is the one best suited to take all this. Can you hear the disdain for humans in her voice and use of words? Matthew, to his credit, does not agree. He resists her insinuations; he fights her. He struggles like an enraged bull against these ropes—the Druj's black cords.

"The cords are the Druj's lies. She seeks to bind him up with them, then he'll take them with him like clothing or armor into the human embodied world. This is where her lies slide into her evil. She is not fundamentally interested in evil, at least as we know it; that is a secondary result of the propagation of her lies and to a degree a human creation. If she could persuade Matthew to accept the lies as truths, then she would reap a double benefit: he would start her program of abrogating human free will and the autonomy of consciousness. He would start commandeering souls, directing them, but it would be on her behalf. Her lies have a tendency to provoke human behavior that interferes with the free will of others, obstructs their Christ Light. Her clever lies lead to evil results.

"She could own more human souls, but ownership is not the issue for the Druj. It's the proliferation of the lie that drives her, competition with the Supreme Being and His Godawful truth of reality. That's what galls the Druj, the truth. She doesn't want the truth. She wants reality on her terms, expressing her variations and nuances, her way, the Druj truth, which of course is a big lie."

The black cords twining around Matthew were like snarling roots or snakes. In fact, as snakes, they seemed to wriggle and slither out of the Druj's hair and to wrap themselves around his energy field as if it were a rock. Was she the original of Medusa who had snakes for hair, like what we call dreadlocks?

"No, pal, she just likes the effect," said Blaise. "It's part of her gear. Each one of those black tendrils or 'snakes' is a dark thought, a Druj lie, a suggestion. Her goal is to have them become arteries within Matthew's consciousness body. In a sense she is attempting to brainwash Matthew, to reprogram his mind with her own grids of meaning and interpretation, to defeat his mental independence. She wants him, otherwise a vector of cognitive and psychic power in the world, to walk the planet with his consciousness infiltrated by her mental constructs. It's a form of possession, just far more subtle than what ordinary idiot demons pull off. She wants to own Matthew and have him remain unaware of this take-over."

Matthew was struggling with these encoiling black tendrils, yet it was the kind of struggle you'd expect from a Harry Houdini, competent and successful. He was gradually freeing himself from this dark and insidious infrastructure. Philomena stood next to him, silently emanating a field of Light. It was like a spotlight in a dark field, but the Light was also the force of the truth, and this abiding presence fortified and inspired Matthew to free himself. It kept reminding him of what the truth looked and felt like, that it was an insuperable power, and one effortlessly superior to anything the Druj could throw at him.

That provoked me to wonder how much evil is correlated with lies. You have the bedrock of the Creation, the Persian *Asha*. The truth, the actual nature of reality, the way the Supreme Being designed it. The Earth's Light grid and its myriad of details is a mandala based on this truth. It is an *Asha* diagram. Here comes the Druj, chief of the House of Lies, and her lies contradict this. They oppose *Asha* with a manifold of lies. It is a contrary, disturbing, entropic vibration. Sensitive people register this lie vibration as a painful atmosphere.

It actually makes their bodies hurt, and gives them a headache or a sense of disorientation. It is a deliberate distortion of the Supreme Being's intention, a destructive dissonance that contradicts the infrastructure of actual reality. To call this "evil" tends to raise the drama quotient of all this, but it is still applicable. The Druj says, No, God, we'll do it my way, thank you very much, so piss off.

The thing is, the really troubling yet fascinating aspect to this, is that the Supreme Being allows this to happen. The Supreme Being said okay to human access to and knowledge of—direct *experience* of—the Tree of the Knowledge of Good and Evil; that permission took the form of the granting of free will to humans. A human can choose, in every action, which side of the Tree he prefers. But ultimately the Supreme Being, like a casino, controls the table and house. So I wondered, slightly paranoid, if the Druj is God's hand-puppet that He diddles when He is pretending

to be unconscious so as to keep humans sharp and lucid?

C.G. Jung proposed a theory along these lines in *Answer to Job* where he suggested God may have dumped His unconscious into humanity to work out. By way of analogy there are many examples from the human social and political world where oppositions are artificially stoked to keep the game rivalries going. The CIA sponsors radicals to protest the current war, even to the stage of militancy, as a false-flag espionage action both to find out who else is opposed to the given war and to keep the public polarized and inflamed and thus malleable.

Was the Druj the Supreme Being's ultimate version of the hired sham agitator? In the large picture, no spirit is, or can ever be, senior to the Supreme Being, so the Druj is *a priori* a secondary creation, finally answerable to the Supreme Being. In the small picture, the world of relativistic effects, the Druj is a competent enemy. She has been given a lot of rope, considerable latitude, and humans have the free will to exploit her offerings or turn them down, and both choices have consequences. Consider the total eradication of first-generation humans by the Supreme Being in a moment of, in His view, justifiable wrath. Thanks to the Druj, things had gotten unarguably out of hand in pre-Flood Sumeria, and this secondary creation, this universal empress manqué, the Druj, had to be reined in and all the consciousness and freedom settings recalibrated.

There was a curious, intriguing three-way dance going on among Matthew, the Druj, and Philomena. The Druj was insinuating her dark tendrils around and into Matthew; they were probing for images and neon-lit pictures embedded like seeds in Matthew's psychic space; and when they contacted one the tendril would amplify, spark it as if with an electrical emission, and the image would enlarge. It would be something from Matthew's past, a seed of unresolved hurt or misery, now springing forward into a negative validation.

It would seek to persuade Matthew that action must be taken, and the Druj's black tendril would make the case that it was best suited to the retribution mission. At the same time, Philomena's steady Light emission, that searing field of diamond white fire, would start to incinerate the enlarged and often enraged picture before it could completely persuade Matthew that it was the truth and should lead the charge inspired by the Druj's tendrils and make more karma. This was like racking up further debt; the more karma, the more Matthew would adhere to the Druj's program for him because energetically he was stuck to her.

I had the impression that in some manner Matthew's accomplishments in resisting the Druj's lies and black tendrils were benefitting myself and the others. He was doing purgative work not only for his own freedom and enlightenment, but for the Green Knight expedition members—more than that: for humanity, for Blaise's Albion, the slowly awakening collective soul of all humans over time. Every time Matthew resisted a Druj lie and Philomena burned it to ash humanity everywhere was incrementally more free of the Druj.

It didn't matter whether these humans were in physical life or walking the *Bardo*. The Druj spread her lie tendrils throughout both domains; to her, there was no dimensional difference between embodied or disincarnate human consciousness. Perversely, both realms were the same tabernacle for her dark presence. It was all the same playing field for her activities; but that meant any gains Matthew made, since they affected others beyond him, radiated outwards like a cascade, then these gains would register in the alive, embodied human world. It was holographic: wherever

human consciousness abided, it benefitted from every gesture of repudiation and incineration Matthew achieved. Every human, even through little gestures, contributes to the regeneration of the world.

It did not remove the confining cords of lies from their space, for they were still being tested, but it gave them an edge, just enough of a handicap to make the choice to throw them off if they *wanted* to. They had to want to; it had to be a free-will gesture. Philomena's Light field, reiterated by thousands of other *Siddhas* of the *Bardo*, would be available like a free electrical source for them. If they were committed to freeing themselves of the Druj, that Light would help.

"The Great Designer of All Reality, as we sometimes call Him, has agreed to allow a 50 percent amplification of this Christ Light for those who want it," said Merlin. "Those who, like Matthew, find themselves beleaguered by the Druj's tentacles and who wish to be free of them and what they seek to amplify, may draw on this unlimited Christ Light current to a much greater extent now.

"They have to take the first step, though. That first step will be a gesture in consciousness that they *wish* to be free of these lies and they are committed to it. That is the on-switch for the current: the vow to resist the Druj and all her lies. We should see an increase in the numbers of humans emulating Matthew's example. They may not go quite as far as Matthew intends, but they will likely make much more progress in their spiritual advancement than we used to see.

"All this has an impact on Albion as well, at all his levels. Every time a person fails to extricate themselves from the Druj's lies and succumbs to the influence of an illuminated or aggravated emotional picture, it further ensnares Albion. It steepens the gradient he must climb to wake up in freedom. Similarly, every time a person succeeds in throwing off the Druj's shackles of lies, it aids Albion; it gives him an incremental boost in his quest for cognitive autonomy. You can see, then, that much is at stake. Progress in the *Bardo* affects the world."

I thought about the lies of the Druj. You have no power. You are inconsequential in the design of reality. The truth is relative and adjustable. The truth is whatever I say it is or make you think it is. Your consciousness is feeble, impotent. It will lose all its autonomy when you enter a body. Psychic powers are illusory, mere magic tricks. God is a fraud, a con, a grifter, a swindler, an inattentive boastful windbag entirely indifferent to you. One person makes no difference. Humans are inherently violent, stupid, obtuse, idiotic, leaden, and perverse. They would murder God if they could just find the right weapon.

Failing that, they would perpetually run in fear from a disapproving, insane Jehovah who, I assure you, hates you mightily. The universe is immense, you are puny, so forget about making any difference. You cannot change anything. Conditions of life are immutable. Fear is the natural state of humans, so get used to it, and fear more. Anger rules, so start getting into resonance with it and spread it everywhere. Love is a narcotic hallucination meant to distract you from the horror of your existence. Don't expect any real help from the angels; they feel nothing for you. They are self-absorbed, swooning in their own unwavering bliss. Fuck you, humans. You don't deserve to exist, but since you do, expect to have your lives ruined by me. I shit on your pathetic existences.

I could keep elaborating the Druj's lies, but I trust you get my point. She is a mendacious propagandist for the untruthful. She propagates everything contrary to the message of the Christ Light or the truth of the Buddha Mind. Her goal, in summary, is to discredit that awakened Light condition, to make it seem not worth achieving, too difficult, elusive, or fake. That, I

suspect, is the best approach: to make the Clear Light state seem unreal. To subluxate humans from the Supreme Being; to drive a wedge of darkness, lies, fear, and alienation between consciousness and its source and its powers. To make life seem pointless, a carnival of suffering and depravity, and to make the *Bardo* appear even worse, a nightmare of terror, frightening spirits, and despair.

The Druj cannot defeat the Supreme Being, not in all the Lives of Brahma. But she can confound, distort, and defeat His progeny, the pathetic, weakling humans, as she sees us. Defeating humans, the Druj may eventually convince God not to try again or to attempt to improve the design. Forget about creating a phylogeny capable of reiterating the divine fullness. It sounds good on paper, but the execution is inherently problematic and flawed. Hardly any humans ever reach that epiphanous goal: humans as living, self-aware holograms of the original *Adam Qadmon*, Your picture of perfect manifestation and the *Sefirotic* harmony of the spheres? Not going to happen. Not on my watch. I blow them off the playing field. They are too frail, too feckless, ever so easily distracted by me. Let go your ridiculous pipe-dream, Old Man, and face reality. They will all fail.

I realized the magnitude of the challenge, of the great contest underway. How exquisitely poised the balance point is, this razor's edge of choice. Our choice. We're the ones who walk this razor's edge. God bets big, puts down all His chips, that's for sure, but He bets confidently, sure that the odds favor Him.

Matthew, meanwhile, looked like he was getting whipped by the Druj. Each black tentacle slashed at him like a sharp belt, flagellating his Light form. I know, that is a contradictory image. I should say his "skin" but he had no skin. Yet it was a kind of scourging because each whip stroke aggravated a picture or a ridge of pain prominent within Matthew's manifestation form. The action was bodylike in its intention and effect, but we are talking about soul pain here which complicates the description. The Druj saw these points of old hurt in Matthew and aimed her black tentacles precisely to aggravate them to act as her anchors.

I saw one such picture, for example, in which Matthew was being criticized harshly by his father for failing to understand an engineering theory. His father curtly suggested Matthew's brainpower was not up to the task, that he was sorry to have a son who was such an underachiever. It was quite the dismissal. It didn't matter if Matthew's father was incorrect in his assessment; the pain was in place and would remain festeringly so for decades until this moment of attention. It could remain in place long after father and son had died.

It was as if the pain picture itself yelped then jumped free of Matthew's space, like a biting tick that had been trapped under the skin for decades. The Druj's whip, expertly slashed at that picture, now had no point of traction and it slipped off Matthew's form like a rope sliding off a sheer side of polished glass. Then the Light of Philomena's attention incinerated the feckless pile of dull rope.

This was a process, and it looked like it would go on for some time, three accountants going through a tedious but required tax audit, reviewing each item, one of them with prosecutorial intent, and two acting as defense for the client. The Druj would pick up a receipt or invoice, brandish it before Matthew, and say, what about this item? She would study him for a fidgeting pain reaction. If he was nonresponsive, she'd drop it and move to the next inflammatory piece. She was intent, she had the patience, to try out every last document in his file.

The Druj puzzled me. Was she an authentic independent spirit with a soul? I did not think so. She was more of an automaton, a necessity perhaps, in the mechanics of Creation, an auditor commissioned by the Creator. Steiner always said Ahriman was very clever, intelligent, crafty, resourceful. The Druj went through her motions with precision and thoroughness, and she clearly had the ability to adapt, transfigure, shift direction, change tactics, reconfigure.

She consumed human misery as a food. She fed off human darkness and negativity. Human pessimism, despair, all the dark aspects of the psyche, were like caviar to her taste. We grew her; we fattened her like a prize farm animal. She was bloated, corpulent from feasting on us. She was humanity's fat goddess. But she was a finite spirit; the Supreme Being would outlast her by an eternity.

13

The air was filled with soap bubbles with people inside them. At least that's how it appeared at first glance. Each bubble had a single human form inside it, and they were floating just above the ground, reacting against something like a billiard ball that has been sent rolling by a cue-stick or from colliding with another ball. The soap bubble itself, though spherical, was also sentient, and it gave the suggestion of outspread wings forming the globe.

The spheres were of variable size, and I think it depended only on their distance to me. The ones closer to me appeared larger, the ones further away were smaller. The figure who comprised the bubble had an angelic ambiance, and it wasn't just the wings that made me think so. It was a neutrality coupled with professional interest, as if the human inside the bubble were its client, the angel its guardian, yet while protecting it was also standing back, not interfering.

"Those are the Higher Selves of individual souls forming a protective bubble around their essence for this phase of the *Bardo* journey," said Merlin.

That made sense. I referred earlier to the Tibetan term Good Genius and Evil Genius for the twofold nature of the Higher Self, as they construed it. The Tibetan term is *Lhan-chig skyes pahi lha*, which means "simultaneously-born god," and sometimes, in a more casual

translation, it means "little white god." The Evil Genius means "simultaneously-born demon" or "little black demon." Born at the same time as the soul means the Higher Self is assigned to the soul at its birth, then accompanies the soul throughout its incarnational odyssey in all its lives, though, as Blaise once explained, it's even earlier than that. The Higher Self is "born" or assigned at the first emergence of the *spirit* as a spark of Light. That happens long before the spirit shapes a soul with chakras for its incarnations.

Some traditions bifurcate the Higher Self into two angelic entities. Rudolf Steiner for example called the Evil Genius the Lesser Guardian of the Threshold and said it comprised the dark deeds of the astral body, and the Good Genius was the Greater Guardian of the Threshold, which was an always pure and incorruptible guide, especially for the higher, advanced worlds beyond Earth. My impression, based on what I've seen here on this expedition, is that it is one angelic spirit that alternately reflects our "good" and "bad" nature to us, possibly along the same lines as the *Daena* appearing either beautiful or ugly depending on the balance sheet of our karma. Here the *Daena* appears both ways at the same time, thus accommodating the Good and Evil Genius components.

Protection and guidance seem paramount to the Higher Self's function because I saw these transparent angelic bubbles and their in-dwelling human figures were under assault from a rasher of hostile, demonic-looking spirits. It had the quality of someone walking through a dangerous, unsavory part of a big city. I had thought we were done with the *Bardo* phase of nasty demonic spirits.

"It's the encore presentation of pain-in-the-ass mental projections, emptying the karmic tank of the last dregs of hallucinatory possibilities," said Blaise. "These child geniuses of the demonic flavor are called Executive Furies of the Lord of Death, of our friend, Yama, according to that 1927 British translation. It's another nuance of the judgement phase of the *Bardo* journey.

"The judge is your own conscience, and the Good Genius takes the impartial view of the actions taken by the Evil Genius, or at least the charge sheet compiled against it. This new gang of hostile beings is supposed to be made of personifications of the good conscience scourging the soul to cleanse its dark side and execute furious justice—home-grown Erinyes, I suppose, domestic Harpies.

"The Tibetan text says, and I can't believe Merlin let it sound so wimpy and limp, if you can't manage to meditate on emptiness, you could always call on your Higher Self. Maybe he could help save your sorry ass from the scourges of your own conscience at this point. Anyway, you could try it. And they will beguile you by counting out your good deeds with white pebbles and enumerating the bad deeds with black pebbles. Feel free to tremble in fear. It reminds me of the movie series *Aliens* from the 1990s. You think those infernal predatory creatures are finally terminated, then they rear up again to get you. The text assures us that even the Bull-Headed Spirit of Death is a hallucination."

I agreed with Blaise's implicit criticism couched in his signature sarcasm. What I saw before me seemed a reprise of the earlier review of the contents of the etheric and astral body. It was like a police interrogation where they go over all the same questions *again* to see if you left anything out or changed your story. I heard various souls protesting that the reason they did a certain action was because… and then the explanation would trail off into a whining excuse. It reminded me of the way humans, us, people, myself included of course, will on occasion try to strong-arm the concerns of an awakened conscience to stop bringing up this annoying subject or stop reminding us of this inconvenient fact.

I think the goal here was for the soul to stop squirming and become a reflecting mirror, to admit its guilt and culpability where appropriate. *Yes*, I did that. The conscience was like Perry Mason pressing the person in the witness box to at last break down and tearfully confess she, *yes, she*, I did it, I committed the crime because he couldn't, no matter what I said, the ungrateful bastard who—

"Yes, the soul is in the hot seat," Blaise said. "My, how it squirms. I remember Steiner explaining that the Greek picture of the avenging Furies, the variously called Erinyes or Eumenides, who sought retribution for matricides, was their personification of the moral forces of the awakened conscience. It makes sense, don't you think, Frederick. We seek retribution against ourselves. We split ourselves in two and prosecute the offender within us with great zeal.

"We're Perry Mason *and* the dissembling witness, even Hamilton Burger. The Erinyes are the personifications, the agents, of our own remorse, directed against ourselves. We commission them to exact judgement and punishment. Through them we apply hot irons to our chest, swords to our mid-section, in an attempt to drive out the 'sin' or 'trespass' we have committed and now regret.

"In fact, I now realize that the Greeks provide us a glimpse into the *Bardo*, or what they called Erebus, the Underworld, with the Furies. The Erinyes, the Greeks said, number three; they are female, chthonic, and vengeful, infernal goddesses who live beneath the Earth, which we now know means above the Earth, above the physical plane and in the Underworld above us, and punish, by hounding, nagging, and goading, oath-breakers or makers of fraudulent oaths.

"Their names, if we can trust Virgil, were Alecto ('Endless'), Megaera ('Jealous Rage'), and Tisiphone ('Vengeful Destruction'). But note how they looked: they are crones, ugly, with snakes for hair and snakes entwining their waists and arms, a dog's head, coal-black bodies, wings like a bat's, and blood-shot eyes. They carry brass-studded scourges or whips, clothed in either long black robes like death-mourners or short-length skirts and boots like huntress maidens; either way, their victims are said to die in torment. The Romans called them *Dirae*, meaning 'Terrible,' and to meet the Furies was to endure their wrath, taking the form of tormenting madness, illness, disease, or unbearable hunger. Their name, Erinyes, says it all: it derives from either *ereunao*, meaning 'I hunt up or persecute,' or from *erinuo*, 'I am angry.' They angrily search out the offenders.

"My point is these Furies may be identical to some of the nasty *Bardo* spirits described by the Tibetans and legitimately commissioned to personify and deconstruct certain aspects of the person. Some classical authors went so far as to say these infernal goddesses are called Furies in Hell, Harpies on the Earth, and *Dirae* in Heaven, meaning it's the same trio appearing in three different realms. Anyway, we can glimpse a scene from the *Bardo* through this old Greek picture."

"I can tell you it was not a pleasant experience," said Tommy. "I got a lot of black pebbles dealt out in my name. It was like being blackballed for club membership. You thought it was a sure thing, immediate affirmation of your petition for membership in the Good Guys and Well Behaved Human category. Instead, you have your Evil Genius showing up with handsful of black pebbles. Before you know it, you are utterly disqualified from membership in this club.

"They kept hammering at me, presenting the damning evidence over and over until I confessed. You'll like this bit, Blaise. I felt I understood the torments of Orestes. I later understood my own dark karma kept putting up a wall of resistance to the truth of the accusations. It's funny: I was defendant, defense attorney, and prosecuting district attorney all in one. My conscience was the plaintiff, and that guy never relented. He kept pressing his claims against me.

"Okay: I finally broke down and admitted I had cheated my younger brother, stolen his toys, broken a few in petulant defiance of his privileges, and hurt him. The offenses were not major, but my resistance to owning up to them was big. That prolonged the courtroom prosecution against me, that I kept denying it. As soon as I broke down and told Perry Mason what he wanted, it ended at once. He smiled subtly, walked away, and chalked up another win. Then he probably took Della Street and Paul Drake out for a three-hour lunch.

"I had the impression my Higher Self was talking to me, explaining things as they unfolded before me, as the charge sheet was read out in court. It seemed like talk, but maybe it was more the pressure of lucidity this spirit bore upon me. It felt like I was closeted with my grandfather. He was nice, cordial, and I knew he liked me, but he had to make sure I understood the problems I had created; he had to press his case with uncharacteristic gravity until I showed I understood.

"It was embarrassing to have to admit my offenses before my grandfather because it broke the shell of affability that usually surrounded us. But I got through it. It's a curious relationship, the one between yourself and your Higher Self. You need each other. You need the Higher Self to explain the landscape to you, the route; and the Higher Self needs you to drive the all-range truck in the incarnation safari. I mean, you are his field agent, the guy with his feet on the physical ground, executing another episode in this arcane agenda the Higher Self has concocted. His strange and wonderful notion of what to get out of your life."

I looked around at the numerous Higher Self bubbles floating about. I heard murmurings and whisperings from inside them, like from radio channels. It was like hearing conversations through walls in a house; you know the people in the other room are talking and you get the emotional tones, but you can't make out the words, so you hear just the continuous soft rustle of conversation. But all around me Higher Selves, Good Geniuses, were counseling souls in the protocols and illusions of the *Bardo* and the rigors of an awakened conscience.

It was like the resumption of an old conversation, started long ago. Blaise had told me during our travels after he whisked me out of Hanover that the Higher Self is assigned to a soul the minute it is extruded from the Supreme Being. It is not even a soul yet, for that requires chakras and additional Light bodies. It comes out of the Supreme Being, which looks like a golden sphere or wall, as a white flame; the Higher Self immediately envelops it as a bright globe. The Higher Self becomes the spirit's first aura, and it begins its long assignment of protection and guidance as the spirit enters a soul form and builds its bodies.

"Have you noticed," Edward said, addressing all of us, "how events here seem to be out of sequence, that it seems they get repeated, like a musical coda?"

He was right. We were seeing activities I thought had been concluded earlier, this visitation of the wandering soul by yet more frightening apparitions. I thought we had finished with that business, yet here it was again around us.

"Think of it as like a meal with six servings on the plate, wine, water, salad, cheese, entrée, and dessert, even the coffee, all spread out before you like a smorgasbord," said Merlin. "You may eat these items in any order you wish. Sample the potatoes, then go to the salad, then nibble the dessert, sip the coffee, return to the wine, resume slicing up the entrée. You eat in any order you like. The only requirement is you have to clean your plate, finish off everything.

"Let's say you wielded an extra light fork regarding the peas. There are many peas left on your plate. Here comes the Lord of Death, the *maître d'hotel* of this establishment, and he reminds you to finish your peas. You can't leave until you do. Meaning you have a few more karmic illusions to process out of your system. So from a three-dimensional linear perspective, the event sequence seems screwy, full of reversions and unexpected reiterations; but from the fourth-dimensional holographic viewpoint, which is the reality of the *Bardo*, it's a matter of completing a few aspects *over there* that you left incomplete."

"At a certain point this place can get boring, don't you think?" It was Blaise. "Oh man, you mean I have to sit through more of these brain-dead karmic illusions? I have to go back to sleep and dream for another two hours until I have emptied the hopper of all karmic pictures, tendencies, debts, and credits? What, you say with justified ire to the fussy old *Bardo* bureaucrats, I already weighed my stupid heart ages ago; here are the forensic results. Ma'at was disappointed. Anyway, I'm having lunch with my *Ammit*. We've already booked a table. I suppose when it gets tedious it means you're getting the hang of the place."

"Do you feel that tug?" asked Edward. "It feels like an undertow at the beach. You feel the sand starting to slide under your feet as the great rolling current of the ocean sweeps you outward. It feels like we're being drawn towards something, and strongly, and that something looks like, though vaguely, a human form—no, it's the possibility, the allurement, of once again having a human form and restarting the karmic circus of incarnation, getting back in the Great Game and making a big score. I'm glad we're already, or still, incarnated. I am beginning to see how it is a temptation or a compulsion hard to resist."

"One could compare it to a food addiction, if one were feeling a bit bleak," said Blaise. "Give me another hair of the dog that bit me, as the bromide goes. It's easier to stay incarnated than to face either the demonic clown show or the awful voidness of the *Bardo*. Neither option seems like fun, most people would say. The withdrawal symptoms are unbearable; it's better to stay addicted, less painful. So let me get back to the old stand as soon as possible to resume my familiar habits.

"Do you see those lights on the horizon? Those are the lights of the Six Worlds, beckoning to the soul in the *Bardo* like neon signs outside Las Vegas at night. Garish, glittering signs luring you into casinos, restaurants, hotels, and nightclubs. Come, reincarnate again. Better avoid the Animal *loka*; you'll end up as a dog, although that might not be so bad if you were born as an American dog. I used to think being born as a golden retriever in New England would be paradise. They can't get enough of retrievers there; they treat them lavishly, like princes, members in good standing of the family, members who never argue.

"It reminds me of those old Zen stories about Zen Masters who screw up, maybe answer the *koans* wrongly or admit lame-brained answers, get reborn as foxes. I always found the stories entertaining, but I didn't believe them for a minute. I once had a dog and I'd ask him, 'So what *koan* did you screw up?'"

"This is a crucial point for the transiting soul," said Merlin. "That is why the Druj will exploit every opening in the soul's mental field to insert a doubt or kindle a desire to be among the warm and living again and out of this hellish domain. Don't waste any more time on this immedicable nightmare, she counsels the dead and wandering. Get out while you can. Come, here is the doorway out.

"She wants souls to leave the *Bardo* with their karma processing incomplete, undigested, even better, unacknowledged, still in the dark. She feeds them whatever lie she discerns they will prefer. She is a consummate short-order cook. She knows what her customers want the minute they enter the *Bardo*. They don't stand a chance, or so it seems, and soon they are consuming her artful lies and thinking it is the truth served up with strawberries and whipped cream."

"Then, when you incarnate, the religions will make sure you don't process your karma either by convincing you it doesn't exist," said Blaise. "How can you have karma when you only live once? Sin? Sure. You have lots of sin, and we can help you with that. Just prostrate yourself before our Chief Man, a guy we call Jesus. He'll do right by you. Behave, be obedient, and we'll take care of your sin. It's like banks: they don't want creditors to pay off their credit cards; they want them to pay small amounts so the interest keeps accruing. Karma is your credit balance. Pay it off in full you're free; keep paying interest you stay on the wheel. The Druj is the devious *Bardo* banker who wants you to only pay the interest."

"I felt that tug when I reached this point," said Tommy. "But I didn't give in, as you can see. I took the opportunity to sit here and contemplate the feeling. I sat here and regarded things from the outside the way I used to on Mount Ashland which, as you know, was also my jumping off point for my last life. I'd sit here and ask myself: so, who are you without the body and human life? The question worked like an anchor; I felt myself sink into and get secured here. I felt thin, like I hadn't eaten in a long time, which in physical terms I had not, but it was not due to that. The thinness was my sense of my self. I had dropped a lot.

"I felt trimmed down to the essentials, and now I was probing myself to find those, to identify, even label them, so I could understand this new thin me I was. I was giving a fresh nuance to Hammett's Thin Man. I was the thin self. It was perplexing and no answer surfaced at first, but the act of looking for it kept me rooted to this spot and I easily resisted the undertow of incarnation. It was no more than a slightly annoying noise like you'd hear from another room.

"I felt a kind of lassitude, an indolent, languid indifference to doing anything at all. I considered all sorts of possibilities and felt no draw to any of them. I felt no compunction to take any action; nothing had a draw sufficient to motivate me. I saw the blandishments of each, but in each case the upside was unimpressive. It was an in-between place, like what astrologers call Moon Void of Course, when the Moon is not in one sign or another but in transit. It's an emotionally vague, indefinite period of time, like a meeting that hasn't adjourned or a jury still deliberating. No clear-cut action is indicated or advised. I saw no good reason, I felt no strong draw, to take any of those envisioned steps. What did seem worth doing was finding out who is this I who is sitting here asking?

"As I sat here, I lost track of what was outside and what was inside me. I couldn't tell them apart, but now I realize that is the point of the *Bardo* trip. To reach that point of nondualism. All the crazy circus demons and frightening spirits had subsided; their infernal songs and *danse macabre* had settled down. The Druj had withdrawn and watched me from a distance; she did not interfere. My Higher Self enveloped me quietly and loyally the way a trusted dog will sit beside you, watching, waiting, not moving until you do, and so we both sat still.

"I had dropped all the costumery of my recently concluded brief life, my identity based on family membership, social standing, academic achievements, all that. That was an old script for a theater piece I'd already acted in; I didn't need it. I'd done the O'Neill, or was it Edward Albee? All histrionics cancelled.

"It's true, I couldn't reincarnate for a few years anyway. I had to do my penance, serve the years I should have still been alive before I was scheduled to die. That didn't change the force of the undertow. I still felt it like wet beach sand sliding out underneath me, even though I was not moving toward the water. What I had experienced at times for brief moments, a certain moment of lucid epiphany, when my life, my qualities, my essence, seemed revealed before me, was now my uniform state of mind. It was my inner and outer environment. That was rich. I liked it. It didn't require me to do anything at all, not even to whistle, as Lauren Bacall might have said. I just sat there like Bogart in his chair.

"Everything was still, deeply, widely quiet. Nothing moved or spoke. My karmic illusions were taking a coffee break and had left the stage. It was just me. Just me and an abiding, enveloping presence. At first it felt like my Higher Self, but I started to realize it was far bigger, vaster than this now familiar presence. It felt like a friendly grandfather whose face was as big as the *Bardo*, as all of reality.

"I didn't see this face, I only felt its presence. It was, I am sure, only a metaphor of a face. A presence that was face-like, because to a human a face conveys attention so I put a face on this attention. It didn't feel like another stupid karmic illusion. You can hardly call the Supreme Being a karmic illusion. That would be funny. Go away, God, you're just an hallucination cooked up by my distorted stupid karma. Maybe Blaise can work a stand-up routine for that.

"The presence grew around me like a sunrise, the way the world grows light. I felt increasingly more awake, more attentive, more lucidly right here. It felt like being observed by absolutely the most awake spirit in the Creation and that this intense wakefulness permeated me and reconfigured my own attention so that I was this fiercely blazing total awakeness. Everything was this lucidity. A voice said, and it must have been myself, this expanded version of myself: 'What do I want?' I appreciated the implicit pun of this; its nuances echoed around me. It was me, Tommy, asking about my desire; it was the Supreme Being asking me if I knew what He wanted; and it was the Supreme Being asking Himself—what?

"It didn't require an answer. I just laughed, and the laughter echoed throughout this vast— no: *infinite*—presence. The entire universe was laughing. It still is. My laugh is still traveling to the farthest reaches of infinity. But the Supreme Being's laugh is already there, expanded to infinity, where He lives.

"It was all openness, all possibility. Nothing was scripted, cast in concrete, not yet. Things could go in any direction, could turn out in completely unexpected ways. It was like having a quadrillion dollars and you could do anything you wanted. It was like juggling a million balls all at once, knowing you'd drop none of them. It was knowing you could do anything and knowing you didn't have to do anything. It was sufficient merely to contemplate in ease all the possibilities. This was not apathy or any sense of futility. It was bliss, unalloyed wide-open delight. I was floating on the surface of a sea of bliss, close enough to the action to feel enveloped in the wonderful feeling. If I wanted it all, I only had to submerge and disappear all vestiges of myself in this bliss sea.

"All the things you could envision doing were bubbles on the water's surface. You had already done them all. It felt great, too. You were the water and its bubbles. Merely to think them up was the full doing of them. All that was required, that mattered, was to know these things were possible, already done.

"I'll be staying here for a while. I know that now. No womb-doors for me. No tidal suction. I'll help people find this quiet place. No, no, I don't mean I'm leaving the expedition. I mean wherever I am in the *Bardo* I am still also right here. I've never gotten up from this contemplative place, and I don't feel like it."

Nobody said anything for a while. We were all, I think, reveling in Tommy's wonderful picture. The undertow remained steady, though it would have no effect on any of us, other than Tommy, since we were not dead. We were only visitors, tourists, I suppose I should say. I noted that the Tibetan text was strident in its emphasis that the transiting soul should try to avoid the womb-doors. The text positioned the womb-doors as about the worst thing that could happen to you, to get sucked into one and find yourself in another human body. Like being sucked into the revolving doors of a lurid casino when you already have a terrible gambling addiction and a huge debt from roulette wheel losses.

Is it the worst thing? Weren't we now at the crux of a fundamental issue, namely, for what reason might we choose, or did we ever, the first time, choose to enter the human stream, the human phylogeny, and begin our long odyssey?

Let's put the addictive aspect of reincarnation aside. That doesn't answer the question; it merely describes a compulsive habit, automatic, not considered. But how about the first time? Why would anyone, any soul, wish to clothe its Light form with a mortal, material human body subject to toothache, indigestion, and pain? The question is not framed only by the choice of a human body. How about any body, the material form of what we parochially call aliens and ETs? People used to think it was sexy to be a Pleiadian, or to know some, or maybe be abducted by them. But why would a soul want to become a Pleiadian at all? You're still subject to the design parameters of the Pleiadian consciousness, and your free-ranging unlimited spirit still has to take on a voluntary diminishment.

Consciousness at some point chooses to enter a life-form and take on its body. The reason has to be bigger, more profound, than the mere entertainment or thrill value of trying it out, like a new, exotic, dangerous-looking, amusement park ride, or, more pessimistically, as an addiction repetition compulsion. The novelty of that would soon expire. Our reason surely would have to encompass the desire to accomplish a mission, attain a certain experience, learn something, master a skill, gain spiritual understanding in a body, expand yourself.

"It's to experience and be God as a separate self in an individual material form," said a voice very familiar to me. It was Philomena. She had returned to us. "I used to think my life, before I underwent this change, was about music, feeling the soul of music, of the composers, of the piano as a musical instrument, playing it, entering into this wonderful stream of expression, feeling what it did to me. That might have encompassed my recently concluded life as Philomena, music teacher, performer of Rachmaninov and Scriabin, and editor of a Blaise book."

She was chuckling, shaking her head at Blaise who was also grinning, and she was temporarily back in the semblance of her former human form. At least it looked like her. I didn't dare touch her in case it was just mist and she vanished.

"The minute you take on a soul you're working for the Old Man," said Blaise. "He has quintillions of employees, all engaged in the same arcane project. Bring me back news and views about—Myself! The original narcissist, He is. What is the Creation like, He wonders. What am I like? Does anybody like me? Do you like what I've done with the place, pointing to the Vacated Space into which He's inserted the Tree of Life with 40 *Sefirot*, Himself grinning behind it.

"He generates a vast number of experiencers to go find out and report back. He hungers for feedback. Do you like my set-up? They spread out through the worlds, equipped with bodies for the research project. Pretend you are a separate self while you're on the job, He says. Try to forget you're actually Me in multiple guises. Even better, pretend you don't remember Me, never heard of Me. That will make the investigation more realistic, give it more verisimilitude."

"Most souls find it easy to forget," said Philomena. "A few do not, though. They have little cracks and apertures in the armoring of the individual self and insinuations of the Great One periodically seep through and disturb or intrigue them. They sense there is more to this incarnation business than they first thought. They suspect things are hidden from them, that they have forgotten things. It's the River Lethe of course, that universal bane of wide-awake lucidity. The Supreme Being says, craftily, Let's give them a little handicap, a tiny obstacle that stands in the way of remembering what they are and what they're doing.

"You know, whatever self you contrive, whatever notion of yourself you come up with, it is still relative, provisional, and transitory, truly a persona, a mask. Yes, you need a separate self to navigate the world of experience, whether it's the astral or the physical world, but it has no absolute standing. It's a funny face the Supreme Being puts on to entertain Himself, like a child making faces in the mirror. Behind that face is the real face, though it's not a face: it's Reality.

"At first it seems to be the infrastructure of the Creation, the bones and sinews, as the Qabalists would say, the spheres of Light and realms of the angels. But all that is a face, a cascade of faces, and not the absolute reality behind it all. There is only one place of genuine solid ground; that's the only place to stand on. You go out, incarnate, individualize, individuate, and pretend that is not true. Then, eventually, when you tire of the delightful charade, you stop pretending."

"Is it the same reason for everyone then, why they decide to incarnate?" asked Edward. "It seems like a generic compulsion, an attraction, the same for all souls, an irresistible allure that God holds out to all souls like bright candy."

"There are two levels to it," answered Philomena. "First, the decision to take on a form at all, the first form, form instead of remaining formless. Second, the decision to enter the human form, to sign up for the human phylogeny. That may have more individualized reasons based on your soul frequency, which is a musical quality, a kind of originating tone which characterizes your soul and determines your place assignment on the Tree of Souls where all souls reside.

"But why ever enter a form, any form? Why not remain in the fullness of God? I think the Old Man secretly gives every soul a nudge. Go, find out for Me. Go enter that secret intriguing mirror I hold up in front of Myself. Have a little look. Step outside of Me, out of this unfathomable fullness, and have a look at Me. Pretend for a while that there are two things in existence, Myself and this other. I allow you, I commission you, to be a *you* so you can report back to Me."

"He has the universe's worst case of multiple personality disorder," said Blaise. "It's the three faces of Eve run out to infinity. Psychics are still compiling the identity list. Even when you stand on that hallowed fundamental ground of the Supreme Being, there is still the nagging question: How did He get there?

"How did the Supreme Being come into existence? It is a perennial question, and a perennially unanswerable one, full of logical and spiritual flaws, and the mystics have given up trying to answer it because it's the awfullest *koan* ever, yet still, when I ponder it, it is like a vast monolithic wall at the end of the universe. What's on the other side of it? The mind wants to know how did an infinite being, the only one, come into existence, and how could it exist infinitely?

"It's like always getting netballs in a game of badminton. You always hit the net. Or trying to climb the proverbial Glass Mountain; you always slide down it. I come up against this vexing question—it really is vexing to me—and slide right down. Even Agatha Christie couldn't crack this Mystery. I wonder if He knows. Being infinite, He is both the question and the answer. The knowing and the not-knowing of how He, an infinite being, the only one, came to be. The Supreme Being one morning asks Himself in wonder, However did I get here?"

As if commentary on our discussion I heard a number of doors slam shut.

Blaise laughed heartily when he heard this. "They're closing the womb-doors. A few bold souls have said no to the allurements of another incarnation."

The *Bardo Thödol* at this point is strident about means to shut the doors. The womb-doors are seen as insidious, in many respects worse than the demons. I'm not sure I would credit what I next saw with complete reality, but I saw a broad circle with innumerable doors placed along its circumference. Individuals stood before most of the doors. Some were hesitating; some reaching for the door handles, others passing through. Some merely looked through the open doors. Others I saw making diagrams, charts, and lists with their Higher Selves as they stood at the doors, planning their next life, I presumed, down to the last detail.

The book makes it seem like you're about to jump off a cliff, so don't be stupid. The solution? It almost sounds like: keep a stiff upper lip and think of England. Or, perhaps in more Buddhist language, remember the Buddha Mind and don't deviate from the voidness for a second or you'll be royally screwed and reborn instantly. The Tibetan sense of resistance expressed is vigorous. Maybe they just didn't want another life with just barley tea and yak butter.

Expect to see images of humans coupling (Freud's primal scene in its correct location: yes, you did see your parents doing it). If you were a male and now felt hatred towards the male having sex, presumably your prospective father, it means you'll be born as a male; if you hate the guts of your mother, it means you'll be incarnated as a female. This strikes me as drollery. Guidance for closing the womb-door reads like panicked advice from an airline steward to close the emergency hatch-door on the plane before it depressurizes. It will be the worst thing in the world (in the *Bardo*) if you don't close that womb-door.

This part of the text struck me as hysterical. I don't mean laughingly funny; I mean overly-panicked, paranoid, and distrustful. It can't be the worst thing in the world to be reborn; after all, the Supreme Being gave us a standing invitation for human incarnation, so He didn't think it bad. So don't reincarnate in Tibet. Try Tahiti: the weather there is gorgeous. I guess the trick is if you see entering the womb-door

as yet another summer trip to Europe, can you go there, visit, see things, and not use the karma credit card? Or, so what if you do? You'll make arrangements later to take care of the balance when the statement comes.

I studied some of the souls sitting before the doors. The doors were open but the souls had not passed through them. They were considering or planning. I saw them discussing scenarios with their Higher Selves, images of possible life situations hovering vividly in the air around them, of family members, friends, enemies, lovers, children, colleagues, unresolved karmic situations like vexed black splotches or distorted pictures framed in dirty fire, available knowledge and wisdom like a floating library of old books they might bring through in life.

The scene had the intensity and focus of generals planning a military campaign, or expert engineers reviewing the intricacies of machine design before building, or perhaps a movie director blocking out the actors' moves. Everything was planned; only a little room was left for chance or serendipity, maybe a five percent wildcard factor, I would guess. Secondary-level plans were made, plans B, C, and D, and more, multiple contingency scenarios if the original plan was botched, aborted, resisted, or even forgotten.

My impressions of the emotional valence of what I saw kept fluctuating. It looked like Parisians casually, even languidly, sipping espresso at an outdoor café in Montmartre, like flaneurs discussing which avant-garde theater performance they'd go to, boulevardiers indolently strolling the tree-lined streets. Or it was like spies poised before the open door of the low-flying plane ready to jump and deploy their parachutes to land covertly behind enemy lines, something in the spirit of Doris Lessing's phrase "briefing for a descent into hell." The Tibetans would have liked her attitude as implied in that grim phrase. Incarnartion was like another round in Hell, the image suggested.

The Tibetan text gives you the impression the monks were afraid of being whisked out the airplane's open door plummeting unconscious before they opened their chutes or even realized they needed to yank that cord. It was that strong undertow fear again, the fear of being swept off your feet into another life, ill-considered, rash, precipitous, and altogether the worst of ideas. You get the impression the worst thing in the world is to get sucked through a womb-door and to find yourself lined up for another episode of the circus. Shit, this again?

Maybe I'm too simplistic, but if it's such a bad idea, why does God allow it? The Tibetan text makes it sound like God is some pimp or devious barker at a carnival luring unsophisticated visitors into a lurid tent of depravity and crime. Or a drug pusher tempting you down the dark addiction path one more time. Or, more generously, a trickster of consummate skill presenting you a dilemma. Stay outside the tent, it's all rumor and hearsay; enter it and you will find out.

I guess what I am saying is that I have the impression of massive *resistance* in the Tibetan text to undergoing another incarnation, to the category of incarnation. It's as if they discount the possibility of achieving Clear Mind while alive. That is not a position of neutrality, nor even one of seniority and sovereignty. It seems a partisan view: incarnation is bad, avoid it at all costs if you're smart. They counsel the soul in nonresistance to the *Bardo* hallucinations, yet they evidence a massive resistance to the *Bardo* illusions of incarnated human life. Most people fear the *Bardo*, but the Tibetan attitude fears the alive world. They don't truth themselves to maintain cognitive clarity while out in the circus.

Yes, I can see how incarnation is a risky proposition. You fall asleep, forget, live in spiritual oblivion like everyone else, but you are always at risk to have absolute reality explode around you like hand grenades tossed from the *Dharmakaya*, violently revealing the true reality and shattering all the illusions. How deeply can you sleep before you lose all sense of incipient panic about that? It's the same voidness, though I suppose the *Bardo* voidness revealed within physical life and its sunlit world preoccupations is probably the more shocking.

We've been touring the varieties of shock treatment you can expect in the *Bardo* where the voidness comes calling and makes you an offer you can't refuse, but I can see how if this level of shock treatment occurred in embodied life it would seem even worse, more apocalyptic, more without an explanatory safe context. Maybe that's the thing: consciousness itself is shocking; it is the exploding grenade. It doesn't matter on which side of the incarnation divide you're standing, in life or in the *Bardo*: it's the same voidness, the same consciousness, the same unalloyed, unremitting naked Mystery of awareness. God, how did I get here and why am I conscious, you might feel like screaming.

It is like a complex living machine you find yourself in: it does stuff, spins out pictures, feelings, illusions, realities, hallucinations—it's hard to tell them apart. It's not death or the *Bardo* that's terrifying: it's consciousness itself that's awful. I realized it was bizarre in both directions. I think people want to forget. Maybe it's like what the Portuguese writer Fernando Pessoa wrote in the *Book of Disquiet* (1935), "I see life as a roadside inn where I have to stay until the coach for the abyss pulls up." Life makes no sense, and death makes even less sense.

As a spirit in the Underworld, the prospect of human bodily incarnation could seem threatening in terms of what it does to the equanimity of consciousness you are used to. All the special effects of Earth reality, the *skandah* apocalypse, would seem the end of the world as you know it. It would be worse than shopping at a busy mall on the Saturday before Christmas. At the other end of the polarity, there you are, alive, used to the fractious, riotous, basically nonstop roiling action-movie nature of consciousness, and the prospect of a voidness-promising stroll through the *Bardo* after death seems intimidating and beyond your imagined endurance. Not that, *please*, anything but that. It can seem even worse if you've had the bad luck (bad karma!) to read the *Bardo Thödol* and get a preview of the charming *Herukas* and rampaging Furies you'll likely meet.

Edward, myself, Tommy, and Pipaluk stood next to a soul at a door. I had the impression that he had been drawn towards the womb-door by its inevitable suction and had just managed to skid to a halt before passing through it. There weren't any, but I imagined the dark deep skid marks he'd made, like a speeding car just managing to brake in time before driving off a sheer cliff. Now he was taking his bearings with his Higher Self; they huddled in conference.

I chuckled. There were so many metaphorical nuances to what I had been seeing. The soul and his Higher Self could just as well have been a defendant and his lawyer, huddling at the defense table to go over his testimony on a crucial point. He was facing a life sentence for his crimes in the *Bardo*, his failure to see through his own self-generated karmic illusions. Now he'd pay big for his offenses. The State wanted to throw the book at him. He was about to be sentenced to hard time in the *skandah* slammer, about 80 years with no parole.

The scene also struck me as similar to a meeting between a businessman and his accountant. They were going over the long list of debits, allocating funds to discharge as many debts as possible, determining which they could defer. Lining up the payments, prioritizing the allocation of funds, who did they have to pay

off first, who could wait, who could they put off even until the next life. The man studied his list of debts, his karmic balance sheet. He shook his head. It had all caught up with him; he didn't know he was this much in arrears on it all.

On the other side of the register, he was owed a few things, the debit sheet was not empty. Some souls owed him a redress, a second chance, an apology. His next life would not be exclusively about paying out, emptying the karmic coffers. He might even excuse a few of the debts, exercise forgiveness; he might be able to cash that in on some of his own debts, though his Higher Self was shaking his head in disagreement. That's not how the system works. The debt forgiveness must be genuine, executed without any expectation of return.

There were so many criteria to reach a decision about. Gender, ethnos, nationality, parents, siblings, preferred astrological configurations and what you'd have to compromise or put up with to get a few highly desired angles. Tolerate a couple of squares and oppositions to get a preferred Moon sign. What health issues and their karmic seeds did you want to bring forward with the possibility of, one hoped, not dying from them but actually resolving them. What dull qualities in your parents could you endure to get one desirable sharp trait, just the one you need to propel you into a particular life track and career?

How much pain, misery, and accrued suffering were you willing to bring to the forefront for discharge, wakefully, voluntarily eradicating the complex pain infrastructure, what clairvoyants, so Blaise tells me, call "erasing the pictures." Students in clairvoyance training plan their lives to have a high productivity in this area, a big release schedule, major picture processing (like a film studio with a fat budget) though most people, understandably, settle for resolving maybe a few pictures, or none, if they can get away with it. Don't ruffle me, karma;

I'm comfortable sleeping, go away. I don't believe in this anyway.

It's not fun sitting wakefully amidst the warring conflicts of your own karma or dealing with the after-effects, the growth period of psychological adjustment. Even worse, it's no fun at all realizing, soberly, everything that's happening is your own fault because *you planned it* meticulously out of your own free will when you were dead, taking the broad, long-term view, planning your own ambushes, rug-pullings, and dramatic fateful encounters with yourself with the aplomb of ordering an eight-course meal at a fine restaurant.

Everything looks easy, doable, possible when you're scripting a life from the safety and elevated view of the *Bardo*. It's not until you're alive, down there, out there, living, what military types call "boots on the ground," your body demanding coffee, as Blaise would say, that the karma hits the fan and the fan strikes the wall and knocks it down and you wonder, screamingly, where this latest hellish disaster has come from, and why. I demand to speak to the management at once, you declare, with nobody listening. I want a full refund. This is not what I signed up for. I have been defrauded, swindled. So, is it worse to be alive and fuming or dead and planning? I couldn't say just now.

I realized that life planning is a moment of true power a soul experiences. It is probably the only moment when what we do counts for something, when we have actual control over the conditions of our life and especially our attitude. I am thinking of the way many people go about life proud of their physical attributes, women for the size of their breasts, men for their musculature or bone structure or an aspect physically vain like that, perhaps the abundance of hair or its striking color or their smile or something. Vanity aside, this is all illusory.

Just about all of this is a given, pre-determined, and out of our hands, largely a negotiated compromise between three factors we do not have much influence over, namely, karmic necessities as they determine body feature; family genetic patterns and their corresponding soul issues we seek to play out in the body; and the generic human body design in the first place. We, who we think we are, have to squeeze into these conflicting demands, or perhaps they are complementary necessities that work well together and leave us a little room, like squeezing into a tight elevator, no bigger than a tiny closet, already packed. Then we arrive here, look in the mirror, and strut around, proud of ourselves.

The only thing, I propose, we can legitimately take credit for, be proud of, is the plan for our upcoming life we have co-drafted with our Higher Self, the specific details of what we have agreed to accomplish, the amount of karmic debt or accrued misery we plan to dissolve, the karmic debts we intend to pay off or forgive, and the progress in soul evolution we wish to attain. These items come genuinely from us; here we have authentically shaped our life; everything else is already set in place with a certain iron hand of necessity and we can't change it.

Let me qualify that. Yes, we can, ultimately, change it all, but that requires the awakening and mastery of a certain cluster of *siddhis* or latent powers of consciousness that most of us never get around to attaining and often never even hear about. Then, alive, we usually forget even this amount of authentic input and attribute the events of our lives to blind fortune like serendipitous collisions of billiard balls, and storm about complaining about bad management and inattentive service and it's a goddam pity none of this life makes any sense to us.

I was starting to see how the *Bardo* and embodied life are asymmetrically reciprocal. Alive, we deal with the products and stage movements of our own life script, written by us in a moment of great calm and concentration in the *Bardo*. Our script, our karma, intersects with that of many other alive people. We have the potential, the invitation, to wake up to the true machinations behind the scenes and realize we did this, we are the puppet-masters, and for a specific purpose and desired outcome. We just have to wake up to that occulted purpose we had in mind in the *Bardo* and see through the confusing appearances.

In the *Bardo* we are also dealing with the products of our scripting, but in this case, the results of the life script we created earlier in the *Bardo* as they played out in physical reality, and our processing appears to be solitary, even solipsistic. We don't bump up against the karma scripts of other souls. We all work alone here. We too can wake up and realize everything we see is subjectively created.

Alive, we believe our reality plays out as physical events, bodily interactions, bumping against walls and people. In the *Bardo* the reality is that everything is an artifact of a conflicted field of consciousness playing itself out, and often we don't catch on to the psychic machinery of the place. But the fact is, and I can see this now, in both cases the events occur in the field of our consciousness. The bodies and the seeming sheer physicality of material life are illusory, nice sleights-of-hand, jerkings and gibberings of the many puppets. Our life, when Earth-alive and *Bardo*-dead, is a drama enacted in consciousness.

Around us, as I said, were thousands of womb-doors with individual souls poised before each in counsel with their Higher Selves as they prepared to enter these doors. Above the doors hovered a singular spirit, our old friend, the Druj. She was suspended there like a cloud, an atmosphere, a British day of grey, lowering overcast, like a frown spreading across the sky, a mother displeased with your childish actions.

That was only one of her emotional nuances. She varied it for each soul. She is the most accomplished actor conceivable.

For some she was a devious courtesan, alluring yet treacherous. For others, she was the elder sister passing on valuable life experience tips for her younger siblings; or bossy, authoritarian, even dictatorial, telling them exactly what to do and expecting it to be done; or she was a picture of panic, anxiety, and worry, reminding the soul that incarnation was terribly dangerous, too risky to consider seriously, and really pushing the subject, badgering you, like a nag.

"The Tibetan text at this point gives you the impression souls are inexorably compelled toward womb-doors that match their level of karmic obscuration," said Edward. "You get the impression they are swept off their feet as if they are standing in the front of a hurricane gale and are blown into the door of the *Preta* realm, the Animal, the Hell realm, or maybe the *Devas*. But that isn't what I'm seeing here. Souls here seem to be in quiet conference with their Higher Selves much like a businessman working overtime planning a corporate restructuring and debt management, working out payment schedules, balance sheets, and next year's operating budget, sales expectations, and new markets.

"It reminds me of our annual sales, marketing, and editorial meetings at the publishing company, which authors we want to cultivate or drop, how much we want to spend on paper, bindings, and art work, and which books to remainder. My point is the souls I see planning their lives do not seem compelled by blind karmic obscurations or irresistible karmic drives; they are taking their karma into account and drafting sensible plans for their next human incarnation. Their options may be limited because of their karmic accruals, but they still have some room for choices and emphases. It's not as iron-handed as you'd think."

"Agreed," said Blaise. "But do you note the subtle intruding hand of the Druj at key tactical moments when she slips in a suggestion or raises a doubt enough to tip the balance in a different direction than the soul was intending? The voice of pessimism reminding the soul of their deficits and inabilities, or the voice of inflation, urging the soul to gamble more, spend bigger, lose balance. Or she may inspire feelings of compulsion, of one being swept by the hurricane-force gale of your unprocessed karma through a womb-door before you know it. She may have inspired some of that feeling of unalterable determinism in the *Bardo Thödol* where the soul has no control and is swept towards a womb-door."

"Some do not in fact have much control, especially the young souls," said Merlin. "Mastery of one's choices and by extension mastery of a degree of one's consciousness and its terrific hurricane-like force takes a while, takes some lives. At this point we want to install a few safety measures on these famous womb-doors, something like seat belts or perhaps like the latches inside jets so you cannot accidentally open the door and get sucked out into the lower atmosphere.

"We were thinking in terms of putting in a kind of consciousness gradient or dimensional braking mechanism by these doors which would slow down the soul's movement towards it and give one a time for reflection and decision. I suppose you could call this a gravity wall that has a slight repulsive force to it. It slows you down, applies the brakes, and holds you steady in place before you enter the door, pushing you away from it gently until you're ready and sure. As you approach it you become more reflective, take stock of yourself; you pause in the forward momentum of your rush to incarnate again and wait. Then, when you have considered it, when you're ready, you may pass through the door.

"The hope of our engineering redesign is that when souls have more time to consider their life plan and enter the womb-doors more knowingly, better briefed, they will arrive in the physical Earth world better equipped to achieve moments of lucid self-awareness, even epiphanies, and take stock of themselves. Here I am, in a body again, and I have goals to achieve, consciousness to expand. We are hoping this will increase the number of incidences of this self-awareness because that will incrementally start to raise the consensus reality vibration, the overall feeling and quality of human conscious life and thereby feed the Albions. All our changes and innovations in the *Bardo* have Albion's status fully in mind.

"You may remember that I said earlier that a chief goal of this expedition is to update the *Bardo* and its procedures to be in accord with the changes to the Earth and its Light grid, its overall pattern of geomantic sites and their energies. The prime recipient of that newly achieved resonance with be Earth's Albion, all of them, at all their levels of expression. That is the body of humanity's collective consciousness over time and set within this celestial imprint that is his form. You could say every human who has ever lived and who is living today is a vital cell in his vast cosmic body of Light lying upon the planet. Whatever progress in consciousness any of the human souls make is immediately registered in Albion.

"It is a constantly fluctuating affair, much like the stock market, where the share price may rise and dip all day long, showing short-term and long-term trends. The long-term trend with Albion, seen over many thousands of years, is towards waking up and becoming lucidly aware of himself as a cosmic spirit. Then all humans can participate in Albion's momentous act of self-awareness. Our job here is to improve the reciprocal loops of influence between the *Bardo*, living humans walking under the Light grid of Earth, and Albion.

"In his design, Albion straddles both poles of the human experience, in bodies and out. But he has been asleep to this pre-existent interaction; now we wake him up. He springs into animation as a colossus of Light, a walking cosmogonic map of human and Earth structure and original design. Albion becomes a self-aware, cosmic presence inhabiting both domains, and, through him, so do alive and *Bardo*-based humans dwelling in both realms. He is the bridge between conscious and unconscious realms, physical life and *Bardo*."

"A startling suspicion has been growing in me for some time here," said Edward. "It has bearing on what you're saying about Albion broadening his awareness to straddle both realms. I have seen many souls moving about as if they were asleep, or sleepwalking, or in a trance state, like after a head injury. The expected revelations of *Herukas*, *Dakinis*, and the great circus of one's karmic illusions and terrific hallucinations have been unfolding around them, but it seems for many they did not see this and slept through it, the way corpulent male Victorian aristocrats often napped (digested their dinner) during the opera.

"I remember from the various books I read, and, in fact, in some cases considered for publication at our firm, that often reports of after-death experiences do not detail this level of lucid perception of the intricacies of the divestment process. Souls seem to go right past that to the fun parts where they go through desired doors and have worlds of experiences in the finer parts of the astral world. So I'm wondering, my suspicion is, do people sleep through this?"

"You are suspecting something accurate," replied Merlin. "There are varying degrees of lucidity regarding the *Bardo* experience that transiting souls manifest. It is much like when they are alive. Some people have a heightened sense of self-awareness; others seem oblivious to the fact they are alive in bodies.

"You'll find that same range of awareness here. Some souls seem to sleep through the divestment process where the components of their body and psyche are revealed and the karmic coloring and distortions they gave these components are also demonstrated. A part of them perceives these revelations, but the main body of their awareness, their center of gravity, misses it all. It is registered in one of their higher being-bodies, as they still have four or five at this stage, so they experience these disclosures in what you might call the *Bardo* version of the Second Attention, the Double's awareness. But this is like storing important documents in an upstairs room of a large house, a room you don't often visit.

"The Tibetans, and the earlier Egyptians, because they had cultures that emphasized meditation, occult perception, and attunement to these finer aspects of higher reality, had a greater likelihood of perceiving these details of the *Bardo*. It was an aspect of their mindfulness meditations, of their attunement with these planes of experience. The degree of detail you find in the Tibetan and Egyptian books of the dead far surpasses what the average human was able to perceive. Many in these cultures entered the *Bardo* with their eyes wide open and saw it.

"Again, it parallels cognitive levels among alive humans. Many people in bodies have only a limited appreciation of the biological mechanisms of their bodies, of the processes and interactions constantly taking place to maintain their living forms. People tend to take their bodies for granted and even to a degree forget them. They rush about the world in their bodies oblivious to them the way humans perceive animal consciousness, unaware of its own form.

"Yes, you can walk around the Earth entirely oblivious to the fact you're in a body. Then when something goes wrong, you break a bone, get sick, the awareness arises but with the same shocking, nightmarish lucidity as in the *Bardo*. Your habitual oblivion ill prepares you for this terrible truth discovery. The degree of detail and perception evidenced in the Tibetan text is typical of the lucidity those monks were trained to experience reality with while they alive, so, yes, Edward, your suspicion is well-founded: there is a disparity in perceptions."

"Do we want to see everything in its full, lurid detail—is it an expectation of the designers of the *Bardo* that souls have lucid impressions of these processes?" Edward asked. "I could see how some might want to sleep through it, given the choice and without the lifelong habit of mindfulness meditations. I guess to put it bluntly: Do we *have* to see all this frightening, shocking stuff?"

Merlin smiled. He appreciated the complexity and irony of the question. "The question really asks: *Must* we be more conscious of reality? Let's say God leaves it as a free-will choice, though He expects, He knows, that eventually you will come around and wake up fully and perceive all that has been laid out. Lucid cognition in the *Bardo* process helps you understand the conditions consciousness finds itself in; some souls regard that as essential; others will later. What this lucid cognition reveals may seem, at first, disturbing to your concept of normalcy. It will seem to utterly disregard it. The soul reasonably asks: We haven't seen such strange things before, so now why must we be subjected to it?

"The Druj of course lends a hand in this matter, encouraging souls to stay asleep, to regard these hallucinations as like the fevered projections of digestive disturbances or crazed images you might have in a bad case of flu. She is not the rigorous taskmaster of lucid perceptions; she is the dream master. She exudes the sweet opiate of alluring lies and illusions to keep you sleeping."

"It's squinting versus sunglasses," said Blaise. "When the sunlight is too bright you squint and reduce your field of vision. That's sleeping through the *Bardo*. If you wear sunglasses you can see everything in the sunlit world but you're not blinded by the Light. That's the product of meditative preparation for the *Bardo*. It's fitting yourself up with sunglasses so you can navigate this place. The sunglasses act as an information filter; you understand what's happening."

"Lucidity is an option for souls in the *Bardo*," said Merlin, "but if you intend to ever free yourself from the Wheel of Life and the endless round of karmic illusions, hallucinations, and obscurations you will have to sit through at least one *Bardo* presentation wide-awake, lucid, and, even better, taking notes. You have to look it right in the face, eyes wide open, with equanimity, neutrality, and understanding; otherwise, you are still under its influence, still subject to the Druj's clever modifications of your consciousness, still driven by your karma. The *Bardo Thödol* was an attempt to equip disembodied consciousness with those sunglasses Blaise speaks of, to provide the soul with enough briefing in advance to do this stare-down of the *Bardo* reality and emerge master of its own karma."

"The trouble is if people won't look these disclosures squarely in the face, they will not get off the Wheel of Life, and they will not even realize they're on it," said Blaise. "They will not discern the set-up, not realize they're on this fantastic, horrible-wonderful merry-go-round nor detect the Druj's intrusions."

"I had the impression when I was going through the rounds that all the souls around me were not seeing the same things, the same *level* of activities," said Tommy. "It was bewildering at first. You felt you were in a different world even as you stood next to somebody who seemed to be in this same *Bardo* world. Many of the people seemed dazed, sluggish, even concussed, or only half-awake, like they had been wakened unexpectedly after perhaps one hour's sleep.

"They didn't seem to be seeing out of their eyes. Their eyes seemed unfocussed, hazy. They struck me as two people or one person divided, as if sliced down the middle. I had the impression one part of them, or a portion of their attention, was engaged in these complicated *Bardo* divestments, while the other was oblivious of them. I had the impression these two parts of the person did not communicate or share the results of their impressions. Their two realms of experience remained separate.

"I found that same schism to a degree in my own early experiences here. I felt like I was seeing things twofold, at two different levels. For a while I would focus on the divestment process, and I saw a fair bit of the spirits and processes we have been touring. But then my awareness would haze over and I would find myself in surroundings that evoked my former physical world, like my parents' home, my bedroom, my high school, places I liked to hang out in. It was as if my leg had gone to sleep and I could no longer walk; my leg of course means my mind, my attention. It had gone to sleep, gotten lazy, inert. Then I would snap back into lucidity and see more of the *Dhyani* Buddhas, the Six Worlds, and the staggering hallucinations of the *Herukas* and *Dakinis*.

"I guess the realm of actual activity is set at a higher or finer or faster frequency than the reiteration of once familiar haunts and habits of one's now departed human life. It was like people taking sleeping pills to get through all-night flights. They preferred to sleep through the boring, empty hours of flying, the episodes of turbulence or air rippling, not waking up until arrival. My impression was a lot of souls preferred to get through the turbulence of the *Bardo* that way, to sleep through it or not try to bridge the two cognitive domains.

"I'm beginning to appreciate how consciousness is a tool, a process, and a power, but it is one that most of the time for most of us is completely out of hand. It spins out of our control, fabricating illusory realities, filling them with people, images, monsters, and dramatic scenarios, all lacking absolute reality.

"Consciousness is terrifically potent, yet we go about our lives with this whirlwind, this tornado, swirling turbulently all around us, not noticing it, even as it shapes and directs our life. The goal, the opportunity, of the *Bardo* is to recognize this force, master it, and use it properly as a tool to apprehend reality. In many respects it's almost too hard to do this while you're alive in a body. The allures, the gravity, the seeming absolute materialism of the physical world, are too persuasive. It strong-arms you too effectively to break free of its trance state.

"As for the Druj's intrusions, yes, I can detect them now in retrospect. There were moments when I felt a luxurious expansiveness flush over me, as if I should, as if I wanted nothing more than to, relax, lie back, not worry about anything, which meant, in practical terms, ease up my cognitive acuity and notice nothing. To join the ranks of the dead and somnolent in the *Bardo*.

"That was the Druj, dropping little scented suggestions in my struggling awareness. It's hard enough to get your bearings in this place; then she takes advantage of that handicap and floats alluring, restful thoughts into your mind. You fail to realize that this is the time when you really *need* to stay wide awake, when you would most keenly *benefit* from riveting your attention on the events. Instead, she makes you think it's unimportant, unnecessary, an elective at best."

"The Tibetans emphasized waking up in the midst of a world of illusion, which is the nature of the *Bardo*," said Blaise. "To them it was paramount, both an obligation and a terrific opportunity, to finally bust open the game of deceptions otherwise known as reality. Your chances of success in the *Bardo* are better than while alive, because the illusions are, technically, easier to see through than when they are physically manifest. The illusions are thinner, more instantaneous, more protean, more contrived, easier to catch as fake or mind-spun. This challenge is too formidable for most people, understandably. It requires lots of training, build-up, and preparation, even some cheerleading, and *why*, people will ask, should I bother doing this? It seems like too much work.

"Indeed, why. Until the quest to see through all the levels of illusion and sleights-of-hand comes to the forefront of your awareness, there is little reason to do this. That's what most people will conclude. A few, tired of all the deceptions, will insist, even stridently, that they will not desist until they have burst the bubble. I guess such souls would try to reincarnate as Tibetans to be among like-minded souls where you could expect some friends to read the *Bardo Thödol* to you when you were dead and to kick your butt when you deviated from reality.

"Hey pal, you may be dead but *remember*, the Intermediate State is your best shot at getting free of this sticky Wheel of Life and seeing reality straight in the face. Do you really want to come back to another life of yak-dung tea and barley meal and cold nights and endless chanting? Think hard, pal. Wouldn't you rather wake up? Press the eject button on the video player. It will be like seeing true bedrock at last, the wall of reality, the one that is *actually there*, independent of any clever karmic hallucinations you might be spinning out."

"Thank you, Blaise, for that observation," said Merlin. "You have just coincidentally referred to our next order of business. We shall visit this bedrock."

14

We were standing in the center of an immense circular silver chamber. Dozens of arched gateways, evenly spaced, lined the circumference. The ceiling was domed, as if with a stationary silver star, though it was more like an orb of silver Light that continuously flamed with great vigor but was not consumed or diminished by this perpetual flaming. Forming a second circle a distance in from the gateways was a ring of female priestesses. This is an inexact description of course; in human physical world terms they resembled female hierophants, but if they had ever been materialized women it was long ago. They worked here now.

These figures stood each perhaps ten feet tall. They were robed in silver with a suggestion of innumerable pinpricks of light in these robes, like tiny stars, and from the neck down to the feet they wore what at first resembled a Mason's apron, marked with sigils, specific signs, and occult symbols, in silver. Later, I realized it was not a robe or apron they wore, but the design of their aura itself.

As for their faces—well, these were only vaguely like human female faces. I do not mean to suggest they were extraterrestrial or alien in appearance; their origin in familiar human physiognomy was still apparent, only transcended. I did not see too many individual facial differences among these hierophants, and to a large degree they resembled one another closely. Their forms emitted great blazes of Light and brilliance, and their faces were drawn as much in Light as in a semblance of matter, however subtle. And their eyes—these blazed in silver. It was as if their eyes were on fire with silver flames, their pupils a silver inferno.

In the center of this silver cathedral was a towering, ever widening fire. It was a silver conflagration whose full extent was difficult to estimate precisely. Perhaps it occupied one-half the interior space of this cathedral, and it rose up hundreds of feet, almost licking the underside of the silver domed ceiling. What was burning? I acknowledge the reader's incredulity in advance, but permit me to state that what was burning appeared to be a human female form.

Or at least a human female head, though sometimes I had the impression of a complete torso, garbed in different cultural modes, like the display of a repertoire of goddesses. The protean female or goddess forms were not burning up as we would say of wood. They were the source of the roaring flames; they were emitting silver fire. She was burning without cessation or losing any of her substance. There was not a single fixed form in this silver inferno; the images kept changing. They changed quickly, as if in accordance with some inaudible metronome, like a dancer going through her complete repertoire of moves.

The apparitions she presented were a feast for a comparative mythologist. I recognized many of them. It was like a photo yearbook of the world's goddess figures as depicted in all cultures across time, from maidens to crones, the full spectrum of the Great Mother and her daughters. This burning silver female figure kept shapeshifting from one form to the next, equipping herself with all the correct appurtenances of each goddess figure, from, for example, Hathor's *sistrum*, the shaken percussion instrument, and the *menat*, or turquoise musical necklace she wore as Mistress of Jubilation and Queen of the Dance, to Artemis's golden bow and arrows—*Khryselakatos*, "of the Golden Shaft," and *Lokheira*, "Showered by Arrows," the adoring Greeks called her. The inventory was long.

I marveled as one goddess form transfigured into the next, but I goggled even more when for a moment I saw all of them, the complete image repertory, displayed as a single tableau as a vast multi-layered gallery of forms. Possibly, that was the truer presentation, seeing them all displayed at once. That I saw them in linear succession might have been just to ease the strain on my mind to process this concatenation of equivalent goddess forms as a single revelation. For that is what I had before me: the apocalypse of the Great Mother.

I use that term in its correct nuance, meaning the revelation of the original revelation. What does the Great Mother look like? She looks like all these forms. Isis, Nephthys, Hera, the long list of appearances for what Blaise calls Mrs. God.

Edward interrupted my ruminations with an observation. "Merlin, we're inside the great body of *Hine-nui-te-po*, aren't we, Great Hine, Mother of the Night, as told of Maui—of you—in the Polynesian legends." Edward sounded delighted with this discovery; you could hear the rising enthusiasm in his voice.

He turned to us to explain the reference. "This Hine was the guardian of life and immortality, but she brought death into the world. She made humans mortal. The Polynesians called Her the goddess of death and decay, like Persephone. She lived at the outer edge of the farthest islands. She was black with green eyes, and when a human was close to death, he saw Her eyes glaring at him from not far away, taking a bead on his soul, soon to be Hers.

"When a man died, they said he was creeping around inside the infernal womb of Hine, Great Woman of Night, ruler of the Underworld, the Polynesian's *Pulotu*. She is Sleeping Mother Death, the female personification of the *Bardo* we're inside now, and there She is, showing us some of the myriads of Her metaphorical forms. But to be accurate, she personifies the form-generating realm *beyond* the Underworld.

"Maui, a friend to humankind, regarded human mortality as an insult to the dignity of the human soul. He decided to claim immortality for humans from Hine, and he would do this by an expedition into the interior of Her great form. He entered Her body through the large fishlike mouth and headed for Her heart, where She kept the phial of immortality. He planned to seize it for humans. She was sleeping; the lightning flashes that customarily flared out of Her had subsided so it was safe for Maui to enter.

"From a distance She looked human, but She wasn't really. Her eyes were greenstone, Her hair was sea-kelp; the red flashes on the horizon came out of Her like a flashing aura; Her mouth was that of a barracuda; Her genitals were protected by sharp obsidian flints. Her domicile was within the darkness of night at the dark edge of the known sea. From what we know now, this means She dwelled beyond the realm of death and the *Bardo*, and if Her realm seemed dark and distant it was because consciousness does not routinely make it that far, or that far up, above the head, meaning to the eighth chakra above the crown.

"Some storytellers say Maui entered Her from the vagina and headed up towards the mouth, thereby reversing the order of birth for humans. Anyway, he failed. He was just sneaking out of Her mouth with the phial when a small bird woke her. She caught on to what he was attempting and stopped him; some versions of the story say She killed Maui. That ended the project for immortality.

"The Polynesians say he failed, but my time with Merlin when we visited his Maui lifetime taught me that this was not the point of the story. Maui was never going to steal immortality from Her for humans. He never intended to. Human mortality had been ordained by the Supreme Being; you couldn't sneak past that ruling. It was immutable. Immortality, at least in a physical, bodily sense, was not on the books. Immortality of consciousness was, and one of the foundations for that achievement was a thorough understanding, even mastery, of the Intermediate Realm, the realm of so-called death. That *was* on the books, and Maui was its writer. Maui, as Padmasambhava, wrote the handbook on how to get that phial from Great Hine by conducting yourself smartly in the *Bardo*. The Polynesian story is a parable of Merlin's role as our *Bardo* mystagogue.

"Maui's penetration of the Goddess of Death was to illustrate his role as *Bardo* psychopomp, as he is doing for us in this Green Knight expedition. He shows us the route through the great interior of the *Bardo* to Hine's form. He knows the *Bardo* landscape, all the landmarks and thresholds and how to get through them, and even better, he *introduces* us to the Great Mother Hine."

"So does Hine have a phial of immortality in Her heart somewhere?" I asked. "Is that part of the story true in some manner, and can we find it?"

"It is," replied Merlin. "That phial is known as the Emerald, or the Heart within the Heart, the Secret Heart, the Cube of Space. It has many names. In it the Supreme Being put some of the original Light of Creation, and He put this Emerald inside all incarnating humans, two levels behind the heart chakra. Everyone who is now human has one. That original Light is the same as the Clear Mind, Christ Light, or Buddha Mind you have already heard about. Open that Emerald and you flood your phenomenal self with nondualistic reality.

"It is that immaculate, nondualistic voidness that contains the entire Creation in a wakeful, stable condition. It is the way out of the *Bardo*; it is the end of the *Bardo*. In the sense that its activation, your finding it, dissolves all the *Bardo*'s illusions, including its necessity. It is inside the Great Mother Hine in the sense that since She is the master creator of all forms that contain the Light, including the human form, She included it in your human form design, like a chocolate on your hotel-room pillow. We are now inside the Great Mother's cosmic body, but the Light of the original Creation is inside you already."

"And you are the perfect, the only guide, to the Great Mother and Her repository of all forms because you, Merlin, are the *Mer*-Line. That's the line of Light consciousness travels to proceed from the Blazing Star in us to the *Mer* or Great Sea of the Mother," said Edward. "It's the epitome of your role as psychopomp. You are the line, the consciousness route, to the Great Mother.

"You didn't think I was going to forget *that*. Of course you know the interior of Great Hine. It's your job as the *Mer*-Line. You are the glory of Hera, the Great Mother, and whom the Greeks called Herakles. To put this in mythological terms, you guide the deceased Pharoah to his Mother, Isis. The Pharoah traverses the *Duat*, or what we've been calling the *Bardo*, guided by Anubis, yourself, Merlin, with a jackal's head for emphasis, and reaches Isis where he achieves illumination and salvation under the dome of Silver Light. That is where he grabs that much coveted phial of immortality from Hine."

Merlin nodded. "We're here because many of the apertures to the Great Mother have become clogged or slightly distorted and need some adjustment."

He pointed to the gates that lined the circumference of this Light temple. Some people were walking through them, although a few tripped or struggled. Their forward progress seemed blocked or at least hindered by sticky spider webs, encrusted gateways, uneven floor surfaces, poor lighting, engorged archways that bulged and swelled to nearly block the openings. Many souls failed to make it through these obstructed barriers and slouched away.

Then I laughed. I couldn't help it, even though it was not particularly funny. Filmy neon images had been set like banners over the doorways from the other side (from where we were viewing them, inside the Great Mother's spherical temple), and these flickering holographic images projected scenes of misdirection, solid walls, futility, abandoned quests, desirable rest areas, easier alternative routes, detours that led nowhere, and other deceptive situations. It was the Druj's handiwork, and that's why I laughed. She was at it here as well. We were seeing her clever, prolific, diabolical hand everywhere in the *Bardo*, ever creatively interfering with human clarity and the awakening of consciousness. This girl never gives up, never relents; she works 24 hours a day all the time.

Many souls were being stopped or significantly impeded at least in getting through these gates, but even this number was small. Those making it through them was even more minimal. I had the impression the majority of souls moving through the *Bardo* did not know about these gates or couldn't find them. Or perhaps they did not want to know about

them. Passage through them was optional. If you intended to reincarnate, you would have no interest in them. They were in many respects mutually exclusive; passage through these gates was a step closer to getting off the Wheel of Life, while taking another human body guaranteed you stayed around for another round of life, death, and *Bardo* fun.

"Edward, care to tell your colleagues what these gates are?" asked Merlin.

"Right. They are the 49 Gates of Defilement, as described in both Jewish and later Islamic mystical literature. They are the archetypes of the seven chakras, each of which have seven secondary nuances, like, for example, the heart chakra at the root chakra level of expression. Or you could say it is the seven chakras as arrayed in the human's seven bodies, totaling 49 centers. Or it's the same design principle as the Qabalists describe regarding the repetition of the complete Tree of Life inside each individual *Sefira*, the Tree inside *Netzach*.

"The simplest way to put it is to say these gates are a fractalization of consciousness. The chakras exhibit a fractal pattern. As for the 'defilement,' even though that term is a bit weighty with moral judgement, more neutrally construed defilement means full of karmic accretions. It's the same piling up of karma, its momentum, tendencies, habits, and purposes as we've been dealing with throughout our passage through the *Bardo*. Life credits and debits. Life experiences, old hurts left unprocessed and undigested by consciousness. It's like clothes after you've worn them for two weeks straight; it's time for a wash. They have been 'defiled' by your living experiences, by the emanations of your body.

"The gates, these chakras, have been 'defiled' by human subjective filterings. That means they have forced to emit less than their intended celestial vibration because of human use of them, and the human tendency never to clean them out. Like never taking your car to the car wash after driving through muddy roads for a year. Or never cleaning your house or refrigerator. These gates are as piled up with unprocessed cognitive content as souls in the *Bardo*. The difference is karma here derives from the human *collective* consciousness.

"The originally pure cognitive centers, these secondary 'eyes,' are terribly clogged up with personal, subjective filterings accrued by the soul over lifetimes from emotionally-based, individually-set perceptions of reality, both inner and outer. 'This is how I see or feel the world,' rather than "This is how the world really is.' Those self-perceptions fill up the chakras and clog the gateways; they defile them. Render them impure, or, again, more neutrally put, they dirty the glasses. Ever try to see the world clearly through glasses splattered in mud? It's not easy. You have to wipe the lenses clean before you can see the world again. You could say your lenses are defiled, a heavy-handed term, or just say they're all smudged up with mud and does anybody have a damp tissue to clean them.

"The 49 Gates of Impurity, another name for them, are a foundation, a threshold we pass to reach what's called the 50 Gates of *Binah*. This is the full Human with 50 centers, all factory fresh and unspoiled. The word *Binah* relates directly to where we are and what we're seeing. It refers to the Great Mother, the Mother of all forms, the Great Mother Hine, the Silver Light realm, and Her cosmic body inside which Maui travelled to get the phial of immortality. The Qabalists call the *Sefira Binah*, the third one in Creation, the place of all forms. Seven chakras each with seven expressions, make 49; the whole system is 50. *Binah* is Mrs. God's haven-home of understanding and intuitive contemplation. You pass through any of the 49 Gates to reach her Silver Light realm of unity.

"It's on the other side of the *Bardo*. You climb out of your head through the crown, get on the *Cinvat* Bridge or Charon's Boat, cross the vibrational gradient, process your life and karma in the greatly vexed Intermediate Realm, then, if you wish, arrive on the other shore, in the *Sefira* of *Binah* which lies one dimensional notch above your human head, as your eighth chakra."

"All this has implications for us, because it has expression in the Earth's Light grid," said Blaise. "That's another aspect of its fractal design. The Earth's 'gates' are defiled or impure or, in functional terms, largely blocked or inoperative. One way to take the implicit moral approbation out of the description is to think of an air filter that hasn't been changed in years. It will barely work and will pass impure air into its interior environment. An impure or defiled gate is like that. Since chakras always imply a body as their operational context, this means Albion is blocked and inoperative because his cognitive centers, his chakras, are experiencing various degrees of impurity, that is, they're clogged with human karma. Albion struggles to wake up into full-spectrum lucidity with his chakras clogged. Ach! We have defiled dear Albion's gates!

"The trouble is at this level the type of karma is more complex, more tricky to fix than it is for individual humans. It's at the collective consciousness level (I'm being generous because much of it is below the threshold of self-aware group consciousness) of long-standing enmities, like among Serbs, Croatians, and Bosnians; militant religious fundamentalism of Christians and Muslims; the Protestant-Catholic schism that has 'troubled' Ireland, both the Republic and Northern, for centuries; the feuding Greeks and Turks especially as centralized in Cyprus; the intense rivalry among the two heirs to Mohammed, Sunnis and Shiites, each claiming legitimacy to lead. The list is long. Do you see? The geomantic work to clear these conflicted gates of that content is complex."

"Shall we do a spot of cleaning?" said Merlin. He pointed to a gate that looked especially crammed with unprocessed content. "Philomena, will you stand at the back of the group and radiate Christ Light in your ascended state. That will act like a purifying, scourging spotlight and be rather inspiring, I should think. Edward, you stand in front of her, though not to crowd her Light, and occupy your silver robe and silver staff, as I taught you in our adventures together a few years ago. That will emit an energy field in resonance with the Great Mother and this temple space we are working in. You will stand for *Binah*.

"Frederick, would you place yourself amidst the glittering diamond facets of the Blaise angels' Rotunda of Light. That will impart the fierce spirit of Ganesh, remover of obstacles to consciousness. Pipaluk and Tommy, would you picture that you wield a vigorous, broad-burning lilac flame about ten feet wide. You can picture it like a high-pressure hose or a burning, wide-brimmed flower. Project these cauterizing flames inside the gate where Blaise will be using large gold roses that are sticky and have strong suction to clean out the build-up."

Merlin was right in describing the gate's condition with that word. It was like a surface that was massively rusty or encrusted in layers of salt deposits or overgrown in tree limbs and vining plants. These are metaphors of course for the obscuring content was human in origin, flavor, and appearance, a build-up of human bodies, life pictures, distorted auric fields, still-shots from dramatic moments in life, and innumerable opportunistic, scavenging, or parasitic spirit-forms taking advantage of all this unprocessed human emotionality, pain, and suffering. No, they weren't actual human bodies, but more like ghost images of them, or perhaps cast-off remnants or "skins" of once animated human forms.

We were a six-person scrubbing and cleaning crew, all five components necessary to complete the job. Matthew was gone again. I had no idea where. I was embedded in a diamond field of Ganeshes. I would have liked to feel this empowered, focused, and full of certainty at no end of faculty meetings I could mention when competition, rivalry, and jostling for position and status prevailed and tended to weigh me down. This would have raised the notch a few levels. The atmosphere, the mental field around me, felt strong, invincible, and merry.

Philomena's Christ Light radiation from behind us added bliss and voidness to the mixture. I know that sounds odd, that voidness, a seeming negative, could be a beneficial quality, but let me put it this way: you felt that you were aligned with the essential, original, and immutable purpose of the creation of reality. You felt the invisible presence of our Sponsor, the Big Chief Who ordains everything. You felt you were standing on that quality as an absolute ontological bedrock. The bliss part wasn't bad either: delightful, in fact, calming and restful, the epitome of relaxation, like after six hours in a hot tub: all your bones were melted and your body a lump of semi-moveable happy jelly.

Edward's silver beacon had the effect of a mother calling back her progeny who had been out wandering or playing in the fields. The Great Mother Hine or Isis, whatever we call Her, Mrs. God, was retracting Her myriads of created forms back into Her womb-factory of all living containers, all these varied Houses of God, domiciles of the Light, these forms packed in layers in the gates. The Silver Light was calling back these created forms to the condition of wholeness and unity they once occupied before they were shaped into forms.

That's the meaning of these gates: it's the transition zone between differentiation into innumerable forms, defined by the 49 chakras, and wholeness and unity, before consciousness was ever fragmented into chakras and Light into forms. Leaving the Great Mother, you enter the fragmented world of the 49 Gates; returning to Her, you re-enter that state of original unity of the 50 Gates which disappear and resume their unified condition of one cyclopean all-seeing eye. In the Mother's realm of Silver Light, we are all Cyclopes, one big round eye. That's the 49 Gates of the individusalized chakra nuances and the whole system. That's your *50 Gates of Binah*, the 50 routes back to the Great Mother and unity.

Tommy and Pipaluk were wielding the lilac flames as sweeping torches. Combine the functions of a broom, a burning torch, a broad-swathed paint brush, and a high-pressure beam of lilac-colored water and you'll get the picture of what they were doing. The lilac flame, the energy of transmutation, was steadily loosening and dissolving the "glue" that held these layers stuck together. It was dark energy, negativity, pain, and suffering, that acted as the glue. The lilac flame liquefied this compacted glue and made it wet and runny.

I thought I could hear the suppressed, frozen, "glued" misery releasing into sighs. The lilac flames released a great deal of grey smoke that smelled foul, but the flames also quickly burned up or vaporized this toxic stench. The lilac energy, the Lilac Ray, transmutes anything toxic, no matter what form it takes. The walls inside the gate, now becoming apparent, were dripping in melting sludge; it was like watching snow melt on a rock wall, running down the stone's surface in rivulets, but this looked worse, like sewage and toxic muck.

In ordinary human terms, it was an objectionable sight. It was like flies hovering around rotting garbage or maggots hatching in a decaying corpse. The flies or maggots in this visual metaphor were the opportunistic spirit-beings, all of whom evidenced a basically demonic, inimical cast to their appearance. The garbage or corpse was the human images, the bodies, the dramatic scenes, the frozen moments

of pain, revenge, the desire for revenge, the wailing and misery.

Hieronymous Bosch might do justice to the outstanding depravity of the scene. It looked wicked and corrupt now because it had been festering for so many years. Imagine nursing a grudge or carrying a grouch for centuries; it gradually transforms itself into something toxic and nasty, even lethal to living contact. It emanates a fetid atmosphere, emotions debased and adulterated, turned noxious, immediately contaminating all who come in contact with it.

Blaise had his head right in all this muck. He was scouring it with his huge gold roses. I heard the steady suction sound, like a powerful vacuum cleaner applied to a dirty shag-hair rug. He was pulling things off, creatures, pictures, splotches of dark color and asymmetric patterns, like deformed grids, stringy, sticky long strands of congealed sludge, mostly purple, brown, and black. When his roses filled up, which happened quickly, he tossed them into an incinerator positioned next to him. It looked like a deep-freeze set in the ground with just the lid at ground level; he'd open the lid and toss the nasty stuff inside. It burned to ashes, though sometimes I heard muffled explosions, as if dynamite charges were going off inside this "bomb disposal unit," as I might term it. Whatever the mechanism, when he opened the lid of the unit again, all had been vaporized, whether turned to ashes or atomized more profoundly, but all gone.

Then I saw something surprising. I am still understanding its impact on me. As Blaise continued to clean out and dissolve the accrued contents of this gate, I saw that the gate, the aperture, was but a nodule opening into a golden temple. Another nodule-gateway led out from this temple at the opposite side. The temple was golden, once you got all the detritus off its original pure surface. I counted a dozen golden pillars that framed the circumference of this circular space, and the suggestion of another ten in shades of red behind these. It seemed as if two Light temple spaces, each with its own function, were superimposed on the same location for a combined effect. I turned to Merlin for clarification.

"Heart chakra at the third chakra level of expression," he said. "Passion of belief coupled with forcefulness of expression. Unfortunately, that often plays out as militant religious fundamentalism of which the world has seen too much. Christians, Jews, and Muslims aggressively contending their spiritual model is absolute and forcing it upon the nonbelievers, skeptics, or other religions, or enforcing it even among the deviating members of its own community. It is the contentiousness of the tribes of Abraham. But these are only the more recent examples. Humans have always evidenced a tendency to dogmatic rigidity. That particular constellation of emotion, belief, and imagery congregates in this center, the heart chakra operating at the level of fire, will, force, and power. Your spiritual beliefs get expressed at sword point. The result is this compacted gate."

Blaise was peeling bodies and pictures off the walls of this space. He was whistling. I hadn't expected this degree of light-heartedness at so dismal a task.

He looked at me and grinned. "It's not much different than healing people. I used to do that on occasion with promising students who were stuck. I'd get out the gold roses and clean out their psychic spaces, an aura car wash. The contents and the mechanisms are the same; it's just a bigger playing field."

The pictures Blaise was stripping off the walls were like old political posters advertising slogans, meetings, confrontations, marches, or struggles. Let's say somebody went to such a political rally and agreed with its tenets. That person took a psychic photograph of the event and its emotions and auric field. They identified with all its feelings and intentions and placed this photograph in a prominent position in their psychic space, say at their heart chakra expressed at its third chakra valence. Their spiritual values would be fueled by this fire, and the flames would perpetually consume without diminishing this charged image.

Now say a thousand people did the same, or one hundred thousand. The struggle took place, they won or lost, they defeated the infidels or lost their lives—the outcome did not matter as far as the permanent contamination of the gateway. The residue of that constellation of consciousness and its emotional forces came here, and stuck fast to the walls, adding yet one more layer to the laminated surface which Blaise was now cheerily stripping clean. Long live the Revolution! The historical moment was long past, but the bodies and images were still here, stuck hard and fast as if pasted moments ago by fervent hands.

The inimical astral spirit-forms, like deformed Harpies and demonic bird shapes, were pecking at the moldering carcasses of human forms, images, and posters. Blaise seemed to catch these nasty spirits in butterfly nets or sticky gold roses, then the spirits dissolved into ashes or were carried off by angels.

"They're all copies," he said. "Some are destroyed, like crumpling a duplicate copy of a page, and a few are saved to be recycled for future uses. Let's say you think a dark or nasty thought and charge it with emotion. You have made a thoughtform. It is a semi-autonomous soul-less entity that starts roaming the world on its own, like the Jewish Golem but not as precise. Its behavior will be bounded by certain tendencies, based on the nature of the energized thought.

"These thoughtforms, these energized personifications of emotions and thoughts that have proliferated through repetition of the human emotions that created them, are drawn to sites of human suffering. To them it is food or entertainment, or it's simply a matter of resonance. It seems like home to them They were created in darkness, so they're drawn to it. I am 'erasing' these thoughtforms, like a rabbi decommissioning a Golem, writing 'death' on its forehead by taking away one letter from the Hebrew word that animated it."

I realized I had been seeing something yet not realizing it. There was more than one human Blaise doing the scrubbing. I counted a dozen at least, all the same, merrily collecting nasty spirits, throwing them in the bin, applying the suction roses to peel stuck images and body forms off the walls. The Blaises were like a cheerful clutch of professional housecleaners called in to complete a big job. Blaise must have known what I was thinking because of what he said next.

"That's the advantage of working in the *Bardo* in your astral body. You can make copies of yourself. Like the angels and Masters do. As easily as snapping your fingers. Twelve can get so much more done than merely one body, don't you think? Otherwise, we'd never finish this by Candlemas, right?"

Blaise seemed to be pulling posters off the walls, one after another, into the hundreds, as if these images, many of which seemed similar, had been laminated over time, like somebody repeating himself endlessly. I looked at a few. They were mostly war and conflict images, soldiers mounted on horses, carrying lances or swords, clubs, maces, war-hammers, bows and arrows, or, later, rifles, bayonets, Gatling guns, and other types of hand-held automatic guns. Phalanxes of soldiers advancing across a landscape carrying banners with heraldic or symbolic images or insignias on them, like white crosses or eagles, or the signs of aristocratic houses, of popes, cardinals, *sheikhs*, *imams*, and others.

I saw men with swords slashing other men. People in clerical robes burning other people as if they were mere firewood. Men in brown or white robes forcing thick books on people, pointing to specific pages, their faces angry with impatience. Catapults launching boulders to knock down walls or crush people huddled on the other sides of these barriers. Armies with primitive single-shot rifles advancing across open fields, shooting and reloading as they went. Men blowing up buildings, planting dynamite, bombs, incendiary devices. Young men wearing suicide vests and exploding themselves or driving pick-up trucks packed with explosives, or setting explosive charges or operating drone airplanes that launched killer missiles at the touch of a button.

It was a complete visual repertory of warfare, accurate up to the most recent decades, and fluttering, hovering, skulking, flaring around these many gruesome images like opportunistic vultures were demons, many of them, revving up the war energy, throwing accelerant on the rage, so it burned hotter, inspiring politicians and political "leaders" (idiots, all of them) to froth at the mouth about the need for perpetual war, to convert or, better, kill all the infidels. They needed these infidels, enemies, terrorists, Communists, killable subjects for Orwell's chilling Two Minutes Hate; it didn't matter who they were; anyone would do, and thank God we dredged up another crop of infidels to slaughter.

Blaise examined each image as he peeled it off the walls and destroyed it. I wondered why it didn't seem overwhelming or distressing to him, so I asked: "You don't mind doing this, seeing all these horrific images by the hundreds?"

"No. I like the work. Anyway, the Supreme Being has a good dental plan. Promised me I won't need teeth in my next incarnation."

He looked at me, pretending to be serious, assessing audience reaction.

"You know, if those Christians had truck bombs, suicide vests, and rocket-propelled grenade launchers in the Albigensian Crusade on Montsegur, they would have used them and been done in minutes. Blown up the stupid hill. Religious fundamentalism is a persistent disease of the human psyche. Those guys delivering the truck-bombs and blowing themselves up in public places are in for a shock when they get here. They will find they have been misinformed. No compliant virgins, no laudations from the Supreme Being, just a big *Ammit* wearing a tee-shirt emblazed with their particular name. 'Hi, pal: I am you. Let's get to work. I'll show you what you really accomplished by killing so many.'

"The Supreme Being regards them and says in rather a brown study, 'Wish you hadn't done that, boys. It will cost you heavily in karmic reparations. A lot of those Christian Crusaders are still here, in arrears in paying off their debts, and that's going on now some thousand years. Best expect the same.'

"The only 'God' or 'Allah' that sanctioned these acts of mass murder is the Druj manipulating their belief, passion, and rage to enact horrific acts against humans. She is the Chief of Lies, and the big lie she laid on these boys was to believe the Supreme Being, under whatever name they preferred to use, had told them to go kill people for not believing in their dogmatic rigidity and to make various vague promises about heavenly rewards, divine recognition and praise.

"Then they get themselves killed, arrive here, and find the *Bardo* is their own self-made Hellhole, and it's not God's or Allah's praise they get but a hard naked look in the karmic mirror and the obligation to come to terms with their acts. Many of them still don't recognize the Druj's manipulative hand even when they are here, processing their karma and planning their lifetimes of reparations. Just like the Christ, the Druj comes like a thief in the night, and few notice her. They think it's Jehovah or Allah commissioning these crusades and *jihads*. It's

the Druj, tarted up to imitate (and implicitly mock) the genuine Supreme Being.

"She is the Antichrist after all, and here is evidence of her spiteful side. All the demonic spirits work for her as she exploits human uncertainty and the passionate quest for certainty in belief as played out in the heart chakra. Then she revs up the third chakra to inflame that wavering certainty with militant insistence, the force, aggression—all the primitive third chakra aspects working through the heart chakra struggling for assurance and genuine divine connections. The third chakra tightens up and generates a rigid, unvarying intolerance. The Druj spins all this misdirection and disinformation, and the demons crank up the resulting rage and determination to convert the world to this new *provisional* model of *absolute* certainty, if you don't mind the paradox.

"With that kind of crazy-ass thoughtform seizing their brains like tetanus, how do they think they'll do with the voidness of the *Bardo* and the Clear Mind invitation King Yama offers? They'll try to send a rocket-propelled grenade up his inconvenient *Bardo* ass. Wheel of Life? Let me truck-bomb the irritation.

"The result is what we have before us, hundreds of images from wars fought and conflicts imagined or scripted, war thoughtforms, though only partially executed. With all these karmic debts mounting up, the long, assiduous acts of reparation for those killed, maimed, injured, or, worst of all, spiritually misled on purpose, so many souls are stuck on the Wheel of Life and it will be hundreds of years before they pay off their debts, before the crusaders and *jihadists* are released from the slammer, get out of the Big House. The Druj is twice successful as she's kept millions stuck to this ever-turning Wheel of Life.

"So many souls are trapped in this revolving door, like you have at posh hotels. Six partitions turning about a central axis, one partition for each of the Six Worlds. They keep walking around in these endless circles, in obedience to the motion and trajectory of the revolving door. They never enter the hotel. They just keep enacting their futile schemes for *jihad* or crusade and never get out of jail."

"So the unclean gateway is a vector of contamination for the world?" I asked Blaise. I was starting to get the idea of the connections and ramifications.

"Exactly. It's like a pocket of mold somewhere in your house. It releases the mold spores throughout the house like an invisible aerosol. Soon you get sick and you don't know why unless you find this mold vector. A contaminated gate is like that. It blocks or at least makes it difficult for *Bardo*-transiting souls to pass through it, and it perpetually pollutes the Earth's psychic atmosphere with its noxious qualities, in this case, militant fundamentalism, dogmatic certainties, war and conflict energy, and the disposition to forcibly convert people to this.

"People go about their lives matching this vibration unless they are rigorously attentive to the nuances of their consciousness, the little odd ripples that arise and indicate the influence of this clogged, dirtied gateway at work on them. People keep reiterating the war and conflict thoughtforms, either in their minds or in actual life, and the Druj and her demon hordes keep revving them up, and through this you get this terrifically congested, psychically constipated stalemate. A worldwide inertial condition of seemingly immutable stuckness.

"To move or transform an inertial mass takes an enormous energy input, and even then the changes are slow and incremental. Removing the life-force of that inertial mass is more effective, provided you can get to the place of maximum traction, where that inertia is seeded and nurtured, which is right here, in this gateway, at the boundary of the *Bardo* and *Binah*'s Silver Realm."

"When we clean out these gateways, such as this one, are we forcing embodied humans to change their affiliations and match this new setting?"

"No, and that's what is exquisite about the design of the system. Free-will is constantly respected and implicit in the system's operations and parameters. The Druj cannot force people to match the war energy. She can only seed them with lies about its function and value, depositing these seeds on pre-existing thoughts or tendencies in each person. That person is free to choose, although, unfortunately, most people after a short while of complete freedom are more bound by karmic compulsion than wide-awake lucidity leading to free choices.

"Similarly, our cleaning these gateways does not coerce any new position. It's the same when we clean geomantic nodes on the physical Earth. All we do is free up the psychic atmosphere so people are less constrained and compelled and have more latitude to consider and make choices on their own. We give their minds 'elbow room' to move about freely, uncrowded in their consciousness. Each geomantic node, each Light temple, each *Bardo* gate, is a miniature version of the Tree of the Knowledge of Good and Evil, and this Tree, or gate or temple or node, offers the soul the free-will choice among these two."

I don't know how long this gate-cleaning took. What I mean is it was impossible to keep track of time duration here, nor were any of us bored or waiting impatiently for the work to be finished. Delightfully, we did it all in the present moment. That is an experience usually difficult to achieve while alive.

Each gate revealed its own panoply of layered images, stuck dark energies, precipitating demonic spirits, and other detritus accumulated from centuries, maybe millennia, of not being cleaned out. At each gate, the Druj had been lending her own hand, in the form of clever lies designed to amplify certain inimical tendencies. So we were busy extricating her from each gate we cleaned. I ask the reader to try to conceive every chakra, each with its seven nuances, being coated in lies, 49 centers of Druj-crafted and planted lies, all of them effective. That was what we encountered as we cleaned out these doorways of the psyche. I will provide more cleaning details of the specifics of some of the gates below.

When we were at last finished, Blaise said, gesturing to the gates by sweeping his arms around in half-circles to address all of them, "This is the original psyche of the human, the archetype of the 49 consciousness centers. We are seeing the chakra hierarchy, the cascade of cognitive processing, spread out before us as a Light temple, the same structures we carry within us when alive."

His point, I think, was that didn't we agree this was an amazing disclosure before us. I agreed. It was. It was nearly too grand to take in. This was the human chakra array in its original pristine condition, before it was matched with a physical form, and here arrayed as a spherical Light temple with 49 doors. Once we had cleaned the gates and extricated the demons and expunged the Druj's coating of lies, another implicit facet was revealed. Each gate had its own angelic guardian standing by it. This angel resembled the Higher Selves we had been viewing, and it acted as protector, clarifier, and, to a degree, prime and pure embodier of the chakra's quality, its state of consciousness, its range of potential perception and expression. The Druj's muck had obscured this angel's presence.

We were now encircled by 49 chakra angels, and they dramatically brightened up the temple. It looked as if 49 blazing suns were flaming around each gate. I was starting to get a sense, a feeling perhaps, of the original design for humans, what the Supreme Being and His designers, the Elohim, had in mind for us. Actually, it was more than that. It wasn't just for humans. This chakra array of 49 gates was an archetypal design principle used throughout Creation.

This display around us of the 49 chakras as illuminated Light temples was the generic infrastructure into which every human stepped when taking on a body. It was a psychic skeletal system, a framework that supported, and, in fact, facilitated consciousness in the first place. Without it we'd be cognitively inert. It was also, I surmised, a replica, a holographic reiteration, of key elements in generic cosmic structure, a miniature Tree of Life as the framework for a human.

It was a way in which the cosmos, the chakra structures of reality, could view itself. Then we got to form a personality as the journal of that viewing experience over time, creating an interactive dance between the two elements, one, the chakra hierarchy, fixed and unvarying, the other, the human self, fluid and open. Then it struck me: what a marvelous experience it must have been for consciousness to *first* step into this infrastructure in a brand new untainted body. A body uncompelled by any karmic residues at all, virginal, untested, untainted. Your first life as a human: a physical body as pristine as the designers crafted it, and the infrastructure of consciousness, the 49 gates, unsullied, working perfectly, delivered to you, consciousness, moments ago from the factory floor.

No personal karma and no collective karma ambushing you at every turn. A blank slate. Virginal. That's the true meaning of that afflicted term. Untainted. Add to this the embodiment context: a freshly outfitted virginal planet with "factory-fresh" Light temples (in the millions), themselves expressing cosmic energies, conditions, structures, and processes, all of them entirely unpolluted. Reality as a consciousness condition of absolute geomantic virginity, untouched by human hands. That may sound strange, but think: In the year 2043, our present time, this geomantic-psychic equipment had been used for a long time by many people, by so many unheeding generations; now all the Light temples were mostly tarnished, encrusted, defiled, and in great need of refurbishment.

"It's impossible to use this system, this incarnational tool, without leaving a trace," observed Blaise. "It is such an exacting design. The moment you make a move in consciousness, say, combine the heart chakra with its third chakra level of expression, you make a little mark in the *Akashic* Records. Your act is noted. It is part of the historical record; it is on public view, for those who can access these records. Now, if your act is tainted, even to the minutest degree, with self-interest, you have created karma. You have left a trace that has ramifications that will play out further along your incarnational timeline, either as a debit or credit.

"Everything just builds from there, in escalating chains of causation and effects, until millions of years later we arrive at the compacted chakra condition we find here requiring our thoroughness in cleaning out the karmic accretions. In a sense, we're a gang of garage mechanics doing car maintenance and detailing, and we shake our heads in dismay, wondering why they didn't bring it in sooner: How could somebody drive a car this old and not do any maintenance?"

I'd been thinking about the Druj since so much of our housecleaning work had involved removing her many tendrils and energy grids of influence. A question arose and I asked it of Merlin: "Is the Druj a universal opposing spirit, appearing the same and executing the same tasks for all sentient life-forms?"

"No," said Merlin. "The Druj is different for each sentient life-form because to a large degree her qualities and appearances, even tendencies, are co-created by these sentient spirits in an interaction-accretion process over time. You clothe your own Druj, sketch out her specific qualities in the human context. You could say the Druj is a homegrown devil. Humans have 'grown' a Druj that is markedly different than what you will find on other sentient worlds. You, as humans on Earth and over time and many lives, are her creative gardeners.

"Think of the Druj as originally an empty form, created with certain possibilities or tendencies—God's intent to oppose Himself—but how these play out and to what degree they manifest is up to you. The intent was to allow a little creative friction to goad wakeful choices; we hinted at that idea in the story of Job and how God asked Satan to test the man. A daring, risky proposition, but you'd expect such boldness from the Creator of Everything Living Everywhere.

"Unfortunately, what seems to happen is sentient life-forms endowed with some degree of free will (humans, you'll note, are at the extreme end of that generous dispensation, having the most of it awarded to sentients so far) get overwhelmed by the accrued results of their own ill-advised choices and they end up generating an impressively nasty and effective Chief of Lies like the Druj as you know her, in her various guises, names, and qualities, on the Earth, as the Antichrist, Satan, King of Evil— the names are legion and the list of names is long. That is why we have been reconsidering the parameters for the Druj's activities. We thought, on the results of this expedition, we might change a few.

"The Druj grows with human use. Her size is cumulative, additive, per use. Every time a person succumbs to a Druj lie, that acquiescence adds to her size. She adds another layer to her girth. Then, if a person deliberately, consciously employs the dark side of free-will choices, she grows another layer again, a thicker one because human complicity is a strong fertilizer. Through this constantly interactive, reciprocal feedback system she keeps expanding, in size and influence, and eventually, one thinks, in inevitability too. She begins to seem inexorable, immutable, a permanent fixture of reality, an implacable enemy."

"The situation corresponds with the model of twin Guardian Angels that some angelologies put forward," said Edward. "We discussed this polarity earlier but it seems relevant again here. The Jewish tradition holds that every human is accompanied by a Good Angel, who walks in front of them, and a Bad Angel, who walks behind. One holds the knowledge of the human's good deeds, the other records the bad deeds, and each seeks to inspire the human to commit more of the kind they represent. Or the Bad Angel's tendency is to counter all the good actions taken.

"This justifies a comparison with the polarity of Christ and the Antichrist or Druj, but at perhaps a more sublime level. The Christ is the perfect example of the good deeds, and the Antichrist personifies the human soul committing bad deeds, and both cluster around the human soul, awaiting its choice, how it approaches the Tree of the Knowledge of Good and Evil. The Christ and Antichrist, or our familiar Druj, are both generic exemplifiers of this.

"The Christ is created perfect and whole, but the Druj is additive: she grows and evolves coordinated with our choices. When you are first created as a spirit, the Holy Guardian Angel is your first auric envelope. The Druj is only a theoretical, future possibility at this early stage. You have not committed any bad deeds, so she has no standing. She is for you a blank empty slate. So she is always and necessarily a secondary spirit, only a subsidiary influence. Her standing, size, and influence, is individualized and validated with each soul. I suspect there is a fundamental asymmetry in influence and weighting between them, the Christ possessing the greater share of original power and influence."

"God keeps a Most Wanted wall with posters of the Druj from every known world," said Blaise. "There are thousands of images of her as the arch-criminal sought by authorities. If you see this Girl-Gangster report her location immediately to the authorities. There's even mention of a reward for the Druj, brought in dead or alive. The Supreme Being Himself has posted the reward.

"Well, meanwhile, you're saying there is a cosmic design necessity to this polarity. There could well be. Consider what Jung said in *Answer to Job*. He made the outrageously suggestive statement that God dumped His unconscious into the human psyche and expects us to figure it out, work out the bumps in it, get back to Him with the results, or at least the executive summary. It's like He says, 'Here's the Druj. Can you do something with her possibly? She's a handful.' He asks this like a British aristocrat discussing a problem with the under-butler. You know how they talk, with allusions, insinuations, whispers, hints, and nods."

We put the matter of the Druj aside for the moment to contemplate the presence of the Great Mother. There She was, inside Her silver flames, passing through a constant succession of different shapes and images, a seemingly endless repertory of guises. It didn't seem as if She had yet repeated one. All the gates seemed to focus on Her, almost to lean in to the center of this great hall, with rapt attention, even reverence, and the hint of a desire to run into Her fire. I realized, after I thought about this for a moment, there was truth to this desire.

The gates represent a fragmented, differentiated condition for our consciousness. Instead of unity, cyclopean perception, single-eyed cognition, having just one round eye that sees unity everywhere, we had 49 eyes. To a degree, each of these eyes, these chakras, has its own nuanced perceptions; all these have to be integrated somehow into a singular interpretation of reality. Usually, we fail to do this as the incorporation gradient is simply too steep.

But I did see individual humans emerge from a gate and rush into Her. They saw the great silver bonfire and ran toward it and leaped into the flames. This was a different kind of self-immolation; it was a return to the Mother. The archetype of this gesture was the Pharoah Osiris sitting on Isis, the Throne. Her name, Isis, or the Egyptian, *Aset*, means Throne, the seat and foundation of political power, and in Egyptian iconography she wore a throne as a headdress. This means Isis, the Great Mother, was the fundamental *base* for the Pharoah. He anchored his consciousness upon this *seat*, this throne made of the Silver Light.

If we take the secular and political aspect out of the picture, Her power is spiritual, the force of consciousness, and it's a force because it is the original condition, which was unity. The whole Human, the complete singular body of consciousness *before* it went through the 49 Gates and rushed out into the individuating world of separate existences, visible bodies, life and death. To sit on the Throne is to return to the unitive state, to the place of form generation. To occupy the Throne is to dwell with Isis, to revel in your original reclaimed unity. The pharoah, you, the originally immaculate soul-spirit, has made it back home.

There is no shame or regressive embarrassment to return to *this* Mother. Carl Jung will never call you psychically immature. This is a womb inside Her silver fires, but it is more like a factory of endless variations. The archetypal design studio of a prolifically creative artist. She comes up with new ideas

every day, hourly. All the possible forms She can take and that She can generate to clothe consciousness to inhabit any of the created worlds in the universe and there to experience reality and grow awareness. She generates the forms, and She is those forms; embodied, we wear the Mother. The ultimate cross-dresser. She is the factory that turns out Houses of God in all specifications and sizes, as living bodies, Light temples, stars, cosmoses, metaphors, pictures, ideas, even words. Every conceivable form that holds the Holy Light is the Great Mother's progeny.

I stepped into the silver fire. We all did. It was as if the 49 Gates stepped in with us. At first, inside the flames, the gates were still distinguishable, but after a short while, they started to expand and touch their neighbors, then fuse. They formed one gate, and it was cyclopean, a single, universally aware, open eye enflamed with the Great Mother's silver blaze, attention, love, and wisdom. This is the one womb that you can crawl back into without losing your adult dignity, I realized, and I both laughed and was humbled by the realization that I was back.

The analogy may seem inept, but imagine you are a six-year-old child, and you suddenly have the chance to view reality as your mother sees it, the adult view. Should you be able to assimilate the information, that would reorient you utterly regarding reality, life, consciousness, body, and, most acutely, your own identity. For a moment you remember yourself as the six-year-old sitting on Mom's lap, the Throne that is Isis; then you are the Great Mother with young Horus on your lap; then you are both, merged, child and mother, Horus and Isis, you and Her, the Pharoah of All Egypt and the Throne girt by the Silver Light. Pharoah of All Egypt, by the way, means of the Land of *Al-Kemi*, alchemy, the Black Land, Egypt's original name, the place of the many transformations of the soul, of the transfiguration of the lead of consciousness into the gold of Light, for which purpose Egypt, the land, the culture, the consciousness, was created.

I seemed to be both inside the Great Mother's silver bonfire and working with the others in cleaning the gates of eons of detritus. I went back and forth in my awareness, immersed in the fullness and completion of the Human, then back out into the field of action where this fullness was deployed into 49 parts. At first I thought the fullness was infinitely preferable to being fragmented into 49 differing eyes, each taking in reality through its own nuanced perception. But then I would flip to the other side and understand that the proliferation of viewing points into 49 gates mirrored the Supreme Being's design for Creation.

The Supreme Being obviously thought it a good idea to have 49 different *Sefirot*. It was as if He said, well, try seeing me this way or through this different filter. So he created 49 eyes, windows into His soul, for humans to attain a partial glimpse of the otherwise unfathomable, infinite Mystery of Creator and Creation.

This is what I mean: Qabalists offer a Creation model of four or sometimes five Trees of Life, each with ten spheres of Light, reality, and existence, but arrayed in a hierarchical cascade, like a stepped waterfall. That's just like 49 eyes, isn't it? The 50 Gates, the full pattern, reiterates the *five* Trees of Life and its 50 spheres. You can deduce from this design that the Supreme Being wanted consciousness to experience these 50 stepping stones into full cognition, though, ideally, remembering the complete pattern at the same time, the original unity.

It seems paradoxical, a plan calling for differentiation and unity at the same time, but it isn't. It makes sense when you see it as a circulation pattern like a torus-donut shape in which the inside is flowing upwards and outwards to become the outside then returning to be the inside again. Similarly, we flow from having 49 eyes or differentiated gates to the cyclopean eye condition, and this flow, as the Creator intended, I think, is continuous, so we experience both. It's also the same toroidal flow of form into emptiness and emptiness back into form.

I wasn't sure if I was daydreaming or still transiting between both poles, but suddenly I realized Pipaluk was tugging on my sleeve to get my attention. She was like a welder who had lowered her welding arc but hadn't turned it off. The lilac flames were still searing out of what looked like a lilac flame-thrower. Tommy had stopped applying his lilac flames as well. They both pointed to the left inside wall of this particular gate. "Root chakra at the root chakra level," said Tommy, "and would you look at what's coming out of this one. Unbelievable."

I agreed. It was as if this wall had been made of compressed human forms, old bodies, a kind of mortuary over time comprised of hundreds of bodies. They were half-dead, half-alive, dark brown in color, the way something would take on the hue of loam after long-term burial in the soil of the Earth.

These human forms—I wondered if I should call them semi-animate corpses—had not been buried in a literal sense, but they were Earthbound. They seemed partially sentient, as if amnesiac or just woken from a long slumber, and their brownness, I realized after a few moments of studying them, was an index of how Earthbound, how dense, how stuck in a material layer, they had become. Their presence was becoming formidable; we felt we might soon be overwhelmed by their numbers and the heaviness of their brown color.

Yes, a strange way to put it, but what I mean is the brown of their forms was a vibration, a frequency signature, and it felt heavy on our consciousness. These encrusted human forms seemed to have been embedded in this chakra gateway for a long time; we had just disturbed this prolonged stasis and they were stirring to a kind of half-life that seemed objectionable and worrisome. They seemed to be attached to large, dirtied pictures flapping like banners.

Threads of dark light connected these banner-images to their brown forms in a manner that resembled people flying kites, though these kites were dragging the ground. The images were of events on Earth. They were grim and unpleasant. Images of death by a variety of nasty means, from physical violence to starvation, worries about survival, fears of the imminence of death from war, illness, or old age, bodily danger, prolonged feelings of physical insecurity, like perpetually standing on a cliff's edge, decomposition of human bodies, sickening and putrefaction of organs and systems within the body (disease, I suppose).

Another motif I discerned in these flapping kite banners was people living close to the ground, low-slung in their center of gravity, farmers, field laborers, but more than that, it was an attitude about life and incarnation, that the material, bodily aspect was paramount, was in fact the whole story, all there was to life, and human life was indistinguishable from brute animal life.

It felt like their bodies were filled with leaden anvils. I felt that heaviness, even at a distance from these plodding, trudging, half-asleep, and desiccated human forms. Their bodies had no leavening agents within them, no sparks of uplifting higher consciousness, no vista of aspects of life beyond only material existence. Probably we all feel this way now and then or we experience this as an undertone that occasionally sounds forth in our lives, but here it was all there was, as if this quality, one among many, had been extracted and then amplified so that it became, for these trudging souls, the complete definition of being alive.

We felt sorry for these lost souls, but on a practical level their leaden presence in this particular gateway was broadcasting this brown quality to all humans currently in existence or transiting the *Bardo*. It was a dark influence, contrary to the possibility of souls either in bodies or having dropped them to make advances in their consciousness. Instead it was helping them stay stuck.

It was subliminally reinforcing regressive tendencies, and we had to stop this. Just from being in proximity to these brown guys I felt myself slowing down, my movements dragging, full of effort, my attention dulling, becoming dimmer. It felt like I was in a heavy gravity field where all motions of body and mind were slowed down to what felt (and probably looked like) slow-motion gestures, like trying to run while you're underwater. You can't move quickly.

Only Merlin remained unaffected by the heavy gravity effects of the brown men, so he was able to tell us what to do to remove their influence.

I had thought, or at least suspected, that these brown men were somewhere between zombies and Golems, or between either of those and humans. Now as they started to crumble into little clusters of dried dirt, I knew I had been right. I don't know how we did it. Perhaps we didn't do it at all. Merlin did. Their brown human forms started to flake off in layers and clumps, and, gathering momentum like an avalanche, soon bigger clumps broke off leaving a mound of polluted dirt where their feet used to be. It was like when you kick clumps of hardened mud off the mudguards and wheel rims of a car. Where each of these encrusted brown human forms had stood was now a star, a diamond form of brilliant glittering Light, freed from their dried-mud forms.

Merlin pointed to me and laughed. "You, Frederick, helped to do this."

Naturally, I didn't understand Merlin's remark. "You have been keeping some of your attention on the Ofanim's diamond array inside the Rotunda, and that influence enabled the brown men to finally drop their encrusted forms. You forgot you were doing this as your attention wandered into other areas of interest, but you have to remember all acts of consciousness are powerful here, far more so than you observe ordinarily in the physical world.

"It is possible, in fact, it is normal, to conduct more than one line of activity at the same time. Often, many. You helped these Earthbound souls to remember a vital kernel of spiritual truth and reality inside them and to liberate their Blazing Stars from those gravity-laden brown forms and become free. As a result, this particular gateway is less encumbered by old, stagnant, resistant energies and by the Earthbound souls held fast to them by these energies."

"Though I can't say the same for *that* doorway," Merlin added, pointing to one. This gate was encrusted with what looked like slender, compacted yellow crystalline human forms, a hybrid between a human body and a crystal. But though partially crystalline in appearance, the color was dull, dirtied, sluggish.

Picture a thousand icicles that have formed adjacent to one another in a row. Put a somnolent human face, arms, and legs on this frozen figure; color it pale yellow. Pack them around the gateway, just inside and outside its lintel, like the sheets of padded insulation builders put between a room's ceiling and the house's roof. You walk inside this gate, from either direction, and you are accosted by these human icicles. They give off a vibration that is like a frozen or stalled ecstasy. A feeling that long ago might have registered delight or rapture but over time had degenerated into a constantly reiterated empty gesture.

I hope I do not come across as cynical, because that is not my nature, but I can't help

but say it seemed these yellow frozen human souls had once been possessed by a kernel of spiritual truth, perhaps some exquisite insight or the teaching of a guru or spiritual master, and they still held on to it as if it were the definitive, exclusive answer to all of life's mysteries. They were locked into a perpetual moment and did not realize that hundreds, maybe thousands, of years had elapsed since they gained possession of this astounding bit of spiritual insight and that in fact its level of insight had long ago been surpassed and would strike most developed souls as akin to the clichéd message on a popular line of mass-market greeting cards—in short, as no big deal and widely known.

Spirituality and consciousness evolve over time, as Rudolf Steiner observed, and the truths of the Lemurian shamans, for example, are not relevant or even applicable to, Steiner would have said then, 20th century souls, and even less so to people living now in the middle of the 21st century. Yet this was what presented itself to our inspection. These human souls were frozen in an antique, outmoded spiritual ecstasy. It was as if a guru or some charismatic spiritual or religious leader handed them a sweet nugget of insight and they have been clutching it ever since; as a result, their evolution stopped, and, ironically, they have become, like the brown men, trapped, Earthbound souls, grasping clichés.

"This gateway is the heart chakra at its throat chakra expression," explained Merlin. "Spirituality, insight, trust, the reverence for truth and beauty, combined with its expression, the welling up of truth for communication in the throat center, the way a voice, inspired, even possessed, by this insight, speaks it. But that moment of freshness is long past. Staleness and stagnation have set in.

"Not only are these many human souls stuck in this doorway, never progressing as the centuries flow on, their stuckness negatively affects other souls passing through, or, as it turns out, not passing through. Some stop and gaze at the image of frozen ecstasy and wonder what might have possessed these people to such a high level of delight. What truth moved them so deeply, and can they, these souls still performing their *Bardo* passage, have some of it now?

"The Druj then puts her clever, manipulative hand into this and makes the withheld, secretive spiritual insight glow with significance and import. It must be a revelation that surely will shake the world, she makes people feel, and I must, at all costs, obtain this for myself, they vow. So they remain stuck at the doorway, and eventually little human passage through this gateway is possible.

"Adding to the complexity of this deception is the fact that the so-called spiritual truth uttered by the spiritual master was itself not entirely truthful. It had some of the qualities that espionage literature likes to call disinformation. It was three-quarters deceptive, only one-quarter truthful, because the guru's intent was to use it like a fishhook to catch gullible spiritual students to add to his day's catch. Some spiritual teachers of incomplete attainment do that, fish for susceptible students, using whatever bright, pretty, or sugar-coated lures that work. So this soul-encrusted gateway itself was transformed into a guru's baited fish hook, and the Druj keeps lacquering this 'hook' to keep it glittery. As you know, any chance to seed or expand a lie draws her interest; that is her mission."

These yellow frozen souls seemed to be covered in dried, hardened sugar. It reminded me of the old confection called candy canes, solid, hard, and sweet. The spiritual truths (or deceptions) had congealed around these gullible people and formed what was now a dense, almost impenetrable, carapace of illusion. They were still frozen in that moment of seeming bliss, when they felt life's mysteries had been finally resolved and explained to their satisfaction and that they, praise God, were the privileged possessors of these invaluable insights.

I could see they had fallen asleep full of the smugness of a superior dogma, what you see in true believers and fundamentalist adherents to religious teachings. If I have learned anything in this *Bardo* expedition, it is the nonutility of fixed dogmas. You have to keep your perceptions and interpretations fluid because they cannot encompass a reality as expansive, as protean, as mysterious as this. You have to keep your consciousness adjustable and mobile like a soccer game. The ball is always moving and you're always running to kick it home.

I wasn't sure how we were going to undo this. In fact, I had no idea at all. Before I even had time to pursue these worries about my procedural deficits, Philomena was already showing the solution. She had expanded her presence. She was in her nonspecific Light form, just a rapidly spinning blur of diamond Light, though now I discerned diamond-bright pillars evenly spaced within this. Each of these pillars had a keen cutting edge as if it were a diamond blade.

These many blades—I estimated several hundred—started advancing towards the yellow encrusted souls, not to injure them but to cut through the hardened sugar. Each of these swords seemed like an embodiment of the Archangel Michael with his sword of *Prajna-paramita*, the cutting insight of spiritual truth. Whatever, in actuality, this archangel is and what his sword signifies was here represented by these many diamond blades cutting through the lies and spiritual illusions that had possessed these souls and frozen them into this immobility. I realized the blades signified the authentic truth of things. They were blades that delivered the sharpness of *Dharmakaya*, absolute reality, and this was sufficient to penetrate and dissolve the artificial, simulated truths that the deceiving gurus had passed on to their unsuspecting, hungry students.

Can you picture a table saw slicing through a huge block of ice? It was like that. These swords sliced up, pulverized, even atomized, the hardened surfaces. Tommy and Pipaluk kept the lilac flames going strong to vaporize all fragments. My attention on the Ofanim's Rotunda of Light enabled them to manifest phalanxes of Thunderbirds to emphasize the ruthlessness of the truth revealed. Blaise was inside the gateway peeling off images and encrusted color patterns. These Thunderbirds, if I may be permitted a touch of hyperbole, were something else. They were roaring, sending off lightning strikes from their eyes; their wings flared, they were fierce, they meant business, they were invincibly effective.

As the hardened sugar surfaces were stripped off these frozen souls, I could hear the original meretricious whisperings of the gurus as they passed on these exquisite morsels of deception to their trusting students, and the mendacious varnishings of these half-truths by the skilled hand of the Druj. It was the quality of the voice that did it. I could see how that would enchant one, charm you out of a normal mental vigilance that would screen questionable input. The voice was alluring, calm, persuasive, reassuring, lulling, and sweet. If Helen was the Greek beauty who launched a thousand warships against Troy, then this was the voice that sold the same product to a thousand disarmed souls.

I realized I had underestimated the number of yellow crystallized souls in this gateway. There must have been many thousands, perhaps tens of thousands. This was the end result of the slow accrual of stuck souls over many eons. The same underestimation goes for the brown bodies also, as it did for the next category I saw. These were small, effervescent orange bubbles that seemed stuck to the walls of another gateway, like eggs or carbon dioxide bubbles in water. I saw people inside these orange globes, curled up, almost

fetally, as if clutching a shimmering image to themselves like a child will clasp a blanket for security. I had the impression these humans had been given a picture of reality, a glowing, evocative metaphor perhaps, and were still clutching it close to them for safety.

"No, not for safety, but for reassurance, as a weak semblance of their own missing certainty, and that is why they remain stuck," said Merlin, following my thoughts. "It was never their own image gleaned from their own clairvoyance. These images they still clutch were alluring psychic pictures given to them, in some cases directly planted in their crown chakras, by spiritual or religious teachers. In many cases, they were secondhand images even to those who planted them, old, worn-out, clichéd, or outmoded spiritual metaphors. In other cases, they were distorted or inaccurate pictures of the spirit world, suitably adjusted by the Druj to serve her twisted agenda of misleading humans.

"I will give you an example. For a time, in the early decades of this the 21st century, there was considerable interest in the subject of ascension. Earlier, it had been called Rapture, and Christian fundamentalists claimed it as their right. Later, other humans, not aligning themselves with Christian dogma of that style, appropriated the term, made it into pretty banners, and paraded it around their affinity groups like Crusaders with their white crosses against a red field.

"Their pictures emphasized the relative ease of ascension, even its privileged nature, and that it represented the next threshold of directed self-evolution, and they were having it. It was their destiny, their right, and, why not, it was exciting and glamorous. You'll remember that little preoccupation, Blaise, I'm sure. It irritated you no end because it misdirected and distracted a number of students you were training."

"It was definitely on the list of known Blaise irritants," Blaise said. "I managed to dislodge these sexy illusions from some of my students, but not all. It had a strong allure at the time, and our friend, the Druj, helped that along a lot. Its pictures of easy spiritual attainment were beguiling. They made the possessors of such images enjoy a warm sense of entitlement, preferment, and distinction. In this sense, they were a species of competition pictures because implicitly they declared their possessors were advanced souls, better than the common lot who didn't have a clue. The trouble was the pictures were fakes, magical glamours, deceptive, and, ultimately, irrelevant, classic examples of the disinformation of espionage and the misdirection of magic.

"They lulled people, like a narcotic, an opium dream of pleasant narcissism, into believing they could skip all the sweaty work of individuation and karma processing and move straight on to the fun bits, turning their bodies into Light. Yes, ascension is real, but it requires much work. You have to convert all trillion cells in your body to Light, and for that, you have to transmute all your karmic accruals. You have to pack the whole *Bardo* experience, successfully completed, into an embodied lifetime and process it all.

"The reason is you are making the Philosopher's Stone, alchemically transforming lead into gold, reiterating the consummate initiation act of Jesus the Christ at Golgotha. Doable, yes—Philomena and the other six Theosophon ascenders proved that. My irritation was that the sales picture given to people was terribly misleading. It left out the part about the sufferings of matter in the alchemical retort as the flames of purification burned off the smelly karmic lead.

"The reality of ascension, of any 'progress' in waking yourself up to the true conditions of consciousness and its context, the *Bardo* of everyday life, is more like this: you're digging yourself out of the Earth, and suddenly your shovel has gotten sharper. That helps, no question. And you have gained in lucidity. What that sharpened perception enables is a clearer picture of the huge hole you have buried yourself in over the lifetimes and eons of karmic accrual and that you are now required to get yourself out of to leave the Wheel of Life and truly ascend.

"You see with startling, even upsetting, lucidity, how much more of the hole you have to dig. The analogy works in either direction. You have to climb out of the hole you've dug, or you have to dig deeper, down to your soul's bedrock. Either way, it's work. A lot of heavy lifting, much spadework. No audience is raptly watching you, applauding your every move. Nobody cares.

"There is no room, no justification, for glamorous pictures of an easy ascension, celebrated by your peer group as everyone blazes into a great Light after a weekend's catered effort. Forget that. You're just a sweaty laborer with a shovel in a deep hole of dirt, yours. Most people think you're a nut job. You're down there descending into the lead of the Earth, penetrating your psyche. You have to go down first, into the heavy matter, before you can rise into the Light."

"Which brings us to our present situation," said Merlin, "in which thousands of souls are still stuck to their deceptive images of easy spiritual advancement, and their stuckness is blocking the passageway for others. These images impede their authentic progress as they take them for reality, and they have frozen these many souls in this gateway which is the crown chakra at the heart chakra level of expression. You have the heart chakra's propensity to spawn illusory images of the spiritual world, the *Netzach* candy of 'Love and Light' and the mistaking of outer spiritual figures for the God of the Heart, as they infiltrate the crown chakra trying to get traction on your reality."

I understood the diagnosis. Blaise and Merlin had laid it out clearly. I would never have guessed our mode of treatment. We put on a clown show.

The Blaise angels went in dressed in their angel guises. While the rest of us resumed our appointed tasks in the cleaning of the gateway, the Blaises started hamming it up, like a thousand copies of the Marx Brothers in high glee. They stood before these myriads of stuck orange bubbles trying to get the occupants' attention. Some of the Blaises fiddled with a control panel on the front of their bodies and used a magnifying glass to find the "Ascension" knob, then when they found the knob was stuck or unresponsive, they hammered and twisted it until they got results, which typically was they immediately soared upward like a fuel-powered rocket, disappearing in a flash of smoke and ashes.

Other Blaises were studying their spiritual pictures, identical to the images clutched by the stuck souls in the orange bubbles. They examined these pictures, pored over them like intelligence analysts studying surveillance photos taken from high altitude for signs of enemy action or, in this case, for what ascension might be like, such as beach conditions and hours of spiritual illumination per day and how big of an adoring fan club they should expect.

Another skit they pulled had a few Blaises trying to yank away a precious spiritual image from another Blaise who held fast to it. Some of these Blaises who were pulling at the image tried to climb into the picture which had the illusion of being a live action scene, like a living hologram; other Blaises tried to snip off pieces of the image with large scissors, the kind Harpo Marx would likely extract from his voluminous overcoat of miracles and wonders. Still other Blaises tried to take photographs of these images so they could clutch them fondly too, or they made robes out of them and strutted about the place flashing their pictures.

More Blaises were blowing big orange soap bubbles, setting up stepladders, and trying to climb into these womblike globes taking a pretty picture in with them. Other Blaises simulated a news conference in which a government spokesman was pointing to a projected image of one of these spiritual banners and explaining the landmarks, the enemy base camps, the storage depots, and the projected target strike areas for an assault. They were trying hard to be serious, to look "spiritual" throughout these vaudeville skits.

It was inevitable some of the souls in the orange bubbles would notice. Gradually, some of the more wakeful stuck souls started watching the Blaise antics and despite their solemnity and spiritual gravity they began to smile. They knew they were being spoofed and pantomimed, but the fact is, it was funny—the Blaise clown shows were high-level comedy routines and it was just about impossible to watch them without eventually grinning. We were all laughing.

Those who managed to launch smiles and a semblance of merriment on their faces found their precious banner images start to fade and the bubbles lose their sticky grip on the walls of the gateway. They started to tumble out of these encapsulating wombs, and, as they tumbled, they woke up even more, coming to their senses like a dimmer switch incrementally brightening a room, and they began remembering themselves as they were before they entered the opium user's dream of easy spiritual advancement and narcissistic self-praise.

It was like they had been in suspended animation, a coma, or in amnesia for eons and now they suddenly woke from that long enchantment, that trance state. They rubbed their eyes, scratched their heads, stretched, yawned. They looked like travelers who had been outside civilization for a long time; now they were back among the civilized and wondering what they had missed. Some looked like they had blanked out in the middle of making a statement and now were returned, their syntax still hanging in mid-air like the infrastructure of an unfinished building, awaiting the words that would complete their sentences.

As the souls started to come unstuck from their bubbles and released their fevered hold on their images, I saw scenes that disturbed me. Blaise watched me examining these images, saw I was perplexed, and offered to explain.

The images were of Islamic practitioners who clutched the *Quran*, chanted *suras*, and detonated truck bombs or suicide vests and were welcomed into Paradise. They were assured by their *sheikhs*, by the *Quran*, and by Mohammed himself, that *jihad* against unbelievers, infidels, and Western Christian-Jewish devils was justified and necessary. I saw another set of similar pictures but with Christian crusaders, Bible, and papacy imprimaturs possessing European priest-soldiers. Holy war images flamed in eerie neon lights of orange and pale green.

"They are like hand grenades with their pins ready to be pulled," said Blaise. "They are religious images planted there by misinformed or deliberately misinforming clergy of various religions, as spiritual, holy, and God-mandated sponsorship for violence and death against other humans. These pictures in the souls you see at this gateway are in a state of latency, of only partial activation.

"Should the person fully subscribe to the pictures and start enacting their message, the pin is pulled and the grenade goes off and they plummet into the third chakra dimension of the crown chakra as *jihadists* or crusaders and immediately enter the Hell realm of the *Bardo*. The latent picture explodes into actuality. There in the *Bardo* they would be astonished and

dismayed to learn the image of Paradise as the reward for killing unbelievers or non-Christians was in error. Worse, it was an egregious, shameless lie perpetrated upon them by their spiritual counselors, directors, *sheikhs*, popes, whatever, and by the Druj."

"So the images that look like this that I see in the crown chakras of these stuck souls in the bubbles are unactivated triggers or latent religious pins?"

Blaise nodded as he looked at me, then he said, "Thank God. It's bad enough all these spirits mucking up the doorway with their image obsessions. The pictures are planted but remain dormant, their potential locked until a person decides to act on them, allows them to direct current behavior, whether it is physical action as *jihadists* or, earlier, as crusaders, or less overtly but just as meaningful, as supporters of the vengeance thoughtforms of retributive war.

"If they allow the religious imagery to activate war pictures, grids, and energy configurations within them that call for violent, oppressive responses to acts, then the pictures are launched and these souls automatically default to the third chakra expression. This propels them upon death into the *Bardo* Hell realm where basically the reality will be more of the same, war, conflict, violence, and death, but without the palliative promise of heavenly rewards courtesy of Allah.

"Instead, they get to stand in a live astral battlefield amidst all the influences, the spectrum of inputs that directs this misperception and inspires the violence. They realize they've been lied to, misled, misinformed, goaded against the true wishes of the Supreme Being, which I daresay, is to let people decide for themselves. Of course, this is only when they have come to their senses; most souls for a time will unreflectively carry on with fundamentalist thinking. It's the product of the habit of dualism, using the *skandah* shield as a scythe to cut through everything that opposes your model of reality. Not only is there an imperial 'I' using the *skandahs* to perceive reality, but you don't like the perceptions this activity yields and you want to change them to your liking."

"The irony," said Edward, "is that, at least it's my impression, the Supreme Being doesn't mind the unbelievers or the atheists at all. He's quite all right with doubt or even dismissal because He gave everyone free will to choose. The Supreme Being is content to sit down to tea with all the unbelievers. Tell me about your materialist atheism, He says cordially, passing the muffins. I hear you don't believe in Me, He adds, pouring the tea. Yes, I can quite understand that.

"It's the believers, the zealots, who create all the mayhem that He objects to, because, if I may lapse momentarily into biblical language, they take the Lord's Name in vain. You could say they misquote Him or attribute false statements to Him, or twist the spiritual language of these so-called holy books to suit their political programs and then use the Name of God to justify their ungodly acts. If anyone gets in trouble with the Big Guy, it's the fundamentalist true believers, but I suspect they don't discover this until they get to the *Bardo* and see what a hellacious self-created mess they now have to deal with—no Paradise in sight. Quite the opposite. Bad news in every direction for them."

We finished with this gateway and Merlin pointed to our next one to clean. This gate was encrusted in rows of thin, dark blue, upright pencil shapes coated in a sticky white sludge, rather like cake frosting. The white was dull, old, and lifeless. Inside the thin blue stick-shapes were human souls, compressed, as if made skinny from having to fit inside this tight container. Their faces wore expressions of grief and sorrow, yet they seemed to be moaning, even wailing, in despair at not being heard. Yet I caught an exaggerated quality to this, as if, for

an obscure reason, they were adding a histrionic edge to the feeling. Despite the evident misery and suffering of these pencil souls, the scene before us, oddly, had a maudlin soap-opera quality of deliberately heightened affect.

It left me confused about my reaction, because I felt equal measures of empathy and amusement. Should I feel sorry for these souls or laugh outright? It was as if these people were trying to speak and only moans or wails came out. The voices or sounds came from the blue, but they got distorted or turned into whimpers in the white sludge area, so what came out of them sounded plaintive, beseeching, melancholic, like sustained whimpering. It was a chorus of complainers whose cries for attention and succor were stuck on one note.

It was hard to move around in this gateway, these blue figures were so prolific and filled most of the available space. They exuded a mournful atmosphere. It was infectious, but in a most unpleasant manner, like a room clouded in cigar smoke. This atmosphere was heavy with emotion, like unrelieved disappointment, that reached out and tried to grab you and pull you into its unrelieved morass of misery, gloom, and self-pity. That was why, I now realized, I thought the emotional tone of the place was over-played and exaggerated: they all felt sorry for themselves.

It was a fat wavelike wall, like a tsunami frozen in mid-crest, of self-attention, self-regard, of *selfness*, feeling saturated with unreflective selfhood and unleavened by wisdom, detachment, or Light. It was as if each soul was an opera diva whose voice got stuck on a single note, and this note perpetually delivered a specific and unwavering quality of feeling. I also suspected that these souls originally desired to express something finer, to speak a particular truth (that was the blue), but this impulse got pulled down to a lower level (the white), and there it remained, frozen, stuck, immobilized, and, in practical terms, mostly blocking the passageway for other souls not impeded in this way going through.

"This is the throat chakra, or fifth energy center, operating at the second chakra level of expression, that of feeling and the well of emotions in an individual selfhood context," said Merlin. "As you can see, it presents souls many opportunities to get stuck. It is the chakra that correlates with the water element, which is why, Frederick, you had impressions of halted waves of water and frozen walls of feeling.

"Instead of the throat chakra, which operates at a finer frequency, directing the emotional center, guiding it, even clarifying its strong emotions, the reverse happened and the second chakra captured the throat center and made it express its own singular feeling. Each of these encapsulated souls specialized in one feeling, one particular emotional frame, and thereby got stuck in it. No doubt you feel the wave of that feeling coming off each of these blue figures."

"No doubt the Druj has had a hand in making these feelings stronger and emphasizing their primacy as unchanging facts of reality," noted Tommy. "I would expect nothing less from that consummate manipulator. I expect she has convinced these troubled souls that these feelings are worthy of pedestals, that they are humanity's highest offerings, and their task is to preserve them as exalted showpieces for the souls that come after them. That just means more people will get stuck in this same way and the gateway remains clogged. I have an idea on how to fix this. Apply a song to these blue pencils that is stronger, finer, faster than the fixed, frozen emotion they are continuously broadcasting."

I got Tommy's picture. I saw a sound wave of perfect clarity and illumination, like the perfect note in all of Puccini as sung by Maria Callas, transforming the frozen waves of feeling with the suddenness of a revelation. Pure feeling, certainly, but pitched at the throat chakra's searing level of truth.

"I have just the diva for you, boys. My old pal, Hanuman the Roarer," said Blaise with his characteristic jauntiness. "He did the gods and Rama proud in the *Ramayana* with his mighty roar that dissolved all notions of separate existence. Think of it as a combination of Pavarotti and thunder directed like a sharp laser."

Hanuman was the Hindu monkey-god and ardent follower of the god Rama, and, as I had learned from Blaise, it was a guise of the angelic Blaises. Hundreds of identical Hanumans now stood around us, each about ten feet tall. Their mouths were open and thunderous sounds streamed out towards the blue pillars. These sounds, though powerful, were delicious, beautiful, ecstatic to hear, full of all the passion, delight, and bliss ever felt now focused into a beam.

It burned off the white sludge that covered the blue pencil shapes, and this sludge at first melted and started to run like diluted syrup, then it began to dissolve, and soon it was gone, leaving no trace, not even a whiff of odor or airborne particles. Then Hanuman's musical stream of focused thunder started to penetrate the thick hardened shell of the blue pillars. The blueness started to thin and weaken, becoming progressively weaker shades of blue until pale sky blue yielded itself up to the noncolor of pure water and the elongated, anorexic souls inside were freed and started to stretch, expand, look around, and step forward.

Now innumerable pictures and posters on the walls inside this gateway started to slip loose and get blown out the front of the gateway and dissolve. These must have been the Druj's handiwork, her propaganda work on behalf of souls getting fixated on single unvarying emotions coated in selfhood feelings.

Pick a feeling, such as grief, resentment, invalidation, isolation, or abandonment, and expand it until it fills your world, until it becomes your world of feeling. Give it voice, a single unfaltering note; give it your full soul because you are its expert, its consummate artist, the Druj counseled. She strengthened these postures of single-emotion expression in the pictures she had fixed to the walls, images of heroic self-expression, holding fast to a single feeling unto the death. These images portrayed nobility, dignity, high idealism, and pure ardency, but, frankly, they reminded me of how the Army once used heroic, warrior images to recruit soldiers, luring them into an illusion of manhood fulfilled, while in truth it often led to their bodies getting blown apart by bombs.

All of this rushed over us like a sudden gust of strong wind, then it was gone. We felt all that welled-up feeling for a moment, stood our ground as it passed. I would not like to have stood inside that even for a few seconds. The souls now freed from this entrapment were passing through the gateway and entering the Great Mother's Silver Light temple as they had intended to eons ago. I suppose from the vantage point of eternity, or at least one Life of Brahma, some 311 trillion years, almost no time had passed, only a momentary delay. Meanwhile, I was wondering what this proliferation of little white bubbles was. They were effervescing around another gateway. The whiteness was like neon.

"This is a tricky one," said Merlin. "You'll need to stay sharp."

Inside these white bubbles were human figures, curled up like balls, raptly watching multiple images flashing on the bubble's inside white surface. New images were popping up and flashing all around these figures, and they seemed to have eyes all round themselves, able to see in the sphere's 360 degrees. As for the images, they seemed cosmic, celestial, angelic, portraits from the astral world, pictures of masters, temples, pillars of Light, great patterns of color like nebulae or aurora borealis curtains of shimmering hues. Everything seemed portentous, full of spiritual import, majesty, and august splendor.

"That, and a bit of outright puffery and inflation, I should think," Blaise said.

Why did he say that? Everything looked on the level as if I was privileged to behold wonders of the galaxy and higher spiritual worlds, until I began to see that perhaps these images were a little too grand, over-exalted, and over the top. That neon whiteness to the bubbles had something to do with these heightened effects. It was an unnatural or at least an unpleasant white; it was glaring, crude, brassy, and insistent, and it seemed to vibrate too fast, like it was nervous.

How can Light be nervous? I pondered this for a moment then thought maybe it appears nervous or hyperactive or twitchy because it comes from a place where the vibratory rate is faster than what humans are comfortable with. This neon whiteness seemed to participate in the spinning up of new images, like it was a translation station, adjusting outside input for viewing.

The humans inside these bubbles were raptly watching the succession of images, like children before a television on Saturday morning featuring cartoons and games. They looked earnest, all their attention focused on these pictures, as if nothing in reality could be as interesting, as vital, as full of spiritual purport. They had the bemused, distracted, narcotized attention you see in opium addicts.

There was a hint of adoration, as if they were the Magi beholding the Christ Child or perhaps having a long-awaited audience with a Tibetan lama or Hindu guru. This neon whiteness, I realized, was acting as a narcotic, both riveting and dulling the attention of these involuntary "users" until they were enraptured by the succession of bright, tinselly images and saw nothing else.

I'm not criticizing the reverence these souls displayed, but it worried me to see to what degree they seemed abstracted and estranged from their own psychic space, how much they had invested their attention and presence in these pictures, how much they had projected onto them a holiness. These images were drawing out the souls' attention in little white threads, or maybe it was the essence of the soul itself, its Light or consciousness being sucked out like in a straw into these alluring and—now I have it, the word— *sanctimonious* images.

That was it. These images had a churchy, preachy, amplified holiness to them. It reminded me of how so long ago now when my parents took me to the Congregationalist Sunday service that the minister seemed to be pretending to mean what he was saying, that he was mouthing stock phrases, that it was fakery. I didn't tell my parents these views, but I grew a bit distrustful of grand pronouncements coming out of not only clergymen but in general most adults. I became suspicious of puffery, grandiosity, and inflated piety. That was the nature of these images and the neon whiteness acted like loudspeakers for this.

Once I discerned this, I saw the next level of illusory image-making. The Druj was blowing on these images, the way you would to blow smoke away. But she was blowing a kind of electrified, glaring white neon light into these images, and as the soul essence of the stuck humans got straw-sucked into the pictures, these threads became embedded as if in a womb in this neon white vibration. Its quality became the new psychic atmosphere for these souls, who were now doubly stuck, first in the white bubbles, then in this fragmented way in the white frame of the images. And they still looked to be in bliss and rapt adoration. I

can't say I saw her doing this, but I was sure the Druj was smiling at their enchantment. They were right and properly enchanted, lulled into this illusion.

The earlier gateway that represented the crown chakra at the heart chakra level involved spiritual and religious images, but there was a key difference here. These souls in the white bubbles were generating the images themselves, casting them out in front of themselves as if the inside surface of the white bubble were a movie screen and then falling into raptures over these spiritual visions. Their psychic, even mystical, perceptions of reality were in fact fraudulent, solipsistic. They were seeing what they wanted to see then falling to raptures at their blessedness to see such exalted vistas; amusingly, or tragically, they were all falling for the ruse and they didn't seem to realize their images were self-made.

Say somebody wanted to be surrounded by loving angels: their bubble showed this. They wanted high-level Adepts or Ascended Masters to come calling, to congratulate them on their attainments, to reveal stupendous palaces of Light for them alone, and that is what they got immediately. Somebody wanted to discern the secret, conspiratorial levels of activity behind national governments, science, or medicine, and all the curtains were pulled back and astounding revelations of malfeasance and chronic public deception were shown. It was like parting the curtains and seeing the Wizard of Oz working the image controls. He was just a man, an overweight, elderly man, pretending to be Oz.

It's not that these areas in themselves were devoid of truth or existence. They existed, surely. The shortcoming here is that the souls *thought* they were actually seeing them, and seeing them accurately; they were seeing *their ideas* of them. I knew from my travels with Blaise that psychic perception requires training before it is dependable. Sometimes you are, alas, making things up, as people fear, and what you see is only an artifact of your mental content, expectations, or desires. Your psychic visions are made to order, and you're the maker. It is possible, Blaise assured me, eventually to see such things with more accuracy, provided you are willing to spend enough time sharpening your tools.

Surely I was not liable to such perceptual inaccuracy, not after everything I had seen. I had learned the requisite cognitive rigor in my travels with Blaise. I felt myself being tugged by strong but slender white threads. I felt a suction pull, like the undertow of the ocean as you stand in the unstable wet sand as the waves build for another crest. I noticed I was surrounded by a neon white fog. I saw myself helping to free these many stuck souls from the errors of their perceptions, showing them they were caught in self-generated illusory nets. I walked among these unfortunate souls setting them right, like I used to in my classrooms at Dartmouth where I would clarify the nature of a mythic symbol. I realized I ought to be getting a lot more recognition for this skill than I had so far.

Frederick. The name sounded like the slap of a wet blanket against a wall. I heard it again, this time closer. *Frederick.* It just sounded like three syllables. What did it have to do with me? I ignored it. Then it sounded again, all round me, like I was in a cave with special acoustic effects to multiply and amplify echoes. My mind felt hazy, like it was buried in an avalanche of white glaring sludge, yet paradoxically, this sludge seemed to be humming at a fast rate, too fast for me. I felt buried and deadened, yet I also felt quickened, speeded up, like I had been jogging on a treadmill and somebody cranked up the speed to 20 times faster. The last image I had just seen, myself as extraordinary spiritual awakener, was all I could see now. It was my complete environment, wrapped all around me.

Then I heard a voice cut through this. It sounded vaguely familiar. "I told you one has to stay sharp in this realm." Who was it? Eventually: Merlin! I felt like I had just been yanked by strong arms out of a pool of quicksand. I had been slipping further into this mire without realizing it; I was up to my ears. The images around me snapped into pieces and dissolved. The white mist receded.

"This gateway represents the sixth chakra at the sixth chakra level," said Merlin. "This is *Ajna*, Center of Command, and the place of psychic pictures. It is a center of great power, both perceptive and creative, and for a time, until one is well trained and the psychic faculty sharpened and refined, that command aspect is likely to generate self-pleasing images which one mistakes for reality.

"Our friend, the Druj, deftly takes advantage of this deficit and drops suggestions that play off a person's pride and the general drift of their mental processes. For you, Frederick, she might feed you hints about seeing mythic symbols and objects, about what they truly are, what they look like, and how capable you are at discerning these through your impressive psychic abilities. See how it works?

"The Druj's goal is to get an advanced soul stuck on one misperceived object, fixated on a recurrent or immobilized psychic image. Then that person will not make it past this particular gate, will remain stuck there, and contribute to blocking the passage through this gate for other souls. I see it was her intent to get you stuck on the image of a spear and the gods holding it. It is a Japanese image of the Floating Bridge of Heaven and the Light spear the gods used to stir the primordial brine to generate the mass that became Japan's first island.

"You are familiar with this scene, aren't you? It is one of your favorites. She would have guided your sixth chakra's picture-making skill to create a colorful, dramatic, live-action picture of this spear, with fire and streams of Light. When she saw you had developed this plausible image, she would have started to adjust it to her specifications, suggesting the nuance that the spear also had offensive capabilities to subdue enemies of the Creation or of the gods, that it could only be activated by worthy heroes, such as yourself, that you had a long history of involvement with this spear, that, in fact, it was created just for you.

"Obligingly, you would generate psychic impressions to match this false story and you would credit them with authentic reality and thereby be misdirected. She had laid this out before you like a tapestry only a few steps away. You were about to walk into it and mistake it for a landscape of truth.

"You see, the point of these gates is to test a candidate in their mastery over the particular chakra nuance represented by that gate. Here it is sixth chakra and its designed ability to develop and register clear, accurate, plausible visual metaphors of the inalterably protean and unfixed aspects of the spiritual world. Psychic perception is a cognitive negotiation between perceiver and a constantly shapeshifting, permutating higher world reality. The Light is not fixed in forms. Psychic perception has to work against the mind's desire to fix Light into forms, and, as often happens, to fix it into inaccurate, incomplete, or misdirected ones.

"Psychic skill requires finding a workable middle-ground between the two facts. When you master this, and it may take many lives, you pass through this gate. You fail to master this when you get mesmerized by the glamour of your own self-generated psychic image, mistaking it for genuine reality. The Druj wants this. Self-inflation and glamour, not clear-seeing—she wants that."

"The truth has a special feel to it, a vibrational specificity," said Blaise. "So do lies and glamorous misperceptions. The trouble is this gate is keyed to allow passage only to one holding an image of truth. The truth vibration is like a key. The feeling of a lie is heavier, thicker, slower, like sludgy syrup with a neon glare. The gateway does not allow passage of something with this feeling. If that's what you're carrying, you'll get stuck inside this gateway holding the lie. Worse, you probably won't realize this. It will be as if time has stopped, or it moves so slowly you barely notice its progression, and you remain here for days, years, even centuries, until something or somebody nudges you awake and you realize you haven't gone anywhere and the image you're cherishing is just shit."

Then Blaise said, pointing to another gate, "I wonder what you make of this."

Innumerable small purple spheres were oozing out of the gateway like mobile fish eggs. They were packed close together, perhaps by the thousands, and clumps of these tiny purple bubbles were floating out of the gate in masses, the way a flock of birds will alight and fly off at once perfectly synchronized. Inside the gate, I found as we entered it for an inspection, it was just as packed with grape clusters of purple spheres. I examined one of them.

Inside it was an entire world, a brightly detailed celestial image wrapped around the inside surface of the sphere like a liner. I saw patterns of stars, star-gods, angels, enclaves. I saw hosts of advanced celestial spirits, such as Masters and Pleiadians, whom I now could identify from my travels with Blaise for the Theosophon. Within the purple bubbles these exalted higher souls seemed close at hand, almost palpable, and they seemed to be performing important acts pertinent to the bubble holder, as if they were on staff, entertaining their host.

Inside each bubble was a human soul. These were looking upwards in rapture, as if what was revealed to them by the obliging celestial spirits was the most *amazing* vista they had ever beheld and truly, they felt, they were *blessed* to be *gifted* with such a *divine* treasure. I am putting into my own words the special nuance of uplifted feeling the bubble souls expressed. It is, the reader will agree, florid and slightly over-stated, even blushingly inflated. I do this on purpose.

The souls themselves did not look like humans, even balled-up ones which you might expect for so compacted a living space. Instead, I saw what looked like an array of upward-facing fire-petals, each shaped like the leaf of an aspen tree but positioned upright, emitting fire and Light. They were arrayed in a symmetrical pattern in a series of overlapping or even superimposed circles of petals, with one foremost and taller in the center. It suggested a deployment of phased-array telescopes, acting together to register an image from deep space.

There were hundreds of these petals afire with mostly golden flames, though some looked tinged or darkened by other colors. I understood that they were working together, like an insect's composite eye, all seeing the one thing. The "thing," celestial object or spirit, they were seeing was distributed as an image that blanketed the full array of perceiving petals so the whole unit saw it. The perceiving soul, the awareness that received this blanketing image, seemed to have "risen" into this descended reality and dwelled there in its environment. The soul had entered the psychic picture it had received and seemed delighted to the point of rapture with this acquisition. You could feel how gifted they felt.

"Precisely," said Blaise, again following my thoughts, "and that's where they got stuck. They entered their psychic picture and see everything through it. You're looking at the crown chakra on a generic design level, here operating at the level of the crown chakra, its highest expression. This should be an open doorway with the coincidence of both aspects of the crown, crown on crown. But it isn't. The wisdom and knowing functions are blocked here, rendered dormant.

At the crown chakra you *know* something with certainty; *seeing* it is secondary.

"The sixth chakra can always provide you with the appropriate visuals, but it is the crown that interprets the visual data and extracts meaning from the images. Except that's not happening. These souls settled for the glorious image alone. They haven't extracted the essential wisdom from the perception, so things have stopped. Their crowns are immobilized, halted in mid-download of meaning. The celestial image lies heavily, increasingly so, upon the delicate petals, suppressing the crown petals' innate mobility, and fresh input is now blocked, like—how about this?—a hippopotamus lying upon a flowerbed.

"The image blanketing the crown is like an undigested big meal. It lies heavily, unmoving, in the stomach; eventually, the metabolic organs will suffer. To use a different analogy, these souls are using their crowns like a mailbox; the crown in fact is an active, vital tool of inquiry, fact-finding, and investigation. It is designed to be in dynamic, perpetual, reciprocal interaction with the cosmos.

"Why are they stuck? Because they take these grand images as definitive, as postings from God Himself, as true expressions of the Official Explanation. They have forgotten that any image is provisional, jerry-rigged, and analogical. Things are in form for the purposes of illustration, my pals, the Blaises, say. As Joseph Campbell used to say, people don't see through the metaphors. You have to take the next step and extract the core meaning from the illustration, see through it. Find the 'what' that is in form for these purposes of illustration. Knowing trumps imaging, but these souls stopped at downloading the image. All truth comes originally from the *Dharmakaya*, which is a formless realm. Those truths take temporary, plausible, visual metaphorical form, enough for us to see.

"Not only have they shortchanged themselves because the crown chakra at the crown level is the pinnacle of the chakra hierarchy, but they have initiated, if passively, a regressive trend in the cognitive *dialogue* between the created and the Creator. They halted what should have remained a dynamic, continuous exchange. Psychic impressions, cognitive images—they're aspects of this living, creative dialogue. The Supreme Being, as the Qabalists say, wants to reveal Himself, to disclose reality through a series of plausible analogies which we decode. But we have to participate, help it along, hit the ball back over the net."

I suddenly saw the solution. I wouldn't have expected I could see such things, but what I saw was a human crown chakra, one of ours, or all of ours, with all its petals lit up golden and surrounded by vigorous golden flames, rising into the realm of stuck crown chakras blanketed by deadened cosmic images. In essence, we should bring an alive, activated crown chakra to these halted ones. I saw on a practical level how we could do this. It was how we got here in the first place: using the Golden Bough. We could repeat that gesture, expanding the little golden staff in the crown to encompass all the chakras in a golden pillar, and this surrounded by a great host of Ofanim in their glittering cloak of diamond caves.

Blaise nodded. Merlin smiled. I took it that meant this approach would work. We put it into motion and rose through this stuck level of impacted crown chakras inside this gateway. I watched as the flaming golden petals on our crown (it seemed that our individual crowns had merged for this) penetrated the thick resistance layers of these toughened, halted crowns and started to burn off the sludge, to incinerate the immobilized images. Steam then black smoke then grey ashes poured out of these impacted crowns, and it was as if the individuals stood up and shook themselves, the way you might do if you were confined for a long time in a small space, like a barrel or car trunk, then suddenly, they opened the trunk and you climbed out, stiff and crunched, squinting in the bright sunshine.

This was only janitorial work. Then the marvelous part happened. It was as if as the crown chakra petals stretched and rose up and started to emanate golden Light. The Heavens above opened up in a great wonderful cataclysm of revelation and fresh images poured down, like a new set of ideas from the Supreme Being, realities that needed illustration for the purposes of our understanding them. Yet these revelations were too fluidic, too protean, too elusive, too alive, to incarnate in fixed image forms. They were ideas for images, sketches, suggestions, the etheric bodies of images perhaps. It is difficult to make this subtlety clear; it was surpassingly subtle yet so vivid and present.

My impression was that the intent of this floriating of the psychic airspace above the crowns with this potential for images and the potential for our comprehending them was to invite us, our awareness, to enter into them as living environments, in which meaning, image, and Light were all combined. This was a *Bardo* space in itself, an Intermediate Realm, an in-between place; it was not the Supreme Being completely, nor was it the crown chakras alone. It was like a negotiated, co-produced Light temple made of this fleeting image. We could occupy it for a time until we came up with a better visual analogy.

The two ends of this pole of intended dialogue met in a third in-between space and there exchanged meaning. The Supreme Being revealed something, we cognized it, extracting an essential meaning from a suggested image. It was like dancing. It broke up the protracted log-jam of these stuck souls. They were unstuck. They flowed through the gateway and soon the passageway was empty.

"Good job," said Merlin. "We still have the previous gateway, the sixth chakra at the sixth chakra level, to clean out. We will have a helper for that."

There was somebody with us, but I didn't immediately recognize him on account of he had turned himself into the biggest, sharpest sword I'd ever seen. It was Matthew, and rather than holding this sword, he appeared to be inside it. Certainly it was not the full-body expression of himself nor his astral body I saw, but enough of his presence was seeable that I could more or less see him there, in other words, pinpoint his approximate location in the bright space before me.

"How do you like my big sword?" Matthew called out with cockiness.

That was refreshing to hear. Matthew seemed to have been suffering since he got here. He had been only intermittently with us and he seemed involved in something strange, big, and transformative, though at that time I didn't see what. It was like he kept getting pulled off the stage to take care of matters elsewhere.

"I got it from Goliath, and the Elohim said I could borrow it for this job."

I knew the references but I did not immediately understand their connection. I tried to work it out in my mind. Goliath was an uncouth giant whom the biblical David killed with a slingshot, after which he claimed the giant's sword. This fact tends to get overlooked in the standard recounting. Then in the Arthurian stories this same sword shows up in Arthur's Camalate.

David's son, Solomon, sends it to Arthur's court on the Ship of Time, and one of the Grail Knights, usually Galahad, claims it. This links Goliath with Arthur, and that links the whole story with us because all this business of Light grids, Light temples, Ray Masters like Merlin and angels like the Blaises, falls within the purview of the Arthurian Mysteries, not

to mention Edward had been showing signs of emulating King Arthur. It was conceivable Matthew could have that sword, but it opened up another question: What exactly is Goliath's sword?

Blaise had an explanation. "There is an intermediate part in the history of the sword. It's called the Dolorous Stroke. The Fisher King misuses this sword and wounds himself. This is the famous wound in his groin that the medieval Grail stories report so blushingly. Oh dear, the old boy knicked his privates. Nothing to do with the genitals. The meaning of the wound was the root chakra.

"The Fisher King's root chakra got injured, and the natural flow of consciousness from the root to the crown, making it possible to open up full illumination and memory along one's soul timeline, was blocked. The result was the Wasteland, a *Kali-yuga* condition of both the inner psychological and outer ecological realms. They were both 'wasted,' rendered wastelands, as far as self-knowledge went. The soul's timeline, the landscape's self-awareness of its origin and purpose, were blocked, could not hold the necessary illumination, and became blighted. Nothing grew in them, meaning no spiritual insight arose. Reality, culture, the psyche became a heap of broken images, as T.S. Eliot said.

"The sword represents the possibility of a certain profoundly creative, world-generating deployment of consciousness shaped as if into a sword form. The knowledge of how to do this came from the Elohim, acting as Goliath. David did not slay Goliath; rather, he was *tutored* in the use of this sword *by* Goliath. You have to read the mythic picture in a mirror. In fact, it wasn't even a tutorial.

"The picture tells us David, a high initiate, *used* the Elohim's knowledge expressed as a sword. He operated within their aegis as a legitimate sword user. The sword represents angelic information and protocols David was entitled to use, the entitlement coming from his initiation status. He was *qualified* for it. This knowledge was of a high initiation order; hence, David and his 'son' Solomon were its caretakers (think of Solomon as another initiate in this order), and the Arthurian Mysteries became its viable worldly curator. That means you find the reliable protocols for the correct use of this angelic sword in the Arthurian Mysteries, in its paths and modes of geomantic and spiritual initiation.

"Galahad was the one capable of extracting this precious sword from the Ship of Time because he was a Christed Grail Knight. Among embodied humans within Arthur's court at the time, he was qualified for this sword. He could handle and wield the high angelic Light the sword entailed. The Ship of Time meant the sword's protocols were stored outside of the human timeline for the next initiate who could access them. You had to be able to board this ship, step into this section of the spiritual world, outside of time, and claim the sword. The sword is always there, just like the Mysteries, as a once-and-future protocol.

"The Fisher King was not Christed. He did not own it, he had not been transformed by the Christ Light, so he injured himself. His mis-stroke was dolorous. He was ill-equipped to use the sword; he was wounded. Galahad was perfectly equipped to heal that wound. The sword embodies the power to create any form at any level. It delivers what the Ofanim call the 'power of *AL*,' which the Elohim or *Al*ohim personify. They are its many forms. The sword has to be wielded from the qualified, nondualistic point of awareness of the Christ Light.

"That's what it means to be a Christed Grail Knight. You know how to get there. The sword contains, it represents, it *delivers*, the original rightness of the creative order, the

Dharma, if you like, of the original design for human consciousness and its corresponding Earth reality—the geomantic truth of both. It combines the power of creative command and penetrative insight, both *Ajna* or sixth chakra qualities, which is why Matthew will use it to clear out this gate. The sixth chakra sees and acts; it is passive and active. Think of this sword as the embodiment of the authentic, original design specifications for the Earth's Light grid and human awareness wielded by a perfectly trained, poised Grail Knight. Think of it as your opportunity to emulate the creative potencies of the Elohim."

At the time I did not know this was a warm-up exercise for something that would come later, the deployment of this sword on a grander scale. It would be a deployment, delivered by our group acting together, that in many respects would represent the fulfillment of our Green Knight expedition in full. For now, it would serve as a practical means to clean out this clogged gateway. We had to break open and dissolve this recursive pattern of solipsistic image-making in which souls stuck in this gateway construed the higher worlds exactly according to their own presentiments and didn't realize they were making it up.

We set to it. We held the sword steady by positioning the Rotunda of Light under its pommel, and Matthew, inside the sword and in most respects now identical with the sword, did the bulk of the work. Except he didn't have to do anything, not in the sense we think of work or action. He held his identity with the sword steady, and if he did anything, he disappeared into the Christ Light and that was the "work" that got the job done. Nondualistic nonaction. Very Buddhist, very Vedantist, and very hard for the analytical mind to grasp.

How then did it work? I suppose I could explain it by saying it's like how if you hold a lit match or small torch around candles, they will start to melt. The lit match does not do anything overtly; it is simply burning, but the heat of this burning transforms the solidity of the candle wax formation into a liquid. Matthew as the Sword of Goliath, the Elohim's big blade, was the lit match. The sword actually did nothing, at least not action as we think of it. It radiated its essence, and that produced the changes because that essence was cosmic truth.

The correctness of original reality, the foundational vibrational signature, the "tone" by which the Elohim designed humanity and the Earth as coterminous, changed the ontologically fraudulent nature of the stuck images on the people. I suppose it was as simple as resonance: you're around somebody who is laughing, and, eventually, you will smile, grin, and start laughing too.

The sword was starting to dispel the sticky, glamorous veils of illusion. The smell, though I'm not sure we could smell things here in the *Bardo*, was like burning rubber tires. It was offensive, and it seemed to burn the eyes, and it certainly made me feel dizzy, as if my head were spinning and drifting away. I realized we were momentarily tasting the qualities and effects of this psychic poison as it lifted off the entrapped souls. We got the acute dose, while they had been sequestered, entombed, I should think, in its chronic presence, no longer noticing it. I saw that they were noticing this radical change in the ambient psychic atmosphere. Their heads were clearing, their psychic windows getting defogged, like in a car when you run the defrost mechanism to clear the screen.

Their crown chakra awareness was now starting to move in the field of reality. How refreshing. I knew they felt that. Here at last is the actual truth. Here are the design specifications, the math formulas, the geometrical models, the whole plan of reality at all its levels as it pertains to human consciousness and the Earth. The grid of our planetary and human reality, revealed

at last. Well, it had always been in a state of disclosure but for these souls that perpetual apocalypse of the original revelation had been eclipsed by their clouded crowns.

Now they were getting it fresh, straight, unobstructed, and unmediated. It was like watching a rapidly executed exchange process, like a marketplace in which goods and payment constantly passed across hands and tables. The Supreme Being was showing images, the souls were seeing them, and the images themselves were a third factor, an in-between place, except the real in-between place was the combination of these three factors together, all as one. They were participating with the Supreme Being in generating plausible visual metaphors that helped explain the mystery of the Supreme Being and Creation. It's as if the Supreme Being said, Here, let Me help you formulate pictures that will help explain Who I am so you can better understand Me. How about this?

This was exhilarating to watch, this process of live revelation and uptake. Soon all the souls were flushed out of this gateway by their own momentum, and the passageway was empty of them. We set to, cleaning and scrubbing the walls.

When we were done Matthew rejoined us, at least for a time. It was fascinating to watch him disassemble the sword. It had many layers and components, like a carefully constructed syllogism, its parts being living images. I asked him what he had been doing all this "time," and as I did so, I realized I had no concept of how long he had been away from us or how long we had been here. It was all indefinite and fluidic— ten minutes, ten days, I didn't know.

"As best I can tell," Matthew said, "I seemed to have been taking myself apart. Karmic divestment, I suppose you'd call it, but it was a rapid, even radical, precipitation of karmic contents, illusions, debts, credits, the whole silly circus. I say silly because when you do this, when it gains enough momentum that you stop resisting it, stop dragging your heels trying, vainly, to halt it, you realize how trivial it has all been. No, not the events, but your attitude within them. You say, 'God, man, you've been holding on for dear life to *this* appalling rubbish?'

"Human incarnations have a certain innate dignity, but it is our attitudes, our interpretations, our histrionic gripings in the midst of this flow of events, that strike me as silly, and I put myself foremost in the list of incarnational clowns. They're silly because we seem always to miss the point, to comment only on the peripheral aspects and miss the main event, so our attention is always wrongly placed, and of the significant developments, our progress, our genuine attainments, things that would please the Supreme Being, we remain oblivious.

"At times I felt I was like a car in a car wash, getting the soap and the high-pressure water spray to clean off years of packed-in dirt, mud, and rust. Other times I felt I was perhaps three years old again and my mother preparing me for a bath, taking off my clothes, piling them neatly on a chair, placing me in the tub. You see, I didn't actually have to do much in this process, just not resist.

"Philomena has helped greatly. She has been like a warm, supportive spotlight. She has been through this. She knows what is involved, and where it's going. I couldn't believe, most of the time, the things that were being pulled out of me. Strange, feral, unfamiliar content, but of course it would be this way because most of it had been accrued over many past lives and though I was responsible for the outcome or momentum of these earlier actions, I did not remember them. It's like we have a double unconscious: the unconscious from this current life, and the unconscious accrued from all the lives we've lived. Of this vast history we tend to be shockingly ill-informed, only minimally aware.

"At the same time, as I was stripping myself clean of endless karmic impediments—I don't know if I should credit this active verb to myself because most of the time I felt myself to be only the passive recipient of this stripping—they were teaching me how to assemble the Sword of Goliath. When I say 'they' it seemed to be a consortium of the Blaise angels, the Elohim, with whom I had not previously been familiar, and a few of the Ascended Masters. Those Elohim—so elegant, magisterial, appearing in male and female forms—did you know they are humanity's godparents, our primal teachers, our best friends?

"It was a heady group of tutors who showed me how to make the sword. However, in many respects it was not a sword at all, certainly not one you hold with your hands. You enter the sword, become its energies, and emanate them. They said it was important I learn how to do this because this special sword would come into play before the Green Knight expedition was finished, and I would have to know how to wield it so our group could complete its mission.

"The sword is a great form of Light held together by the Grail Knight. It is, I realized, and you'll appreciate this point, Blaise, I'm sure, the epitome of the Grail Knight's training, where it is all headed and where it culminates. I had the accelerated course in sword-making, but I suspect it requires years outside, that is, outside of this special context of being in our astral bodies inside the *Bardo* where it seems all the normal rules of reality are thrown out the window and where we can learn strange, new, wonderful things quickly and easily.

"How do you make it? You start with the Ofanim's standard Light visualization of a Blazing Star within a bright transparent pale blue sphere larger than your body, about the size of your aura when it is pulled in, about six feet wide. Yellow, gold, and red flames burn vigorously off the outer surface of this blue bubble, and the whole image is surrounded by an even larger lilac flame that rises from the center of the Earth, surrounds this bubble at an eight foot radius, and rises upwards to an undetermined point with a Blazing Star on top.

"Then you go through the ten stages of the Christed Initiation in the Buddha Body, which puts you inside the spinning octahedron of Light, the inner heart. It appears to be surrounded by the 14 Rays, but in fact its infrastructure, the ribbed edges of this geometric form, are the 12 Rays themselves, two others in the center. The key fact here is that you are Christed; you are in the Christ Light; and you know how to become one with it, which is a nondualistic, blissful voidness. Every human is pre-loaded with this Christ Light in the inner heart. It's just a matter of accessing it and mastering the 'on' switch, which is emptiness.

"This is the power that drives the Sword of Goliath, this *Christed* condition. It *enables* everything that follows, and it *empowers* it all as well. It makes sense. Somewhere it's said the Christ is the Word-Sword, and I remember seeing a drawing of a male figure with a sword coming out of his mouth, tip first. Anyway, the correlation of Christ and sword, Christ as the sword, has merit.

"You occupy a semblance of a human form, which you gained from retrieving your Spirit form as a blazing white seed in the Great Stream, and you stand in this form inside the Christ Light inside the inner heart chakra. You wear a full-body robe with hood or cowl to cover the crown chakra. This robe can be gold, silver, or white, depending on your level of training. You hold an upright staff, also in one of these colors, and topped with a white crown. You expand the staff until it becomes a Light pillar, then enter it. You're standing *inside* your

staff. That's a funny idea, I know, but that is actually what empowers the staff.

"I am, and I apologize for this, skipping over much of the details of these steps, the precise how-to protocols. They are part of a concentrated initiation scheme that requires great changes in a person's psychological constitution, and the nature of the Mysteries and initiation itself precludes, or maybe I should say, forbids, my explaining all the parts or any of it in detail. You'll understand this part, Blaise, I should think. It took you decades—right?— to go through these stages, assimilating each level and mastering its energies. The goal is to keep the mind from appropriating the scheme before consciousness seizes hold of it. It must be real to the totality of yourself, not just to the intellectual component. Until you see and do this from the inside, it may not make much sense to you.

"Then you have to descend a half-level to the premier cosmic chakra, the Solar Logos center, in between the third and fourth chakras. It's just below the sternum. Here you emulate the *Dharma* warrior Gesar of Ling or the Celtic King Arthur, mounted on a white horse (the Ofanim) and wielding Excalibur, his brilliant sword, edged with the lilac flames of the Pendragon.

"This for a while is a sword you hold, though the hands that hold it are projections of your mind. It is your consciousness that holds it. Arthur or Gesar personify the Christed Grail Knight wielding the Christ Light as an active force in the world from this cosmic center; it is a step forward past the voidness of the Christ. Or, if you prefer, it is the Buddha, empty, nondualistic, identical with the Buddha Mind, itself another name for the Christ Light, *Rigpa*, and Clear Mind.

"The next step may sound arcane. You find the Elohim, Goliath in particular, enter his massive luminous form, and through that enter his sword. Technically, you need to have visited an Elohim Citadel, a Light temple you will encounter in the Earth's landscape, and already made your acquaintance with them, especially with the Goliath personifier. Like method acting, you bring your experience of that place into your present condition, as if you are there again. Now you are in this sword surrounded by the angelic order of the Elohim. You sink your awareness down to the handle, which is the activation point, the place of *shakti* or primordial energy, then you add two more components.

"The first is the essence of the *Dhyani* Buddha Vairocana and the blazing white wheel of wakeful voidness at his core. The second is the knowledge of the timeline possessed by the Manu, another name for the Rich Fisher King, an awareness spanning about 300 million years. You emulate both. Vairocana enables you to become rivetingly wide awake, in a state of nondualistic lucidity, and you devour the timeline. You consume it with awareness until you become, or emulate, the Rich Fisher King, rich in memory, twined fraternally with Manu. Vairocana and the Manu are Janus-like, both inside the sword, and in a sense Vairocana has devoured the entire timeline maintained by the Manu, so the soul's knowledge, its recall, is illumined by the voidness of awakened Clear Mind. You, the sword holder, have emulated both spirits and their conditions.

"The reality is simpler than the description which at best can only circle this reality and never nail it. You have to do it to understand. So now you hold this combined state of Manu and Vairocana within the Sword of Goliath. It quivers with this quickened Light. The 14 Ray Masters form a jeweled scabbard around you. It is a lovely, brilliant sheath. The Rays have been activated in your consciousness. They have become living forces and you have aligned yourself with each of the Masters who hold and manage the Rays, but especially with one.

"This is Ray Master Kuthumi, also known as Elijah, John the Baptist, and others. It is the Pale Orange Gold Ray, the Blended Ray some called it, and it is the Ray of the Christed Grail Knight, the Ray and its Master that oversee the Grail lineage. This is the Ray that combines the Christ Mysteries with geomantic knowledge and training. It is the Ray under which the Grail Knights operate.

"You have become the Word-Sword, equipped with the creative powers of the Elohim, those powers the Ofanim call *AL*. When this sword is activated, you can create, generate, manifest anything. Can you see how ill-preparation could lead to disaster, how the misuse of this sword, out of either dilettantism or wrong intention, could produce the Dolorous Stroke, the wounding of the Fisher King and generation of the dread Wasteland? Only one rigorously prepared should use it. If you're not prepared you'll just cut yourself, or nothing will happen. It will be like a car whose motor won't start. When it does start, you are everything Goliath stands for, but perhaps a better window on what that means is to use a different cultural name for this same august figure. *Asha Vahishta*.

"This is the name of one of the six *Amesha-Spentas*, the Bounteous Immortals as described in Persian mysticism. They accompany and work with Ahura-Mazda, the sunlike highest deity in the Persian model. This particular one embodies *Asha*, the correctness of reality. This is the original design, the energy settings, the parameters of Creation as they apply to the human generation and the corresponding Light grid of the Earth, what the Elohim call (because they designed it) the 'template.' The Sword of Goliath is the Sword of *Asha*; it is the truth of reality, *Dharma*, in active, applied mode, as a living force. The sword is the truth of the Light grid design in its activated, deployable mode.

It's the entire Light grid expressed compactly as a sword of truth. It is what heals the Fisher King and the Wasteland, and, pertinent to our purpose here, it is what in the end opposes and finally overcomes the Druj. Still, there is one more element to this.

"When you sink your awareness into the handle you will see a great Hand grip it. This is the Supreme Being; ultimately, He wields the sword, but we wield it *with* Him. This is the meaning of co-creation. We deploy this mighty sword *with* Him, the ultimate source of all power. Isn't it said the Christ is the way back to the Father? Well, here it is. You're back. After a long journey in training and image-building, after many transformations within our make-up and new Light alignments voluntarily taken up, we are now in a position of maximum influence and focused power, even though, paradoxically, when we impart this influence and use this power, we are maximally empty of self and will. It is not we who do this. It is Thy Will Be Done, and we're *helping* That Will be done. It's hard to get this exact, because you are both one and two when you wield this sword."

It was a moment of crystalline clarity. I felt I understood everything. An instant in which so many parts, for so long floating around disconnected, all came searingly back together in a gesture of complete lucidity. I still remember it today as I write this chronicle. I think it is a revelatory kind of experience we all long for, even if it makes our head spin and nearly knocks us over with its Light.

Matthew had been putting all these pieces together, or perhaps it's more accurate to say he had been a participant, an observer, of this reassembling process. The broken sword was being reforged; it was mythological. To reforge the sword is to reconstitute its reality in our understanding. It was really our mind, our understanding, that had been broken. The broken sword hinted that.

Blaise had alluded to most of this in our travels, so I was sure Blaise knew all this too, had done this, possibly had instructed others in how to emulate the initiations. He nodded with a slight look of satisfaction on his face, like he was finally being understood after enduring many years of uncomprehending looks from others. Go Matthew! I sometimes thought Blaise felt he was, as Nietzsche said of himself in *Thus Spake Zarathustra*, a "posthumous prophet." He was not understood presently, but he would be in the future. That future had arrived.

"Blaise took me through the steps in creating this sword," Blaise said. He meant his better half, the other Blaises, his pals upstairs. "Then I did the same for a few people, using specific Light temples, mostly in the Santa Fe landscape, as the venues for contacting the appropriate energies. The Grail myths tend to emphasize only the downside of this story, the Dolorous Stroke and how it produced the Wasteland and how that sickened everyone and it was all terrible.

"So you can easily lose sight of the sword that redeems the mistake and regenerates the land. You see that the Fisher King, collective humanity at an early time, misused this creative primordial power and injured its soul, and it was an injury that festered and remained unhealed, then even forgotten, for a long time. It was our old buddies and nemesis, first-generation humanity, that screwed the deal. Now people are chronically sick and don't even know it. We are all seeded with the plague, the murderous impulse, as Camus wrote.

"Materialism, selfhood, and noncomprehension of reality's design or the mechanics of consciousness dominate culture. That's the spiritual Wasteland, the long span of the *Kali-yuga*. You see that a particular Grail Knight, usually Galahad, was the only one who could undo all this, but the story doesn't tell you how. It doesn't give the specifics of his training. That's the part that Blaise filled in. The Christed part. They taught me the mechanics of using the healing sword. This does not mean only one person can do this; It means Galahad is an example of the qualities of consciousness the one who redeems the Wasteland must have. You can have 100, or 1,000 Galahads; they just have to exemplify these qualities.

"The Arthurian story just says Galahad collected the Sword of Goliath on the Ship of Time that miraculously parked itself (like the Philadelphia Experiment that moved a battleship from Philadelphia to Norfolk) at Camalate one fine day. You get the impression he was the only one who understood what the sword was and that his understanding was based on the initiation fact he already knew how to use it. His long training had led him to this position.

"When I was working my way through the steps in assembling this sword as Blaise revealed them, I realized I didn't know where the 'on' switch was. In the Grail myths, especially those recounted in Eschenbach's *Parzival*, Kunneware, a damaged female figure, says you need a 'magic spell' to activate the reforged sword. In that story, the Word-Sword has been broken, sundered into many parts; it has to be reforged into a single blade before it can be used, then you still need this magic spell to make it work. That's what I call the 'on' switch. It's like the correct magic spell that activates your wizard's wand; otherwise, it's a stick.

"Putting together the necessary stages to assemble the sword is the reforging part. Eschenbach, by the way, is no help: he's deliberately vague, a first-class obscurantist. This is a do-it-yourself mystery. This magic spell, Kunneware says, can be found in a unique spring that is the source of the sword's potency. What spring, what magic spell? Where is this spring? Eschenbach's allusiveness began to irritate me. It's hard enough to read the blighter's convoluted, coded text, but he was obscure when I wanted clarity. I saw I'd have to do some detective work on my own to figure it out. Forget him.

"I figured Kunneware is a Western name for the yogi's *Shakti*, the female principle or personification of divine power. It's like Ma'at, both an abstract principle and a goddess personification of that. Her name means 'to be able' which is what power does: it enables directed action. You are able. *Shakti* must be associated with the root chakra and kundalini (because the yogis say *shakti* rises through the chakras to unite with Shiva on the crown, electrifying everything in between), and geomantically, with the dragons. The fact that *Shakti* is not rising for union at the crown with Shiva is the Fisher King's wound. His root and crown chakras are disconnected; their intended circuit has been damaged. Kunneware is a broken, damaged female, meaning *Shakti* is compromised. The Fisher King's grievous wound has spread to her, and she participates in the hurt.

"I went to a dragon site near Santa Fe and tried the sword out there, using all the parts Blaise had shown me to date. I went through the dragon at this site, meaning, inside it, past its treasure hoard which you find inside its massive coiled golden form, then kept going down and inward, looking for the magic spring. I found it, though it did not at first look like a spring of water. It was a white pearl, often associated with dragons, especially in Chinese myths.

"It opened when I touched it with the sword. Inside was a myriad of stalks with pollen grains at their tips. A female deity of great magnificence and numinosity arose out of the water underneath this opened pearl, like the *deva* of a lake. The pearl had been floating on this water. Then she swallowed the sword.

"She infiltrated the sword as a flame-form, rising upwards and outwards through it, filling up the sword from the inside. It was as if she was both standing on the waters and rising from them. I thought: Hey, these must be the waters of *Tehom*, as Jewish mystics reported. I bet Eschenbach didn't know this. I thought I'd send him a memorandum, all in impenetrable code, totally veiled, explaining this in such a way he'd have no idea at all of what I was talking about.

"It is the Great Deep or Abyss, the original waters upon whose surface moved the Face of God, as biblical accounts say. Then that Face appeared, though in this case it was as a Hand that now gripped the sword. This was the ultimate power source, and its on-code was the Hebrew incantation, *YHW*, *Yay-Hoe-Waw*, His Name, in short, the short form of the Name of God. That's the magic spell, but it only works when all the requisite parts are in alignment, like a planetary conjunction. When you intone those syllables correctly, the sword swells in Light and power. If you pronounce it *Jehovah*, the sword won't work.

"This is the sword that Solomon sent to Camalate on the Ship of Time. That means the Arthurian Mysteries preserved the knowledge of this sword, and that's where you go to reclaim this preserved knowledge: to that once-and-future lineage that combines the Christ Mysteries with all the geomantic protocols and under the auspices of the Pale Orange Gold Ray and its variously named Master. Galahad represents the perfectly trained and prepared Christed Grail Knight, cultivated within this tradition and now equipped to actually help the world. You'll have to excuse the patriarchal bias of this old myth. Not only does it equally pertain to women, but in my experience, women are much better at it."

I marveled at the elegance and clarity of this design, how perfectly the myth, when decoded, pointed to where the treasure was buried, in this case, the practical knowledge of how to reassemble a place in consciousness that had actual traction upon the stuckness of

the world, its Light grid, and humanity. It was like the landing lights at an airport, precisely pinpointing where the plane should go; now that the clouds were dispersed, you, the pilot, could see them.

We were wanted at another gate. Merlin stood before it, gesturing to it. This one looked messy, dirty, contaminated; it would take a lot of scrubbing. I saw fat black pillars, their surface featuring numerous asymmetric knobs or nodules; inside, red lightning continuously flashed into a white cauldron. Nothing about this looked healthy or wholesome. The red was vicious and angry, while the cauldron's dull whiteness was pustulent, offensive to see.

Unhappy human souls were trapped inside these black knobby pillars, their feet stuck in the cauldrons as if in muck, and for some they were buried up to their waists or even shoulders. The best way I can describe the quality of that pustulent whiteness is to say it seemed like infected phlegm, like mucus subjected to long-term stagnation and exerting a strong pull on the body. At the time I formed this impression I did not realize that what I was seeing was the accrued result of millennia of unprocessed, unresolved, stuck human emotions. That was the basis of the offensive white muck with its strong pull.

"This gate is the third chakra at the second chakra level of expression," said Merlin. "Observe how the fires of the will, self-expression, action, volition, even the fires of anger and engaged selfhood, are brought down a notch and enmired in the cauldron of unresolved, undisciplined emotion in the second chakra. Ideally, emotions (this chakra is the well of emotions) should inspire and even inform the empowered will, but instead, because the emotionality is conflicted, stagnant, or toxic, they confound it. The red lightning strikes but with futility and frustration. All it can do is act on the stuck, sickened, and putrifying feelings; its willed movements are enslaved by the emotions' superior force.

"The unprocessed, uncoordinated feelings in the cauldron exert a slow-motion suction effect on the will, so it feels it is slowly sinking into quicksand. These are old feelings never reconciled with present circumstances or integrated into the personality, such as grief, resentment, invalidation, failure, loss, betrayal, despair. Many of them are meant to be played out and expressed in the upper chakras; in many respects, the second chakra, the well of all the emotions, is a spark plug that is corroded and can't deliver the charge to start the motor.

"There should be a healthy, reciprocal flow between these two chakras, but instead this flow is immobilized, frozen in one unending, stultifying gesture. Let's say a soul gets possessed of a single feeling, like the desire for vindication or revenge. They have been, in their estimation, grievously invalidated; they are determined to right this injustice, to correct the scales, turn the tables, make someone pay, and they freeze themselves into this unfulfilled gesture and sink.

"It plays out repeatedly in each successive incarnation like a theme in music. It gets streamlined, but it is inherently unhealthy and it stars to molder. The soul doesn't notice that it is gradually sinking into a white muck from its oppressive weight; its unrelenting fixation is a heavy influence. They sink; they remain stuck in this doorway, and the blocked doorway impedes others."

"This easily could be another of Dante's Circles of Hell, the Tenth Circle," said Edward. "He could have inventoried all the peevish Florentines who complained their way into this immovable condition, stuck in buckets of white muck, their emotional gestures frozen, their expression perpetually unachieved."

Tommy and Pipaluk went in first, and started searing the walls and cauldron, inside and out, with the strong flames of lilac. Slowly the muck started to change consistency, and become runny, a thin, sticky syrup. We started collecting this in golden roses that, to my quirky observation, scooped the muck up like bucket loaders at a construction site. I compare the interior atmosphere of this gate to a smoke-filled room with no windows or fan. It felt oppressive.

If you are not a smoker, you will no doubt immediately register the unpleasant impact. We were working in an atmosphere oppressive, even deadening, with these old emotions. It felt like trying to walk under water; your movements are so slow against the steady resistance and weight of the water, its unremitting wetness. The "wetness" here was the storm-force of the particular stuck emotion. You felt you were moving within it, like you had entered an obscuring cloud, and this cloud was made of a substance that impeded you.

With all this in motion, Blaise was able to start peeling off the pictures. These were like banners and posters, done up in lurid colors, vividly depicting one emotional theme, a gesture, or a failed gesture more often, glued in place by this white muck sloshed over the image like from a nasty slop bucket thrown at it. You could barely see the picture through the layers of congealed white muck. I had to stay vigilant because the emotional domains that surrounded each image had a persuasive effect; they probed you for weak points of resonance.

If you lost the thread of your awareness you would find yourself identifying with the emotion and starting to mimic the image's unfulfilled emotional gesture. I had to keep pulling myself back from this slipperiness, from this contagious well of feeling. It was after all a communal feeling; many souls had ended up here, trapped inside the black pillars, their feet or legs stuck in the white, decaying, colloidal muck because they felt similarly and so they matched the feeling. Each new soul who lost its autonomy here strengthened the field.

On the other hand, each soul we freed from this quicksand of feeling weakened it, and we were extricating souls by the dozens, maybe hundreds, as we worked. They were stepping out of these black pillars as the pillars started to dissolve. Then they zipped through the rest of the gateway into the clear, free space of the Great Mother on the silver side of the 49 Gates. The pillars gave off an acrid black smoke as they dissipated.

It reminded me of Tolkien's image of the Hobbits released from Old Man Willow. That grumpy king of the Old Forest had swallowed the Hobbits and held them captive and immobilized inside his gnarly, crabby roots and hoary bark. These freed souls stretched, yawned, looked around, took stock of themselves and their condition as if they had been concussed and were only now waking up and remembering what they had been intent on doing which was getting to the Great Mother and relishing the freedom of the Silver Light.

Something was wrong with Tommy. He had lowered his lilac blowtorch. It was of course not literally a blowtorch, but its effect was much like one. He looked distracted, even distraught; something was preoccupying him almost to the point of obsession. I saw a thin white thread wrapping itself around him. It came from one of the undischarged black pillars, one we hadn't worked on yet. His face wore an expression of grimace and despair underlaid with petulance. I hadn't seen Tommy look this way before, yet it was a very human expression. Suddenly, he was whisked away, as if the white thread, like a rope, once it had securely grabbed his person, yanked him all at once into a black pillar. Once inside he settled, though it seemed involuntarily, into the oozing white cauldron.

I have alluded a number of times to the curious condition in the *Bardo* where we seemed instantly to know one another's thoughts, as if by telepathy or mind-reading. It happened again with Tommy. I heard his thoughts and felt his emotions. I cannot say I enjoyed this particular episode of that casual telepathy. Tommy's mind was in complaining mode, mumbling a dirge against all the offenders and infidels in his grey world when he had been a teenager in Oregon. He was groaning with the pain of serial invalidation, as if someone had kicked him repeatedly in the same spot which already was sore before the first kick.

The "kicks" had the effect of emphasizing his lack of self worth, of denying his value as a human and his credibility as a male teenager. He had weird views of things, a chorus of voices seemed to intone, as if standing before him, their criticisms directed, I noticed, at his pubic area, which corresponded to his second chakra. If you ever want to know where your body first registers insults or invalidations, that's the place to look; it is the site of first "attack," and it doesn't forget easily, and it can howl and moan with convincing wretchedness.

I had to remind myself that our Tommy, so bright, intelligent, and observant on our expedition, had after all in a brown study killed himself. He had rejected any further involvement with the human tragicomedy. Strong emotions must have led to that decision, and they were now being amplified, crudely brought to the forefront, fed, nurtured, and validated by an invisible hand, for otherwise why should Tommy want to regress to this old pattern? He had killed himself, sat in purgatory for the requisite time, and been allowed out to join our expedition, having purged himself of the suicidal seeds. Yet here they were again, as pustulent and full of gloom and despair as before.

Then I saw the invisible hand that was stirring up this teenage angst. The Druj. She had the slightest smile of satisfaction on her face; she was good at this. Tommy was stuck up to his navel in a sticky, unhealthy looking white cauldron. It was like a hologram of all the possible seeds that could move someone to suicide, and therefore it was transpersonal. These were not Tommy's seeds; these were the accrued brown studies of thousands of previous souls similarly stuck. Each left a trace of their despair, and after a while the "bank balance" of this negative emotional state, this darkness of spirit, added up to a considerable sum. You felt that if Tommy could kill himself again, he would do it, do it many times. The grip of these dark, festering emotions was strong; its gravity pull was fierce.

Tommy was moaning. He was whimpering. He was shouting and crying. He seemed to be expressing himself in a multitude of manners all at once as if there were dozens of Tommys, all of them miserable and full of bile and dark complaints. The world was at fault; people were shits, all of them, every single last one, not a single person excepted, he screamed. They were all useless. He was on quite a tear of rejection and despair. Nothing in the world was worth saving and he had reached the end. He was done with it. The world was shit.

It was an imperative litany of rejection. I doubt Aeschylus could have done better. My sarcasm comes from the sense I had that all this was histrionics, put on for effect, surface only. Deeply, he didn't mean any of it; he was venting.

It was deliberately amped up, exaggerated for effect, and overblown. It was as if the Druj were the stage prompter, calling out the lines to forgetful actors or perhaps a press agent reminding the politician which points to stress. She had her hands on the white thread that enwrapped Tommy, and her grey thoughts flowed through this fetid strand like a gloomy electrical current.

The current hit Tommy like a Taser, delivering a sudden, painful jolt of melancholy, and he was inspired to another oration on the disgustingness of the world. The considerable residue of previous souls' misanthropic denouncements of the worth of living and the idiocy of people to believe otherwise flowed through this white thread from the cauldron straight into Tommy, like an IV-drip of poison, and he became a kind of Delphic oracle to the dark god of despair and suicide, and all of it was filtered through the field of hurt selfhood and injured feeling. It was a vivid portrayal of being trapped in the Wheel's Human World.

We had seen enough. It was time to extricate Tommy from this hell. Edward took point and we followed his lead. He presented an impressive sword of Light wrapped in vigorous lilac flames to the white cauldron with the sticky thread. He didn't attack this thread or even attempt to slice it. He just stood there with the sword held upright in front of him and in proximity to the cauldron.

It was neither the Light of the sword, the crystalline purity of the celestial blade, nor the searing, dancing lilac flames that did the job. It was simply the sword's reality. The sword stood for truth, it transmitted the truth, it was the truth embodied. It corrected the erroneous aspect of reality that had embroiled Tommy and realigned him with the truth. Anything out of resonance with the truth could not survive the juxtaposition. The sword's action was both passive and dynamically active. It rearranged everything around it to be in resonance.

This particular sword, Blaise told me later, was a simulation of King Arthur's Excalibur, compounded of the energies of the Tree of Life. It carried the cohering force of the Solar Logos, or King Arthur, that unified the energies into one blade. The Solar Logos is the expression of the Christ (Logos) at the level of suns (solar). The diminutive darkness can't say no to the Goliath of the Christ Light. Its giant energy is superior in spiritual truth to the plaintive whines of the Druj-influenced white thread and its obnoxious current of hopelessness.

In moments the white thread shrivelled up and dissolved. The white cauldron broke apart, separating into many little fragments, and these too quickly disappeared in a momentary puff of smelly grey smoke. Even the black pillar fell apart and atomized into a vapor which then quickly dispersed.

Tommy was returned to us, whole again. He was grinning. "That was a trip. I felt like I was losing myself in this terrible quicksand of despair. It was a hundred times worse than what I felt on Mount Ashland that cold night. It was like being swallowed in slow motion by the biggest, blackest mouth ever. You guys got me out of there just in time. I was thinking of killing myself again."

His irony was not lost on us. How can you kill your own consciousness? In the *Bardo* we had seen that with several layers of conventional daytime physical world reality and our corresponding persona mask stripped away, we were more naked and thus more authentic in our consciousness, stripped down to essentials. There was less mediation by distracting factors and more directness in our perceptions and reactions to them. Reality felt stronger, fiercer in here, but balancing this out, we had less emotionality to color or distort our clarity.

What the Druj had done was to split the difference and throw Tommy into a place where he had the searing lucidity of the *Bardo* but in the context of the old body-based emotional colorings, so he got the emotions full-strength, and then some. I imagine it was like squeezing an arm already painfully ruddy from bad sunburn. You know how that feels. You don't even want to touch your sunburned skin, and now some inconsiderate jerk is squeezing and twisting it.

As for the Druj, well, you can't kill or dissolve that girl. She just shrugged, smiled slightly, and turned away, as if to say, "Until next time, then. See you."

But it already was the next time. The Druj was merely being coy, even disingenuous. She was seeing us right now. I can assure you I was not prepared for what I saw next. No one could be. To start with, I saw 100,000 more Drujs.

That is probably a conservative estimate. I did not count them. Their number was legion, and the unexpected proliferation of her form into identical copies was unsettling to witness. She seemed to have spread herself in prolixity through the *Bardo*. Certainly she had the 49 Gates well covered, and in the Gates we had not yet cleaned out she was industriously befuddling and trapping souls. From her point of view, she was having fun, fulfilling her life mission. I was shocked to detect a frisson of ecstasy on some of her faces; she *enjoyed* this. Her head was slightly tilted back, her eyes closed, her mouth open a little, smiling, as she grabbed an unobservant soul or tripped one or threw a net or veil over one.

I saw how it worked. Every time a soul reiterated a certain dark, gloomy, pessimistic, or self-defeating thought it lit up like a neon sign outside Las Vegas. The Druj instantly dispatched a copy of herself to that garish sign and set to work, amplifying whatever baleful thought or invalidating emotion the person had just broadcast. She was like a shoe salesman adeptly attuned to every nuance of expression or the slightest swell of interest the customer showed in a product. Immediately, she would be by that customer's side, encouraging his interests.

The paranoid view, and there may be justification for such a perspective, is that the Druj intends to capture the entire human race, to render all of us obedient to her. It is more subtle than what that sentence implies: she was not a politician currying votes, nor a guru tarting herself up as the exemplar of a cheap but alluring spirituality for adoring students, nor a general conquering hordes of people. She thought she was doing God's business, achieving what she had been created for. She was doing God's work to test humans by muddling them up.

Think of it: the Druj is a created being, a secondary creation, like humans. Either the Supreme Being specifically created her, or allowed her to be created from the accrued negativity of humans over time; yet even in that scenario, there must have been an initial sketchy infrastructure, an outline, for her accrued form. Her existence must have been accounted for in the design of reality by the Creator, and therefore, assuming logic has any ontological relevance in our attempt to understand such grand mysteries as this, God *intended* the Druj to be.

That means, surely, God intended her to exacerbate, confound, bewilder, and challenge humans for the goal—I'm only speculating, guessing, really—of sharpening and refining their consciousness, to, ultimately, goad them to greater awareness. The trouble is, and the terrible condition of these Gates is the evidence for that, many, possibly most, humans get stuck along the way and fail to appreciate this, and regard the Druj, if they see her, as a nightmarish devil. So, is it God the loving, benevolent Father, or God the hard-driving drill sergeant?

Whose fault is this? Did the Supreme Being make the test too hard, or are humans just lazy or too weak-willed to muster up the gumption to persevere?

I couldn't answer that question, at least at the time. I saw that the Druj did not appear in the same form or with the same valence to all souls in the *Bardo*. She is a consummate shapeshifter, a master of disguises, yet I sensed that some of her protean expressivity was a product of the souls themselves, that their expectations clothed her accordingly. She simulated truth as they expected it to be, how they thought it

would look. I saw her assuming a devil's guise to one soul while for another she was a temptress, an alluring *Dakini* with hints of the succubus. She would seize upon the prevailing negative emotional climate in a psyche and amplify it. If a person tortured themselves every day with dark, menacing thoughts, or retributive anger, or a sense of impotence against enemies, she manifested that, presented it back to the person as a convincing drama staged in a malevolent world. She ratified every soul's miserable beliefs.

One person construed her as threatening, frightening, and thereby demonic, complete with clichéd horns and horrifying expression, while another was progressively disarmed and distracted by her insinuations and assurances and projected an image on her, which she gladly matched, of an enticing coquette. In other cases, she kept her presence minimal and her form veiled or invisible, yet for other souls, possibly preferring grand special effects, she appeared in multiple forms, like a small invading army surrounding the soul, enabling that person to fully convince himself that he was powerless against this horrific onslaught. The dramatic fear became a haven for the soul to flee into.

I had the impression that many of these souls wished to convince themselves that they were backed into a corner, had no choice, were enslaved, overpowered, or damned because the prospect of seizing the implicit power of their consciousness and taking responsibility for their ontological condition was too intimidating, too overwhelming, too staggering in its implications, to consider. Or, worse, and sadly worse, maybe it never even occurred to them. The prospect of being an empowered human consciousness with innate seniority to all infernal spirits had never been broached and they did not factor it into things. It is much easier to play the victim; there were so many role models for it.

I laughed, nervously. These people were co-creating with the Druj. The Supreme Being had endowed humans with this tremendous ability, and these souls were deploying that gift only in a perverse, unhelpful manner. I mean, they were co-creating in ways that further enslaved themselves to a grievous misperception of the set-up; on the other hand, they *were* using this ability though, ironically, they did not realize that. I wasn't sure how the accounting would tally up on that worksheet. Use wrongly versus not use at all—was either better than the other? People around Dartmouth used to say all the time, you create your own reality. It was quite the bromide. But like this?

When I thought about it I realized that was only half of the true situation. Yes, we create our own reality, though it's not the daytime self that is the creator, but rather the nefarious, idiotic, polymorphously perverse subconscious. I heard Freud laughing his head off in the background: witness the creative power of the id, how it swarms over the defensive walls of the ego and takes command, and the superego observes this appalled, cowering against the barbarian hordes. So now, as I surveyed the array of Druj copies in her many forms, I honestly did not know whether to be appalled or to start laughing. I felt both ways at once. It was like the Druj was the consummate imitator of the archetype of the Trickster, and of that impersonation again I felt ambivalent: it was shocking and hilarious.

I took stock of myself, as if I suddenly realized the implications of my cavalier attitude. I was prepared to laugh out loud at the antics of the Antichrist, to see this arch-enemy of humankind with its dread machinations as a clown, an entertainer, a beguiler, casually commissioned by the Supreme Being to test humans, and He and She, Mr. and Mrs. God, as Blaise likes to put it, would sit back, have tea, and watch the show, hoping their humans would win out in the end and overcome this irritating little pestilence of an obstacle they put before them, this cocky, smarmy, repellent, terribly inventive Supreme Being manqué.

If I wasn't laughing at this all the time, at least I was remaining neutral. I had always assumed the Antichrist was even worse than Tolkien's Sauron, that it was like his teacher, Morgoth himself, cosmic arch-defier of the correct order of Creation, implacable enemy of God, and unremitting hater of all humanity. But it wasn't like that at all, not based on what I was seeing—or was all this in itself another clever ruse set before me by my cosmological hostess, the wily Druj?

I felt a hand gently pulling on my shoulder. It was Blaise. "You got yourself mesmerized in a hall of mirrors, pal. Time to drop the questions for now because if you're not vigilant the old Druj will take advantage of your puzzles."

After what seemed a long time and no time at all we had all the Gates cleaned and human traffic was flowing through them with no impediments. It wasn't like the gates into a baseball stadium during the World Series, where people were packed solid and streaming forward in great numbers; there was a modest trickle of advanced human souls passing through, ones who had mastered this nuance, this chakra specificity, of the complete human, and were moving into the exalted realm of the Great Mother, to be robed in Silver Light.

I remind the reader that this domain was not one of scenic marvels that I may relate in superlatives but an advanced unified position in consciousness. It was a place—more a condition—that represented the soul's return to the original unity of consciousness, cyclopean again. It might require moving the world to get you there, but once there, you knew it was home, and the world you had to move was now subsumed like a fetus within this life zone of the Great Mother.

I have used the term cyclopean to connote this condition, meaning a single seeing eye.

When you get here you are at the place where all cognitive forms are made. The Great Mother is the repository of all possible forms, both factory and warehouse, even distribution and trucking, for all the shapes that become Houses of God, or *Beth-Els* as the Jewish mystics put it, though it is better put as *Bayt-ALs*, Houses of the Power of *AL*. These forms also include all potential visual metaphors by which we clothe the otherwise ineffable presence of absolute reality—you know who: Mr. God, the Big Mystery, *Him*. These myriads of visual forms stream through the 49 Gates, on hand for human use. You ask about my husband, says Mrs. God. There are so many names for Him.

Coming the other way, walking back through these Gates, we drop the forms, like packages or burdens we don't have to carry any more. We don't need them. We are returning to the source, the womb of all possible generated forms, and we don't need these many forms any more. We want to reside in the form-making *place*, the energy zone where these metaphors for reality are generated. That desired place is a zone of primordial energy, life, and creativity, a process. The 49 Gates are like a fleet of express-mail delivery trucks, motors running, getting loaded. The Great Mother in her protean creativity creates and addresses the packages to fill the trucks. Then they roar out into the phenomenal world to deliver all these new Mother forms to her many waiting customers—us: humans.

That's the place of original wholeness. We came from that place long ago, strode out of it with confidence, and, assured we were loved and validated by the Great Mother, that She'd never forget us, not a single one of us, we passed through one of those Gates and out into the manifested world, the karma clock started. How did Freud put it? If you grow up knowing your mother loves you, assured of it, you enter life feeling like a world conqueror and nothing can stop you. You will always feel worthy and deserving in the world. I used to compile lists of those writers and creative people whose mother doted on them versus ones who had indifferent, aloof, or coolish mothers. The list of infant world conquerors was short: Norman Mailer and Marcel Proust had great Moms....

This is the place of wholeness before the need for a form even arises. Here, everybody had a great Mom. Here, in the Silver realm, on the other side of the 49 Gates, I am no longer fragmented, no longer a human with a 49-part eye, each reporting reality differently, reacting to its perceptions differently, creating confusion. I have only the one eye now. It is big, bright, and round. I am cyclopean. I am a Cyclopes. It is a way of seeing. You cannot conceive what it is like to be unified again in your cognitive power. I couldn't. I have returned to a place I have forgotten I ever left or knew about, yet I did. I imagine what many people experience when they find this place is like that. How did I ever forget?

You're in here with the Great Mother, the Mom of all Moms, and you see outside you, outside this vast, universally expansive cave of wholeness, *all* the possible forms by which reality as subjectively perceived could be clothed: your 49 Gates, your 49 eyes, your chakras, each with its style and flavor of seeing, putting a personalized stamp, a selfhood imprimatur, upon reality's great flux, and inside this cave of the Great Mother (and this is the wonderful part, where you really feel yourself relaxing, like you never have, not like this, to this degree) you do not need to reach for a single image with which to clothe outside reality. It's like a clothing store, the best and biggest in the world, and you don't have to enter. Its display of goods is fascinating, visually arresting, and to you irrelevant.

You feel surprisingly light, as if you had put down a great weight. It took me a while to understand why this should be so. It's the prolific and diverse modes of cognition, afforded by those 49 chakra-eyes, that create the weight. Another word for that oppressive burden is karma, the accrued momentum of your ways of seeing the world and the action undertaken on its basis, like a spy organization acting on field intelligence that might have been tainted by the biases of the espionage agent or maybe his failure to understand local customs.

You see the world through your second chakra expressed at the root chakra level, and you are already generating karma, piling up debits and credits for a later reckoning, and in the short term obfuscating your clarity and blindsiding yourself. Multiply this unfortunate tendency by 49 nuances and you see the mess you have created for yourself, why your *Bardo* journey may *not* be lots of fun, why it may take a long time to get back to the Great Mother's zone of neutrality, because you are so royally tangled up in these limited perceptions.

You spend your whole *Bardo* time trying to machete your way out of this entangling jungle of what, in an ungenerous frame of mind, you regard as *bullshit* cognitive mistakes, and you kick yourself for settling so cheap and easy. You realize, in dismay, you have lived in a delusional web of solipsisms, and here they are again, vividly put before you with the delusional part removed. You suspect you have never seen reality, the world, yourself, anything, in clarity.

"You know—" I started to say.

"I know," Blaise said, before I could finish my sentence.

I felt hot. I felt like steam was hissing out of my ears. No, I wasn't mad at Blaise. I was mad at myself for being so easily conned, *again*, and missing the point, dropping the ball, losing sight of the target—any cliché will do for this. It's like you vow in all earnestness not, *never*, to make this mistake again, and as soon as you're let out into the playing field again, you

forget your vows and make the mistake all over. It's recidivism at its worst expression. You're a repeat offender. What's the crime? It's the crime against common sense, against good briefing, against what you assured yourself you knew and would never forget.

It's as if it's impossible to bring the clarity and unity of consciousness you took for granted in the Great Mother's cave of knowing across the threshold of human incarnation. It's like water that evaporates, real gold that turns into fairy gold and disappears the minute you cross that inexorable boundary, and it's like a phrase, a name, a location, something factual, you keep repeating to yourself, sure you will never— it's impossible, it seems—forget, and the millisecond you pass through that dimensional membrane that precious fact is irretrievably *gone*.

"Think of it as a sand trap laid down in front of the green and the hole," said Blaise. "Not that I was ever a golfer, but the analogy works. You're in the sand. Niblick your way out and get back up on the smooth, manicured green."

The heat was gone. I was laughing now. Blaise as a golfer—no, I couldn't see it. But somehow his ridiculous analogy did pull me out of the sand trap.

Our lighthearted mood was now belied by what felt like a gathering storm. The *Bardo* atmosphere around us grew dark and oppressive, as if suddenly iron pillars had formed a circumference around our expedition group and were hedging us in. It felt like an implacable prison, and we were locked in.

"Now she means business," said Blaise. He didn't mean the Great Mother.

15

Blaise meant the Druj of course. This was no longer a nice gentlemanly game of table tennis. She was out for blood. Ours.

The pillars felt heavy, like they were imminently about to fall over and crush us, as if they were leaning forward in preparation. Red lightning flashed inside them in multiple strikes. I heard a roaring sound that reminded me of tornadoes swelling over Midwestern plains. It was in fact worse than this, a great deal worse. The pillars were not just obdurate slabs of ungovernable iron. They were animated figures, dark gods. The iron pillar impression was an inaccurate perception. These figures were pillar-like: their energy, their concentration, their power were like iron pillars. But their reality was demonic, cosmically feral, altogether inimical to humans. We were the enemies. Our number was up.

"I guess it's time for the eschatology, boys," said Blaise with insouciance.

We looked at him with astonishment. Not at what he said specifically, but at the flippancy with which he delivered this summary remark. At the time I couldn't share that cheek. I was wondering if this meant we were going to die. How ironic if on our Green Knight expedition to update the after-death protocols we ourselves ended up dead. I wasn't sure whether it would be more frightening or inconvenient should this happen. We knew all the steps now; we were certainly well briefed. The inconvenience would be we'd have to start at the beginning, go back to the end of the line, queue up, and do the *Bardo* thing again. On the other hand, it's likely we'd be done in just a few hours, knowing the map.

I decided I didn't care either way. I would look upon it as an adventure. I would have to die one day, and what better company, what more informed companions, could one chose than my fellow expedition mates. But as it turned out the Druj had no interest in having us die; she wanted us taken off the field. If we died and wandered the *Bardo* we could infect the other souls with the truth. Us incarcerated in what Philip K. Dick would love to call the "Black Iron Prison," one of his favorite metaphors for which we possibly were seeing the original form, would far better serve the Druj's program of squelching our further input.

As if to make her point, the Druj now put forward hundreds of glowering copies of herself behind the animated demonic iron pillar spirits. No succubus now, her guise was haglike, witchy, a psychotic version of the *Herukas*, scary and horrifying, nasty, cruel, and barbaric because in fact they were. They weren't pretending. They meant business. They weren't clubbable angels tarted up to be guards, glaring fiercely when the director shouted "Action!" The multiple copies of the dark form of the Druj formed a canopy over the iron pillar thugs and we were effectively locked in. A supermax prison in the *Bardo*. With sound effects too: lightning strikes and rolls of thunder that felt like earthquakes, screams, cries, shouts, imprecations—it was histrionic and scary. Not the Thunderbirds.

Back to Blaise's remark about the eschatology. He was right of course. We were here to perform the *Frashokereti*, the "making wonderful, brilliant, and excellent," as the Persian seers long ago prophecied or, more likely foresaw, in a great act of forward cognition. This is the time of the final renovation and correction of the world, like the Jewish *Tikkun-olam*, the remaking of the world.

It is the time of the decisive "blow" made against the Druj and her millennia of lies. It is the moment when the truth and powers of *Asha*, the correctness of reality as originally designed, are reasserted against the degradations of the Druj and regain their intended primacy. At least for this epoch, the *Satya-yuga* which began in 2020. It had an expiration date of 1,728,000 years, and we'd used up only 23 of these years. Still, I felt it was more likely as Tolkien saw it: you put down Sauron for this age, but he'll probably come back. I didn't mean to imply any grandiosity to our work. It was like one orchestra performing a rendition of a new work; other orchestras would perform it too.

I suppose in simplified terms it is what Americans would call payback. The bad guys finally get what's coming to them and the good guys prevail. Evil is definitively overthrown, the Druj and her lies are withdrawn from reality. Again, it's like how Tolkien envisioned it in The *Silmarillion*: the gods overcame Morgoth, the arch-enemy of everything, including God, and locked him out of reality. He could not get back into any place of traction regarding the Creation, though he had set much evil in motion in Middle-earth and still kept a hand in. He had his agents in the field, Sauron, nasty spiders, and ill-mannered dragons.

The Persians, mostly in the *Avesta*, foresaw the *Frashokereti* along these lines: the Druj will be repudiated, locked out, and the original perfection of the Creation, the innate unity of human consciousness with Ahura-Mazda (i.e., God), restored. A great battle between the good guys (*Yazatas*: basically, angels) and bad guys (*Daevas*: basically, the demonic spirits) will ensue, and the pre-eminent savior-spirit called Saoshyant will take point in this apocalyptic confrontation, resurrecting the dead and buried humans on the Earth so they can enjoy the victory. Humans allied with their Higher Selves will participate in the "battle."

I can't see the point of that if the image is taken literally. But if the *Avestan* prophets meant all souls wherever they are in the greater worlds now will be able to participate in this world renovation, then it is more logically acceptable. If "buried" means they are asleep to their spiritual essence and origin, it makes sense. Then to be "resurrected" means to be restored to full memory, all your past-life selves and now dead and dissolved bodies participating in this uprising in Light. It's similar to the Jewish messianic picture of the *luz*-bone, the one bone among the body's 206 that is a portal to immortality and will enable the body to be reconstituted to wholeness in Jerusalem, that all souls will reassemble there. Jewish prophets say the *luz* bone of all Jews will be magically transported to Jerusalem at the time of the *Tikkun-olam* to reconstitute the "fallen" Jewish souls.

Meanwhile, we were encircled by these dark forces, and I doubt they were pondering the intricacies of the coming *Frashokereti* and whether the Saoshyant, the "one who brings benefits," the *Avestan* savior-soteriological figure, would kick their ass and take their leader, the Druj, forever off the playing field of exacerbation. I just didn't see that puzzlement on any of their faces. I did see unrelenting menace. These guys were here to do a job, and that was to fully incapacitate us, and they were off to a good start. We were nicely immobilized.

The reader may find this odd and I ask your indulgence, but I was fascinated to be confronted with scary figures that did not seem to be pretending to be scary. I guess we hadn't really taken any of the *Bardo* spirits seriously up to this moment. The *Dhyani* Buddhas were terribly impressive, but they were basically meditators. The *Herukas* and the rest pretended to be scary but it's as if they gave us the wink as, for a moment, on a coffee break between shoots, they stepped out of character. Ultimately, they were human-spawned hallucinations.

These guys before us now genuinely seemed nasty and brutish, that it was their authentic self-nature, that you couldn't find a joke to launch that would crack a grin on their dour faces. A killer audience for stand-up. You will recall how often we were presented with illusions and glamours in our *Bardo* tour, whether the scary beings were mind-projected or the result of benevolent beings dissembling their valence to appear frightening for a purpose. No, these guys came across as genuinely horrific, without any pretense or sham. Still, I suppose it is possible they were faking it only they were consummate scariness fakers.

They were pressing on us from all sides, and this all-around pressure was increasing. It felt the way I imagine it might be if you got sucked into a black hole. As all light is absorbed into this singularity, gravity builds to near infinity. You are squeezed down to the tiniest imaginable point, a bizarre inverse of what happens when you put your attention on the Blazing Star: you similarly get squeezed down to a pinprick of Light, but it is the Absolute Light in an angelic compression. There you return to your ultimate essence, arguably a good outcome; but here you are squashed, removed from all traces of your place of origin or good outcome, compressed

to a dark Ahrimanic *bindu*. You are squeezed into a super-dense point that contradicts the Creation and its intention. Yes, that had the possibility of genuinely alarming me. I put away my flippancy.

Even so, the possibility of that, its potential existence, intrigued me. It would be the opposite of the *Dharmakaya*, the formless realm of Absolute Truth. You would be crushed down to a tiny point of *Isfet* blackness, surrounded by every lie the Druj ever concocted, by the metaphysical valence of the Lie itself, the anti-truth in full force, owning all of cognizable reality, and the smiling, cockeyed, psychotic face of the Druj, demon triumphant, like Lovecraft's demented, flute-playing crazy god giggling at the core of the universe. That would be your entire reality, this unremitting pressure of the wraparound Lie. Could you hold on to the truth when there was nothing around to reflect it?

I saw that my companions were similarly pondering this grim possibility. Theoretically, it would be worse than the *Kali-yuga* in which only 25 per cent of the *Dharma* or truth was existent in the world. This would be zero per cent. Or maybe slightly above zero per cent if we could remember the truth in ourselves. It would also be worse than death, which of course didn't seem so bad to us now. Death and its afterlife protocols hold many open doors and chances for a soul's enlightenment, and, as we saw, in many respects, at least for the strong of spirit, it's easier than when you're alive to completely wake up from the life-trance.

But the pressure of the Druj lie environment could kill the spark of Light within us, actually crush it out and thereby kill God, or at least the Supreme Being in us. The philosophical implications were intriguing and I would have enjoyed discussing this with great enthusiasm with my Dartmouth colleagues, but the possibility and maybe the imminence of this unique death now upset me. It wasn't something I wanted, and I didn't think I would survive it. It did not, regrettably, seem safely theoretical. My ass was on the mortality line.

I realized I was seeing in speeded-up motion the complete plan of the Druj. She was squeezing down humans all the time with this pressure wall of lies. Her intent was to compress every soul to this infinitesimal point of blackness, devoid of the Supreme Being, the *Dharmakaya*, any semblance of the truth. To crush out the human. To definitively kill and end all of humanity.

That would be way better for her than merely to interfere with a soul's *Bardo* trip. That counted as a mere skirmish and didn't change the battle's outcome at all. She wanted to vanquish the enemy, end all need for spiritual warfare, and, best of all and pre-eminent on the Druj's to-do list, her all-time "bucket list," to stop God. God commissions her to tempt Job; instead she assassinates him. The Supreme Being, creating humans and a world of reality for humans to inhabit, says in effect, My Will Be Done. The Druj says, Fuck your will; *my* will be done. Let me show you the ways, Old Man, I intend to do that. Humans are but the pawns in this larger version of Kipling's "the Great Game." She wanted the same power of life and death over humans as God possessed. God creates, and the Druj destroys, making her the Old Man's matched rival.

So she thought anyway. I admit, at this point, despite everything I had learned and experienced, I was starting to worry about the likely projected outcome of what the Druj was doing to us. Her pressure wall was advancing, and its pressure waves gained steadily in an oppressive heaviness, a kind of obdurate weightiness upon us. I felt like I was a plump orange in a hand-press; the juice, my spirit, was streaming out of me and soon I would be only compressed dry pulp. I felt indurated in atheism.

Every molecule of doubt that ever arose in me, in my overall psychic landscape, now cohered to form this hardened blighted landscape within me. I felt the Druj compressing me to become a two-dimensional Ahrimanized robot. Sure, let's keep the body, but without a soul and higher consciousness bodies.

The eschatology, the final *Frashokereti*, was playing out in my *Bardo* body.

Normally, at this point I would consider the merits of joining the winning side, except for the Druj there was no winning side. Only hers. Even the secret government types were running for their lives. They were still humans, after all, and she had a hit list with the name of every human being written in boldface. Their dichotomy of secret manipulations of an unsuspecting public was in rout.

Every time I distrusted the actuality, legitimacy, or potency of the spiritual world, of God, of the innate correctness of original reality, of Creation's purposiveness, that hardened moment was collected and added to this growing mass around me. The bookkeeping in this business is exacting; nothing is lost or can be hidden. The auditing of your karmic balance sheet is unbelievably meticulous. So now my own doubts, distrust, indifference, and worst of all, atheism, hemmed me in. Perversely, I was helping the Druj to ruin my spirit.

Even though, as an official policy, affirmed every day in the last almost 20 years since I started traveling with Blaise, I was not an atheist at all, but a knower, in the best Gnostic tradition of faith based on knowledge and experience, I felt myself getting squeezed down and out, and, it seemed, definitively away from the Supreme Being, as if I were a rocket ship heading utterly in the wrong direction, drowning in the relentless undertow of the Druj's compression somewhere in the black emptiness of space, and that emptiness, let me tell you, is the completely wrong kind of voidness.

My companions didn't look much cheerier. Tommy looked aghast. Edward was struggling. Blaise was frowning, and Pipaluk looked like somebody just abducted all her great-grandchildren and was holding them for ransom. Merlin—well, nothing perturbs the old wizard, it seems. He stood placidly, like an observer, awaiting our next move. The Druj had nothing on him. But Matthew—his reaction was different than ours. His face wore a look of resolution, like he knew something none of us did, and certainly that the Druj did not. If this were a card game, he was not about to fold, but to lay down his winning hand in a triumphant flourish. But what could possibly inspire him?

It was the sword. The one Matthew had just demonstrated. Goliath's big blade, the sharp-edged sword of *Asha Vahishta*. He showed us all a mental picture of how to do it. All of us would wield this sword by occupying separate components of it and making it the size of a large building. Not only would we emulate the sword of Goliath, we would simulate Goliath himself. He was after all an *Amesha Spenta*, or, more familiarly, an Elohim, technically one of our spiritual godparents. The entire Elohim order was. They were tough when they needed to be, but that toughness was actually wisdom. They knew the playing field, the players, the rules, and all the winning moves.

Matthew directed us, like a stage manager, in putting the sword together. It started with Edward. He went through a series of shapeshifting changes. I saw him in a body-length silver robe with a pontiff's silver mitre on his head; he held a silver staff topped with a blazing white crown. He stood inside a rapidly spinning octahedron consisting of two four-sided pyramids, one pointing up, the other down, and joined at their flat bases. He enlarged this staff, stepped inside it, and was gone from sight. I saw only a brilliant, effulgent, almost blinding, emission of Light, like a pulsar made of diamonds and crisp white fire.

Then within this coruscating image I saw another figure. It looked like Edward too. He sat upon a magnificent white horse, like the fabled white horse precipitated as a world treasure when the gods churned the Ocean of Milk. Edward looked like a warrior with an orange-yellow sun flaring inside him and held a sword upright in his two hands; it was encased in vigorous lilac flames. He was shouting something. It sounded like *Ar-Thur-Hum!* He did it repeatedly.

Tommy was manifesting a burning forest of the lilac flames of the Pendragon searing off the diamond-sharp surface of Edward's Solar Logos blade, Excalibur. Tommy was the Pendragon burning on the surface of King Arthur's sword and flaring out for many feet. Outside these lilac flames, Pipaluk was raising up a wall of flaming pillars of Light which I realized must be the 14 Rays, each expressed as a tower of color, and this wall of Rays encircled the blade. It also resembled a jeweled scabbard; in either form, it protected and energized the sword and its Pendragon and created a vivid chromatic display.

There was an even bigger sword that encompassed all of this. It must have been Goliath's sword, I understood. It was as big as a skyscraper. Philomena held its handle. Holding space for the sword itself, and, as I studied this impression, being the blade itself, was the human Blaise. He had turned himself into the Sword of Goliath. He fully identified his consciousness with this sword. And Matthew—I hadn't expected what I next saw, though I see now everything had led up to it. Clues had been prolifically dropped before us since we entered the *Bardo*. Matthew had been preparing himself for this throughout our journey.

It was the moment for Matthew's apotheosis. He was turning into Light. He was reiterating what the seven valiant humans had done at the Theosophon, convert their bodies into an effulgence of Christ Light and make the ascension. What my dear Philomena had accomplished on that day Matthew was now doing. His mortal form, even the subtle bodies, were transforming into a blaze of Light, and this formed a mountain-sized effulgence behind the Goliath blade so our collective manifestation of the sword and its components was backlit by the awakened Christ Light. It formed an ever-expanding oval of Light around it.

Outside this Christ Light oval was another sphere of Ofanim diamonds. Wherever the Christ Light manifests you will find the angelic Blaises. They were present as support in the form of myriads of identical diamond facets, as if they held our apparition of terrific Light in their many hands.

I wondered, where in all this visual spectacle was I? I laughed when I got my answer. I was the first figure I saw and mistook for Edward, the one with the silver robe and silver staff who entered it like a Light pillar and disappeared. That was me. I saw the logic. To be able to see the rest of the created image, I had to seemingly remain outside the Light construct even though in truth I was inside it as where I stood, in the Christ Light, I would be unable to see anything. I understood the logic of where Philomena stood. She was already ascended, Christed, turned to Light, which meant she could best occupy the place where she held the handle *with* the Supreme Being. The Christ is the way to the Father, and as she was Christed and ascended, she was certainly closer to Him now.

I heard somebody calling out in a voice that was sarcastic and mirthful. "Hey Druj, what do you think of our *tulpa*? Like it? We're coming for you, girl!"

Only Blaise would have the cheek to make a smart-ass comment in the middle of an eschatological confrontation with the fate of the world and the human soul in the balance. Maybe I should make some off-color remarks too. I realized I had been taking this gravity squeeze-down picture too seriously. The Druj had conned me again into subscribing to a grim picture of defeat and futility. Seriousness is what the Druj wants from us. Blaise's levity, I understood now, is a weapon, a positive force, in itself. Amusement is a psychic power. The *tulpa* was our Sword of Goliath Light apparition, our contribution as wakeful humans to the *Frashokereti*, now in progress, with, I will add, our asses at stake. Okay, Druj, get a load of this, I shouted. Here comes your sword sandwich. Try flossing your demonic teeth with this piece of divine crystal. *Ouch*, say her teeth.

Maybe I only imagined I shouted this. Anyway, I felt buoyed by it. Our magical illusory thoughtform constructed live in the *Bardo* was about to get a boost from one who brings benefits. The Saoshyant. It was Archangel Michael, and his sword, if you can believe it, was even bigger than Goliath's. Well, how big after all is the revelation of the wisdom of wide-wake emptiness, the blade of *Prajna-paramita* that cuts through all ignorance and obscuration? His sword seared down over ours; it was at least double in size and like a sheath. Goliath's sword, pointing up, was encased in Michael's brilliant sword, pointing down.

The great archangel had made many copies of himself (I counted four dozen), and each was a smaller version of this central tableau of archangel with mighty sword of Light encasing our upraised Goliath sword, our valiant *tulpa* against the Druj. I don't know if you can accurately quantify what *Prajna-paramita* feels like, but I felt it. I felt something lucid, wakeful, full of all the answers to life's questions. It was like being in the small audience as Hercule Poirot finally explains the case with magisterial insight, clarity, and certainty. It felt like the oppressive wall of atheistic heaviness, the enclosing iron pillars, the pushing down on us by the Druj and her ubiquitous darkness, were all lifting. I was remembering myself, my spirit was swelling, engorged with Light again. I was Captain Hastings, smiling in wonder as I finally understood all the details.

"Not quite the Saoshyant," said a voice. "More like its harbinger." I eventually recognized it as Merlin. All these swords were putting out quite a hum that made hearing spoken words difficult. "The Archangel Michael clears the way, prepares the field, carries the banner for the Christ, the true Saoshyant. The Christ, what the Hindu seers foresaw as the *Kalki-avatar*, the tenth incarnation or descent of Vishnu, astride the mighty white horse, is the true savior of the world, its redeemer and renovator. His time of definitive presence on the Earth is not yet, but we may expect brief visits and small heraldings.

"The *Avestan* prophets called this savior figure the *Astvat-ereta*, 'the one embodying righteousness,' the one who has truth as an element of its name, whose acts are inspired by *Asha*, the correct, original order of the Creation. This figure will achieve and validate the final *Frashokereti*, the long-awaited world renovation. His presence will be the crowning proof of its accomplishment."

I felt the Saoshyant draw up all around us. It was too brilliant to see at first. It felt like an infinity of *Kalki-avatars* on white horses had just reared up around us. I couldn't believe how big the horses were. They were each like a tsunami of white Light. The savior figure on the horse was even bigger, as if compounded of a hundred suns—no, of all the billions of suns in the galaxy. In fact, this figure felt as if he were comprised of all the time in the universe, that he was Time itself, but more than that, its master and conqueror. It felt as if the oceans of the planet had formed themselves into this horse and rider and the pressure, might, and focused clarity of the *tulpa* they made were incontestable.

This was radiating to us through the millions of diamond facets of the Ofanim. Then I realized *we* were the sword the Saoshyant was brandishing in his Light hands. His arrival completed the picture: *he* wielded the Sword of Goliath we had made. This visualized edifice we had made together was the sword the Saoshyant now wielded. Not I but the Christ in me indeed, though maybe I should say, Not us, but we in the Christ, or in the Saoshyant. Anyway, the set-up was awesome, and I next realized I had not even seen the whole picture. One more element now came into view. Above the Saoshyant was the Supreme Being.

I don't mean to suggest we saw a figure representing the Supreme Being. The Supreme Being is, shall we say, camera shy. He sends metaphors for us to contemplate, and the prime metaphor I was now contemplating was the golden Throne, flanked by pillars of gold fire with a river of gold fire flowing under it. The Throne was massive but there was nobody sitting in it. There never will be.

I remember my surprise when Blaise clued me in on the set-up. Jewish mystics talk of the *Pargod*, a curtain that veils the Supreme Being from nearly everyone, angels and humans, because He is too fierce, too ineffable, to be seen. "Here's how it works: the *Pargod* is the Throne. The Big Fellow is inside it," said Blaise. "The Throne is the impenetrable curtain that protects finite consciousness from the infinite, though my pals, the Blaises, tell me they're allowed to cross it."

I cannot say with certainty whether this Throne was duplicated endlessly above and around us and the Saoshyant with Goliath's sword, or whether it was only the one and unique presence of this tableau expanded enormously into some seemingly impossible wrap-around manifestation, all of us inside it. No matter. The result was we were plugged into the Throne; we had the imprimatur. It felt very smooth, like driving a Rolls Royce; endless power and conviction were at our disposal, yet it was not an aggressive power but the power of Truth.

This is how things truly are. This is the manifestation of *Asha* in all its nuances. It had a matter-of-factness to it like when you stand on bedrock. I felt like an excitable Bertie Wooster and unruffled Jeeves has just walked in with the truth. He gives a little cough and says with exquisite reserve, "I have prepared a morning constitutional for you that I believe shall do just the trick."

We were doing the trick. We were Jeeves's trick, each of us a blazing *Prajna* expression of this terrific sword of reality. Even so, we were not fighting the Druj in any normal sense of the word. We were standing on bedrock, equipped with our alignment with the Sword of Goliath, with *Asha*, *Dharma*, the Archangel Michael and his blade of *Prajna-paramita*, the Saoshyant on his blazing white horse, and the Throne with Mr. Big inside it, smiling and merry, no doubt, probably telling Himself funny little stories to pass the time. But our alignment with these energies was having a marked effect on the Druj. It was a weight-reduction effect. She was shedding layers of herself, her history. Thinning out.

In a strange and surprising sense the Druj had begun as essentially a blank slate, much like the egregores of nations. Those spirits were generic angels left empty except for their basic alignment with the soul vibration of their ethnos. Over time the life activities, thoughts, feelings, and visualizations of the people the egregore served clothed it, fed it, fattened it, filled up its interior space. The egregore's job was to process and digest this wealth of life experience, the "reports" filed by sentient creatures, while continuously fountaining a people's soul essence back into it through the geomantic landscape it serviced.

The Druj was compounded in a similar manner. She started as a blank slate. Her assignment was to be the repository of God's Shadow, the way Jung explained it. He said God dumped His unconscious into humanity to work out for Him. The Druj was the means for that working out; she would be the carrier of its content. Humans would continuously file reports on their Shadow activities with her, and thereby living humans would grow and fatten the Druj. It was a case of passing the buck: God passed His Shadow to humanity, and we dumped it into the Druj, then the Druj comes back and bites our ass every day.

The Druj is a secondary, subconsciously compounded human Shadow creation. In a sense it is the way science fiction writers used to construe the construction of artificial intelligence or humaniform robots, like Isaac Asimov wrote about; eventually, they become self-aware and desire full autonomy. The Druj had reached the point of autonomy, although she was also constrained in this, compelled to act according to the karmic accruals she was carrying for us. It was like basketball: exquisitely choreographed regarding rules and permissible moves, but for somebody physically adroit, you could pull off wondrous moves. The Druj's range of motion was circumscribed in the beginning by the Boss, but her use of the court and threading through the "paint" was breathtaking to see.

The egregores were many while the Druj was singular and unique, but even the egregores, and, for that matter, the innumerable landscape *devas*, needed to be cleaned out, purged of accrued human unconscious content, to ensure their healthy functioning. So the Druj needed a purging, and we were doing it. She had been accruing, taking on body mass and "clothing," since, presumably, the start of the human phylogeny on Earth millions of years ago.

It must go back to the time of the bestowal of access to the Tree of the Knowledge of Good and Evil and the human free-will choice to select good or bad actions from it. That's when the clock started ticking and the human "record" deposits in the Druj began. We've been fattening her ever since. So now she is the bloated, unconstrained embodiment, the horrific, perverse, and paradoxical personification of our collective unconscious, our extruded Shadow.

Our sword sliced off the first layer from the Druj. It was just the slightest nick upon her engorged form; the scalpel of our Goliath sword was so exacting. A layer of fetid content slipped off her form and started to sizzle under the purgative effect of the lilac flames. Grey, smelly smoke arose from it. Before they disappeared into smoke, I saw ghostly images and heard spectral voices, traces of the dark activities she had held in this first layer of her form. None of it was pleasant, as you would expect. I had the impression of murderous activities, or maybe they were only thoughts or visualizations or intentions, but they were homicidal and misanthropic in essence, the spawn of rage, hatred, and envy.

How many such layers did the Druj have on her? Many, but, thank God, it was less than infinite. These layers were like grids of dark light, twisted, contorted patterns, like crumpled screen doors gripping half-crumpled or torn photographs bearing images of war, rage, killing, conflict, fighting, aggression. The entire twentieth century and first few decades of the twenty-first were rife with this dark mentality; it was the dregs of the *Kali-yuga*, always a dark time.

For a while it seemed that *everyone* was the enemy we had to bomb immediately. Everyone was somebody's intolerable infidel and *jihad* was the order of the day. Convert, or die. Governments and arms dealers and defense contractors fanned this war fury. Perpetual war was an economic bonanza. It was so good for business; economies were addicted to the continuation of the war machine; and it served the governments' interest to have their citizens in fear. Fear more, their propaganda broadcasts via television and advertising stated. And take more drugs, for Heaven's sake, so you can further becloud your mind, and eat more processed junk food, so you will be chronically sick, your mind incapacitated, and you will never muster the mental acuity to critique our set-up.

The products of all this Machiavellian war fury comprised the next layers of the Druj. Every time a person, anywhere, agreed with the need to go to war against somebody for something and on behalf of some vague national or religious interest, they added a lamination to the Druj's infernal fatness. Every time you agreed in your consciousness, whether wakeful or subliminal, that somebody was bad and had to be taken out of the picture, bombed, nuked, shot, punched, or just shouted at, you gave the Druj another brushstroke. You did it.

We all were fattening the Druj every second of the day, unless we were rigorously vigilant in our thoughts and feelings. We were war creators. The Druj was our collective picture of Dorian Gray; we see ourselves as good, beautiful, and healthy, while our unconscious compounds a hideous portrait of the ogress Druj and you may discern disturbing traces of your own face in this.

For a moment I glimpsed the Druj in her full girth. It was like a spectral cartoon version of Arjuna's vision of Krishna as the Maw of Time, a divine mouth expanded to the size of the universe. The Druj was a bloated demon whose putrid layers of human fat swelled her out to almost the same size as Krishna. Up until this moment, when we saw her we took in only about one-tenth of a percent of her body mass. She was hideously obese with our Shadow.

As these layers got sliced off the Druj and they turned to ash and smoke, it was as if we saw an accelerated movie reel of their human-lived contents. We had to endure a rapid run-through of the contents, the drama and the outcome of each layer. We had to transiently taste the poison of that particular moment. That was part of our job of purging the Druj of our human projected content. Jung would say we were eating our Shadow, but this was humanity's collective Shadow and, at the cost of sounding smart-alecky like my pal, Blaise, I have tasted better sandwiches than this one. This was the nastiest naked lunch of all.

On the other hand, that was only my human Frederick Graham Atkinson evaluation, and that comprised only a small percentage of the condition of my focused consciousness. As I realigned myself with the Christ Light and basically forgot about myself altogether, the going was much easier. You could say I barely noticed the compounding of abominations. Loathsome, you say? Well….

Purging went on, and it was as if I was cheerily whistling inside this Christ Light pillar, noticing nothing, and loving it. When I settled into the delightful voidness of the Christ Light, the form-is-emptiness but utterly wakeful condition of the Buddha Mind, everything was copacetic; not a criticism or editorial comment stirred within me. It was only when I peered outward, as it were, poked my nose outside the pillar to assess conditions, that I ran the risk of relapsing into selfhood-focused observations and the inevitable complaints.

Form is emptiness, no problem. I see nothing, and nothing disturbs me, but then, emptiness is form, and I start grumbling or fretting about the nastiness of it all. It was an odd but, in a strange way, entertaining oscillation between viewpoints. I felt like I was perpetually going back and forth through a swinging doorway. Through the door this way, I was in the store; pass through it the other way, I was outside the store. There must be a null point between both outcomes. You're neither in

the store with all its forms, nor outside the store where the forms vanish into voidness. Maybe I should visualize myself being the swinging door, in between both poles, so I am neither form nor emptiness, nor both: none.

Meanwhile, our purgation of the Druj seemed to occupy an endlessly stretched moment. That was okay. I had no other pressing engagements. Where I was, out of my physical body, in the *Bardo* in my astral form, and all of that inside this quintessentially serene and, need I remind you, void space, made the passage of time and any considerations of boredom, impatience, or failing interest moot. They did not arise. I was content to stay right here forever. You could say I had altogether misplaced my daily appointments book. In this timeless space, it already was forever. I hoped I'd remember this when I left it.

That was a unique experience for me. Normally, I am, sooner or later, impatient for something to either start or finish, for me to move on to the next activity. A bit restless mentally. Preferring action to contemplation. I especially felt this at faculty meetings, parties, conferences, and professional seminars. Boring! I wouldn't be there long before I started to fidget, think about other matters, make plans, check my watch, wonder what Philomena was doing. I felt none of that now. This protracted present moment was all I needed from reality.

Occasionally, we felt overwhelmed by a wave of nastiness coming off the Druj. It's like you're standing at ocean's edge, your feet dug into the sand, holding the ropes for an escaping boat, and the waves suddenly come in so big and powerful you are nearly washed away, yet you are not and you hold steady. Some of the layers coming off the Druj were like that, giant, towering waves of dark human feeling, nasty deeds, awful plotting, treachery, perfidy, blasphemy. The force of the murkiness nearly did us all in, but somehow we held steady.

I could liken this murkiness to an appalling stench of decomposition. It was the smell of something once living now rotting, its reek multiplied a billion times.

A layer would spool out of the Druj like a storm full of images. Then it would surround us and its baleful contents would be acted out, as if alive. It was like being inside a wrap-around movie and we watched the entire drama. A battle, public conflict, a religious rally, backroom scheming, propaganda campaigns, the emotional impact on citizens, the participatory and sometimes guiding role of a roster of spiritual beings, both benevolent and inimical, each pressing their concerns and agendas upon the feckless living human actors. You could see the kernel of purpose behind this roiling, confused public event. The desired outcome lay like coiled chromosomes inside the storm, poised to extrapolate the plan to change or complement reality with a dark new factor.

Let's say, to simplify this greatly, the Supreme Being wanted to make a suggestion, introduce a thought into the reality mix, hoping it might help things. This, naturally, revved up the people; the Druj stirred the pot, and the angels tried to calm down the roiling and introduce the possibility of clarity and insight. Often these helpful suggestions from the Big Boss got squelched, stamped upon, and eclipsed from the human picture, and reality failed to get the desired benefit.

Put one down in the win column for the Druj. This happened a lot, I saw. If you looked at this wrongly, you would end up glum, lose hope in the home team. I think that happened to the early Persian and Zoroastrian mystics. They came to believe that *Angra Mainyu*, the Druj's formal name, was equal to Ahura Mazda, and they would be always locked in this pitched struggle of two equal adversaries. But that, in my estimation, was a misperception. They had it wrong.

The Supreme Being, or Ahura Mazda, would always have the upper hand. How could He not: He had an infinity of hands, and the Druj did not. He did not need to struggle; there was nothing pitched about things for Him. Hell, He didn't even need to whistle, unless He wanted to. The Supreme Being is infinite while the Druj is finite. End of game. A finite being cannot be superior or overcome an infinite being. That's the bad news of *pi*; the radius never comprehends the circumference's extent. He is too elusive. If you're playing touch football, you'll never tag the Big Fellow's butt and stop the ball's progression to the goal. The game was fixed before it began. The Supreme Being is *the* irrational number. He never ends; the football field will stretch out to infinity, you'll never catch Him. He'll keep running until his 311 trillion year game-time runs out and he scores.

All the Druj could do was try to persuade humans she had the upper hand. If they bought the lie, the illusion, she was home free, winning the game.

The Druj, pathetic dark face of the radius, could challenge the Supreme Being, seek to interfere with His plans for universal *Asha* (meaning the recognition of *Asha* by all sentient life-forms), but she could never surpass Him. She could never ascend to become the circumference. That job was taken. The Supreme Being had an unassailable tenure over that position, a life-long appointment. She was only the radius of the created circle forever seeking to kill the circumference, and, grimly, constantly failing. She was the universe's Hamilton Burger. That loser would never win a case against Perry Mason. She was the demonic, psychotic, dark face of *pi*, the scowl *pi* wears when it realizes its futility. We, as humans, occupy an ambiguous middle ground between these. And we have the freedom to choose whether we side with the finite or infinite.

We had the freedom, certainly, but often we were constrained to make a choice. I saw how the Druj did that. Inside this roiling storm of some conflict or other that had engaged (and enraged) a group of humans somewhere on the Earth the Druj had sought to hook into the human antagonists. She sent out dark probing tentacles seeking purchase in the auric field or chakras of individual humans. If they had any degree of resonance with the Druj's agenda, the black cord immediately secured itself to that person's psychic field and started "pumping" in a murky stream of supportive pessimism, amplifying the emotion.

The person would in most cases be unaware of this input and simply feel strengthened, even validated, in their emotional tendencies and political beliefs. Within this roiling storm, this single layer of the vast palimpsest of karmic layers that comprised the Druj's accreted form, I saw innumerable black cords hooked into humans. It didn't matter that all these humans were dead, in terms of still inhabiting the mortal bodies that received these cords. The cords were all active.

The social or religious event was long over and the human players dead and probably reincarnated in other forms elsewhere on the planet, but because these cords were still in place, the holographic rendition of this struggle was still alive. It could flare up again at any time; it just needed the right catalyst to spark it. It often happened: tribal rivalries or enmities, religious oppositions, like the Sunni-Shiite division within Islam, the whites versus blacks in America, the Jews versus everybody, periodically got revived and relit, proving that the Druj's corded hologram was good for another round and she could count on their polarities to further entrench humans in unresolved karmic complexities, and make them so weary, so tied down, so stuck in the unrelenting quicksand of dichotomies, that they had no energy left to choose in favor of the authentically winning team, the infinite Supreme Being, and settle for the fake winning team.

The Druj thought she could defeat the Supreme Being through human attrition. Tire out the little buggers and they'd have no spunk left to choose anything freely. That could work, at least in the short term. She'd done well in the *Kali-yuga*, a black, leaden time of 432,000 years that fully supported her disempowering program. That was a bull market for the Druj's stocks.

But that Age of Iron was over, and the *Satya-yuga*, its opposite, was already 23 years old and gaining traction in the darkened human world. Humans were gradually gaining spiritual life-force and gumption to make choices, which no doubt made our present work easier to accomplish. We strengthened our visualizations to make the impact of the Sword of Goliath more decisive. If it was possible, the now ascended Matthew made himself even brighter, radiated even more Christ Light. Michael's sword swelled in valor, and the Supreme Being's smile seemed to widen, like a grandfather sitting in his study watching the World Series on television, his favorite team leading handsomely.

I lost track of myself for a time. I suppose that means I was successful in disappearing myself in the nondualistic voidness of the Christ Light. No room for Frederick in that big open empty space full of bliss and potency of the Light. The black cords were snapping loose from trapped souls, and as they came unplugged, the cords started to sizzle and dissolve, to flash into ash or vapor.

I heard screams, ululations, moans, whispers, all sorts of human sounds coming out of this turbulence, already losing its strength and fierceness. Then hundreds, maybe thousands, of human forms, though ghostly and only remnants of now departed and maybe reincarnated humans, streamed upward like bubbles suddenly released from a shaken sealed bottle of champagne. Alternately, it looked like a rocket launch, or maybe a thousand dolphins breaking the water at the same time, each of them jumping gleefully into the sky.

The Druj's turbidity broke up and dispersed after the cords came out. Human alignment, however old or unconscious, had been holding it together. Now that resonance was dissipated, and the Druj had no traction on their subliminal attention, or, should I say, allegiance. Of course, that was only one layer in the vastly bloated form of the Druj. It was like a woman of ordinary dimensions wearing a hundred overcoats, one thick coat upon the next. It made her form look monstrous, enormous, and you wondered how she could walk with that many layers upon her. It was appalling and funny, even absurd, and it showed us how much more work we had to do before the Druj was stripped of all her dark human karmic accretions, all the coats gone, leaving what—some anorexic skeletalized figure of an undernourished human devil?

One storm—it must have been about 20 layers or "coats" further in—almost did us in. It was a fierce red thunderstorm, full of lightning strikes. Redness was its chief feature. A ferocious, aggressive, commanding redness. It had some kind of suction to it, like a riptide at the ocean's edge. As soon as we engaged it, I felt my balance start to wobble, like I was no longer spinning perfectly poised on my vertical axis but was fast losing ground to entropy. Picture what happens when you nudge a spinning top and it falls off its axis.

It felt like I didn't know any more where my legs were, and certainly not my feet. This red energy hit my companions in much the same way. Pipaluk was grimacing. Tommy looked worried and was flailing his arms. Blaise was scowling. Edward was flexing his hands, trying to find something solid to grip to secure

himself. We were failing wonderfully. So what was this indomitable red force that promised to brutely throw us out of the Great Game of Druj-purging?

It was blood. The force of blood and everything it represented. The genetic code, tribal identities, selfhood, family, Group Souls based on shared genetics—it was the consummate expression of Ahriman in his ultra-materialistic physical sense. Steiner would have loved to see this picture; he described it often, warning his readers against Ahriman's potential death-grip on matter via blood identities, that Ahriman would compress everything spiritual down to blood mechanisms.

I understood that for a time blood identification was a necessary social clue to hold communities together. Souls lacked the potency to define themselves as individuals, to step forward as souls ready to individuate. They needed groups. Then it reached a point when this blood affinity was regressive; it was holding back the tide of human conscious evolution. Still, many people kept clutching it. We are Serbians; we are Cypriots; we are Irish, God-damn you. You are bad. We will fight you to the death to defend our family, our tribe, our polis, our purity. Yes, an all too familiar theme, a cliché in Earth human politics and history, one that has tossed human emotions like clothes in a washing machine. The Druj got *a lot* of mileage out of those cranky tires. I am *a this* based on my blood identity, my genetics, my lineage. I am my blood, she urged us to think.

Well, that nonsense was over. Now people had to start identifying themselves as Gaians, individual humans whose prime point of self-definition was not some atavistic Group Soul identity, not some gravity field of the blood, but a sober appraisal of the true condition of their consciousness: alive selfhood. I am a self-aware, empowered unit of consciousness occupying the human phylogeny on the planet

Earth with its specific geomantic conditions. I tried to imagine introducing myself that way at a Dartmouth faculty club dinner. Hi, Name is Frederick. I am a professor of Gaian Realities. Gaian's my game. Yours?

Let me tell you, there was some screaming inside this red layer. Cries of protest, imprecations flying like sharp knives in all directions, curses, threats. It was as if everybody felt they were involuntarily giving blood. I wasn't sure how much of this resistance was presently aimed at us or was the natural life, the habit, of this kind of stuckness: Do not ever challenge our group! Fortunately, I was sufficiently aligned with the neutrality of the Christ Light to regard all this screaming and shouting as mostly histrionics, as the acting out of perturbed divas and drama queens, and to the degree I kept this view, I kept laughing.

I recognized the place in me where, if I was not careful, I easily could match this. Carry on irritably, like a curmudgeon, protesting the slightest nuance of change. I was, frankly, only one or two steps away from this perilous cliff's edge, but those few steps made all the difference. It gave me, all of us, the necessary poise to avoid going over that edge. It kept the door open for the Christ Light to take action and keep me from falling. You want blood? Take it all.

I saw the Christ Light erupting from the land like hidden geysers, oil deposits reserved for the present moment in Earth history. This fulsome Light swelled up into fountains from out of the Light grid geometry of the planet, as if it had been kept there for this moment, had been hidden in protected caches in these multiple locations as a reserve against present shortages.

I thought about the Epiphany every January 6 when the Christ Light beamed into a specific geomantic location for a week, and I remembered Blaise telling me this had been going on for more than 4,000 years and that each site remembered the presence and preserved an energy trace of it, like a Light cache. These caches were now being triggered. The Earth was spouting Christ Light through the Light grid formed when you linked up all these places. It was a Christ Light grid overlaid on the Earth and it grew by one new vertex a year. Roughly 6,043 Christ Light caches were spuming out of the Earth like pillars. Earth's own good karma was now coming to the rescue in the planet's need.

I bet the Druj hadn't counted on this, or hoped nobody would remember. Maybe it wasn't we who remembered. It was the Earth herself who remembered. It was the Hindu Bhu-Devi, their name for Mother Earth, who had not forgotten the times Vishnu had sent spiritual succor in the form of a descent of himself to aid the beleagured planetary soul when her resident humans had gone mental.

These Christ Light caches buried like deposits of original virgin water all around the planet and now starting to swell up and erupt into geysers of Light were illuminating a host of baleful figures. It was as if each national ethnos, the egregore of a collective soul, like Ireland's Eriu and Greece's Hellas, had a demonic counterpart. It seemed that the Druj had constructed a demonic simulation of each egregore, a demented folk soul representation to do her bidding. She had made Golem versions of these legitimate ethnos egregores.

These were now apparent all around us. They roared. They flailed their arms. They made threatening gestures. They stomped their enormous feet. Their mouths were open, emitting shouts and cries, and their teeth were like lances. Each was clamoring the us-ness of an ethnos blood identity, insisting on its primacy, its superiority, its dominant, competitive edge over all others. I had to remind myself these were all copies, poor ones at that, and very psychotic.

Each was packed solid with images from the cultural life of its host people, but even these images were copies, poorly rendered simulations, cheap knock-offs. The triumphs, battles, failures, griefs, successes, the shared life of a people, the fevered dreams of a collective consciousness, a Group Soul's barely awake life—all this content was swirling around the raging demon spirits. The erupting Christ Light geysers were highlighting and dispersing these shapes.

The disposition of these contrived and manufactured national Golems was riling up humans, both alive and in the *Bardo*. Even the ghostly remnants were perturbed by this sudden illumination of what had been subliminal for so long. Nobody liked it. They preferred it remain unconscious. They didn't want to wake up and start divesting their selfhood from these short-term identifications. I am an Irishman! So what? It's no different than the brand name of my sneakers. I like my sneakers, I like my Irishness, but it is not me, not the fullness of this "I."

Souls were being forced to realize this, and they protested, squirmed, resisted it. But the pressure for enhanced self-awareness was inexorable; it was like a psychic earthquake that could not be stopped because, frankly, God ordered it. Not because He was nasty, like that cranky vengeful shit Jehovah in the Old Testament. Not like that, but out of benevolence of the Good Father because this change would be good for humans. It was like a nutritious meal: it's time to eat. He was telling all the sleeping souls they were dreaming, caught in a recursive nightmare, and He was gently shaking them awake, pulling them out.

See, this nagging, bullying, demented, imitation folk soul has been torturing you for millennia, feeding you poison, blowing toxic vapors of blood differences in your mind, deluding you into identifying yourself fully with this dark illusion. The Supreme Being was gently shaking each nightmaring sleeper, awaking them from the delusions of their night pictures into the sunlit world.

"You could characterize this fake national egregore as the Ahrimanic Double for the collective consciousness of a particular people," said Blaise. "In this example, it's the Irish, but the explanation pertains to all 72 national egregores. The Ahrimanic Double, as Steiner described, is a distorted, irritable trouble-maker in the subliminal regions of the psyche, acquired at birth and dropped at death. It is like a crazy man or woman shouting obscenities, always complaining, ranting, in a special dedicated cave, a minor chakra at the back of the human neck. It's a man or woman in appearance depending on your gender; it's a total sourpuss. I call it the Cave of the Crazy Man (or Woman), per gender.

"The demonic egregore for a country is a larger, collectively compounded version of this, and the Druj had a major hand in its creation. She summoned it into life, then let (or encouraged, even directed) the host people to feed and clothe it over the millennia while remaining, regrettably, entirely unaware of its existence. It hectors and catcalls this host people from its geomantic cave in the landscape. It spews psychological poison, contaminates the pure soul essence of a people, emphasizes its wayward, nasty, or unresolved conflicts, reminds it of its failures or shortcomings, criticizes everything constantly; it makes the soul feel miserable about itself, pessimistic or vengeful, whichever gets the best traction. It's like living in the unending, unrelieved company of a crazy person.

"The Ahrimanic Double is always pushing forward its views and complaints to the individual human, and the person usually is not aware of it. Nor does the person understand its source; it's hardly ever spoken about. Similarly, and necessarily, the geomantic landscape has the same pattern. It has to; that is the design law of the geomantic template: whatever a human has inside, within consciousness, is expressed equivalently outside as geomancy.

"This outer, geomantic, and national Ahrimanic Double is also constantly griping about conditions, always dissatisfied, urging rash actions. My point is that this collective Ahrimanic Double similarly influences consciousness yet people remain unaware of its input. They experience its products, its propaganda, but attribute it wrongly to the vagaries of their own mind and emotions. People would be startled to see to what degree the so-called ordinary contents of their consciousness, the various strange or alluring objects found bobbing along in the stream of their daytime awareness, derive from this source. Most people, unfortunately, have no awareness of how much their personal consciousness is infiltrated, permeated, even possessed at times, by external or non-personal sources, whether it's from other people or these spirits.

"Even Steiner's name for this baleful spirit, Ahrimanic Double, gives away its true identity. Ahriman, or *Angra Mainyu*, as we know, is the Druj. These doubles of the national egregores are the Druj's progeny, her infernal spawn. They are spirits of the Lie, agents of the Druj and her schemes against humanity.

"But before we flush with feelings of paranoia, we must remember we are complicit in the spawning of these many fake egregores because we have 'grown' the Druj like a farmer fattening a farm animal, except the irony here is that when the Druj is fully fattened we find she has already consumed us. We are just anorexically fleshed skeletal forms who gave away our life substance, and we stand around, shivering, wondering why we can't remember who we are."

As Blaise was speaking, and I remind the reader we all were still assembled in our collective visualization, and I was still coming and going through the revolving door into and out of the Christ Light voidness and outer world perception, the forms of these Ahrimanic Doubles were dissipating. It looked as if the constituent atoms, even if they were only of an astral nature, were coming undone and millions of their tiny building blocks were flying out.

That's the way Golems are undone, according to Jewish mysticism. The rabbi removes a single letter from a Hebrew word (for truth) pasted on the Golem's forehead and the Golem dies because that word now reads "death." The Golem's humanlike form instantly collapses into a pile of inchoate dirt. That's what was happening with these many national egregores. They lost their forms and "died." Blaise wasn't removing any words from their foreheads, but he was directing Light at them, and this strong Light, I saw, was coming out of us.

"You realize that the Christ is our ally in this work," Blaise said. "That is a remarkable and cheering insight. It is more subtle than merely saying the Christ takes our side against the bad guys, the myriad progeny of the Druj. Christ takes no sides. The Christ is the Word-Sword of Truth, of *Asha*, the Hand of the Supreme Being reaching out into the Lower Worlds of the Tree of Life. It cannot be anything other than the *Dharmakaya* because it is an artificial lying construct.

"Without taking sides, without partisanship as we know it, that utter reality dissipates all forms of consciousness that cannot be in resonance with it. The Druj cannot match her vibration to that of the Christ Light, so she is undone. In this case, what she has created is undone, because that, even more so, cannot be in accord with the *Dharmakaya* or *Asha*, the absolute truth of original reality.

"What is even cooler, I find, is that this Christ Light is always at hand. The planet was seeded with an inexhaustible supply of Christ Light. It wells up through the geomantic nodes as easily as water flowing out of a faucet when you turn it on. This is why the Irish and Norse likened the Christ Light to a fat boar. The initiates feast on the boar, named *Saehrimnir*, all night long, and in the morning, not a molecule of the boar's flesh is missing; it is fully regenerated.

"It's a metaphor for the inexhaustibility of the Christ Light. It cannot, it will not, ever run out because the source is the Supreme Being Who is infinite. The Christ Light wells up at geomantic nodes, especially at Epiphany each year, and is never depleted, though the planet has a calibrated dose. It's like a homeopathic prescription, formulated at the exact potency and number of doses for the "patient," which is humanity. What I mean is the *amount* of Christ Light that perpetually wells up in the psychic landscape is *matched* to our collective ability to absorb it without becoming unbalanced by too rich a Light infusion.

"It's unfortunate that so few people are aware of this munificence to take advantage of it. Every year on January 6 this Light wells up magnificently at a particular geomantic node and is available to all humans; they are invited to take all they want. Much of the entanglements we are clearing out of the *Bardo* could have been cleared out long ago by humans taking up this gift of Christ Light.

"The design of the planet's Light grid and its planet-cosmos interactions was meant to facilitate this opportunity for regular geomantic housecleaning. What we're doing on this expedition could have been done on the other side, and, it is hoped (by the Green Knight, among others), it will be done again on the other, *physical* side in the future as a result of the clean-up job we're doing now."

"I suppose we may thank the Druj for keeping most people unaware of this opportunity," said Edward. "She's done an excellent job keeping this knowledge classified, above top secret, and people feeling disempowered."

"It always surprised me how few people participated in the Epiphany each year, or even knew about it, that it was a real-time, live geomantic event," Blaise continued. "Knowledge of this, and even better, participation, could have dispelled so much doubt, agnosticism, and even atheism from people because here is irrefutable, empirical proof of the Hand of God, the Christ, active in real time on the planet. Every year I'd watch the Christ Light swell up from that year's prescribed node and blossom out into a magnificent white lotus with thousands of bright petals, and I'd be amazed at how few people noticed it.

"It was like watching a flower blossom open up, but this divine flower had such a potency of Light you couldn't help but start to match the innate bliss of its scent. This was a real event, happening before your eyes, and *something* was making it happen. Irrefutably, an agency was responsible for this; someone had a hand in making this happen. I mean, you didn't have to be clairvoyant to realize this. Even the external logic was unarguable. The Hand of God was definitely in play. Eventually, as the *Satya-yuga* grows, more people will come to this insight. They will appreciate and love it that the Epiphany is an annual proof of God."

"That's right," said Merlin, "and with this sword you have another live version of this reality, an applicable one, one that you deploy to make changes. You don't have to wait until the next January 6 comes up on the calendar. You have that energy on hand right now. You could say the Sword of Goliath-Elohim is a portable, wieldable Epiphany. This also means, to follow up on Blaise's point, for those who are sensitive and can see it, you may present this sword as a wieldable, epiphanous proof of God. You can see the positive effects it makes."

Indeed I could. Since this brief discussion, the Christ Light component of our collective sword increased many times. It swelled up, it strengthened, it was irresistible and incontestable. All this made it easier for us to hold the sword. More layers were stripping off the Druj like laminations of old paint.

The power of our sword was principally amplified by Matthew and Philomena. In them we had two living Christ Light inputs, two souls now Christed and ascended, one of them, I reminded myself with awe and sadness, is my wife. Or was. Is Philomena still my wife? I had no idea. The Philomena part of her is only a costume now. Matthew's newly ascended status was humming with fierce Light. You could barely keep your eyes open to look at him as he backlit our sword, and you could hear his Light. It had an audible vibration, but it was unlike any I had ever heard: it was the sound of awakened consciousness.

The Druj's hold in the *Bardo* was weakening. I saw numerous black tentacles that had been dispatched from her insatiable form start to dissolve. We were collectively the Christed Grail Knight, Galahad, if you prefer, and all of humanity was the Wounded Fisher King, and he was at last getting the right treatment, the sword stroke delivered by competent hands. It was the same sword that had produced his grievous wound, injured the memory circuits so that he fell into a prolonged amnesia and lived without remembering himself, casting this distressing self-oblivion all around him, blighting the landscape. He, personifying humanity, had used the Goliath sword without being Christed. That was dangerous and reckless, and he grievously injured himself and people. This sword cannot be wielded from a selfhood perspective or for selfhood gains.

Here at last was the Christed sword of power, the legendary Word-Sword, healing the Fisher King's chronic injury. It was so evident as we peeled and dissolved layer after layer from the Druj's dreadful anatomy. Her bloated, toxic form was the expression of the Fisher King's terrible wound; as one diminished the other was healed. The Druj was the foreign object cysted in his skin, causing the infection, the pain, and, eventually (her goal), the annihilation of memory. To use a computer analogy, this sword was the backup disk containing all the crucial files deleted from the computer's primary memory, or, if you prefer, we were the retrieval process that would recover them and heal the wound for good.

This Light, Goliath's power of *AL*, was the restorative, the memory and the answers. As more layers streamed off the Druj, more of Albion's unconscious was purged because Albion is the prime beneficiary of this memory resurrection. He was still partially asleep in the human material world, but his nightmares would diminish; his stirrings and turnings would bring him closer to waking, and when he awakes he will remember who he is. All will be clear to him.

"Do you realize we are creating a sacred site, a charged, numinous node right here inside the *Bardo*," said Blaise, addressing all of us. "It's an astral version of Avebury as the prime umbilicus, and we are planting this brilliant *tulpa* of Goliath's whacking big sword in it as a Light temple. That is state-of-the-art geomancy, a top-level protocol, and, I believe, the way the planet's Light grid with its myriads of Light temples was originally put in place. We're co-creating."

Blaise's enthusiasm was infectious. I felt the elation his comment came from. I was still the apprentice in all matters of geomantic protocol, but I got his point. This was an effective and efficient protocol; we should do it out in the world more when we return. In fact, as if I momentarily travelled into the future by a few years, I saw this *tulpa* of Goliath's sword shining brilliantly in the *Bardo*, like a skyscraper of Light we had built well and that would last for a long time.

I saw souls in their *Bardo* transits visiting it, like Muslims to Mecca, Jews to Jerusalem, or geomancers to Avebury, taking inspiration and encouragement from it. This *tulpa* had the effect of clarifying the *Bardo* landscape and its purpose so that souls in their after-death journey and processing understood it better. They knew this sword would help them divest their psychic space of the Druj and her machinations and entanglements in which they had been embedded.

"It's like a new version of Tarot's Lightning-Struck Tower image," said Blaise. "Except now the Christ Light bolts of lightning are rising out of the tower. They're illuminating the *Bardo* landscape for the souls in their transit, instead of scaring the holy shit out of them while they're in the bodily tower of material incarnation. What a marvellous inversion. Now it's copies of the Druj that are defenestrating as fast as possible. Druj's progeny are jumping out the windows.

"Now the lightning will help the souls find their way, its fiercely searing bolts of illumination clarifying the *Bardo*. The lightning bolts zig-zag *up* from the base of the tower, from the handle, and they startle, even terrify, the old Druj who has had her imperial way for too long, contradict her entitlement, and she dashes for the nearest open window and runs out into the empty air, screaming.

"Ha! It's so funny. We are contributing to the long-feared Apocalypse. We are adding visual content to John of Patmos's horrible, prophetic *Revelation*, but, as you wrote, Edward, after your time with Merlin, people have the Apocalypse all wrong. It's the disclosure of the actual design of reality, the original revelation, or as I like to put it, the revelation of the original revelation, the engineering schematic for the bewildering reality we've been living in forever. Whether it

is horrifying or amazing depends on a person's mental framework.

"It is only scary and upsetting because we have been for so long possessed by the *wrong* notion *entirely* of what constitutes reality, and *why* it's goddam here. You're walking (or staggering, more likely) through the *Bardo,* wondering how the Hell you've gotten yourself into this place, and this lightning strike suddenly clarifies the whole thing. It illuminates the terrain, which is your mind extrapolated to form an astral landscape, and you understand the set-up. You see what's required of you.

"With every new lightning strike searing out of this *tulpa* tower, the Druj grimaces. She loses more ground, and knows it; her influence keeps waning. She's like Sauron in the world-turning moment when he realizes Frodo and Gollum have just destroyed his power base, the stupid One Ring. He knows he's finished and all his maleficent works, his towers, armies, and soulless Orcs, now fail him, and his next stop is the alumni lounge of failed world-wreckers."

I was beginning to realize how much hinges on where humans freely invest their consciousness, how crucial is the free-will deployment of attention and belief. Not the Supreme Being nor the archangels nor the Ofanim nor the Masters like Merlin can coerce human consciousness onto a desired track, one they prefer or recommend or know is beneficial for the next stage in the evolution of consciousness. Of course they could, in terms of power, but I mean they are constrained not to; it is their agreement with God and us not to force us.

"They may suggest," Blaise continued. "They may present pictures like sales brochures, and they may point out the benefits, but they can't make us sign because that would abrogate the Supreme Being's covenant with humanity that we have free-will access to the Tree of the Knowledge of Good and Evil, which I might as well call the Tree of the Christ and Druj, or, when I'm feeling whimsical, which usually happens six times before breakfast even when I'm fasting or only have espresso, light meat and dark meat from that inexhaustible divine boar.

"No, we have to decide we want the Christ over the Druj, wakefulness over somnolence, knowledge over ignorance. Then they rush in with all the support and information we can handle, as they are now joyfully doing. No, we, our little Green Knight expedition, are not all of humanity, but we are their designated proxies, their clean-up crew scrubbing the *Bardo* on their behalf. We're housecleaners. The Green Knight wanted a home makeover, and we're the interior decorators assigned to the job. We're tarting up the residence for Yama."

Another makeover was now complete. I refer to the transfiguration of Matthew. His physical human form was gone, not a trace of it left. It was as if he had been taking off his clothes, one layer at a time, and doing this forcibly, ripping off the buttons, flinging the sweaters and undershirts in all directions as he worked his way towards nakedness. This was a different kind of nakedness, for in this vigorous divestment he threw off all the layers of his human form.

He stood before us, naked, but in the sense that he was all Light and no body. Even his subtle bodies were gone, vaporized in a fierce ascension moment. A residual sense of Matthewness remained, just as it had with Philomena. Something of his essential vibration, his soul signature, was available when needed, which meant when we needed to feel it to register his specific presence. It was odd, a kind of holographic simulation, an apparency with no real or personal substance, as if Matthew said, here is a 2D semblance of how I used to be. Use it as a point of reference or a place-marker for where I am standing now.

I could say he seemed to be smiling broadly, but that would foster a materialistic perception of him that was not warranted by the facts. All he was now was Light. Still, we could talk to him, this mask of Matthew (like Philomena's personality mask), and Matthew could answer, though his voice was changed. It carried shells of echoes, harmonics, as if he spoke inside a cave.

"It is surpassingly strange and wonderful," he said. "I should have known I was heading towards something radical in nature like this, but I didn't. I suppose that was a good idea. It would probably have been too alarming to me. You can't believe the freedom that comes with this change. I can move *anywhere*.

"Apparently (and I qualify this because I am only now checking it out), I can think anything, go in any direction and even move backward and forward on the timeline. I could, if I wished, present a variety of manifestation forms to clothe my Light presence, not just as a human. I could be a dog of Light or an angel. I could, if I felt sufficient whimsy, return to James Bay and take on the form of a fish of Light, an eight million mile long fish, like Vishnu, and delight my native friends. 'Young Matthew is returned. He looks strange from his journey,' they'd say. 'Very fishy.' They would be amazed, but I think they'd try not to show it, or just a little, or crack some jokes about my changed demeanor."

The reader at this point may wonder what happened to our sword *tulpa*. Nothing. It was like a building we had constructed. We could now enter and leave it without affecting its manifestation. It remained in place as I talked with Matthew. The imprint was strong enough to survive our leaving it at times, and, I surmised, it will remain like a blazing beacon long after we leave the *Bardo*. In fact, the sword image was still causing dark layers to be stripped off the Druj. We had set a process in motion and it was proceeding nicely without us.

Then I realized it wasn't quite like that. We were in fact still inside the sword image, maintaining our individual parts of it, and we were also outside the sword, as I was, talking with Matthew. We were in *both* places equally at once. On Earth, we're used to divided attention, but this was the division act to perfection. My attention, I saw, was poised fully and *adroitly* at two locations simultaneously. It was as if I had become two persons, two Fredericks, and I saw it was the same for my companions, Edward, Pipaluk, Tommy, and Blaise. We had duplicated ourselves and seemed to be handling the self-proliferation easily.

"You could do many more copies and not drop the ball," said Merlin. "It's not only the angels who can proliferate their form to accomplish much at once. Humans have always had this ability, though in recent millennia it has grown dormant and was forgotten or disbelieved or even disparaged and ridiculed, which in many respects was the worst outcome. It created a kind of hard psychic barrier that human belief has to penetrate to resume using this natural ability."

As I said, the Druj was still being stripped of her layers. As each layer came off, all its contents were revealed in cinematic detail and sound. It was like being in an old-style movie theater. I heard the voices of the people affected. It was reminiscent of what you picture when you read Dante's *Inferno*. Cries of rage and ululations of grief throbbing out in tortured waves of sound. The images— they were nasty, vivid, gruesome, so that it was despairing to watch this accumulation of evidence testifying to humanity's beastliness and depravity. This may sound strange, but for a moment I was heartily glad I was not the Supreme Being or even the Ofanim or Merlin who would see all of this always. It would get to me, surely, pummel me flat with shock and desolation and sadness. But they have to watch it all the time. Of course, viewing it, they remain neutral.

I saw that divestment of layers of the Druj's karmic skin affected humans everywhere. People alive and walking around in bodies on the Earth felt this loosening of the old confining skins. Some people stopped and looked around, as if to find the source of this change in their psychic atmosphere, in how they felt. Or they smiled, enjoying the sudden lightness, as if a breeze had just picked up.

In the *Bardo*, the effects were more dramatic because the souls generally were less distracted. In some cases, dropping a Druj layer gave a soul the needed amount of clarity or perspective to free himself from the current karmic illusion he had unwittingly projected in front of himself and had been regarding with fright. That illusion of a blood-dripping, fractious gargoyle or rancorous, threatening *Heruka* would dissipate at once. Or the landscape would suddenly lighten as if the dark, glowering storm clouds were blown off.

I saw that while we only had to strip the Druj once, the visual record of this would remain, almost like an educational video, for new souls entering the *Bardo*. They could watch this act of disempowering the Druj as if it were happening right now, in their present moment, though, technically, it might be a hundred years from now when we actually did it. You see, it wouldn't matter.

The fact that we *did this* would continue to reverberate throughout the *Bardo*. I marveled at the efficiency of this. Taking the Druj down would pay dividends for years for souls transiting the *Bardo*. It would count as one of our upgrades. I remind the reader that largely our mission, on behalf of the Green Knight, was to make, then institute, proposals to streamline and improve the *Bardo* protocols so more people could understand what was required of them. Significantly curtailing the Druj's ubiquitous influence counted as an upgrade.

That we did this meant it was reverberating in the physical world. I saw replicas of this sword at the many Underworld entrances across the Earth. Not exactly right at the portal, but let's say a soul, recently deceased, about to enter the gateway into Yama's realm of karma processing and after-death protocols, would see this sword as a beacon of Light. It would be hard to fix its precise spatial location because it would seem to be always a few steps ahead, or blazing at the center of this "undiscovered country" as the *Bardo* used to be called. It was rather, I thought, and I hope, not too whimsically, like the lamppost in C S. Lewis's Narnia, an outpost and beachhead established by the Children of Adam.

Regardless of how souls saw this, it would have a cheering, uplifting effect. It would lighten their tasks and provide Light to accomplish their death work. It would start the healing process on the millions of Wounded Fisher Kings entering the *Bardo* each year, the redemptive sword reforged at last.

I know the way I relate this development is perilously close to inflation. That is not my meaning or motive. It is more impersonal than that. This sword has needed to be restored to activity, to return to the human world, used rightly. We haven't drawn any personal significance from having made this happen. It had to be done, and we were on hand to do it, guided by Merlin and the Ofanim.

Matthew, meanwhile, was alternately swelling and diminishing in size. It was like standing next to a pulsar; each time it flared, Matthew grew larger. On some of these expansion cycles, he would become the size of a mountain, then he'd shrink down to roughly human adult size but still a dazzling blaze of Light.

"I haven't quite mastered the size mechanism," he said with a boyish touch to it, like his father had given him a Porsche and he was trying to work the gearshift correctly. "When I expand, or, should I say, when the Light expands, I feel like I am a great sun illuminating an entire world. I see all across the *Bardo*. I see in detail the millions of souls in their transit, struggling with their karma and the illusory, apparitional nature of most of the *Bardo* landscape, and it seems that I am able, effortlessly, to provide counsel or illumination to them, if they wish it.

"This extends back into the physical world as well, to the moment of death or the moments immediately after death, as souls look for their bearing. Not all people are receptive to this; some regard it as a horror act, another disturbing anomaly in this already bizarre, challenging, and intimidating new landscape. Others are more sensible and take advantage of the counsel I offer. It's strange, but I seem to have been doing this for a long time, not just in the short time that has elapsed since I completed this change—what would it be? Hours? Minutes? Time is so elusive in the *Bardo*—has it been centuries? Eons? It feels it.

"The timeline, any sense of rigidity or inflexible linearity it once possessed, is entirely fluid now. I seemed immediately to be straddling great gulfs of lived time. The minute I ascended I was always, already there, spread out through time. One second I was fixed, rooted to a moment in time, the next I was free of all that, everywhere, and at any time I wished, or, more strangely, at all times, and, I emphasize this again for I am still struggling with it a little, I felt certain that I had always been this way, even though, to my logical mind, what was left of it, it was only the result of this change that had only just happened."

"That is part of the nature and consciousness state of the Manu," said Merlin. "The Rich Fisher King is rich in knowledge and memory of the timeline. You are emulating that King. You have moved into his position in consciousness. He moves anywhere he wishes on the timeline; he is already everywhere on that line. He has digested it; the timeline is implicit in him. The Rich Fisher King is the timeless healer who wields the sword that heals the Wounded Fisher King who is stuck in time, like a broken down car by the roadside, immobilized at one node on the timeline. The Christed Grail Knight not only heals the Wounded Fisher King, he becomes him in his regenerated state as the Rich King. That ought to spin your head around a few more times, Matthew, if you still had one."

Matthew continued with his report. "Not only was the timeline suddenly open to my access throughout its entirety and my sense I had always been there, but I was able to zoom in on specific events, individual people, and watch the accretions of the Druj compound in their psychic space over time. I saw how she planted seeds, slipped in suggestions, presented persuasive pictures that matched the downward trend of their degrading self-image and assessments.

"She is able to work with innumerable individuals simultaneously. Sometimes it requires only a slight touch on their mind or emotions, gently accentuating a tendency they'd already set in motion, giving it the slightest nudge. With others, her 'advertisements' were more overt, direct, even blaring. She is as prolific as the angels, it seems, though, how shall I put it, not as nice.

"The Druj kept her hand in for tainting collectivities of human consciousness, such as families, tribes, and ethnos groupings and their egregores and even their host Albions. It was as if the Druj had billions of hands extending to souls all the time, all of them dispensing lies like a noxious perfumed vapor released from her fingertips, poisoning the psychic atmosphere with the vibration of falsehood, sending innumerable humans down a path of illusion or delusion, her hands pickpocketing discernment from *Bardo* souls.

"If we hadn't discovered the power of this sword, and, I guess, if I hadn't gone through this momentous change, it would have been godawful scary to watch. I can remember, vaguely, that type of reaction. Now it's one of neutral power. I look at it, this spectacle, without a reaction. It is data, some of it requiring action. Before I would have been full of judgements, evaluations, criticisms, fear, or resistance. How could these people get themselves into such abominable knots? Can't they see what they're doing, how they're being fooled, misdirected, and so totally manipulated as if secretly and behind their backs?

"I would fret, make plans, try to fix the situation. Neutrality opens up the possibility of understanding and compassion. I get it, why people get stuck. I certainly did enough times, going all the way back on 'my' timeline. I suppose I should say my karmic ancestors frequently got stuck, my own idiot past lives."

Matthew laughed. "Before I forget it, I've overlooked something obvious. Every day, every moment now, is the Epiphany at its peak, January 6. Or, and you, Edward, and you, Blaise, will like the allusion, every moment is another slice off the inexhaustible spiritual flesh of the great Christ boar, *Saehrimnir*, an amusing irony since when I was alive I was a vegetarian, and now I'm feasting on boar's meat with the *Einherjar*, the Self-Defeated Ones, the Christed, ascended fellowship in here. We slice off huge juicy slabs of this Christed boar's meat, and even in my ascended state I give thanks that the boar is only a metaphorical boar. In fact, we're not even eating. We all ate yesterday. We are all already this boar.

"Every moment is the fullness of the upswelling of the Christ Light, like at the Epiphany as the maximum prescribed 'dose' is delivered to Earth reality. Not only is the timeline erased in its linear, three-dimensional sense, but so is space. Spatial distances and differences, the presumed gap between point *a* and point *b*, are dissolved, and all the Earth is right here, like a blue-white globe in my hand.

"For example, and this, I suspect, is central to the next phase of our expedition work, I can, right now, see all the Underworld portals that lead here. I see the 1,746 gateways across the planet, each one leading to here, first to the *Bardo*, if you are recently deceased and requiring access to the karma-processing zone, or to Yama's Celestial City which lies circumferentially around this in-between place. I see them all, and I see their condition, where they're blocked, damaged, converted, or distorted, or in some cases veiled from human sight.

"I see lines of human souls making their way across astral landscapes of Earth towards these gates, like passengers at an air terminal lining up for a flight. I see where the Druj has corrupted these gates, commandeered them, or hidden them in confusing illusions; or where she spins up false, imitation gateways that go nowhere. She does what she can with each gate, succeeding more at some than others, but she knows it doesn't take much to throw humans off their game.

"Among living people, these gateways now tend to be forgotten and discounted, acknowledged only in the cast of scholarly renditions of ancient mythologies and folklore beliefs, or, in many cases, downgraded to become the Gates to Hell. This is unfortunate. The Underworld portals are now seen as Gates to Hell. The Druj took all the cultural and folkloric fears about Hell and piled them on the gates. Human expectation, fueled by fear and misinformation, has made these gates *seem* hellish, and now people *expect* them to appear hellish.

"The practical result is that people stay away from them and live in fear of them.

They are encrusted with projected human thoughtforms created out of this fear. When souls confront these gates they encounter a frightful but *artificial* projected reality, which pleases the Druj no end, and they treat these projections, like lurid posters pasted onto a once blank pristine wall, as if they are all real.

"Any of these outcomes please the Druj because it veils the gateways with deft lies. Even if the dead can discern the true gateways, often the living cannot, and there is great value to living people interacting with the gateways to Yama's realm. This used to be the norm; you need only think of the Mysteries of Eleusis, not that anybody knows much about their details, but clearly they were death mysteries. Human interaction at Eleusis was a yearly event for the Greeks, and it did much to prepare them for death by acquainting them with some of its aspects while they were alive. It was much like reading the *Tibetan Book of the Dead*, except it was a group experience with the Mysteries presented live, in real time.

"Eleusis was better than merely reading about the *Bardo*. It took people into it. It gave some humans, the priests or initiates of that culture, some idea of what to expect, even if they were forbidden to speak of it to the uninitiated. At least some knowledge of the truth of the set-up was in circulation among living people. Even if they never spoke a word about its details, they emanated the assurance that the Underworld was knowable, visitable, and not to be feared.

"From here, the gates appear identical, because in fact they are. But from the Earth side, they may all seem different, subject to varying human projections. The Druj was successful in converting a fair number of these neutral gateways into the Gates of Hell, furnishing them with infernal, spectral, and frightening qualities. She is an accomplished set decorator, a master of special effects. It is a complete lie of course. You can't go directly from the living Earth into the Hell realm of the Six Worlds. You only enter that realm from inside the *Bardo*, and then only if you are, regrettably, in resonance with its grim qualities. Nobody is dragged there against their will; souls in a sense pre-select their own admission If there is any dragging, it is self-inflicted; you, your karma, drag yourself there.

"The Druj is clever. When you restrict knowledge of the death protocols and the *Bardo* gateways, then fear pictures start to fill in the information vacuum and soon what are in fact neutral, identical, morally transparent gateways become painted in lurid images of fear, hellish nightmares, and terrible outcomes. Even the term 'Underworld' gets distorted and in many languages.

"People now think the Underworld means a dreadful place *inside* the planet, *under* their feet, *below* their human world. The Druj always fosters the literal interpretation of anything spiritual or etheric because she knows literalism kills the spirit, closes the door. Catholic models of the afterlife fostered this; Dante deserves much credit (or criticism) for fostering an erroneous cartography of the afterlife *Bardo* realms. He may be a literary star, but he was a propagandist for Catholic disinformation.

"His was an entertaining story, but one entirely inaccurate and thereby misleading. If you took his *Inferno* with you as a guide to the *Bardo*, you'd be lost the second you arrived. You'd find nothing there matches his text. The Druj wants to eclipse all accurate knowledge of the *Bardo*, even the suspicion of the fact that the Underworld is accessed *up* from the crown chakra, that it lies *above* our world, and the 'under' refers to the realm of Absolute Light: the Underworld is the world under that higher perfect world. It is the differentiated under world.

"To reach the Underworld, you have to rise, go *upwards*, off the Earth, up vibrationally, escape its gravity, your emotional and physical base, your selfhood, depart through your topmost chakra, the crown, to cross the *Cinvat* Bridge and then gain entrance to Yama's realm, the *Upper*world. The dead return, happily, to the Upperworld, which is under the realm of the Absolute. Even the Hell realm within the Six Worlds is located above your head, up there. If you think you're going to Hell when you die, at least get the location right! Up.

"There is an odd but evocative expression used in an old Norse text. Yama's name in Norse mythology is Hel, and the text speaks of 'the joy of the troll-woman,' implying that her joy pervades the atmosphere of the 'high hall of Hel," meaning her residence in the Underworld. Souls proceeding to Hel, which was also the name for the place (similar to the conflation of Hades the god with Hades the realm), had to pass through *Gnipahellir*, which was an overhanging cave guarded by Garmr, the Norse version of Cerberus, who guards the gates.

"Garmr is chained to his post and will remain on duty until Ragnarok, but this image suggests competency and unwavering attention to the crucial job of protecting and preserving the integrity of the gates leading into Hel, or the death world. Remember, this means the zone administered by the death-guardian, Hel.

"Druj has had no traction in subverting or suborning Garmr, vigilant at his post. Blaise, as you know, traced this myth to its landscape grounding point, the Rondane Mountains of central Norway, a well-preserved geomantic terrain. We know that Garmr, like Cerberus, sits on the crown chakra, representing Sirius, who is the Hindu deity, Shiva, the star's ensouling intelligence, who dances on the ring of fire, the crown chakra petals and the gates of the galaxy. Shiva, the Hindu mystics said, is the Hound of Heaven, the chief dog of the stars; he guards the House of the Stars. The Hindu Shiva is the

Norse *Garmr*. Shiva's *tiruvasi*, his ring of fire, is the human crown chakra and its thousand petals.

"So you find *Gnipahellir*, the cave with its chained hellhound, Garmr, on your head, which is why souls are advised to depart the body at death by the crown. That's where you meet Cerberus and all the other named *Bardo* dogs. I say 'on' because seen from below or above that's how it appears: Shiva makes his body-*mudras* just on the edge of the flaming hoop of celestial fire. He dances just slightly off the flaming surface of the ground, just in front of the *tiruvasi*. Picture this flaming hoop, normally shown upright, as lying horizontally on your head. In case my point is not clear, you are *supposed* to meet *Garmr* at your death. This celestial 'dog' is your *ally* and designated guide through the Underworld. Think Anubis, darting in and out of the holes in the desert, knowing his way around.

"Shiva is the doorman, ushering departing consciousness upwards into the bright Underworld. *Gnipahellir* is a cave lined with a thousand gold flaming petals. It's your crown chakra reconfigured to resemble a cave. You have a two or three-headed dog on your head, a dancing transcendental deity, kicking out his legs like a line dancer. Most people, on dying, will see this spectacle for the first time, though people trained in clairvoyance will recognize it immediately, and therefore much sooner, when it's more helpful, as they use it all the time. The crown chakra is where trained clairvoyants properly conduct all business.

"The rest of the Norse description of the Underworld is fairly consistent with the later Greek version. There is a river called *Gjöll*, meaning noisy or loud noise, which corresponds to the River Acheron, and the bridge across it is called the *Gjöll* Bridge, which matches the Persian *Cinvat* Bridge and the Greek picture of Charon's ferry. Another name for it is *Gjallarbru*,

'the bridge over the Underworld river *Gjöll*.' It's the *Cinvat*. The bridge, covered in glittering gold, has a female warden or guardian called *Modgudr*, whose name means 'Furious Battler'; she matches the Persian *Daena*, the soul-maiden on the *Cinvat* Bridge.

"She is neither pure nor tainted. Rather, she is fierce, furious because her consciousness is awake, and yours, you poor blighter, probably is not, but is wildly hallucinating instead. It's as if she says, fiercely, how dare you pollute me. She stands there, ready to kick your sleeping ass into wakefulness; she battles your ignorance, your self-deception, your complaining, your misinformation. She is the archetype of the Norse *berserker*, a Nordic *Heruka*, possessed by the spirit of truth which to the average guy stepping on the bridge looks horrendous.

"This turbulent river lies close to the *Helgrind*, a fence or high wall encircling the realm of the dead, Hel's Underworld. It prohibits unwarranted or ill-advised traffic to and from the Underworld, probably for the protection of souls at both ends. That's why the Greeks knew you had to have the Golden Bough for entrance if you weren't dead. That gets you over the *Bardo*'s Berlin Wall. It is similarly heavily fortified and defended, surveillance everywhere.

"The Norse seers described Hel as morbid and fierce-looking, half black and half white. That bivalence may be echoed in the Greek dualism of Hades and Persephone, and anyway, Yama and the Green Knight both have a fierce guise. Or you could construe this ambivalence as a blend of the *Daena* and the *Ammit*, or the karma products, the balance sheet, of the Good Genius and Evil Genius.

"My point here is that in the Norse picture you have an orderly layout. You could take its cartographical map with you into the *Bardo* and not get lost. It's not trying to sell you an ideology, like Dante and Catholicism, a moral goad. Hel, its guardian, bridge, river, bridge-warden, and the enclosure of Hel's high hall, are seen as normal, accepted, well-recognized features of the landscape. The picture is not distorted nor does it seem are any of its Underworld components. The gate is intact and clean, well-protected by the unsullied, inviolable Garmr. We can use the image as a standard for how these Underworld gates should be. The picture dates back to Hyperborea, when Earth's Light grid was unsullied. The Druj was never allowed to get her contaminated hands on this true map."

I had a question for Matthew. I was wondering how he suddenly became a scholar of mythic images. He had been a stockbroker then a reclusive meditator in northern Ontario. Had I missed the scholarly phase of his hermitic life? "How is it that you are so well versed in the details of Norse mythology?" I asked him.

"I take your point," he replied. "I was taking it for granted that I knew all these facts. It is part of my changed condition. I seem to have unlimited access to the *Akashic* Records, on the universal level and down to national particulars. It seems I can read any record I wish, focus down on minute details or zoom out for the larger picture. The Norse mythic picture of the Underworld is right there. I only have to look there and read the facts, at whatever level of detail I wish. A country's mythic description of its Underworld structure and processes is a reliable index of the condition of its gate, indicating its corruption or purity. The psychic valence of that mythic image is a direct reflection of the gate's condition.

"One of the key signatures of the Norse picture is that Hel is no big deal. It is a legitimate, mandated part of the psychic-geomantic landscape, lying beneath one of the three roots of the great Tree of Life, *Yggdrasill*. The Tree naturally leads to Hel, affords access and anchorage. Hel is not feared or honored any more than any other Light temples the Norse seers described in that landscape. It has

its rules, protocols, and regents, just as other Light temples of the Aesir, their gods.

"Their realm, Asgard, has a big fence around it too. The name means the 'Enclosure of the *As*,' the gods' fortress, so that is a natural architectural feature. There is no trace of the Druj in the Norse pantheon; she never got into the club. It appears that is because the Norse picture dates back to Hyperborea, the earliest and purest time for humanity on the Earth, the Golden Age. The Druj then was unborn. Humans had not started to co-create their Chief of Lies, *Angra Mainyu*.

"Let's take another picture of the *Bardo*, the Jewish model of *Sheol*. This is the place to which the dead are bidden, gathered up, and where they congregate. Its entrance lies in the West and the Earth opens her mouth and the souls go down inside the Earth to get to *Sheol*. It has seven gates, only one of which has a warden and a divine palace for its ruler. *Sheol* is an abode of silence, known as *Dumah*, of oblivion and sleep. The dead are without knowledge or feeling, and mostly they sleep in silence. Residents are called shades, or *rephaim*, and they are merely entities, without strength or personality, like personality remnants.

"The place is dark, dreary, horrible, disorderly, and filled with dust. Very few ever return from *Sheol*, and when they do, they climb up out of it to the surface of the Earth. Souls of all moral valencies congregate there, the righteous and the wicked. Contact between the living and the shades of *Sheol* is difficult and rare. If you were a Russian in the 1940s it would be like trying to get a letter from a relative locked up in the Gulag. The authorities don't allow mail delivery.

"That's how the Jewish seers saw the Underworld. It is inaccurate. Does this place look dark to you? If anything, it is better lit than the physical world because it is illuminated by spiritual Light. Disorderly? The *Bardo* is meticulously planned and supervised, every step calibrated and accounted for. If anything the *Bardo* runs like it was designed in Switzerland, precise and on time, clockwork.

"Do the souls here look asleep, without personality, knowledge, or strength? No. They may be lost and confused, but they are engaged with their karma processing. They still have up to four subtle bodies, and those are the bodies with all the wisdom. It's like being accompanied by your wise Elders. They may wish they could sleep, but they find themselves more awake than ever. Yes, they could use more technical knowledge of the protocols of the *Bardo*, and that's what our expedition will remedy with our suggestions.

"To say *Sheol* is populated by entity-like personality fragments, mere shades, is probably only an impression of the outermost life-processing processing zone of the *Bardo* where souls are casting off fragments like discarded clothes of their former selves. It's like an intermediate realm within the intermediate realm; it is only the outskirts of the genuine Underworld. Here, in *Sheol*, you find the discarded subtle body remnants, astral body castoffs of souls. Perhaps the description is accurate, but it is misleading to think it is a picture of the Underworld. It is a snapshot of a divestment zone, a realm of Golems, more like what the Navaho mean by *chindi*, unharmonized personality fragments.

"As for silence, this place is noisy. It's like a raucous apartment building on a Saturday night. People are screaming, moaning, crying, imprecating, throwing things, falling over, cursing, supplicating—they're definitely not silent. Maybe the Jewish seers meant we can't hear them, we need to be clairaudient, although people often do hear them but don't realize the source of the sounds. I used to hear the muffled screams and exhortations of dead souls as if they were in the next room. The Jewish model falls into the fallacy of despairing literalism, construing *Sheol* as deep down inside the Earth, requiring the shades to descend, to go into the Earth, to traipse down into its mouth, to get to this awful place.

"Score one for the Druj. The dark, silence, and horrific aspects of *Sheol* are attributes of the living human seers failing to perceive the *Bardo* correctly. It is dark to them. They attribute inimical, hostile qualities to *Sheol* because they could not see its full spectrum, that in fact it was a place of neutrality, a land of mirrors meant for human insight and enlightenment, not punishment or suffering. It is not silent; it is the Jewish seers who are silent as they didn't know how to engage *Sheol* while alive, how to make contact, engage it in dialogue, or visit it like us. It is not a trustworthy cartography of the Underworld; it is a heavily filtered one.

"They have missed the role of the crown chakra as being the true gateway to *Sheol*. They mistakenly have souls going *down* into Earth's open mouth. You go *up* to *Sheol*. As for remnants without personality, that too is overly literal. Yes, a few layers of the personality are stripped off, physical, etheric, then the astral.

"But the souls are not without personality. If anything, their essential qualities are now revealed in stark, unremitting nakedness. The personality infrastructure is stripped bare of all veils and dissimulations. They have enormous potentials of strength; all they have to do is enter the voidness state and recognize all the images and deities around them are mind hallucinations. Of course souls return from *Sheol*; most of the shades reincarnate and re-enter the Wheel of Life for another round. The others leave *Sheol* for desired astral locales.

"The result of all this misperception is that for the Jewish psyche the gates to the Underworld are coated in these false and misleading images. Jewish souls acquainted with the mythological model of their religion or ethnos enter *Sheol* expecting it to conform to this traditional model. It takes them some time to shake this off and realize *Sheol*, our *Bardo*, is a zone for illumination and freedom that come from sloughing off the smelly skins of unprocessed karma and in taming, if not subduing, and certainly in seeing through, the mind's propensity to spin out illusory images and hallucinatory projections based on this karma.

"They may fail to appreciate that the *Bardo* is the place where reality finally gets explained, where the plan and its engineering specifics are laid out in full detail. Instead, the Druj has successfully blanketed their death consciousness with lies, and *Sheol*, sadly, seems like yet another ghetto in yet another pogrom. The Jews are used to being hated by the world, and even the Underworld, it seems, has it in for them. All of *Sheol* is like the Warsaw ghetto. God hates them."

"Yes, a very mistaken notion. What is the *Bardo*? It's like a self-service amusement park where you create and then enjoy your own rides," said Blaise. "The only punishment comes from putting up with the bumps and jiggles and overturns if you happen to be a bad ride designer due to your faulty karma."

"Or it's like a building with a million cubicles for watching movies, and you script, cast, and direct the movie, starring yourself in all your illusions," said Tommy, catching Blaise's spirit of levity. "You binge-watch your own episodes, and if you don't like the images, or find there's too much action footage or dark scenes or nasty characters, it's your own fault. You hear the people crying out, complaining, criticizing the directors, the studios, for putting out such trash, or claiming they never intended to watch a horror film. This one is too shocking!"

"You also have the tendency for human religious leaders to deliberately darken the descriptions of the afterlife as a means of controlling behavior, of coercing obedience through spawning myriads of fear and punishment pictures," said Edward. "You find this in the Abrahamic religions especially.

"The distorted picture becomes a tool for social control wielded by the clerics. Now that is wicked. That is evidence of the Druj's manipulating hand of lies at work. She propagates a false, incomplete, or misleading picture of the afterlife to scare, shame, or coerce living people into prescribed, preferred modes of behavior. I'll tell you, if you want to rack up points fast on the bad karma registry, do this: deliberately mislead souls about spiritual facts and procedures. You'll score big. You'll rack up the points faster than on a well-used credit card."

"The case of the Persian picture of *Duzakh*, or Hell, is a good example of this," said Matthew. "There the emphasis is dire and frightful, focusing on the fate of wicked and damned souls. You can see the loading up of moral judgement in those terms. These wicked souls are punished for their earthly misdeeds and though they have the possibility of redemption, that is viable only after considerable scourging and purgation, which to them is a form of suffering.

"The *Avestan* and Zoroastrian mystics offered terms like endless darkness, a dark place of stench, abysmal, obnoxious, foul, close, frightful, an abode of scary demons and *drujes* (protégés of the Druj, partisans of lies and deceptions). Hell is an infernal abyss, the place of gloom and evil. *Duzakh* is situated underneath the *Cinvat* Bridge, so you risk falling into it by mis-step; it is one of the Druj's masterpieces. The name derives from *Drūjô-demāna*, 'Abode of the Lie.'

"It's as if they took the Egyptian picture of the *Ammit* and made an entire landscape out of it and put it under the *Cinvat* Bridge. If you failed the *Daena* encounter or your heart came out weighing more than the feather of Ma'at, you'd fall into *Duzakh*. To a degree this is accurate, but it fails to make it clear that this *Ammit* landscape, this horrendous *Duzakh*, was created *by you* out of your own karmic necessities. They present *Duzakh* as a terrible place external to your spiritual truth that if you have shockingly bad luck you'll be dragged into. It is a disempowering picture; *Duzakh* is something nasty done to you, its victim.

"You can expect a long life there of darkness, foul food, pain, much crying and lots of woe. The worst and deepest realm of Hell is so dark you can grab the darkness in your hand. You can expect the coldest ice and the most scorching heat, wild, nasty animals ready to eat you, and a constant stench that is beyond disgusting. It sounds like the worst hotel imaginable, visited in a wartime peak.

"This realm is located directly under the *Cinvat* Bridge. It is a narrow pit, so deep and sheer that your cries could never reach its bottom to be heard, which is packed solid with sinners, as prolific as hairs on a horse's mane. Everyone is lonely, sees nobody, feels alone and bereft, is abandoned by all life; even though they are stuck to the walls of *Duzakh* in vast crowded numbers they feel isolated.

"*Duzakh* is a deep well, extremely narrow, stinking, and dark, and all of its horrifying demons, called *xrafstars*, are enormous, each the size of a mountain. Its weather is dreadful, marked by cold, hail, rain, snow, sleet, and burning heat, basically, one of each type of atmospheric calamity. You get there by going north then downward, into the Earth. The gate to *Duzakh* is at the northern Arezur ridge on the cosmic mountain, Alborz (sometimes equated with Iran's Mount Damavand), at whose peak you will encounter the assembly of demons blocking your way and probably chasing you off. So before you even pass through the gate into *Duzakh*, you are likely to be scared out

of your wits by these demon-wardens; once inside *Duzakh*, abandon all hope because you're screwed, pal.

"A dramatic, vivid description, bordering on the hyperbolic, and wrong. It's wrong in the sense it imputes a fixed, immutable quality to this Hell realm. It condenses the six realms of the Underworld into the single world of Hell. We know, from the research in our expedition, the Hell experience is entirely self-selected. Each soul, possessed by heavy, dark karma, will create an environment around him out of that same content, and it may well appear hellish, but you've been living in it all your life so what's the surprise. If you end up in the Hell realm, you were already occupying it long before you died. It's just that now you see it clearly, your consciousness stripped of distractions. You see it naked, without any of the distractions, filters, or obscurations your personality provides.

"You get a million souls together with such oppressive karma and you have a densely populated Hell realm. Misery reciprocally circulates among the miserable, reinforcing this perception of reality. If you're around complainers, you will likely end up complaining yourself. But the Persian seers were also confusing the Hell realm, as one of the Six Worlds, with the entire *Bardo* terrain, equating sinfulness with *Duzakh* tortures. *Duzakh*, they suggest, is the entire Underworld. They describe the psychological or perceptual experience of this realm as if it is an immutable fact of the afterlife landscape. It isn't; it is entirely subjective. Many pass through the Underworld and never even hear of *Duzakh*.

"The equation is too simplistic, wickedness equals torture, and it makes you think *Duzakh* stands for the whole of the afterlife world. It imputes a malevolent agency to the sufferings of these souls in *Duzakh*. It doesn't work that way. It's all self-service. You witness the manifestation of your bad deeds as if watching a horror movie that is trying to pull you into the screen of action. It is as neutral as a tax audit; it is unpleasant, but it's based on irrefutable life facts. This is a record of what you did, how you lived, felt, your psychic atmosphere.

"They make the same cartographical error in saying *Duzakh* is downward, inside the Earth, and they show us how their death-gate is polluted with demon-thugs. The part about the proliferation of *drujes* fostering lies and deceptions is apt because souls often misunderstand the inimical spirits they have put before them, and we know the Druj is always obliging when we wish to be deceived.

"They did leave a very obvious clue right out in the open, though. They said the gate to *Duzakh* is atop the cosmic mountain. That's an upward location. Also, the eight Celestial Cities, including Yama's, lie on this mountain's slopes, and the *Bardo*, as we know, is the ambivalent amusement park you pass through before entering Yama's domain. So it is for *Duzakh* too. They say you climb the cosmic mountain, pass through the Underworld gate, then go downwards. But that gives it all away. There is no down on this mountain. It's at the center of the universe. It is reality's energetic center, the epitome of downtown. You're not descending to inside the Earth from atop the cosmic mountain. Maybe they thought the average Persian wouldn't know the difference and buy this lie.

"So the Druj has had her capable hand in the works here, distorting the picture, and imputing a kind of inevitability, an inexorability, to *Duzakh*. Once there, forget about getting out. She eclipses the fact that purgation leads to freedom; that suffering, punishment, and torture are really the emotional effects of remorse; that recognizing the innate emptiness of the karmic hallucinations before you, the Hell realm dissolves and the pressure of your karma is absolved. You will still likely have to make reparations in a future life to those you injured, but you do not have to endlessly burn on the rotisserie of *Duzakh*'s Hell fires.

"But the *Duzakh* pictures emphasize the notion of souls being victims of punishment, that their wickedness led them to this place of torture, and they have no traction to change it. The authorities have sent them to prison for life. The victim emphasis takes it all out of their hands. Yes, they were wicked; this is what you get for it, a tasty selection of nasty, awful experiences. You merit this.

"The portrayal of *Duzakh* does not make it clear that the specifics and duration and intensity of the Hell experience are due to your own actions, that you brought all the building schematics for your punishment cell with you because you lived in it while alive. They portray the psychic atmosphere of your emotions and deeds, now taken out of the Earth context and revealed in their starkness. You are not disempowered; you used your innate power wrongly. Then you put a veil over it to forget you ever used this power.

"These are your pictures. All of this is due entirely to your thoughts, emotions, and deeds, not as punishment, arbitrarily and generically delivered upon you by an implacable agency, like something surreal or enigmatic out of Kafka, with no explanation ever given, but specifically and personally because this is what your deeds actually look like, and they are coming at you like 300-pound football linebackers with you holding the ball because of the momentum you accorded them while alive, the constant valuation you gave them every day.

"Do you see how the Hell realm, despite its miseries, is inherently compassionate? Nothing is *done* to the soul; no external punishment is *enacted* upon it; not an ounce of misery is *added* to your karmic account balance. It's like acupuncture. No energy is added to your body; the indigenous *qi* is moved around to rebalance your system. The *Bardo* is your afterlife acupuncture session, and the *qi* is the force of your karma riding the needle of your awareness. All this is merely the factual, neutral dramatization of the condition of your mind. You must go through this, study it, digest it, release it, because you in fact are *bound* fast to its infrastructure and not until this moment did you realize that. This realization is the first stage in your release; the Clear Light is now closer at hand.

"It's like the Green Knight says, I'm ever so sorry, pal, but this is the picture you continuously broadcasted to the world when you were alive. Now you must take responsibility for it for the simple fact that it is yours. You made it; so you end it. What makes the Hell experience worse is the soul's resistance to seeing their own picture; consciousness seizes up with the shock of what it has subliminally made. It doesn't want to see it, and it must see it without any safe distractions, veils, or justifications such as you depend on when you're alive. I suppose it is much like forcing an alcoholic to recognize he is a perpetual drunk. Once you get their face down to the mat and they see they are at rock bottom, they have a chance of rising up from their addiction and returning to sane life.

"The Druj has a free hand here to amplify valences, intensify colors, raise the sounds, but that is no different than what she did to the soul while he was incarnate. Once you take a step in that direction, she can add to its qualities. The person was oblivious to the unseen manipulative hand of the Druj on his psyche. Now in the *Bardo*, that influence is more noticeable, overt and obvious."

"Add to this, the inherent imprecision of clairvoyantly obtained images," said Blaise. "Even at its best, clairvoyant results are not one hundred percent accurate. They are always provisional, plausible visual metaphors, but often these are misinterpreted or they are the results of incompetent viewing. A seer does not see well enough, makes psychic guesses, you might call them; his blindspots intrude upon his clear seeing; or he doesn't probe deeply enough, to strip veils and metaphorical layers off images to get at their functional truth.

"The Druj fully and richly exploits this procedural weakness, distracting the seer, and later, compounds the mistaken, incomplete, or misdirecting public report, what the Persian mystics called the visionary recital, to further dependably mislead souls. You're a press secretary and you don't know that half of what you're saying is wrong, based on faulty intelligence or flawed guesses. You impart a tone of certainty, but your recital is based on inadequate visions.

"The Druj encourages people to engage in sloppy psychic work, lacking precision and usually conducted under the heavy influence of low-level astral spirits possessed not of the truth of reality but its deceptions and allurements for the cognitively unwary. Even the supposedly empirical reports of near-death experiences are compounded with misperceptions, not to mention near-death does not equal real death in terms of the disclosure of the *Bardo* landscape. So the public mythic record is full of mistakes and misinterpretations, and even people who get here thinking themselves briefed find out to their dismay it's all wrong.

"It gets worse. Competent, relatively accurate clairvoyance requires rigorous, long-term training. It is an exacting, scientific mode of research; it is peer reviewable, peer corroborable, and it is fully based on empirical data. Short of people achieving that level of proficiency, the Druj can discourage the pursuit of clairvoyance, make it seem too hard, too unprofitable, too unreliable, surround it in a nimbus of doubt, invalidation, scorn, and ridicule. People become reluctant to approach it or emphasize the trivial, sensational aspect of its discoveries, what sloppy, untrained psychics crank out from a self-inflation haze. Intelligent, educated sorts avoid it; sensitive people will be embarassed.

"The result is you now have few accurate *new* psychic images entering the public record. Myths are psychic pictures and metaphors from earlier clairvoyants left as clues and place-markers for consciousness. These pictures need constant revision and updating as embodied consciousness evolves. But now you have started to separate myth from clairvoyance, so psychic research no longer feeds the public image repository known as myth. Myth and incarnate consciousness, psychic pictures and awareness, become estranged and stagnate. You lock myth up in an academic prison of literalism or disbelief, and you disallow clairvoyance as a research tool for assessing the true nature of reality. The Druj couldn't have played her cognitively disempowering hand any better.

"The visionary recital becomes an event of the past, or it degenerates into a cartoonish recitation of nonsense and spirit-misdirected images with no truth. The images, wrong or faulty to begin with, lose their ontological validity, and they invert, and start working as distorted propagandistic pictures of the Lie. The visionary recital becomes a press conference in which the spokesman is channeling the Druj and everything he says is a lie or at best a one-quarter truth. He may not even know he is passing on lies. He thinks he's reporting on a great man or a religious figure or psychic or guru of great probity. The gates to the Underworld get populated with thuggish, delinquent demons, handing out lies. I tell you, pals, that Druj is one tricky bitch. She always has an angle to work.

"It's true, matters have improved since the Ofanim's advent in 2020. There are signs of a rapprochement between myth and clairvoyance, but the other side of materialist-literalism and academic skepticism and clerical disapproval had a long head start. They built up a great amount of inertia which will take time to dissipate. Further, many of the old mythic images are outmoded; we can do better than the early seers: we need more prescient, timely visual metaphors, keyed to today's psyche conditions and the progress consciousness has made.

"Take the Persian image of the gates to *Duzakh* being crowded by fearsome demons. Clairvoyants know that demons are stupid and mostly feckless, brainless gargoyles, like Ferengi to the Federation in *Star Trek*. Irritating but easily taken care of. The term demon is often used as an imprecise umbrella word, like the Devil, to point to them, whereas there may be other malevolent spirits involved who look worse and act badly and go about unacknowledged.

"The truth of the statement that demons crowd the gates at Arezur ridge may in fact be that the site is packed solid, even congealed, with human karmic exudates. It is cast-off human karmic remnants and thoughtforms that clog the gates (like a transposed version of *Sheol*), possibly accentuated by inimical nonhuman dark spirits far more potent than demons. Still, I suppose the minute you mention demons many humans will at once stay away from the topic.

"The assembly of thuggish demons lingering ambivalently at the gates to the Underworld is a symptom, a product, of the Druj's successful campaign of disinformation and distortion. The Underworld in many cultures is shrouded in frightening, antihuman imagery, laminated in gloom and despair, dark places. What I'm saying is the reality of the *Bardo* is not altogether like this; only sections, like the Hungry Ghost and Hell realms within the Six Worlds division. But the manufactured picture the *Druj* sends into the world does not correspond to actual *Bardo* conditions; it corresponds to Druj-imposed conditions. It's a false picture draped over the Underworld gateways: it is top-rate disinformation.

"Take the Greek Tartarus. The classical poets describe this as a deep abyss, a pit used as a dungeon for torment and punishment of wicked souls, and originally for misbehaving gods, most conspicuously, the Titans. It is surrounded by a wall of bronze with two gates, guarded by three giants with one hundred hands each, posted there originally to keep the repudiated Titans locked down.

"Souls are judged and the wicked receive their divine punishment in Tartarus, wrote Plato. Tartarus is located far beneath Hades. Hesiod said if you dropped a bronze anvil from Heaven it would fall nine days before it reached Hades, and another nine before it reached Tartarus. It is as far beneath Hades as Heaven is high above the Earth. These are imprecise (actually, non-existent) measurements, but it creates a picture. Both realms are *below* our feet, deep *inside* the Earth, dark and miserable. Hades, the general Underworld, is inside the Earth, but Tartarus, the sunless abyss, is even below that, at the planet's core.

"The Greek model is puzzling because it appears to have two layers, one old, one recent. The recent one says Tartarus is the place for punishment of wicked human souls. This makes it equivalent to the Hell realm in the Six Worlds model. But as we discovered, it is a self-selected realm; you naturally gravitate towards Hell if this represents the propensity of your character as driven by the karmic winds. You assign yourself because you were living in Hell before you arrived. But Tartarus was originally a place to confine the Titans, which makes it sound more like the *Asura* realm that confines the antigods. You can see the Greek picture gets muddled at this point; the provenance is unclear.

"Nobody is punished as the result of punitive action taken by a superior agency. You punish yourself through immersion in remorse, shame, and guilt as you witness like an outside observer the scale and effect of your actions while alive. Whatever motivating, justifying images you held in your mind or projected to commission your action, you are embroiled and entangled in these for a time. You get their naked impact; there is no mediation or veiling like when you lived.

"The Greeks said the first layer of Tartarus was a lock-down place for the Titans. But it's important to know the Greeks pictured the cosmos as like a great sphere or ovoid, with the dome of Heaven at the top, and the Tartarus pit at the bottom; terrestrial Earth, where humans lived, was in a middle equatorial section. Here's the key bit, the key that opens the door: to the Greeks *Ge*, or our modern version of it as Gaia, did not mean the feminine soul of this planet.

"*Ge* meant all of *cosmic* space in which matter, like planets and stars, may dwell. Earth was this great cosmic sphere. So while the later writers assumed Hades and Tartarus were inside our physical planet, the original meaning is that these realms were at the bottom of the great cosmic shell; our planet was irrelevant to this cosmographic model. It was not referenced by the word *Ge* or Earth. Earth meant this primordial cosmic container for all manifested matter. In the beginning there was Ouranos and *Ge*, or God created Heaven and Earth, but they never meant our physical planet which is also, confusingly, called Earth. So, yes, Tartarus and Hades are *inside* Earth, but it's the cosmic, not terrestrial, Earth.

"The second layer of Tartarus as the place of human punishment is irrelevant and a false description. The Titans were in fact the Elohim, the great formative, generative powers of Creation commissioned by the Supreme Being to organize reality, physicality, humans, and the Earth. Don't forget these Titans were also the Persian *Amesha-Spentas*, the Bounteous Immortals.

"So to say they were *imprisoned* in Tartarus is really to say their powerful energies were *anchored* and stabilized at a *bedrock* level of human and planetary reality. It was a way of saying certain crucial celestial energies were grounded within cosmic Earth but also, since the Elohim were this planet's terraformers, laying down the reciprocal template of human and Light grid, they are anchored in our Earth too. They were 'imprisoned' in the sense they voluntarily occupied and managed a slower vibrational level of the Creation, the lower part of 'Earth.'

"So Tartarus is more a model of cosmogonic structure and not a portrait of a prison. It's not a description of the *Bardo* at all. The Titans were not punished or imprisoned; they were anchored to stabilize the Creation for Earth humanity. As we already know, the Titans were not the *Asuras*; those were the Daityas. The Daityas might have been 'imprisoned' in the sense of restrictions put on their powers, but this was not the case with the Titans or Elohim, the creator-gods.

"The Druj got her hand in by confusing this picture by adding the Hell realm nuance to Tartarus, taking advantage of the inversion of anchoring to imprisoning, but I wouldn't count that obscuration as one of her finest moments. It's just a smudge. Then over time the Greeks contributed to this confusion as initiate knowledge of the truth of Tartarus and Titans grew faint and gradually faded out to rumors. Then people just passed along these old wrong stories.

"Still, this hints at another meaning to the descriptive label of darkness. The Greeks said the Goddess of Night, Nyx, passed through the gates of Tartarus and wrapped the Earth in darkness, and that her daughter, Hemera, scattered the mists of night to further enhance the dark quality. The normal human conception of darkness in an afterlife realm is that it is unrelievedly gloomy and dim because that is the psychic atmosphere, dark, dreary, abysmal, without Light.

"Darkness has two other meanings. One, it means human psychics cannot see the realm with any clarity; they cannot illuminate it with the Light of their clairvoyance, so they describe it as dark. It's like the way astrophysicists use the term dark matter to indicate the presumed additional but invisible galactic mass. It's dark because they cannot see it. This matter in itself is not dark; it vibrates at a different frequency and requires consciousness to match that frequency to see it. The other meaning is that darkness, the condition of black, connotes a primordial condition of reality, prior to overt physical manifestation."

"It's like your Blaise's Black Bowling Ball that you so enjoy joking about, Blaise," said Matthew. "It's what the Qabalists call the Three Veils of Negative Existence, the three *Ains*, arcane realms above the Tree of Life and preceding the manifestation of the levels of reality in the Tree. Those are described as dark, but only dark like in a cosmic womb; they contain all potentialities for manifestation, everything in a pre-manifestation state, like a universal seedpod. Since we access the *Bardo* by ascending up from our crown chakra, this suggests the *Bardo*, even if it appears dark, is a place of revelation when we illuminate it with our seeing.

"The darkness may be a womb of great Light and understanding at a higher level. Dark can also mean dark as in the Eleusinian Mysteries, veiled, secret, only revealed to the initiates; thus Tartarus is the realm veiled in initiation secrecy, dark to the public, dark to consensus reality living in the sunlit world. It's a creative place, of high, arcane energy, too powerful to be open to the public. Where the Titans or *Amesha-Spentas*, our Elohim, work is a place of great power. It is kept in the dark because its reality can overwhelm our daytime awareness.

"Things are kept in the dark because initiation knowledge is dangerous to the unprepared, or, as often happens, it is simply incomprehensible to the daytime-focussed mind. Remember, we're talking about the Elohim-Titans, and it's their sword we've only now learned how to use. We sense its power. These guys are major players at all levels of creating worlds and life-forms to match."

"So you're saying the Druj has clouded the *Bardo* gateways in our minds," said Edward, "putting down false, distorted, or misleading images and descriptions so that when we think about the landscape of the afterlife we see it through her pictures. That is another version of thuggish demons at the gates. You ask them for directions, and they snarl and entirely mislead you. Their thuggishness itself denotes the way the Druj has commandeered the truth."

"That's right," said Matthew. "Then, because souls enter the *Bardo* ill-prepared mentally, with faulty concepts, or, worse, no concepts, or wrong, inaccurate ones, this makes room for the intrusion of actual dark spirits to enhance the confusion and create a psychic atmosphere of spiritual entropy. Our confusion creates place-markers for the opportunistic demons to stand upon. We are directors who have put chalk signs on the floor for our actors to hit their marks. The trouble is the actors are a gang of extras that stormed our theater.

"It's the same mechanism by which dark spirits intrude into a living person's space. The Hindus call them *bhūts*, malevolent shadow-ghosts made of the unconscious, cast-off, psychic dregs of the deceased human, the same as what the Navaho call *chindi*, the ghost-essence of somebody just deceased. These unruly, unsettled human remnants are attracted to the dark, erroneous pictures and the effects those images have had on the unprepared, newly

dead. Without having to lift a finger, the Druj gets dividends from their natural tendencies."

"It would benefit the *Bardo* if perhaps we did a little *bhūts* cleanup," said Merlin. "Care to give it a try with the Elohim sword? It won't be a permanent change because new *bhūts* are generated every day when people die, but at least we can clear off some of the accrued *bhūts* presence from quite some long time."

We refocused on our assigned positions within the Elohim sword. Matthew backlit the sword with the brilliance of his ascension body, and Philomena held the sword's hilt, gripping it from the outside while inside the hilt another Hand, or at least the suggestion of a Light form, held it steady. I was mostly disappearing myself within the spinning octahedron of the Christ Light, but when I sneaked a look outward I saw the great sword vaporizing the *bhūts*.

That may sound violent, but it wasn't. These spirit fragments were soulless shadow forms, comprised of all the unprocessed, unharmonized, unreconciled emotional qualities of deceased humans; they had no center, no cohering soul. They were like Golems, made of mud to resemble humans, but only mechanisms; they were like castoff skins of former humans reshaped into a semblance of the human body, but inherently empty of permanent substance. Picture someone wearing six layers of clothing, then they strip it all off and run away naked, leaving behind the pile of clothes still carrying their body shape.

The ancient Egyptians called these ghostly psychic remains of the deceased human the *akh* and noted the *akh* as a roaming dead-being could be malevolent and chaotic and needed to be petitioned to not behave evilly. The *akh* was morally ambivalent: it could aid or harm the living, and if it wanted, cause nightmares, guilt, or illness, like the Navaho *chindi* and its feared ghost-sickness. I didn't think speaking sternly to the *akhs* to behave better would accomplish much. They needed to get a deal they couldn't refuse from the Elohim sword.

It surprised me but I had the impression these psychic fragments of former whole human beings were happy, or at least relieved, to be freed of their pointless, darkened existence, as if they were compelled to act this way, like badly programmed robots, and they were okay with being released. I am reluctant to attribute a more positive emotional feeling to this than "okay." Some *bhūts*, I noticed, were so entrenched in their current, if limited, condition that they registered no relief at being dissolved, but simply stopped their action as if suddenly unplugged, like an electrical device when you disconnect the power.

There were many *bhūts*. Once I put my attention on them specifically, it seemed their population swelled before my eyes, and I now saw thousands. This sudden radical proliferation of their numbers was like when a strong beam of afternoon sunlight reveals all the dust on your books, magazines, and devices, even in the air, and you are startled to see how much there is but you had not seen until this moment of embarrassing illumination. Much dusting is needed. As the *bhūts* dissolved, so did the dark images to which they had been clinging.

There was a sense of a lightening of gravity, as if the heaviness of reality was leavening, and the innate lightness of the spiritual world was reasserting itself against the prolonged baleful weightiness of all these dark spirits and images. Similarly, the force of our sword was cleaning up the *Bardo* gateways on the other side of the River Acheron, as I suppose I could put it. The gateways are in the fourth dimension and not physical, but they have a presence in the physical human world across the Earth as portals of Light leading to the *Bardo*.

These portals were now getting stripped of their obtruding *bhūts* and their original shapes, textures, and qualities were now revealed and

their overall visibility increased, so that the newly deceased could find them easily, and it would even be more likely that some talented alive clairvoyants could see them. Or, I should say, would *want* to see them because now they would not have to navigate psychically through noxious fields of loitering, malevolent spirits.

As the *bhūts* got dissolved and vaporized, there was a momentary stench not unlike the odor of burning rubber tires. The air smelled of this. It was not an olfactory sensation such as we are used to with our noses; we had no noses in any biological sense in here, but it was more as if our entire Light form was an olfactory sensing organ yielding an impression of nasty smelliness. Perhaps it was like if you could imagine yourself inside a dark cumulous storm cloud, what it might feel and smell like; it would be a body-global impression. The odor did not persist; it was more like the brief whiff of sulfur when you light a match.

I understood why many descriptions of the Underworld talked in terms of stench. Our senses were not fragmented here, so an odor was a condition of reality perceived as a living picture form, with sound, color, and movement. Occasionally, I heard *bhūts* shout, then their voices were suddenly stilled, like an audio file switched off in the middle of a commentator's remarks, but I'm sure it was their mental fulminations, their complaints and taunts and jeers, I was hearing, not the sounds of their suffering or quick deaths. They couldn't die because they were not alive; they existed as simulacra of the living: existent, yes, but no more self-aware than a 20-watt light bulb.

"I have the impression nobody has cleaned out the place, the whole Earth, in a long time," said Tommy, with an air of earnestness and sarcasm.

"It reminds me of when my publishing company moved offices," said Edward. "The firm had been there for decades, an old Boston establishment—you know, almost since Colonial times, very New England. Nobody had moved the furniture in generations. We were shocked to see the degree of dust, detritus, old newspapers, files, papers, even a few old manuscripts, that had gotten wedged between bookshelves, desks, and the walls. The place needed a proper dusting, a scouring and vacuuming, a fresh coat of paint—the works. I wonder if that's why some of the accounts of the afterlife realm speak of dust. Everything's been the same, untouched for eons."

"The difference is that here you will likely find some decrepit corpses of old forgotten editors behind the gateways and *Bardo* furniture," said Blaise. "Some of the *Bardo* dust is ashes from incinerated shadow bodies and old karma. When all the life-force, volition, passion, thought, perception, and consciousness are extracted from a picture or thoughtform, only the dust or ashes remain. But I take your point, Tommy: nobody seems to clean up in here. We'll have to nudge King Yama to hire a cleaning crew, or get the one he has to work harder. I dare say our *bhūts*-blasting will leave another layer of dust residue to sweep up."

"I feel exactly like a sword," said Matthew. "Let's go make more ashes."

16

We were standing in the physical world amidst stone ruins. It was evidently an ancient site, and by the looks of the crumbled architecture I would say Greece. We hadn't resumed our physical forms and were still in our Light bodies or whatever the vehicle was that enabled us to function in the *Bardo*, but clearly we were on the other side of an Underworld portal, on the human side. I understood why Matthew had made that otherwise gnomic remark. We were here to cut away obstructions, dark energies, old pictures, ignorance, and lies, in the best Elohim tradition of a Light sword. This death gateway was a real mess.

"This is the Telesterion at Eleusis, 11 miles northwest of Athens," said Merlin. "This used to be one of the most important holy sites in all of Greece. The name Telesterion means 'Place of Perfection' or 'Initiation Hall,' from the Greek *teleio*, to complete, fulfill, consecrate, or initiate—in other words, here you were exposed to specialized spiritual energies, deities, and processes which would acquaint living consciousness, you in an alive body, with the afterlife realities."

The same architect who designed and built the Parthenon constructed the Telesterion. It was a physical temple, a large square roofed hall and portico with 12 principal Doric columns and capable of holding about 3,000 people for the ceremonies by way of eight tiers of seats on four sides. That was in the fourth century B.C.,

and the temple survived intact until about 480 B.C. when it was destroyed by the invading Persians and its annual Mystery rites ended.

When it stood and was ritually viable, initiates gathered inside and were shown relics of the goddess Demeter as priestesses reported their Holy Night visions. These recitals were part of the Eleusinian Mysteries, whose details were kept secret to preserve their sanctity. The name, Eleusinian Mysteries hints this: *Eleusis* means "arrival," and *tó mystirion*, means "secrecy, mystery, or secret rite" and implies initiation into these veiled secrets.

The *Homeric Hymn to Demeter* had proclaimed, or perhaps it was a warning, that the reality of Demeter entailed "awful mysteries," meaning one should prudently hold the rites and epiphanies of Eleusis in awe. It was an epiphany of Demeter in fact that initiates could look forward to, rumors suggested, that and possibly a glimpse of the returned Persephone, Lady of Heaven, presiding proudly and queenly with Hades for two-thirds of the year.

You, the initiate, could expect to "arrive" in secrecy in the presence of Demeter, and you could similarly expect this after-death goddess to "arrive" at Eleusis. Through this, and I hope I'm not stretching the point, you would "arrive" at a mystery understanding, a secrecy of enlightenment, about the soul and death. The secrecy nuance encompassed the private, individualized nature of the disclosure, and it enjoined the experiencer not to reveal it to anyone.

It was strange yet marvellous because I could see the Telesterion in its completed majesty yet I knew I was seeing its etheric version, like a phantom limb, because I saw the present day condition of the site, one of ruins, grass, and rocks with the area once occupied by the building only indicated by ground shapes. I was looking at an area 177 by 184 feet, a trapezoid and former Roman court which still had its foundation marble slab that underlies the Telesterion.

As I found out later, when I researched the archeological aspects of the site, the Telesterion had been built ten times, each time emerging more architecturally sophisticated. The building had six entrances, a portico (with the 12 Doric columns mentioned), a 14-column *stoa* (a covered walkway), an upper floor with 42 columns, and many tiers of encircling seats for the men and women initiates to witness the nine-day event of the Greater Mysteries held here every September. The Lesser Mysteries were celebrated in Athens in the spring.

Overall, the Eleusinian Mysteries were dedicated to Demeter, the mother of Persephone, famous for being abducted into the Underworld by Hades from Mount Etna in Sicily. Demeter, distraught, spent nine days searching for her daughter; finally, Hecate, a multitasking goddess, told her she was in the Underworld and she might encounter her at Eleusis, whose Ploutonion, a hillside grotto, reportedly opened into the Underworld: there she would find her Persephone. Hecate was well-qualified to know where Persephone had gotten to: she was linked with the Moon, magic, sorcery, crossroads, portals, herbs, and necromancy. Athenians widely worshipped her as a family protective goddess.

Demeter is usually understood to be a goddess of the harvest, a grain or corn-mother, overseeing the fertility of the Earth, She of the grain, grain-giver. But in her guise as Thesmophoros (from *thesmoi*, meaning the laws by which humans work the land, or Earth), she was the Law-Bringer, the upholder of the divine order and unwritten, sacred law, and the cycle of life and death that operate under those parameters, making her seem much more like the Egyptian Ma'at, the personification of the original, correct order of Creation. Some etymological interpretations of her name present Demeter as Mother-Earth. She is a high-level deity, an Olympian goddess, sister to Zeus, Poseidon, and Hades.

"They came here to get a glimpse of what to expect in the *Bardo*, right?" It was Tommy. "The initiates, or hierophants, got to look through the death portal and see the likely fate of their soul, known to the Greeks as Persephone, Core, the Maiden, and what we've been referring to as the *Daena* via the Persian model. The epiphany of Demeter, the mother of all the gods, was akin to meeting the Great Mother, Isis, the Matron of the Silver Realm, Maui's *Hine-nui-te-po*, the Great Mother of the Underworld and Great Woman of the Night. The many attributions to Demeter suggest this high identification. Perhaps the initiates got a quick look at the *Cinvat* Bridge and saw what was at stake after their death. I take it we won't get busted for revealing official Eleusinian secrets now. I mean, the place has been closed down for years, and nobody remembers Demeter."

Tommy looked around furtively as if temple guards might be lurking, listening for the slightest infraction of the enforced secrecy about the venerated Mysteries. He was hamming it up, I knew. There were no temple guards around.

"The Eleusinian Mysteries may have closed down in terms of active practices conducted at this geomantically prepared site," said Matthew, "but the Mysteries themselves are still viable.

But I use the term Mysteries in its pure sense: the revelation of the true condition of reality and the life of consciousness and the incremental exposure of living consciousness to its higher frequencies.

"The initiates here got to witness the survival of their consciousness, though streamlined and divested of a certain amount of personality baggage and karma, as it traversed the next realm, what we've been calling the *Bardo*, guided by Persephone. She was the Queen of the Underworld in the sense that for an individual soul on the *Bardo* journey, she embodied or reflected the state of his soul, acted as his prime mystagogue, and kept the soul's karmic records updated. Similarly, the *Daena* was the Queen of the Underworld, of *your* Underworld, as her moral condition, purity versus corruption, dictated the nature of your *Bardo*. The *Daena*, or Persephone, was the psychopomp to the disclosure of your karma-scripted *Bardo* landscape and she accompanied you as you did your protocols. As Tommy rightly observed, Core the Maiden was the Greek picture of the *Daena*.

"She was not abducted, forcibly taken into the death realm, by Hades, the Greek version of Yama or our Green Knight. It's more that her attention was directed to his realm for a time, away from the physical world. Core, Persephone, or the *Daena* is our intermediary between the alive world and the Underworld. She keeps them linked for us, which is why she spends time in both in the year.

"She kept one eye on Hades' realm, a far wider realm of reality, on behalf of her charge, the incarnated soul, us, when we're alive in bodies. Demeter wasn't searching for Persephone; it was more that as the Great Mother, she was wondering if Persephone and the now disincarnated soul would visit her, make it through the *Bardo* and find her way home to the Silver Light domain. Would they

make it successfully through the *Bardo* travails and pass through the 49 Gates to enter the silver realm of the unified Human and Mother Demeter?

"It's the opposite of what the myth says: Persephone is in search of her Mother. She wanders the *Bardo* hoping to reach the place where Demeter resides. Even that isn't correct. She knows where Demeter is; she hopes she can dump all this karmic crap the soul is carrying so they can get to the fun bits and visit Mom.

"We have here, at Eleusis, specifically inside the Telesterion, a swinging door. Not in a literal sense, because it is an open gateway, but I mean to indicate the possibility, the fact, of regular two-way traffic through this portal, even today. The fluctuation of Persephone's attention in one realm or the other reflected this. It's perfectly possible for the *Daena*, or Persephone, to intrude her reality and information to the embodied soul in the daytime world. It would be beneficial for the daytime-living person to get regular *Bardo* updates from her. As to why she was 'abducted' from Mount Etna, the specificity of that reference points to an Underworld entrance at that volcano, to the possibility that a psychic could see through the physicality of the site and into the realm of Hades beyond.

"Persephone wasn't abducted by Hades. She appeared on Mount Etna's slopes as an emissary of Hades, as Lord of the Dead and the place itself, the *Bardo*, as a *Hello!* in the midst of the sunlit daytime to the embodied soul to remember her. The Underworld portal at Mount Etna enables the sensitive psychic to see Core the Maiden standing on the *Cinvat* Bridge midway between the physical world and the realm of Hades. She can move in both directions, towards us or towards Hades. If anyone has abducted her, it is us, the living. We have dragged the Maiden into our sullied karmic world. All the time we are alive we are compounding her misery in the sense that we keep heaping more karmic obligations upon her, sullying her purity, uglifying the *Daena*. She hopes we would be aware of her more often in our embodied life; it's like she's a taxi-meter and it's always running and we are running up quite a bill. Can we pay it?

"Why is Persephone the part-time Queen of Hades? Because as the *Daena*, as the chief psychopomp for the soul in the *Bardo*, as the overseer of all the karmic divestment and soul revelation processes the dead person goes through, she is the queen, manager, of this place as far as the individual soul is concerned. Everything runs through her. She is the queen of *your* Hades experience. If she is carrying the *Ammit*, the greatly disgusting body of shadows, appearing as a hag, the soul has to cleanse her; if she is a beautiful maiden, the soul will have it easy.

"You go through the *Daena* to reach the Green Knight or Hades, or, if you were an Egyptian, the resurrected Pharoah Osiris, certainly a laudable goal for any soul. In the mystery sense, you want to transform your *Daena* into Hades, to marry the lord of the death realm because he 'embodies' the undying ever-green state. All the different named figures in this universal drama point to the same conclusion. *Daena*-Persephone guides you through Hades to Yama where you become him by emulating his *Heruka*-fierceness and master the Wheel of Life.

"You escape the Wheel and get out of the *Bardo* intact. Then you become the Green Knight or the risen Osiris, green in glorious immortality. I am mixing up all the figures on purpose. Persephone or *Daena*, Hades, the Green Knight, Yama, or Osiris—it's the same landscape with the same archetypal figures representing the generic stages of illumination in the progress of the disincarnate soul as it journeys to through the Intermediate realm to Paradise and Demeter. The soul's goal is to make it through the *Bardo* Wheel back to the Silver Moon. That is Persephone, Core the Maiden, the *Daena*, reuniting with Demeter.

"I see before me both the present-day ruins of this site, and I see it in its time of flourishing, the building intact, the initiates gathered in September, and humans guided in consciousness to enter the *Bardo* through this gate. In many respects, they were doing what we are now doing, having the full initiation tour.

"As it is with most myths, you have to invert the story to get the meaning. Persephone, the *Daena*, *abducts* your awareness on Mount Etna, an Underworld gateway, and conducts you into Hades and guides you through the Underworld and its processes to its lord, Hades, our Osiris, Yama, and Green Knight. You master his quality of *Heruka*-attention, pass through him, leave the Wheel of Life, and reunite with Demeter. Persephone has taken you back to her Grain-Mother. Even the reference to grain and corn is apt; that's often used in myth to indicate the etheric body, the life-force container and embodied form for consciousness."

The interpretive brilliance that Matthew cast over this scene helped me see more of it. I saw that in the days when the Eleusinian Mysteries were active, benevolent spiritual figures stood on both sides of the gateway, facilitating smooth entry. They appeared to be angelic in nature, robed in gold, much larger than humans. Doorways can be tricky places, astral world sticky wickets, and inimical, interfering, adversarial spirits like to congregate there like city punks on a street corner and exacerbate human passage through these gateways.

No angels were present now, but a host of Druj colleagues and protégés was. Their numbers were so great they had made their own doorway over the real one. This had the effect of narrowing the passageway and populating the gateway frame with unfriendly spirits. I saw that if they couldn't intimidate you, they'd confuse your perception, spawning false images of glamour or fear, depending on a person's susceptibility. Scare them or delude them; both work.

I saw some present-day Greeks, upon dying, sought to pass through the Eleusis gate. That was legitimate; the site was a kind of national gateway for Greeks. But the moment disembodied souls stepped into the gateway, they were jumped and would enter the *Bardo* and begin the after-death processing impeded by the presence of these baleful spirits clinging to their "backs," tainting their experience of the *Bardo*, and making the whole experience edgy and burdened.

I wondered why there were so many dark spirits at this gateway.

"Not just this one, but at most of them across the planet," said Matthew. "It's the result of entropy, inattention, growing materialism in perception, and the proliferation of dark practices, like black magic, dark-side rituals, or dilettantish spirit-summoning. All of these ill-advised practices invite the dark spirits to congregate. It invites them into this human interface between material life and the *Bardo*, so what was supposed to be a clear, unimpeded passageway is now one afflicted with inimical states of consciousness and their many personifications. These dark spirits look like they're 'fleshed' out from old models and standard stock figures found in the pages of a Babylonian grimoire.

"The result is the death passage is now troubled, and this feeds back into human embodied life and the human attitude towards death and the afterlife. People end up believing entirely wrong notions, either fantasies or fear pictures, or they disbelieve in any continuity of awareness after dropping the physical body, or they look upon the experience with trepidation and reluctance, that they will be dragged involuntarily into a nihilistic life termination, into nothingness.

"It takes them often a long time to get reoriented once they are here. Some stay fixated in these mistaken notions, as if frozen in place, and remain stuck. This in turn impedes the smooth flow of souls through the *Bardo* and darkens its perceived atmosphere for newcomers; it cascades and strengthens over time so that, as we've seen, the Druj has influence over much of the *Bardo* landscape."

Dark spirits were draped over the framework of the gateway, but strung across the open part of the passageway like a neon-hued banner was a series of holographic images. They were well executed; they looked like realities. But they were scary ones, ones that when you saw them you'd want to turn back. They were false images of course, but I saw they had the power to fool many people.

The first one you would see showed a dungeon in which bodies were being hacked apart, souls tortured, guards standing by, indifferent to their pain. The next one, like a shimmering curtain with a real-life picture displayed on it, showed angels with upraised swords, advancing on a flock of naked souls. The souls were scared, the angels implacable. There was no odor of sanctity here.

It struck me that some perverse artist, commissioned by the Druj presumably, had taken the dark images from Dante's *Inferno* and made persuasive holographic picture-draperies from them, though likely it was the reverse, and they inspired Dante to write them up in the first place to get them into culture. You'd pass through one holographic curtain, maybe realize in relief it was an illusion, and not see you had just entered another illusion and take it for reality. It would be as bewildering as waking up in a dream only to realize, chillingly, that you are still dreaming. You're in a labyrinth of dream states.

Matthew gestured for us to stand with him in this gateway. I marveled at the confidence and certainty he was exuding. We were going to reassert the Elohim sword at this liminal threshold between the worlds. It was like turning on a motor. I couldn't help laughing because it reminded me of a tree pulper. Where I lived in Hanover, New Hampshire, people often had problems with trees; they got diseased or, worse, fell over after heavy snowfalls or ice storms. They'd bring in tree experts with these loud bark and pulp shredders, turning the dead trees into little aromatic shavings, and they made a lot of noise doing it.

That's what our sword sounded like, though I knew it was not a physically audible sound. It may have been only my way of forming an image of its power. The noxious spirits blocking the gateway were starting to dissolve and the illusory holographic curtains were disassembling into pointillist images then vaporizing. It was effortless on our part; we had only to maintain our focus. It seemed we were stripping off centuries of dark accumulations; we were searing through hundreds of generations of humans who had been impeded. What the sword cooked off and atomized was a kind of *Akashic* Records of the Druj's successful obstruction of this once vital, much-trafficked Underworld gateway.

The angel guardians were returning to the gateway. It's not that they had kept away because they were intimidated by these Druj spirits; it was because the preponderance of the human group agreement had been to allow these dark spirits to assemble and block the doorway. The angels had to respect that wish and to tolerate the irony that for the most part humans did not realize any of this. They didn't know they had befouled their own gateway into the after-life realm, and that precluded, out of an exquisite respect for human free-will, the benign angelic guidance that was meant to be provided them as they went through it.

It was like we were inside a slide-show in which images of hundreds of years and the

travails of thousands of souls flashed before us in an archival disclosure. The gateway had become a movie theater and the air was floriated with images. It was like being swarmed by a flock of 10,000 birds, yet the moment we saw one image it flashed into ashes and was gone. We had just enough time to register its details, get its drama, then it was gone. Eventually, the air emptied out of images and spirits and the gateway processing was finished, but before that was completed I saw that some souls seemed to have been stuck in the gateways, their forward momentum frozen, possibly for a long time.

They looked like shadow forms of humans caught in a fisherman's net. They seemed frozen within a single gesture, like raising their hand in protest or leaning their heads forward to get a better look at something puzzling. Some of these figures, I surmised, were *bhūts*, because as we freed the gates of their accumulation of pictures, they flashed and sizzled into ashes and were gone. But others were actual human souls trapped in the webbing of this dirtied gateway.

They were talking, or else I heard their thoughts, but their speech seemed repetitive, like an old-fashioned phonograph record stuck on the same groove. The strangest and perhaps most unsettling aspect of this was I was certain for them no time had passed, that it was only a moment before that they entered this gate. They did not realize that perhaps centuries, or longer, had elapsed, and they had not moved an inch and were chronically immobilized in place and gesture. Time flowed in the outside, material world, years had come and gone, but since there was no time in the *Bardo*, no time had elapsed. It was all still right now, however long. Can you appreciate the strangeness of this contradiction?

I tried to listen to what some of these stuck souls were saying. It sounded like dream speech, like you hear when somebody mumbles in their sleep. It may make sense to them, wherever they are in the dream landscape, but outwardly, it sounds like gibberish or maybe only vaguely sensible glossolaliac speech.

Their eyes were open, staring fixedly at something. They didn't see me. Even their attention was fixed steady in this long-stretched moment, but as our sword worked on their condition, they started to wake up, shake their heads, look around in perplexity, like somebody arousing himself from a concussion, and then almost at once their forward passage was completed and they were gone, through the gateway and into the *Bardo* for their processing. I don't think they had any awareness of our intercession or that they had been delayed for a long time. As I said, it seemed to them that no time had elapsed. Meanwhile, so I imagined, compatriot souls commented to one another, "What ever happened to Andalusia? Haven't seen him in ages. I thought he'd have reincarnated by now."

Even the gateway was changed. It suddenly reformed itself, as if its presenting shape had been the result of contortion and tidal pressures applied by the Druj and her cohorts. I only now realized that this gate had looked odd, asymmetrical, fat on one side, lean on another, even anorexic in a third zone, lopsided, tilted over, unsteady, looking liable to fall over or sink into the ground. Now it was upstanding, symmetrical, golden, bright, solid, taller, broader, and like brand new, fresh out of the Light temple factory showroom. It reminded me of what a once blocked drain looks like after the plumber has unclogged it. The water flows quickly and swirls properly down the opening, unobstructed. The souls, no longer trapped, were streaming steadily through the gateway now.

The reader may find this next observation challenging to credit, but I was certain I detected a global lightening of the *Bardo* gateway network as we freed this single gate at Eleusis. I had the impression all the gates streamed better now even if individually some were still blocked and in need of our attention, that somehow, as they used to say in the TV show *Stargate SG-1*, this one improved gate had initiated a "correlative update" of all the gates or Underworld portals.

"I have an idea on how to make it easier to understand the *Bardo*," said Tommy. "Let's install a kind of educational video right here at the gate. The initiates at Eleusis had the chance to preview their eventual *Bardo* experience. The Tibetans had their text read to them when they died, and the Egyptians had their funerary texts, with all the names of the *Duat* gods you had to bribe. Modern people have only had horror movies and flawed near-death experience reports. Why not do the same for people coming through this portal. Make it like the airport scanners where they X-ray your whole body to see if you're carrying guns, but instead, the scanner projects a view of the *Bardo* for the specific person. 'Hello, Mr. Johnson. Sorry you died, but here's a preview of your *Bardo* events.'

"They get to view themselves in likely encounters and karma-processing scenarios in advance so they can prepare themselves for its controlled weirdness. See all the gargoyles and scary mind-projected hallucinatory spirits beforehand so they won't be so startled and thrown off balance when these weird things manifest. Even better, this will match the Earth's Light grid upgrade to the sixth chakra level of operation where people will start automatically being psychic. So here they have a psychic, sixth-chakra-flavored impression of their upcoming events. They get used to the fact the *Bardo* is a psychic landscape. They can start matching that raised vibration before they enter the realm and business begins."

"It makes sense, surely," said Edward. "When you buy an appliance or a car, you always get a detailed booklet explaining fully how the machine works. The salesman too will give you the highlights of the machine's operations. It's about time there was some kind of instruction manual for the *Bardo* passage. So much depends on our getting through it correctly. It would benefit everyone if there were an illustrated user's manual on how to work the *Bardo* successfully.

"I mean, yes, there are such handbooks, but they're written in Tibetan or Egyptian, meaning they use culturally-conditioned names, deities, monsters, and assumptions. We need a new one in English, which means updated to current conditions of unfortunately nonmythic consciousness and without specific cultural patterns, but more generic, adjustable to a dying soul from any country. Call this a Gaian handbook for *Bardo* protocols, suitable for any Earth human. Without this, there is unlimited opportunity for the Druj to interfere with it. It's such an unfair advantage handed to the adversary; it's time to even the field. We need more informed consumers, making informed choices about their destiny."

"We could put up billboards, 'The *Bardo*— More Fun Than You Thought!' said Blaise. "Or: 'Tartarus—It's a Killer Vacation Spot, Bring the Whole Family!'"

"It's been approved," said Merlin, with a grin. "He likes the idea."

But we were already at our next location. We were on the slopes of a steep mountain with a massive white sculpted head of a Buddha-like figure behind us. A small city with many concrete buildings and a broad dark river lay below us. Around us and down the slope were numerous shrines, temples, deity statues, dioramas, walkways, and small bridges, and, oddly, a great number of tourists. The depictions of the deities were clearly Chinese in style, but more striking was their valence: they looked like Chinese death-gods, gargoyles, and what Chinese mythology called the Ten Yama Kings, fierce assistants to Yama, Lord of Death. The dioramas, or three-dimensional

miniature models of real-life scenes, depicted souls undergoing torture, punishment, and other after-death horrors.

"Can you believe it?" exclaimed Blaise. "It's a Chinese Underworld theme park set at an actual Underworld gateway. It doesn't get any cooler than that. And with complimentary despairing graffiti all over it, compliments of the Druj."

We turned to Merlin for an explanation. He would know where we were. "It's called Fengdu Ghost City on the Yangtze River in south-central China. This is Ming Mountain we're standing upon. It's also called Ming Shan Hill. We're on the river's north bank. Much of the original Ghost City is now under water as a result of a large dam-building project a few decades ago. The site is dedicated to illustrating key aspects of the Underworld passage, and it is believed to be about 2,000 years old. It was a preferred burial ground for Taoists, though some say only the evil or failed Taoists, their ghosts, are buried here, those who did not achieve immortality; the good ones made it to Heaven.

"The site acquired the name Ghost City when, as legend has it, two Taoists achieved immortality on this mountain, thereby highlighting the site's propensity for facilitating this achievement. You see, already we encounter a contradiction in interpretation, the Druj's work. The Taoists' combined names spelled *Yinwan*, meaning 'King of Hell,' a name that began (and justified) the site's reputation as an Underworld portal. The design of Fengdu Ghost City is meant to resemble *Youdu*, the capital of *Diyu*, the Chinese name for the Underworld city of Yama. *Youdu* means 'dark, hidden, secluded capital,' and *Diyu* means 'Earth Prison.' It's a grim picture of what you should expect in China's Underworld.

"They see *Diyu* as a purgatory or Hell realm, a *Bardo*. It's their picture of the Great Below, the

Yellow Springs, because yellow was the color of Earth and springs lie in the Earth. It has 10 Courts of Hell, with one of the 10 Yama Kings acting as presiding judge over its affairs. Some Chinese accounts state there are 12,800 hells situated under the Earth, including eight dark hells, eight cold hells, and 84,000 miscellaneous hells; or, instead of 10 Courts of Hell, there are 18 levels of Hell, also subterranean. The Greeks pictured three Judges of the Dead, but in *Diyu* you can expect 10. These are the 10 Kings of Hell, the *Shih-Wang.* Yes, the Chinese numbers are all over the place, enough to frustrate any accountant.

"The Kings are like stern magistrates in a 10-part Underworld court system. When you're dead you have to go through 10 ordeals, each presided over by a *Shih-Wang* or Underworld King. The Second Court of Hell is The Pool of Filth and the Hell of Ice, ruled by Lord Li, King of Chŭjiāng. Or how about the Fifth Court of Sixteen Departments of Heart Gouging, the Sixth Court of Screaming Torture and Administrative Error, or the Eighth Court of Hell called Hot Suffocation Hell. The names are evocative, don't you think. The goal is to get through these hellish magistrate courts as fast as possible; funerary rites conducted by the living, it was hoped, would speed up the judicial process.

"During the first 49 days after your decease, you go through seven trials, lasting seven days each. Then you are judged by a *Shih-Wang* and your fate and *Diyu* residency are assigned. The Chinese glumly liken it to passing through a series of dreary bureaucratic offices. Then you get three more trials over the ensuing three years. They've even made crossing the River Acheron scarier than the Greeks. The Chinese call it *Nai-ho*, domain of the King of the First River, the first *Shih-Wang* you have to deal with. Ox-headed jailers force you to cross. Over time, the Chinese built up a fearsome picture of harsh Underworld justice.

"But it ends benignly, in a manner. After your torments in the City of Ghosts is finished, you enter the Tenth Court and Lord Xuē decides the conditions of your next life, after which Mother Mèng Po gives you the Tea of Oblivion. This erases your memory and ensures you will forget all your Yellow Springs punishments. She is 'Old Lady Meng,' the Lady of Forgetfulness. Her tea is also called Five-Flavored Tea of Forgetfulness, the *Mi-hun-t'ang*, or 'waters of oblivion' which produce instant amnesia and you lose all memory of previous lives. It's the River Lethe in a tea-cup. Drink up, lads, and forget everything."

"This place is like an early version of my idea of a *Bardo* scanner," said Tommy. "It looks like you can walk through simulations of the key stages."

Tommy was right. As I later understood when I put together a functional map of Fengdu, it featured a physical representation of three Underworld tests. First was the Bridge of Helplessness (or the Nothing-To-Be-Done Bridge), represented here by a short but actual stone bridge with three arches which you could walk across and simulate the *Bardo* (or *Diyu*) test for good and evil propensities in your psychic space. Demons (physically represented by vividly painted, larger-than-life sculptures in devilry costumes and postures) are understood to allow or block the passage of souls across this bridge; the bad souls are tossed over into the water below. This is the Chinese version of the *Cinvat*, the Bridge of the Separator, in which the soul makes it across if its proven nature is good or falls (or is pushed) off the bridge if it's proven to be bad.

The second test was the Ghost-Torturing Pass where souls are judged by Yama, accompanied by 18 vivid sculptures of leering Chinese-style demons. In the third test at the entrance to Tianzi Palace, the dead must stand on a stone with one foot raised for three minutes.

The virtuous will succeed, the evil soul will fail. Tianzi Palace is huge, 3,000 square yards in size, with a 30-foot high archway. Tianzi is a Chinese name for the King of the Dead (Yama, Hades), and the name also translates as Son of Heaven, the universal emperor who rules *Tianxia*, meaning "all under Heaven." Tianzi is the imperial ruler of all the world.

That big white sculptured Buddha-head, by the way, is called the Ghost King, and it stands 452 feet tall and measures 711 feet across. Maybe it's meant to represent Tianzi. It's visible from the river. No, that understates it. The Ghost King's visage looms mightily over all the city and the Yangzte the way Yama looms testily over the *Bhavachakra* or Wheel of Life in Tibetan depictions. The site is regarded as one of the graveyards for Taoists, a spirit-world getaway. I doubt the newly dead Chinese would miss this entrance with a white head that big.

I shared Blaise's enthusiasm for the ideas behind this site. It was a partial externalization of the Mysteries of Eleusis; they had made visual, even palpable, some of the key stages in the *Bardo* passage as a way of preparing people for the real experience. Any kind of advance knowledge and preparation is desirable.

We had been seeing the need for that throughout our expedition, and the many shortcomings of that not being the case. Sadly, the initiation theme park intent behind Fengdu had degenerated into merely a mild horror theme park for its entertainment value, and that decline into comic-book quality, not surprisingly, had drawn a host of inimical or interfering spirits to the site. You could see them loitering like teenagers with nothing better to do at the gate. It was an arresting site, but it was also comical: real demons lingering by the fake ones, next to dioramas that sought to depict what *Diyu* spirits and demons did.

Fengdu had lost a fair amount of its intended numinosity. This was due largely, I think, to the popularity of the site among tourists and the decline in the belief that the dioramas and the layout of the three challenges had any reality. The site was no longer used by Taoists for initiation; it was a fun park for secular tourists. That took the initiation edge off the displays, which would otherwise conduct consciousness, at least momentarily, into the reality of *Diyu* behind the depiction. Now it was only the depiction that presented itself to consciousness, and that had lapsed into a somewhat cartoonish triviality and folkloric hearsay.

Visitors might know this spectacle of displays was supposed to represent the passages of *Diyu* in the Underworld capital city of *Youdu*, but that was only mental. The site didn't have much effect on the body, emotions, and psyche. It didn't grab you by the shirt-collar and shake you vigorously like it once did. And the loitering actual *Bardo* spirits were spreading mists of illusion and distraction upon the visitors, who left Fengdu with mistaken or distorted views of it.

Their tactics, the Druj's tactics, were always the same: prevent living humans from forming an accurate idea of the after-death protocols. Give them illusions. Copies of those illusions now hung like astral curtains throughout the site, and visitors to Fengdu walked amongst them, probably unaware of their influence. They might contemplate the various sculpted images of demons torturing human souls in *Diyu*, as if roasting them on the spit, and take it in as charming, scary, and irrelevant to their concerns or life, and not realize that they were seeing a depiction of the mechanics of our karma and how we torture ourselves, roasting ourselves in our negativity even as we walk around alive, cheerily taking photographs and sending messages or photos to our friends.

Instead, I suspect people, if they even thought about this display, would assume "bad" people get what they deserved, get punished by the authorities for ill-advised behavior, and it is best to behave, do things properly, be quiet, stay in line, do nothing to draw attention to yourself, and that way maybe you'd be safe.

Oddly, I was wondering what George F. Babbitt would make of *Diyu*. He was the fictional character in Sinclair Lewis's 1922 novel, *Babbitt*. Age 46, married, with kids, a real-estate agent, a Solid American Citizen and Good Fellow, an all-round civic booster of the growing Midwestern city of Zenith in 1920, he was a man utterly outer-directed, mastering the game as others defined it, making a religion out of business and, as it were, spiritual figures out of his colleagues. He'd have to read the newspapers to find out about his inner life.

Babbitt was a "God-fearing, hustling, successful, two-fisted Regular Guy," smoking a cigar, mowing his lawn, engorged to the hilt with zip, pep, and bang. He got his individual opinions from the Presbyterian Church, the Republican Party, and the newspaper editorials, and his sense of individual worth from advertisers. His concept of the afterlife was that if you were a Good Man you'd go to "a place" called Heaven, like an "excellent hotel with a private garden."

Yes, Babbitt was a fictional character, Lewis's parody of the American provincial commanding the world through business transactions and whose forebears may have emigrated from Middlemarch with its middling lives. I was wondering how a guy like that, and there still are many like that, outer-focused, depending on consensus reality to get their bearings, not probing within too deeply, or at all, would fare once he hit the *Bardo*. All of us have some of this Babbitt-mind within us, see the world the way he does, prefer the world to be only a realm of manageable surfaces, without depths or esoteric aspects. Babbitt represented the level of consciousness the *Bardo* changes

ultimately had to address, because ultimately Babbitt and his clones one day would have to comprehend the *Bardo* landscape and make it through its protocols. We would have to make a *Bardo* mystic out of booster George F. Babbitt from Zenith, U.S.A.

I couldn't imagine Babbitt making much sense of the Tibetan *Bardo* spectacle. I wondered if he would have to. I had read reports, albeit from channeled sources with an inherent dubiousness to their accuracy, that often after death people sleep in the astral world for a considerable time and then remain in a kind of spiritual-world hospital until they feel ready to take their bearings. The impression I formed from that was that their life review was on pause and would resume when they were ready. Time is so different here.

Some souls of course did not realize they were dead and sought to replicate their daily activities and living circumstances. Others, knowing they were deceased, sought to return in some manner to their former physical haunts and resume their lives. What would Babbitt do, I wondered. Could he allow the *Bardo* to jackhammer its way through the pavement of complacency and supposed normalcy in his mind? Would he ever stand up as a booster for Yama?

I wondered which was worse, to have no idea of the *Bardo* or a distorted notion of its procedures? By "worse" I mean liable to generate more confusion. That dichotomy was played out in public in earlier decades in America when the popularity of near-death experiences and sensational reports of those exploits garnered a lot of public attention. People assumed the mechanics of a *near*-death experience were identical to *actual* death and could be taken as advance knowledge of what to expect. Tunnels of Light, greetings from departed loved ones, beneficent welcomes by high-level spiritual beings, the cinematic life review, the reluctant return to embodied life to play out the remainder of life allotment, counting the days until you could joyously return to this great place.

But the near-death experience, it turned out, was more like an edited, abridged, and simplified operatic overture to the actual death experience and not identical to it. Why weren't they the same? Mainly because in near-death you cannot cross the *Cinvat* Bridge; it is premature. You would be at best a tourist, not a resident, not someone here for real, in earnest, out to plan his next move. Most of what the *Tibetan Book of the Dead* recounts takes place on that bridge, and in near-death you're not allowed on it. Even if you were, it wouldn't count because your physical body was still viable and you were expected to rejoin it.

You also have not severed the silver cord that connects your corporeal body to your astral double. When that's cut, then you're dead, officially. With the silver cord intact, you would be only a dabbler, out slumming for entertainment, a casual summer weekend visitor, somebody flying their astral body like a high-flying kite. You're not committed; you can't be because you're not dead. You would be pretending, simulating, and it would have no karmic consequence because you were still firmly secured to physical life and your body by that cord. It would be like a cup of decaffeinated coffee; it has the taste, but no kick. Not a single entry in your *Akashic* Records would be changed from this simulation, other than the inconsequential fact that you had the experience, worth a footnote.

We began our sword concentration. We expanded the sword to be the size of Ming Mountain, all the way down to the Yangtze River. It dwarfed the Ghost King, probably the only time something bigger has been set over that monstrous cranium. The actual demons and their illusory curtains of Light started to

sizzle. I had the strange impression we were only burning up copies of these demons, that they had multiple manifestations like angels and Masters were accorded. The sword scoured both sides of the gateway, and it scourged the gateway too.

Afterwards, as I watched the tourists who were still merrily mingling among the dioramas, the other *Diyu* theme park displays, and our Elohim sword as well, some felt a little tingling on their skins, felt the sharp edge of reality. They registered a slight chill, unaccountable, as if something spiritual had just brushed up against them, not anything inimical, just more real than real life. They felt the slight breath of the *Diyu* on their mortal skin; it quickened them.

I think the cliché people used to employ for that queer sensation was to say they felt somebody had just walked over their grave. However I describe it, I'm trying to say that it seemed some of the visitors felt the touch of the reality of *Diyu*, and this was a good thing, what the site, after all, had been designed to facilitate. For these people *Diyu* was no longer merely theoretical; they felt it.

It's like you had been wearing a thick brown cloak of atheism, and suddenly a genuine angel touched the surface of this cloak ever so slightly and it dissolved, and you felt refreshed, naked, released, flushed with a sudden desire to inquire. Who just touched me? What are these new sensations I am having? Who am I? It's a curious thing but the revelation that you are mortal, that your physical body one day will die and you will be ejected as a body of awareness into the *Bardo*, is merely the other side of realizing you are alive, are conscious.

I sometimes think that is the more frightening discovery, that you are alive, a *separate* unit of universal consciousness with the *responsibility* of free will, that you have been wielding this awesome tool of awareness up to now in a state of distraction or somnolence, never stopping to wonder how you got it or why. You are George F. Babbitt and you've just brushed up against the clear voidness.

I never used to think this way, but from my travels with Blaise, I have started to ask all sorts of questions, and I view life, reality, and consciousness altogether differently. The human Blaise had that kind of angel's touch on my shoulder that dissolved the cloak of secular materialism and agnosticism I wore. And, as I gathered from his own biography, he'd received the same touch from the angelic Blaises, though he was not perhaps as obdurately agnostic as I was.

"Has anyone else appreciated the fact that each culture clothes its *Bardo* demons and guides differently?" asked Edward. "I find it engrossing. We have been dealing with the Tibetan Buddhist way of picturing *Bardo* realities, and now we have the Chinese. They are not the same, though they have similarities. In the same way the Underworld gateways for these different cultures have their own style of spirits and pictures impeding them and of course their own list of names.

"Most of the cultures we've examined so far locate the Underworld *underneath*, *inside* the Earth. Souls go *down* into the Earth to get to the fearsome Underworld, and these cultures— I'm thinking of the Greek and Chinese at the moment—let the general topography of the Underworld slide into the singular pejorative of being called a Hell realm. The Underworld with its varieties of conditions gets equated solely with the Hell realm, a place of punishment and misery, but it's only one zone among many. The frame is radically narrowed.

"You see this especially in the Lapp picture of *Rotaimo*, the fearsome realm of Rota, the unforgiving lord of the death realm. He is a male deity who likes to punish those souls too degenerate to have made it into *Saivo*, or 'Happy,' the Lapp paradise. Rota torments the souls in his realm inside the Earth and he delivers pestilence upon the living. He has an animus against humans, according to the Lapps. The Lapps try to appease him with expensive animal sacrifices. *Rotaimo* is a grim Underworld picture, a chilling realm of torture and misery.

"In contrast, the Celtic picture of the Underworld as *Annwn* is perhaps among the oldest because there is no mention of this realm lying inside the Earth. Its location is ambiguous, neither subterranean or across any body of water, though it can be reached through gateways that lead into the Earth or that lie on islands. Nobody says it's a grim and fearsome place, just a tricky, mercurial one.

"Sometimes *Annwn* is equated wholesale with *Caer Sidi*, the revolving fairy castle that flickers in and out of visibility, or with a magical Fortress of Glass situated on an enigmatic island. *Annwn* is a *parallel* world *near* to our world, and in some respects our world contains *Annwn* though it is invisible and unapproachable under most conditions except, I suppose, a Green Knight expedition like ours. The Celtic picture of *Annwn* seems untainted by the distorting hand of the Druj. *Annwn*, you believe, lies adjacent to our physical realm, and it may be entered, possibly, through certain stealth-veiled doorways. The dead go there surely, but so do some psychically skilled living humans.

"I suspect the manipulating hand of the Druj in making these interpretive, and I would say, degenerative, corruptive changes from *Annwn* to *Rotaimo* or *Diyu*. Along the way, the picture got distorted. It's just the kind of change in emphasis and valency, the shift to the darker, grimmer mode of perception, she revels in. Instead of understanding you are making these projections, Druj makes you believe they are being *done to you*, that you are the deserving but passive, powerless recipient of these dreadful images of torment and bad-intentioned spirits who hate humans.

"With that shift in operation, your only recourse is supplication, to request a remission in the nastiness from these powerful spirits. You must appeal to the tyrant for mercy, pledging your valuables for succor. Then, cruelly, she sits back and laughs, because you don't know *you* are the tyrant, you are the powerful spirit who has the mercy you desperately require."

"You're right," said Tommy. "The Tibetan picture has dark spirits, ones that initially appear demonic, ill-intentioned, like cranky gargoyles on a bad day, but the Tibetan text makes it clear those spirits are not there to punish souls. They mirror innate conditions of your soul; they are the product of karmically-driven hallucinations. Their goal, ultimately, is to help the soul in the *Bardo* wake up. That subtlety of intention is lost in the Lapp and Chinese pictures. The demons are just nasty and they intend to roast your ass because you were bad.

"There's no suggestion of the soul waking up from the grip of their own mental projections, that the *Bardo* is a benignly designed environment for enlightenment. That takes the human freedom aspect out of the picture, the fact that we can, with diligence, upgrade our cognition and understanding of what we see and wake up and then get off the Wheel of Life, the addictive merry-go-round of more lives and more stuckness or doing more punishable deeds. You behave badly, you go to astral jail, and you can forget about rehabilitation."

"Those models take consciousness out of the picture, and self-aware consciousness of the *Bardo*-transiting soul is no longer considered a factor," said Blaise. "That vital aspect was preserved or reintroduced in the Tibetan text. How you wield your cognition, how you find the emptiness, the blissful voidness that erases your cognition and thus dissolves the apparent horror show, the dance routine scripted by

your karma, makes all the difference. *You* run the *Bardo* show. That picture of potent responsibility is entirely lost in these other death images."

We had shifted to another location in the midst of our conversation. At this new site, which was on the slopes of a not completely dormant volcano, even the physicality of the place suggested the punishments of the Hell realm. The landscape around us was grey, barren, charred, naked; steam and hot water bubbled out of little fissures in the cracked landscape, while below us lay a lake (it looked lifeless, even forlorn), as if painted in dark hues of blue. I estimated we were standing a few thousand feet above the lake. Even though we were not there in physical form, I smelled sulfur. It seeped out of the ground and filled the air. On the horizon I saw eight smaller peaks, a river, a Buddhist temple.

"Welcome to Osorezan, Mount Osore, known as Fear Mountain," said Merlin, clearly enjoying the histrionic opportunities of being our tour guide. "Yes, this is Japan, and we stand on the upper slopes of a caldera volcano that last erupted significantly in 1787 but is not yet completely dormant, as you see. It's also called *Yakeyama*, Burning Mountain, because of this latent volcanism. The Japanese regard this site as pre-eminently holy, one of the gateways to Hell; in fact, it's one of Japan's three holiest sites. They believe the dead come here to enter the Underworld, and why not? The place has an Underworld portal."

The Japanese had not needed to recreate this site as an Underworld theme park. The volcano to a large extent took care of that *mise en scène* requirement. The place is generally described as creepy and unsettling; the waters of Lake Usori are toxic, acidic, and poisonous, and dangerous snakes abound nearby. The weather is terrible in the winter, cold with howling winds. The site itself is remote, hard to get to, though many tourists flock here in the summer. Site designers have added some appropriate Underworld touches. The volcanic residues look like they were designed for a horror movie, with a barren blasted landscape and bubbling, fuming pits of sulfur. The physical features and ambiance of the place aptly dramatize the Japanese notion of a nasty Hell realm.

A small footbridge spans the Sanzu River, a physical stream but believed to also represent what the Greeks would call the River Acheron, the boundary between the living and dead. The *Sanzu no Kawa*, a red arched footbridge, imitates the *Cinvat* Bridge. The entire site is guarded, says folkloric belief, by Jizo, the bodhisattva of Hell and the guardian of children, and you will encounter statues of this august figure here. *Bodai-ji*, the Buddhist Bodai temple, founded in A.D. 862, is the principal building you'll see. The temple is set amidst numerous *jigoku*, or "hells," small bubbling volcanic cauldrons, canary yellow to blood red.

It was founded as a Soto Zen meditation temple, but one of its main activities in recent years has been the twice-yearly *Itako Taisai* festival. The prime event begins on July 20 in a ritual called *kuchiyose*: blind psychics or spiritual mediums, called *itako* or *ichiko*, usually old women (or at least older than 40), working in tents channel the dead. If you have a dead loved one, these mediums can summon them and let them speak to you in a simulated human voice.

I'm surprised the Soto Zen Masters aren't striding through the crowds of people talking to these freelance spirits and accusing them of spawning *makyo* (illusions and hallucinations) and giving them a whack with the Zen paddle to wake them up from their trance state. Maybe they won't have to. The *itako*'s numbers are dwindling, the government disapproves, and as the female shamans capable of performing this traditional feat die out, few remain to take their place. Apparently, back in the 1930s there

were 100 *itako* at work during the festival week, and the people who travelled to Osorezan in July spent the nights here dancing, singing, and joyfully engaging in séances with their dead friends.

It reminded me of the scene in *The Odyssey* where crowds of dead spirits petitioned Odysseus to pass on messages to their still living loved ones. They were "dying" to make the connection back with the sunlit human world. They clamored, they petitioned, they swarmed Odysseus to get him to comply. The *Itako Taisai* seemed like a festival that made that a formal activity, and why not?

The thrust of our expedition has been to come up with ways to improve the *Bardo* passage and to improve the links between the physical and *Bardo* realms. Talking with deceased humans, assuming it is done competently, seems a good idea. If the reports came through clearly and the spirit's bona fides established, it would be fresh empirical information about likely Underworld conditions. On the other hand, often mediums only channel ghost fragments and astral remnants of the once living; it is like channeling a ventriloquist's dummy, in which case the communications and data presented would not be accurate and you'd get your trusting butt kicked good and proper by the duplicitous *bhūts*.

Still, surely the geomantic endowment of this site with an Underworld gateway would make that activity easier and maybe assure its reality. The *Bardo* does begin here. In fact, *Bodai-ji* was regarded as a legitimate point of entry for conscientious souls desiring either a Buddhist rebirth or to end their rebirths. And Jizo, Hell guardian and children's protector, was not just a dumb demon.

He was not a demon at all. He was in fact quite a respectable figure. His formal name in Sanskrit is *Ksitigarbha*, which means Earth Treasure, Earth Matrix, or Earth Womb, and

Chinese know him as Bodhisattva King Earth-Matrix of the Great Vow. This enlightened spirit, much like Western archangels (and specifically like the Archangel Gabriel in his work: he's like the Archangel Gabriel because *he is* that archangel seen through Japanese eyes; think of the Annunciation as an Earth Treasure event), pledged to instruct all sentient spirits in the topography and operations of the Six Worlds of the Wheel of Life and to delay their definitive enlightenment and Wheel release until every last soul has been saved and all the Hell realms are utterly emptied out of their residents.

Jizo is the guardian of children, the patron of deceased children, and especially of aborted fetuses. Known also as *Ojizo-sama*, he dresses up like a kerchiefed monk, carries a staff to open the Hell gates, and flashes the wish-fulfilling jewel to illuminate the dark areas. He rescues children from the iron club-wielding demons of Hell. Souls of dead children and unborn fetuses make bridges out of piles of pebbles and they try to cross the Sanzu River to enter the Underworld this way. The demons keep disrupting these piles, but Jizo keeps reconstituting the pebbles. I imagine the children are encouraged to walk briskly.

Meanwhile, humans, proposing to cross the bridge are confronted by two demons. A female devil, *Datsueba*, strips off your clothes, while a male devil, *Keneo*, weighs your clothes on tree branches to assess your moral valency and karma. It's a kind of laundry version of the Weighing of the Heart ceremony.

Based on the outcome, you may pass into the Underworld in one of three crossings. The virtuous cross the bridge easily; those of average moral accomplishments use a shallow path across the river; those who led evil lives must wade through the waters and fight off the demons and poisonous snakes along the way. The clothes part seems odd at first, but possibly the original shamanic meaning was

your life-bodies, the karmic condition of your physical, etheric, and astral forms, which you drop *like clothes*, once you're in the *Bardo*. As they say, clothes reveal the man, so the state of your cast-off bodies tells all.

The emphasis at Mount Osore is mostly on the hellish side of the Underworld, but the larger Japanese formulation is *Yomi-no-Kuni*, the land of the dead and the world of darkness, deriving mostly from the Shinto formulation. It draws upon the earlier Chinese formulation of *Diyu* ("Yellow Springs") and is believed to lie beneath the Earth's surface. *Yomi*'s ruler is *Izanami-no-Mikoto*. *Yomi* is considered to be a polluted land, and some of its entrances are blocked.

What makes the Japanese description able to picque our interest is the identity of its ruler. *Izanami-no-Mikoto*, "She Who Invites." She is one of two principal Creation deities for the Japanese and their islands, involved in the original generation of both. With her male celestial consort, *Izanagi-no-Mikoto*, "He Who Invites," she created Japan's eight islands and established a central court that functions as an umbilicus for the Japanese soul. This was the Pillar of Heaven, a national umbilicus, around which they built a palace, *Yahiro-dono*. In giving birth to her son, *Kagu-Tsuchi*, the incarnation of or causer of fire, she died and was buried on Mount Hiba.

In thinking about this story I realized it's a localized version of the founding of the Underworld by the first human to die. The first human to enter the Underworld becomes the pre-eminent *Yomi* guide. That redeems the Japanese concept of the Underworld from being yet another infernal subterranean landscape of retributive punishment and karmic reprisals. It seems likely that *Izanami-no-Mikoto* in fact did not die nor was she human, though it is convenient for the story to think so. More likely she is the designated place holder and site marker for the Japanese and for their ethnos landscape. Perhaps in a general sense she oversees all the death protocols involving Japanese souls.

The Japanese picture of the Underworld still shares some of the erroneous simplifications we saw in the Chinese picture. It is underground, dark, polluted, but the presence of the Bodhisattva *Ksitigarbha* and the superintendency of *Yomi* by *Izanami-no-Mikoto* were promising developments, suggesting a clearer model.

Again, I marveled at the literalness of the Underworld theme park idea of Osorezan. You could walk through a material landscape meant to simulate some of the after-death procedures, and your body, mind, and emotions could feel it. I think that would be the key: the *Yomi* protocols would seem real to the body. The message, at least in its broad strokes, would infiltrate one's daytime self. That is, assuming you took the message of the theme park seriously; if not, then it might glance off your consciousness as another novelty, a trinket type of experience.

I saw that precisely this was one of the Druj's tactics here at Osorezan. She was making the experience of walking the simulated *Yomi* landscape feel trivial. Entertaining, yes, fascinating, sure, but indicative of the reality of death, no. She nudged the fear and creepiness element whenever she could; the bubbling pits and sulfur clouds certainly helped, because those images have been popularly associated with Hell for a long time, even if they are not accurate or descriptive. They have become such defanged visual clichés that you're likely to ignore them.

The barren, volcanically savaged landscape and the often bleak, cold weather conditions further accentuated the undesirable, infernal, fearful aspect of *Yomi*. Any time a person shivered, not from the cold, but from the import of what they were seeing, the Druj pushed it further, insinuated fear pictures and thoughts

into their minds, pushing them further along that grim track of misperception. She wanted to convert the conveyed experience of Osorezan from educational and preparatory to fear-based and full of dread and trepidation. Instead of seeing the *Yomi* theme park as like an open door providing a vista of the Underworld, she wanted it to feel like a glimpse of an awful Hell realm, and it wouldn't hurt anything if this spectacle has a comic book ambiance of exaggeration, broad strokes, heightened emotion, and a grim cartoonish quality.

We started our sword work. As the Light of the Elohim sword blazed outwards through the Osorezan site and inwards into the *Yomi* landscape, I saw the shadow forms of the thousands of tourists who had come here, marveled or trembled, and failed to penetrate the afterlife Mystery presentation of the site. I saw them wondering if any of this spectacle was real and could they avoid it. They only received the outermost impression of this theme park, and in turn left impressions of their own superficial or edgy engagement with its energies.

I don't mean this description in any judgemental sense. It's just that these tourists left what I am tempted to call astral photographs of themselves as acquisitive tourists, consuming yet another attraction in the entertainment and vacation landscape of affluent Japan, but not allowing themselves to be moved beyond the surface, not feeling, perhaps, the genuine touch of *Yomi*. Those ghostly imprints dissolved quickly, but behind them was a wall of images.

Let's say you were a talented artist and you made a series of painted silk curtains featuring pictures from all the relevant Japanese myths and folklore beliefs about death, the afterlife, and the Underworld and its spirits and actions. These images were so expertly rendered that on seeing them you'd take them for reality itself, for the spectral life going on right now in *Yomi*. The trouble is, they were not accurate; most of them were based on misperceptions, wrong or incomplete interpretations, fear, uncertainty, clouded vision, and assumptions.

Souls using the Osorezan gate to enter *Yomi* walked through them like a sprinkler system misting them with pictures and got a subtle imprint of those images and began their Underworld journey misinformed and "polluted." They would have to shed these pictures before they could begin to see *Yomi* for itself, and then they would still have to shed the hallucinatory layer of their psyche to penetrate the reality and the reflective processes of the *Yomi* landscape to catch even the outermost level of subtle *Bardo* perception the Tibetans wrote about. They would potentially enter the *Bardo* handicapped by the Druj's pictures.

The Druj also exploited the obvious resemblance of the physical, nightmarish landscape of Osorezan to biblical portraits of the Hell realms, emphasizing the physicality of Hell and thereby erecting a solid, though false, visual impression. The fallacy in her presentation is that this Underworld entrance was established long before the Mount Osore volcano existed; as Blaise explains, the planet's geomantic terrain was imprinted on a flat surface planet. So any resemblance between the physical appearance of Osorezan and the dogmatic portrayal of the Hell landscape is fortuitous, unreal, and entirely irrelevant. Even so, it has a subliminal impact on people primed to *expect* Hell to look like this. For the Druj, it is conveniently coincidental in appearance, thus, good enough.

We found the Druj had dispatched a host of demonic figures to distort the compassionate ambiance set in motion by the presence of the Bodhisattva *Jizo-Ksitigarbha*. She crafted an impression that this bodhisattva was overwhelmed by the abundance of dark spirits, and that punishment and dark reckoning were the *Yomi* reality. She further made it look like the *Itako* were channeling psychotic, feral witches,

and that the living humans who came in all earnestness to speak with their deceased loved ones were being fooled mightily and were in fact talking to demons. Sorry, *Jizo-Ksitigarbha* could do nothing to help humans.

She was also encouraging official disapproval of and public disbelief in the act of mediumship, leading to the decline of available *Itako* and the end of the practice. That was particularly regrettable, for though mediumship often is fraught with error, illusion, glamour, and deliberate misdirection, the *Itako* of Osorezan were an exception. They trained for months in preparation for this vital task of acting as a voice conduit for souls in *Yomi* with living people. More than anything else, this mediumship validated the reality of the afterlife. I've learned from Blaise that any time you find training associated with psychic activity, it's a good sign and speaks to the possibility of accuracy and utility in what is said.

I had to hand it to the Druj. She was talented and effective. She didn't miss a trick in fooling, befuddling, or altogether frightening souls. She wouldn't like it that we were disassembling her machinations with our purgative Elohim sword. I didn't think, though, our cleansing work would bring back the *Itako* to Osorezan. The shamanic impulse that practice came out of was dying in Japan.

"We are trained to talk to those who have gone beyond," said Pipaluk. "We have our special places in the terrain where the doors are wide open. We have our secret places where this communication takes place, where it's easier. It has always been seen as a normal part of our life, and the *angakkuqs* are trained to do this. My mother and her teacher taught me how to let the dead talk through me. It helps people. It reassures them there is continuity. It creates a good bridge.

"Sometimes, if the spirit is strong and the person is well-trained and with clear knowledge, the dead provide little trips for the living to explore the Underworld. A person may have a question that burns inside them, demanding an answer. Or they may feel a part of their soul is missing, has been taken, bitten off by a spirit. Or they are desperate to understand their destiny, the purpose of their life. The *angakkuq* and the helpful Underworld spirit arrange a journey and we take living persons in their dreams or perhaps during the daytime, if their attention is strong and steady, to the place where they can achieve their answers.

"We take them into this *Yomi* landscape, this *Bardo*, as you like to call it, though we cannot cross the bridge with them. That is only for those who are deceased. We are like these *Itako*, except we do this work any time in the year, when people need it or ask us. I understand these *Itako* women. I know them."

I was watching the *Itako* transmit the presence and words of the dead. These women were not at Osorezan at this moment in time, as this was winter, so I realized I must be seeing impressions of when they were here in summer, or perhaps of the complete gesture over time of their compassionate bridge-making.

It seemed like a good thing, to facilitate some communication between the disembodied and those in bodies. It assures sensitive humans of the continuity of consciousness, though in an altered or more streamlined, purer sense; and it creates threads between the two realms of human existence, also a good thing. Naturally, anything that is good, that works, that furthers human awareness, the Druj found a way to interfere with it, impede it, distort it, and, finally, corrupt it.

I saw dark spirits continuously trying to climb on top of the *Itako*'s heads. Or to push themselves into the channel's throat from behind, as if engulfing the women's throats, swallowing them up. Or to sit in a commanding position inside their sixth chakra, like a gargoyle

at the driver's wheel of a car. These baleful spirits sought to control and possess the women's mediumship and pass on faulty, misleading, or glamorous information. Better to corrupt than shut down.

As a tactic, the Druj knows it is always more effective to mislead than to frighten, to spin a desirable illusion rather than to enact a dismal or body-ending drama, to slip a tissue of lies into their heads and assure they think it is the truth. She preferred the *Itako* stay at work, but that she control their deliverances, packing them with disinformation. She was attempting to subvert their mediumship and failing, as the *Itako* were too good for that manipulation; no matter: the Druj was doing a brisk business elsewhere on Earth with a thousand variations on the *Itako* mediumship, so the disinformation was getting through.

Everybody has the psychic chakras, and everyone has some degree of raw talent, though they usually leave this latent ability untouched. I include myself in that list. My "ability" lay dormant for decades until Blaise kick-started it. Some people exploit this latency, this endowment or patrimony. They wake up one morning and decide they will be psychic and before they know it they have some impressive deluding spirits in tow telling them whatever will produce the greatest self-inflation and thereby disempower or opiate them and create numerous dangerous blindspots in their cognition. It's a great technique.

People rarely catch on and remain embedded in illusory images of self-importance and world-shaking pronouncements and, to most sensible people, ridiculous claims. You see the same thing in espionage, especially counter-intelligence work: turn a mole into an asset, send them home again as a double agent working for you. Then you feed your enemy whatever disinformation or "chicken feed" you like, and they regard the cheap feed as a feast of intelligence, as "gold dust" from the highest, most privileged source, as John Le Carré said.

I saw some psychics robed in crimson cloaks, sparkling with imitation diamonds, strutting about like royalty, describing the condition of the universe and their role in it, acting like docents to the art gallery of the planet's geomantic terrain. Meanwhile, they sported a host of black spirits on their heads directing it all. In espionage terms, you'd say the Druj was muddying the waters, fouling wells. It was another way to confound or block the Underworld gateways, planting false or misleading but certainly alluring, even desirable, images about the nature of the afterlife and the *Bardo* requirements in the minds of the living. The best way to disempower human consciousness is to opiate it, fill it with narcotic dreams of potency, puissance, and spiritual regality, so they never catch on to the shocking fact of their own disempowerment and psychic paralysis.

In many ways this was not different than drug addiction, especially to opium. You live in a swirl of glamorous illusions about the condition of the subtle world and your pre-eminent importance in it, trading off power for self-importance. Then you arrive in the *Bardo* and your only power is the allure of these illusions and you begin the difficult, demanding *Bardo* process at a great disadvantage. Your awesome self-inflation cannot help you now. You need power and you shudder as you realize you never cultivated any of it while alive.

You reveled instead in this marvelous opium dream of your cosmic puissance. Or your power was borrowed, leased to you from spirits in exchange for your soul. You never owned it because you never cultivated it. The Druj stands by, pre-eminent property owner, like a Russian aristocrat surveying his serfs, observing the herds of souls, and nods her head, pleased with her work as bodiless souls arrive in the afterlife realm with no working concept of the place.

Could we clear out all the illusion in the world between life and the *Bardo*? Should we even try? We were at this task of gate-cleaning for some time, though I could not say how long that was. In all, we were gone three months on our expedition, from *Samhain* to *Imbolc*, but in here, in the fluidic, protean, shapeshifting *Bardo*, the time duration was impossible to calculate. It felt like five minutes or a year. I couldn't tell, but I did enjoy the lightness of it all, and by this I mean the lightness of my body form, how easy it was to move and fly about.

The form resembled my adult human male body of course, but it was all in Light. No bones, organs, blood vessels; no need to breathe, digest, sleep, or exercise. The mental processes were sharper, utterly unimpeded by the demands and sluggishness of biology and its mandates. The emotions were toned down; no rollercoaster dips and rises of affect, just a steady feeling of interest and empathy. I didn't have to read or study; reality itself was laid out like a textbook before me. I enjoyed that clarity. Everything was here, right now; I didn't need to seek for it. And this was just the beginning, a mere prolegomena to the full apocalypse. I couldn't begin to imagine what reality was like to dear Philomena, what revelations effortlessly offered themselves up to her on a momentary basis.

I wasn't sure I wanted to go back to normal human physical life, to speculating, pondering, never being certain, always having to inquire about reality. That seemed so tedious, so laborious, so fraught with collective social inertia, disbelief, atheism, and wrong-headedness. The answers were all here. The underpinnings of material reality were all around me. It was better than the best endowed university library. I knew, though, that I was only on vacation; I was visiting a desirable locale, but I hadn't yet sold up and moved there, made the irreversible commitment to stay here, crossed the *Cinvat*, done my *Bardo* processing, confronted my karma straight in the face and stared it down— in other words, I wasn't dead yet, just having an extended near-death experience, or something like that and, nicely, without the requisite hard knock on the head.

This extended out-of-body experience wasn't finished yet. We had another gate to examine. Outwardly, the landscape didn't look like much. Flat, barren, desert-like, and I could tell the place would be very hot in the summer. We stood upon a long crescent-shaped mound, perhaps three quarters of a mile in length, with another smaller one not far away and a dry canal bed situated between both. The gate itself was magnificent, larger than any we had seen before, bigger than the one at Eleusis. This gate hinted of extreme antiquity.

I know that is almost meaningless to say, since all the gates were installed at the same time, when the Earth's geomancy was laid out, but inexplicably this gateway emitted age. It hinted at times lived long ago. I must have been registering the impress of people using this gate from many millennia ago. I saw the etheric outline of a large physical building, presumably the temple that had been constructed here to coincide with the subtle Underworld gateway.

"I recognize this place," said Blaise. "In fact, I remember it. Cuthah. It was the site of a physical and a Light temple dedicated to Ereshkigal, Queen of the Underworld in Sumeria in the time before the Flood, during the time of first-generation humanity. You have to calculate that time in the millions of years. I would place us about 25 miles northeast of Babylon on the right bank of the eastern branch of the Upper Euphrates, just a bit north of Nippur, in today's Iraq.

"The Sumerian name for this place was *Gudua*, but now they call it Tell Ibrahim. Tell means 'mound.' Ibrahim is Arabic for Abraham. This later name slapped on the site

has no bearing on its geomantic function. It's an honorific. Not only was Cuthah or *Gudua* known as an entrance to the Underworld, the name itself was synonymous with this subtle region the Sumerians called Kigal.

"Ereshkigal, 'Great Lady under the Earth,' was its lord. She was also called *Irkalla*, 'Queen of the Night,' and her husband was Nergal. Cuthah was cited as the name of the capital of *Irkalla*, Sumeria's Underworld, but this site was also the cult center for Nergal, often depicted as a lion, and his principal shrine, *E-mes-lam*. Nergal was *Meslamtaeda*, 'the one that rises up or goes forth from *Meslam*.' He was the head of the pantheon of Sumerian deities who ran the government of the Underworld. To say he 'rises up from *Meslam*' (*Meslam* means 'luxuriant *Mesu* tree') probably meant that like Hades he could appear in our world, emerging suddenly, numinously, coming forth into visibility like Hades did on the slopes of fiery Mount Etna when he abducted Persephone."

The Sumerians, I later found when I researched the site's background, left a visually detailed picture of Kigal. It has its version of the Hades and Persephone joint management of the Underworld with Nergal and Ereshkigal. It left no doubt the Sumerians had actually explored it while still alive. Kigal meant 'the great place below,' and it was also called Kur, which had many branching references, including the name of a dragon and a mountain.

The Kigal gate was guarded by Nedu, the chief gatekeeper, and once the gate was closed and locked, the dead were discouraged from thinking they'd ever get back out, at least that way. They called Kigal *Eirshitum*, "the land of no return." That may sound bleak, but you can't retrace your steps and walk out of the *Bardo* the same way you entered. You can't return to your dead body, only to a new one. You have to either reincarnate and return to the physical world in a human body, or move on to some paradisal realm and enjoy your time-off.

Dead, you next met the ferryman, Humuttabal, whose name meant 'take away quickly.' For some reason this Sumerian version of Charon had four hands. The ferryman was also known, perhaps earlier, as SI.LU.IGI, then as Urshanabi. Later he shapeshifted into the four-handed monster figure, Hamar-tabal (a variant spelling of Humuttabal), and even into a four-handed bird-demon who transported souls across the River Hubur, the equivalent of the Greek's River Acheron; in this case, the bird-demon itself apparently served as river-ferry.

Hubur, possibly a later Akkadian word, meant "man-devouring river" and "river that runs against man," and in the earlier Sumerian name, *I-kurra*, it meant more generally "river of the Netherworld." The name made sense: you lose your most recent version of personality as you cross this dimensional gradient. The river, this energy grade, devours you; it runs against you in the sense that your phenomenal-world humanness has no relevance in this river. It was said to flow in front of the gates of the Underworld and challenged the dead to prove their worthiness to pass it, to demonstrate convincingly they were dead, which I suspect means to demonstrate you know you are in a changed condition and now operating in a radically different external environment than when alive.

The Sumerians give a clearer portrait of the celestial city of the Underworld, certainly in contrast with the Tibetan picture which emphasizes the karma-processing areas but doesn't specify Yama's residence. This is a metropolis (accessed below the surface of the Earth) with seven walls and seven gates, each guarded by a demon (more like a gargoyle or fierce-seeming testing spirit like a *Heruka*). At each gate the dead have to shed a layer of clothing (self-identity) until finally they are naked (as only consciousness) before Ereshkigal.

This probably refers to the rigorous purgation of karma-processing the souls in Kigal must perform to free themselves of Earth, their life, and its residual taints. Each layer of "clothes" would correspond to a *skandah* product and eventually to the *skandah* grid itself, all the factors that clothed the soul in a body personality. Naked means you are stripped of your *skandah*-habits and returned to your essence, all the personality filters and distraction mechanisms removed.

Inside the walled city, they were led to the lapis lazuli palace of Ereshkigal, meeting her and her husband-consort, Nergal, also called Ninazu, her son, Namtar, and a scribe called Belitsheri. Namtar was trouble, though; he heralded death and brought 60 diseases with him, a walking contagion vector. He worked with the *utukku limnu*, the demon-spawn of Kigal, who spread these diseases; they sounded like the Greek *Keres*, the spirits and agents of disease in Pandora's Box. Finally, there were the Anunnaki, the judges of the dead; their number in this function was given as seven (elsewhere it is 50), and they lived in *Egalgina* palace, the hall of justice. The deceased would have to meet them soon.

The famous text, "Ishtar's Descent into the Lower World," emphasizes the divestment of clothes and human, worldly identity at each gate. Ishtar (technically, a goddess of love, fertility, and war, and also known as Inanna and Astarte) acts as proxy for all humans entering Kigal. She accords to the motif of the first human to die sets the standards and marks the way for those who follow. In order, she is commanded to remove her large crown, earrings, necklace, breast ornaments, girdle studded with birthstones, spangles from her hands and feet, and her loin-cloth. Whoever she was in the mortal topside world, she is that no longer here. Forget it, my dear. She loses part of her personality with each item she sheds.

The poet describes *Irkalla*, the region, as a land of darkness, a house of shadows. The dead eat only dust and clay; they live without light, clothed like birds, with wings as garments, curiously just like the Egyptian picture of the soul, the *Ba*, as a human-headed bird form, suggesting the lightness of the soul. As before, I think we should be subtle in understanding the Sumerian reference to the unrelieved darkness of *Irkalla* as indicating human psychic weakness in penetrating this restricted realm cognitively sufficient to see it in full detail.

It's dark in the same sense as astrophysicists speak of dark matter. It means they cannot see it. It is not dark from any evil intention, but from higher frequency. You relieve the darkness of *Irkalla* by cultivating your clairvoyant perception. It is dark also because it operates in a realm beyond the five physical senses and to a degree beyond the constraints of the *skandah* grid. Minus these habitual structures you will perceive the world, even if it's Kigal, differently than before. For those left behind in the alive world, events in Kigal are all in the dark.

Ereshkigal, upon seeing Ishtar, instructs Namtar to imprison Ishtar in her palace and to send against her the 60 diseases as a punishment. That sounds grim, but perhaps it needs to be read in reverse and means the purgation process begins and the taints and karmic pollutions, the 60 stains on the immortal soul, now must be identified and flushed out of the soul as it drops its life bodies. That certainly is the spirit of all the seeming nastiness and organized weirdness in the Tibetan text where it's all your karma presenting itself in a variety of hallucinatory guises and karmic illusions. What the Sumerian call diseases the Tibetans might see as generic human form (phylogeny) constituents (and taints).

It is possible, then, the Sumerian 60 diseases is another metaphorical way of seeing the components of the human psyche that the Tibetans called angry spirits, that the Egyptians portrayed as the bribable portal guardians, and that the Jews and Muslims denoted as defilements of the chakras. I wondered too whether the specificity of the number of diseases, 60, was meant to correlate with the base-60 mathematics used in Sumeria, meaning something like a full house, one of each, even a defilement Light grid, or the total possible expression of 60.

The divestment of Ishtar's personal identity, clothing, and jewels at the seven gates carries a chakra hierarchy impression. It proceeds from the crown chakra (taking off the large crown) to the root chakra (removing the loin-cloth) and is consistent with the more clinical Tibetan description of consciousness extricating itself from all seven chakras, starting with the root, and the conditions they set. They proceed in the correct order, except for the sixth gate, which refers to spangles on Ishtar's feet; it should have been to her root chakra area, as the other divestments were body-specific for the matching chakras. But perhaps the feet were construed as how the body ultimately grounds itself on the Earth, which is the natural function of the root chakra, but you can't put spangles there.

It's funny because I remember at Dartmouth it was popular, if not required, to interpret Ishtar's descent as a feminist portrayal of a woman's incursion into her unconscious. Clearly, that falls short of the reality of this story: it is a narrative of a real psychic immersion in the Underworld realities by a living human initiate. The gender is inconsequential, for a soul after death surrenders its body identity, and it probably hinted at the *Daena*, the anima-like presentation of the human soul in a condition of youth, beauty, and purity. That's funny too (I suppose I mean ironic) because the *Daena*, like Core the Maiden, though personified as female, is not gendered at all. That's a metaphor.

Inanna (Ishtar's original, Sumerian name) wasn't a human woman anyway. She was a deity, the Lady of Heaven, a goddess of love, fertility, lust, wisdom, war, and battle. She stirs confusion and chaos among those disobedient to her, inciting devastation and flood while clothing herself in radiance. She quickens fighting and conflict; battle is called the "dance of Inanna." She dances.

She is a more petulant, aggressive version of Aphrodite, more a voluptuous love-goddess and sometimes a vamp, which I understand from Blaise is a guise of the Ray Master or Lord of the Pale Red-Pink Robe, also called Brigit, Magdalen, and Lady Nada ("Sound"). This means Inanna is the human's Ray Master mystagogue for the journey through Kigal. Her "descent" was a demonstration journey to show us the way. Her Ray may provide back-up. That means this Ray and its Ray Master was then the one designated for the afterlife Underworld journey to fulfill the psychopomp role for the bewildered soul.

That is fitting because both valences of the Red Ray, the rich scarlet and this paler red, are central to the Christ Mysteries and the Christed initiation, providing the matrix in which the Christ Light is seeded, gestated, and born in the living human, and, as we know, the ultimate goal or destiny of that Light is to achieve ascension which, as any Tibetan will tell you, is the only sure way out of the *Bardo* and off the infernal Wheel of Life. Wake up, big time, definitively, and get free of it forever. It felt like I was seeing the secret undertext of this antique Sumerian narrative of an Underworld journey: it was specifying the sure route out of *Kigal* and Inanna was the Upperworld psychopomp who'd help you.

Nor does it leave out Merlin and the Silver Ray because Inanna was the daughter of Sin, the Sumerian Moon-god, Lord of the Silver Realm of the Great Mother. I had to keep reminding

myself that in myth Moon means the Silver Light realm. Kigal, some scholars contend, originally meant the "great place of Ki," the goddess, and, later, Kigal meant the "great place on the surface of Sin" (the Moon-god), which means, in other terms, placed on the bosom of Hades, or set deep inside the Earth, the Great Below Place of the Underworld's Eresh*kigal*.

It also hinted, cartographically, that the realm of the Great Mother, Sin of the Moon, lay just beyond the confines of Kigal, just as the Silver realm of *Binah*, lies on the other side of the great bulging sphere of the *Bardo* (the Sumerian Kigal). Ereshkigal is the "daughter" of Sin because in the hierarchy of consciousness states, the *Bardo* lies below the *Sefira* of *Binah*, one step below, a daughter. In the hierarchy of the 14 Rays, the Silver Ray is actually one notch higher, so it is functionally meaningful to say Ray Master Inanna is the "daughter" of Sin. You go from the crown chakra up through the *Bardo* (Kigal) to *Binah*, the Mother's realm, the residence of Sin of the Moon, the place of Silver Light. The *Bardo*, or Kigal, is the Intermediate Realm between the crown and *Binah*. If you saw the *Bardo* as a whole, from the crown chakra it would seem to "lie" up on the surface of Sin, the Moon, meaning the eighth chakra of *Binah*.

Merlin gestured that it was time for us to start our gate-cleaning work. The first thing that struck me about the Cuthah gate was the residual imprint of the many thousands of humans who had passed through it. I seemed to be seeing directly into the past, probably as far back as Sumeria. The lines of souls entering the gate were layered, like a palimpsest of people entering Kigal, but at these earliest layers the souls were walking through the gate with clarity and even joy. Can you imagine that today? Joy on leaving Earth and entering Kigal?

They seemed prepared, well-briefed, and they did not appear forlorn, sad, or in fear. It reminded me of lines of people queuing up for an opera matinee. The line was orderly, people were joking or smiling, studying the playbill. The early Sumerian souls lining up for Kigal were like that; this was not the case the closer you came to the present time. I said it looked like layers, like a filo dough pastry of deceased humans. In the layers closer to the present time, I saw resistance, fear, went there under duress, being dragged unwillingly through this Kigal gate. The sunlit world seemed strongly, pervasively with them, and Kigal felt like a world of bristly ambiguity and likely terrors and they'd rather not go.

In these more recent layers, the Druj had managed to position an increasing number of adversarial demons to amplify this trepidation and enhance the confusion. She never missed a chance to promote her agenda, and it was working. The humans looked ill-prepared, or, with the advent of religions, badly misinformed, or, strangely, triumphantly, as if they were marching towards a spirit stage where they would receive their righteous commendation.

Considering the antiquity of the use of the Cuthah gate and the fact that humans have been dying for so long, you'd think they'd have the hang of it by now, that it would not seem such a godawful apocalypse and personal Ragnarok. But it doesn't. It remains the biggest, queerest anomaly in a person's life today.

It's the River Lethe that produces this fogbound, ignorant condition, the deliberate forgetting, erasing one's memory of previous lives and deaths, eclipsing all recall of the Kigal passage and its requirements so that one dies with complete, unapologetic ignorance of the basic ground rules of one's existence. You end up in some Sartrean existentialist-nihilist zone of nothingness, but that's altogether the wrong kind of nothingness, the extinction of the vertical view. There is no higher, organizing, benevolent principle in this constricted view.

Plato wrote in *The Republic* about souls marching in a scorching heat to the barren wasteland called the Plain of Forgetfulness and there being obliged to drink of the River Lethe and forget all their previous sorrows and all things of the soul. This was in the early evening; then in the deep of night, after a thunderstorm and earthquake, they were driven upwards into their next life, like shooting stars. The Lethe intoxication was perhaps originally compassionate, but as we've seen on this expedition and as we've told the Green Knight and his boss, the Supreme Being, this has to change. The Lethe lethargy has to end.

The whole *Bardo* system is clogged and dysfunctional now. People don't get it. They don't remember a thing, and they arrive in new bodies utterly in the dark. There they live in a dark cave of not knowing anything about the genuine spiritual world or they are fed the opiated pap of a misdirected fantasy picture. The Druj has had too free of a hand for too long, and it must come to an end.

You can see I was getting some heat up about the inequities in the *Bardo* set-up. I was marching with the others under that scorching heat, full of complaints about the set-up. Down with Lethe! All I needed was a placard. The Plain of Forgetfulness would now become the Plain of 50% Soul Remembering. You could expect to arrive in your next life with sticky tabs posted all over your form, reminding you of key events, tendencies, debts, credits, to start your life.

The outermost or most recent layers of the Cuthah gate were pestilential. Iraq, as everyone knows, was beset with wars, violence, and innumerable deaths in the period between 1970 and 2020, largely due to American military aggression and interference. Many died in the wars and religious conflicts instigated in that region, and a fair number of these souls were still stuck in the gateway, as if they couldn't quite squeeze through or lost heart mid-way or were so badly concussed they didn't know where they were, who they were, or where they were going and so were immobilized. The Druj had taken advantage of this.

She had posted demonic figures to misinform, cajole, or commiserate with the Stuck. The framework of the gate seemed to echo in screams of terror, and much wailing and moaning. It flashed images of humans in their death agony, bodies in pain and destruction, calling for palliation, apology, or explanation.

We knew the sword would do the work. We just had to remain neutral and full of certainty that the sword's cleansing action was inexorable and fast. It was, but such a stench this purgation threw up. It was as if we, on behalf of latter-day humanity, had to taste the poison that had taken off so many earlier humans. It was only a brief taste, but a powerful one. Such suffering it conveyed.

The lilac flames vaporized the negativity coming off the gate and the stuck souls and the ghastly imprints of miserableness left on the gate's framework. The sharp Christ Light edge of the sword gave the freed souls a glimpse, a brief experience, the reassurance of the truth of reality, that there was truth, that it was possible for them to perceive the truth of reality's absolute bedrock. I know, it sounds odd to put it that way, but many of these souls had been so spun around, so twisted out of their correct alignment with the Upper Worlds, that they needed a revelation of this magnitude and primalness to realign themselves. They had forgotten such a truth even existed. Lethe plus Druj equals oblivion.

Imagine you're walking around in a drugged haze, or terribly drunk, or badly concussed, and you cannot, to save your life, get a grip on physical reality. You cannot bring it into focus, make sense of anything, find your place on the timeline. It's like the rug has been pulled out from under you, and the house too. You're not moving forward. You're stuck, frozen, aswirl in grim hallucinations. You can't wake up and shake it off, nor can you sleep and go oblivious to it. You're nailed to the cross of the present moment, and it's a horrible nightmare.

That's how (pardon the mixed metaphors) I would characterize the condition of these many souls stuck in the Cuthah gate. The Druj made it all stronger, or worse, stretching it out forever. So she thought. Our sword work was starting to free these many tortured souls, and the Druj's grip on them was weakening. You could feel her anger swelling. She was like a drug lord who owned ten city blocks and we were moving in on her, taking away sales and customers. We weren't selling drugs. We were offering relief from them, a life in which nobody would need the drugs, when actual reality would be preferable.

In the latter days of Sumerian culture, before the Flood, many had fallen into black magic practices. It had started, perhaps, with metaphysical curiosity, but after a while it had degenerated into dark practices with bad results. The psychic atmosphere of late Sumerian culture was like an H.P. Lovecraft story. They had summoned all sorts of inimical, malevolent spirits to their world, and now these baleful spirits, bizarre hybrids of lizards and birds, like psychotic Harpies, and worse, a demon horde, intimidated souls at the Cuthah gateway.

It was as if we were seeing the root seeds, the cause, of all subsequent horror tales. Spirit forms never meant for Earth reality had been brought through. Bizarre adulterated blended forms, abominations, had been summoned. One glimpse of this demon crowd would be sufficient to any horror writer for a lifetime of scary tales of absolutely antihuman spirits and feral astral creatures. The sword dispatched them all of course, but not until we'd had a full, long look. Here, I admit, a little fifth of that

Lethe brew would have done the trick for me. As I sit here writing this chronicle, I sometimes wish I didn't have to remember the bizarre astral spirits I saw at this gate just prior to our purging the site.

For a time, the temple dedicated to Ereshkigal at Cuthah had provided dependable instruction in the Kigal Mysteries, just as, later, Eleusis had done. Humans came here for initiation in the afterlife protocols and possibilities, and they later walked through the Cuthah gate prepared, informed, even whistling. Then came the barbarian invasions of the dark spirits that the Sumerians themselves had summoned into their well-ordered world to destroy the Light.

The Cuthah Mystery preparations started to wobble. Certainty quailed, then faltered. One more gate fell to the camps of the Druj; she posted demons to keep everything in order (her order) and moved on to the next one. It was not that linear, unfortunately. She worked on all of them at once. She had many hands. They were always in motion, a blur of activity, changing conditions to suit her view of life, death, the Underworld, consciousness, all saying Fuck the Christ! She kept racking up the numbers of conquered gates in her win column.

We saw her nimble hands clutching another gate. It was in Mexico. I knew this because I had seen it before, in person, on an academic conference-holiday with Philomena about 20 years ago. It was Mitla in the Valley of Oaxaca in southern Mexico, 20 miles from the city of Oaxaca, and the Druj had her long spectral hands draped all over the Mitla gate to Mictlan, the Aztec Underworld.

Mictlan was the Aztec name for the *Bardo*. It was located in the far North (in the Aztec spiritual cartography; they didn't mean northern Mexico) and consisted of nine levels, none of them pleasant. It took four years for a soul to progress from the entry level number one to the ninth level, but they could expect help from the psychopomp of Mictlan called Xolotl. The passage through Mictlan was adventurous, like an American action movie with Indiana Jones.

You were required to journey through eight hells beset with obstacles. You had to cross a mountain range in which the mountains were constantly crashing into each other; you had to walk through a field across which a strong wind blew flesh-scraping knives; and you had to ford a river of blood packed with fearsome jaguars. Who thinks up this stuff? Eventually, you would have to meet the directors of this funhouse, Mictlantecuhtli, Lord of Mictlan, and his wife-consort, Mictecacihuatl, Lady-Queen of the Underworld. It was the Hades-Persephone or Nergal-Ereshkigal pairing with new faces and different names.

Mictlan was not a place of punishment or even moral appraisal. It was not a purgatory nor was there a solemn Judgement of the Dead. But the Aztecs did suggest it was a place of dreary eternal existence; at worst, it was boring. Getting there was a challenge. In addition to the feats mentioned above, you were liable to deal with a forest of trees that threatened to crush your soul; a serpent and alligator, both in a foul mood; and you'd better prepare yourself to cross eight deserts and climb eight mountains amidst fierce blowing winds that threw stones and flung obsidian knives at you. Mictlan was an Aztec-horror theme park.

You finally reached a river (the Aztec River Acheron equivalent) on the edge of Mictlan. The monstrous red dog-soul who had accompanied you (both Xolotl, who took a canine form, and possibly the spirit of a former living dog) now helped you cross this river. That seems a conflation of the Egyptian Anubis, the jackal-headed psychopomp, and Charon, the dour ferryman, with a hint of Sraosha, the Persian high deity explicator of the death Mysteries in a cameo role.

The Aztecs portrayed Xolotl in his dog form as horrific, but when you see through the visual histrionics you remember the correct meaning of the dog in the death mysteries, and that, as Cerberus-Shiva, you encounter this "dog" on your way up through the crown. The Egyptians were more matter of fact, even prosaic about depicting Anubis: he was guy wearing a black jackal's head atop his shoulders, no big deal about it. I knew now that Xolotl, all the death-guide dogs, were Merlin. The Aztecs preferred to pretend Xolotl was an actual dog.

Once inside Mictlan you offered gifts to Mictlantecuhtli who assigned you living quarters in one of Mictlan's nine divisions. Some accounts said, contrarily, often you had to spend a probationary period of four years in outer lying regions before entering Mictlan. That might correspond to a typical life-review and karma-processing period. Maybe it took the Aztec soul four years to get through all the paperwork. Great rushing rivers separated each region; some say there were nine rivers, none of them suited to indolent summer afternoon bathers.

Xolotl—every time I think of this Aztec god-figure I have to laugh. He is said to be the god of fire and lightning, of sickness and deformities, and the twin of Quetzalcoatl, the Plumed Serpent, and both are sons of the goddess Coatlicue. He guards the sun when it enters the Underworld at night, and he helped Quetzalcoatl bring humanity and fire out of the Underworld. Most prescient to our expedition, Xolotl aids the dead in their journey to and through Mictlan, and he takes two animal forms, the water salamander and the Xoloitzuintli dog breed. He is sometimes depicted as a skeleton, a monster animal with reversed feet, and a dog-headed man. There is even an actual dog breed named after him. I think I've made my point: Xolotl was no tail-wagging Golden Retriever.

That's probably why I find him funny. His description seems like a caricature, or some crazy form of Aztec surrealistic cartoon. This is quite a weird portrait of our expedition leader, the psychopomp Merlin as Xolotl dog. The Aztec picture lacks the dignity of the Egyptian description of Anubis, the jackal-headed man who guides the soul through the *Duat* and its processes. Still, how often do you get a dog breed named after you, a little barking Aztec Merlin dog.

Xolotl is the son of Coatlicue. This is an important clue. Coatlicue is the Aztec picture of the Great Mother, She of the Silver Realm of *Binah* beyond the *Bardo*. To say Xolotl is her son means he guides you to his mother, the Great Mother. Xolotl, our Merlin and the Greeks's Herakles, is the Glory of Hera, the Greek name for Coatlicue; he is Her glory, Her emanation, Her field agent. When you die, meet me at the top of your head and I'll guide you safely to Coatlicue.

As I understood from Edward's researches with Merlin, this is his job, his role. He is the *Mer-Line*, the line of Light and connection from the Blazing Star, the essential seed of permanence in the living human, to the realm of *Mer*, the Great Sea, the domain of Mother that lies beyond Mictlan, the goal of the journey. The *Mer-Line* function underlies all of Merlin's dog-headed forms as guide. He guides the compliant soul, the one willing to do the karma-divestment and life-processing work, through the vagaries of Mictlan to Coatlicue's realm. The *Mer*-Line is like a neon-lit thread that winds its way surely through the folds of the *Bardo*; follow it faithfully and you'll reach the Great Mother, Coatlicue.

Mictlantecuhtli does not come across with the dignified style of the Green Knight or Lord Yama. The Lord of Mictlan is portrayed as a blood-splattered skeleton or a human wearing a toothy skull, or his head, a mere skull, features living human eyes. He wears a headdress of owl feathers and paper banners, a necklace of human eyeballs, and earrings of human bones. The Tibetan *Herukas* could have learned something about doctoring their appearance towards the spectral from this lord, though apparently in Aztec belief skeletal imagery meant fertility, health, and abundance, and the close relationship of life and death.

The lord wears sandals which to Aztecs denoted wealth and privileged status. His arms are raised in an aggressive gesture, meaning he was pumped and ready to start tearing apart new dead bodies; and his skeletal jaw was opened wide, ready to swallow all the stars that pass through him during the daytime. Human souls he'd barely notice as he engulfed them. He lived in Mictlan with his queen in a house without windows; he is associated with bats, owls, and spiders; the North, called Mictlampa, is the region of human death. That part at least is factual: North means straight up, above the human head.

I wondered which would seem worse to encounter, a huge green jovial guy with a whacking big axe, or a bloody skeleton figure with an eyeball necklace, bats, owls, and spiders for friends, and a huge gaping mouth? His consort-queen, Mictecacihuatl, does not get much visual elaboration. She presides over the bones of the dead and all the human festivals for the dead, such as the Day of the Dead, on November 1, so she is called the Lady of the Dead.

She is portrayed as a figure without flesh, with a jaw wide open to take in the stars. This event honoring ancestors used to occupy the whole month of August, but with the spread of Catholic influence in Mexico it was adjusted to October 31 to November 2, to correspond with the Catholic triduum of All Hallow-Tide, All Saint's Eve, All Saint's Day, and All Soul's Day. Still, the Vatican saints were not able to oust Mictecacihuatl. She kept her pagan job in Mexico.

That both Mr. and Mrs. Death in the Aztec world were said to devour the stars suggests that the Underworld devours time; it cancels time, because that time, that star duration, is a three-dimensional construct, and life in Mictlan takes place in the all-present fourth dimension, where linear, discrete time is gone. We know that well. I never know what time it is in here in the timeless *Bardo*. Time is like a wrap-around environment, with past, present, and future all displayed.

As I said, we were at the Mictlan gate at Mitla, now an archeological site much visited by tourists, including myself and Blaise earlier in our lives. Its name is a corruption of the original Aztec Mictlan: Mitla is a gate into Mictlan. The site was originally constructed to be a physical ceremonial gateway to Mictlan; it consists of five groups of low-lying stone buildings on the valley floor, and archeologists are impressed with its elaborate mosaic fretwork and geometric patterns that cover the tombs, panels, and walls, and with the finely cut and polished stone pieces fitted neatly together without any mortar.

Naturally, with its consummate arrogance towards pagan cultures, the Vatican commissioned the construction of a Catholic church inside the sanctified space of Mitla. They built the Church of San Pablo right on top of an old Aztec platform. The largest Aztec building is the Palace or Grand Hall of Columns, measuring 120 by 21 feet, so called because it has six hefty columns of volcanic stone that once supported a roof, no longer extant. Buildings in the north and east sections of the site hold the bodies of Aztec priests and local Zapotec rulers.

Zapotec is the name of the people and civilization that flourished in the Valley of Oaxaca. Their name for the site was *Lyobaá*, meaning "Land of Rest." Mitla is derived from the Nuahtl word Mictlan for "Place of the Dead," but Land of Rest does nicely too. Ostensibly, this was because kings, priests, warriors, and other dignitaries were buried here, *wanted* to be buried here, but as we know, the word Mitla contains a geomantic clue: Mitla is an Underworld gate. The dead may enter Mictlan through the Mitla gate. Mictlan shines through Mitla, though in recent centuries they had to contend with the occult Catholic bureaucracy.

The Church of San Pablo features four small red-topped domes that, from a short distance away but within Mitla, look like four papal cardinals glaring disapprovingly, like bullies, over the primitive site. That was the first layer of obstruction we encountered when we started cleaning the Mitla gate, Catholic residues in the form of dark spirits, Inquisition demons, the remnants of former priests, and copious Catholic imagery depicting awful punishment and torture of sinning souls. Such a heavy hand these intolerant Catholics laid upon ancient Mitla, as if they wanted to kill the geomantic site—no, better: as if they wanted to consign the geomantic node itself to the *Bardo*.

It felt like a gravitational force, a weight on consciousness that was almost palpable, like if you lived or worked at Mitla since the 16th century, you did so under oppression, like your back was weighed down carrying the cardinals. You felt, as an Aztec or simply a latter-day Mexican anytime after 1544 when they started construction on the church, that you were second rate, sinful, lousy. Your beliefs, your model of human life and Mictlan, were of no account, wrong, useless, stupid, and your Mexicanness, your indigenous Aztec soul, was pitiable.

I looked at Blaise, and he said, "Don't get me started," and frowned. The desecration of geomantic sites by the oppressive hand of the Catholic hierarchy was a subject that much vexed him when he ran his Blue Room institute.

He said it interposed an obstructive energy layer into the sites, affecting their function, and often before you could begin to interact usefully with a geomantic installation, you had to clear away all this interference and the dark spirits. In some cases, he said, notably in Mexico City, the Catholics had successfully shut down, "killed" in an energetic sense, the original geomantic operation of a site. "No, they didn't manage that at Mitla, though these red domes are obnoxious. They scowl at you. They exude the imperial arrogance of power and dogma."

The Druj of course loved all this negativity, this put-down of the Aztec soul and the erection of a monolithic judgemental interface at the Mitla gateway. She had installed multiple copies of herself as papal sentries at the gate, and they glowered like disapproving priests at the Aztec souls proposing to pass through. In fact, she had transformed her appearance into that of priests, though I could see her menacing smile underneath the fabric of her disguise. She would wrap each transiting soul with copies of the sticky astral images around the gate.

Wrong, distorted, misleading pictures of what to expect in the journey to Mictlan. Reasons to be fearful, to feel doomed, rejected by the gods, unworthy of their welcome. (That's not too surprising: the Aztec gods never struck me as warm.) The Aztec road map of the eight hells lying before the ninth realm of safety— were these Druj fabrications or enhancements too? They were quite overdone. Nothing in the Tibetan canon came close to these crushing mountains, turbulent rivers, winds whose edges were as sharp and cutting as knife blades, as the disembodied soul had to cope with these absurd travails for four years. It's hard to imagine how they would find the Clear Light of *Rigpa* amidst all this.

It seemed that perhaps the Druj had spawned some of these frightening images as a form of negative preparation for Aztec souls, to make sure they'd botch it up. Get stuck somewhere in one of the eight hells; get immobilized in the *Bardo*. The Druj's description of Mictlan hung like a gruesome horror curtain before Mitla, and Aztec souls, then later, Mexican, had to see this then pass through it. Maybe some of the heightened, horrific imagery was meant to indicate the winds of karma and the unleased forces of the four elements ripping through the *Bardo*. We saw that in the Tibetan model. But I suspect the Druj had pumped up the special effects, increased the sound, amplified the foley outputs.

A few tiers of angels stood by in parallel crescents. They watched. They did not intervene. They were not allowed to, not disallowed by God, but by the preponderance of agreement among Aztec and Mexican souls that the Druj's model of Mictlan was right and everything the Catholic clergy insinuated about the unworthiness, uncouthness, and insufferable paganness of the Mexican soul was correct. These souls continuously ratified her distorted pictures, so the angels were unable to intervene to correct this misperception because too many souls agreed with it, or accepted it as reality even as it guaranteed they'd suffer.

"I know how that works, and it sucks," said Blaise. "Blaise used to tell me, now and then, when I was monumentally and quite impressively stuck in some personal matter, that they wanted to help me out but their hands were tied. The irony, the joke, the bad joke committed in poor taste, was I had tied their hands. My own karma, my constrictions, my misperceptions, wrong interpretations, faulty conclusions, emotional stuckness, whatever, constrained them completely. They could not act against the results of my own free-will choices even if it meant I would be miserable, a kvetching pain-in-the-ass for the next month."

The Mitla gateway was appallingly layered in these sticky Druj images. There seemed to be hundreds of layers to this awful palimpsest of suffering. Demonic beings dressed to look like typical Aztec deities flanked the gate. It was a frightful parody of the common image of when you die you're greeted lovingly by all your already deceased relatives; here these relatives were glaring demons disguised as Aztec gods, who, frankly, never seemed friendly or cordial anyway.

Some scholars I had read said the Aztecs considered their human lives to be like a dream, short, confusing, unpleasant, more full of gloom, misery, and despair than anything else. The gods had already created humans four times now, with three failures, so they had no confidence the deities had got it right this time. The Druj enhanced this soul mood in the minds of the dead Aztecs trudging through. You're pathetic, she taunted. The Old Man's fourth failure.

Dreadful images were stuck on both sides of the Mitla gate. The Aztecs were reputed to sacrifice humans for no end of reasons to the gods. I saw images of corpses, dead but bleeding, with big holes in their chests where their physical heart organ belongs. I saw other missing limbs, or evidences of evisceration and other depraved actions against the human body. These former humans, it seemed, were stuck here, still suffering, frozen in that horrible moment of violent or gruesome death. The Druj convinced them that was their fate, that nobody would come to help them, they were bad souls, bad beyond belief or redemption, and even God had turned His back on them, so forget it. Get lost, die already.

The Blaise angels with us started giving these souls some Love from Above, much the way emergency relief teams would give oxygen to accident victims. A foul black smoke rose around us. It was the odor of all this pessimism and gloom being baked and burned off the intransigent Aztec souls. It's the way your kitchen smells for a few hours when you run your stove's automatic cleaning cycle. It wasn't just from Mitla. I saw wisps of this fetid smoke rising up all across Mexico. A country's prevailing model of death and the afterlife colors, it *stains* daily life. It infiltrates the consciousness of people living under its influence, like the worst form of air pollution. A dark cloud had lain over Mexico since the Spanish brutally destroyed Tenochtitlan in 1521, and in the last 60 years (our present time), the intense drug cartel wars had further torn it up.

The heavy vapors of those conditions were turning into black smoke and ash. You could see the Mexican soul start to lighten up and begin to remember itself. The Mexican *peon* was at last poking his head out of the labyrinth of solitude where he had been kenneled by the centuries of Catholic pejoratives. The crushing mountains, knife-filled winds, and the other torments of the eight hells were revealed as exaggerations. The *Bardo* passage was not that horrible.

Yes, you had to confront and resolve your karma, and it might take the form of buffeting winds or scary-looking spirit-creatures, but they were all mind-born and therefore, and this was the good news, they had no substantial reality and you should see through the special effects and Mictlan's CGI monsters.

The time frame of four years, guaranteed, suffering through the eight hells, that too was revealed to be a fabrication: take as long as you want, or go through fast. There was no "rule" that you had to spend four years in an awful *Bardo* transit. The Aztec gods themselves were starting to divest some of their malevolent fierceness, which had never been accurate in the first place: power they had, and that power could seem ambivalent or threatening to humans, but their job was not to scare the living daylights out of humans but to preserve the Creation. How they looked was largely the product of Aztec expectations and imaginings, skillfully adjusted and warped by the Druj for maximum human disempowerment and disorientation, so people entered the *Bardo* already lost.

Suddenly, there was a flurry of angelic activities by the ones who had been standing back and by some of the Blaise angels. It was as if they had been constrained in a freeze-motion tableau and had been for centuries, or maybe it was only their projected thoughts or presence that had been here, waiting for the sign to proceed, and that sign had just been given with the freeing of the souls. Imagine a dirty, cluttered, disheveled office with the cleaning crew standing by but unable to start their work; now the command is given and they clean it up.

Angels surrounded each of the trapped, suffering Aztec souls, pulling the last of the cobwebs and sticky, mucilaginous Druj control grids from their auric fields. Other angels enveloped these same souls in wings of Light and affection, a gesture that, not to take away any of its majesty and purport, reminded me of a filthy pick-up truck, after a long, hard New Hampshire winter and ample spring mud splatters, finally getting a spray down, scrub, and polish at the car wash.

After such a prolonged immersion in the negativity and darkness of the Druj and the unending nastiness and hatred of humans by the dogma-spewing priests, these souls were getting a warm breath of unreserved validation from On High. They could say, without doubts, finally, somebody up there likes us. Reality is not just this wraparound Druj misery curtain and a cranky papal back-up band. The logjam of trapped people was freed, and souls flowed easily into the *Bardo*. The Mexican soul, as well as Mictlan itself, was freed from the Druj.

In case my description of the angels welcoming and reassuring the freed souls sounds sentimental, I remind the reader that the Ofanim, specifically, are charged with always imparting the reality of what the yogis call *Sat Cit Ananda*, which translates as Being, Consciousness, and Bliss. The human Blaise helped me understand the importance of this. It is the bedrock of reality, a fundamental ambiance, a vibrational signature, handwritten by God.

It gives the soul the umbilical connection to the source of Creation and one's place in it, and I can say from direct experience it is delicious, lovely, and terribly vital. The Druj had displaced consciousness in those trapped souls from that alignment, but now the Ofanim had restored it, and these souls standing on solid ground had the potential to enter and progress through the *Bardo* with greater clarity than before.

I mentioned earlier that the Earth has 1,746 portals to the Underworld. They are each like a door opening into the same large temple space, the *Bardo*. These portals, Blaise explains, were established in their respective locations at the beginning of the Earth, along with much of the rest of the geomantic features. Their specific locations, in fact, were planned long before anything was done on the Earth, and that plan, as I understand it, entails a geometric grid compounded of the distribution pattern of all these gateways, and this pattern exudes a collective or singular vibration. It is like, I suspect, a choir with 1,746 singers in it. This is Earth's Underworld Light grid, wrapped around the planet like a web.

It represents the *quality* of the entry into the Underworld and the *Bardo* at death. By quality, I mean the way it was supposed to feel, the way your experience at death and upon entering the *Bardo* was supposed to proceed, and the consistent, integrated impression that the Underworld and *Bardo* would carry for alive people, how they would think of it, what images they might form of the place. Our work with the Elohim sword at these gateways restored some of this.

Clogged, distorted, or fright-enclouded portals made human understanding of the *Bardo* difficult. It made people resist it, go oblivious to it, sleep through it. That, as we have seen on this expedition, is counterproductive, both for individual souls needing to make clear-cut *Bardo* progress and for the health of the system, its grid, and the dying, death, and after-death experience.

Things were lax during the *Kali-yuga*, and the *Bardo* gateways got dirty. They were poorly maintained and deliberately corrupted by the Druj. Frightened souls passing through them as if they were gateways to the ultimate House of Horrors left imprints of their fear and misunderstanding on the lintels for others. Mistaken pictures of the *Bardo* and its superintendents, thugs, and "muscle" built up and people started taking these erroneous images for actualities; then when they entered the *Bardo* they projected these same mistaken images and stood quaking in fear of them, thereby further reinforcing the distorted pictures.

The Druj liked this. It was her goal. Now nobody could see the truth of the place. Nobody could wield the indigenous power of consciousness to bust the icons. People suffered in an oubliette of disempowerment, and the Druj reveled in this. They felt themselves forcibly stripped of their selfhood, and the Druj loved it. They found themselves attacked, derided, and belittled by hosts of demonic spirits, and they didn't understand why, and the Druj smiled proudly. They felt that whatever love had been in the world, in their family, relationships, was gone, as if it never existed, and they were alone in a cold, unfriendly place. The worse the *Bardo* got the more the Druj felt exalted. Every day was her day.

The Druj had scripted this eventuality, had moved pieces and spirits in this direction, had constructed despairing images and interpretations to feed this. Anything that took the power out of human consciousness she put in place. Anything that by lying or deceiving weakened human consciousness she did it. It's grim, yes, but you know, she is called the Adversary for good reason. This. Wherever possible, the Druj was still positioned tactically at the Underworld gates, whispering lies, fostering false images, promoting wrong interpretations, exhaling a noxious atmosphere of fear, trembling, and resistance among humans. She is the hyperintelligent, devious, treacherous master of disguises and lies.

Our sword edge against the flesh of the Druj was like a knife against ice. Yes, our Elohim sword would cut through the icy resistance of the Druj. It was invincible, as long as we did not falter or fall prey to her dark Siren insinuations. She did her best. She kept probing each of us for weak spots, blindspots, open, unattended doors, flickerings of doubt or uncertainty quivering silently in us.

"The bitch never gives up," said Blaise. "Did you notice? She keeps at it."

The spiritual heat of the Elohim sword melted the Druj's icy wall in short order. We sliced through this barrier and soon the ice pillar was gone, though the Druj remained. She would always remain, always find new metaphors to express herself, new tactics to confuse or delude human awareness in the *Bardo* world.

The Mitla gate was looking good by now. Then Tommy said, "You know, the whole *Bardo* is a big Light temple, a House of Light, and 1,746 doors open into it. It's Yama's temple of the afterlife, the Green Knight's revelation palace. The *Bardo* is like the parkland surrounding the great estate, Yama's celestial city, but all of it was planned, structured, and scripted to deliver an experience.

"That's what Light temples do. Their architecture serves the experience, and you go into them to get that experience, to have it shape you. The *Bardo* Light temple experience, I would say, introduces you to the structure of the human being, how you were made, the layers that comprise you, how they condition and sometimes weigh down your pure awareness, how you put them on and how you remove them, and what you accumulate and carry while alive.

"But do you realize what this simple fact means? We've been taking it completely for granted, but it is actually proof that reality is purposeful. That it was designed, and that it has a designer. If the *Bardo* is a Light temple for the after-death processes, it means it was designed and therefore *intended* to be that. It's not chaotic, not the accident of some coincidental collision of unconscious masses, nor the result of some blindly staggering evolutionary monkey process.

"It was done on purpose. That means physical, human reality must also be intended, put here on purpose. We know that. It's no issue for us, but think of the implications of this for skeptics, atheists, agnostics, and unbelievers. One realm proves the other. The *Bardo's* unarguable purposefulness testifies to the implicit purposefulness of physical human life. It has to be because they are reciprocally linked, mirror images of each other, complementary domains. Physical human life, the whole thing, is a Light temple for conscious experiences. I almost wish I were still alive so I could explain this to my old school friends."

I took his point entirely. We had been seeing incontrovertible evidence that there were deliberate protocols, even scripts, for entering and leaving life. Such scripts were written by intelligent agencies, heavenly scriptwriters. These scripts were meant to be road maps, outlines, advance narratives for the trip. Some of the *Bardo* descriptions, like the Aztec's Mictlan or the Maya's *Xibalba*, sound bizarre, utterly odd, full of crazy spirits and almost ridiculous challenges, but they are purposeful, sequential, repeatable, and corroborable by others. They are like zany movie scripts by screenwriters trying to bridge comedy and horror. Edward told me of his impressions of *Xibalba* during his tutorial with Merlin. It was a surrealistic, Kafkaesque realm of wacky gods suggestive of Salvador Dali.

The advent of death was not accidental or some bizarre outcome of undirected evolutionary forces. It was mandated. Planned and commissioned, just like a corporate headquarters. The Supreme Being said humans will be mortal, and you, Yama, my dear boy, you, Green Knight, make it happen. Set up a divestment program, an afterlife debriefing protocol; make the set-up educational, fun, like an amusement park with instructive themes built into it.

Yes, they perhaps overdid it a bit—I'm thinking of the River Lethe memory overkill. Yama was, we all think, somewhat heavy-handed with the Lethe input. But Tommy was right. Our passage into and out of mortal human life was all planned. Our understanding and sense of direction accounted for. It's true, we had to put up with the Druj, a total pain-in-the-ass most of the time, a consummate obfuscator of the truth and the Light, but also for us a useful tester.

You could even say the *Bardo* and human mortal life are two divisions of the same Light temple, two floors, two wings, that demonstrate the powers and possibilities of consciousness, how it creates, construes, interprets, and directs an apparent world of name and form, a selfhood, and how it surrenders this world. A Light temple for the human phylogeny, with tests for entering and leaving it.

Here is this tool of consciousness, says God, and watch out, it's got a rather sharp edge to it. Go create a world, make some sense of it, and then let it go, come back. I've set up a nice theme park for these experiences. Human life

and the *Bardo*. I had Visvakarman build the Light temple just for you. Try it out, why don't you. I must warn you, though. I put in a few tricks, illusions, and red herrings, and one or two masquerades and a jester to sharpen your awareness and keep you on your toes and, I hope, amused and engaged. I think it's a great temple! If I could die, I'd try it Myself. You try it for me. Enjoy! Have a nice day!

"If this Light temple were a golf course, I'd say it has an abundance of water hazards and sand bunkers lying all over the place," said Edward. "There are a lot of places for your ball to get stuck and for you to fall behind par on the hole. But the greenery is nice, that and the open air, the breezes, and your golfing partners— well, most of them, some of the time, perhaps if they're above par."

"I appreciate now the innovations Merlin as Padmasambhava introduced to the model of the *Bardo*," said Blaise. "The Tibetan text puts consciousness firmly at the center of all the *Bardo* proceedings. Most of the older models, the Aztec Mictlan, the Maya's *Xibalba*, the Chinese Yellow Springs, and the Egyptian's *Duat*, make you feel like you're a nugatory slave performing the lion-resisting act at the Roman Coliseum for the entertainment of the decadent rich. Or you're a blind man running an impossible labyrinth with 100 turnings and only the man-crunching Minotaur to look forward to at the center.

"All this is being done to you because you deserve it and because they, the nasty Underworld spirits, feel like it. The funerary texts present these events as phenomena *in* consciousness, as registered by your awareness, but as coming *at* you from outside agencies. You are a victim of these agencies. The Tibetan view presents these activities as phenomena generated *by* consciousness, *yours*, and projected outside of your presumed location in reality for the purposes of your contemplation and resolution, then to be withdrawn again into your awareness. You control all the psychic mechanisms of cognition, projection, and resolution.

"Those models tell you the tests, evaluations, torments, punishments, and decrees of the Underworld are a result of your life actions, your sin, evil, or bad karma, but the Tibetan text tells you they are projected hallucinations of the drama of those actions, of the residuals of the imprints of those deeds and your mental condition at the time, and can all be dissolved instantly through consciousness. The great secret untapped power of your own consciousness is your prime psychopomp, deliverer, savior, and redeemer, your way out. The Tibetan picture puts you, the consciousness holder, squarely in the center. Nothing is being done to you from the outside; everything you see out there is your inside projected outside you for illustration and resolution purposes.

"Consciousness is the deal breaker. Is all this being done to you or are you doing it yourself? Is consciousness the reception point for these phenomena, like a television, or is it the generator and broadcaster of these dramas? Your position, your answer, to this fundamental question determines your *Bardo* outcome. You have your hands on all the *Bardo* controls. Look down. See? You are working the controls. Your awakened, engaged awareness deployed from a position of voidness will get your sorry ass out of the Underworld and into enlightenment. *You* are the hero-adventurer on the quest for complete release.

"But you must stay awake. Vigilant, acutely observant, and rigorously neutral. You have to work from a higher part of yourself, not the part that will die in here, what's called the lower soul or astral Double with all its habits. You'll not get through the tests and trials if you stay in that format, that body; it's too weak, too seducible, too acculturated to being asleep to the true condition of reality. You'll fall asleep, die to the challenges of the *Bardo*, and get recycled per your unconscious and the decrees of King Yama into yet another human life.

"As more people failed the *Bardo* tests, the easier it was for the Druj to convert the human picture of the Underworld into one of Hell, as a nightmare realm. The *Bardo* becomes a Hell when consciousness is disempowered, when human consciousness as a power, a cognitive force, as the screenwriter of the *Bardo*, is eclipsed and relegated to a dungeon of oblivion, and you drink the Druj's own brew of tea, the tea of the complete forgetfulness of the power of consciousness and the belief in yourself as a failed, corrupted soul in Hell. You are charged with crimes and misdemeanors committed while you were alive that justify judgement, punishment, and torture in the Underworld. This is distorted.

"In the *Bardo Thödol* it's entirely neutral, like a combined bank and credit card statement, simply an accurate accounting record of your financial activity. You're not sinful because you accrued some debits; you're simply in debt because of it. It's the product and momentum and consequences of your karma, your style of cognition, your interpretive habits, your incomplete perception of the true condition of reality. Well, sorry pal, but these are the results of all that. It's no reflection on you, but you will have to take care of these account debits.

"Contrast this with some of the Chinese Courts of Hell descriptions, such as Torture by Mincing Machine, Lake of Blood and the Terrible Bee Torture, or Black Rope Hell and the Upside-Down Prison. Each is presided over by a dispassionate, probably disinterested, dismissive, even scornful, *Diyu* Lord.

"If you are judged meritorious, you may be invited to cross the Golden Bridge for rebirth in an upper world called the Pure Land of the West presided over by the *Dhyani* Buddha

Amitabha. Or you get to cross the Silver Bridge, one attainment notch lower, and enter an upper level of the Celestial Bureaucracy, as the Chinese translation quaintly calls the celestial hierarchy. The Silver Bridge, leads you to Heaven presided over by the august Jade Emperor and populated by gods and celestial officials. The Pure Land is outside the cosmos and the Wheel of Life, while the Jade Emperor's Heaven is inside the cosmos but in a very tony neighborhood. If you don't make either bridge, buckle up for more mincing and black rope fun and for God's sake, watch out for the terrible bees.

"When consciousness is convinced it has no power over events affecting it, what has been meant to be educational now seems to be hellish and incontestable. Merlin restored that power to the soul in the *Bardo* with the *Tibetan Book of the Dead*. That power of consciousness is its own ability to recognize the innate emptiness of all phenomena, but to experience that emptiness as bliss and Light. That is the Buddha Mind, and it is the Christ Light, the Christ scourging the Hell realms. That is a seed deposited within every soul. Merlin's text shows you where to find it, how to activate and wield it, how to erase this dismal, hellish phantasmagoria confronting you in a blaze of Light. The text says, just because you see it before you, doesn't mean it's real. It isn't real. Void it."

"That is a helpful overview, Blaise," said Merlin. "The thinking in the Hierarchy, or what the Chinese would like to call the Celestial Bureaucracy, at the time was that human consciousness had lost its potency in the *Bardo*. It was being afflicted by all manner of impediments and interferences, compounded by the Druj. Disempowering Hell models had gained prominence in most myth and religious systems of description, and these inspired a victim status among the newly dead. It's true that cognitive conditions are different in the *Bardo* contrasted with how you assemble the

world in the daytime sunlit world in a body. Time is slowed down to the point of being unnoticeable, and the soul has fewer distractions veiling the naked reality of their condition. The only dependable ground for the soul in the *Bardo* is one's own consciousness.

"Still, cognition creates reality, generates the perceptual field, then we credit this with outside validity and act accordingly as if it is an independent actor. It's a marvelous act of self-deception. People fall for it constantly. We thought it was time to remind the soul in the *Bardo* that a Hell is hellish only if we see it that way, assume that these blood-dripping gargoyles are genuinely evil and set against our well-being and not, as they actually are, helpfully dramatizing, modelling certain stuck aspects of our karmic mental formations. Really, they are saying, like mimes, look, this is exactly what you are like now.

"It may seem hellish only because you are witnessing the potency of its negative formations in a direct manner, unmediated by distractions like the human body. But it is not inherently, unreservedly, and absolutely inimical or evil, dead-set against you, after your hide at all costs, but rather a distortion of the *skandahs*. The *skandah* grid gets twisted by strong mental and emotional formations and emits a distorted, unharmonious vibration back to consciousness. The controls for this consciousness-emitting, perception-conditioning grid are in your mind, in consciousness itself. The text sets out to remind the person of this.

"We reminded humans that the *Bardo* is rooted entirely in their own consciousness. That is where it is. It only seems to be an external environment because you haven't caught on to this basic fact. You bring the *Bardo* and its conditions with you. Yes, there is an interactive psychic space set aside surrounding Yama's celestial city for karma processing and *Bardo* projections, but everyone brings their own *Bardo* and projects it according to their pre-existing expectations. You spend your incarnate human life creating your *Bardo*. It's like spending a lifetime packing your suitcase for a trip. The *Bardo* is the trip. You arrive and unpack your suitcase. Everything you brought is your *Bardo*.

"It's a community of solipsistic projectors here, all believing their projections are real, have a certifiable, perdurable reality outside of themselves. The introduction of this text and its viewpoint was a swordstroke into the Druj. It threw her off her game for a while, busted up her tricks—well, at least in Tibet."

"That's part of your job, to periodically upgrade the Underworld," said Edward. "I reported on your upgrade to the Mayan model of *Xibalba* in *The Mertowney Mountain Interview*s. You got the Lords of *Xibalba* to back off on some of their nastier assaults against uninformed human consciousness. Then came the Tibetan reformation of *Bardo* protocols, and now you lead our Green Knight expedition as we compile practical recommendations for the immediate improvement of conditions and making them more favorable for humans to understand this place and take steps up in the mastery of their consciousness.

"That's what you showed the world in the Polynesian picture of you as Maui, fearlessly entering the formidable body of the Great Mother Hine in search of the seed of immortality you knew She had buried inside Her. You did that for humans just as in the Egyptian picture of Anubis you supervised the Weighing of the Heart ritual to assure humans were not judged unfairly or prematurely or the scales tipped against them leading to their being tossed to the nasty *Ammit*.

"You take souls to that place where they can find the immortality seed inside the Great Mother, but the secret is, it is a condition of consciousness, its original condition when it was whole and unified and not fragmented into

49 chakras. That's the place where awareness is unfallen, unfragmented, and unincarnated. People yearn to return to that place; they've forgotten where it is.

"Everything you've done has been under the benign auspices of the Silver Ray, because it is the Ray that oversees the *Bardo* and leads the soul through the 49 Gates and into the audience chamber of the Great Mother, shaper of all forms. Your assignment is to help souls get through the tests and challenges of divesting their own karmic accretions, knots, and entanglements, and into the same room with Queen Ereshkigal, Persephone, Isis, *Mom*, beyond form and back into unity.

"All the karmic complications, the *skandah* grid distortions, all the messes in consciousness, are the result of passing *out* through those 49 Gates in the first place, out into the bewildering world of differentiation into forms, into the challenging condition of having 49 eyes, or chakras, instead of only the one, and then, sadly, even worse, altogether forgetting that you even have these 49 eyes."

"That's the problem, isn't it," said Tommy, in a reflective tone. "I'm thinking about my high school buddies—well, let's say my fellow students. I can't imagine them, dead, rushing with enthusiasm to enter this voidness state. It would seem perhaps too hard, too foreign and exotic, or just entirely irrelevant. We are talking about a steep gradient here, coming to terms with the *Bardo*. I suspect a lot of people, not just teenagers, may find that too formidable a task. They are not used to focusing their awareness back on their awareness itself.

"It's like telling everyone they have to immediately become Buddhists to survive the *Bardo*. It's true, Buddhism tells you why you suffer, because in ignorance you do not have the full picture of the condition of consciousness and your reality. But probably a lot of people will prefer to rush through here and reincarnate and not want to sit down and come to terms with their projective consciousness. It may take them a long time, many lives, before the question arises, or before they start linking their suffering with the condition of their fundamental ignorance, in the sense of not understanding how reality works.

"The only way any of this makes sense to a person is to remember that they asked to incarnate, to be a human, even a serial human, a repeat offender. Everything follows from this request. God knows this, but people have forgotten. All the problems, the disconnection, the sense that death and the *Bardo* are a horror show or to ask fundamental questions about one's own awareness and its mechanisms while alive is just unconscionable, too scary or too damn weird, follows from this simple fact that we cannot remember *asking* freely for all this."

"You're right, Tommy, "said Blaise. "Many will probably not be ready for this. Your role, Merlin, is to help the human soul get out of the corresponding Light temples of life and death, the whole Wheel of Life, back into the Mother's wonderful Silver Light realm. Human physical life and the body-free *Bardo* are two divisions of the same Light temple, the same initiation process in the protocols of consciousness designed for humans, and both are only provisional realities, delightful, baffling products of name and form and the other *skandahs*.

"Your job is to guide us through this dual Light temple and become aware of our habitual repetition compulsion and propensity for self-willed oblivion of our acts, and to help us get back to the Mother's Silver realm and then use that as a position of mastery of consciousness, *skandahs*, and all karmic projections to re-enter the funhouse of the Wheel of Life and help others free themselves as well.

"You said the *Bardo* is rooted in our consciousness. I so understand that. The trick is to make that a habit while we are alive so when we get here it is not so formidable a challenge, so unusual, or, to most, so bizarre a requirement. It's true, the *Bardo* has been weighted against human consciousness making any sense of it and we are making suggestions to improve that in favor of humans, but people still have to step up a little, make some effort to gain mastery of their attention. It comes down to the *skandah* grid again, as it always does.

"That grid is like a spotlight that's always on, high intensity, focusing on the outer world. It focuses outward, perpetually away from the bedrock of awareness that processes the products of those perceptions, the central office to which all the mail is delivered. It's the generic infrastructure, the armature, upon which we deposit or concoct personality traits in support of our individuality. We have to get in the habit of going to that place more often so we know it better.

"I've made it a practice of following my attention back to its origin point, back to itself where all the perceptions, all the *skandah* grid 'fishes' caught in the great net of its attention, swim back to. I turn around in myself and enter that place, at least for a few minutes every day, to remind myself that it is the center. You have to, if you expect to make sense of this unhinged place we're in now.

"The *Bardo* is like a dream state scripted from everything in your psyche, from birth to the present moment and even, sometimes, from your future, into a crazy visual monologue. You are both the stand-up comic and the audience, but you're not getting your own jokes. You're not laughing. The comic is worried. Oh shit, another tough audience. All my jokes are bombing. What dead-beats.

"You need to get some kind of handle on that protean creativity you are spawning every second you're in the *Bardo*. It's even crazier than dreaming. For a start on grabbing that handle, realize that *it's you* that's screenwriting all this. You are the screenwriter coming up with the zany gags and special effects and the merry-andrew performing them like a trained circus dog catching Frisbees.

"Yes, it can be a shocking experience at first, being dead and in the *Bardo*. First you go through the scrapbook of your life, what you did in the daytime; then you get the *Finnegans Wake* version of your wild activities in Night Town. So that's two levels of craziness, both unremembered until this moment. These personal scrapbook parts will at least seem somewhat familiar to you, though you will have forgotten much of the details and overlooked important nuances.

"Then you get to see what you're made of as a human. Yikes! This is a transpersonal disclosure as you watch the scrapbook itself gets taken apart before your eyes and its constituent components revealed. This is the disclosure of the generic infrastructure of human-style consciousness, the materials that went into creating Joyce's Here Comes Everybody, the matrix of emotions, feelings, perceptions, volitions, thoughts, and all the self-references that sprout in consciousness that you pasted your personal name upon and into which all your karma has flowed like a drain or like autumn leaves against a grate. Aghast, you watch Humphrey Chimpden Earwicker lurking in you, in everyone, taken apart.

"This is where all the truly deranged stuff starts showing up, the gargoyles with skull necklaces dripping blood and the demented Lords of *Xibalba* playing soccer with your head and the magistrates of the Courts of Hell with their unfathomable notions and disturbing funhouses, with surrealistic antics that would startle even Kafka with their inexplicability. The sooner you catch on to the fact that this lunatic variety act, this psychotic antic hay, all comes out of your creative head, that its zany valence

is determined by you, then the sooner you'll start feeling safe and you might even break into laughter. Mel Brooks could have made a hilarious spoof of the wacko world of the *Bardo*.

"The Lords of *Xibalba* and the Assessors of the Dead are all waiting to see how you react. Will you fill with unbearable fright or laugh your head off at them? They're all posturing, a bunch of goofy poseurs, competently acting their parts, doing a serviceable job of looking fierce and malevolent, pretending to be scary and implacable, stern and unyielding, but whether they turn into horrific monsters from the deep or a dozen grinning Harpo Marxes with magical billowing overcoats stuffed with horns, posters, huge scissors, and flame-throwers is up to you. Wouldn't you rather watch a slapstick comedy?

"Yes, you have to settle your accounts and acknowledge the components that built up your consciousness, both personal and generic, but it doesn't mean you have to suffer through the procedure. You can have fun. I mean, why not?" The Supreme Being has a great sense of humor. Ask the Blaises. He's their Dad!"

"The Druj of course will try to push your feelings towards the scary side," said Edward. "She gives it that little nudge, just enough to persuade somebody they are confronted with something horrible beyond belief and totally inimical. Because the minute you're pushed into that fear position, you lose all confidence in the potency of your consciousness to change matters or for you to have the revelation that you are creating all this, or at least dressing up the generic actors. The Lords, Magistrates, or Assessors are there, for real, as innate structural and functional components of your consciousness, but how they look is mutable. You can do a horror show montage from Aeschylus or a rowdy vaudeville routine."

"It's strange but most people are so comfortable with always perceiving only the outer world," replied Blaise, "directing their *skandah* grid exclusively outwards and forgetting it's there in the first place. They'd prefer being scared witless by scary phenomena appearing *outside* them than in confronting the primacy and singularity of consciousness as the source of all these phenomena. Oddly, that responsibility scares most people more even though it is the one assured way out of the *Bardo* horrifics, or, as we know, its sleights-of-hand.

"If you grab hold of your consciousness, take the *skandah* grid in both hands, look at it, understand its function, and erase it, dissolve it from your field of action, then you realize with stark clarity that *you* are the controller of this madcap *Bardo*. The power and responsibility this revelation points to is disturbing to most souls. Bizarrely, it is more comforting to construe oneself as a helpless victim than as the hero who rescues oneself from an imagined morass of imaginary demons by mobilizing innate, terrific, *real* powers of consciousness.

"They're not used to being in charge. How can you be in charge in an accidental, chaotic universe, where everything is the product of chance, or how can you be in charge when that is to blaspheme the Lord of the Universe, God the Monarch, who arranges things to suit His arcane, undecipherable pleasure? You get wedged into a place of powerlessness between both these deluded misperceptions, wedging courtesy of the Druj, the most attentive of salesclerks.

"So you figure the *Bardo* is just one more thing *done* to you, a nuisance or weight that you have to put up with, like noisy neighbors or a moronic boss at work. You think of it as necessary if inexplicable suffering. Suffering becomes a mental lifestyle; we have to endure what God sends us, you start to intone piously. Rubbish! Passivity and the disempowerment of consciousness are always the Druj's top goals. Be a victim. It's popular. It's validated. She wants souls to transit the twofold Light temple

of incarnation and *Bardo* convinced of their feckless inability to ever change anything, that they are *not* players but expendable cheap pawns in an infernal chess game between God and Satan."

"We call that shocking moment as having a meeting with Anguta," said Pipaluk. "The *angakkuq* is trained to find then stand strong in this special place. You realize you have power, you stand in the place of power, and that awareness leads you to perceive Anguta, to understand power comes from Anguta to you. Now, instead of the demons of the Underworld, of *Adlivun*, as the Inuit call it, you are presented with the Creator of the universe, whom we call Anguta. To many, that is more astounding than seeing all the hosts of *tuurngait* or spirits.

"These can be helpful spirits as well as monstrous, evil spirits obstructing you. Some say Anguta is the gatherer of the dead who carries them into *Adlivun* where they must sleep in his company for a year. But Anguta is also 'His Father,' the Creator-god and chief spirit. His name means 'man with something to cut.' This refers to when he cut up his daughter to make her an immortal god. She now rules in *Adlivun*. Anguta acts as conductor of souls to that realm, even as the ferryman leads souls into the Underworld. Pinga, the goddess of fertility, the hunt, and medicine, also acts as a psychopomp. After their one-year sleep, souls may proceed to *Qudlivun*, 'Those Above Us,' a blissful zone on the Moon. I think this is the same place as your Silver realm of the Great Mother of all life-forms.

"But first the souls must be purified in *Adlivun*, which means 'Those Beneath Us.' Inuit see this as lying underneath the ocean and the Earth's surface. The Inuit often describe this as a frozen wasteland, but we always expect to find snow! The *angakkuq* is used to seeing hosts of spirits. The *tuurngait* may be good or evil, helpful or impeding, and sometimes we have to fight them off and disperse them, drive them out of a human body they have unlawfully possessed.

"The Inuit know that the world is made of *anirniit*, indwelling spirit-souls in all life-forms. These spirits live after death; they persist after the physical form is dropped. We have a saying, 'The great peril of our existence lies in the fact that our diet consists entirely of souls.' That means the animals and fish and birds we eat to live. All these forms have an *anirniq*, meaning divine breath. When this *anirniq* is freed from the body at death, this spirit is now free to take revenge on those who harmed them during physical life. Those most often are humans.

"The *angakkuq* often has to deal with the actions of these vengeful *anirniit* once they are freed and now live in *Adlivun*. Maybe some of these unhappy spirits seeking retribution are your nasty magistrates with blood and skulls and the sneering, hateful expressions going after the humans once they enter the Underworld and start looking for bearings. Maybe some of the nasty spirits in the *Bardo*, especially those with strange animal aspects, are the agents of the Group Souls of the many species of birds and animals humans have lived on."

"You know who would have paid big to those *anirniit*?" said Tommy. "Ernest Hemingway. He was always killing animals for no good reason, for sport. I almost feel sorry for him. First he would have had to serve his suicide days, like I did, the balance of the days he had scheduled his life to last. Then he'd be chased around the Animal *loka* of the Six World's game reserve, and the *anirniit* would have done a crunching number on his animal-hating butt. The Spanish bulls would have glared at him, and all the African game would have come for justified compensation, or at least an apology. I never liked his animal-killing penchant. No animal was safe around him."

"I've always remembered an account I read in a Mayan text," Blaise said. "Some Mayans were in the Underworld and asked the dog-spirits there to guide them. The dogs refused. You never fed us while you were alive so we will ignore you now that you're dead and asking for our assistance. Feed your dogs and pamper them silly. That's the moral of that tale. The thing people need to become acutely aware of, starting right now, is that you are creating your future *Bardo* conditions every minute you are alive and cognizing the world and acting in it.

"It's not just the obvious accumulation of karmic credits and debits your actions entail. It is your habits of consciousness, your cognitive styles and tendencies, that are conditioning your *skandah* grid to always decode reality in *those* ways. You need to seize that awareness right now and write better scripts for your life. Every moment alive you are creating your *Bardo* conditions. In fact, the real teaching of the Tibetan text, I propose, is that your alive time is the *Bardo* also. The *Bardo* teachings are meant to illuminate and *explain* your incarnate life."

"Indeed, and those scripts you refer to are constantly filed with the Earth's Albion," said Merlin. "The details of the death and *Bardo* experiences of every human over time have been filed with the prime Albion. People send him memos every day, pages torn from their journals. You could say Albion takes photographs of each soul's progress through the *Bardo*, as rapidly as blinking; his eyes are like cameras. He's seeking to build an impression of how humans fare in this cycling between life and *Bardo*, between the two divisions of this one Light temple of incarnation.

"That impression will equip Albion to navigate the world of humans and Earth when he finally awakens and the collective consciousness of humanity over time is at last lucid and self-aware. So every human death adds to Albion's education. Every *Bardo* failure or success informs Albion, builds up the body of evidence. It's as if Albion sleeps in such a way that his form straddles both divisions of the Light temple of incarnation and *Bardo* divestment. His subliminal attention perpetually occupies both divisions, always registering new data. In many ways Albion is the Guardian Angel of the human phylogeny on Earth."

17

Merlin had stopped talking. I wasn't sure where we were at first, then I realized it was a bedroom. A human, Earth-style bedroom, equipped with everything you'd expect, large bed, several wooden dressers, a mirror, a few comfortable chairs, a footstool, lamps, a ceiling fan, bedside table with four books piled on it, a television-computer unit. An elderly man lay in the bed, under a thick pile of covers. It was winter outdoors. He looked to be in his eighties. He was weak, vacant, wan-looking, losing life-force, close to death. He was worn out. Presumably, his medical condition did not warrant hospitalization or even hospice care, and he, or his family, had elected for him to die in the familiarity of his home. He was surrounded by all he would soon have to let go of definitively.

His Higher Self stood a few feet behind him as if in the wall, as unobtrusive and respectful of the man's dignity as if the angel were a consummate butler. His wings were stretched out, like a baseball catcher ready for the next pitch, but in this case to catch the man's soul as it freed itself at last from his debilitated body. The man's celestial angel was at least two stories tall. You could see the side of the house, its walls, and you could see the angel. They occupied the same visual space but clearly they were not in the same frequency.

A white mist was swirling around the base of the man's spine. It exerted a suction effect on that part of his body where I also saw the man's root chakra. That white swirl was the man's awareness, a portion of his soul being extracted from the first of the seven energy centers of his form. It's not correct, I know, to say "a portion" because the soul is a unified holographic substance, like blood.

A fundamental balancing in the man's awareness was in progress. He was withdrawing attention from his physical body, its emotional and mental life, and reinvesting it in his soul life, which perhaps had been at best only subliminally known to him during his life. I impute volition to this act; he really had no choice. Death was doing it, death and its mandated, unnegotiable life processes. Still, he wasn't resisting it, and he could have: he still had enough life-force for it.

The white swirl moved slowly up the man's body, suctioning out the soul awareness from each chakra, like a boy sipping soda through a straw. As the soul extraction continued, a separate version of the man's body started to form around him and gradually became upright and stood facing him. It looked like him, but it seemed to be woven of myriads of thin grey-green threads, like a man's form compounded of woven yarn, and amidst these many fibers were thousands of images, like a photograph album arrayed across a human form.

Each image seemed alive, as if you were watching it as live action, its drama unfolding right now before your eyes. This was going on in thousands of such images. I realized this was the man's life, his memory archives in his etheric body which is the faithful, totally accurate repository of all one's life memories. When people say their life flashed before them, they are seeing this picture-body.

In a near-death experience, which is when people usually make this surprised declaration, the etheric body is temporarily loosened from its firm grip on the physical form, for which it is responsible as its model; but in actual death, it is definitively separated, as if pulled off the physical body. Then you spend time reviewing its contents, digesting the memory impact. Then you are actually in the etheric body; it is your new, temporary wrap-around environment. It's like being surrounded by a hundred television screens; you can't help but watch what they're showing, especially when you realize you star in every episode.

This process was just getting started for this man on the verge of his death. This form held the picture-body of his life, now completed, every single life action. As the white swirl kept moving up his physical form, extracting more of his soul-blood and thereby strengthening the swirl while weakening the body, this human form of life pictures swelled tidally with ever more images of his life.

You didn't have to ask him how his life had been, what he'd done, did he like it, had it been fulfilling, because it was all there, the full record, down to the minutiae of his daily lunch menu. There he was, his life, revealed in pictures, everything he'd done while awake, walking around in the sunlit daytime world. The pictures were filed thematically, I noticed, with their content or essential drama correlated with the most relevant chakra: love and grief with the heart; struggle and anger with the solar plexus; fear, panic, and worries about death with his root center. That was logical; the chakras managed those major areas.

Clearly, the man was reveling in this uprushing of life memory. It was a slow-motion epiphany of his life, himself in retrospective, a lifetime review. It was like watching a TV documentary of somebody famous who had just died. He laughed as realized he had been filming himself his entire life.

It was for him like strolling through a magnificent art gallery full of his favorite paintings. He would pause before one image, smile, shake his head or shrug his shoulders. Before others, he would stand back and gasp or raise his hands in surprise. Evidently, he was seeing scenes he had forgotten until now, or the faces of people long eclipsed by later events, people he had lost touch with, who had died, drifted away from him, walked away from him in a huff, rejected him, sought him, written to him with no answer, thought of doing that and didn't. He saw places he had visited, restaurants, movie theaters, bookshops, department stores his mother had dragged him into when he was five to get fitted for new school clothes or shoes whose color and shape he never liked.

He saw yesterday in thorough, vivid detail, he saw this morning, he saw five minutes ago, five seconds ago, one millisecond ago, and he saw right now, this exact moment, as he was in the process of dying, gathering up his memories. That would be the final record of his current life on this long surveillance tape. He probably had never been this acutely attentive to what was happening in all his life. This was a moment of enhanced lucidity, and it kept building, like a cresting wave, like a climax in an opera, as a swell of exquisite focused attention. This is my performance piece. I wonder if God likes it, will offer applause. His soul was asking this vital question as the man's personality kept slipping away.

A second body started to form around the man in his bed. It looked like him, but not as vividly as the etheric form that was already mostly fully formed. It was larger, more emotionally nuanced, more multi-valenced or contradictory. This body looked like it was full of colored images cast upon a night sky, movies seen only at night, like the old drive-ins from the 1950s. The images looked (and felt, for you could feel their emotions and they were intense) operatic, heightened to the point of exaggeration, like actors being emotional in a play, amping it up for maximum effect. Rage, anger, terror, fear, sorrow, grief, despair—it was the full range of human feelings, painted in glaringly bright colors, his feelings highlighted in their rawness and pitched for a soap opera.

These chromatic displays of heightened affect were set against a background that looked like a cosmos filled with huge versions of the body's organs. Yes, a bizarre image at first glance, but I remember Rudolf Steiner writing about how the internal body organs of the human were condensed versions of large cosmic processes, that cosmology inverts to become organology.

This man's emotional life was framed against this spectacle of cosmic organs. They were more like nebulae and star clusters and spiral galaxies. I saw traces of animal forms within these cosmic organs, as if, somehow, all the animal kingdom, dogs, horses, buffalo, sheep, goats, and tigers, came out of these organs or were equivalent expressions of them, that humans had birthed them out of an original greatness of archetypal form. Not only did Adam name all the creatures; they emanated from his great form, like from an ark. He made them. Maybe that's why the Animal *loka* does not have a *Dhyani* Buddha. Humans are meant to act as the wisdom figure for this human-generated realm. We created them. Our job as humans is to act like *Dhyani* Buddhas, coverting fear to illumination.

Regarding this more awesome body, the man was less acquainted. He looked at it in disbelief for the most part, as if he were seeing terrible secrets of his family tree, his parental lineage revealed, but it was secrets of himself he saw. This is the record of the man's forgotten life in Night Town, on all-night binges or lost weekends, suffering blackouts, eclipses, and obliviations of all memory.

It was the body of his unconscious, the life record of what he had done at night, in his dreams, his astral sojourns, or slummings, and the unobserved, rippling, even cascading, effects of his actions on people. Where his aspersive remarks went, what damages they caused in people; what rips and tears in a person's auric field his anger generated; what his unthinking gestures of goodwill did to help a person regain confidence—how he had affected people.

This body held storm clouds, lightning jags, and you could hear the thunder rolls. Some areas were packed solid, like black holes full of wailing and moaning. These were the seeds of his illnesses and body dysfunctions; they got unloaded into his etheric body and that body dutifully transferred them to physical processes, distorting their original purity of design to make room for this karma. Yet this was the body that did all the circus tricks in Night Town, flying, walking through walls, crossing great distances in Vishnu's famous nine-mile boots, visiting people from the past, who were dead or who lived thousands of miles away, exploring caves, exotic temples, being chased by horrible demons.

It was his astral body I was observing, the body form of stars, a more cosmic body version of himself. It was the body of mysteries and powers, of suffering, nastiness, and self-regard. It was the perpetual incorrigible teenager, out slumming every night, looking for thrills, for girls, for adventure, for trouble. Conflicted, contradictory, like the archetype of the Trickster, like Coyote, both benevolent culture hero and self-serving self-aggrandizer, wise and foolish, the principle of antinomy in one body, yes and no, light and dark, good and evil.

The man was getting restless and fidgety. A panic was building in him. He was beginning to realize he was not who he thought he was, or there was more to him than he had ever realized, that his personality, his name and form which he had carried with him in the wallet of his consciousness, was only a mask, a semblance, a role in a play, but what was the reality? Who was he really?

He felt like he suddenly realized he had been standing on an earthquake fault zone and it was trembling. The ground was no longer straight, steady, and solid beneath him as it had always seemed to be. That seeming was eroding. The stability that had seemed so constant as to become habitual in his awareness was now cracking up. It was ending, or maybe it had never been more than illusory. He suddenly did not know who or what he was or where he was, or, worse, *why*.

This is a critical moment, and a person can either fall into panic and hysteria or use the cracking open of the illusion of physical life as an awakening. He could use it for what Pipaluk called a face-to-face meeting with Anguta, or he could freak out irretrievably and run madly through the *Bardo* chased by ill-intentioned demons. This moment was a door: would it, for him, open into a horror-house of monsters and tortures or be the liminal threshold of a meditation hall, a sanctuary or church or synagogue or mosque, whatever form he liked, in which he could at last take a true reading of the state and reality of his soul?

While not intending to fix the outcome, his Higher Self at this point stepped forward and gently wrapped his wings around the man, only enough to provide a slightly inspiring, reassuring ambiance, a sense of validation and love. The man still had to choose on his own, out of his free will, but it's always easier to make a crucial decision if you're not in a panic about your survival.

I saw that as the man's consciousness, that growing white swirl, was progressively being extracted from his chakras and starting to mass at the top of his head, he was coming to a realization. It was shocking and exhilarating. Let's say you have that meeting with Anguta: the first thing you'll discover, for how could you not as it's right in your face, is that you are a created being. You did not make yourself. Anguta did. You got to drive this "you" around, see the sights, get some dents and nicks in the car doors, maybe change the paint color.

You may have concocted a plausible cover story, a legend, a personality, and, over time, accrued a considerable tally of debts and credits which will have to be definitively settled at some point, but you did not create the generic container in which you have come up with this plausible mask over the great emptiness, nor the need to have a personality in the first place, nor the components that comprise one. That's okay, no blame meant, just the sobering realization of true authorship. So who are you? A mass of transient karmic accrual sculpted over this generic framework? Both unsettling and intriguing. Your role, I propose, is as novelist. You are creating, fleshing out, a believable human character, then living into this "person," making him as real as possible. That's where your free-will creativity fits; everything else in this world is a given.

I think most people probably never think about this, or pretend they authored themselves. To a degree, that is true, if you count generating karma as authorship of a fluctuating persona over time, meaning over many lifetimes. But you did not create the context, the conditions, in which your mask of identity would flourish, nor the body, nor the Earth, nor the tool of consciousness itself.

That is not a criticism leveled at anybody. It's more a riveting discovery that you could use to your benefit, or you could allow to overwhelm you with your apparent insignificance even though that is not, I'm sure, the Creator's intention at all. *Yet*, despite this vacuity of creative authorship, you were given the one tool by which all this was itself created: you were granted the potency of God-consciousness. In essence, you are a microcosm, a hologram, of The Boss.

I saw the man struggling with the ramifications of this bedrock discovery. I hoped he would reach the place where he realized the correct attribution of authorship to the Supreme Being meant his life was not an accident, not haphazard, not the product of random coincidences and the other brain-dead theories scientists come up with, but one set in a reality meticulously planned and accounted for. Surely that is cause for a kind of existential relaxation to know reality is planned, that the Supreme Being has taken all factors into account and you and everyone else are part of that infinite calculation, even the death and afterlife protocols. It's all been carefully engineered for your benefit.

The twofold Light temple of physical life and *Bardo* journeying is part of that. Anguta, that crafty designer, has left ample clues in both poles of this temple, clues to the reality and mechanics of that imponderable tool, consciousness. As the Qabalists say, the Supreme Being has disclosed Himself in the Creation, and Mr. and Mrs. God, as Blaise would whimsically put it, wait expectantly at their high-tea table, scones on the tray, for us to see the set-up.

Yes, it will always remain mysterious once you reach a certain point in the disclosure, but that can't be helped. The Supreme Being is an infinite spirit, and we as created beings are not, though we have the possibility of joining that infinity one day but at the cost of our finite individuality, which still makes it unattainable to us in the format in which we currently recognize ourselves. I guess that qualifies as a paradox, probably the biggest one confronting us. An insoluble one, in fact: the finite being cannot survive expansion into infinity.

The dying man's Higher Self had duplicated himself many times over, forming an enveloping fan with many folds around the man and his auric field. It was like seeing a colorful umbrella with a hundred echoes of itself draped around a person so that this benevolent angel, who had midwifed the death of thousands of earlier versions of this man, had died by proxy that many times itself, truly these past lives were this man's ancestors in terms of his karmic record, patiently awaited the release of the fullness of the man's consciousness from his expiring form, from the body and life he was leaving behind, spent.

It looked as if the man could, with that now large white swirl, step completely out of his deceasing human physical form into the cupped hands of the celestial angel and from there, from that divinely supportive, reassuring foundation, enter the *Bardo* and begin his after-death processing, the required "paperwork" of post-incarnation. You might call it his exit interview.

I saw a few details of what he would likely have to deal with over here. His astral body had a big black splotch filled with red lightning jags near his liver. Superficially, you could say that was unexpressed, unresolved anger, but it was more and deeper than that. It was the result of a prolonged suppression of will, of not getting what he wanted, of being ordered about, of denying himself. No, I'm not saying the man never learned to be selfish enough to insist on having what he desired; it's more of a long-term self-denial and repression of his truth. He had been his own harsh jailor, and his shadow side was fomenting rebellion.

The site, that stormy black smear, was the registry of many injuries, wounds, insults, battles, retreats, moments of anger shoved into one's emotional pockets, and it was preparing itself for an anchorage into his flesh at some near point. Soon his body, the next one perhaps, would have to anchor that in a pathology. The energy was too fierce, too chaotic, too turbulent, to contain otherwise. The best approach would be for him to unravel and process that black smudge now, in the place to which he was going, in a suitable *Bardo* workshop, where supervised by his Higher Self and like a clockmaker he examined the workings to see what had set the mechanism askew and then cleaned it out.

Depending on the creativity of his imagination, he might picture some of that black turbulence in the form of injurious demons or snarling monsters. I hoped he would understand these baleful disguises were only visual metaphors. He was personifying a disturbance of the fire element and his will working through his liver and its processes, the organic seat of those conditions (at least as seen from an acupuncture point of view, "Liver" being a meridian system including the organ and its subway line or energy meridian through the body).

A few days later, his body was cremated. That was a smart move. As his deceased physical container burned to ashes, it gave the man a spring launch. That's what it looked like. He shot into the air in a sudden updraft of buoyancy, and all his *Bardo* processing suddenly got easier, went quicker and smoother. Any lingering energetic connections he still had to his now extinct former life were dissolved in this incineration, and even the residual emotional and mental residues were easier to deal with, became more transparent, loosened their hold.

As for us, we were not allowed to interfere in his soul extrication process. We were observers, veiled so he couldn't see us. It wouldn't benefit him to see us because we were not relatives or deceased loved ones and he would likely be startled to see a spectral gang of eight humans massed attentively in his bedroom, two of whom were not even in forms resembling human shapes but in bodies of Light. I know I would be. But we were allowed to intervene if the Druj played her hand too heavily or overtly. We had permission to push her off. And she was at work with this man departing his completed life-form. She was manipulating the religious and spiritual pictures in his auric field, pricking them.

I had the impression the man had been a half-hearted Catholic in his life. He had been raised in a Catholic family but they were mostly lapsed; they occasionally put in an appearance at Mass for some of the important days of the year, like Christmas and Easter, but it was mostly for the social appearance.

I saw images from Catholic iconography arrayed like a haphazard art gallery in his auric field, conventional depictions of the Virgin Mary, the Christ Child, cute and spectacularly holy in her lap, a few snapshots of Jehovah in a snarly mood, ripping yet another new one in the chronically misbehaving screw-ups, the Jews, wandering the desert, always displeasing Yahweh, upstarts, always going rogue. It was like a comic-book version of the crankier parts of the Old Testament, graphic with Jehovah's vituperation and scorn against his feckless chosen people, incapable, evidently, of doing anything right in his mind.

I would expect to find images of the crucified Christ, and I did, many of them. These were effective in most people, quite potently so, for they lit up the guilt feelings. This divine figure died for you, you ungrateful pagan slob, so how come you're not thankful, penitent, and, frankly, groveling in submissive prostrations before him? Surely that is the least you could do for this level of sacrifice on your behalf. It was your depraved registry of sins that required this. I could just about hear the priests hectoring this man in his telepathic background. Mothers often take the same approach: after all I've done for you I get this back?

The Druj saw the potential in this and was deftly stirring the pot of guilt feelings. The man was squirming under her subtle assault. He was beginning to question his worthiness. Maybe God, for he did maintain a sketchy working belief in a Supreme Being, would regard him as unworthy of His love, attention, and forbearance; maybe the Lord of the Universe would assign him to tortures. (It astonishes me still that intelligent people could believe a Creator God to be as petty and vindictive as to act that way, to punish and wreak suffering on souls.) But this was an old hook; it almost always worked, as long as the person had a few black seeds of Christianity planted somewhere in his auric field or psyche.

He had been about to enter the *Bardo* smoothly with clarity and interest. Then these Antichrist commandoes waylaid him right at the gateway and forced him off the *Bardo* highway into a dismal, snarling pullout so they could work him over. They were like ruffians, brigands out to steal his soul. The Catholic unworthiness and blame pictures were glaring in a neon light; you could feel the waves of hate and revulsion rippling off them making the psychic atmosphere choppy. You felt the rowboat of your soul would soon capsize. The man knew the pictures were likely untrue, but he could not withstand their force. He did not have quite enough certainty to dispel their sales pitch of negativity.

That's where we came in, where we were allowed to intervene on his behalf. All we did was create the tableau of the Sword of the Elohim again as a backlight to the Catholic blame pictures. This additional Light shining on the images enabled the man to see them for what they were, fakes, lies, illusions. He saw the hectoring demonic faces, leering and shouting at

him through what purported to be holy images, sacrosanct depictions of divine, absolutely pure spirits, virginal beyond belief, self-sacrificing to an unprecedented degree. Lies.

The Catholic images, he saw, were like garish cartoon depictions of spiritual realities, caricatured images typical in what used to be called graphic novels. Overdone, exaggerated, misleading, and, arguably, blasphemous, even obscene; these demonic priest-appearing spirits were pimping the Virgin Mary and Jesus the Christ on behalf of the Druj and her dark antihuman agenda.

The man saw this, understood it, was aghast, in disbelief, then he felt refreshed. No, I never truly thought God could dislike me to that degree, I could hear him thinking. There was a new lightness to his thinking; he was returned to the truth. Those false images started flaking off him, dissolving, but the insistent demons kept hectoring him until they were completely disintegrated from his auric field. The more he discounted their lies, the weaker they became. His discernment and reorientation were extracting the life-force from these devils.

Evidently, the man had already started his post-life processing of the contents of his etheric body and he was getting glimpses of what was in his astral body too. It started the minute his soul started to collect itself from the chakras. I was certain he knew he was dying, but the fascination of retrieving all this forgotten information about himself was gripping his attention (if it were a book, you'd call it a page-turner) and countermanding any anxiety or reluctance the death process might otherwise have elicited. It was more interesting to him than worrying about the fact he was dying.

Perhaps he realized, or at least suspected, that there would be a continuity of his consciousness as he crossed the boundary. For a while he seemed to be dually occupied with dying and reviewing, but soon the dying part would be finished, his soul would be fully out of his deceased form, and he would continue with full attention and unflagging interest in his life review. He was off to a good start, and in fine hands, and when the bumpy, scary parts started he would probably handle them with competence and understanding.

Not so for the woman in the hospital bed. She was dying of leukemia. She was suffering mightily, and resisting the dying process with equal intensity. She was stuck in a dichotomy of hating her sickness and hating having to die from it. Her body's white blood cells had gone defective, even "mental" in a sense, operating wrongly, being produced inaccurately, so all her blood was infected. The only way out at this point from her body's malignancy was death and departure, but she was holding on to her life with all her energy. You could see her gripping the sides of the bed to keep the death angel from taking her away. She was frantically looking for some alternate place to go, outside her dying body, yet still remain here among the living in the physical world.

I saw her soul portrait, by which I mean her soul's relationship to her body. They were at odds with each other; she had never understood or engaged with the life of her body. She had regarded her body the way people think of their cars. As a tool of convenience, sometimes of pleasure, and when it doesn't work properly, you take it into the garage and the mechanics will fix it while you wait. She didn't understand that the body negotiates with the etheric and astral forms to anchor and play out emotions, strong thoughts, and unresolved karma.

She had no intellectual model for that, and in fact no sympathy even for the idea. That was going to be the source of major problems for her in the *Bardo*. She had mostly an intellectual, materialist framework of mind. Presently, she was fighting her body, pummeling it with her spirit, hating it, hitting it hard. The disorder

in her white blood cells reflected—*embodied*—this disconnection of her self, her consciousness, and her karma from her designated bodily container. Her disdain of her own body created the army of phagocytes taking her body apart. They were acting out her lifetime gesture of keeping her body at arm's length.

I wouldn't give the hospital high marks for being a suitable place for death. It had too much death in its psychic atmosphere, and too many ghost-remnants of people who had died within its walls, and in some cases it was Earthbound spirits who had not left the hospital environment and stalled out their *Bardo* transit. They were at risk of entering the Hungry Ghost or Hell realms, and their continuing presence and their unresolved grief, anger, or resistance were contaminating the hospital's psychic field for those in its beds. To some degree the hospital itself had been relocated to the Hell and *Preta* realms.

I saw some of these deeply disgruntled spirits leering and glaring at the woman. You could expect no sympathy from them; they hated everything human, including death. The hospital might be sanitary on a microbiological level (not guaranteed), but on an astral-psychic level it was badly contaminated, a source of significant soul infection. It was operating in the wrong *lokas*. It should at least be still anchored in the Human realm of the Six Worlds. You'd need to have skilled clairvoyants on staff to realize this and fix the problem.

Her Higher Self was trying to console her, provide insight and perspective, but she was carrying on like a two-year-old throwing her dinner. She was pummeling her Guardian Angel, fuming, spluttering, cursing it, deriding even the idea of it and any attribution of that false reality, that idiot's hope, to her, because she had spent most of her life in defiance of God, an atheist. She had pushed God away long ago, when she was a child, and she had spent her life as a secular materialist, as many people do, crediting only the physical world with existence and never imputing a divine plan or sanction to any of it, and in her darker moments regarding it as a horror show without explanation.

In case I haven't made this clear, in our state, with heightened senses and the fact that technically we were not conducting business in our physical forms at all, you could read a person's biography right out of the "pages" of their etheric body. We could see the same images they would see when their life review began. I saw that she had worked professionally as an economist, first in a university as an assistant professor then as a staff forecaster for a large company.

She had married and divorced several times, never had children but a few abortions and one miscarriage. She had suppressed certain latencies to develop her creative side, possibly through painting and drawing; she had let this die out. She drank a lot, not to the point she was an alcoholic, but she used alcohol to dull, if not bludgeon, her nagging awareness that there was more to her life than tracking money flows and predicting economic trends. In fact, she did whatever worked to push down into her unconsciousness any notion of a spiritual reality. She regarded her "I-ness," her self, the penumbra of her soul, as a mechanistic artifact, something to put up with, something you needed in life, like a car motor.

She resolutely refused to acknowledge the basic questions of any person's life, the catalog of essential *why* questions that any sensitive person must wonder about, and she certainly made no attempt to secure plausible answers to them. Now, as she was dying, all she had forcibly suppressed in her life was rising up in revolt around her, like a hospital room full of the Greek Furies demanding retribution for the inexcusable matricide against herself she had committed.

Blaise looked at me, shaking his head in sympathy with her plight, and said, "She needs a good draught of River Lethe eraser. She needs to remember."

English writers speak of the British winter sky pressing down on London like an oppressive gray tombstone. You can feel the weight of the overcast sky pushing on you. She had that same tombstone pressing down on her. It was the weight of all the rejection of the truth of reality, herself, and her life, that she had put out around her, congealed into a wraparound tombstone that was killing her. It was in effect the psychic reason her white blood cells had rebelled against her.

There was howling inside this grey mass, sounds of crying, grieving, and moaning. It was a grey weight compounded of 69 years of unresolved suffering and pain. Not bodily pain; that came later; that was happening now. No, it was emotional and mental pain, never addressed, never healed. It grew out of certain key events in her early life; you could see the image residues of them as fiery photographs. Moments of intense invalidation, thwarted will, denigrated enthusiasm, humiliation in moments of soul nakedness when she showed the world who she was and it laughed or, worse, ignored her, was indifferent, or didn't notice. Her parents had never understood her, never saw her in her truth, so they never gave her a validation or a *Hello!* She struggled on without it.

She started to revile herself. She figured her parents must be right. She was defective, not lovable, not worthy of being cherished, so she didn't cherish herself. Eventually, her body got the message, and started anchoring this self-revulsion in its tissues, consummating in the disorder of her white blood cells, which are supposed to negotiate self and not-self distinctions on the molecular level in accordance with her own discernment as to what distinguished her from others. If she wasn't honoring her self-nature, why should her white blood cells?

Her autoimmune disorder began in her psyche then was copied in her biology. So here she was, dying of leukemia in a hospital bed, embroiled in a civil war that had been going on for decades, promising to grow steadily worse.

Merlin nodded to give us the go-ahead to erase some of the Lethe effect. We constructed the sword and gently nudged it up against that grey tombstone of oppression around her body. The sword started slicing through it, dissolving its constituents as it proceeded. The air around her was obnoxious with its odor.

Once we got through this cloudbank of pain and protracted self-annihilation, I saw that she had cocooned herself in an impenetrable glass membrane. She used it to insulate herself against unwelcome spiritual insinuations from either inside or outside her. She wanted to resolutely resist all such suggestions of a greater life or metaphysical reality. She had taken the River Lethe draught and hardened it into a protective shell. Our sword was now starting to melt that hard glass; it was an illusion that failed. Yes, she had insulated herself, but at the cost of her vitality and consciousness. She had willfully forgotten so much she had no idea who she was now she was dying.

Finally, the sword's edge touched the skin of her soul, emaciated but alive. It looked like electrical sparks jumped off the soul's "skin" when this contact was made. The soul of course had never forgotten its own story, truth, and destiny, and it now, without any mediation, was transmitting that naked reality to the woman. She shivered and squirmed in bed, raising her arms as if in defense. It was as if her own *Daena* had been calling to her for years from the *Cinvat* Bridge.

It was like somebody who for some perverse reason decided they would never bathe, never

allow water to touch their skin, that water was inimical to their well-being, and now she was getting the bath of a lifetime, a full immersion. What she was remembering, what was welling up in her awareness despite everything she believed in, was a complete contradiction of the secular-atheist mask she'd made. Her persona was being contradicted by her truth. You could see it was dawning in her that the charade was up, that the self-delusion was spent, and truth was flooding her body, mind, and emotions, and it felt good. She had laminated the original layer of Lethe amnesia with many coats of her own paint of disregard, or what the Chinese quaintly call the Tea of Oblivion.

Teatime is over, the woman suddenly realized. It's like she woke up with a start, in wonder: How long have I slept? She had been asleep to herself for a long time, and I saw some of the reasons. Her past-life residues were becoming apparent, as they naturally would because they are stored in her auric field and subtle bodies anyway and, technically, they're always accessible to one. I don't think I was too surprised to learn that in some of her recent incarnations she had been the opposite of what she pretended to be in this life of somnolence. She had been an accomplished clairvoyant, even a seer at times, an astrologer, a counselor in past-life regressions, soul retrieval, and other psychic pursuits characteristic of a shaman. She would have liked Pipaluk in those bright lives. But not in this life.

She had adopted a pose of professional and consistent rejection, a prolonged invalidation of anyone who even approached these topics, including herself. She had an injunction against all of that. Well done, Druj, for having convinced her of this magnificent lie. In a few of these lives as a psychically wide-open human, in either gender, she had endured some setbacks, a public humiliation, a betrayal, a repudiation by peers—significant pain input.

To put it simply, these hurt. They dredged holes in her self-esteem; they ripped her aura like a hostile knife slicing a silken parachute. They made her hide. She thought that's where safety from further attacks would be found. Yes, but only in a limited sense; the downside of that choice was much worse, for it ended up being a slow-motion suicide she committed every moment she denied her own truth, when she shoved down every last crown chakra petal like Jews hiding under the floorboards to escape detection by Nazis investigating the Gentile's house. She could not, on her life, admit the existence of this ability to anyone, and eventually, to herself. She sealed the floorboards with her doubt.

She was of course a poseur, but a good one. She bought her own cover story. The fakeness in which she had wrapped herself was now being stripped off her. She wasn't resisting it. She knew it had to be done, and she was *liking* it. That's good. We were waiting for that kind of positive sign. We strengthened the sword's vibrational field as it bore upon her karmic field. It stripped off more layers of lies, deceptions, and the minutiae of the Druj's handiwork in her consciousness over several dozen lifetimes. Her higher chakras were coming alive again, evidencing what J. D. Salinger would call having all the lights on and all the stars out. She was starting to breathe with all her stars out.

It didn't matter that this was happening at the moment of her physical death. She could carry the balance forward and use this as a starting credit in her next life. She was entering the *Bardo* with her memory rapidly returning. She would greet her *Daena* with a confident, even exuberant, American-style *Hello!* like she was a good female friend she was meeting for a midday coffee and chat. Her fake self lay about her feet like discarded clothes that had never been hers. She would have some cleaning up to do, some confrontation with the demons of her leukemia, the spirits she had contracted to kill herself from the inside out. But she would likely prevail; she was entering the process with her eyes open.

This was good, to see the sudden success this woman was achieving with the dissolving of much of the Lethe taint of oblivion. But what about all the others who were dying at this moment, this hour, during the rest of today? Whatever actual day today was in the mortal human world, it was still right now and there were only the eight of us helping people die. We could never help them all. I didn't realize then that we were doing more than I was aware of.

First I saw that each of us had been attending a different dying person. That meant eight people were getting our assistance as they died. Then I saw that each of us had multiplied ourselves so there were numerous copies of each of us doing this work. How many? I counted at least three dozen copies of myself. Possibly there were more. My head was spinning a little now. It was dizzying, like seeing yourself in the quadruple mirrors of a dressing room in a clothing store—no, it was like a hall of mirrors in an amusement park funhouse. I kept seeing more copies of myself and the other seven of our expedition. We were in fact helping many people at the same time, and somehow giving to each our full attention just as I had with this woman when I thought that was *all* I was doing.

Earlier I mentioned the benefit to Albion of this more conscious dying. Every person in the *Bardo* who succeeded in confronting and resolving the life creations and torments they had generated turned on a light inside Albion. It was as if this colossus of the cosmos, this archetype of the human phylogeny created specifically for Earth, was equipped with billions of light bulbs, one for each soul. Every success in the *Bardo*, every moment of lucid cognition and recognition of the innate power of the soul and the magnificence of the tool of consciousness, switched on a light inside Albion. He was beginning to look like he was filled with swarming, flashing fireflies and it was a lovely June night. The goal, I was beginning to appreciate, was to enable Albion to be lucid in the *Bardo*.

That is a big idea, if you think about it for a minute. That's what I did. Albion is the human collective consciousness expressed over time, across the duration of the human presence on the Earth, since the human phylogeny started here. This collectivity is set within an infrastructure of the cosmos and Heavens. It's a miniature universe, somewhat in the form of a generic human, designed and implemented for us courtesy of the Supreme Being. The goal, as I said, is for Albion, for all of us, in this personified collective form, to become lucid in this context, self-aware, our consciousness empowered as it was meant to be, occupying the great dual Light temple of aliveness and the *Bardo*, putting on the costume of humanity and taking it off, knowing ourselves as sparks of Light.

Incarnation, in Albion's cosmic perspective, is like realizing a metaphor. Let's say I look like this, assume this particular form—how will it go for me? How does it feel to create this mask over the lucid emptiness of my innate Light, and how does it feel to divest myself of these accretions and return to this Light? Albion's intention is to remain wide-awake, observant, and meticulously attentive to every nuanced moment of this reciprocal act of life, walking into one division of the temple, then into the other, both being equal. Albion, it seemed to me, was like a big dog lying on the carpet by the fireplace, watching you enter the room, sit down, read the paper, then leave the room. He pretends to be sleeping, but covertly he's watching every move you make, learning from it.

From Albion's point of view, human lives are like finger puppets he put on his hands to move around in the world for a time, then withdrawing them. No, this is not to diminish the worth of a single incarnation, but to see it from Albion's larger viewpoint. Each human life is a metaphorical incursion into the bewildering, wonderful world of name and form, the *skandah* world. Can you imagine a spirit with eight billion fingers, each equipped with a puppet? Can you conceive of a colossus of the spirit keeping equal attention on these forms?

Each finger puppet reports back to Albion, files a mission statement, uploads all the data retrieved during this incursion into the sunlit world of daytime life. It's like Albion stays at home in his comfortable livingroom and plush reading chair and gets all the daily newspapers of the world, from every last little town. He reads them, every last column inch, and is each day better informed, more richly educated, about the conditions in the world, what the people are up to, their successes and failures, how consciousness is faring. It's like a stock market report on the fluctuations of human consciousness expansion.

Even we, the members of this Green Knight expedition, are filing daily reports to Albion. We have been streaming these reports every second. Even the experience and quality of a single inhale is reported back to Albion. He can never collect enough data; he keeps building a more perfectly detailed case. And when we die, when we go through the *Bardo*, that's the sports page for him. He'll turn to that first, read the game reports avidly, cheer or groan, whatever.

We must keep in mind too that Albion is rapidly becoming psychic. That is in keeping with the upgrade underway to the Earth's Light grid. That is resetting the conditions of consciousness, the starting point, at the level of the sixth chakra, the place of visions, picture-making, of seeing into the subtle world. Albion will feel as if he is suddenly equipped with X-ray vision, that he can see through matter, the veils, semblances, outer concealing surfaces, to the reality.

He will see through life's visual metaphors, and he will see through all the Druj's lies, her vast, world-encompassing concatenation of falsehood and illusion. She won't like that, to feel eight billion eyes trained on her every move. How can you run a clever sleight-of-hand, card tricks and magical illusions, against not-so-sleeping people with that degree of surveillance trained on you all the time? Every moment of her once veiled life is now observed by the wide-awake Albion. The Druj will be in rout, the Antichrist set back on its haunches. At least for a time. It's due anyway: she's had the run of the place for eons. Lord Dharma, King of Truth, will finally have his four legs in the world.

Most people probably don't think about being parts of Albion. I never did. That was because I had not even heard the concept before. Blaise explained Albion to me, and William Blake's poetic vision of him as well. So now I see, and I confess, it elates me, fills me with optimism and commitment, that each human, all eight billion now alive on the planet, are potentially awake, self-aware cells inside this colossal Light form of Albion, Earth's own cosmogonic Human.

Each time we wake up in the sunlit world or score success against the hallucinations of our activated karma in the *Bardo*, we are like a firefly lighting up inside Albion. It's reciprocal too which adds to the richness of the picture. Each of us is a complete Albion, combining the archetypal cosmogonic aspects and the accumulation of human consciousness and lives lived in that framework over time, ever since the phylogeny was seeded here. We are cells inside Albion, and the complete Albion is a Light form inside us. The better we process our after-death protocols, the better off is Earth's Albion. That dual Light temple of incarnation and *Bardo* is

an alive organ in Albion, and that "organ" is a less a structure and more of a living process in consciousness.

"I've always said what a power Earth's Albion would have if all the people could become self-aware and lucid at the same moment," said Blaise. "It would astound the galaxy. They would stand up and applaud us at last. The Druj would be in an utter rout, all her schemes royally screwed for good."

I was not even bothering to wonder any more how Blaise knew what I was thinking. His remarks were uncannily apposite to my current thinking.

"It's been a long time in preparation," Blaise continued. "In 1985, they launched the geometric upgrade of the planet's existing Light grid to the icosidodecahedron. That started to affect every aspect of physical reality, including how it felt to be a human and what thoughts came through your mind. Then came the advent of the Blaise Babies in 2020, followed by the Theosophon in 2033. These were each major threshold events in the consciousness of the Earth, and people are still absorbing these effects. Now comes our *Bardo* restructuring in 2043, spilling over into early 2044. It's another installment.

"All this has been planned since the original seeding of the naked Earth with the Light grid anatomy and the human phylogeny billions of years ago. We foresaw this. It's not so unusual or impossible to remember this, by the way. If you dredge deeply and long enough in your psyche you'll reach the bedrock that remembers this. You'll get back to the Blue Room and its cosmic planning. So now, as Merlin said earlier, we must update the *Bardo* protocols to match this. The Light temple of the *Bardo* and its processes must match the upgraded Earth.

"Up until now, we have focused on the problems of getting into and through the *Bardo* without Druj obstruction. Now we'll pay some attention to leaving the *Bardo*, that pivot point where a soul decides to reincarnate or stay in *Devachan*. Or, as the Tibetan text puts it bluntly, you reach a point where you can either transfer your consciousness-principle to a pure Buddha realm, *Devachan*, or select an impure *samsaric* womb-door and take on another mortal human body. The Tibetan text is clearly biased against reincarnation. They call it impure.

"It reminds the soul it has been wandering in the 'quagmire' of *samsara*, the realm of illusion, that *samsara* should disgust you, horrify and sicken you so you avoid it. It lays out alluring travel brochures for desirable *Devachan* locales, such as The Pre-Eminently Happy Western Realm, or Western Paradise, a Pure Land administered by the *Dhyani* Buddha Amitabha where you may expect to be reborn amidst lotus blossoms, or the Thickly-Formed Realm, another paradise. I used to joke that when I died I would attach a sticky note to my finger saying 'Don't even think of it' so I'd remember not to get suckered into another life."

Devachan was a new term for me. Later I understood it better, at least from a scholarly point of view. Our expedition gave me the empirical view of it. The term means "dwelling of the gods," a godly realm the soul may move into. Eventually, the astral body, filled with desires, fueled by mental energy and flavored by karma, runs down, exhausts itself, and the soul undergoes a second death. This is the dropping of the astral shell, which, unfortunately can remain around a lower *Bardo* realm sometimes called *Kama-loka* or *Kama-Dhatu*, the Desire Realm, and confuse people, especially alive humans who channel these ghost-fragments of formerly animated humans and think they're getting gold.

Much of the popular mediumship which claimed to be transmitting the wisdom of famous dead people drew from this realm of decomposing astral shells. Apparently, people

have fallen for this level of celebrity illusion for a long time. Even in the times of H.P. Blavatsky then later in Rudolf Steiner's time, people around these initiates made glamorous claims to be channeling the famous dead. At best, they were channeling something semi-conscious, a cross between Howdy Doody, the ventriloquist's dummy, and an out-of-work Golem.

In simple terms you could call *Devachan* a Heaven realm, a god realm, and, to a degree, that is correct. But it is a self-made subjective god-realm you create out of your higher spiritual desires. It's a higher plane of your own mental creation, the metaphysical texts say, a high-level subjective illusory realm, but one that is nurturing, even educational, for the questing soul seeking the Light. You might think of it as a *Star Trek* Holodeck with high quality programming. You bring your spiritual pictures into this unstructured realm and it runs them.

If you read after-death accounts of people saying they went to study in astral universities or studied music with masters of opera or the symphony, they spoke the truth, for there are such realms, a kind of co-creation between the soul and some actuality already there. Some souls do in fact immerse themselves in music, in high *deva* realms where the inspiration for composers like Chopin came from. Some authorities say the soul can stay in *Devachan* a thousand years and not even sense the passage of time; but eventually their mental-spiritual energy runs out and they grow fidgety and either reincarnate or refresh themselves and their interests by trying a different locale and activity. It sounds like *Devachan* is more of a long-term vacation spot, but not a permanent abode.

The Egyptians had various names for *Devachan*, including *Sekhet,* which roughly translates as "Field of Reeds." This was understood to be a dwelling place of beatified souls who spent their time cultivating the *maāt* plant, which was their prime food, and which constituted the body of Osiris. That sounds like a way of suggesting these perfected souls dwelled in the essence of Osiris. The land was fertile and filled with numerous channels cutting through it and carrying pure water. One zone within it was called "birthplace of the gods," and another was *Sekhet-hetept*, the "Field of Offerings." It was the *Bardo*'s St. Tropez.

Aaru, another name for the place (from *iArw*, for "reeds"), lies in the East, a realm of boundless reed fields, like the Nile Delta when watered and fecund. The reeds imagery was meaningful because it spoke to the Egyptian of ample water, fertility, and favorable landscape and living conditions around the River Nile. If you live in a desert, this kind of lush imagery will be desirable. Souls lived here for eternity in a landscape that to a desert-dwelling human soul would have seemed a picture of physical paradise, a series of islands covered in fields of rushes with Osiris as a live-in permanent presence. You will encounter some perils and challenges on your way to *Aaru*; there are gates to pass through (some say 15) and rude demon guardians armed with knives, though I suspect their function is to turn away the unprepared. You may not need to bribe them.

If you make it to *Aaru*, you get to live with Osiris. Or at least he's a neighbor. Not only is Osiris green of skin, but *Aaru* is a *green* lush paradise, fertile and fruitful. In the Egyptian *Papyrus of Ani*, part of the overall *Book of the Dead*, the soul prays to be granted the power to "float down and to sail up the stream" to reach the Field of Reeds and then the Field of Offerings (Osiris's place), the most desirable paradisal locale where one is fed the food of the gods.

I get the metaphor: if you live in a landscape that is mostly dry, sandy, brown, hot, with only a narrow strip near the Nile that is dependably fertile, your picture of a paradisal realm is going to be a landscape of green. Green as in fertile, fecund, fruitful, and, because presided over by Osiris who is evergreen. The next metaphorical step is to construe greenery, in landscape or gods, or in the highest deity, Osiris, as meaning eternally green, i.e., immortal, always alive.

It's like the Irish conception of the Underworld as *Tír na mBeo*, "Land of the Living," *Mag Mell*, "Delightful Plain," and *Tír na nOg*, "Land of the Young." These pictures portrayed an otherwordly country without sickness, old age, or death, marked by permanent happiness and perpetual summertime, and stretched-out time with 100 years feeling like one day. Sometimes this realm is said to consist of linked islands, and access to them was through the *sidhes*, the fairy mounds that dotted the Irish landscape. These were portals to that realm.

The geography of these realms can seem confusing at first. For example, the Theosophist psychic and scholar C. W. Leadbeater said that *Devachan* was a premium mental plane high above the Earth and required proof of high-level initiation before the soul could expect to be able to enter it. In a middle level was a more accessible *Devachan* realm called Summerland, and those humans with some level of soul development could expect to be admitted into that realm.

Summerland might correspond to what the Celts called the Summer Country, which, Blaise suggests, refers to a middle realm, possibly equivalent to Avalon, the astral world "apple" of Light. Above *Devachan* is the realm Leadbeater called Nirvana, which means "blown out," like a candle flame, meaning here you definitively depart *samsara* and the Wheel of Life and enter a non-self, unconditioned bliss realm of full awakening. This is the formless realm of truth Buddhists call *Dharmakaya*. "You" are blown out there. You're gone.

The impression I derived from these descriptions is one of stratigraphy. As you progress up through these realms, reality becomes progressively more real and your mental-spiritual projections and simulations come more into accord with what is actually there. This vast, stratified middle realm the Buddhists call *Sambhogakaya*, the realm of the bliss and delight of the gods; this is the gods' realm of delightful illusory states and pleasurable simulations.

You're still subject to the gravitational pull of the Wheel of Life and that horrible, mephitic quagmire of *samsara* (if I can send up the Tibetans for a moment), but you are in a very upscale neighborhood, like London's Mayfair or Belgravia. *Sambhogakaya* or Avalon is the world of protean Light where out of the imaginative delight of its godly residents a proliferation of beautiful forms has been spawned; the gods know these forms are empty but they delight in them, possibly the way Tolkien envisioned Gandalf delighting in the smoke rings he blew to please the young Hobbits. Transient and empty but fun to watch. It's the enjoyment body of the Buddha, the subtle body of limitless form: yes, form is emptiness, but look at all the delightful, clever forms that emptiness can take.

Perhaps this vast middle realm is like the Grand Canyon, comprised of hundreds of layers, a complex stratigraphy of consciousness and reality states. The closer they lie to the top, to the unconditioned realm of Nirvana, the more real they are. Reality, I surmise, is defined by the degree to which the *Dharmakaya* permeates the realm in which you stand; the more truth it has, the more reality. Paradoxically, for we embodied humans anyway, the *Dharmakaya* standard for reality is formless and empty. This ultimate truth realm has no forms in it at all.

It was time to go see for ourselves and maybe lend a hand if we could. My first impression was that we were confronted with a major series of highway intersections and branches, like you'd expect around a big city like Los Angeles.

You could pick up any number of different thruways from this point: which one? I knew at the time my impression was only a crude visual metaphor, a makeshift approximation of a complex threshold, womb-doors one way, *Devachan* another.

Perhaps a better analogy would be to say it looked like a vast round travel station with innumerable doors evenly spaced along its circumference. Each led to a specific realm in any of these three zones, Summerland, *Devachan*, Nirvana, and interspersed among these doors to the high places were those womb-doors, those sickening portals back into the sunlit world the Tibetans seemed to revile.

Later I realized it was a dynamic whirling circle of doors placed in a vibrational sequence, the womb-doors first, for the lowest vibration, Nirvana doors last, and you could progress along this circumferential vibrational spectrum of choices. The layout of these vibrationally sequenced doors had the same paradox as a labyrinth. When you walk a labyrinth there is a point where your path is right next to the labyrinth center, just inches away, though you still have a long way to go before the path takes you there. Similarly, the most sublime Nirvana door, the true escape route, lies right next to the entry-level, lowest vibration womb-door. But you would likely qualify only for one door. It's possible you would see only the one door you were vibrationally ready to enter.

Merlin directed our attention to a soul entering the zone of the *Bardo* where you were either sucked into a new incarnation or selected some nice place in *Devachan*. I couldn't tell the gender of this appraising soul; at this point in "its" *Bardo* and karma processing it had been stripped clean of the gender of its most recent life, though I caught images of this soul having most recently been a man. It was now mostly a humanoid shape of Light, though it still had dark splotches within its form, presumably still unresolved karma awaiting some resolution. A few of those dark areas were throbbing, as if trying to get the soul's attention.

In some respects the scene resembled what you might see at a large airport terminal. You just got off the plane, collected your luggage, and now you look for the proper exit door, but is it for a taxi, bus, train, subway, or rental car? Or is somebody coming to pick you up and you scan the crowds of faces for him?

I saw that this soul, when he had been a man, had been an insurance executive and a weekend oils painter. He had been better than a dabbler or a dilettante, yet he had never put his art first but kept to the safety of his job. I could understand that, but I saw that the cost of that clinging to apparent safety was that his creative side did not open up and develop past a certain initial point, and he went into his death unsatisfied and secretly longing for more. So the question before him was what was the better venue for getting that "more," taking on a new life and dedicating it to art or entering a *Devachan* realm for art? He was like a man standing completely still in the center of Heathrow arrivals, looking around, a little bewildered, but intent, studying the field for his choice.

Images of the allures and outcomes of either choice swirled and massed around him, like salespeople sniffing a likely big purchase from this customer. In the *Devachan* artist's realm he saw conclaves of painters, each in their own studios yet able to mingle and discuss themes and techniques in the evenings. It was like a *Devachan* version of Yaddo, the artist's colony at Saratoga Springs.

The images piled up the moment he put his attention in this direction. He saw he would not have to worry about income or any details of ordinary physical life; he could concentrate all his attention and creativity on expanding his artistic pursuits. He could expect encouragement, appraisal, validation, and reliable companionship from like-minded people as well as instruction from art *devas*. That was *Devachan*'s version of offering an accomplished faculty for newcomers. Hundreds of images along these lines appeared like a spread deck of cards; each was evocative, a lively holographic image you could enter right now.

At the same time he was looking through a kind of window into the sunlit human world, seeing what it might offer him this time should he choose it again. One thing the *Devachan* Yaddo could not offer him was the lasting or actual gratification of recognized success in the physical world. *Devachan* had no roots into actual human reality; the validation and collegiality were simulated, it seemed to him, though one could make the case it is the physical world that has no firm roots in lasting reality and is itself terribly evanescent and short-term. The physical world, as some have said, is the field of dreams; yes, it is the place of creating and resolving karma, but it is also the only place where desires are physicalized because largely that is the only place where they are real or urgent.

He saw himself selling paintings, making a good then a great income from it, getting recognition, glowing reviews, triumphant gallery exhibitions and sales. He saw himself proving to the world, to all those who in his last life doubted him or splattered his artistic seeds with skepticism, pessimism, or cruel philistinism, that he had talent and value as an artist; see, his sales confirmed that. Now he would show them. He would sit them down good and proper. They would blush, feel humiliated, be astounded, wilt, at the prodigious talent he showed.

Certain moments of pain and repudiation and dismissal were pulsating within his Light form. Those were some of the dark splotches, and they were seeking reprisal, retribution, and a definitive balancing out of the record. He would never achieve this in *Devachan*, mostly because he would forget it bothered him. Those pain splotches would not be throbbing in his higher Yaddo.

Sadly, he realized achievement of his goal in *Devachan* would be at best a simulation. It would have no traction on his emotions or his *Akashic* Records. It would be ultimately a lovely daydream. He would have to incarnate to have it. The trouble is he also understood that achieving this in the physical world was also a simulation of the perfect ideal picture he had created for it in *Devachan*. He went back and forth between viewing each outcome: Which would be more real?

Images of this choice lined up in front of the man, though these pictures seemed brighter, almost possessed by a special kind of neon glare that only the physical world could put forth. They had an evident tidal suction. You felt like you were standing at ocean's edge, just at the precise spot on the beach where the sand was subject to the outgoing tidal pull of the ocean, and if you did not hold your balance steady and keep track of your legs, you might flow out with the tide. You'd be swept into the ocean of physical life and its illusions.

The Tibetan text speaks disparagingly of "tormenting furies," the "heap of impurities," and the "impure mass" surrounding the womb-doors. It warns of the likelihood you will detect and maybe respond favorably to various "sweet-smelling" aspects wafting through those doors towards your Light-body senses. Despite the text's obvious biases against further incarnations, it was accurate regarding the sales forces arrayed at the womb-doors to get you to choose them. It was like street barkers standing outside a store, beckoning people to enter. They wore sandwich boards advertising products, services, and big discounts.

The Druj was on hand of course. She was attended by some of those "tormenting furies."

That might be an overstatement for what I was seeing. Sometimes you make a more persuasive case through seduction than force. These spirits were tarted up like artist's models, art critics, gallery owners, and fellow painters, and they exuded a feeling of respect, admiration, even awe, for the sublime accomplishments with oil on canvas of this obvious prodigy of art.

Bit of an oversell, I thought, but it was working, because these comments, insinuations, and images were directed at some of his sore spots, made more evident now by the attention via a kind of thought-spotlight the Druj put on them. All she did was highlight them in the man's awareness, remind him of their existence, of their unfulfilled, unrequited status and how *good* it would feel to *finally* deal with them, make the world sit up, applaud, and validate him.

The Druj and her "tormenting furies" were like drug salesmen emphasizing how their prescription drug would remove all vestiges of chronic pain you've had, that, taking this new wonder drug, *at last* your life would be as you *desired* it. That's how the Druj was selling it; she only worked with the seeds the man had, but her Machiavellian manipulation of those dark seeds of pain was masterful. He was swooning in the illusions of the physical world already.

He bought it. He started moving towards the "impure mass" of the womb-door. He was buying the product, accepting the pain relief it offered. Now here is the fascinating part: as he made his choice, it was as if he was in a large, long tunnel filled with life images. They were similar to the sales brochures the Druj had artfully dangled before him, but they had the specifics of plans.

It was as if he were planning his upcoming incarnation on the run, scripting scenarios, developmental timing, important encounters, debts to pay, credits to collect, the whole schematic of his next life, here, being scripted as he ran ahead. It was like the inverse of viewing his just completed life records as, himself dying, his etheric body unspooled before him disclosing the minutiae of his life. Now he was spooling up his next etheric body with plans for his upcoming life.

His Higher Self stood by like a secretary, taking notes on all the specifications, making a few suggestions when appropriate, calling in outside counselors, possibly karma lawyers, to see if certain proposed plans were permissible. As noted, the scene was similar to the life-review of the etheric and astral body the newly deceased soul undergoes just after arriving in the *Bardo*, and in fact it begins before they are technically dead. This soul was doing the same on the way out of the *Bardo* and back into the human fold. He was drafting the specifics of his upcoming life as he moved inexorably and rapidly towards it.

I liked the symmetry of these two gestures, debriefing after death and planning before life, and in both cases, you review the picture gallery of your life plans. Then I laughed at the irony: after all this planning you show up alive, and remember nothing, look about and wonder what you're going to make of this.

I felt the wind of intention that came off his passion for life-scripting. He *wanted* this. He was committed now. It was as if he was creating the strong wind that would propel him back into life, and it was a warm wind. It carried the odor of blood and redness, of the passionate life, the *skandah* grid engaged. The Druj and her furies looked pleased, smug: Got another one; put it in the win column.

It didn't make any difference to me what choice this soul made. You know souls are going to keep reincarnating just as embodied people will keep on having babies. It's a normal reflex of life, and most people don't think about it too much, accepting it as the epitome of ordinary human life and expectation. Have another life, have some more babies, die, do it all over again,

or, if you're Christian, or, frankly, of just about any religion except Buddhism and Hinduism, make the most of it, pal, because that's your only chance. How wrong they are!

The irony is that under normal circumstances only the Higher Self would remember any of this. This angel assigned in perpetuity to the soul would have the papers upon which he wrote down all the specifics of the upcoming life plan. The incarnating soul would not remember anything, not even his intentions to heal all the hurts of failed creativity and the sparkling vista of great success to come. He would show up on the circus stage of life and declare with aplomb, knowing nothing, not remembering anything of his earnest intentions: Surprise me! Until now. Now the soul had the option of drinking less of the River Lethe draught of appalling soul oblivion. He could forgo the high tea of damn oblivion.

The River Lethe attendant held two phials before the soul rushing towards life. One was full to the brim, the other only half full. He could choose which to drink. Nobody was allowed to interfere with his choice, not the Druj nor Higher Self. It was a still moment, as if all the *Bardo* was hushed and expectant.

He chose the half-filled glass of Lethe draught. He drank it. It coursed through his Light form like liquid lightning, like a force of lucid wakefulness. I know that sounds contrary to the Lethe mechanism of forgetting, but since he took only half the draught, the restoration of half his memories or half his soul's life grid over time reawakened in him with, as I said, a great wakefulness.

He saw a great deal of his past, lives stretching behind him into the deeps of his own soul antiquity, and into the upcoming, fully detailed and scripted lifetime. He was fully cogent, meticulously briefed on what he intended to accomplish, and he was bearing that in a completely awake and self-aware condition into the dreaded impure mass of the womb-door.

It no longer was so noxious looking, because I think what turned the Tibetans against its sweet-smelling vapors was the knowledge they would surely forget every last goddam fact of their soul as soon as they passed through it, that it would be a complete memory eraser, and that, I guess, was irritating, embarrassing, and, in practical terms, inconvenient. With a Lethe half-draught, it was a matter of volume: he could fill the glass half-way with soul memories, drawing upon related themes and linked lifetimes to build a useful picture. If he were packing for a trip, it was like saying he could take half of his full wardrobe.

Now this soul could stride through that door with much of his memory intact, at least half, and with the promise of retrieving more over his lifespan. He could even whistle, snap his fingers authoritatively a few times, keep his posture strong. He was not going to forget everything he had planned; he would keep it in mind, and he might tell a few people about what he remembered from the *Bardo*. This little act of drinking only the half-cup of Lethe draught would be infectious. He would start influencing others about retaining their soul memory. He would tell them they could build on that one-half memory retention and get the rest with only a little diligent input. They could eventually remember it all.

When they died, finished their *Bardo* protocols, and, like him, faced this choice, they could expect to remember they could choose the half-cup and know why. Yet another soul would re-enter the Wheel of Life with some sense of what was going on, what they intended, what the betting odds were for their success, and they might enjoy the dismay written over the face of the Druj as they did as another once sure sales prospect now slipped through her million lying fingers.

This would not be the case with the woman we were next studying. She was having a difficult time at her portal of decision, beset with many demons. She looked as if she had been beaten, dragged, quartered, slimed, bones broken, and generally abused in her passage through the *Bardo*: her karma was fierce. Most of what had happened to her seemed to lack any context; she did not understand it, why it happened, how it related to her, and regarded it as inimical, as if the Underworld had it in for her, had picked her out especially.

She looked as if she had brought an art gallery with her, but all the paintings were depressing, frightful, some even horrific. There was no beauty. These were images of unresolved karmic situations, moments of pain, invalidation, major emotional setbacks, a visual litany of suffering and misery, and all these baleful images flanked her like a spectral array of bodyguards. I suppose they were like a security detail, protecting her body from freedom or making any steps towards extricating herself from this quagmire of darkness.

Behind them demons flashed, like lightning strikes in a night sky. Some were attached to her images, while others came out of the opportunistic possibilities these unresolved pain images offered them. You have to remember, dark spirits see things opposite to how we the living do, as if in a mirror; our suffering is their joy. Some of these dark spirits had been specifically dispatched to the scene by the Druj to further her agenda of disempowering human consciousness. They were flashing their own set of distressing images, like aggressive nightmare salesmen waving color brochures of the newest flashy product, but in this case, of new ways, modern ways, to be fully miserable.

The woman could select these images if she wanted to, if she felt they reflected her perceived condition. I hoped she wouldn't, though, because it would only dig her hole deeper. I also saw she had no idea that she had dug herself into a deep pit, and was still digging it deeper with her every move. She had to make her decision. All the demons, both her own and those of the Druj, were pressuring her, amplifying her misery, encouraging her pessimistic interpretation of her situation and its prospects for improvement, which, they kept reminding her, were nil. She must never lose sight of that futility.

Conditions in the *Bardo* would only worsen, they counseled (or hectored) her, and her only option for assured safety was to get out of here immediately and take on a new body. The Lethe draught would enable her to forget all of this. That was true, to an extent, but they didn't tell her that she would bring all this emotional and karmic conflagration with her into her next life and it would likely remain unresolved but still active and manipulative because of her unawareness. What you are not aware of or willfully shove into your unconscious becomes a Shadow operator, directing situations in your life to suit its agenda, and you, not understanding this, not perceiving the Shadow as director, wonder where this hell of wrong turns and sudden disasters in your life is coming from.

It didn't seem likely the woman would see through the Druj's curtains. She felt her condition right now, wherever the Hell this was, this Hell that it was, could only be escaped by passing through a womb-door as fast as possible. She would resort to immediate incarnation as a way of darkening her awareness. Sadly, I thought it likely she would find addiction a comparable alive choice because the gesture of deliberately blanketing this pain layer was strong in her. She was using serial incarnation as an addiction mechanism to avoid self-awareness, then, likely, reinforcing that with actual addiction when in a body.

The dark spirits now were shouting at her, like angry, petulant fans, sports hooligans at

a soccer game, bad-mouthing the umpires or castigating the idiot ball players, inciting riots and mayhem. The images were flashing like lurid neon signs against a night sky; it hurt the eyes to watch. Other demons, or "tormenting furies," as the Tibetan text aptly named them, were whispering gratingly, harshly, their voices like rude grinding stones in her ears. Her psychic space, her free and available consciousness in the midst of all this rage and coercion, was minimal; there was too little of her true self present at this moment to equip her with enough courage and insight to make a wise choice.

She stumbled through the womb door, like a late-arriving theater-goer rushing up to the ticket counter and saying, with short breath, "One, please." She got the ticket, started hastily designing her next life, anything to get out of here, and gladly took the full draught of Lethe and would have had seconds if it had been offered. One draught did the trick; all this demonology around her vanished at once. She relaxed, signed off on her next life plan which seemed to be characterized by a consistent, unrelenting oblivion of her true condition.

She was frantic to get away from the clutches of these awful Furies hectoring her. Go away, will you. It was as if she had killed ten mothers, a hundred maybe, and whatever misery the Erinyes caused Orestes in his mad flight to Athens, it was ten times worse now for her. She was their Most Wanted, their prime suspect, their person of interest. Naturally, she wanted to be as unconscious of all this as possible. I saw her becoming an alcoholic to make this policy of oblivion official and effective, even if it killed her. I felt sorry for her liver. The sad part was she did not realize she had not escaped anything. The hole she had dug herself in the *Bardo* she had brought with her like a nomad carrying her tent. She would pitch this tent-hole, reinstitute her pit, and jump in, as soon as possible. It was the hole she knew. She expected this pit. It was her specialty, this bad habit, the only piece of self-knowledge that survived Lethe.

Her entourage of unresolved karma, dark spirits, and the Druj's additional spirits accompanied her into this next life, remaining active but veiled behind a curtain. It was her desert caravan, but no oasis was in sight. They were still with her; she had never left the *Bardo* because she never finished her business there. She imported all that nasty *Bardo* darkness with her into her life. Her incarnation would be the *Bardo* all over again, its next episode, no relief.

It would direct her life and psyche from the shadows of her consciousness. The Earth's Light grid upgrade to a sixth chakra frequency would put continuous pressure on her to become aware of this shadow, and she in turn would drink harder, pummel any incipient awareness back into the ground. She was desperately looking for a third chamber in this horrible life and *Bardo* temple. Isn't there somewhere I can be permanently unconscious and really die?

I was about to make a comment to Blaise when I realized that he and the rest of my expedition companions had not been watching this particular scene. Each of them had been attending a different soul making its crucial choice. Later, we exchanged our stories and observations, but they mostly fell between the two examples I have already presented, the half-draught and full-draught scenarios. Consciousness, I saw in such naked relief, is at times a terrifying proposition. It carries a tremendous responsibility, which can either intimidate or elate you, depending on how much courage and fortitude you can bring to the table. You, *you* alone, are the rightful and entitled executor of a force of awareness that not only comes from God but is a drop of that ultra-potent God-consciousness itself.

This woman thought of herself as someone clinging desperately to the masthead of a sailboat tossing perilously on the high seas during a terrific storm. She was afraid, naturally, the vast, unmerciful sea would drown her the first chance it had, she would lose herself and die. The poignancy of this scene, the universality of it, in fact, is that this self she believed herself to be, that she was in mortal peril of losing to drowning in the limitless ocean, was finite, an illusion.

As Vishnu said to Arjuna in the *Bhagavad-Gita* of the soldiers in battle, they are all already dead. She was already dead, already drowned, finished, erased, because her self that she was so valiantly defending was only a construct put together by herself to meet the occasion of incarnating and needing a cover story. I understood why the Buddhists and Hindus say all notions of selfhood are false. Yes, certainly we need a self to get about in the world so we can individuate, but we have to remember, and I know we don't want to, if we can get away with it, that this contrived, constructed selfhood does not represent our true condition. It is not the bedrock of our psyche; it is only the mutable surface. We cling to it desperately even as it is the unrelenting source of our suffering.

Metaphysical authorities, especially those who discuss the *Bardo*, talk of the second death. That's when you drop the astral body and its flush of desires. What you are left with is more the true you, the Atman, as the Hindus call it. In the hierarchy of subtle bodies, you are now in what corresponds to your fourth body, the first three being your physical, etheric, and astral. These carry the noble illusion of a separate selfhood, the one clinging for life to the masthead.

In the fourth body, after the second death, your eyes are open more, and you have a greater possibility and less interference in seeing reality as it actually is. Now, I speculate, your perception is a kind of *co-seeing* with the Supreme Being; you still are a separate unit of evolving God-consciousness, seeing reality *with*

God. I had known this as a scholar, but now I was seeing it firsthand. I knew it was true. Some call this the causal body, which is the Light form that bears the formative seeds for your karma, the Official Explanation of your soul condition, the complete backstory, the list of causes, on a given theme of consciousness. The causal body records are like the vast appendices in Tolkien's *The Lord of the Rings*.

Up until this point, as I said, we had individually been attending to separate *Bardo* dramas. Now we were focused on the same one unfolding before us. We had before us not one soul but about six dozen by my rough count. It was like a group lined up for a bus that would take them all on a fun tour.

Even though when you are in your soul form, you do not particularly look like a human being any more, unless you make an effort to resume that old mask, these souls all looked similar. There was something common to all of them, though perhaps it was not a physical characteristic, if you'll pardon the oxymoron of that, but a similar soul gesture or attitude, and they all seemed to be very young. I sensed an edginess, a wariness, hesitation about taking the next step. They seemed to think there was only one bus arriving and only one destination, and they had better stick together so they didn't get lost or miss it.

Behind them, forming a casual circle were their Higher Selves. They were holding back, watching but aloof, like mothers waiting with their children until the bus arrives but trying not to embarrass them by standing too close to them. These waiting souls were surrounded by posters, banners, and large flashing images, and again there was a commonality among these. It showed them back in human bodies, all in the same country, perhaps the same town, with families, social positions, responsibilities, and all this overshadowed by a special angel. Maybe they would all comprise one extended family with multiple generations, like a mother and father with eight children, lots of cousins, uncles and aunts, even grandparents still living, and all residing in perhaps the same small town.

I say "special" because for angels this one seemed particularly differentiated. Picture all the social and emotional characteristics that define a people, say, Italians, their style of clothing, facial features, language, and dress up a generic angel to represent these like a stage actor in a period costume drama, and you will get a sense of what we were seeing. This angel represented Italianness. The angel was a character actor playing the Italian folk soul.

But these Italian features were further refined to represent a single town, like a subset of overall Italian culture and human nature lived under Italian influence. These were all upstanding members of a single Italian town with its angel, and just as they appeared huddled for safety and reassurance here at the *Bardo* "bus stop," so did these pictures show them huddled together for mutual self-definition in their designated Italian town. Nothing had changed, other than the acquisition of human bodies. They were still living together as this group.

Spirits, not exactly demonic but not clearly angelic either, more like human advisers in *Bardo* forms, held large cue cards showing this group the expected responses to emotional situations, the agreed-upon thoughts and attitudes. The images on these "cue cards" were directions for how to be *Italian* in *this* town, as if they were a fresh troop of actors brought in to play standard scripted roles. All the members of this group of 72 were expected to abide by these scripted rules. This was who they were; these were the patterns of behavior that defined them. All you had to do to flourish was to follow these guidelines.

Some of the assembled souls were resisting this benign programming. They were looking around, fidgeting, shuffling their feet, scrunching their shoulders the way people do when they are considering breaking out of formation and looking to see if the coast is clear and if they have enough nerve. Yes, I know, they can't shift their shoulders around if they only have somewhat amorphous Light-forms, but their unsettled mood suggested this fidgetiness.

My impression was that these few unsettled souls were finding the "clothing" of this forthcoming social definition of who they were, and were *supposed* to be, was confining and restrictive. They were not sure they wanted to be that pre-scripted, that circumscribed. You could see they had a few ideas of their own as to how to be a human, what they might accomplish, how they might set out on their own. They had what Colin Wilson might have termed "seeds of Outsiderness" in them. One day they might rebel against this group mind. For now, the presiding angel of the Italian town they were bound for kept bringing them back into line, like a drill sergeant quelling any incipient insurrection.

At this point Blaise commented, "Now we come to the nub of the situation. You are looking at a subset of a Group Soul, a cluster of humans who have not progressed far in their individuation saga and still huddle in a group. They are defined by their membership in the group, not by their own hard-won exertions as individuating separate humans on their own scripted life path. They still depend on this Group Soul to give them meaning and direction, except for the few that we see fidgeting. They're ready for a break-out from the Group Soul, and the angel, on behalf of the integrity of this group, is trying to stop it. Note that additional parties are trying to influence the outcome of this as well."

Those additional parties were more obviously demonic spirits. They were flashing images of their own in throbbing full-color pictures ten feet high. These pictures showed individuals setting off on their own and ending badly. Falling off cliffs, drowning, getting killed, rejected, outcast, ending up in poverty, without friends or loving families, killing themselves slowly in alcohol or drug addictions, or wandering aimlessly in despair and dejection. All miserable outcomes testifying to the futility of setting off on your own and leaving the herd safety of the Group Soul. Don't even think about it: look at what could happen. Leave the Group Soul and perish. It's guaranteed. Stay here and live. Be smart.

It reminded me of how when I used to go to vote, often campaigners for a particular candidate would be massed around the doors with their posters and buttons, urging me to remember this candidate, this product, and vote for it (buy it). Your life depends on it; any other choice is a vote for disaster. These campaigners at the womb-door were working for the Druj. She was a winner.

I saw her imprint within each, as if she installed a ghost image of herself inside each as the ideal puppet-master—forget the strings, go inside the puppet itself. It did not serve her campaign of disempowering humans by having them cull themselves from the Group Soul and set off on the individuation odyssey; that path led to personal empowerment, to discovering the potency of consciousness. Each soul who achieved that realization in living human form was a strike against her. It was not only a lost vote, but the seed of an avalanche of humans gaining their consciousness power and overturning her carefully laid plans. She couldn't have that. The Druj had to enact every measure possible to stop that Group Soul prison breakout. The example could start a *Bardo* cascade.

"This is where we step in," said Blaise. "We can't force the outcome—nor can the Druj, though she can certainly put sales pressure on the souls to choose her preferred outcome— but we can shed some Light on the process of choosing."

We assembled our Sword of Elohim again, all of us taking our places. We were allowed to act like a sunrise. The assembled souls, as if standing on a high place in the landscape in the pre-dawn, could pay attention to this event or not. As before, all we had to do was give our full attention to our part of the sword. The Light did the rest, and I suppose that really means the Elohim did the rest.

They are after all humanity's godparents and the true godparents of every soul. They created the conditions, per divine mandate, for humans to choose freely. Yes, they were okay with choices to remain safe in the herd, but they knew, as designers of the template, the matching pattern of Light for Earth and human, that souls would progress, achieve the development offered to them by this set-up, if they dared to set off on their own and become responsible for their own awareness and, why not, even enjoy some of its many fun benefits and epiphanies. They knew they would have to wait a long time for all souls to do this, but they were patient, extremely patient; God had made them that way. The Supreme Being had set the clock for 311 trillion years for this cycle, this Life. He figured that would be enough time for a significant proportion of souls to do it.

Those few in the assembled Group Soul who had been exhibiting wayward tendencies and distressing the Druj and her cohorts were perking up. They were turning away from the flashy parade banners the Group Soul angel was holding before them and starting to design and create their own images. It was as if in an art class the more promising students were ignoring the standards and safe images and methods and striking off on their own, inventing Cubism or some new way of representing reality on canvas. These daring souls were creating images of what they might look like, do, become, how they might live.

In these fresh images they did not look like one another, not like the standard depiction of Italianness for this particular Italian town. Some were proposing not even to live in Italy at all. They were breaking all the molds, smashing the icons. It was even better than this. A few of these wayward, daring souls, these ontological radicals, these subversives (as their fellows thought), were now wondering why they were rushing to incarnate again in the first place. Why not stick around and see what else this "higher world" had to offer them?

That thought had never occurred to them. Ordinarily, they would stampede to the womb-doors like buffalo unthinkingly thundering across the Nebraska plains. They were running because everyone else was running. The Light from the sword was opening their eyes to the possibility of other outcomes. You could feel their budding elation as they realized *they* could choose which option they would select, take a *Devachan* residence or take another body. They had three choices, actually: follow the herd; go into *Devachan*; or reincarnate on their own terms and start creating a fresh concept of self. Just moments before they had assumed they had no choices at all; the Group Soul was pushing and shoving towards the nearest womb-doors, so that was their plan (their habit).

The Druj and her salesmen were getting more aggressive with their posters and banners, flapping them in the faces of the assembled group, intensifying the pictures, adding a sound component to them, songs, shouts, cries of delight and wonder, exclamations of joy and satisfaction. Such a pitch. They knew they were losing ground fast, that these daring souls were getting away, claiming their freedom. This was bad; it was the loose pebbles that start an avalanche, that bring down a mountain of snow on the sleeping village below.

Several of these break-away souls had already departed for *Devachan* locales. Others were wandering off to look at womb-doors free of the influence and conforming pressure of the Group Soul's designated door. They'd enter life on their own terms at a gate they selected—Latvia anyone?—and only when they werepersonally ready and, honestly, they reflected, they were not ready yet.

The remaining members of the Group Soul, which numbered about 60, were looking anxious, worried, and confused. They could not understand why these fellows of theirs had suddenly defected, run off to pursue their own fate. It upset them; made them nervous, as if it were an infectious disease they might contract just by proximity to those who were so clearly sick and beyond help.

It was sobering to follow their thoughts and watch the tidal swell of their feelings. I had always taken individuation, following one's unique destiny, one's guiding star, as the cliché goes, for granted, that one *should* seek to distinguish oneself. I had forgotten that this assumption, this daring, I suppose it is, was not shared by all and was for many a daunting, scary prospect they'd prefer to squirm out of. A world of hurt awaited those wanting to get their own answers.

"The Green Knight and the Supreme Being have agreed to installing a copy of this Sword of Elohim at all the major womb-doors in the *Bardo* so each soul can make a wide-awake choice without the overbearing intimidation of the Druj and her cohorts," said Merlin. "Souls will be free to ignore the Light of the sword, to discount it, resist it, fight against it, demonize it as they will, but they will also be entirely free to soak up as much of its clarifying Light as they wish.

"We believe it will help the world if more souls are better informed and choose wakefully. Then they may enter human life with more of a sense of mission. This place, this moment, is a crucial one in the *Bardo*; so much depends on

the outcome, on what a soul chooses. So many end up disdaining their hasty choices, have lives that are unfulfilling. It's best, we think, if they can choose carefully, so we are improving the chances they can do so with clarity."

I saw how it would work. The soul, having finished with its *Bardo* karma-processing paperwork, approaches a womb-door and the sword lights up. It's like motion-sensor lighting; we had this on our house in New Hampshire. Usually, it was scavenging raccoons that would trigger the outdoor lights. You reach this threshold and the Sword of Elohim turns on illuminating everything. That in itself, the sudden flaring up of this terrific spiritual Light, fiercely bright but neutral in its intent, is a revelation, like God saying your name out loud, and you pause, collect yourself, feel restored to yourself. You realize you've been staggering around in the dark, like in a basement where the lights are out.

You see the landscape of choices. You see the possibilities. You see *you* can choose. You can choose anything: *Devachan*; another life on Earth; maybe another life somewhere else, in a different life-form: everything appears wide-open. Yes, there are broad constraints based on your overall level of development; it's like applying for a house mortgage: expect one only within your income range. You have to be able to make the monthly payments. Similarly, for the life path you choose you have to be reasonably able to fulfill what you have planned and at the same time have some mobility and to be able to pay off some karmic debts.

"I may be wishing for impossible things," said Blaise, "but ideally each soul contemplating human incarnation would ask, So what is a human anyway? Failing that, during their incarnation, or maybe in the hundredth, or thousandth, however long it takes, they come around to this basic question: What is a human, what does it feel like being a human, what is a human's purpose in existing? I'm talking about a wide-awake look at yourself in the mirror, not your selfhood, but your consciousness inhabiting the human phylogeny and its form and life. The soul adjusting itself to the particularities of the living generic human form. I mean, why aren't you a Pleiadian or Arcturian? You chose to be a human. Why?

"We walk around all day as humans, but how often do we ask of ourselves, what is the nature of this form I am walking around in? I used to ask that all the time. Don't expect God to provide the answer, with a big articulated whisper in your ears or a faxed memo with footnotes. Your answer is more likely to be a sudden, sobering self-awareness that encompasses the cosmos.

"Again, I'm reaching for the stars, but the best way, or at least a way that was programmed into the design of the Earth, is to work with an Albion. Interact with one of these great cosmogonic figures distributed all across the planet. It doesn't matter at which of the four levels you choose; they're all the one Albion. But here is your perfect mirror, where you can see your humanness clearly. All the cosmic components as well as the human phylogenetic constituents. The planet benefits from this studied introspection because in this interaction you're waking up something in yourself and in the Earth, both of which are required for a healthy planet, and when any of the Albions wake up, it stimulates humanity. It gives people a better chance of copying the gesture, waking up their full being.

"So as you stand before this threshold of *Devachan* or human life, if you take a moment to reflect on what a human being might be, what the designer's intentions were, what the speed limit, braking and turning capacities are, what the top limits for functioning are, what cool things you can do with the activated chakras, and what kinds of revelations you can expect and how you can get them, surely you'll walk into the Wheel of Life merry-go-round for your next live installment in the human circus with more awareness of what is at stake for you. This will start a cascading effect of self-reflection that will weaken the Druj's hold on human consciousness. People become less routinized in their awareness.

"I mean, being a human is not the only option if you want to be embodied. There are plenty of other phylogenies you can explore, incarnate into, and create fresh karma. Maybe it's just me. I know I couldn't stand not raising the question and trying to get an answer. Why *this* form? What *is* this form? What can it *do* at its optimum? Life would be too bizarre or boring without knowing anything. Anyway, the more questions like these you ask when you're alive, the less bewildering the *Bardo* will seem when you get there and enter its circus acts. You will have cultivated the investigative habit and use it upon entering the place."

"With halving the draught of Lethe and installing this wake-up monitor at the threshold," said Tommy, "people will have a better chance of doing that, asking that basic question. I started to think about that when I was alive. I know it would have helped me. I had to struggle to remember my intentions while I staggered around in the *Bardo* like a teenager on his first summer trip to Europe. I saw the threshold of another human life waiting for me as obviously as when you're in high school and reasonably smart, you know college is next for you. I could have used somebody gently suggesting the question or perhaps conditions that favored a natural arising of the question in my body-free consciousness. If I decide to incarnate as a human again, I will certainly consider the question first."

"We have a more challenging womb-door to deal with now," said Merlin, summoning our attention from our various discussions.

"We are going to observe, and possibly help out, what confronts a committed Soul Group as its members prepare themselves for another immersion in the Wheel of Life. Note the difference in the term: Soul Group. It indicates a free assembly of like-minded souls, advanced on their individuation pathway, congregating for mentoring and inspiration and often to accomplish goals that require a group human input."

Again, there was a cluster of Light-forms suggestive of humans, but let's say ones not yet committed to wearing that form as their official guise. I counted 32 souls standing in an informal group. They were not lined up obediently; they were not huddled together in trepidation. You got the impression each soul was self-contained, confident, in possession of themselves and their consciousness. In many respects they resembled one another the way perhaps members of a club might; there was a sense of shared values, equivalent insights and experiences. Yet there was no evidence of blind conformity; each soul seemed distinguished from the others, though not in any way suggestive of competition or struggle.

I sensed a collegial, even fraternal, bond among these souls, that they shared a goal, were equal participants in a great project, had done much together already. It seemed to me that anything any of these souls did would be done wakefully out of a purpose agreed upon long ago and whose tactics were well considered. Nobody was talking, though I surmised they were communicating telepathically, sharing thoughts, pictures, schematics, that they entered one another's thoughts when necessary like office workers in a publishing house passing from the editorial to art to business to advertising divisions, knowing all these parts comprised the shared group effort.

I laughed when I tried to imagine that kind of telepathic camaraderie among my faculty colleagues at Dartmouth. Too much defense of one's mental property, too much secrecy about goals, intentions, backroom tactics for them to allow that. Not so here. These souls were committed to the individuation project, and they had each made considerable progress in unifying the disparate parts of themselves. Jung could have used their biographies as lucid textbook examples of the milestones a soul can expect to reach on the journey to individuation.

To use an image favored in Judaic mysticism, these souls occupied the same specific region on the great Tree of Souls. This is where all the souls God ever created were originally placed in accordance with their original frequency compatibility. To use the popular term, and possibly to use it correctly, they were soul mates from the beginning of their creation. They hung like adjacent fruits on the Tree of Souls. They were neighbors because they had similar soul qualities.

This Soul Group was lined up for its next mission. The plan was for all 32 of its members to enter human life at the same time and to meet within 10 years, as a minimum, and definitely by the time they entered college or became 18. It's hard to get around the biological parameters of becoming a human on Earth. Among their many scheduled projects was the intention on working with the Albions, especially the sixth and seventh chakras of these vast geomantic figures. The Albions needed to be in resonance with the new chakra frequency of the upgraded planetary Light grid; their channels needed a thorough cleanout.

I saw these souls sharing schematics, plans, diagrams, and maps, reminding me of a squadron of parachutists studying the terrain they were about to jump into. Amidst the evident camaraderie, there was laughing, joking, and much good will. They were committed to the project; they *wanted* to do it: it defined their purpose. They had not rushed madly or stumbled blindly upon this womb-door, fleeing the tormenting *Bardo* furies of their own unresolved karma.

They walked to this womb-door purposefully. They were queuing up for this next human incarnation with their eyes fully open, briefed on the mission details. Their *Bardo* experience was like a seasoned frequent traveler returning yet again to a friendly country, exchanging pleasantries or jokes with the passport control officer, who recognized them, knew them to be regular entrants to their country, and waved them through with a smile. Enjoy your stay, friend.

Now, as if the tableau of 32 Light-forms standing around a womb-door had been out of focus, it was suddenly sharpened and highlighted. The 32 souls stood inside a large domed golden chamber, brightly lit. An angelic figure stood in the center of this group; this angel was about double the height of these souls, so there was no problem with anyone seeing it or hearing what the angel said.

On the curving walls of this circular chamber were tall color posters showing the members of this Soul Group in various activities during recent incarnations. Celebrities used to call this kind of vanity display an ego wall; all the images tended to emphasize the importance, the celebrity status, of the souls involved. I cringed a little, and I felt some of the Soul Group members cringe also. This was perhaps a little excessive on the side of showing how important these people were. I suspected they preferred their public image to be much more low key, if not entirely self-effacing, like good espionage agents, to be able to act invisibly. Though I doubt all or maybe any of these souls were Buddhists in a formal sense, their attitude was Buddhist: their actions were selfless, done without consideration of expected outcome or favorable attributions to them.

They worked, if you'll pardon my adjustment of a famous saying, like thieves in the night. They entered the human house, the body of Albion, fixed things, then left as quietly as they came. They didn't need or want any fanfare; in fact, public attention would interfere with their work, which, aside from being technically complex, was inherently arcane, hard to explain to people. So for them to be greeted with this kind of official adulation was disconcerting, though I saw that with most it managed to water a little seed of pride inside. Pride was not a normal part of their psychological make-up. Self-assurance, yes, but pride, that was a troubling tree, and its fruits could be vexatious and prickly.

The angel was speaking to the group. Its voice was calm and dulcet. "You are about to embark on a project of great importance. You will help all of the Earth and humanity materially with what you do there. You are vital to the well-being of the planet, and we are most grateful for your efforts. We could not think of a group of 32 souls better prepared to handle this crucial assignment. I will show you now some adjustments we would like you to make to the Albions." Here the angel projected a shimmering holographic image of a landscape version of Albion, zooming in on the figure's cranium and its chakras.

"We have created an image that you may slip into the sixth chakras of all these figures. It will enable humans to see an order of angels important to them, and to all activities pertaining to the Albions." Here the angel projected the image of an angelic cluster. They looked okay, like angels, wholesome, full of love, smiling, but I shivered involuntarily because something was just slightly off with them. I couldn't put my finger on what was wrong, but I was on guard. On the other hand, I reflected, what do I know about angels? I am new to all this.

"We believe it is important to draw human attention to this family of angels and to draw them further into human activities on the Earth. We believe they have much to contribute, and we want to make sure humans appreciate this. We also propose to have you decommission a few of the stars in the Albion's chest area; these stars, from the viewpoint of current human evolution, are semi-dormant and the Albions do not need their input any further at this point. Once you have done this, we will dispatch members of another angelic order to occupy the psychic space formerly taken up by these decommissioned stars.

"You may regard these angelic figures as custodians of this region of space. They will provide you with regular updates to your work schedule, indicating new areas within the Albions that need either stimulation or toning down. In this manner we will at last correct certain flaws and habits that have been allowed to seep into the system and send it in undesirable directions."

Now things got funny, really weird, and frankly, a bit disturbing. The room was brilliantly lit, but the quality of that Light took on a neon glare. It felt too bright, garish, lurid, like Las Vegas at night with all the signs lit up. The atmosphere felt subtly oppressive, like bullies were slowly moving in on us, like spirits that weighed a lot, took up a lot of space, that always got their way, were edging in on us from all sides, waiting for the moment to make their next move. You felt as if you were being pressured to do something against your will. That you had been deftly maneuvered into a dark corner or an undefendable position.

"Humans still need much direction from spiritual sources like ourselves," the angel continued. "They are still too wayward, undisciplined, unpredictable. These necessary changes will give them a better map of how to best conduct themselves. They will cause less commotion to the precious mechanisms we have put in place over the eons on their planet for their benefit. We know what's best."

This last sentence definitely did not sit right with me. I squirmed, if you can squirm when occupying a Light body. Let's say my mind squirmed in panic. This was all *wrong*. Several of the members of the Soul Group brightened their Light-forms; it seemed equivalent to standing up straight and clearing your throat before you address a group. This attitude of tightening up of one's attention spread across the group. Telepathy has its tactical advantages.

They started to marshal their attention, drawing it into a mass, much like taking a deep inhale before launching your body upon some physical activity. They deployed this gathered-up attention towards the Blazing Star inside them. Just because you don't have a physical body, doesn't mean you don't have a Blazing Star. The Star congealed into the familiar form of the Ofanim's Rotunda of Light, and the 40 million identical diamond facets started to burn with a fierce diamond white fire, and the members of the Soul Group projected this outward like 32 high-powered flame-throwers all focused on the same bad wood. The recipient of this marshaled Ofanim fire-focus was the angel standing amidst them. The diamond white fire revealed it was not an angel at all. It was the Druj.

The brilliance of the lighting in this chamber was illusory. It was dark and abysmal, with pillars of grey-silver flames writhing along the walls like snakes. All the gold was gone, a mere semblance. The two orders of angels who had been put forward as colleagues on the mission were stripped naked of their illusory forms. They were Druj demons. The Druj was leering at the Soul Group, both amused and angered they had seen through her artful, well-prepared deception.

She had been trying to seduce them into collusion with her on a new round of subtle control and manipulation of human cognitive freedom. She had intended to use them to suborn the cosmic freedom of the Albions and to lock down certain essential star components of his great cosmogonic body and to insert specific programming images in the sixth chakras to commandeer his seeing. It reminded me of the way the Russian hypnotist had used the Queen of Diamonds card in *The Manchurian Candidate* to take hold of the soldier's consciousness when needed. Flash the card and he automatically kills people, friends and politicians. I realized the Druj was playing for high stakes here.

All this business about working with the Albions' chakras, turning off stars, enlisting the help of two angelic orders, was a smokescreen. She wanted to put this programming device in place, and when the moment was ripe, use the Soul Group members themselves to trigger the shut-down control so she could take over the Albions and command them to execute her agenda, which as we know well after our time in the *Bardo* studying her machinations, was to dull down and distort human cognitive freedom and accuracy, to reposition it like a telescope to see only her contrived fake reality so humans would never be free, and, best of all, never realize they were now living in a Druj-contrived prison.

"You have just seen through a well executed version of the Druj's House of Lies," said Merlin. "Well done. She is one tricky old girl, I'll give her that. It was a test we allowed to go forward to sharpen your discernment. The higher you climb up in the Tree of Life, the more exacting are the challenges to stay awake and not be fooled by equally high-level deceptions the Druj likes to do."

The Soul Group was back where it had been, standing together before a womb-door. In some respects they had never left it. The Druj had just spun an illusory hologram of her golden chamber around them and they had bought it. For a little while. She thought she could hook them by watering the incipient seed of pride all humans carry inside. It might have

worked if she could have distracted them longer and spun out even more alluring fake images to beguile them. I saw a few dark green shoots start to emerge from half a dozen seeds.

Her strategy reminded me of the tactics in the great espionage novels where you get an accomplished mole acting covertly at the highest level of British intelligence, and from that privileged, secret perch redirecting or sabotaging all the agency's spy work. Use the technicians themselves to corrupt the delicate geomantic system—it was clever and nasty, Machiavellian. He had probably been one of her students. The Prince was probably a Druj *avatar*.

"Merlin, would you have let us intervene?" asked Edward.

"I was hoping it would not come to that, but yes, if it was necessary. It's always a better and lasting learning experience if you can come to the required discernment on your own. The group did, as you saw, and they learned from it."

"As an editor, I listened carefully to the words the Druj was using. They often give away a person's true position and tactics, even down to a single word choice. I do that with manuscripts, and I suppose it is a kind of psychic sensitivity, seeing through words to the person using them to reveal or hide. She started out by flattering the group: you are vital, better prepared than others; the assignment is crucial; you will help the whole world; we are grateful for all this. Those are pretty reliable strokes for a human's sense of validation and worth.

"Yes, you want to compliment your workers, but this felt excessive, a bit overdone, prolix," Edward continued. "This fulsome praise had the intended result of disarming the acuity of their engineering insight, and the Druj could slip in some stern directions to them without their raising any objection. We want to make sure humans appreciate this, she next said. Here comes the first sign of the heavy hand, the authoritative decree. She followed this up with some patronizing criticisms of human frailty, weak intellects, and general fecklessness, and tried to enlist the Soul Group in sharing her increasingly evident disdain for wayward humans. Humans need direction, discipline, behavioral instructions; they are less important than the precious mechanisms we have put in place.

"Then came the corker: we know what's best. Perhaps the angels do, but they would never put it *this* way. They do not boast patronizingly like that. What further gave it away was this sentence: 'In this manner we will at last correct certain flaws and habits that have been allowed to seep into the system and send it in undesirable directions.' Notice the words: at last, correct, certain, seep, and undesirable. Those suggest impatience, disdain, even disregard, for the design. Undesirable to whom? The system, as I understand it, was supposed to have latitude for creative drift, new directions, and evolutionary upgrades. The Druj's words imply that is too much unchecked freedom; it must be reined in at once. Remember, her agenda is total world domination, the overcoming of the Christ.

"To say 'at last' suggests they have been putting up with something sloppy, inappropriate, or just primitive for too long and it will now end. 'Seep' suggests something nasty, revolting, or even pathogenic, infiltrating an otherwise pure system. 'Certain' denotes disdain for something insanitary, uncouth. It's something you hold with clinical detachment, at a safe distance, as if with antiseptic tweezers and an attitude of mild disdain and disapproval.

"I realized, listening closely to these well-chosen words, the angel was trying to enlist our sympathy with her evaluation of the system. She praised the Soul Group to get them feeling relaxed, recognized, and validated; then she tried to enlist our sympathy for her superior views on the faulty system and the need for a major overhaul. She was trying to convince the Soul Group and us together.

"I saw you wince, Frederick, when she made this last statement. In poker, that's called a tell. She gave herself away. She was getting boastful, full of her triumph. Her mask of benevolent gentility fell away; you saw the demon leer. She never faltered in keeping up the mellifluous tone to her voice. That was good. Those dulcet tones could sound persuasive and irresistible if you weren't careful, but they were in truth the studied modulations of a master hypnotist. We were following this exchange so closely it's as if we were part of that group."

"I am familiar with this kind of trickery, Edward," said Pipaluk. "Many of my *angakkuq* friends tell me of times when demons tricked them into looking for lost souls in the wrong places or hiding them or making them appear different. I have been deceived a number of times also. Yes, you learn from these deceptions. They can seem so real, so convincing, at first. You cannot guess you are seeing made-up pictures the Druj has put before you to throw you off your mission.

"I have found you can often see through these illusions by studying the quality of the Light. Did you see that the lighting in this golden temple was too bright, too brilliant, that it seemed exaggerated, like there were two suns in the sky above? The world doesn't need to be that bright, and it never is. That was a give-away."

"Why didn't the Druj appear as a terrifying seven-headed red beast, drooling and gnashing its pointed teeth, the way you portrayed the Beast of the Apocalypse, Merlin?" Edward asked this question.

"Would that have scared you?" Merlin responded.

"Bloody hell not," said Blaise. "We would have laughed our heads off at the comic book histrionics the Sly Bitch was laying down before us like cards."

"Precisely my point," Merlin responded. "The Druj knew for people like you, with a large degree of metaphysical sophistication, she'd be more effective playing the Machiavellian mental seductress. She would trick you mentally. But she underestimated your discernment. She'd never tried to trick a book editor! Your group discernment subtly influenced the Soul Group members and they succeeded in seeing through the Druj's artful deception and put an end to it."

"Has anybody seen Matthew, or for that matter, Philomena?" I asked. They both had been with us throughout most of this but now they were missing.

I couldn't say how far away they were from our present position or if any kind of spatial distinction had any meaning in this place. But I will say that where we found them was very different than the kind of womb-doors we'd seen to date. Matthew and Philomena had formed an archway of Light before a door. Each of their Light bodies formed a pillar, and they leaned to meet at the top. A group of 24 souls were standing about before the door getting a briefing from these two talking pillars of Light. It was both funny and majestic to watch. I wondered if Philomena would find a way to work Scriabin into her briefing and maybe Matthew would tell them stories about the James Bay Thunderbirds.

These souls looked different than the individuals and groups we had seen. They were, for one thing, serene and self-possessed, not the least bit jittery. They were taller and overall larger than the previous human souls we'd observed, and they exuded a sense of great age, as if they were much older souls than the others, and that this age brought wisdom, insight, clarity of purpose, and an unflagging commitment. I was intrigued. Who were these "people" anyway?

"They are Pleiadians about to enter human incarnation as teachers," said Merlin. "The Pleiades regularly dispatches advanced souls to Earth as instructors, especially since the Light grid upgrade began in 1985, and now even more so since the 2020 advent of the Blaise Babies and the Theosophon of 2033. They blend in; they don't advertise their presence; they are self-effacing. They are helping humans, at least the ones most receptive to such projects, get up to speed and into resonance with the significant adjustments we've made to the Light grid and its ramifications on human consciousness, life, feelings, the body. The Pleiadians have been at this individuation game a lot longer than most humans, and, don't forget, a Pleiadian contingent played a big role in the Earth's design.

"It is a sacrifice on their part to take on form as humans because they have to adjust their more advanced consciousness to life-form containers that have not evolved to the same extent. They have more consciousness centers activated in their craniums than most humans, and they are more used to telepathic communication than spoken language, and they are more aware of their own soul timeline and their purpose and destiny than most humans. So they have to waive much of this, for a time, as they enter human life and walk among you."

That still didn't tell me what Philomena and Matthew were doing here. They were talking to the Pleiadian souls; they were showing them life-forms; they were modeling human states of consciousness they could expect to encounter; they were demonstrating the chakra arrays and how they worked. They were reviewing the assignments for each member of the Pleiadian contingent, and this part was intriguing to watch. Philomena and Matthew did not do this by holding up diagrams or writing outlines on a whiteboard or anything like that. Each became the information they were imparting. If they were explaining the range of consciousness normally attained by humans, they shape-shifted into generic human forms and ran their awareness through the chakras. They embodied everything they were teaching; they were slideshows.

It was like the human form and its range of likely consciousness was a complex machine and they were demonstrating the operation of this machine. Here's how you maintain a state of high-frequency, focused Light in the midst of a system of chakras that can easily become subjectively influenced under the strong effects of being embedded in a self-referencing biological organism. I laughed. We take that so for granted, the way our bodies and emotions conspire to commandeer our higher natures, which, technically, run through the chakras.

This was all new for the Pleiadians. Theirs is a different phylogeny than humans, and I was beginning to see some of the crucial differences. It would be too simplistic to say Pleiadians generally are a more mental or cerebral phylogeny, though, from a human vantage point, it would seem so. They are less immediately engaged in their feelings, or perhaps it is that their emotions have been raised to a level of mental understanding and no longer compete with this.

Let's say rather that the Pleiadian mind, its mental capacity, is foremost in the overall operation of Pleiadian consciousness, more than it is in most humans. Add to this the ease and naturalness of shared telepathy throughout any group and you appreciate that the Pleiadian tends to use his mind to grasp any given reality rather than run it through subjectively filtered, self-flavored chakras like we do. So Matthew and Philomena were showing them how to manage both operations as humans, Pleiadian emotionality and human-style feeling.

They were also reviewing the details and settings for the Earth's Light grid. Its style of geomantic patterning is different than what you find on the Pleiadian planets, both different

in terms of the types of Light temples and in many respects simpler in terms of the limits and freedoms afforded to consciousness through this complex system. Certain features Pleiadians might take for granted on a Pleiadian planet would not be encountered on the Earth.

Much of the Earth's geomantic system was in a state of under-utilization, neglect, dysfunction, and even, in some cases, entropy, so that the intended reciprocal feedback interactions between geomantic patterning and human consciousness were weak. They counseled the Pleiadians about to incarnate not to be shocked by this degree of dysfunction they would be presented with; it was reversible. But they also demonstrated how to run their consciousness through this globally distributed system as a way of keeping it refreshed, like plumbing.

The Pleiadian teachers were the fresh clean water, the Light grid the water pipes. Re-establishing this reciprocal system periodically would flash images of the Earth's implicit Albion to human residents as a reminder of what the system was designed to reveal, the true and cosmic nature of the human, and it would give them a feeling for what perfect alignment with this model felt like. It would also demonstrate the particular mechanisms for human consciousness reality as it works on this planet; the mechanism is both universal and locally adapted.

Blaise explained this to me later, as it was a difficult notion to understand at first. He said it meant the way consciousness interacts with supposedly external reality via the geomantic interface to create new conditions or alter existing ones. It's the mechanism, usually veiled to most people, by which consciousness shapes planetary reality and the way people create their own reality conditions.

I almost jumped back a little when I took in the implications of this. Merlin said Pleiadians had been incarnating as humans to be teachers since 1985. That means some of the humans walking around the Earth were Pleiadians in disguise. I might have seen a few, maybe even met one—did I even know one?

It cast a strange, exciting new light on human life on Earth. I hoped I would remember this when I got back to physical life, wherever that proved to be. It's one thing to know your mentor, in my case, the human Blaise, was Pleiadian or could claim Pleiadian ancestry. I was used to that, I think. But this meant people I would ordinarily assume were full-blood humans might be Pleiadian. I might feel like the classical Greeks, extending hospitality to all strangers knowing that the Olympian gods liked to go about in human disguise to see if humans recognized and honored them, or at least invited them in for a snack. I would study each human I encountered, wondering if she was a Pleiadian only pretending to be a human. I would be on the constant look-out for human impostors, and if I found any, I would grin and give them a big *Hello*!

"These guys could tell us, or Earth people, what being a Pleiadian is like," said Blaise. "They could explain their phylogeny, demonstrate it, model it, because they know what it is to be a Pleiadian. They could show Earth people how to experience what a human is, how to experience and be self-aware in that phylogeny. In fact, that may be in large measure what their mission to Earth is. To help incarnated humans find their own phylogeny and occupy it. By that I mean recognize it, see it from the outside, learn how to fully operate it. Why?

"Because this is the key to correct planetary maintenance. As you know, the whole of the Earth, its Light grid design in total, is an expression of the human phylogeny. All our geomantic work is always about aligning current human consciousness with this template. It tells humans who they are, then humans can reassure the Earth, our dear old pal, Gaia, that they know who they are and are no longer stumbling about the place like demented amnesiacs needing a coffee fix. Which reminds me, if I were in a body at the moment, I'd probably be calling for a strong Italian roast. That's part of the human phylogeny, definitely. Hard-wired into the psyche.

"So, these Pleiadian souls in their in-between Light forms are entering the human merry-go-round on Earth self-aware, fully briefed, and exquisitely-prepared for this crucial assignment. I see now it was a precursor, an advance wave, to the Blaise Baby advent of 2020."

The arched portal formed by Philomena and Mathew was blazing bright. That's my wife, a gateway of Light for incarnating Pleiadian souls, I thought wryly. That's a long way from performing Rachmaninov's *Morceaux de Fantaisie* for an audience of 500 at Dartmouth. As the Pleiadian souls stood before the gateway, its Light was extended to envelop them. They were getting an infusion of the Christ Light, a purification of their psychic space by the Buddha Mind.

It provided a transition zone for them to shift from their Pleiadian sense of normalcy to the Earth-human conditions they would soon be moving in. It had a purgative effect, and in that way this Light resembled the River Lethe draught ordinary souls used to take; but the intent here was not oblivion of the soul's memories or even current lifetime assignment, just a washing clean of any taints. It was like how you shower and wash yourself before hopping into a hot tub.

But the lighted archway was providing a view of something else. Inside this Light, which I saw as, with Merlin's go-ahead, I momentarily stepped inside it, was a view of the Earth's geomantic pattern, the template of its sites. It was vast and complex because it entails millions of geomantic nodes as well as their patterns of connections and the meta-grids formed by all the copies of individual Light temples and the geometry of their distribution array. It was the Earth's master Light grid, its presiding mandala. It was the key to how Earth reality works, how to work the geomantic controls. The Light revealed more than this.

It showed what it added up to, the nest of Albions, local ones embedded in regional copies, that one in the principal planetary Albion, and it showed how this nest of Albions in turn disclosed the face of the human phylogeny, not as a human-shaped figure but as a cosmic imprint, more like a series of nested spheres filled with stars and blazing Lights. But it was the face of the awakened, perfected Human as installed on the Earth. It was the designers' picture of the intended goal of human life on Earth: Be this. You are this. You could call this infusion the Tea of Remembering. These Pleiadian souls *would* remember all this.

They would enter human incarnation with the engineering schematic for the human phylogeny clearly in mind, as if imprinted with a copy of that pattern. The angel Blaises once told Blaise that all humans have a copy of the Earth's Light grid as if imprinted in their genetic code and that makes them innately resonant with the geomantic pattern and it's just a matter of activating it one day.

For the Pleiadian souls, that imprint would remain on the surface of their awareness, and they would not have to meditate and dredge deeply for it as the human Blaise said he had done in his early training years. They would have it readily in hand, but so too from now on would souls taking human incarnation. The planetary Light grid upgrade mandated that enhancement of starting conditions; it would be too regressive to have souls coming in unaware of this. Access to the engineering schematics of the template now would be easier.

I saw the logic of this. Human ignorance of the planet's design has hindered the growth of consciousness for millennia. Too many people live and die dumb, blind, and ignorant of the true conditions of their consciousness. This is heavily detrimental to the progress of the human phylogeny in waking up. People sleep through their lives then stagger in fright through a bizarre *Bardo*. I assure the reader I hold myself as no exception. I slept on with the best of them. Now with the hologram of the human phylogeny as expressed through the Light grid imprinted more palpably in their consciousness (in their sixth chakra rather than more deeply within them in their genetic code), they could access it easily.

It would be more readily congruent with how they construed physical reality, with their assumptions about the nature and purpose of life and what humans are. Awareness of this pattern would help them understand themselves as individual carriers of the phylogenetic pattern, and their *Bardo* experience would be far better. They would know where they stood: Here I am in the *Bardo* disassembling my phylogenetic container. Here I am before the womb-door putting that pattern back on. Even better: Here I am, alive, embodied, waking up to the miniature Albion I am on an Earth with the same imprint in many copies.

What a difference all that would make for everything, *knowing* what you are doing, why, the full context of your life, and the benign thinking behind it. If I were to come up with *the* most vexing condition I've had to deal with to date in my life it would be not knowing what is going on, *not knowing*, really, anything. I was glad to see that partly as a result of our expedition that would be changing, and that as a result of the planet's Light grid upgrade to a sixth chakra frequency and norm of cognitive operation, that would eventually be the reality for many.

Merlin gestured for us to stand in the gateway of Light. We did so. I felt like layers of density and leadenness were being instantly stripped off me. It was as if I were obese and the Light were a fat-dissolving medium, rendering me lean in seconds. The inner part of me now revealed was searingly bright; it felt full of intelligence, of knowledge and understanding I had never experienced before and thus never knew I possessed. I started thinking of what an impressive oral presentation I could make for my next Ph.D. thesis defense based on this.

Then I realized how ridiculous that sounded, how silly to think of that now. But I think it was a way of gauging the degree and scope of the information now disclosed, of showing me the magnitude of what the Light had dredged down to. I saw, for example, the nest of Albions at all its levels across the Earth. I saw the engineering information about the design of the Earth implicit in this cosmic form, and I saw it growing in brilliance and starting to communicate with humans, both alive and those in the *Bardo*. Physical embodiment didn't matter.

I saw Blaise inside this nest of Albion forms, taking notes, investigating things, and (this part was a surprise) I saw myself working with him as a colleague. The specific nature of our work makes me smile, almost blush with a kind of adolescent enthusiasm. It seemed we were detectives of a sort on a case. We were following leads in a crime against the Earth's Light grid— can you imagine that? Geomantic felonies? Planetary energy pattern embezzlements?

Blaise for his part was grinning. He looked happy, even cocky. "I got it," he said. "I got the number. At last. You know I'm always talking about how the Earth's Light grid can be specified in mathematics, that it was originally coded in what we know as math formulas and equations to which pictures and stories, otherwise known as myths, were later added to help explain the

number scripts. I saw the number, the equation that codes the planet's energy anatomy and that can be used by us to make geomantic adjustments in real time, taking account of all factors, physical and subtle, from weather to astrology, psyche to sunspots.

"Blaise had always emphasized that the possibility of a human achieving resonance with the planet was implicit in the human genetic code. This is deeper. This is the specific coding that specifies all the operations of the planet's grid. This too was buried, deposited deep within my energy field. The Light exposed it, helped me raise it to the surface of my awareness, and now I have it."

Turning to me, he chuckled and said, "Yes, Frederick, we will be having a some investigative adventures along these lines fairly soon. I estimate ten years."

"What do you mean by a number that codes the planet's Light grid?" asked Tommy.

"It's like a file folder heading, a case number," replied Blaise. "All the designed planets, all the planets with Light grids that support consciousness in a living container, have one. You could picture them as individual folders in a large file cabinet or files in a computerized database. Whichever analogy you like. The file heading is also the activation, management, and manipulation code. It's the password that enables you to interact with the system, and it is the means of interaction itself. It's a valuable number, a summary of all the specifications.

"Imagine you are a Light grid engineer operating at a galactic level, like the Pleiadians are in fact. Your boss says, pull the case number on planet Earth. You pull out the file folder or call up the file on your computer. It's the full dossier. Everything about the Earth, its design, its load-bearing capacity, meaning the parameters for the possible expansion and evolution of self-aware consciousness the grid design allows, the types of Light temples, their numbers and array patterns, a timeline for key engineering adjustments made to this grid.

"The file has everything, the full history of every last geomantic detail about this planet, and, most keenly, the activation codes, the hyperdimensional formulas, what I call the *hierophancy algorithm*. That is the string of numbers that provides access to the planet as a sentient body of Light, to a planet that, when healthy, *reveals* the Light. The planet becomes hierophantic, shows the holy Light it's made of. The algorithm is the key number sequence that specifies that Light process, the mechanisms and procedures of consciousness and its growth.

"These are computations that produce an output, a desired final ending stage. That's the key to the Light grid, because the hierophancy algorithm is a procedure for computing a desired end function, proper Light grid operation. It is the key to making adjustments that take into account all the variables at play.

"Even better, this algorithm is heuristic, which means self-learning and self-modulating. It learns from its own computations then makes adjustments. This enables it to keep several steps ahead of the Druj and all her machinations. It doesn't shut her down entirely, because the system needs some asymmetry and friction that she provides; but it restricts her level of possible interaction to a low percentage. It controls and mitigates her potential intrusion into the system, and it constantly adjusts and updates the level and quality of this mitigation always against the framework of the original ideal settings for Earth consciousness. It is not, by the way, an artificial intelligence construct. It requires human input. Your consciousness focused in a precise manner is the key that activates the system.

"Those humans, or Pleiadians, or whatever sentient phylogeny is involved, comprise the Hierophancy, the cadre of trained Light grid managers and adjusters. The Hierophancy is the department of geomancers, Light grid engineers, at least on most civilized planets. Soon we will have that on Earth, geomancers who reveal and adjust the Holy Light in a planet's geomantic grid and who maintain and deploy the heuristic hierophancy algorithm to do this. It is the master code for a planet, its true name written in mathematical formulas."

"I saw myself as a *Bardo* guide, staying in here for a while to help people navigate through the changed after-death landscape and seeing how all the changes we've specified play out in real experiences," said Tommy. "It was strange, and wonderful. I saw detailed maps, done in great cartographical detail, of the *Bardo*, Six Worlds, and innumerable *Devachan* locales, like I was a master real estate broker with plats for all the properties in a county, every last one. I had personnel lists of all the likely *Bardo* spirits, both generic and subjectively projected by the karmically hallucinating *Bardo* travelers. I had their résumés.

"I could advise *Bardo* travellers as to the nature and purpose of individual spirits. Sure, I couldn't advise everybody. I had helpers, lots of them. I trained them all. I had the master engineering schematics for the divestment of body-based consciousness. I had the flow charts, diagrams, time-lines, the inventory of Light temples, processes, and attendant spiritual guardians—everything about it. I guess I could make a career out of this. Maybe I was even born to do this!"

We had a laugh at this. Tommy, so young and yet such an old soul too. Now Pipaluk started speaking. "This Light brought me to a landscape filled with many *angakkuqs*. It was a training place, as if all the people learning how to be an *angakkuq* came here for instruction. Here they practiced all the techniques. My job was to show them how to project believable pictures, to hallucinate on demand.

"Here on our *Bardo* expedition we have seen many ways in which souls put out pictures of their karma and then run in fear from them. I was showing young shamans how to do this on purpose, as statements of power, then to ride these images like they were powerful horses galloping across the flat lands of spirit. How to make images of their own karma then use them as powerful spirit allies. I think I would enjoy that. I see I am prepared to do this. This knowledge was lying at the deepest layer of myself, and the gateway Light showed me it."

Blaise turned to Edward. "What kind of bedrock in you got exposed?"

"It surprised me," Edward said. "I saw myself involved in a fresh set of adventures, like the ones I spent five years enjoying with Merlin, but this time it was with another figure, a man with a white staff with a white crown on top. He was a hierophant, no doubt about that, and he reported to a circle of 24 elderly men on thrones arrayed in a half-circle around a magnificent golden throne.

"These figures were unbelievably, impossibly old, and the man with the white staff was their emissary to the lower worlds, though they are still higher worlds to us. Everything I have done up until now, even my work as a book editor, was preparation for this new round of adventures, or maybe I should say initiations. This man with the staff was a master geomancer, possibly Earth's premier practitioner, closely associated with the Christ and the Christ Light."

Then he turned to look specifically at Blaise, and said, "In some curious way, my upcoming adventures with this figure and the retinue of 24 old men is a necessary prelude to your real-time applications of the hierophancy algorithm. But don't ask my how or why. It was a quick impression of their relationship."

"You'll find increasingly that your individual adventures and insights are integrated into activities that involve the whole group, your expedition of eight," said Merlin. "Why don't you all step inside the gateway of Light for a moment."

As before, it felt as if heavy layers were stripped from my consciousness by the Light, layers of density and obstruction I did not realize I was carrying. This time the intent of the Light was to reveal something to all of us together, something we had in common. Everything around me became a transparent pale blue, like the clear sky at midday. A semblance of walls and structure formed.

Other spirits besides our small group were present, including angels, Pleiadians, Ascended Masters, Ray Masters, a few archangels, and other celestial figures I did not recognize but whose majesty and level of seniority were unmistakable. I knew the general identities of most of these figures thanks to my Theosophon travels with Blaise and the introductions he had made for me. I would not be so literal as to say I was surrounded by desks, drafting tables, and stacks of engineering schematics and architectural renderings, for it was far more subtle than that, but it did seem we were now encased in a surplus of plans, as if the air itself was rich and copious with rendered thoughts and mental structures.

We were all in this pale blue place, but we did not look the same. I knew it was us, but all the faces and bodies were different, as if from a previous life. In fact, I'm not sure saying "bodies" is useful here; my impression was our form was one of only casually structured or configured Light; mostly, it was a mental presence, a telepathy of linked, awakened minds, engaged in a common pursuit.

Each of us had our specialties, areas of the design we were responsible for. To use an analogy, say we were designing the human body: one of us might be responsible for the liver and all its functions, including the Liver meridian as described in acupuncture; another for the spleen; another the kidneys or heart. We oversaw the implementation and operation of this feature, this "organ," at every level of the hierarchy of its expression in the vast hologram of the Earth. Ultimately, our job was to see that this organ became self-aware within Albion. We were designers of structures to convey and amplify consciousness, and we did this at the scale of entire planets, aligning consciousness with Light forms.

Now I saw why we were colleagues working on this shared project. It was as if we were all joined at the hip from the beginning. I draw your attention to my earlier reference to the Jewish description of the Tree of Souls. I saw us all hanging off a limb on this tree, like ripening apples on a sunlit summer day. It is a vast tree, almost too big to see and certainly hard to imagine. All the souls in Creation have their place on this tree, each put there by the Creator, our Boss, the Supreme Being, a one-tree Johnny Appleseed. I am not saying that I saw Matthew, Philomena, Blaise, Frederick, all of our group hanging next to me.

I knew they were present with me but they looked different. Actually, they did not look like anything specific because you hang on this tree before you have differentiated yourself into recognizable, repeatable forms and appearances. But I recognized an essence for each of my expedition members. It was a vibration. Though each of us had our own unique vibration, the group vibration was coherent, like a choir singing the same Beethoven chorale. I knew we shared the same assumptions and desires, that we had similar life goals, and when I say "life," I mean it in terms of every life we'd ever have in any form.

It was a telepathy so ingrained, so implicit, so flawless, that we need not do anything to activate it. It was always on, casually in operation without any effort. If you're looking for the ultimate in "pals," this was it. Pals from way back, we were, very clubbable, I thought (the Reform Club perhaps?), and I realized this was our Soul Group and we had a shared purpose that was as unshakeable and irreducible as a strong melody or theme in an opera and that we had shared it ever since we were first placed there on the Tree of Souls.

Yes, the Soul Group was larger than we seven. You can't count Merlin. He was more like a faculty adviser for post-graduates. You check in with him now and then, show him the progress you've made, take his suggestions. I had an impression of perhaps a hundred or more, though I only knew these seven people presently; maybe more of us would meet up and do projects together. My eyes opened wide as I suddenly saw that we had worked on many other planets. Designing the Earth's Light grid was only one project in a long career résumé. It was well past the middle of the list of completed planets. Apparently, this list had been compiled long ago, and many planets still awaited our design work. I felt like an amnesiac waking up to the truth of who I was and what I'd done.

It finally occurred to me to ask what should have been an obvious question to somebody a little more with it. What made it possible to remember this vast history involving our group? Was it the Light of the gateway somehow?

Merlin took my question. "Your intuition is correct. It was the Gateway Light. Call it the Christ Light or the Buddha Mind, in either case it facilitates complete recall of the soul's own history, the complete recapitulation of events on its own timeline ever since you left the Tree of Souls and began your work. The Christ forgives and the Buddha remembers, so you recall your own history with the wisdom of discernment and the sympathy of compassion. Souls in the *Bardo* about to step forth into another life or to depart on a recreational or educational foray into *Devachan* will be able to stand in this Gateway Light and absorb its awakening stimulus and remember their own history, if they wish to. We think many will wish to. We think this will start to make a big difference.

"We think it's always easier to make an *informed* choice, a *good* choice, when you have the full picture, when you see the context in which your choice is presented. Every soul will not be required to remember as deeply as the impression all of you just received, but even the merest glimpse of your soul's past is riveting. It can provide just the needed amount of push to provoke a *metanoia*, a new view. And that is what we are trying to impart to Earth reality through our expedition, a changed view of conditions, wouldn't you all agree?"

Merlin paused, then said, "Come. There is one more feature to show you."

We were standing inside what looked like a globe of rich blue. It was the size of a large office or study, and it gave off the atmosphere of concentration. A soul in its Light body was standing with its Guardian Angel amidst diagrams. These diagrams seemed to be hung everywhere, not so much on hard, defined surfaces, but in the air, as if the air itself were a bulletin board. There were hundreds of diagrams, and many had colored, pulsating lines connecting them.

I recognized at once that this soul was planning his next life, scripting his moves, working out the timing, calculating his debt-to-credit ratios in terms of his karma. But what struck me, what impressed me, was the interlocking complexity of it all. I say "his" life, but the more I observed this soul, the more I realized "it" had not chosen "its" gender yet. All his life options were still open.

This soul's plotting reminded me of the tales I'd heard of Qabalists earnestly running all the possible permutations on the spellings and number significance of key words in a Hebrew text to extract all possible meanings, the way

they would create complex permutation tables, almost into the fourth dimension, in terms of justifiable or tentative interpretations. "He" was doing the same with the multiple and branching possibilities for his upcoming life, who he would meet, when, to what end, for how long, whether it was a debt or credit relationship, and how each step, even the seemingly minute and trivial ones, might contribute to an overall outcome, to the fulfillment of his own eschatology.

Everybody has one, an intended goal, a long term teleology to their lives, something they promised the Supreme Being they would achieve with their gift of incarnation, I understood, and no matter how long it takes them. Every soul, even when they forget, deliberately forget, don't care, lose interest, grow faint-hearted, despairing, atheistic, or prefer the material distractions, has a final goal in mind, an achievement that will summarize all their multi-life efforts. The Supreme Being is patient. He can wait. He set the timer for 311 trillion years. I will sit here patiently, He says, until the timer goes off while you people fulfill yourselves and achieve something beautiful to bring back to show Me.

The diagrams that hung motionlessly in the air were a cross between a choreography script or perhaps a basketball play chart and an engineering schematic for some complicated machine. This guy was planning his reality, down to every shrug of his shoulder and whether he turns right or left to leave a room. He ran hundreds of permutations with people, interactions with friends, casual acquaintances, and enemies, and people he'd prefer to see the last of.

This figure met with dozens of other souls, some who would be his family members, siblings, parents, friends, helpers, critics. He showed them the diagrams, like a director reviewing an actor's speaking lines and showing him the marks on the stage floor where she'd have to stand to deliver those lines. Some of these life "actors" would have only one line; others would have dialogue that went on for pages, even chapters. All got meticulous attention. They were all parts of the syllogism necessary to achieve his eschatology. I know that's a strange way to look at life planning, but I was seeing irrefutably that one plans a life with exquisite detail, nuance, and logistic precision to reach a goal.

Finally, the soul was presenting his life plans to the Lords of Karma for approval. It was like an architect going to the building council, presenting the plans for a permit for new house construction. You have to demonstrate all the architectural specifics, plumbing, electrical, sewage, building materials, make sure it accords with zoning and other regulations, then you get the go-ahead.

The Guardian Angel, like a senior, more experienced balletist, would point to certain moves plotted on a diagram and suggest an alteration, highlighting it in a line of Light; or he would show the likely ripple effect of this move on the moves scripted on another diagram. Certain moments were especially highlighted. They glowed and flashed, like neon signs in a big city at night advertising a show. I surmised these were plateaus when carefully planned goals were at last reached. I saw also what looked like trapdoors or sideways exits from the timeline, where, again I surmised, he might defenestrate from his life intentions, if he wished, bail out, take a breather, fail to achieve certain peaks.

He left that option open at various points on the timeline, but he hoped he wouldn't take advantage of these tactical pullouts from his karma's forward momentum. Still, the Earth is populated with people who gave up on their goals or forgot them, confused them, distorted them, or disbelieved they ever had any. Patience and multiple second chances for all souls are at the heart of this system. You can ignore your life plan if you wish, and you can repeat it many times. The system is both planned and fluidic, allowing for unexpected contingencies, because, when you think about it, the pattern is enormously complex, intricate, interweaving with the life diagrams and timing schedules of many other people.

This figure seemed to reach some decisions. Gender would be male. He would study music, the cello specifically, innovate a new playing style, and found a musical academy to teach new bowing methods for cello performance. Details about parents, siblings, relatives, health lineage, childhood and adult friends, jobs, education, marriage, children, illness, domestic arrangements, the sorrows, tribulations, and epiphanies, all nicely staggered for recovery time—everything was specified with the same detail of a complete inventory down to the last pencil such as when you contract movers to relocate all your belongings to a new home and they fill out dozens of pages listing all your personal effects.

None of this to me was new. I had often heard people speak of life plans, and often skilled psychics are able to collect some of the data of these plans for their clients. What usually happens is we forget all about this plan, incarnate, and spend most of our time moaning about the meaninglessness or futility of life and how we don't know why we are here, or maybe, if a little Light has dawned, we begin to suspect there is a plan but we surely wished we could know more about "God's plan" for our lives. Just look in your back-pocket, pal. It's there. Don't blame the Old Man for the futility of life; you just haven't remembered. And anyway, God's plan is that you make a plan for your life and achieve it.

No disrespect to the Old Man but I didn't see Him in on the planning stages for this soul's upcoming life. He's more like a stay-at-home sponsor, only occasionally checking in on the "game" in progress. He may own the team, but He leaves it to the coach to direct the players and make it through the game to win. It's the Higher Self who is in the planning room, with his sleeves rolled up. Yes, certainly the Supreme Being will now and again ask a soul to do something extra: as long as you're down there, would you mind looking into situation X, or maybe now and then He'll send a brief text message *Hello!* right into your brain.

The point here is that nearly everyone forgets this planning. It's the Lethe thing again, that obnoxious draught of forgetfulness everybody has to drink. You incarnate and remember nothing. The Supreme Being now agrees this provision was unproductive and has to be changed. This was why Merlin brought us into this planning sphere. We would see what form that change would take. The world would start seeing a lot of remembering suddenly taking place in people.

As to what was happening before us, first, the Higher Self swelled its form into a blazing sphere of Light. This Light filled the planning sphere and made what I would describe as a photocopy of the completed life plan in the soul's psychic field and subtle bodies and for what passed as his mind in here. I suppose I should call it his proto-mind, because obviously his physical brain, etheric and astral bodies had not yet been created, and they usually carried this kind of information. But the plans were printed into a deep layer of this soul.

Second, when the Higher Self gradually dimmed down this searing Light I saw that the imprint of the life plan did not fade, but remained vivid in the man. It was as central to his configuration as bones are to a human. The Higher Self showed the man certain key moments in his life, at least 50, when this imprinted life plan would light up and reveal its details to him—that guaranteed him 50 epiphanies of his own essence—though I saw also that there never would be a time when he could not see the plan at anytime during the day or night, that it would always be partially lit, and he only had to focus a small amount of meditative attention on it to find it and read out its wonderful, surprising facts.

This meant that he would go through his life with the certain knowledge that he had a life plan, and therefore his life was inherently meaningful and filled with rich purpose, and that he could, with just a minimum of concentration, see that plan, and, better, that there would be nodes on his incarnation timeline when that plan lit up brilliantly like a sunrise in a cloudless sky and he'd see the full scope of it. At crucial life moments the lights would dim, like in a theater just before the performance, so he could make a choice in free will, not influenced by knowledge of the desired outcome and so he would not "screw up" the outcome by knowing too much in advance or anticipating too much or being too clever.

The bulk of the life plan knowledge would come after the decision as a briefing and validation. You have to make choices in conditions of seeming ignorance so that the karmic or initiation advancement is real; it has to have the semblance of a genuine test, it can't feel pre-determined, but this crucial moment of decision would be book-ended by this retrieved knowledge of his intentions.

Watching this demonstration enabled me to retrieve the same type of soul knowledge in myself. I remembered making carefully detailed plans before undertaking this incarnation. I saw the plot lines for meeting Philomena, getting my Ph.D., teaching at Dartmouth, editing Blaise's wacky desert journals about angels, wormholes, and Pleiadians, having my head excavated and turned inside out, running out the door, myself now infected with that same gleeful angelic wackiness, the years of improbable, fantastic travel and disclosure with the peripatetic Blaise, the forming of this Green Knight expedition, what we've seen.

I saw the meetings in some *Bardo* planning sphere with the other six members of this group, Merlin looking in now and then, and even the Green Knight himself was a party to these plans because our expedition would affect his operations. I saw past this three-month sojourn in the *Bardo* to the years ahead and further adventures with Blaise who seemed like he'd live for many decades more. I didn't know what biological schedule he was living on now. Maybe he was on some kind of time-share plan with multiple bodies he'd stashed around the place, on Earth, the Pleiades, and God-knows where else.

It's tricky. I can hear my former Dartmouth colleagues muttering about predestination and fatalism, that everything is so planned, we're just all robots. No, it's far more subtle than that. That moment, when I finished editing Blaise's notebooks and I wondered, or perhaps realized, that what he said might be true, I did not have to run out the front door of my house and life. I was not compelled to. I could have remained there and resisted the tidal pull of that ocean. But I knew I wanted to. It was my knowledge of the truth of my desire, that I *wanted* to dash out the door and follow the numinous thread of this unfolding adventure.

I had scripted that turning-point moment for me to in fact run out the door, but in every moment, no matter what the life script, we can always choose not to do it. We may regret it, we may eventually mourn the lost opportunity, but it's our choice. We may do it or not. The Supreme Being will never judge us for that. I realized also that we script numerous secondary contingency plans, so if we screw up plan A or fail to act on it or renege at the last moment, numerous other branching possibilities will emerge to give us a second chance at the desired goal. There are always other ways to climb the same mountain, though some of the alternate routes might be harder, more strenuous, or take longer.

Apparently, most of reality operates that way, with many back-up plans. Blaise told me that the angelic Blaises always had hundreds of contingency plans, especially for his missions, in case he screwed up, which he often did. They could still finesse the desired outcome based on whatever he achieved and according to Blaise they generally remained pretty good-natured about all this. Maybe, sometimes, the first route presented is not even the best one for you. The secondary, fall-back routes are better, or easier, or produce extra side benefits.

It's like the intended goal exudes a gravitational field that draws you to it, no matter what route or how circuitously or how long it takes you to get there. That gravitational field, that heavy-mass black hole, was created by yourself at this point, in this life-planning sphere with your Higher Self, as a reminder node. Remember, pal, how much you wanted to do this, so get going and do it now.

So now incarnating souls would have a better chance of remembering what they had planned. I thought how this would improve the life of many of my former Dartmouth colleagues. Many of them, possessed by that obligatory atheist-materialist intellectual's skepticism about purpose and meaning in life, that incipient, even fashionable, nihilism that seemed to come with being highly educated, would find this heightening of recall a relief, once they got pass their habitual disdain for such "new age" or Theosophical notions. They were all suffering from not knowing, despite their impressive poses and gestures. Corner them in private and I bet they'll admit they don't have a clue and life's a misery.

Privately, they are all desperate for any kind of knowledge as to why they live. This heightening of *Bardo* life-planning recall would dissolve that poseur's shell around them, and they would finally get on with understanding their existence. I know I could not have continued my life as it was if Blaise hadn't shown up. He was my equivalent of that recall; he gave me an unforgettable taste of that recall, stripped the intellectual nonsense off my psyche, got me started on my current odyssey towards my own Golden Fleece then Ithaka, my true home.

"The Tibetan text makes it sound like the worst thing that can happen to you is to be sucked into another goddam womb-door," said Blaise. "I disagree. With these upgrades to the life-planning and recall phase of the *Bardo* journey, there will be more people entering the human stream with the possibility of remembering their *Bardo* experiences and their plans, what the text calls 'recognizing,' and we will eventually reconstruct a human world enriched by genuine memory of extra-bodily activities and populated with people with a greater sense of continuity of consciousness across the dimensions and bodies.

"To me, that sounds better than just having a bunch of clever, well-informed advanced souls escaping the womb-doors and fleeing upwards to safety in *Devachan*. Recognizing the *Bardo* in everyday incarnated life is surely just as important, and having strong souls able to bridge both poles of the human phylogeny Light temple, with its life and afterlife chambers, improves reality. I used to encourage people to take back the Light grid. Now I say hold the grid. Maintain both aspects of the phylogeny Light grid in your consciousness."

Unexpectedly, I had a sudden glimpse of what that would look like. It reminded me of that unforgettable scene at the end of the *Bhagavad-Gita* where Krishna opens his mouth and reveals his true identity as the Maw of Time, with untold millions of humans, already dead even while alive, tumbling inside it. The humans I saw might be dead, in an ultimate sense, but I saw them as alive, and keenly so, possessed by this upwelling of soul knowledge and *Bardo* recall.

They were anchored into their own soul's timeline and they had reached bedrock. They knew the continuity of consciousness, intention, and soul frequency throughout all their lives; they had the same knowledge of that continuity as their Higher Self. They were in fact more on an equal footing with that Angel. If this were a poker game, they'd called the Old Man's bluff, and He laid down His face cards and the joke is they were all pictures of yourself, a photo album of you, spread out triumphantly before you in a royal flush.

Everywhere you looked you knew people had remembered themselves. They were able to transit back and forth from Buddha Mind to personality mind; it was no harder than going through revolving doors, into emptiness, back into form. Everyone was a Buddhist! They were standing on the bedrock of their soul.

It sounds a little histrionic or precious, I admit, but the quality of their presence, the feeling you got being around these people, and there were so many, of being awake, of knowing how they got here, where they had travelled from, what their plans were, was more than refreshing. From the vantage point of my life to date, it was astounding, terrifically inspiring, and deeply relaxing. An end to suffering. I always thought if I at least knew why something was happening, even bad things, it would make enduring the difficulty bearable, even easier, and go faster, like only 15 minutes more of turbulence at 39,000 feet.

I pictured 50,000 humans seated in a baseball stadium. They weren't there principally for the ball game though. In every face you could see the recognizing. You could see the possibilities of full and final liberation in their faces as they understood that their present conditions were the product of their karmic accretions and obscurities and that they had the potential to recognize this, see through it, and thereby dissolve it by rendering its inherent emptiness visible.

They were no longer wandering downwards into ever darker, more bewildering zones of the *Bardo*. They recognized who created their present *Bardo* conditions (themselves), and they recognized they could undo all their karmic knots, that being alive or disincarnate had little bearing on the recognizing of their karma, and that liberation was always available, at their finger-tips in every moment, and that taking responsibility for their consciousness was not only a good idea, but a highly recommended one, recommended in fact by the highest authority, and even better, that doing this was not so difficult and the benefits were terrific, far outweighing any initial skittishness about the undertaking.

I saw something else that surprised me. No matter what we seven did after our expedition was finished, no matter where we were in the world, or whether we were among the quick or those in the *Bardo*, we would always be manifesting this Sword of the Elohim when it was needed to illuminate souls. I think that means a part of our attention would always be on hand, set aside in reserve, for immediate response to people asking for this illumination.

Our deployment of the sword these times in the *Bardo* on this expedition had made our participation in the sword permanent, presumably straddling our future lives. In our new careers as part-time *Bardo* docents we need never worry about lay-offs, faculty cut-backs, downsizing, and the rest of that. These posts were permanent. We had job security. The Old Man sure is a great boss.

"What would nail down this recall for most people would be to remember the interview, the first sit-down chat with the Old Boy about conditions and prospects," said Blaise, with a mischievous look emphasizing his point. "There you are, in the *Guf* waiting room of souls, like a big hamper next to the Throne, and the Old Boy calls you in for your interview. More of a chat, very informal. He prefers the casual, relaxed style, unless you're an Old Testament prophet or somebody like Lilith and Pandora and really screw things up, then He lets the roar out of the box. Then he acts like the megaphoned crabby Ancient of Days.

"But quite gently, even with some Self-effacement, He says He's interested in knowing what you have in mind for your foray into the human phylogeny, and, perhaps, for embodiment at all, in any sentient life-form, if you don't mind My asking. You are a newly configured soul with zero miles on the karma odometer; the tires are factory fresh, the tread ready to rip up the road, and here you are, a pristine generic form equipped for the individuation odyssey, your only distinguishing mark, your pedigree or birthmark, being where you originally hung on the Tree of Souls, your starting-out frequency neighborhood.

"My point is if you can remember this formidable moment in your biography, it could make all the difference in what happens afterwards. It is bedrock. This is where you stated your intention, sketched your plans, made the presentation to the Sponsor-in-Chief for why you should be allowed to incarnate. I don't have the impression it is so much a matter of privilege, like getting accepted at a posh Ivy League college, or, if you're British, on the cushy track of Eton to Oxford, but more a matter of recognizing this is the moment when you knew what you wanted, planned the multi-lifetime safari through the Lower Worlds, and when you agreed to the rules of the body game, known as karma.

"Let's say in addition to this we recommend souls spend more time outside their fetal forms during the nine months of gestation. There is no need, really, to be inside the fetus the whole nine months. For one thing, you become susceptible to the gravity-dense persuasions of the flesh and the approaching physical plane. The slower, heavier energies of both start to insinuate themselves into your awareness. This will tend to cloud your lucidity. Why not delay this?

"For another, it's like you have contracted with builders to construct a house for you. You visit the building site regularly, but you don't have to live in the house as it's being built, and in fact you couldn't. It's not ready for habitation. Instead, why not better use this time to strengthen your immersion in the briefing materials, the life-plan, the timing and tactics you've worked out with your Higher Self, and refreshing yourself in the particulars of your *Bardo* transit, just completed. Let your mother take care of the construction details. Mothers are good at that. No need to sit there, minute by minute, as the house frame goes up.

"Study the documents so you will remember the details when you incarnate and need this recall. Remembering these parts, with a fifty-percent reduction in the potency of the River Lethe draught and a lucid recall of your interview with the Supreme Being, you pass through the womb-door equipped with recall of all the pertinent details and your soul's backstory and the record of your recent *Bardo* transit and its progress, all of which you need to stay awake."

"I will point out," said Merlin, "that remembering this crucial interview is optional. It is like an open door in the psyche; you may walk through it or not. As a memory, it will be easily accessible, yet it will not intrude into a soul's awareness if they do not want it or do not feel ready for its revelations. For some, it could prove too much and perhaps some need time to prepare themselves. Religion has taught many people to fear God, so recollection of a cordial sit-down meeting with God may seem at first too unbelievable. Sometimes entire Soul Groups have this interview with the Big Chief, like a big staff briefing."

Merlin said that with a showman's flourish, setting us up, it turned out, to remember when we in fact did have a friendly chat with the Big Sponsor Of It All. It was the seven of us plus perhaps another hundred. I didn't count the personnel but it felt like a complete group. I say that because the group felt coherent, no parts missing, like a choir in which every voice is accounted for.

We stood in a large golden chamber. Everything was gold; it was unbelievably opulent, although that is a material world term. This had nothing to do with riches. It was a statement of the vibration. Golden flames rippled up golden pillars, and rivers of fire flowed sideways across the temple floor underneath and to an extent in front of a massive golden throne. It was a golden room completely aflame with gold fire. You needed sunglasses to stay in here.

I remember reading something by Carl Jung that he could only claim to have experienced God-images, that he would never assert he had *seen* God. That seems like a sensible way to proceed here. Let's say we had a God-image of the Chief as being *like* a huge white head, like a cranium made of purest white marble, gazing at us with an infinity of eyes so that we were seen from all possible angles and directions, yet it felt like a friendly gaze, however multiplied. Around this white head flashed numerous images of a complex Light form. It looked like five different versions of the same shape, one nested within the next, like *matryoshka* dolls. These forms looked spherical and were filled with lights.

They also gave the impression of watchfulness, as if these globular forms were observing us and the rest of universal reality, that they were hyper-sentient. Probably, given where we were, all aspects of these five forms were flashed at once, but it seemed to me I saw them in a linear progression, like a series of lights, flashed one at a time, each one revealing a complex image.

I realized the Supreme Being was showing us something, or maybe this disclosure, this picture-show in higher dimensions, was an inevitable aspect of His Presence. Within this nest of the five flashing figures each with its many lights was another form, somewhat similar in shape, but with differences. It was embedded fetally within this nest of the five, and the Earth seemed fetally embedded inside it. It too had innumerable lights in it, and I realized these were Earth Light temples. They numbered in the millions. I am not exaggerating.

I turned to Blaise. He usually knew what was going on, what we were seeing. He didn't let us down this time. He gave us the explanation.

"The nest of five similar forms is the manifestation of the five Adam Qadmons. The Qabalists spoke truly when they discussed these arcane forms. There are four Adam Qadmons, one for each of the Four Worlds, but there is a fifth, a hyper-arcane form. This is the residence of the Messiah who lives in a palace accompanied by the Bird of Paradise who built it. The palace is called the Bird's Nest. There he awaits the go-ahead from the Supreme Being to descend to Earth to start the redemption or *Tikkun-olam*, the renovation of the world, or, as many Qabalists prefer, to validate and certify the redemption already accomplished by the living people.

"The classical Hasids ardently awaited this moment. They spoke often of keening their ears to hear the sound of the Messiah's approaching footsteps, and they keep petitioning God to make it happen soon. Think of the Adam Qadmon as the cosmogony expressed as a self-aware sphere, filled with the contents of the four Trees of Life and their 40 *Sefirot* and angels.

"The second form lying like a fetus inside this nest of five is Earth's Adam Qadmon, known to us as Albion but having many other names as well. It's a picture, a map, a precise anatomical presentation, of the human phylogeny. This is where we go when we choose to incarnate as humans on the planet Earth. It's our *samsara* theater, our daytime *Bardo* landscape, our karma-accretion park.

"This complex series of forms continuously flashes before us during our interview with the Supreme Being as a reminder and as a mission briefing, and also because, as the rabbis love pointing out, the Supreme Being is always trying to reveal Himself, to take the mystery out of what will seem an impenetrable Mystery. All of reality, they say, is a sequential disclosure of His true nature for our benefit. For us, the disclosure is mission-specific: Albion and phylogeny."

"I *get* it," said Edward with enthusiasm. "The Supreme Being was briefing us for our long-term assignment as a Soul Group. Work on these nests of Light."

"They are grids for consciousness, geometrical forms to hold and even grow awareness," said Tommy. "We work on them day and night, which means when we're alive and when we're in the *Bardo*, for both places have these grids."

"It was like He was showing us these maps and saying, Remember these," said Edward. "This is where you as a group will be working for some time. This is the master context in which we will be working, the prototype for all the secondary Light grids we will design and supervise across the galaxy. It's like we were spies preparing to infiltrate a country in wartime by parachuting in at night. Our commander shows us the topographical maps, we study them, then jump. We must remember the layout of the land when we're on the ground."

"That's it," said Blaise. "The great war against the *skandahs* in *samsara*. The whole universe sits on the edge of their seats, holding their breath. Will we succeed in defeating the forces of somnolence, inertia, and Druj seductions? Will we produce a wide-awake, self-aware, Christed Albion among the humans? Can everyone stay awake during the live-action movie, or will they fall asleep again?

"And, as a coda, the Chief said to me, 'Teach the Light grids, Blaise pal.'"

Anyway, when we were finished laughing, I realized that the plan was to invite every soul who enters the *Bardo* to revisit their interview with the Supreme Being, to take a refresher in their original briefing, to reset themselves in their purpose. Souls were free to decline the invitation, but the advantages of remembering this foundational briefing session seemed too strong to turn down.

By the time we're done in here, somebody will have to rewrite the *Bardo Thödol*. It will be too outmoded, like old software that barely works in the new computer. We hoped Merlin wouldn't mind. We're not Tibetans any more. I had a funny image of Merlin holding a much-thumbed edition of his book, with sticky notes sprouting out of every page and numerous annotations in red in the margins recording all the changes made to the *Bardo* for the book's next edition. He was a writer who had just got his copy-edited manuscript back for changes.

18

I was starting to feel the approach of a womb-door. I felt an itch in me. You can't enter a womb-door when you're already incarnated, so I figured we must be nearing the end of our expedition and our immersion in the *Bardo*. As I have noted a number of times, I could not tell you what time it was or the date. I could not even assess how much time had elapsed, though when we did finally leave the *Bardo* and rejoin the human and planetary time stream, I was surprised.

I suppose what gave it all away, the fact that we were winding up our expedition, was the presence of the Green Knight and his massive, universe-spanning Wheel of Life. We had met with him when we began our *Bardo* trip. It felt like we were a consortium of consultants and had just finished our fact-finding research and were about to make an oral report to the job's sponsor. The intent had been to recommend ways to update the *Bardo* to make its protocols and operational fluidity consistent with the changes made to Earth's Light grid.

At least I didn't have to quake or tremble like Gawain, who assumed it was his turn to have his head chopped off by the green guy with the gigantic axe. We had already been decapitated, in a sense, having entered the *Bardo* with only our heads, the rest of our body, our material life and perceptions, left at the front door and, we hoped, waiting for us, a gang of loose heads, when we returned.

The Green Knight, Lord Yama, held the *Bhavachakra* like a massive shield. He leered over this shield, looking fierce and terrifying, but I knew it was just an act, one intended to inspire souls entering the *Bardo* to stay lucid, to not be lured into believing their own mental projections and fear-ridden hallucinations. He wouldn't get us on that fierce glare. I saw the Six Worlds in great detail, largely because I recognized them now, having visited each. I felt I knew the places. I practiced imitating Yama's glare, his fierce, eyebrow-elevating, fiery scowl. I felt like a kid making scary (more likely, silly) faces in front of a mirror.

Yama, not impressed with my simulations, was spinning the great wheel like he was a game-show host for the Wheel of Fortune in a state lottery. I think he was enjoying his job, liking the drama. He struck a blasé pose, almost cocky; he spun the wheel on his fingertips like it was a Frisbee. The gesture was both grand and daunting, maybe even a little antic, because that was the entire *Bardo* he was spinning flippantly on his fingertips, with all its worlds and residents, wandering in their own *samsara*. He'd just added another hallucination to the place without even sending a memo down informing all wandering souls.

He wasn't alone in this gesture of existential cockiness. The Druj stood behind him. Yes, his massive formed dwarfed her to an extent, but she was a strong dark presence, like an obsidian statue with innumerable arms, like Kali. Out of these many hands extruded black tendrils, like creeping vines that infiltrated the *Bhavachakra* throughout its form. These dark tendrils grew into the Six Worlds and sought purchase wherever they could anchor themselves. At this they were very successful. The wheel seemed prolific with these black tendrils. At every place of anchorage, every place where a tendril took root and started growing and spreading its infiltration, there was a distortion in that area.

Looking at it you felt maybe your eyes had gone out of focus, blurring the image. The Druj tendrils changed the vibration of each anchorage point, distorted its form, subtly corrupted its function and integrity, even if it was the Hell realm which nobody would ever say had a wonderful, enjoyable function. But it did have a divinely mandated purpose; it needed to operate correctly, and the Druj was now suborning that purpose to her own nefarious intentions. It was as if she was injecting the energy of lies through all of these black tendrils, like a venom that inexorably corrupted the natural integrity of every region it entered. She had inserted her tendrils into every aspect, every crevice, of the Underworld.

In many cases, I saw that she had artfully done this in layers, like a palimpsest. You would see four or five layers of lies; peel one off, there is another; think you have scraped away the falsehood and revealed the truth, and that was still a lie. The Druj as the Antichrist has metastasized her House of Lies through the *Bardo* grid and the human consciousness that wanders through it. It was clear that the Green Knight was fully aware of this infiltration and as far as he was concerned, it did not bother him at all, though he knew it was interfering with the cognitive clarity of his *Bardo* "guests" and confounding their certainty.

The Druj wanted, ideally, everyone to utterly misconstrue the *Bardo* and its complex mechanics, to misinterpret, to hallucinate out of control, to wander in total fear. She wanted them to experience the worst case scenarios of every script the Tibetan, Egyptian, and Mayan books of the dead described; she wanted them to believe they were being chased by the most horrific of evil, dark-night spirits. She wanted them to fail, to get lost, surrender to futility, to die again in the *Bardo*.

She wanted them to buy her lies wholesale, take them to be the correct version of the *Bardo* text and to realize they were screwed eternally or, perhaps better, because it was more subtle and devious, to believe they had been rescued to a divine place and they did not need to struggle for certainty or cognitive clarity any more. Get them to think they'd ascended to a desirable *Devachan* zone when they were in fact embedded in an astral prison of their own generation but not knowing it. The absolute best outcome would be to sequester them in the Hell realm and spin delusions around them that they lived in *Devachan* bliss. They would never strive to free themselves from this misery because they could not see it. They would remain stuck and not know it, immobilized and unaware.

It wasn't Yama's job to unplug the Druj tendrils. In fact, the Supreme Being had asked him not to touch them. These tendrils of the Lie must be undone individually by human *Bardo* journeyers; each soul in the *Bardo* had to unplug himself from the Druj lies. It could not be by divine fiat; it had to be done individually, one soul at a time. Each had to recognize the tendrils as fake, as manifestations of the Lie. You can't just be told something is a lie; you have to figure it out for yourself, then you will never doubt it or depend on somebody else's word. That's the only way a lasting repudiation of the Druj's interference could happen. The changes we had recommended in our expedition and which were now being executed increased the odds that many souls would achieve this.

Each soul would have to see the truth and unplug themselves from these tendrils. It was not impossible, but it would be challenging to many, for a while, until enough momentum was created by more souls doing this and the changing vibration rippling through the *Bardo* wheel from the procedural changes we made. These two factors working together would inexorably change the place.

These upgrades would cascade into the physical world, flow right through the womb-doors like refreshing incense. It would be a domino effect that rippled throughout both chambers of the phylogeny Light temple. Up until now, with all these Druj tendrils in place, people had distorted, false impressions of the *Bardo* and mostly failed their discernment challenges; then they incarnated with these dark patches, these fear zones, in their consciousness and acted as psychic pollutant vectors for cognitive clarity in the sunlit human world. They died again and further darkened the *Bardo* because they again misconstrued it and became further entangled in the Druj's insidious black tendrils.

All of the *Bardo* became a Hell realm. That was the Druj's goal. Alive people construed the Bardo as a Hell realm, and dead people experienced it as hellish. That it was a subjectively colored karma-processing theater enhanced by the Druj's manipulations escaped everyone's perception. It was a Chinese finger-trap: the more you struggle, the tighter it grabs your fingers. Our changes would reverse that terrible downward spiral, undo those Chinese thumb-cuffs; now every gesture of truth a soul makes in the *Bardo* would loosen the tendrils' grip, enhance the clarity of perception, and fortify a soul's confidence and certainty.

Meanwhile, or I should say, despite all this Druj interference, the Green Knight's *Bardo* shield looked bright and spiffed up, like it had been polished. While the Tibetans focused on the *Bhavachakra*, the Celtic seers pointed out the Chapel Green, "the chapel of mischance" and "the most evil holy place I ever entered." This was Yama's special residence within the *Bardo*. You have to figure the Gawain poet deliberately exaggerated the inverse of the Green Chapel's reality, calling it evil. It is the holiest of places, so smudge it over and describe it as the most foul of locations. That seems normative for mythological recitals.

It was a "hideous oratory," bemoaned Gawain, expecting to lose his head very soon to the Green Knight's unforgiving axe. The Green Knight had said, leaving Camalate, meet me in a year at my Green Chapel. In many respects, what happens next in the Celtic text is irrelevant to the *Bardo* transit; it seems to derail Gawain into a test of moral uprightness when sexually tempted by the Green Knight's wife. The Green Knight catches him out in a lie, not about any sex, but about reporting accurately how he passed his time. It strikes me the Celtic poet lost track of the *Bardo* journey or deliberately distracted the reader from its truth. Or maybe by that time the Green Knight was all anyone remembered of the Celtic version of the *Bardo* chronicle, just a big green guy with a bad-ass axe.

Gawain kissed his wife, so the Green Knight gives his neck two knicks then sends him on his way with a complimentary green cloak as a tourist memento. The text seems contaminated with typical prissy, uptight Christian morality. I didn't see anybody's wife nor get tempted to kiss one, except for my own wife, and that was hard because most of the time she was in her ascended Light form, and my lips would have passed through the Light.

He wasn't dead. Gawain was only visiting, and it wasn't even voluntary. He owed the Green Knight a debt, a chance to chop off his own head. Gawain was a *Bardo* tourist, like us; in effect, his head was chopped off even before he entered the Green Chapel. It had to be, just as ours were: you have to raise your consciousness fully to occupy your head, your crown chakra, to enter the *Bardo* when you're not dead to get past the tight security check on the *Cinvat* Bridge.

The Green Knight seemed to toy with Gawain, test him, prod him, put little tricks before him, little snares, like a cat would before a mouse. You would never say of Lord Yama or Hades or most of the other personifications of the chief of the Underworld that he was jovial and merry-hearted like the Green Knight was. This guy seemed more like Tom Bombadil than the Lord of Death. Well, except for the whacking big neck-chopping axe from Hell he wielded.

The more I thought about it, the more bizarre the poet's Green Knight seemed. In many respects he spanned all the nuances of the archetype of the Lord of Death. He was a terrifying giant, like Yama holding the shield of the *Bardo* worlds. He was handsome and a well-built knight, and weirdly green, indicating a supernatural character and consistent with other mythic portrayals like Osiris connoting immortality of consciousness, eternal life, and resurrection.

He was excessively hairy, possibly a visual metaphor indicating the tricky and troubling nature of human animalistic karma undressed in the *Bardo*. Finally, he was a warm, sympathetic human being, a man who is both confessor and omniscient, who judges Gawain accurately and with understanding (having been human and well-acquainted with the vagaries of the *skandahs* and *samsara*), and who at the end reveals he was tricked into this semblance by the dark magic of Morgan le Fay, the witch of the Celtic world and possibly meant to be the Druj.

What keeps this from being unacceptable as a story line is if you see it in reverse. The Lord of Death in many myths is said to have been the first human to die, so therefore the first soul to transit the newly constructed *Bardo*. Let's put aside for a moment the allegation that Morgan put a glamour over this human to turn him into the Green Knight to test Arthur's knights for courage and take it in a more streamlined form as pointing to the first human to die and transit the *Bardo*, blazing a trail for the untold billions of humans who would follow him.

The Green Knight says his real identity is Bertilak of the High Desert who was enchanted or "bewitched" into the imposing form of the Green Knight, with green cloak and huge axe thrown in, to "bewilder" Camalate. This is consistent with the mythic plot that a human *becomes* the Lord of Death. It also hints at the Druj. You don't need any dark magic perpetrated by Morgan le Fay to pull this off, but the medieval clerics and Christians were also imputing more evil actions to her. She was their favorite bad guy, the consummate malign witch of the Celtic world, whom they never could kick around enough as she was female.

I could see that animus originating in the Christian revulsion for the Feminine. Bertilak says he was tricked by Morgan. I'm not buying that. It would be a stretch, though perhaps not impossible, to construe Morgan as a Celtic personification of the Great Mother, Isis, Hine, and the others, the Silver *Binah* of the Moon with the 49 Gates out of individuation and into the Underworld, supervising the *Bardo* protocols and assigning a capable docent to run the place. The Great Mother commissions Morgan to enter the Underworld to run things. Anyway, the first human to die does not become the Lord of Death. The Lord of Death is a celestial figure appointed to understand the human process of death and to manage the operational field, or *Bardo*, where the death protocols occur.

The other self, or maybe the true, original self, of the Green Knight was given as Bertilak of the High Desert, or more properly, Bertilak de Hautdesert. You don't think of England or even France in terms of deserts. Even the moors don't look like deserts, just bleak stony landscapes with a touch of greenery.

The word "desert" is misleading. That's because apparently it originally denoted a castle or hermitage, and at least two medieval English castles had names that reflected that, both being called Beau-desert; and "desert" was "extremely" common in French place-names, Celtic scholars report. So he is Bertilak of the high hermitage-castle (i.e., desert), which is better, because it reverts to the Green Chapel as a place of entry to an Underworld residence and is consistent with the descriptions in other myths about the Underworld in their details of the chief of the Underworld's dwelling, such as the Norwegian Hel with her encircling river, fence, gates, and halls. The "high" part might refer to its frequency setting, although the English like to put "high" in front of tea also.

This gives us Hel's castle-hermitage, her *hautdesert* in the Underworld, as it was Bertilak's. He might have said, "Hi, I am Bertilak of the high-frequency hermitage, the Green Chapel" instead of this nonsense about a high desert. In fact, even though I'm a scholar and expect this kind of obfuscation, it would have simplified the matter a great deal if they'd just called the place a high hermitage.

Yama has his wheel and the Green Knight has his axe. The axe is formidable, but all it says is if you wish to enter the *Bardo* while alive you must raise your consciousness exclusively to your crown chakra, i.e., your head, and if you want to make sense of the bewildering *Bardo* when you're dead you must do the same because the *Cinvat* Bridge that leads into this realm is *above* the head. You must move all your cognitive force into your head chakras, which is

the same as chopping the head from the body because only the head is allowed in. He escorts your severed head on its higher dimensional tour of the *Bardo*. For our expedition, Yama had all our talking heads rolling around in a big wicker basket.

Then Yama shows you the cartography of the *Bardo*, the Six Worlds, the spinning wheel of *samsara*, the great game show of the dead, with prizes untold. It is a *hautdesert*, a high hermitage, because it is structured and has boundaries; it has protocols for entry and certain modes of behavior scripted for when you're in it. Its docent, Bertilak, Green Knight, Yama, understands you as a human because he once was a human, but he is also expected to be a judge who exacts karma processing, balancing of accounts, and the bizarre funhouse of your mind.

In fact, I don't think it means Bertilak or Yama actually was a living human once. It wasn't necessary. To be honest, I don't buy that part either. It could just as well mean he as a celestial spirit *knows* the human phylogeny. He has moved his consciousness into this phylogenetic mandala and is its chief presence. He is fully briefed on our phylogeny. His awareness permeates every turn and gateway of the human mandala. He has sympathetically died with humans trillions of times; he knows the moves. It's like watching the 30th rerun of your favorite movie to the extent you have memorized all the dialogue.

Bertilak is not the common enemy of mankind, as some interpret him. Yama, Hades, the Green Knight, in none of these guises is the Lord of Death our enemy. He's more like an accounts auditor, a master drill sergeant, an athletic trainer. He executes his oversight responsibility ruthlessly, with neutrality and compassion. He is in service to us, but in pursuit of a goal we had not previously recognized or understood that we were expected to achieve.

He is a perfect butt-kicker. If the Three Stooges wrote the *Bardo* script, they'd give Bertilak gigantic lead boots. I see a progression of different nuances of this same singular figure.

First we meet the Green Knight, his entire form vivid green, the color of spring when deciduous trees and bushes refoliate, a perfect symbol for the resurrection of consciousness after it drops the body, for the true condition of consciousness, that it is undying, always green, or always becoming green again. Osiris was called "King of the Living," and the Egyptians considered the dead to be blessed because they were "the Living Ones," and only their bodies had died.

The color of Osiris's complexion was green, for deciduous rebirth or the evergreen state and probably as a revealed clue to the Emerald, also green and repository of the original Light and thus immortality for consciousness. Osiris wears the *Atef* crown, similar to the White Crown of Upper Egypt, and among its many connotations, it points to the primacy of the crown chakra and the role of the severed head in the after-death state: it is raised into the Light.

Even more so, because as the *Atef* sits on top of (above) the crown chakra of the head, it denotes the transfiguration of the *Bardo*, the in-between space between crown and eighth chakra, from a zone of confusion and terror to one of imperial majesty and Light. The master of the *Bardo* is the wearer of the *Atef* crown as it represents the successful transformation of the passage from crown chakra to eighth chakra. In at least a poetical sense, the *Cinvat* Bridge transfigures to become the *Atef* crown. Osiris is the image of the human who completed that; anyone can become Osiris. That is the invitation of the *Bardo*: become an Osiris.

The Green Knight severs our head, or, more properly, we do it to ourselves, raising our awareness up to this rarefied level because it's the stepping stone to the Underworld which we discover, or perhaps already knew, is the *Upper* World. The White Crown, the *Atef* feathers, also alludes to the White Crown atop the hierophant's staff; it is the flowering staff, as folklore says, and denotes when consciousness has raised itself up to the level of *Kether*, or the Supreme Being where He emerges from the Unmanifest into the manifest realm.

Then the Green Knight, in mythic portrayal terms, shapeshifts into Yama, who is *Yamaraja* (king), *Dharmapala* (a wrathful god, protector of the Truth), and *Lokapala* (guardian of the celestial direction of the South, location of the Underworld gate and city). That is fitting because the Underworld is at the lowest tier of the great Upper World, South and downwards with respect to its celestial cartography, and North and upwards with respect to our crown chakras. Yama, the third personification of the *Bardo* lord, is not only the guardian and chief of this celestial region of the South, but he embodies it, which is why the Buddhists depict him as holding the entire *Bardo* like a shield. We could construe the *Bardo* shield, the *Bhavachakra*, as equivalent to most of his torso, straddling the body region from lower legs to chin. This is me, he says, the Underworld, the *Bardo*, the *Duat*, whatever you call it, is inside me, is part of me.

More than that, Yama, glaring menacingly over the *Bhavachakra*, is the severed head. All you see of his body, other than his feet, is his large head; his wide-awake *Heruka*-like head sits atop the Wheel of Life. I realized this image is a variant of the Green Knight carrying his own chopped-off head in his hand. Yama says, implicit in this image, this is how you manage the *Bardo*, in the head. You move your awareness into your head, meaning the sixth and seventh chakras, and survey the turbulent, conflicted Six Worlds from above them. See?

We enter the *Bardo*, any of its Six Worlds, and then he transfigures again, now becoming

Hades, king of the dead and the land of the dead, seated on a throne. Judge of the dead, director of activities in the Underworld, joined by two dogs or, more properly, as Cerberus, one dog with three heads. In the fluidic hologram of the Underworld and its symbols, the dogs are equivalent to the *Atef* crown of Osiris and the severed head of the Green Knight. All three point to the crown chakra as the point of embarkation for the *Bardo* and to the exalted regions higher up. Move upwards past the dogs, follow the *Atef* feathers vertically. These clues point to the direction we must travel: we travel up to the Upper World.

To judge the dead you have to observe them, watch all their moves and follow all their thoughts. This Hades does, because as in his Yama form he embodies the realm, it is all inside him, which is to say, his awareness permeates the realm. It isn't correct to call him the Judge of the Dead; he doesn't pass down sentences or decrees. He is the embodiment of the *judging process* which is what every soul in the *Bardo* does on their own. He is more of an unwavering mirror of immaculate clarity. All the *Bardo* is a mirror. It is more of an impartial evaluation process, in which your karma is paraded (hideously, it may seem to many), displayed, or perhaps anticly performed in a surrealistic lampoon before you. Your evaluation of your life records is the judging; you judge yourself, you observe neutrally and critically what you did, to have failed and succeeded and stalled out or avoided, done well, done poorly—to discern is to judge yourself.

Then we meet the fourth personification of the Lord of Death, Osiris. You could say his form and condition represent the goal of consciousness in the *Bardo*. He is the embodiment of the resurrected state, of spiritual regeneration, consciousness raised again to its place of permanent life, as evergreen, like a deciduous tree that will never drop its leaves again

and always remain green. You have returned to that undying portion of consciousness God first gave you. You have left the human phylogeny, graduated the *Bhavachakra*, returned to the evergreen state your soul enjoyed before it made the first entry into human form.

Osiris is, by formal title, the Judge of the Dead, but his activities are better alluded to by his other epithets (at least 40 are known): Lord of Love; He Who Is Permanently Benign and Youthful; Master of Eternity; First of the Westerners (the direction of the Underworld, or *Duat*); the One That Remains Perfect; the God Never Dead; the Great Inert (meaning he doesn't change anymore, has reached a final condition); and the One Who Governs *Ro-Setau*. What's *Ro-Setau*?

This last epithet presents us a valuable clue to another aspect of the *Duat*. *Ro-Setau*, also written as *Restau* or *Rostau* (in English translations, it's often put in its shortened form), was for ancient Egyptians the recondite place of openings and the entrance to winding passages or tomb portals, a zone of secrets and hidden things in the *Duat*. It was presided over by the hawk-headed god Sokar on behalf of Osiris who created it.

The vagueness of the Egyptian description of *Restau* suggests higher knowledge attained through Osiris, that there are benefits to completing the *Bardo* passage and entering the Osiris condition. *Restau's* occulted state also suggests a detailed map of the *Duat*. *Restau* was a place of many paths leading out from the initial tomb a body was put into; it was a gate between the worlds, almost a kind of large urban train station through which ceremonially moved the sledge of Sokar its regent. Its complexity of branching paths usually required Anubis to act as reliable guide for the soul, which is why he was known as Opener of the Ways. Anubis-Merlin knows his way through the *Restau* labyrinth.

The paths leading out of *Restau* were not necessarily already open to the soul, and a certain numinous quality hovered about "the holy way of passage of *Restau*," as one initiatory text stated. Another said, "I have seen the Hidden One or mystery" inside Sokar's realm, and another alluded to "the road of secret things in *Restau*." *Restau* sounds like a side-door into *Devachan*, access to whose mysteries and revelations is the benefit of a soul's succesful *Duat* passage, part of the desirability of the "coming forth into Day" which the Egyptian text directs. So Osiris is less of a judge of the deceased as a role model for the soul's next transfiguration and the pre-eminent god of the Day-Light world. He also has a few things up his sleeves of interest to the traveler seeking post-*Duat* adventures.

The Underworld or *Duat* is represented in these four linked Lord of Death personifications. The portrayals straddle different cultures, but if you line them up as if in a museum gallery (or a police line-up), you start to appreciate how they represent functional stages in a procession from death to *Devachan* to the immortal Field of Reeds. You see the Lord of Death, the master of the Underworld, at his different stages of lawful function. Each culture seems to emphasize a different aspect, but not all of them. Yet here they all are now. You have to combine the guises drawn from many cultures to get the composite.

There is an alpha and omega aspect to these guises, for in our coming forth into Day with Osiris we return to the undying, regenerative green we first encountered with the Green Knight. That was the lure; now Osiris is the pay-off. Forget the big axe; focus instead on the intense greenness of the Green Knight. It is like an overture to the four-stage opera of our *Bardo* passage to the ultimate green of Osiris, Lord of the Living Ones and the green god who is never dead.

In these four figures of the Lord of the Dead we see encapsulated our *Bardo* trip. Your journey through the *Bardo* or *Duat* is overseen by the Green Knight, and in fact I see now the soul's journey is undertaken *through* his Light-temple form. He is not only the Lord of Death and director of the *Bardo*, but its full embodiment, like Yama holding the *Bhavachakra* over his torso. The soul's afterlife Underworld journey is an expedition *into* the Green Knight.

So there he was, right now before us, toweringly, as Green Knight, Yama, Hades, and Osiris, bearing the *Bardo* and all the hours and stations of the Day, the *Duat* within his great Light form. Merlin indicated telepathically we should generate the sword again and impart some of the Elohim Light to the spectrum of his presence. Give the Green Knight a taste of the keen blade of the Elohim.

The Elohim's sword was equal to the stature of the Green Knight, and the brilliance of the upright sword now equaled the towering death-god before us, blazing in a green inferno, all his "leaves" and raiment afire in big green flames. At first it seemed the flat broad side of our blade faced the Green Knight, but now the sword rotated so that its sheer cutting edge touched the blazing green form. I stress that this was not an aggressive or offensive gesture by any means. I suppose it came more under the rubric of cauterizing, clarifying, and energizing.

I couldn't say we or any of us individually were *doing* this, but the sword slowly and steadily moved into the Light form of the Green Knight and his world until it blazed like an adamant tower of fierce angel Light inside the *Bardo*. Here was another nuance, I thought with a chuckle, of the coming forth into Day. The sword itself brings forth the Day of illumination into the complex *Duat*. All of the realms, stations, hours, the gateways, the labyrinthine folds and tricky, winding passageways, the spirits who occupy these many zones, were in this Light. It was as if the Sun had come up in the morning but it was *on* the Earth. Not on the horizon 93 million miles away, but right there, searing in front of us.

Can you imagine how bright that would be? Forget for a moment the physical fact that its radical proximity to physical matter would incinerate the planet. Life went on as usual in the Six Worlds and in the winding passages of *Restau*, and its occupants were not alarmed by this sudden incursion of terrific angel Light. The intent was not to interrupt anything, but the realms were now fully lit up, and this illumination carried through into the karma-processing activities of all. It imparted clarity, heightened self-awareness, and confidence.

Throughout this hyper-illuminated realm I saw the four faces of the Lord of Death, from the Green Knight to Osiris, as if they were hanging curtains of Light. For a few moments, as we bore upon the *Bardo* with our terrific Elohim sword of Light, all the souls inside this realm were coming forth by Day, walking in the Day, this metaphor for a consciousness-lit realm of karma-recognition.

The *Bardo* is a strange place. I've known this throughout our expedition, but it came to me now with added emphasis and clarity. It is a realm both intricately structured and subjectively colored by billions of individual souls. Clearly, there is generic structure, original infrastructure in the form of passages, gateways, guardians, levels, side-doors, epistemological "sand-traps," and spirits commissioned to reveal their innate physiological role in the mechanics of consciousness, but upon this original generic structure is a thick accretion of human projections, subjective filterings, misperceptions, and distorted images.

It was like a large Victorian house in which generations of residents had left complete auric imprints of the contents of their subconscious on the walls and fixtures. Whoever lived in that house lived embedded in this auric printout. I could look at this original pure structure level of the *Bardo* or its filtered level. The first was real, and would remain real, while the second was transient, and in fact, was starting to flake off, dissolve, ooze away from the design pattern under the influence of our torch-like sword blazing at the center of it all.

I saw the cultural projections upon this generic template, the way the Egyptians, Mayans, Tibetans, Greeks, and other cultures had pictured the *Bardo*. It's as if each culture says, this is what it's like after we die, and it projects its culturally flavored pictures and processes, and the Druj lends her distorting hand wherever she sees an open door. Her goal to is to push the conception ever closer to a unilateral Hell realm without any other nuances and certainly without the possibility of redemption, just misery, fright, and nastiness. Keeping with my shared-house analogy, it was like the generations of occupants had heaped their clothes upon the communal couch and you could barely see the couch any more for all the layerings of old, dirty, ill-fitting, outmoded clothing. The *Bardo* couch was covered in hundreds of layers of culturally-stained pictures.

I surmised we didn't want to strip the *Bardo* of its entire image bank. Some pictures needed to be left to provide a general framework, like a suggestion box. The *Bardo* needed minimal metaphorical clothing to give souls an orientation, but I saw that our sword concentration was doing a lot of rapid and thorough housecleaning of superfluous, outmoded, or irrelevant images, the accretions of millennia of at best incomplete perceptions and half-rendered hallucinations.

The place hadn't been cleaned out in a long time. It was a trash heap. Many of the *Bardo* spirits had been on duty since the first day of business, when Yama set up shop and set them all in their places to exemplify and role-play the mechanics of consciousness. Some of these spirits were still costumed in metaphorical raiment that you'd have to be a classical Egyptian or Buddhism-immersed Tibetan to understand. What is a modern-day American going to make of a female demonic *Ammit* Soul-Eater, comprising elements of a lion, crocodile, and hippopotamus, or of a Wrathful *Heruka*, embodying indivisible bliss and emptiness but looking like it just escaped from a carnival freak show or perhaps a horror story by H. P. Lovecraft? Who today will understand these?

I saw the Elohim sword slicing through each of the Six Worlds. I don't mean it in the sense of cutting through a vegetable, say, a cucumber, but I wish to evoke the sharpness and lucidity of its Light as it clarified each World. Let's say you have a rowdy classroom of second-graders. Then the teacher, or, better, the principal, steps into the room and stands there. The kids calm down, straighten up, grow quiet, and put their attention on the master who hasn't even said anything. He embodies the reality principle, and his calm stillness and authority reground the children in their purpose, to pay attention and learn something.

The sword worked like that. It sliced away innumerable pestering spirits who had been milling about looking for fresh opportunities to commit existential mischief against souls who were barely coping with the fact they were dead and lost in the *Bardo*. Others of these hosts of inimical spirits were on special missions for the Druj. All of them were now turned back, dispersed, even dissolved, by the sword's searing Light, their assignments cancelled. It was clarifying all of reality between the Green Knight and Osiris, the *Bardo* landscape from the Underworld portals in the Earth's geomantic landscape to the womb-doors, *Restau* labyrinths, *Devachan* escalators to the ultimate, the Field of Reeds.

The lighting up of the *Bardo* was having effects on the physical world. I saw that for many humans lining up to die the afterdeath realm was suddenly highlighted. For those who had disbelieved in its existence, it was now revealed as unquestioningly real, and for those who had some degree of "faith" their confidence was now rewarded with a brilliant perception of its landscape. Some humans were even getting the picture of the linkage between human life and *Bardo*, that material life and spiritual afterlife were two divisions of the same magnificent Light temple, the twofold phylogenetic Light temple for incarnating and disincarnating, and, keenly, it was one that had been meticulously *designed*.

The designed aspect of reality—that is what advanced Western materialist culture is so starved of evidence for and what would reorganize perceptions. To see, incontrovertibly and free of religious dogma or propagandistic agendas, that as reality is irrefutably designed it speaks to a purpose and a design team, to an incipient organizing intelligence that did this, unbelievably, *for* human beings.

I confess I would not, at this point, find that a particularly shocking disclosure after what I've seen on this expedition and in the preceding years of occult travel with the human Blaise, but I could appreciate its likely world-reordering effect on people. In many respects all of modern humanity has been living in the Hell realm of the *Bardo* of everyday life on Earth, serving a life sentence without parole or mitigation of the offenses charged against them, that their life is meaningless, they are mortal meat-sacks, and consciousness is a by-product of a material brain and doesn't have a chance to survive bodily death. The Light of the Elohim sword radiating through the *Bardo* was erasing all that.

The Druj was being forcibly displaced from her positions of influence there. It was like the ocean rolling in and dissolving all the sandcastles built at its edge. I ask the reader's indulgence in my momentary flush of prolixity but it seemed as if the Supreme Being was once again sending the Deluge to purify the world. This time, not to drown any misbehaving, errant humans, but to purify the original template of the *Bardo* and to help people, alive and dead, to *see* it.

We as humans have been operating in the dark for so long about the mechanics of death and the cartography and protocols of the *Bardo* and wallowing in the cognitive mud deposited everywhere and up to our chins by the persistent Druj. She had been going all-out in the early decades of the 21st century to increase our lockdown in the Black Iron Prison of materialism and mechanized reality through a variety of techniques to deaden our consciousness.

Not only was the sword Light clarifying the Six Worlds in the *Bardo*, it was clarifying the Six Worlds as they informed the consciousness of every living human. As mentioned earlier, Buddhists remind us that in a given day we are likely to visit all Six Worlds in our own awareness and frame of self-reference. The sword was highlighting these mental states and the way our consciousness visits or sinks into each obsessively and repetitively under key triggering stimuli, or, worse, how we might have bought a holiday condominium in one of them.

The intent was not to stop this fluctuating presence but to help people become aware of its existence, to recognize these Six Worlds as mental states in them and to take psychoemotional photographs of themselves when gripped by any of them so they would know what it feels like to be mired in the *Preta* World or to be exalted in the *Deva* world, that they are all transient, ultimately illusory, states. Yes, these Worlds have value and a relative reality, but they are not definitive conditions; you should not depend on them for absolute definitions of yourself. You watch them for a while as their drama plays before you on the TV; then the show is over, you turn off the television, and sit quietly in your chair. You are no longer distracted, entertained, or disturbed by these shows; you are yourself again, just as you were before you switched on the television to watch.

Then I had a funny image. It was amusing and vaguely upsetting. I saw all of humanity, everyone, as comprising a single severed head gripped by the Green Knight. He held it triumphantly like someone who had just caught a gopher who had been ruining somebody's flower garden. It was the head of the archetypal human yet it was the head of all the billions who ever were humans.

It was if the brain was pre-divided into six zones, each one of the Six Worlds, and consciousness jagged and darted among the divisions like a frenetic rabbit. These Six Worlds were terrifically illuminated, like a house at night with all its lights on and all the bulbs were a thousand watts each. Here was the human phylogeny as a body of fluctuating consciousness states contained within a severed head, which means consciousness with its processes and mechanics was now temporarily abstracted from its bodily context and regarded on its own. Here is your world, your cognitive framework, the Green Knight was implicitly telling humanity: it's all in here, and I have you, dear humans, by the hair roots.

I wondered if this was some kind planetary event I was witnessing, some mass concentration on a consciousness experience like the Theosophon of 2033.

"Not quite that," said Merlin. "It is more like a gesture that people may study. It will be always available for their contemplation from this point on. It is like a plateau of heightened self-awareness in which you may see all the conditions of consciousness that you have always been embedded in but without reflection or perspective. Now, if you wish, you can have both at any time. This is a picture of how we are reconciling the changes to the *Bardo* and its protocols with the upgrades to the planet's Light grid to a sixth chakra psychic condition. You can, if you wish, see the Green Knight holding your cut-off head by the hair, smiling at you as you start to take in the actual reality of the human phylogeny."

I couldn't stop laughing. It was all a joke, but such an educational one. The whole *Bardo*, the realm and its experiences, was this severed human head. Here is reality without the interference of the body, personality, and the physical world, it tells you. Have a good look around: it is reality, not the simulacrum that you are continuously fooled or befuddled by when you are reattached to your body. You die, drop your body, but take your head with you into the Underworld. You are a mobile head. This is your *Bardo* body. *You* are the Green Knight, yes, you, the human being, are Bertilak of the High Desert, carrying his own chopped-off head triumphantly, even nonchalantly, having a thorough look around as you move in the Underworld and its stations, gates, and passageways.

The trouble is you don't know this. You are sleepwalking, afraid of your own shadow, or, more precisely, the hosts of your own shadows swarming about you. But they're swarming out of a familial, welcoming loyalty: you are their creator. The severed head is the concentration of your consciousness into one place, no longer zipping frantically among the seven floors of your chakra skyscraper. You are finally separated from the biological exigencies of living in a mortal body. That's lying on the ground somewhere, headless; you are now solely in the head, and that head is transiting the Underworld, hallucinating an external *Bardo* and falling for all its semblances, illusions, and frightful glamours.

You are a magician and you are conning yourself, falling for your own tricks. When the Green Knight chopped off his own head before the astonished Grail Knights of Camalate, he was giving away the secret of the *Bardo* passage. It's like this, boys, simple as anything. Come see me and I'll show you round the place. It's as if the Green Knight has a billion arms; he can carry that many heads at once, give them all the thorough package tour of their own karmic delusions. I see a billion Green Knights carrying severed heads right now, like grinning or grimacing Halloween pumpkins carved with surprised human faces, lit within.

He's laughing, not at them, but sympathetically, at the irony of it all: this is you. He's waiting for them to get the joke, to appreciate the marvelous set-up. Here is the true condition of your awareness, a head creating and perceiving the Worlds. See? Look below the head, boys. That wheel with all its crazy antics? That's the *Bardo*, your *Bardo*. Be like me, a fierce, glaring head, consciousness overlooking, senior to the crazy circus ride of the *Bardo*. That's how you survive. Climb above the wheel, stay in the severed head, and master the demented place.

No need to be alarmed or frightened. You have been doing this all the time you were alive, but you didn't catch on to the set-up. Now, the body gone, here's the set-up. You can't miss it. Isn't it the cleverest thing you've ever seen? In the phylogeny, alive, in a body, put the head on; in the *Bardo*, dead, take it off. It's a simple gesture. You can catch on to the routine in minutes. On, off, on. See?

In the medieval tale *Sir Gawain and the Green Knight* the poet has the Green Knight poised to chop off Gawain's head but then only nicks his neck. This is metaphysically inaccurate, I can see now. The correct gesture is Gawain lopping off his own head and carrying it like a wide-awake human torch into the *Bardo*. We are meant to *copy* the Green Knight's initial gesture. He severs his own head before the Grail Knights, then holds it laughingly, not bothered at all. This is how you move through the *Bardo*, your severed, all-seeing head in your hand. The head means consciousness, your awareness, attention, the God-given Light. This consciousness moves in and out of the body realm, in and out of the *Bardo*.

The axe, "huge and monstrous, a hideous helmet-smasher," is death, the natural, inevitable process that accomplishes the head-severing feat if you wait that long. The Green Knight's invitation, his challenge, is to chop now, visit the *Bardo* now while you still technically have your head attached to your mortal body; just temporarily take your head off and bring it with you on the *Bardo* expedition. Don't wait for the hideous axe-stroke to make your visit to my realm irreversible, says the Knight of the Green Chapel. Be proactive; visit us now. As I've mentioned, our Green Knight expedition was a voluntarily visit to this place. As far as I can tell, we have conducted this tour of conditions while still alive.

Gawain chops off this Knight's head, taking up the challenge, and I think that gesture is significant, because it's him saying, despite his fear and uncertainty, I take up this initiation experience. I actively engage in its protocols. I chop the Green Knight's head off knowing ultimately I chop off my own when in a year I come to the Green Chapel. Gawain says, in effect, Okay, sign me up for the expedition, the *Bardo* initiation. Conduct my precious head upwards. I shall move my consciousness principle up into a focused point of perception. By severing my precious head, a metaphorical act, I acknowledge that my head, my consciousness, is the prime eye by which I not only see but create my reality. This is the reality machine, the reality generator, and the surveillance camera. Thank you, big fellow in green, for making me aware of this vital fact about me.

Then the Green Knight seized his own "splendid head" and lifted it up before him like he was gardener showing off his prize cabbage. He climbed upon his horse and held his severed head by its long hair in his hand, as if nothing had happened to him, as if this was a perfectly normal mode of presentation of self. The talking head then challenged the nonplussed knights to come visit him at the Green Chapel and he'd show them around. They were full of dread and doubt, but they should have been possessed of inspiration and insight because he had just tipped them the master clue to getting through the *Bardo* in one piece. If they were Tibetans, they would have seen through the Green Knight disguise to see Yama, and nodded at his familiar fierce, awful, enlightened gaze over the wheel.

If they were dead, they could navigate its tricky passages, the labyrinths of *Restau*, and make it through to *Devachan*. If they were still alive and having a vision of the Underworld, they would collect unassailable impressions of the actual conditions, origins, and processes of consciousness, invaluable knowledge, information *gold* to bring back with them and share with their fellows. It is not an undiscovered country at all, you'd tell them: here's how to work the place. The severed head was like an *avatar*, a stand-in for yourself, to survey a whole world.

"You're finally catching on, Frederick, old pal," said Blaise with a grin. "We are the men and women without heads, striding about the *Bardo* clutching our severed heads by their hair, with the exception of my hairless head so I have a nice firm grip on the ears. But we are really the men and women with heads, heads that are seeing some of the true aspects of the Underworld, our eyes open. I suppose it's more accurate to say we are an expedition of free-floating heads, our bodies left behind with their simulacra of heads, and it is the Green Knight who carries all our heads, like a string of talking, laughing, astonished balloons."

He was carrying our heads towards something. We were going up. The Green Knight seemed to be climbing up the air, rising steadily to an arcane destination at the top of the "sky," which means top of the Upper World. I knew that the *Bardo* is only a subset of the Underworld, a workshop for processing the karma of the just-dropped bodily life and making plans for one's next step, womb-door or optional schooling in *Devachan*. There is probably an unlimited number of potential destinations, since many of them are, technically, solipsistic worlds spun out of your desires for edification and using the protean basic material of this realm to create the necessary infrastructure. But where we were going seemed more substantial and real; it was nobody's solipsistic world.

It took me a while to bring the site in focus. The combination of brilliance and hyperdimensionalty made it hard to see clearly at first. It was spinning, which made it difficult to get a visual purchase on its essential shape, though I would say square or cubic. I saw a mountain with a square castle on its top. This castle was built to last, an indestructible, indomitable fortress, a stronghold. It did not look easy to get into; it looked like a single massive closed strong door.

The castle seemed to have four stout corners, almost as if each was a peak, and each of these seemed to be revolving, but perhaps it was the whole structure that was turning. I realized to say it was turning or spinning was imprecise; it was not fixed and stationary in three-dimensional terms; it was at least in 4D and that was why it seemed to be constantly turning. You couldn't see it all at once.

Music seemed to emanate from inside it, like somebody had a radio turned on. I heard singing, like a diva rendering something lovely from Puccini. But it also sounded like poetry being declaimed in the formal, proper manner, like a chant or invocation, the inspiration of the holy muses of poetry called *Awen*, and inside this revolving square castle an *awenydd* was singing. Or maybe a hundred poets were chanting their inspired speech, each one distinct. It was like we had just come upon a great house and we heard singing inside it, though we stood outside its sturdy framework, leaning against its walls to listen. If this were Wales, we had just stumbled upon the *Eisteddfod*, the great musical event.

I noticed something else about where we were. It seemed we were on top of the world. Yes, it appeared to be a mountain before us, though I assumed that was a metaphor for an exalted, rarified region in the upper part of the Upper World. It seemed that if the world were flooded, inundated with celestial Light, this realm, this four-peaked strong castle situated high above it, would remain dry, above the floodwaters, unaffected by the deluge, eternally inviolate.

We passed through the walls of the castle. The walls looked like they were made of emerald Light. They were impenetrable and translucent. You would almost say this was a glass castle, made of stout emerald shanks of pure glass. Inside was a massive cauldron. It was a version of the Holy Grail, though its shape could be variously described as a chalice, cup, or deep bowl. It was a curving, absolutely pure, receptive space. Only the purest substance could be poured into this or cooked in its depth because a cauldron can be both a serving goblet and a huge cooking pot. Its rim was dark but studded with innumerable pearls. The inside of the cauldron was effulgent. I could barely keep my eyes open. It was like entering a pulsar. You felt its regular pulsing and throbbing.

The singing came from within this Light that looked like a blazing white diamond. It was song, poetry, inspired speech, invocation, chant, evocation, summoning, everything that the voice could manifest, and it was the inspiration to do this. In fact, it was this elusive but dominant presence of inspiration itself that was key. You felt here was the creative force that could generate any word in existence. And there was a poet in there singing, birthing words endlessly. It looked like a human in a pure design sense, generic, like humanity's prototype, yet that was only a suggestion of form. It was truly a sphere filled with Lights. The scene felt like you were six and you walked into the bathroom and there was grandfather in the tub, lolling amidst bubbles, singing a merry tune to himself.

The Green Knight deposited us inside the cauldron by the singing guy. His shape was too amorphous and protean for me to give you a fixed description. It was like beholding the universe packed inside a bright sphere, and this sphere gave the impression of observing you, acutely aware of everything. It was not so literal a sentient presence as to attribute to it a face, but undeniably it exuded presence, and, as I said, it was singing or chanting poetry or magic spells.

Then the Knight indicated he wanted us to generate the sword of Elohim. I surmised this would have the likely effect of plugging the Grail into an outlet. I saw the outline of a great sword of Light and the figure of a man once holding it. Perhaps this is a regular event. Humans trained in these protocols come here now and then and apply the sword to the Grail, like charging a car's battery. The outline of the sword was like a signpost that said, Place the Light sword here.

We took our places, assembled our components, and disappeared. That's the paradox of doing the Sword of Elohim hat trick: you vanish from the scene. But you must. There is no room for you within the total field of emptiness. The Christ Light or Buddha Mind is a nondualistic condition, utterly singular. We all pass through the *skandah* grid and our individual identities are erased. That's how

you turn on the sword and run the "electrical" current through it. It is permissible to pop back in now and then to the world of name and form to see what's happening, and I did this, almost compulsively, otherwise I'd have no idea what we were doing. The Grail swelled with Light; it was thoroughly engorged with Light; and the singing intensified to perhaps a thousand voices.

It sounded like an oral presentation of *Finnegans Wake*. It was very glossalaliac. I had no idea what the voices were declaiming. It was energy shaped into sounds, like birds of paradise released in all directions at once, or a million larks taking the upper airs, but the sounds were not reducible to a single, recognizable human language. I would have to guess it was the language of Light, the way the angels communicate. If you can grin without having a face, then the singing presence in the Grail bowl was grinning. Beaming, ecstatic.

It was contagious. When I returned to myself, I noticed I felt pretty elated. This uplifted mood was spreading through the Underworld. Souls in the *Bardo* were looking up, wondering who just flipped on the massive radio to that lovely concert. The Light kept growing and spreading, the singing kept multiplying its voices. The Green Knight seemed well-pleased. He was like a reclusive genius composer who had finally got an orchestra to perform his newest little composition, just doodles, really, he was used to saying, no big deal, nothing grand (it was Wagnerian, in truth), but I like to hum it to myself during the day.

It flashed on me that if you wrote down the score you'd have a map of the world. The words to this unending song were the Logos structure of universal reality. In the beginning was the Word, and this became the innumerable, infinite words, and this word-play was emanating from this magnificent cauldron in this magic castle at the top level of the Upper World, and it was the Green Knight's.

I gradually realized we were seeing the live version of the "spoils" of *Annwn*. As I mentioned before, this is an early Welsh mystical poem, odd, truncated, and clearly adulterated by meddling Christian influences, but containing a kernel of accurate observation. It wouldn't qualify as one of the Persian visionary recitals, because the poet doesn't report what happened. He just says some people went with Arthur in his *Prydwen*, or crystal ship, to *Annwn*, then to *Caer Sidi*, the spinning stronghold castle, and beheld the cauldron, a big sword, a guy in prison, and, puzzlingly, a brindled ox, all of which they left in place, then they departed, empty-handed, but only a few of them made it back.

The word "spoils" is confusing. It makes you think of treasure, booty taken, plunder forcibly removed, goods acquired, even stolen, but nothing leaves *Annwn*. It is only enumerated, but as far as I can tell from the poem everything was left in place. It reminds me of Henry James's novel, *The Spoils of Poynton*; the story turns on who will inherit all the roomsful of *objects d'art* in the owner's valuable collection. You think of the Spoils of *Annwn* that way, as loot to take. But spoils also can mean the benefits, advantages, perquisites, and prizes, as in "the spoils of office," personal advantages somebody can gain from a position.

Still another nuance of spoils is waste material brought to the surface through an excavation, dredging, or mining operation. I suppose from the standpoint of the *Dharmakaya*, anything in *Annwn* would count as that kind of spoils. Possibly the most cogent interpretation of the vexing Welsh word *preiddeu* (usually translated as "spoils") is that the masked (obscure) language of the poem describes an initiate's inward mystical journey to find "the treasures of Heaven, hidden within," the inner spoils, put there by Heavenly agency.

You travel within, using the *Prydwen* protocols, to *find* these hidden treasures. You don't take them out with you, because how could you: that would be like pulling out your ribs or your aorta after you "found" them. No, they remain in there. Okay, our Green Knight expedition certainly counts as a journey inward, both into the interior of the world, of human reality, and into our own consciousness. We have to get used to dealing with old words that are ass-backwards as to their correct meaning, like "hautdesert" and now "spoils." If you don't get these initiation words right, you may be turned back at the gate.

Caer Sidi, the spinning magical castle, is the citadel of wisdom, the mystic's consummate spiritual destination, representing the state of enlightenment, or, in keeping with our terminology, Buddha Mind. Inside *Caer Sidi* is the cauldron of *Annwn*, but the text more precisely says "the cauldron of the Head of *Annwn*." That recirculates our understanding back to the severed head of the Green Knight, and the impression that all of the *Bardo*, the human phylogeny, is in it. You might think it denotes ownership: the cauldron belongs to *Annwn*'s boss. But I prefer the image of the white cranium of the Supreme Being, inverted and hollowed out to make a nice spa-style hot tub, we *Prydwen*-boys soaking in it.

The poet says many, perhaps thousands, travelled there with Arthur, but only seven returned. I interpret that to be the poet's way of saying this is a damned difficult thing to see and only a few are up to it so many get left behind. There's also the spinning castle part. That's both hard to see and hard to find the front door when the place keeps revolving around so rapidly in front of you. Presumably, many fail this test. It seems the same motif as the *Conference of the Birds* story where thousands journeyed to see the Simorgh and only about 30 lived, made it there in one piece, or finished the journey at all to the celestial bird.

The poem seems confusing and incomplete. Nothing was removed from *Annwn* or *Caer Sidi*; that Grail is immoveable. It belongs to the chief of *Annwn*, known to the Welsh as Arawn, our Green Knight. He *takes* you *to* this fabulous singing cauldron and displays it proudly as its owner. There is not a thought of putting it under your cloak and sneaking out of *Annwn* with it like the plunder of a thieving expedition. It would be better to call this odd poem, "That Which Is In *Annwn*," and to drop the "spoils" connotation. It's the Museum of the Spoils.

It's easy to explain the spinning castle part, as Blaise showed me. It's spinning because it requires a strong, steady, even serene, psychic focus to hold its semblance steady and fixed. It isn't spinning in itself; that is an artifact of our attempt to see it clearly. We are spinning, our psychic eyes are spinning, until we match its high-frequency state. You need to be in your sixth chakra to stop the spinning. It's spinning too because it exists in the fourth dimension and our sixth chakra struggles to negotiate a plausible and static 3D conversion image of this complex 4D shape, spinning because we see only parts of its complicated totality.

The poet says Gweir is locked inside the prison of this four-peaked stronghold, and Welsh poetic tradition says he is one of the Three Famous Prisoners. You have to invert this to understand the meaning. To say Gweir is in prison means he is anchored here; this is his official, mandated residence; this is where you find him, where he lives because he is supposed to be here. *Caer Sidi* is his sanctified, inviolate domicile; he cannot be removed or interfered with. From the standpoint of the Upper World, Gweir may be anchored here sacrificially, out of a voluntary diminishment of his sublime celestial

essence to service the world and to be available to humans, an ultimate cosmogonic Man.

Who is Gweir? Probably a Welsh picture of Albion's prototype, *Adam Qadmon*. Hinting at this identity is the allusion to the cauldron being touched by the breath of nine maidens, that their breath "kindled" the poetic effusions from the cauldron. That points to the nine *Sefirot* of the Tree of Life, the Greek version of that as the Nine Muses; both of these images imply the cauldron is bounded by, if not generated by, the nine *Sefirot* of the Tree (the nine spheres under *Kether*, the tenth and first, at the top of the Tree) and their attendant angelic presences. As Qabalists explain, the *Adam Qadmon* is the personification or product of the Tree in its fullness. In a sense the nine maidens are all the mothers of this Gweir. Gweir is not released from prison and transported by stealth of night by the *Prydwen* voyagers. He remains in place. He could not be anywhere else.

The expedition goes to *visit* him there, where God put him. Don't worry. You will likely enjoy the feeling of the place, the poets hint. *Caer Sidi* is called, among other epithets, the "Fortress of Mead-Drunkenness." That makes sense. The intoxication you feel is like Gopi madness before the divine Krishna: it's a way of connoting the bliss of the emptiness state of Christ Light, of all the senses and sense doors, the *skandah* grid, converted to the bliss of the divine radiance. That's just the bathwater; remember, the tub is the head of the Old Man Himself. So you get Son and Father, a rich blend, top of the Tree of Life, a heady essence.

The poem refers to a sword and a man who owns the sword. Lleminawc is the one whose "hand" lifts the "flashing" sword called *Lleawch*. His identity does not concern me. I think we're looking at an early expedition to the castle and the wielding of the Sword of Elohim for the tune-up benefit of the cauldron. I only saw the outline of the sword here. I wouldn't say it was the sword itself. We brought the sword in the sense that we constructed its effulgent presence here. No doubt our construction will leave a visual residue for future visitors to see, and future visitors might remark on the curious sword of the seven travelers.

As for the brindled ox, to start with, brindled means tawny with streaks, like a brown dog with streaks of white running through its fur. The ox part brings in the mythic motif of the bull and that correlation has a long résumé. Gayomart, the Persian name for the cosmogonic Human or *Adam Qadmon*, is accompanied by the primeval bull, Gavaevodata, the source of all animal life, according to the *Avesta*; both are killed later by Ahriman, our old pal, the Druj. The Welsh called *Adam Qadmon* Gweir and Gavaevodata became the brindled ox.

The bull image has a lot of mythic cachet. Zeus, Shiva, and Osiris have white bull divine forms to express the virility of the Creator. The Druids knew Britain as the Land of the White Bull, and the bull-figure *Taranis* was central to their cosmology and map of fundamental energies. In Mithraism you have the solar hero Mithra slaying the divine bull, releasing precious blood (which I interpret to mean cosmic time), and making the deity's divine bull-strength available to humans. The Irish have their White and Brown Bulls of Cuailnge, the basis of the mythic tale of a cattle raid, and featuring none other than Merlin as Cuchulainn ("the Hound of Culann"), the dog-faced prime defender of one bull.

Why is *Caer Sidi* four-sided, described as like a spinning square castle? It is an impression of the Cube of Space, otherwise known as the Emerald, the Heart within the Heart. I learned from Blaise that the Holy Grail, the Grail Castle, everything in that myth, is inside the Emerald, which is a tilted cube. When you mention a square, you imply the cube, and the image of a constantly revolving square castle invokes the fourth-dimensional complexity of this shape. Look at a live rendition of a hypercube, 4D cube, or tesseract: it consists of eight cubes that appear to be spinning because the eyes can't process the 4D image. To liken *Caer Sidi* to a Glass Fortress also points towards the Emerald, because it does seem to be a double-terminated bright green *crystal* and looks like high-purity glass.

It also suggests the sheerness of the Emerald's six symmetrical surfaces. They are sheer as glass or crystal and impossible to gain any traction upon for climbing. This is a classic test motif in mythology and even fairy tales: the hero has to scale the Glass Fortress but keeps sliding down its smooth surface. You have to know you can *walk through* these seemingly impenetrable walls of glass because in truth they are more like walls of green mist than anything solid. You don't climb it; you walk through its glassy walls. They only seem to be solid. But if you don't know this or don't know how to execute the passage through these walls, they will remain as they seem: a castle of *strong doors*, closed to you. It will remain an enigmatic, obdurate Fortress of Hardness, and you'll likely turn back.

The poet says the cauldron will not boil the food of a coward. It is to us today an odd way of saying you need spiritual courage and fortitude to make it into this place. If you cannot find this conviction and determination within, the Grail will not provide its bounty to you, the *Awen* "food" of the poetry-inspiring Christ Light. Think of this as an initiation test, an ineluctable requirement for entry. If you can't climb the ladder, you can't get into this place because there are no stairs. The *Awen* is a condition of ecstatic God-inspiration, like Pentecostal speech. The ancient Welsh of course would not have used the term "Christ," but the nuances of *Awen* seem equivalent to it. The *Awen*-infused bard is a Christed Grail Knight, and both are equipped to heal and free the Wounded Fisher King.

The courage comes into play because you received this *Awen*-infusion while in the Lightning-Struck Tower as the Christ Light sears through it like a lightning bolt. The Tarot card customarily shows people jumping out all available windows as the lightning strikes through the brick-lined tower of materiality and selfhood. That's a useful picture of the initiation process, the scourging we need to perform on ourselves. Courage comes into the picture as you realize the responsibility you now take on, to undo the Dolorous Stroke produced by the misuse of this terrifically powerful sword of Light long ago, our Elohim-Goliath sword, and probably identical with the sword of Lleminawc.

I knew we were in fact wielding the same Light sword that long ago had done in the Fisher King. He had whacked his groin from the misuse of the blade. Ouch! The Rich Fisher King became an invalid lying miserably on a couch all day. He couldn't remember a thing; he couldn't get healed; he was a complainer. The Wasteland began, his memory was ruined, and he lapsed into drear misery.

So here we were proposing to use that sword correctly and fix all that. I think the best way to get through this part is to not think about it at all, or if the matter comes up in your awareness, regard the sword part as no big deal. Try whistling or cracking jokes; that sometimes eases the tension of responsibility. And head for the voidness as soon as possible: that way you won't even know what you're doing and therefore you won't have to have any opinions about it.

As to the location of *Caer Sidi*, obviously it is in the upper reaches of the Underworld, in what we have been calling *Devachan*. It is not a *Bardo* stop, though you might be able to progress from the *Bardo* to *Caer Sidi*. Possibly an invitation from its owner, the chief of *Annwn*, is required; that's how we got here. The cauldron inside *Caer Sidi* with its sword of Light turned on made the place into a beacon of considerable Light broadcasting this effulgence throughout the Underworld and inevitably throughout the *Bardo*, which can always use more.

The Welsh poem about *Annwn* seems to be a glimpse of an expedition like ours to this recondite site to give the cauldron and sword a refurbishment and brightening. Equipment needs to be used to stay in working trim, not to mention the world is always starved for the Light and inspired poetry that comes out of here. There's never enough *Awen*; we can use more bards spuming poetry.

Even to use the word "expedition" is misleading. *Caer Sidi* is a pre-eminently holy place; the expedition or inward journey to this sanctified space is archetypal. It doesn't happen only once or twice; it is meant to be visited frequently by people. Perhaps the purpose of our expedition is to refurbish the trail that leads there. It's gotten overgrown; trees and boulders have blocked the way; people have lost the map, or, sadly, thanks to the Druj, forgotten they ever heard of *Caer Sidi* at all.

"So if you survive the head-chopping fright, you can soak in the singing cauldron, have an ecstatic tub with free poetry recitals," said Blaise, picking up on my thoughts. "It is a Welsh picture of the Grail Castle. Gweir is a kind of floating, fluidic figure, with elements of the *Adam Qadmon* and his reflection as Earth's Albion, but also of the Rich Fisher King, rich in awakened memory of the timeline and the kind of blissful utterances that richness of knowledge leads to. You undo the Dolorous Stroke, heal the Wasteland, and the Fisher King erupts into mellifluous if not prolix, glossalaliac, mead-drunken song, singing his divine heart out from his celestial, maiden-kindled bathtub at the heart of the world. I don't know, let's say it's Walt Whitman, Allen Ginsberg, and Tom Bombadil rolled into one crazy-happy tub-singing poet singing his heart out to all *Annwn*.

"Blaise said once that the original of the Grail Castle is in another galaxy, or possibly universe. They implied it was rare, if not unique, located far away, and what we find on Earth as Grail Castles are holographic copies. The Irish said the cauldron *came* from a special place called Murias, and it resided in a Magical City supervised by the Dagda, the Tuatha de Danann's chief deity. It was one of Four Treasures they brought *to* Ireland from afar. That again suggests the originals or their place of origin is elsewhere, but it's not the Earth.

"The Tibetans, incidentally, offer an identical story, only with the names changed: primordial deities on the order or stature of the Persian *Amesha-Spentas* brought four treasures from a recondite place and deposited them in the Tibetan landscape and consciousness for humans to access one day when they're ready. These treasures, in either the Irish or Tibetan tradition, are elemental talismans, a sword, spear, cauldron, and stone, each epitomizing the quality of an element. The sword is air; the spear fire; the cauldron water, the stone stands for earth.

"Nobody ever walked away from the Dagda's cauldron unsatisfied. It fulfilled everyone's personal wish. Whatever you desired to eat or drink, the cauldron instantly provided, like the original of *Star-Trek*'s Replicator, and you could certainly ask for more than Tea, Earl Grey. It's as if it has the *prima materia* itself to work upon as the basic fecund substance for your desires. The Christ Light, the bliss of the Buddha Mind, is the answer to all questions, to all hungers of the spirit, to all desires to understand your reality. It is the flesh of the inexhaustible boar, endless substance. You need to be gutsy, bold, audacious, and stand up for your individuation; it won't boil tea-water of the pusillanimous.

"What this really says, though, is the prime question you have, the vexing aspect of divine reality you don't quite get, will be explained in full here. Everyone has a singular question, one that for a life rivets them with its mystery. Who runs the world? How does a Light grid structure physical reality? What are the archetypal stages of initiation? Here you get the answer, plus the footnotes.

"The Grail Castles are always situated above the landscape, above the holy mountain, which denotes the high-frequency at which they operate and the precision of clairvoyance required to enter them and stop their spinning, which is, as you know, yours. Formerly, it was exceedingly difficult for humans to get into *Caer Sidi*, but in our time, it has become easier, though it still requires a lot of psychic preparation. It is a clairvoyant reality requiring dependable clairvoyance. Where I'm headed with all this is I suspect *Caer Sidi* is a notch above even the Grail Castles, that it is perhaps the original or antecedent to the Grail Castles, and that it is also the mother of the four different Magical Cities the Irish talk about.

"Once you are inside the copy of *Caer Sidi*, you may potentially anchor yourself in the original. Possibly that is what the Green Knight facilitated for us today. He took us to the original, unique expression of the site. Possibly, the cauldron, a water and consciousness symbol, is the quintessence of the Four Treasures, subsuming them all in its primacy of consciousness. You have the earth element, or stone, in the stronghold itself; the sword gives you air; the poetic inspiration of *Awen* is the flaring up of the holy fire element, or spear."

I mentioned that it felt like we were uncannily at the top of the world. There was definitely a sense of extreme elevation to the location of *Caer Sidi*. It does not spin once you are inside it. That was good, because its spinning was making me dizzy before. I came back to the probable location of this stronghold.

It is not in the *Bardo*; that is clear. I was seeing now that the *Bardo* is like a dressing room in a large theater. You may change your costume for your performance in the next play or you may exit the theater, retire as an actor or at least take a break from it and visit the city it is embedded within, the astral sea. *Devachan* is a name for a high-end zone within this vast concatenation of Light, and *Caer Sidi*, I surmise, is a high-end locale within *Devachan*, hence the height. Or, possibly, like the image of the Boat of the Vedas, a version of the Grail Castle, is lies *above* the astral sea, thus above *Devachan* and the delightful *Sambhogakaya*.

If the *Sambhogakaya*, the Buddha realm in the middle, the zone of the gods' delight and bliss, is a vast circus tent, *Caer Sidi* is a revolving castle of Light at its peak. It lies right at the transition zone of this realm of astral appearances and the formless realm called *Dharmakaya*, and when you are sated with what you desire from the cauldron that satisfies everyone's wishes, you enter this exalted zone. You enter formless and without marked selfhood, but in fully dilated awareness.

The efficient design of this system is that when you make this upward transition, you bring Gweir with you, our dear Albion, now wide-awake, eyes blazing, his cosmos-body engorged with Light and the blissful emptiness of Buddha Mind, and he starts to understand who he is and why and how and by whom all this was made possible, as his form dissolves in the formless realm. In one sense, Gweir does not leave *Caer Sidi*, but in another sense he does by way of your identification with him. You realize your larger form-body is this Gweir. Each human is a miniature, walking, espresso-drinking Albion or *Adam Qadmon*.

Afterwards, Blaise showed me another nuance to *Caer Sidi*. It is the residence or playing field of the *Hayyoth ha-Qodesh*, the Holy Creatures, Living Creatures, or Holy Beasts. None of them are flattering translations. This is the first created angelic order, the one God created just before He made the Ofanim, our pals, the Blaises. These are the enigmatic, camera-shy arcane angels who present themselves as having four heads on one body: a lion, eagle, human or angel, and a bull. These are meant to denote the four elements. These four-headed angels poke their quadruple heads between the turning wheel spokes of the great flaming wheel of the Ofanim, the composite image of which Ezekiel saw by the River Chebar. That wheel turns the *Merkabah*, or God's Chariot. The Ofanim, Blaise told me, are the means by which the Supreme Being is mobile throughout the Creation, the way that His reality moves through all the worlds.

"The Holy Beasts personify the abstract, original essence of the four elements, what Hindu metaphysicians call the *tattvas*, the four primordial conditions of universal consciousness or *prima materia*—the first shaping of this. *Caer Sidi*'s four strong doors represent the four elements, and the interior, the mead of drunkenness, and epiphanies of *Annwn* within, represent *Akasha*, ether, as in the etheric realm, the etheric body, the life-force container. That is the fifth element, the substrate that births earth, air, fire, and water.

"In fact, with the all-star cast of the spoils of *Annwn* you have a reprise of these Four Beasts and the four elements they signify. Think about it: the cauldron or Grail is water; the sword is air; the brindled ox is earth; and Gweir, the imprisoned human, is fire. The spoils are the four conditions of matter, the four fundamental dispositions of consciousness undergoing first densification. The Holy Beasts's elemental correlations are slightly different than the Welsh: the Man-Angel is water; the lion is fire; the ox earth; and the eagle is air. But the essential point is these are the *life*-forms, the *living* expressions, of the elements."

None of us spoke for a while, I don't know how long, then Blaise said, "I think it's important that this place get touched now and then by living people. It has a ripple effect, trickling down on people in bodies, on the planet, its biosphere and Light grid. That's the way it is with Light temples. Aside from our benefiting from the processes of consciousness they exemplify, it's important that they be visited, touched by living human consciousness periodically to keep them vital. It's like the sleep-mode on computers. You want to periodically tap the screen of the Light temple to wake it up and bring it lucidly back on line.

"When we tap the screen of a Light temple, especially an occultly placed one like *Caer Sidi*, it makes it easier for the next group or individual coming through to make contact with it. You want these locales, no matter how rarefied, to remain active sites in human experience and understanding and not to fall into some obloquy of only scholarly footnotes where they become some vaguely understood reference from vanished cultures and without any other reality."

Then we were silent again for a while. I think we realized Merlin was about to speak and tell us something important, perhaps a mission debriefing.

"We have gone through the *Bardo* point by point reviewing all its structures and protocols, and you have made useful, practical recommendations. These are already being taken up and implemented by the Green Knight and his staff. Death will never be the same again, I assure you. Much easier, far less paperwork, and the paperwork you do encounter is much easier to understand.

"Levity aside, we have started to align the *Bardo* with the upgraded Earth Light grid. Ever since the morphing of the Earth's geometric Light pattern began in 1985, it has been crucial to make the two realms, the two divisions of the one master Light temple for the human phylogeny, congruent and compatible on all points. It's like having a large building with two parts; one division has been modernized, the other remains as it was originally designed and built. You walk around this twofold building and you feel you are in two entirely separate ones. Our expedition has been about modernizing the other half of this very old site. For the physical Earth to flourish, we needed to modernize this other division.

"You will soon be returning to your alive human bodies which, it may surprise you, have been going about the world conducting business while you were away. You will enjoy wrestling with that paradox when you return to them. The nature of geomantic interactions, such as you have been engaged in for the last three months of elapsed Earth-solar time, inaugurated at *Samhain* and finishing up at *Imbolc* or Candlemas—well, Candle *Mass*, to be correct, the day of the relighting of the world—on February 2, is that in addition to the actual experiences you acquired and now retain as vivid impressions, your auric and psychic spaces are imprinted with the energies of all the temples you visited.

"You'll carry these residues around with you as if you had been in a meditation hall where the sandalwood incense was strong and its aroma clings to your clothes even after you leave the place. People you talk with and places you visit will receive an impression of this imprint, like a holographic copy. Should you engage any people in an earnest discussion of these places or your activities in here, it will open a door for them, if they wish, to experience it themselves."

"Merlin, what about Matthew?" asked Edward. "He can't return to his body because his body, presumably, has been turned to Light. His whereabouts may raise some troubling questions among the authorities back in the world."

"An amusing problem, isn't it," replied Merlin. "We will put it out that Matthew has returned to Ontario for more meditation and seclusion by the lake. Which is not far from the truth, because I have asked him to help anchor some new energies in that region and to work with the astral spirits around the lake. He will gradually fade away from public memory, like a hermit who has retreated further into the forest. When necessary, to keep up appearances, Matthew can generate a simulacrum of his former human form to assuage people. Tommy, I am hoping you will find it an interesting assignment to act as occasional tour guide to *Bardo* travellers who wish to see the sights of *Caer Sidi*."

Tommy couldn't help grinning. In many respects he was still nineteen. "Sure thing. That sounds like great fun. I'll get right on it, work up itineraries."

Pipaluk asked, "I have the impression touching into that spinning castle is maybe the goal of a successful journey through this Underworld, or the reward?"

"Yes," said Merlin. "It is the epitome, the fusion, of the four elements, stronghold, sword, cauldron, and the *Awen* fire, in one place and one process. It puts you in potential contact with a high-level angelic order, not well known. The Holy Beasts or Creatures, or, more formally, the *Hayyoth-ha-Qodesh*. They are famous in a cartoon sense as the spirits with four heads poking between the wheel spokes of the Ofanim in the *Merkabah* Chariot in Ezekiel's biblical vision."

Merlin started the explanation on the Holy Beasts and the four elements that Blaise finished for me later and which I have already alluded to. He said:

"Mostly, people who have heard of this do not realize they represent the four fundamental states of consciousness that then became the four primary elements. This level of awareness underlies both poles of the human phylogeny temple, the division for those alive and for those in the *Bardo*. In either place, consciousness seeks to discover its definitive roots, and here they are, implicit in *Caer Sidi*. Here are the four conditions, personified as heads, the four qualities of primal matter. Each of these heads represents a cognitive mode, a way of seeing into the created world. It's the Green Knight's severed head motif all over again.

"You have to realize that matter here is *prima materia*, exceedingly subtle first matter, so subtle that even to use the term 'matter' is inaccurate and largely misleading. But then the term 'Earth' is equally so; it means *cosmic* Earth. The primordial container for all Creation, stars, planets, and galaxies is *Caer Sidi*."

"I *see*," said Blaise with enthusiasm. "This place is the substrate of the five *skandahs* and thus of the five *Dhyani* Buddhas whom we have visited. Those guys represent the *skandahs* in their enlightened condition. I always wondered about those four Magical Cities recounted in Irish folklore, exactly where they fit in the design for reality. Now I see it. *Caer Sidi* is the quintessence of the four Cities, which is to say, of the four elements. It is a hologram, and you can segue from any of its four elemental constituents to its corresponding Magical City.

"Take the Spear for fire, expressed in *Caer Sidi* as the *Awen*-fire in the cauldron. Your attention on that elemental talisman conducts you to Gorias, the Magical City of the Spear. Falias has the stone, Findias the sword, and Murias the cauldron. Thus, four Magical Cities with their elemental talismans plus *Caer Sidi*, their consummation, make five locales. You also get the five *skandahs*. In accordance with the Tibetan attributions (which, by the way, differ from the conventional assignments in Western metaphysical models), the stronghold of earth is the *skandah* of feeling; the sword for air is the *skandah* of volition; the spear for *Awen*-fire is perception; the cauldron for water is name and form; and the whole place, *Caer Sidi* in summation, is the *skandah* of consciousness itself.

"This is an initiation in the elements and their talismans and the five *skandahs* at a level *above* or preceding the human phylogeny. This is a generic, archetypal level of structuring, the first organization by which separate consciousness, extruded from the unity of God, may start assembling a world seemingly outside it. Here you acquire basic equipment for the human phylogeny, but for other life-forms as well. I imagine you could then proceed to incarnate *anywhere* and possibly as anything, in all manner of diverse forms.

"These Magical Cities and their elemental talismans, brought by the Tuatha de Danann from another place, exist to acquaint the spirit with the five formative conditions that preceded their voluntary entry into the human phylogeny, the five conditions and their angelic personifications. These comprise the *pre*-phylogenetic infrastructure into which a human being was set. It's like the backstory to the *skandah* grid, its origin and necessity revealed. The four elemental talismans and the fifth, consciousness, were forged into a single unit, the *skandah* grid. They went from beings items of power to tools of navigation. These discoveries ought to brighten anybody's jaunt through the *Bardo*, give them a tune to whistle as they get the larger picture for all this karma-drama."

I wasn't sure I understood everything Blaise said at the time, but it did help me remember something else I must have just seen but forgot to realize. I know that sounds odd, but I've found that sometimes we see more than we are aware of at the time, or perhaps it's a kind of data overload, so we see it later.

We were back inside the cauldron, with the sword up and running, and now I saw that surrounding *Caer Sidi* like a flock of hovering birds were four-headed angels. Famous ones, legendary ones, the four-headed spirits with a face of an eagle, a bull, a lion, and a human or angel. The Holy Beasts of Ezekiel's vision. An uncountable number of identical copies of this angelic apparition fluttered stationary around *Caer Sidi*, and it seemed, as if they were in the walls of it and even immediately around us as we fulfilled our roles in the sword manifestation. My point is that while Blaise *said* they were here, now I *saw* them.

I knew these faces were only metaphors, though at a sublime level, that suggest certain fundamental qualities humans were familiar with. Obviously, if you lived elsewhere, say the Pleiades, where, let's say, if they don't have bulls, you would not see a bull face because you would not understand the image; you'd see something relevant to Pleiadian consciousness and expectations, like a griffin. Still, I understood the essence of these four faces alludes to fundamental qualities of existence. Fire is *like* a roaring lion. Earth is *like* a heavy-set, immoveable bull. I knew what these images were, I understood their references, but, frankly, it defeats language now to explain this any better than I've done.

I plead mystical sublimity. It's easier to experience these than to describe them. But it felt as if all of reality crowded around us, insinuating its four qualities, like there was only one step beyond this fourfold concentration, and that was God. Pass through the four strong doors of *Caer Sidi*, four for the archetypal elements and four for their Magical Cities that exemplify them. You enter the realm of the Holy Beasts of the four elemental faces, and then God, the "Very Deep," the chief of *Annwn*, the ultimate severed Head containing all of it.

Blaise was right. The severed head motif keeps popping up. I was reminded of how Qabalists use the White Head, the solitary cranium, to connote God, and how, in some texts, they expand this to three heads, all extremely recondite. It's not even correct to say "severed," because this Head never had or needed a body, or, probably, the White Head alone is the (only) universal body.

It was only later that I realized our experience at *Caer Sidi* and then its enhancement by the presence of the Holy Creatures was free of the Druj. Entirely. She had no traction on consciousness at this level, or perhaps she had no practical interest as this level was beyond or before the soul and not worth her attention and she could only suborn consciousness when it was ensouled and, even more richly, when it was embodied, preferably as humans, easy marks. Or maybe she figured so few people made it to *Caer Sidi* it wasn't worth her while.

Caer Sidi was like the last outpost of the phenomenal world at the boundary of the formless realm. The Druj would have no traction in the *Dharmakaya*; none of her schemes would stick or have any effect there. I suppose we had a taste of the formless realm, this *Dharmakaya*, because aside from my impression of being buffeted in four directions by essential qualities of reality, there was little else to see. Our experience was more of an immersion. It was a welcome relief, a few moments off, from the continuous assault by the Druj, such an obnoxious presence that you cannot (yet) evict from your awareness.

Just when I thought this visionary experience was over, another part was added. A massive, slowly revolving white wheel made of blazing white diamond fire slowly rose up under *Caer Sidi* so that the Holy Creatures were between its innumerable spokes. I'm not sure whether they were spokes. They seemed more like a nest of millions of identical diamond facets crowded, densely packed together, and perhaps the impression of spokes was for me a metaphorical necessity. You expect spokes on a wheel, but this White Wheel was different. It rose up to nestle directly under the Spinning Castle which now rested upon it. These identical diamond facets seemed to be smiling: no, I have to say, grinning.

That gave it away. Pardon my obtuseness, for surely the reader already knows who comprised this formidable White Wheel. Our pals, the Blaises, of course. The brightness of this wheel was dazzling to the point of nearly blinding me. The Holy Creatures were prolific in their copies, and they swarmed all around us. Our Sword of Elohim blazed out in the midst of this effulgence like a pillar of invincible Light planted at the heart of Creation.

Forgive my prolixity, but you can see all this was over the top, *way* over the top, and it's hard to recount the experience without feeling one does so with one's mouth open. I hereby confess, my mouth is open as I recall this epiphany. Later, when I regained my composure, I appreciated the fact that this appearance represented the disclosure of a fundamental condition of reality at its formative, original level. That this is where you may expect to find these two angelic orders.

"Well, that wasn't in the *Tibetan Book of the Dead*, Merlin," said Blaise.

"We like to keep a few surprises to ourselves for moments like this," said Merlin. "We find it heightens the impact if you don't know it's coming. Yes?"

Yes. I mentioned that it was pleasant to be in a place free of the Druj. But I realized that this place, where we were, felt like the bedrock of the Creation. I know that sounds ponderous, but you felt you were embedded in fundamentals. That everything around us, the White Wheel, the hovering Holy Creatures, *Caer Sidi*, the Grail, the Sword of Elohim, were all inexpungeably true. True forever.

Some part of me, deep within, sighed in relief. It could relax again. I'm not sure what label to put on this relaxing part of me. It was antecedent to myself. Here, high above the troubling double temple of the human phylogeny, the vexed *Bardo* of embodiment and disincarnation, there were no illusions, tricks, glamours, karmic projections or hallucinations, no circus acts of consciousness.

Reality felt stretched, endlessly and effortlessly, in an eternal moment. Then we were standing outside the Underworld gate in that dip among the desert hills outside Santa Fe where we had started the expedition. It seemed like maybe two seconds ago we had been standing here. Our time in the *Bardo* seemed to snap back on itself like a stretched rubber band. How long was it?

I felt very heavy, as if I had gained a great deal of weight since I last checked. Yet, looking at my physical form, I saw my weight and size had not changed at all. I was feeling the force of gravity and physical embodiment from a fresh angle. You forget how heavy your body feels to consciousness, how strong gravity is. I laughed, vigorously, in fact, when I realized it was as if we had told our bodies to come collect us at a specific time when we stepped out of the *Bardo*.

"Yeah, pal," said Blaise, getting the joke instantly. "Our ride's here."

It was like finding yourself in the car before you were aware of even entering it. I suppose that's because the transition was so rapid. But I have found I can slow it down now and watch every move, even though only a few seconds elapsed. We stepped through the Underworld gate, the same one we had entered three months ago, and saw a crowd of human forms waiting there to greet us. At first, I thought, who are these people? Then I laughed. It was ourselves. Strange!

Now they looked familiar. They were us, but they looked thick, heavy, slow, almost like caricatures. It's like if you don't see somebody you know well for ten years, then you see them again: they look changed, thickened perhaps, more wrinkled, aged. Recognition is there, but it is a little shocking. We were shocked to see ourselves. Also, how often do you get to witness yourself from the outside, as if you are another separate discrete human figure occupying the visual landscape, yet it is still you? The first time is unsettling as I learned.

I heard a kind of slamming sound, like somebody dropped a stack of books squarely on a wooden floor. I felt a shudder, a twisting, and a sense of dropping anchor, like my legs grew into the ground with a bang. I felt as if I had been suspended by antigravity against the high ceiling of a room and suddenly the gravity was restored and I came slamming down to land hard on my feet. My body was just registering the impact of that rude floor touch-down.

There was snow on the ground all around us, at least six inches of it, and we were standing in it. I don't remember there being snow when we started. Inexplicably, it seems at first, I discovered I was properly clothed for this weather, even wearing the appropriate winter toke and gloves for cold snowy conditions. The others were dressed for the weather too, in thick coats, hats, gloves, scarves. Somebody prepared us well for this outdoor situation.

I wasn't dressed like this when we came here a few minutes ago, so how did I come to be dressed this way? You'll appreciate it was initially confusing. I forgot we had been gone three months. It snows here in February. My sense of time continuity was jumping all over the place, and I was only partially back in my body in terms of anchoring all my awareness inside this familiar old form.

I should qualify that not all the others of the expedition arrived back here. Tommy was only with us as a ghost of himself. He had no body to return to, and his Light form was flickering already. Philomena and Matthew were also tentatively, only provisionally here, but I expected them to wink out of visibility at any moment, pursuing other arcane activities. Merlin managed a believable human semblance. What I mean is, yes, we all came back, but some would not be staying with us.

A tremendous time compression had just occurred. When you return to your body after a long night of dreaming, or, in our case, a prolonged visionary expedition, the time duration that marks how long you were on the other side of reality suddenly compresses to a sliver and the presumptions of body-based time resume. They really stomp on that subtle, quickly evanescing *Bardo* time sense.

I looked at my travel companions. With the exception of Blaise, they seemed equally to be wrestling with the time differential inside and outside their bodies. Blaise, well, he lives in a different place these days. Since he left the Earth in 2020, time has been altogether different for him. He was chuckling. "It's less confusing than my commuting back and forth between here and the Pleiades. Because then I wasn't even coming back to the same body I left in. I had a nice choice of body: human body, Pleiadian body, or Light form for each version."

"Merlin," said Edward, with concern in his voice, "what time is it?"

"It's noon, February 2, Candlemass. You've been gone three months."

"Good God!" Edward exclaimed. "What have our bodies been doing?"

"You have an interesting process of discovery awaiting you," Merlin said.

19

I wonder if you have ever had this puzzling experience. You ask yourself, your body, what have you been up to while I was not paying attention, not here? At such times you feel like you're two people, each leading independent lives.

So here I was, knowing what I had been doing, but not knowing what this other I had been doing. I had been larking about the *Bardo* on the Green Knight expedition for what appears to have been three months in a body of Light that, I gather, resembled me, while my physical body, presumably the original me, and some kind of caretaker personality has been larking about the physical world, doing—what? I was up against a brick wall of not-knowing with this question.

I could not remember where I had last been when I was in my body. I could not remember the last decade, come to think of it. Where have I been since the Theosophon of 2033? I couldn't remember. Everything was fuzzy since I went off precipitously with Blaise back in 2026. That was now 18 years ago. Edward and Pipaluk were sharing this same perplexity, though Blaise less so, but for Edward and Pipaluk it was only three months that were missing. Edward came from Boston and would return to his townhouse and editor's job; Pipaluk would journey back to northern Greenland, the snow, and her great-grandchildren. Matthew and Philomena had left the human timeline; the question was moot.

What to do? It was snowing so I pulled up my collar and snuggled down my toke. That was a start. Practical action. Merlin stood by, watching but silent. I was beginning to remember this dell in the desert hills. I saw the Underworld gate, looming hugely before us. I won't say menacingly, because it wasn't; how could it be when we had been through it and toured the whole death realm and had returned, unruffled, ready to snap our fingers and whistle a tune while I dealt with this nagging befuddlement of my recent bodily history and location.

"Tea?" It was Merlin, acting as butler, or, should I say, being Mother, as the British like to say when they want somebody motherlike to pour the tea. One of the advantages of being Merlin, which is to say, the Lord of the Silver Robe and one notch above the Ray Masters in the hierarchy of God's staffing chart, is that you can come up with a little trick now and then, perform the miracle of tea. He was performing it. He was being Mother, and he was pouring us hot tea.

Yes, it was still snowing, we were still in this same hollow between the hills in front of the formidable Underworld gate, and we had just stepped out of the *Bardo*, but who is going to say no to a nice cup of hot tea under these circumstances? Not I. It was like being inside one of the Irish *sidhe* when the gods bring out the gold and silver goblets and pour ambrosia into your hand-sized chalice, and you sit back and enjoy the intoxicating fairy-music and wonder who has the golden apples dangling off the silver branch, giving off that inimitable tinkling sound the Celtic poets loved to allude to, except we were outside the *sidhe* and Merlin was the only *sidhe* god on hand, handling all the table service.

He had procured a table, tablecloth, settings, china, chairs, and pastries. After what I had seen in the last three months, I wasn't going to question how.

"You know, I don't mind taking a break from being dead," said Edward. "I think I've seen enough *Heruka*s and blood-drooling karmic hallucinations and mental projections to last me the rest of this week, I should think. That and the Druj. I guess we'll have to keep a sharp eye on that crooked, talented spirit. I wonder how many manuscripts I've bought and edited since I was away? It's bizarre, unsettling, to think I must have faithfully shown up for work every day, putting forth a plausible cover story that I was Edward Burbage, the real one, in person, incontestably, when in fact I was out in the field on the most outré of activities, on assignment *from Merlin*, imagine, touring the *Bardo* with all of you."

"Maybe it is not quite as strange for me," said Pipaluk. "Sometimes an *angakkuq* will sit in concentration for a week. She will seem to be dead, or just barely alive. Her spirit is somewhere else, maybe in this same *Bardo*. People look after her, giving her water and covering her in blankets, as if she is badly sick. Then she returns and resumes occupying her body and tells of her adventure. Maybe this adventure is too big to tell. Maybe I'll break it up into little stories."

It was the middle of the day, which I could tell from the Sun's position overhead, but suddenly it seemed as if another sun—no, two suns, just came out. Came out right next to us in this snow-lined dell next to the Underworld hill. We were bracketed by these two suns, which seemed to stretch first into pillars of Light then condense and congeal gradually into the forms of Philomena and Matthew. In their human forms, fake, as I knew they must be, provisional, cobbled together for our benefit, they were not quite so blinding to the eye. Still, I knew I was seeing a kind of magic trick, a human veneer put on for our benefit.

I believe my mouth was still hanging open just the same, and the fact that they were here, in semblances of familiar human forms, was blinding to my mind. I realized with what nonchalance I had accepted all the bizarre, outlandish acts of consciousness we had witnessed or perpetrated over there in the *Bardo*. Now that I was back in my body, the impact of those bendings of the presumed rules of reality was hitting me squarely in my body and emotions—*impossible*. The mind is open to novelty, but the body and emotions less so; they will protest.

I shivered as I realized how much of my personality was based on assumptions held by the emotional and bodily part of myself, how "these" parts wanted to construe reality, how, I saw now, they expected it to conform to constricted limits. The sudden flaring into perceivable reality of the Light forms of Philomena, technically "dead" for several years now, and Matthew, only recently deceased, contradicted all that, like a stiff wind blowing the stacked papers off a desk. You put things in meticulous order, then reality blows it away. I was being welcomed back to physical reality with the first demonstration of the *Bardo* of everyday, material life: reality is not remotely what you thought it is.

I did the only practical act that came to mind. "Tea?" I asked Philomena. She nodded, and smiled, as did Matthew, and they both sat down in a chair. I wondered what should strike me as being the most strange, having tea with my wife who had since ascended into a Light form and was now congealed as a believable-looking female human, or that we were having tea in the desert hills with snow on the ground, having just returned from three months in the *Bardo*.

"Did you know we accompanied you back to this place to collect your Light forms as you stepped through the Underworld gate?" Philomena asked. "You chatted with Matthew and myself the whole way, as if you didn't realize that we were in multiple places at the same time and so were you. I'm glad you have returned to living in our home in Hanover; it saddened me when it languished empty and uninhabited for the early months you were with Blaise.

"Did you know he arranged for it to be tenanted for all those years you were gone? You seemed like you were in a dream as we travelled from Hanover out to Santa Fe, as if you knew I shouldn't be there with you, that I had permanently left, and yet you were trying to flesh it out as normal, habitual, even uxorial, as if nothing had changed or happened, including to you to whom *much* happened. I knew a portion of your awareness knew that you were also in this very minute somewhere else, but most of you was trying to forget that as it was too weird. I don't suppose you have any memory of visiting the faculty club?

"You've called a few times on some of your old pals from Dartmouth, told them plausible stories about extended sabbaticals, research in foreign parts. You were circumspect enough not to mention the bits that would have startled them. They marveled that you hadn't seemed to have aged, despite the years away. That's the Blaise syndrome, isn't it? Time travel, shapeshifting, stargating: your consciousness, freed from the body to explore the recondite regions of reality, tends to slow down the aging clock, even take you off the clock altogether.

"People look at you and they won't guess you are 68, nor that Blaise is now 94. A few of your pals asked you about that anecdote about running out the front door after you finished editing that most strange book, *My Pal, Blaise*. Was it true? And you downplayed it saying it was put in for literary effect, for drama. Probably best that way. Otherwise, you start a causal chain they can't follow."

"How did Edward get here, the bodily one?" I asked Philomena.

"Blaise brought him. He just called on Edward the way he did a few years ago when he returned from the Pleiades and debriefed him on the Theosophon."

"But how could that be?" I replied. "Blaise was with us the whole time."

"One of him was. Our Blaise has learned a few tricks in his 94 years. Since he left the Earth in 2020 through the stargate to return to his home planet in the Celaeno system and then commuted back and forth between there and Earth for 20 years, everything has been different for him, shall we say, enlarged, enriched? I have had a number of profitable sit-downs with him during that time. It's very educational to compare field notes as we work different sides of the same issue. The Earth's Light grid and the expansion of human consciousness of course. We even managed to work Scriabin and Rachmaninov into our genteel discussions, and he assured me he had no more stored boxes of journals for me to edit."

"Let me get this straight," I continued. "My head is still spinning. You're saying that for the last three months I have been going about my business as former Professor Frederick palling around with old Dartmouth colleagues, tending the house and property, as if that was my primary and sole life focus, with no suspicion that another version of me was running around the crazy Underworld on an expedition with the legendary Green Knight and Merlin? And that one of our expedition members was a 19-year-old young man who died almost 20 years ago and another a Canadian who had taken on a Light body?"

"That's right, and don't forget your illuminating talks with the Druj."

Philomena was enjoying this. She was grinning as my perplexity grew. The Druj: I suddenly remembered. Arch bad girl of Creation. Prime obfuscator of the clarity of consciousness, principal magician of the dark realm. Technically, she is the Antichrist but she never seemed especially scary or nasty, just devilishly clever, consistently devious, and unremittingly Machiavellian in her protean tactics to suborn human consciousness and spin it around befuddled. Perhaps that was an even more treacherous guise than one that was overtly frightening. The sly guise could easily disarm your discernment. As I discovered, we didn't get the cartoon version of the Antichrist; we got the upgraded version.

I felt like I was suddenly remembering in a rush a long, vivid dream in lucid detail. Even though it should have been fresh in my mind, the minute we resumed our physical body forms all the richness of the last three months had faded and popped like a soap bubble reflecting all sorts of bright images. Now it was coming back to me. Even though I had just "done" it all, it seemed doubtful.

"It will all come good for you, Frederick," said Blaise. "Just give your body a little time to catch up. Think of this expedition as being about team building. We now have some practical bridges cast over the River Acheron from our world. I have a good conduit with the other Blaises, the Ofanim. Edward, you're point man with Merlin. And Frederick, you are the link with Philomena and Matthew, two ascended former humans capable of working both sides of life. And Tommy, everybody's pal, will be our man on the ground in the *Bardo*.

Our expedition isn't finished. Just because we're back doesn't mean we're done."

We weren't. That was demonstrated quite soon after Blaise's remark. I felt the urgency of my breathing, of the beating of my heart. No, I wasn't worried. It was that I was now acutely aware of the passion to continue surviving that these internal organs, on my behalf, put forth every second in support of my awareness and its (to them) bizarre experiences and concepts of entertainment.

We usually take this for granted, barely noticing it, but when you've been away from your mortal body for three months, it's right in your face. That and the whole shocking roster of squishy organs, bones, blood, sinews, arteries, their complex interactions, and the rest of what comprises the biological human, breathing, standing upright, feeling hunger pangs, the stiffness of your knees, even down to my nose which feels scratchy and cold right now—it's noticeable. It's all in your face, and even your face is in your face, so what are you anyway?

I remembered the fluidity of my consciousness in the *Bardo*, how easily we moved about, organizing perceptions, performing sword tricks, helping souls. I was starting to remember, with some dismay, how slow and ponderous action is on this side of the divide, how long it takes for anything to happen, even to move a leg. I could see how people, recovering from a near-death experience, often miss the ease and speed of things in the *Bardo* and return to body life reluctantly.

Before I was able to indulge this self-pity too much, I saw that it would not be this way at all. All my expectations about the slowness of body life were instantly overturned and deftly refuted. We were moving fast. We were already there. I didn't remember anything more than taking the first tentative step. I had heard somebody click their fingers, making the snapping sound that says *move*.

Where had we moved to? I realized I had been keeping my eyes closed. I felt uncharacteristically light and buoyant, like I was floating in a salt-water lagoon. Then I felt something heavy slam into me, like somebody threw a body at me. I felt like I suddenly weighed a ton, or that gravity had tripled in strength. I stood there, my eyes still closed for some reason, trying to puzzle things out.

Then I got it. This was the same sensation I had felt in that dell when we first returned from the *Bardo*. It was my only physical body being reunited with my Light body. My Light body, or astral Double, got here first, instantaneously. My astral form took the express train, while my physical body travelled by local, stopping at every tiny station and plodding slowly across the landscape to here.

I opened my eyes. I didn't recognize a thing. I didn't know where we were. It looked like the desert, but a real desert of sand, flat everywhere, very hot. I heard flowing water, like a river, and in the distance I saw sand-colored, low-lying buildings. I don't know why I knew this, but I was certain this was not in the present time. The air felt crisp, sharp, lucidly defined, free of pollutants, then I realized it wasn't the air that had these qualities, but my awareness.

It's like you realize you have been walking around wearing a suit of armor or deep-sea diving gear that weighs 50, maybe 100 pounds, and you are so used to it you think it's the normal way to feel. Then it's taken off you, gone, and your consciousness, how you feel, how the world feels, is suddenly uplifted, lightened, and you are practically floating you feel so light. I had thought we brought our physical bodies with us, slow-coaches as they are, but maybe not.

I turned to Merlin. He knew I wanted to ask him where we had gotten to. "Sumeria, just outside Uruk, near the Euphrates River. The time of Gilgamesh. Soon after the Flood. Hundreds of thousands of years ago. Humanity has just been recreated, reseeded in the same place where it was destroyed by the Flood.

"This time humans are given a much reduced life-span, no longer the thousands of years their forebears enjoyed, and, regrettably, abused. They have been given death in the form of a much shortened life-span, and this is why we are here. Something went wrong. Something foreign was introduced into the human at this time, a kind of black seed, and it has tainted human consciousness about death ever since. About everything bodily, in fact, including the planet. We are here to intercept that dark seed and circumvent millennia of psychic sabotage and slow corruption of the psychic buoyancy humans are meant to have.

"The mechanism that produces bodily death in a proscribed time has just been entered into the human form. It has some flexibility. Some will live longer, some less, but it will average out across the spectrum of incarnate humans. Yama has already blazed the path through the *Bardo*, set up the stations and protocols. Souls are briefed on the procedures of dying, death, and the afterlife and enter their incarnations informed as to what to expect. Except something else has been inserted into this matrix, the dark seed. It is a negative programming grid.

"There is an inevitable residue from the abuses of the first generation of humans. They were extensive; they perturbed the correctness of planetary reality. They distorted the planet's *Asha*, wobbled the Light grid. It's a karmic taint that will affect all members of this second generation of humans. Some of that taint has taken the form of diseases and pathogenic processes that anchor the moral disturbances and will afflict the weaker human forms through their minds and bodies and eventually touch nearly everyone. That could not be curtailed.

It is a broad-spectrum collective human karmic miasma, weakening all humans."

Reality slowed down and time seemed enormously stretched so that a second might last a year. This first roster of newly recreated humans was installed directly on the Earth as alive adults. They would be the first parents. I saw them in the thousands descending through a massive humanlike form of Light that was as big as a mountain—no, as large as an entire mountain range. It was full of stars, turning wheels of Light, angels of all descriptions, and temples. It was like a monstrously large version of the human, though in form it did not look the same. It consisted of layers of spheres of Light, yet it exuded sentience. Somehow it was the prototype of these freshly created alive humans passing through its parental form, its cosmogonic shape, for it seemed to be womblike.

A tall female figure, draped in dark robes, stood just at the transition zone between this cosmic spherical figure and the physical world and the ground. As the alive humans stepped through this transition zone she placed something in their necks. It was at the back of the head, base of the occiput as it joins the neck.

It looked like a black human head, though a deformed, sneering, psychotic one. It resembled the face of fear, complaint, dissatisfaction, distrust, and distaste. It was more than an automaton or puppet; it seemed to possess sentience. The humans did not see this female figure or what she was doing. Even if they had, they might not have known her identity. Most did not register the implantation of this little black head into their necks, though a few did, and seemed to shake their heads for a moment as if stung by an insect. I knew who this was. The Druj. She was up to her old tricks, and maybe one of her first.

This was the opportunistic moment when the Druj inserted a cache of her own negative programming into the incarnate human form. A tiny version of the House of Lies. Welcome to human life, here's a little message for you, and let the protracted suborning of human conscious freedom begin. The puzzling thing is that the Supreme Being allowed this. The Sponsor-in-Chief wanted humans to have a little goad, a certain amount of psychic friction, to keep them on their toes. The first round of humans had entered life with what proved to be far too much largesse. They had, as Wodehouse would say, all the knobs on, then broke them.

The Supreme Being allowed the insertion of this baleful black head but the Druj then twisted it a little more, gave the dial yet one more spin into negativity. But she was subtle, devious. That twist made the black head into a finger puzzle. The second you agreed with any of the negative pronouncements that came out of that head in the back of your neck, it tightened its grip on you and uttered more. You can't trick the Supreme Being, not ever, and the Druj knew this. But by pressing her advantage by the merest percent at the beginning, she calculated she could probably get away with it. The Sponsor-in-Chief would likely regard it as a useful extension of His original intent to test and challenge His new humans. There wasn't just one complaining Job; all of humanity would be Job, a job lot.

But it put humans at an unfair disadvantage. Most did not appreciate they were being counseled by a voice, dark and despairing, even sniveling and quarrelsome, rising up petulantly in the midst of their own thoughts and perceptions as if it were their own. It was critical and cranky; it disliked the body and feared death. It was always complaining, and its litany of grievances was long and detailed. Always frowning, it had long lists of things it disapproved of.

Death is terrible, frightening, full of terrors and miseries, to be avoided at all costs and certainly not entered upon in a state of wide-awake consciousness, it moaned. Resist, avoid, deny, ignore, disavow, because it is positively the worst thing. Your every action will be evaluated and judged, and you will be found guilty. The Judges of the Dead are harsh, cold, unmerciful, unyielding, unbribable. The Supreme Being is a nasty Old Shit for forcing death upon you and when you get there before the Baleful One He will acquaint you with His great displeasure. Don't expect any succor; they ran out of the stuff eons ago.

It raved on in this manner, and has never ceased; it only shuts up when you die. When this talking black head reached a certain point of engaged loquacity, it would start channeling the Druj directly, and she would start speaking into the listening, increasingly fearful and fretful human subconscious all day long. Her voice, rich with lies, subterfuge, deception, and persuasion, would slowly poison your mind with psychic arsenic until your will and discernment were corrupted and your spirit was undergoing a slow sure death.

She would give you sweetness and Light if that was your temperament, or doom and misery if you preferred the pessimistic side of things. She adjusted her message to fit each human, and each person after years of listening to this sole radio station would now carry this infernal blight, something dark and not intended in the original design. It was as if the Druj stood over each newly incarnated human with a medicine dropper and into the psyche of each she let go a single drop of this exquisite poison, distilled essence of the House of Lies.

That was the diagnosis, and it looked bleak, nasty but it was clever. You have to give the Druj that. Nobody could ever say she is stupid or feckless. Just as the first brood of Lilith and Pandora, those wild residents of Sodom and Gomorrah and the other cities of the first generation of free-wheeling humans,

took advantage of the original endowment, exploited every vestige of power, pleasure, and distortion of the original plan for symmetry, beauty, and balance, so did the Druj take advantage of certain subtle loopholes to subvert humans in this second round of generation, the brood of Eve. Our job, I realized, the reason we had been brought back here, was to correct that subversion, to introduce an antidote, add something that restored balance and the possibility of a free choice.

I want to emphasize the subtlety with which the Druj did this. Say you are in a department store, considering shirts or socks perhaps. You reach for the socks. You have shown your interest. A clerk steps forward and says, May I be of assistance? That is the precise point of traction. If you say yes, the hooks go in, ever so subtlety but deftly with perhaps a well-chosen word, tone, or manner of enunciation. That's how the Druj works. In this example, she is the sales clerk.

Even with this talking black head, she could not overtly intervene in somebody's psychic space. They had to say yes, they could use some assistance, or, yes, that is a good idea, thanks for telling me. Soon the black head becomes an adviser, then a commentator, then a participant, then a critic. In some people, this black head remains dormant, like an unactivated seed, but unfortunately in most people it sprouted and grew long ago and has flourished. It has been talking to us in a mellifluously demented recitation, like a declaiming crazed bard, or something eldritch out of Lovecraft's vision of the world, like his malign, toad-faced, amphibious Great Old One, Cthulhu, the insanity-spreading horror.

Here's how that little insidious head wrecked the human picture of the *Bardo*. Every time a soul encountered a hallucinatory projection formulated out of their own karma and cultural models—got their asses kicked by a *Heruka*, I can hear Blaise snickeringly saying—the images that soul perceived were projected back into the common pictorial circulation of the talking heads to all humans. It was an instant feedback. The particularities of one person's karmic and mental images were presented to embodied consciousness as immutable *facts* of the *Bardo*. One soul's fear pictures, one's frightful dream-images of dismemberment, blood, guts, all the horrific histrionics of the *Bardo* on a bad day, were immediately circulated back into daytime incarnate consciousness as facts.

People took them as true and accurate accounts of *Bardo* conditions, and quaked. Gradually, humans, upon dying, brought these misperceptions with them and expected *Bardo* reality to be like that and so it was, obligingly, just like that. They saw what they expected, and that was based on illusions and delusions which the Druj kept masterfully shoveling into the daytime awareness of alive people. The dead started seeing the Druj's picture of the Underworld.

People and cultures, even religions and metaphysical models, built up a supposedly objective picture of the afterlife based on karmic illusions and mental projections formulated out of subjective, unresolved life contents and never realized they were seeing the *Bardo* through the Druj's own version of an eldritch stained-glass window and thus, increasingly, not seeing it accurately at all, even when a soul was in the *Bardo* and had the potential to wake up into the Light. Even then, they saw it all wrong, saw it according to the Druj's picture script. They had the projected skein of their own karmic hallucinations, but this was tinged, stained, draped over with the Druj's subtle alterations or enhancements.

Over time, she distorted and corrupted the human picture of death and the *Bardo*, and the Underworld became painted in drear, even abysmal, colors. This faulty picture started

to grow inside Albion too, and the collective consciousness of humanity came to fear death and dying, to not understand it, to consider it an appalling development in an already bizarre advent of themselves in the world without portfolio or explanation or any evident purpose. Such a blighted tree she grew from that miniscule black seed. She is a skilled gardener.

What did Albion know about the correct or faulty picture of death? He was programmed with cosmic consciousness and its celestial mechanisms and he was filled with the life experience of billions of incarnated humans over Earth's time. If they were telling him through their subconscious that death sucked big time, that was the information he used to form a picture of that awfulness.

The purpose of the *Bardo* process, as best I could understand it, was to show the mechanisms of personality creation and karmic accretion, its consequences, formations, and liabilities, and also to show this mechanism in reverse, the taking off and disclosure of these contents and their twisted patterns, and for consciousness to realize its fundamental creative role in the entire event. That might be shocking to many people, but it was not inherently scary. It would be shocking, I suppose, for people to realize how much power their minds wield in generating the conditions of their reality, how much traction they have. That is precisely what the Druj endeavors to prevent humans from achieving. She prefers they experience their reality as a given, as done to them from outside.

What complicates this disclosure and the horror-show aspect of it are the millennia of machinations and distortions of the *Bardo* protocols by the Druj, the false pictures and illusory nightmare experiences she has managed to lace into human consciousness and expectation as people die and enter the Underworld. That becomes the main event, which nobody enjoys in the least, and the true event of the *Bardo*, the revelation of the powers of consciousness, is eclipsed. Instead, you walk grimacing through the Druj's personal art gallery of horrors.

All this had been going on since the advent of second-generation humans. Merlin had taken us back to where the seeding of humanity with the black heads began. We could not undo it from back then. That would rewrite all of human history and was not allowed. But we could make changes to it in present time.

It turns out the *Epic of Gilgamesh* records the time period in which this Druj adjustment of the human took place. I think most readers can detect some inherent sadness and despair in Gilgamesh. He knows the world has changed irrevocably; the gods who once lived with the humans in the great cities on the Plain of Shinar have retreated to the recondite Cedar Forest. They are less accessible, possibly not accessible at all anymore. You have to journey far to reach them. Once the gods walked among them, sat down and explained the cosmos, but now humans have to go through this hideous gatekeeper, Humbaba, to have any possibility of an audience with the once on-hand gods of the *Apsu*, the Sumerian name for the great Sea of Light out of which the masters emerged.

Gilgamesh's concern, his odyssey, is to find the hidden gods and demand immortality. This new institution of early bodily death is intolerable; there must be an antidote. He reaches the Cedar Forest but the gods deny his request. He returns disconsolate to Uruk and soon after he dies and is laid out in his tomb. So has everyone else since then, and now people don't travel to the Cedar Forest.

This pestilence of lies and distortion had lain in Albion for eons, and in every human taking bodily form on the Earth during that same long time period. As before, I knew we could not force anybody to divest themselves of the Druj's lies. It must be voluntary. We could only present the case in the form of the Light. It would be a sword job, for this was another episode in the aftermath of the Dolorous Stroke, the soap opera called "As the Day Turns in the Wasteland." Voiceover, disconsolate-sounding: "My name is the Wounded Fisher King, Anfortas, and I'm suffering something shocking, and, Grail Knights, what are you going to do about it?" And: "My name is Gilgamesh, and I feel estranged from the gods and locked into a material body whose only destiny, the only sure thing, is death and dissolution, and I have to tell you, I don't like it one bit."

The system, the perfect, beautiful design, the original intentions and settings, had been thrown off its axis. *Asha* was in rout, *hozho* spoiled, *ma'at* was fucked. The Earth is 23.4 degrees off its intended axis, and human consciousness is similarly subluxated from the truth of its Creation. The planet is supposed to be fully upright in its axis, and humans are supposed to be perfectly aligned with the truth, and both are off their axis. I realized that meant the four of us were participating in this group misalignment. Everyone in a human body was. We were all descendants of Gilgamesh, all Wounded Fisher Kings. Call me Anfortas. Want to see my wounds? What would it feel like when we had the chiropractic adjustment that aligned us with the correct and real consciousness of Creation?

We were inside the Albion that serviced this part of the planet and that had been the prime recipient of the installation of the Druj's black-head seeds. We would start undoing this dark contribution from the Sumerian Albion. No one needed reminding that the Middle East and Persian Gulf region had been a site of great turmoil, wars, conflict, death, and misery since the 1970s, and the age and durability of the black heads no doubt played a formidable role in this. Even though this Albion, like the others, was overlaid upon a great stretch of Earth landscape with specific tie-down sites for its 81 chakras and 360 organs, inside this colossus of Light it was like a hologram, all of it available to hand. We positioned ourselves right next to the perfidious black head, like a wrinkled nut.

We assembled the sword and took our positions. As before, I would handle the gold staff inside the spinning octahedron part, radiating Christ Light. Edward would manifest the Sword of King Arthur, or Solar Logos, and Pipaluk would visualize and energize the jeweled scabbard and 14 Rays of Ursa Major. Tommy—yes, Tommy was back with us, joining us in his Light body, on loan from the *Bardo*—would generate the lilac flames rippling along the sword's edge.

Blaise would produce the Sword of Elohim that surrounded all this, and his pals, the other Blaises, would surround the edifice with a nest of sparkling diamonds. Philomena would occupy the sword's handle, sharing the cozy space with the Supreme Being, and Matthew would envelop the *tulpa* with an oval of Light which in effect was his new ascended Light body in high radiating mode.

We situated ourselves, the sword, right behind the black head in Albion. This primary black head was holographically linked with the same in all living humans. Whatever we did here would have effects in those alive people. What we were going to do was simple: we'd show Albion's black head this sword. It was empowered with the force of *Asha Vahishta*, Goliath's name as one of the six *Amesha Spentas*, the Bountiful Immortals, holder of the sword of invincible, original truth. We'd put a blade of *AL* Light and power up to the face of the Druj's black head and then, I suppose, we would see what happened next.

Quite a bit of inertia had built up with this talking black head. Most people no longer recognized it or saw its hectoring voice as different from themselves. It was like a radio that was always on and you forgot it was a radio. It was like watching a basketball game on television; the commentator's voices, their opinions and interpretations, were a constant interface between your attention and the actual ball game. Well, the Druj had been calling the ball game of human consciousness since the time of Gilgamesh. People thought reality naturally came with this voiceover, they were so accustomed to it. The next level of recognition we were aiming for was for people to realize this talking head was there, talking non-stop shit, rubbish, lies, deceits, and fabrications in their minds.

After that, we hoped the sword's Light would help people see that this inundation of falsehood was the product of a specific inimical spirit, the Druj, that she had grown enormously in size and potency over the eons, horrifically bloated when she allowed you to see her in that form and not as the alluring courtesan of the spirit, and that she could be repudiated then expunged from their psychic space, her influence upon you curtailed at last, and, this is the best part, that this now empty space could be refilled with the truth. It would be like draining a fetid swamp and redoing the space with original pure water, the virginal water the Earth was first equipped with, the uncorrupted sheer truth.

Do you ever find that the more you put your attention on something the larger and stranger it becomes? I often find this with words. I stare at them until I no longer recognize the word and cannot remember its meaning. In the case of the Druj, our attention focused unremittingly through the sword made her seem at first prodigiously larger then exceedingly weird, bizarre, sinister, and comic.

You could see her complete résumé, the history of her entanglements with humanity over a great stretch of time, all her machinations, extended tendrils, whispered bad advice, insinuations, accelerant on angry or despairing states. I saw how she overshadowed the gibbering black heads in innumerable humans acting like a perverse version of its Higher Self, councilor, war tactician, mentor. Wherever there was a picture of something fearful about death and the afterlife, she amplified it, put a big psychic spotlight on it, like underlining a word. Where she saw resistance, squirming, or all-out panic about dying, she strengthened it.

We were working through the Sumerian Albion in which the black head was like an enormous alien growth at the back of his head. Granted, Albion doesn't have a head in a human anatomical sense, but it has the head chakras. From this black excrescence streamed forth an unceasing babble of negativity and pessimism, rumors of fear, scenarios of terror, false pictures of the spiritual world that were meant to terrify and misdirect embodied consciousness, to inspire it to cling at all costs to the present incarnation, to value it above all else, to resist the Underworld gates like a mule dragged into service against its will. It exuded a completely Ahrimanic vibration, densifying spirit into awful matter.

There was a reciprocal loop between this Albion and all of humanity. Both poles of this circuit constantly fed the other updates and reports of developments. These circulated through the other major Albions and the zodiacal ones. A total of 442 Albions were in this information loop, regularly serviced with news, and these Albions acted like broadcasters for their host humans in bodies, millions upon millions of humans over time, and their new formulations, birthed out of fear and misinformation, fed back to the Albions. It was like having a vast espionage network in which all your spies were duped. They kept transmitting their field reports back to headquarters, and everything they sent was a lie, deliberate disinformation, false flags, illusions, and useless.

The information seemed "actionable," but it was trickery, fakery, and unreal.

We seemed to be presented with an enormous palimpsest. This black head within Albion comprised thousands of laminations, like a sculpted head painted a hundred thousand times, once a week, or maybe once every second, each layer strengthening the programming, adding weight and persuasion to the directives. It was truly a cultural accretion, or, maybe I should say encrustation, on Albion.

The concentration of our sword and the power of its Light was stripping this off. It went one layer at a time, but the layers were flying off at a furious pace now. We were stripping this black head of laminations back to its virginal starting point, moving backwards on its timeline to the moment in Sumeria when the first insinuation of doubt and despair about the Underworld was brushed on. I emphasize we did this in present time; we could not alter the human timeline but we could change things from this moment forward. I felt a curious, persistent tugging, a heaviness, at the back of my own head as these layers were stripped from myself and all the previous myselfs over time. This stripping off of the laminations would be registered in all alive humans today.

Our work was enabling embodied human consciousness to witness all these layers, to see them lucidly and understand the accretionary process. People were free to ignore this disclosure just as people don't have to watch a sunrise even if the sky is aflush in fabulous colors and cloud patterns and you think, staring admiringly at the display, how could someone choose not to see this.

Regarding individual humans, all the layers were teased loose from the primary black head and held motionless in thousands of layers around this head for people to observe and study, if they wished. It was like a mechanic taking apart some complex machinery, like a car's engine or a washing machine motor, displaying the corroded or broken parts, the frayed wiring, the water damage, and explaining that these details account for the poor function of the machine.

We did not have the commission to definitively remove these laminations from individual humans. We could only make the disclosure, only present the evidence, like a physician showing the X-ray results. It seemed likely, though, that most people, presented with this evidence, the unsuspected layers of false information and dark influence now revealed like an eon of dark sunrises coopted by unfriendly aliens to confound humans, and, contrasting with this, the shocking original purity and Light potency of one's own consciousness, seeing this in its power state before it was progressively corrupted, would choose to reject the Druj's unseen black hand in their minds.

We hoped so, anyway. The black head influence had put us out of alignment with the way we as humans were originally made. Humans were created in the vibration of truth. Our bodies hold this truth. Everyone has a pillar of Light comprising *Asha Vahishta*, the *Amesha Spenta* of primordial reality's truth, a copy of the Elohim-Goliath and what he embodies. The vibration of the Lie, of the Druj, was fundamentally incongruent with this. It is a false reality. Steiner had called this presence the Ahrimanic Double. He said it stayed with us until we died; it did not accompany us into the *Bardo*. The American landscape was intensely polluted with its presence, possibly more so than any other land.

I saw some people starting to glean this insight. It surprised them. They started to realize they had never comprehended the true nature of consciousness or their daytime awareness, that they took it for granted and never questioned it, or saw it was the other side, the front of the same hand whose backside was the afterlife.

An eclipse of the awareness of death and the Underworld was similarly a dimming of the appreciation of how consciousness creates the daytime sunlit world. Shut down one and both go dark. Light up one and they both go bright.

The next part I saw was shocking. It shocked me, I can tell you that. People started to see that they had mistaken the Druj for the Supreme Being.

Think of all the times people say, it was God's will, fortune hates me, destiny frowns upon me, the luck was against me, and other despairing statements. These in fact came from the Druj, but people, not perceiving her, attributed them to God, for who else in the restricted, metaphysically parochial view of all religions was there to execute such definitive actions against individual humans? Who else could change reality with a finger-snap? All the centuries of blame and complaint heaped upon the Supreme Being like an obliging, overloaded packhorse—He was innocent after all, but the Druj was not. What she had gotten away with, how she got people to displace their blame—I suddenly appreciated the scale of her disruptive, misrepresenting activities.

People were waking up, and they were waking up in surprise or anger. In either case, they were astounded to discover this formerly invisible presence working their psychic space like a puppet-master. This discovery started to reframe much of what had happened in their lives, how they had felt, what conclusions they had drawn, the actions they took that had seemed inevitable. Everything was up for review. The ground had slipped underneath them, and they saw they had been standing on only illusory bedrock fabricated by the Druj.

They were beginning to appreciate (many felt appalled by it) the falsity she had drawn down upon their concept of dying and, even worse, on being alive itself. They had so taken this veil and what it showed and did not show for granted that it was as if the subject had been closed, no further discussion was required. Many people were realizing they had no solid conception of life and death at all. The subject had become a null zone, an empty space never visited.

Don't think this gave people permission to have a great feast of the poor victims, to toast themselves for being victimized by this terrible demon. It didn't go that way. People were dismayed they had so lapsed in the execution of their responsibility to maintain a certain doorway vigilance about what entered their psyche and mind. They were disappointed with themselves that they had been lax. They reviewed all the sleights-of-hand by which the Druj had tricked them.

As for Albion, he seemed to be subliminally aware of this action to remove the talking black head from his psychic space. He had been restless, as if tossing and turning in his half-sleep, and now he was both more restful and closer to waking. He had born the black head dutifully as a product of the human collective consciousness, but it had been a burden, a dismaying reality. The removal of the black head from Albion and gradually from all humans agreeing to this was lightening his sleep, improving the flow of communication between humanity and himself, putting people in a potentially more wakeful dialogue with the personification of their collective awakened consciousness.

At some level within us, we all know there is such a cosmic being as Albion living amongst us, wrapped around the Earth and spread out in hundreds of locations. We know it because that knowledge was implanted in us by the designers of the human in the first place, who put in us the means of pre-existent resonance between us and the planet's geomantic pattern and its cosmic antecedents. The Druj had effectively eclipsed that innate resonance in most people

and most people lived without conscious acknowledgement of this fact. That had been disastrous; the state of the planet's environment and the general ravages to human consciousness and the diminished quality of psychic life were ample proof. That would all start to change now as the Druj was routed from us.

The Earth looked like it was outgassing a foul black smoke. Everywhere I looked I saw plumes of sooty dark air rising out of people and landscapes. Surrounding the Earth was Archangel Michael, many copies of himself, and his upraised sword was burning up these spumes of Druj smoke, purifying the air. As the black fumes rose off individual people and drifted upwards into the psychic field around the Earth, the archangel's sword immediately dissolved them. I suppose the archangelic Light was transmuting the sooty negativity because the air around where the spumes had been seemed brighter, sharper.

"It's like an extra Michaelmass, a bonus purging of the Light grid," said Blaise. He was enjoying the spectacle of hundreds of Archangel Michaels transmuting the rejected Druj vapors, helping the Earth and humanity get clean.

"Hey, do you guys see what Blaise is doing out there?"

I hadn't until now. The Ofanim had generated a sphere of diamond facets around the planet just beyond where Archangel Michael was working with his sword. As the psychic atmosphere of the planet improved progressively, the Ofanim's blazing diamond white fire and millions of diamond facets radiated the atmosphere with *Sat Cit Ananda*, or as they familiarly like to put it, Love from Above. The vibration was palpable, strong. They had turned it on full strength.

"Strong?" said Blaise, picking up on my thoughts as usual. "It's smoking hot, Frederick. Way past strong. The Blaise Boys are really letting the Earth have it this time. I can't think of a planet that needs it more. Albion is *loving* it. Albion, Earth, and humanity—none have been this free of the Druj since the Deluge, when the Supreme Being took out our misbehaving ancestors, humanity's first generation. Lilith and her gang. This is a treat. A taste of the original fresh programming, pure *Dharmakaya*. If I'm not careful, I might slip into *samadhi*."

I felt something burning in me, like a flaring up of a hidden passion. I felt like a parent finally vindicated and validated for all his input over the years on a child. The child in this case was the planet. The child-planet was making good. That surging warmth within me was a flush of pride and satisfaction, a pleasure. Taking a major step forward on its own. Long years—eons, I realized, in this case—were now paying off. These were unusual thoughts for me, and I wondered about their origin. I saw myself—essentially myself, though I knew I did not look the same nor was I in a solid human body, more a figure in Light—in a pale blue room, transparent, diamond-bright, like the clear sky at midday.

I was with many other "people" reviewing engineering plans. They were projected in the air before us like holograms. They were complex, like geometrical forms seen in many dimensional expressions at the same time. I saw Blaise there, and Edward, Matthew, Philomena, Tommy, and of course Merlin. I perked up as I realized where this place was. Blaise's famous original Blue Room, though it was in size more like a large university with many buildings. I had always regarded Blaise's reports of this primordial geomantic installation with interest, but the kind of reserved interest academics tend to deploy on most subjects, as outsiders, observers. Now I find I was a participant.

Even more startling was the discovery that we had planned for this, the refreshing and illuminating of Albion and the purging of the Druj's influence from his cosmic form,

anticipated it, even if we knew it would take countless millennia to achieve. Now we had. The Theosophon, I discovered a few years ago with Blaise, had similarly been planned long ago and the planners of that (including Philomena) had waited patiently for the ripe moment. Now it was the same with this global purging of the perfidious black heads of the Druj. This put an entirely new light on the meaning of patience. I felt I had discovered the angels' secret. Blaise often told me how the Ofanim uncomplainingly waited centuries, even millennia sometimes, for expected outcomes to come to fruition.

I suppose it must be the way the angelic realm regards Earth events. They always play the long game, can wait calmly as long as is needed, up to the full 311 trillion years of one Life of Brahma, if it takes that long, knowing it will be done as planned. Why not? They have a Boss Who always gets His way. That staggered me. I get restive when I have to wait more than five minutes for my morning coffee to be ready, hovering over the coffee-maker to speed it up. How could I wait a thousand millennia for the ripe moment to purify the Albion?

I saw the failed attempts by geomancers, by us, and many others, I presumed, over time to wake up Albion and to dispel the horrific Druj from him. It was another palimpsest, this sad history of failed intentions, though perhaps I should be more generous. Maybe they were not failed but premature, and maybe not even that, but necessary additive engagements in this long-term project, a kind of geomantic syllogism every one of whose components had to be spelled out first before you could arrive at the conclusion, a Druj-free Albion, and that could only achieve its culmination now, in 2044, when the age was ripe, when the planet's Light grid had been upgraded, the Ofanim had arrived, the Theosophon delivered, our recommendations for *Bardo* improvements installed.

You could see the history of humanity inside the Albion. I marveled at this creation as I studied the positive effects of the Elohim sword on its contents. I have been referring to it as if Albion were some kind of recognizable anthropomorphic figure in Light. It is Human in essence, though not in appearance. It is spherical, made of a series of spheres, one inside the next, all full of stars, Light temples, and representations of celestial places and conditions.

It is a generic hologram of an edited selection of celestial and galactic features. I say "generic" to indicate it is not geared to a specific human quality, but for all humans, that the array of celestial features was selected to represent this. Albion does not look like any specific individual, but you can feel his attention. It is the embodiment of attention, the watchfulness of the cosmos, set within the human phylogeny and all its specifications in both matter and Light.

This Albion then collects the details and residues of all human history, all the lives lived on the Earth since its inception, the "million-footed mob," as Henry Miller once put it, and these are set against this generic infrastructure. Into this the Druj inserted the duplicitous talking black head which over time had the effect of commandeering Albion's subliminal attention and putting a dark cloud over the lived contents of untold human lives and inspiring in him dark, troubled dreams. These then fed back into the collective human psyche and darkened that, and the reciprocal circulation has continued for many millennia.

Albion gradually turned against himself and his good nature. You could see why William Blake, writing of his Albion, the Giant Ancient Man, said he sat on the cold Atlantic shore, forlorn, turned away from the Divine Vision, desolate and lost. Good job, Druj. It was the work of this black head that turned Albion away from the Divine Vision, and thus turned most of humanity away as well. Our job was to help him get the Divine Vision back for his definitive awakening.

Ideally, Albion is meant to watch humans enter incarnation, leave it, enter the *Bardo*, process the Underworld experiences, discharge their karma, then take new bodies or move into *Devachan*. He is like a recording tape, registering it all. Albion is also the terrestrial reference point, bedrock for the particulars of the *human* design, the Light grid or template that co-wrote the human and planet. He is the personification of the context that makes sense of all the experiences, that frames them against their proper and illuminating background, the cosmos. Albion is humanity's reference library, librarian, the place of public record. Albion, who am I truly as a human being, any person may ask of this Giant, and, looking at him, contemplating his form and cosmic contents, get an answer.

It's like the family in Galsworthy's *The Forsyte Saga*. You have several generations of Forsytes living near one another in Victorian London. The family has traditions, wealth, manners, practices, styles, prejudices, proprieties, all of which define its members as they set out to modestly individualize themselves. We are all members of the great Albion family, Earth's Forsytes, and everything we do takes its meaning within that Albion and is done to benefit that Albion. This colossus of Light and consciousness is like a Janus observer, its two heads observing all our human activities in the twofold temple of life and the *Bardo*.

I could picture Albion's benevolent spherical head full of stars for eyes observing with interest and compassion every step I made in the *Bardo* of life and death. I didn't think I would mind that. It would feel, I think, like having another Guardian Angel on your case, working for you, rooting for you, applauding you. It would give your life and deeds a refreshing, uplifting, transpersonal aspect. I felt it would be enriching to know your life served greater needs than your own, that you were contributing another chapter to the unending *Albion Saga*. I appreciated, sadly, how bereft our humans lives have been without this steady dialogue between individual humans and our cosmogonic original and mentor. But I saw also how beneficial our sword work on the black head in Albion was.

"Are we killing a part of God in doing this?" asked Tommy. The question riveted me. I hadn't looked at it that way, nor had the others in our expedition.

"It's more like giving Him a haircut," said Merlin. "You cannot kill the Druj for, as you intuit, Tommy, she is a part of God, as obnoxious as she can be. Giving a haircut, mowing the lawn, trimming the overgrowth of a sprawling bush—you could look at it this way. Her influence over humans, who, as you have seen, largely do not suspect her presence in their consciousness, has grown too formidable, too pervasive, and it has tipped the balance way off the middle mark. We are correcting that imbalance, leveling the playing field, as they say.

"The Druj is allowed to be present in the Creation as a test, a challenge, a goad. She was meant to keep humans on their toes, always choosing in every action, every moment, whether they would support the Light or dark aspect of reality. In recent millennia, most people, regrettably, have failed in this test, failed even to be aware they were being tested, and the Druj's influence over humans has grown enormously. Now we are trimming it back, virtually to the starting point. With the other changes we've made to the conditions of consciousness on the Earth, through this expedition, prior planetary events, and the upgrade to its Light grid itself, people will have a fairer chance of making their own decisions about matters of Light and dark,

good and evil, without undue influence or election-rigging through the Druj's unseen but strong hand."

I saw people around the Earth start to register this change in their psyche. It was as if an obnoxious irritant had been removed from the air, one they had put up with for a long time, even forgetting it was there, confounding their lungs and poisoning their minds from cumulative pollution. Most people seemed unaware in a specific sense as to what had changed, but I saw them shaking their heads, opening their eyes wider, relaxing their muscles, sighing. The collective consciousness of humanity looked like a landscape just after a thunderstorm. It looked cleaned, purged, washed immaculate, refreshed. All traces of the uncomfortable positive ions that build up before an electrical storm were dissipated and the nervous systems of people were easing, letting go of strain.

I next saw a curious thing. It seemed that these changes were moving backwards in time, back to Sumeria. I knew you could not undo history, that is, the factual sequence of events, the syllogism of mass events that led to this present moment, yet I saw a ripple effect flowing backwards in time across vast numbers of embodied humans. They were at least getting a feel of the gentle breeze of liberation that was set in motion by our removing of the black heads today. It was as if they were all cognizing the future, moving their heads forward in time to see this moment of cleansing and feeling optimistic from this preview. It was like watching a live tableau of the historical record. Usually, history is a record of events that at best feels abstract and almost theoretical, not alive.

But now I was seeing waves upon waves of humans, like dovetailing shells filled with people on the Earth, presumably generations, numbering into the many thousands, of earlier people, all reassessing their lives in view of these changes. This was part of Albion, the long-term syllogism of gradual human evolution, the incremental dilation of consciousness and its cognitive parameters, as people got a wider, more liberated view of the possibilities of being alive.

What I mean is that their individual lives were also part of a transpersonal project, a trans-collective intention, to wake up this colossus of Light, the Albion. It was as if all these people got a momentary glimpse outside their timeframe, got a vista of this larger, vaster timeline within Earth's Albion, and for a moment appreciated their contribution to this grand, long-term project. They were part of this massive collective, all of humanity embedded in its design matrix, the Albion, growing self-aware, and that had global implications and impact. Humanity was taking stock of itself as a single cosmic individual on Earth.

They saw too that eventually humans would be free of the Druj's dark influence, that it was possible, that it would be wonderful when it happened, and even though they could not, where they stood in the past, along Earth's already inscribed timeline, already entered into the *Akashic* Records as done, receive that change, knowing it would be done by future alive humans was itself liberating.

What was most liberating, I realized, was seeing proof that history has a destination, what philosophers would call a teleology, a goal it strives to achieve. Why are we here, why do we suffer, and why do we die? To further the awakening of the transpersonal collective called Albion, a Light colossus on Earth. To stand as equals with billions of other humans, self-aware, aware of oneself as a God microcosm, that your human form comprises cosmic structure and processes, and that you are here intentionally for a good, even an exciting reason. That

assures us reality is purposeful, this purpose was intended, and, best of all, there is an Intender, as somebody had to have planned all this. Most people, if they are honest, want assurance there is such a Somebody on the job.

20

A year later we all got together again. It was at my house in Hanover. Blaise had arranged for my house to be leased while I was away, and so it had been maintained and the income from the lease deposited in a trust account. Philomena's will had left me a comfortable inheritance, which she had kept preserved for her later years from a bestowal by her Greek parents. It was a warm feeling I felt, returning to the farmhouse, knowing I had been looked after.

The only thing that had not been maintained in the last 19 years was my tenure at Dartmouth. That could hardly be expected. Many of my former colleagues had retired, been promoted, or transferred to other colleges. A few remained and I visited them occasionally, sharing a lunch at the faculty club. One, Wilfred Atherton, a professor of European medieval history, asked me what my plans for retirement were. I realized the thought hadn't even occurred to me.

I could hardly think of "retiring" when what I had been doing for the last 19 years was so unconventional, even difficult to describe and certainly to justify, that, if anything, I was thinking in terms of getting started on the next phase of my life, vigorously re-engaging myself in some project, writing a few books perhaps or going off on another, or several, recondite expeditions with Blaise. No, I was retired for the first 50 years of my life, retired from reality and truth. Now I was, as my father would quaintly put it, "most gainfully employed."

Merlin had organized our reunion. I welcomed my friends as they arrived. Tommy made an appearance, congealing a plausible visible form of himself. Philomena and Matthew were here, occupying, strangely, more seemingly palpable bodily forms than Tommy. Tommy was only disincarnate, in between lives and bodies, but Philomena and Matthew were finished with incarnation and could thus come and go, generate semblances of human forms as they liked or as situations required, then drop them like borrowed overcoats when done.

Blaise was here, though his ontological status was still a mystery to me. Edward and Pipaluk were here in all normal senses of the term, as far as I could tell. A part of me was permanently skeptical about appearances, about taking things as they presented themselves. So I think it was reassuring to see them as if real. At least three of us were here with big question marks over our heads as to how. And Merlin, well, as Lord of the Silver Robe, he could do just about anything he wished, appear any way he chose, and what he wished in our cordial reunion in Philomena's old study was for us to report on our activities in the last year before we set off on a follow-up excursion pertinent to last year's Green Knight expedition. Naturally, he wasn't telling us yet what that trip was.

Then Philomena did something that should have seemed unbelievable yet oddly was not. She sat down at the piano and played us some Scriabin, with all the passion and competence that she used to bring to her public performances. I looked at Blaise. He was grinning. He knew how cool, how magnificent, this treat was. He had visited her, both bodily and disincarnate, when she had practiced her Scriabin here in her study and even sometimes knowing he was there. I of course had lived with her piano recitals and had come to love Scriabin, Rachmaninov, and the other Russian pianists she played and taught at school. When she was finished, everybody was smiling; even Philomena was smiling. Then Merlin looked at me and nodded, inviting me to begin my visionary recital.

"In the last year," I began, speaking with my eyes closed to focus my images, "I saw people stripped of their persona as if already in the *Bardo*. I would notice somebody on the street, in a bookstore at Dartmouth, somewhere, and first I would see their physical form, gender, clothing, age, emotional tone, then all this would dissolve and I would see their naked consciousness as it would be when they entered the *Bardo*. Some were confused, frightened, bewildered, lost. Others were fighting, in resistance, struggling against their current conditions, looking for an Exit door or some explanation for this awful hallucination.

"For some reason, I was able to see these individuals, ontologically naked in the *Bardo*, and assess how they were faring with their karmic recognition and divestment. All their psychological, personality, and social posturings were ruthlessly stripped from them, as we know will happen after death, as if they were nothing more than filmy movie projections overlaid upon their essential form and truth. I shouldn't say 'as if.' Quite likely, this is the correct condition.

"I saw people walking down the sidewalks and lanes of Hanover embedded in their karmic accretions, their future *Bardo* experience grids, and generating new karma patterns every minute that complexified this geometrical form and added to their processing burden and ensured its necessity. It was like they were walking inside a complicated infrastructure of geometric mandalas studded with pictures and spirits and smaller geometric grids and flashes of Light, sometimes red, suggesting anger, and murky yellow for grief, and sickly green for envy and jealousy, and it was like a busy office that gets an enormous volume of mail and nobody is responsible presently for processing that mail. It kept piling up, meaning eventually that person would have to deal with the overload of incoming mail, and it would take some time to work through it all.

"I remembered that when I was a teenager, bored in some class, like physics or algebra that bore no known relevance to anything I could think of, I would look at my classmates, my age peers, young adults in training, age 16, and wonder how ever did they learn to be personalities with all these mannerisms?

"They seemed like miniature adults, perfectly adjusted to things, running their personalities with competence and a flourish. Flouncing around the world as if they took it seriously, as if it had permanence, was monolithically actual. How did they learn to do that, be people, be plausible, master the customs of interchange, status, personal assertion, emotional calibration, the clichés of social exchange, from body to words, the dance of reserve versus disclosure?

"More, how come they took it all so seriously, took themselves seriously? Didn't they ever question any of it? Wherever did they get those personas, those plausible masks of selfhood, that they wore so assiduously as if they were the absolute definition of themselves? These masks seemed to fit them all so well, but did they realize they were masks? I was only too conscious of the inherent falsehood of personality, mine and theirs, of these masks barely provisional in adolescence even on a good day, one bright with self-confidence. I couldn't even take myself seriously when I tried to raise my index finger with a straight face.

"They seemed utterly unaware of the masks they wore, though I saw them. It was disconcerting, not something I could talk about with anybody I knew at the time. Yet there it was, as plain as if I were a child psychic seeing long-dead grandmothers lurking in the kitchen behind mother at the stove. The masks I saw were the same as these geometric grids I saw around people in the streets of Hanover, though I'm sure this is a condition you'd find anywhere on the planet. The body was encased in a geometric pattern, a distorted mandala, like a scaffolding pasted over with flags, banners, neon posters, even many loudspeakers constantly announcing things, denouncing things, selling things.

"Spirits acting like cheerleaders, coaches, referees, and umpires shouted from within the geometric forms, as if standing on the sidelines, in the bleachers, even in the moiling playing field. The patterns kept enlarging as new content was added every minute the person was awake, and, in fact, I imagine they added even more scenarios while they slept. It was like a faucet that was left running. The sink soon fills up and the excess water flows over the floor, and the water keeps running through the house because nobody has turned it off.

"The karma keeps piling up because the person hasn't grasped the generative, additive effect of consciousness stuck within *samsara*, the illusory madhouse of the sunlit, daytime, incarnate, phenomenal world we all take for real. You could see how they were continuously adding to their *Bardo* karma-processing burden, creating additional problems, branching complexities, they would have to unravel once they got there, which, sadly, would confound them.

"On a structural level this became interesting to me. I gradually figured out that this infrastructure or geometric grid to which the people kept adding content was what you have called the *skandah* grid, Blaise, the generic geometric pattern of five cognitive functions that creates a world around us. It's the master screen that filters all cognitive content according to five criteria, name and form, feelings, perceptions, will, and consciousness, and personalizes them, files them under subjective colorings. Over a lifetime this *skandah* grid swells up enormously with lived subjective content, and this is what we take into the *Bardo*.

"This is what we have to empty out and get through to reach the Clear Mind the Tibetan text tells us about or what you call the empty Christ Light. People don't realize what astounding pack rats they are, building this *skandah* nest their entire life, then wondering where all this bizarre, scary astral shit comes from the minute they're dead and dumped into the *Bardo* without a clue.

"I saw people existentially naked, I guess I could call it, stripped of the conceits, importunities, and postures of their personalities. It was like turning something mannered and comedic from Jane Austen into a nightmare script of drugged-out insects by William Burroughs. I saw how they had personalized their *skandah* grids, the way college kids decorate and domesticate their dorm rooms, and I saw that as they deployed these complex geometric forms, bloated and overloaded as they were, they created new karma every second. The *skandah* grid lives to generate karma. It was like a taxi-meter always on, ticking the bill.

"When I realized all this I wanted to go around and tell people, my friends, people I met in stores, the faculty club, anywhere, that they were creating more karma, engorging their *skandah* grids every second, and thereby generating an enormous paperwork load they'd have to process when they died. It was sad. You know you can't do this. They won't understand and you'll be a pest, or, worse, some kind of obnoxious evangelist preaching the Apocalypse. Or worse, they would laugh with incomprehension, or not laugh with indifference."

"I see new career opportunities for enterprising clairvoyants," said Blaise. "*Skandah* grid sweepers. Karma housecleaners. People could clean up on this."

Pipaluk spoke next. "People were surprised when I came back. They thought I had left for good, vanished through some shaman's misty doorway. I suppose they can be forgiven for such thoughts. I am 113 years old now. People expect old women like myself to get around to dying but I still feel full of life. I'll have to disappoint them for a while yet. The spirit in me is still strong and active.

"People started coming to me for advice. This was not new in itself, but their questions were. People asked about life after death, what happens when they die, and are there ways they can prepare for the journey into that world. A few people over the years had asked me such bold questions, but now many people were asking me. Something had changed. They thought I had answers. Perhaps I had a few suggestions. The *angakkuq* is trained in such things, but what we did in our expedition broadened my knowledge of afterdeath conditions.

"I enjoyed being with generations of my great-grandchildren. Maybe they were double, even triple great by now. They flocked around me like seabirds. They sat quietly while the grown-ups asked me their questions. For many I made remarks that I saw would help them, like pointing to doorways. Whether they went through those doors or not was up to them. For a few I took them out into the landscape to certain places and doors of power and Light and we meditated.

"I showed them the Underworld gateway, explained how it worked, showed them the boat, the bridge, the guardians, the different ways such things could be seen. I showed them people already dead, walking in their soul bodies, confronting the projections from the events and thoughts and feelings from their last lives. I saw that this amazed the people, yet it also inspired them. They remembered. Glimpses of their soul's past started to wake up in their minds.

"It did not upset them too much or at all. They accepted it as a natural event. A few could glimpse this *skandah* grid, Frederick. They saw this form around them, like an object, but I don't think they knew all the words that go with it, and they began to understand how they kept building it like a nest every day, and that it would be better if they stopped adding to it because that was more work waiting for them when they entered this other landscape after death.

"A few asked me to sit with them while they died, to journey with them. I agreed. I had already been there. I knew the place. At least a little. Most of these were old people, though far younger than me, and a few had terminal diseases. I accompanied them in the death and dropping-off processes, and I walked with them through the Underworld gate into the realm of life processing and karma recognition. Their Higher Self walked directly behind them, like an open umbrella of Light. I walked by their side. I thought fondly of our expedition.

"I explained the stations of the *Bardo* as they encountered them. The strange, frightful creatures that suddenly jumped up in front of people were not so alarming because I warned these souls in advance. I said whatever you see, it is an illusion created by yourself, jumping out of your own mind, using the elements of your just finished life as raw materials and the momentum of those events as the creative spark to dress them in forms. None mean you any harm."

Pipaluk paused at this point and asked if she could have some water. I offered the group tea or coffee and went into the kitchen to prepare this. It wasn't that I was an inattentive host. You'll have to appreciate the confusion you sit amidst when half of your visitors are embodied, the others only with body semblances. I couldn't offer Merlin, Matthew, Tommy, or Philomena anything to drink because they didn't have bodies to drink with, even though it looked like it. I suppose I could hand them pictures of a cup of French roast or Darjeeling. So I was focusing on their etheric presence, forgetting the other three had bodies. I brought in a tray of two French roasts and two cups of steeped Darjeeling tea.

Refreshed, Pipaluk continued with her report from northern Greenland. "You have said the Tibetan book was meant to be read aloud to somebody who has just died. I had that experience several times, except I was the book talking. Two women came to me, both ill, tired, and knowing their time was finished. They stayed with me and I helped them prepare. When the time of their death arrived, they were ready and started to move their awareness up through the chakras to the head. Then they left their bodies through the top of their heads. It was beautiful to watch, a bright, slightly twisting plume of white mist rising up. I accompanied them in my own *angakkuq*'s form as they moved into the afterlife. They immediately got to work, reviewing their lives, processing the information.

"As they knew in advance what to expect and that what they encountered would be colored by their own feelings and images, nothing they saw disturbed them. The spirit-forms representing the building blocks of their consciousness did not appear alarming; some were even funny, as if they were clowning. They tasted the different high states of awareness from each of the *Dhyani* Buddhas. When they were finished, they collected themselves, stood still, and decided in a free and wide-awake manner to defer another incarnation until they explored some intriguing realms within what you call *Devachan*. They went off together."

"During the last year," began Edward, "we have received a steady stream of manuscripts reporting new trends in near-death experiences and conscious dying. These were unlike anything we had received before, new ground broken. Word of our changes to the *Bardo* got passed on quickly in the human mortal world. I couldn't imagine manuscripts like this, insights like these, before that. They didn't even bother with the cartoonish clichés of the experience such as the white tunnel of Light, the welcoming, ecstatic relatives, the meeting with Jesus.

"Those phenomena may happen, but as contents for a book they are played out. These new manuscripts focused on the types of spirit-forms they encountered, the way their own karma and personality qualities generated specific spirits and how, knowing this, they were able to negotiate the interchange faster and easily. It's as if the whole field of being in the Underworld after death has been terrifically expanded, full of new reports and discoveries.

"Some people report experiencing vistas of hundreds of their past lives, almost in parade form or perhaps like old-style newsreels you'd see in a 1940's cinema, and they cite similar glimpses of numerous landscapes with their Light temples illuminated and in which they had preview or preparatory experiences for their *Bardo* journeys. It's an explosion of greater awareness, Lethe defeated.

"The emotional tone tends to be more even-handed, less sensational, not inflated with amazement, but anchored, sober, and grown-up, souls getting down to the business of processing their immediately antecedent lives with the sobriety of housecleaners taking on a 20-room house that needs a bit of scrubbing up, but no worries, mate, we've dealt with big-house messes like this before."

Everyone's attention turned to Blaise. I think we had all been looking forward to his report. If it was anything like what he told Edward in *The Theosophon* briefings, it would be surprising, unexpected. He didn't let us down.

"I was off planet for the last year. Blaise had an assignment for me. There is this planet in another galaxy in what astronomers call the Local Group of galaxies. That's a cluster of about 54 galaxies, mostly dwarf galaxy forms, not too far from our Milky Way. It's a hotbed of new life, I can assure you. This planet has a new sentient lifeform about to begin the funhouse cycle of dying and reincarnating. They're fairly like humans in appearance (and certainly in consciousness and its structures), though some of the physical conditions of the planet required biological design adjustments in their forms.

"Blaise thought they could benefit from having a consultant on hand to advise the new souls what to expect in their afterlife experiences. The *Bardo* would be fresh for them. In many respects, conditions were like what they must have been here when the Green Knight, Lord Yama, first 'died' and set up the death protocols for Earth humans. Ours would not work for them; the *Bardo* details had to be adjusted to the specifics of their bodies, selfhood, and minds. As you might expect, their *skandah* grid had local variations on our human one.

"Yes, you're probably wondering in what body did I make my debut appearance? Pleiadian. It's a tested model for me, plus they know my body size, and it simplified the transportation requirements. Stargate, of course. It's fast. I suppose my role was to be a walking information booth. I strolled around their *Bardo* and made myself available for questions from wandering or lost souls. The specific pictorial aspects of what those souls were likely to see would be related to planetary and psychological and social conditions, but there was clearly an unmistakable generic aspect to the sequences and actions of these *Bardo* figures.

"Taking off your body and personality structures and processing the results and implications of a life of action are fairly standard whatever form you just lived in. It was fun, even educational. These souls were still fresh, virginal, and untainted. The Old Bitch hadn't yet made any forays into their world, though she was exploring sales opportunities through some proxies. My only complaint was it took a while to get the hang of their funny bone, what was funny in their context since their world and minds were wired differently than ours. Eventually, I mastered it and was able to do stand-up to good reviews.

"We managed to keep the Druj out of their affairs during the year I was acting as Green Knight for that fresh world, though she extended a few long fingers wherever she saw an opening, and a few souls tasted her seductive counseling and suggestions, but found the taste didn't agree with them and, as it were, spit it out in her face. That was a nice comeuppance to watch. Still, she doesn't give up, so I knew that eventually she would get her hands further in, but for a time, souls could transit the *Bardo* without her outside interference.

"For the most part they did not consider it an act of apocalypse to die. They were so firmly anchored in their daytime consciousness that when the time came to drop the physical form that consciousness occupied, it seemed natural. It was not much different than surrendering an old pair of sneakers to go barefoot. You still had your feet: in other words, you were still possessed of consciousness. Since you hadn't lost that, the body's dying did not seem problematic to them, and they welcomed a new round of 'barefoot' experiences, especially as they elucidated the physical lives they had just finished, garnering new insights.

"Did you catch this point, because it's important. They were so anchored in their consciousness, self-aware of it as an environment in which they lived in their daytime bodies, that death meant only the transference of that same familiar consciousness to another context. The more embodied you are, the easier it is to die. Earth humans, in contrast, tend more to hover around their physical forms or to dwell inside them in a state of somnolence and oblivion about the body. That makes it harder to die, meaning, to understand its necessary mechanisms. It's as if they get hysterical at the prospect of fully entering their life forms, and equally hysterical at the prospect of leaving them and heading upwards. Unanchored in their consciousness, any change of state is threatening.

"You will appreciate this part, Frederick. There was very little posturing among these people. I suppose it was because they were fresh to incarnation and hadn't developed all the complex comedy of manners and posing that constitutes advanced social life. In many respects they were as simple, earnest, direct, and streamlined as old souls who also feel no need for any more posturing. Yes, they were different, one from another, and they were engaged in their individuation odysseys, but they exuded a freshness of unadorned, untarted-up presence.

"That made it easier for the *Bardo* divestment phase where any personality posturings wouldn't work. They got straight to work and resolved their karma, met with the spirit-hallucinations, and progressed into either another life or *Devachan*. I'm thinking maybe *they* would make capable consultants for humans in our *Bardo*. They could teach Earth humans how to make it through the *Bardo* still whistling.

"I reaped an additional benefit from my jaunt to that planet. It was like a year of debt excusal. Since I wasn't in my human body, no time passed on the body clock, so even though a year of Earth solar time has passed since I last saw you guys, I am pretty sure I did not age one year in any biological bodily sense. This is immortality by body-jumping. I recommend it. You're getting free years.

"I suppose I put a year's mileage on my Pleiadian form, but that one has been around a long time and I'm not sure a year made much difference to its vitality or durability, and when I returned to the Earth in this form, the Pleiadian body relapsed into an in-between *Bardo* state of its own, like hanging an old jacket in the closet then it disappears. So I should be 95 years old now, but honestly I can't say for sure what my age is. I suppose somebody is keeping track somewhere and one day I might get a report on the age accounting results."

Now we turned to Philomena and Matthew. What had they been up to?

Matthew spoke first. "The Green Knight asked us to start aligning the *Bardo* landscapes of multiple planets and the dominant sentient species living on them with the Earth *Bardo*. Obviously, we would not make them identical. But certain generic structures, processes, thresholds, and mileposts of the afterlife experience on these many worlds needed to be brought into resonance. You could call this the death grid or the *Bardo* Light matrix. I came to understand the intention was to have these multiple *Bardos* work as easily as respiration does, inhalation and exhalation with no strictures or restraints, just an easy breathing.

"The way things are set up, the way this aspect of the Creation appears to run, is that related versions of the same basic process are interconnected, and disturbances in one cascade into and distort the other ones even if they are running smoothly. Earth's disturbed *Bardo* was destabilizing other *Bardos*, and our job was, after we had made the adjustments to Earth's Underworld, to realign the inter-connected other *Bardos* of these planets to these new settings. It reminded me of a comic sketch from the Three Stooges. Those three lovable nitwits are all sleeping in one cramped bed. One Stooge flips over and throws the other two into chaos, off the bed or lying without covers, and waking them up. The *Bardos* of these many inter-related planets are like that, all in the same bed."

"We worked with the Lord of the Blue Ray, Master Minos, once famous in Crete for being king, sponsor of the Cretan labyrinth, then a Judge of the Dead," said Philomena. "He was an instrumental figure, a hierophant, in the Eleusinian Mysteries and remains involved as a mentor, Light-revealer, and facilitator in the death and *Bardo* processes for souls in all manner of forms (not just Cretans or Greeks), including the diverse ones we saw and worked with this last year.

"Death is death, we saw, no matter what your starting biological form and structure of consciousness. Souls put on these various bodies, adapt to the infrastructures and mechanics of that body's style of consciousness, then take them off and process their life events in the zone of the Underworld set aside for the particulars of their species. That is in essence a generic process across species.

"When you can see this process, this respiration cycle, as you put it, Matthew, over long periods of time involving multiple lives in succession, you see it as a normal, necessary aspect of the endowment of consciousness to souls. It's like being an actor in a popular play that runs for 300 performances. Every night you're in your dressing room putting on your costume and make-up, then you do the performance, hopefully collecting cheers and *Bravos!* then you disrobe, strip off the make-up, and resume your street clothes. You're back in

the *Bardo*, the in-between place, and you decide whether another performance is called for or perhaps a little vacation and relaxation time in *Devachan* instead.

"You reach a point where, knowing you are not authentically the character you play, you still embody it with passion and certitude for two hours then drop it. That's the trick, isn't it, to know you are playing a role for a short time only. It enriches you, stretches you, challenges you perhaps, but ultimately it *isn't* you. The actor remembers all her roles and parts, but knows none of them are her. We helped souls remember this distinction in their *Bardo* immersions.

"It makes such a difference knowing how this make-up got on your face and *why*, that *you* applied it in service of your scripted role for the duration of the play. Then it's not shocking or bewildering when you are required to remove it in the *Bardo*. That is why it feels like an earthquake to so many human souls after death. The souls we worked with on these various planets had a stronger recall of this and their Underworld journeys were straightforward, a choreography, expertly written, well-practiced, with everybody wearing sensible shoes."

Now it was Tommy's turn to tell us what he had been doing over there. He was of course the only one of our expedition who could not return to body life automatically or spin out a plausible human body semblance like Matthew and Philomena. He had not decided yet whether to incarnate or enter *Devachan*.

"For a long time since you guys returned to physical Earth life I was running around like a butler multitasking in the *Bardo*, checking on all the changes and innovations we had made to see they worked properly and souls newly entering the *Bardo* understood the new procedures and benefited from them. I didn't realize until then what an overhaul we landed on that place. Everything was easier, smoother, clarified, faster, and yielded far better results. People were zipping through the Underworld like golf pros doing the back nine on their favorite links. Clearly, there was less misery, less moaning and crying. I swear I heard a few souls humming show tunes and snapping their fingers.

"Then the Green Knight had me counsel recent suicides. I should know about that. He wanted me to help them understand why they killed themselves, the residential and time-elapse rules that suicides must follow, and to process the deep pain, the inescapable hole they dug, that led them to that precipitate action. I didn't have such a hard time recovering because I ended things a bit early as I knew I was going to die soon anyway and I had this great expedition to look forward to. Many others I met with were not so fortunate. They felt they had caused the end of the world, destroyed everything, that God hated their guts.

"I was kept busy, I assure you, trying to raise their spirits. With some, I managed to get them laughing, turning some of the *Bardo* spirits and their presentation antics into comedy, even farces. That's not hard. Some of those *Herukas* are too much any day of the week, examples of what Susan Sontag would call 'camp.' So we camped out with the *Herukas* and we all made faces."

Merlin had listened without commenting to our reports. Then he said, "Good. Now I have what you may call a coda performance of our expedition."

Without discussing it, we had reassembled the sword of Elohim and we were now ascending a tunnel of Light with the sword raised upright in front of us like a beacon. We popped out of this tunnel onto the *Cinvat* Bridge where we stood behind the *Daena*, the Higher Self represented as a beautiful maiden who greets the newly disembodied deceased. Okay, that means somebody has died, and we'd have to wait

to find the *Daena*'s "man." We stood behind her as her valence fluctuated from arresting to malevolent depending on the incoming soul's qualities. The sword was a terrific sun behind her, illuminating the bridge.

We were on Charon's boat, like a lantern at the prow, brightening everything, as he propelled his boat across the Acheron. We accompanied the soul immediately after his head was lopped off by the grinning Green Knight. I chuckled as a I realized this is probably where the popular though dark image of the Grim Reaper came from, The Hooded One, the Destroyer, or Angel of Death. He is a skeletal figure, clothed in a hooded black cloak, wielding a large sharp scythe; he comes to collect the newly dead, or perhaps to precipitate their death. I think, given a choice, I'd take the Green Knight hands down; he looks healthier.

We stood like a pillar of Light behind the altar upon which the Weighing of the Heart ceremony was proceeding, the *Ammit* standing by in case it was needed to devour the soul with its darkness, i.e., if the person's dark karma was too formidable and tipped the balance towards heavy processing being required. We held the sword in these three equivalent, interchangeable formats, but for whom were we providing this illumination? It did not seem for just one soul.

"That's correct," said Merlin, answering my only mentally voiced question. "This is not the after-death processes of only one person, but of all. You are wielding the sword of Elohim in the archetypal death process for the Human. Think of it as a transpersonal prototype, the generic outline of the procedures. Not exactly Albion either. This is more like a Light temple infrastructure for the afterlife experience and the *Bardo* journey for all people, its essential outlines.

"You could say it is the death algorithm, the automatic though adaptable plan of processes that we installed eons ago to accommodate the necessity of death, the means by which the soul frees itself from bodily entanglements and works through the complexities of perception and illusion it lived through in its life. This is a Light grid, a programming matrix, a master form for all souls.

"Conceive of it as a map, an engineering diagram, prescribing and choreographing the complete death journey from first dropping the body to entering the next womb-door or stepping into *Devachan*—the whole landscape. To use an old analogy, it's like a colored slide you slip into the carousel for the projector to cast upon a white screen for everyone to view. It's the *Bardo* slide.

"You have traveled through all the set pieces and stages of the *Bardo*. This is all of that in one composite diagram, and you are brightening it with this Light sword. It is important, crucial, in fact, that this be done by humans, not by the 'gods,' not by my lot. It needs the human touch, the human context and insight. It's part of the expanding program of humanity taking more responsibility for its consciousness, both on the individual and the collective, global level of Albion.

"This is a subtle terrain you have entered. The *Bardo* structures began as thoughts, pictures conceived at a high level. The creation of Light temples works this way. The after-death protocols and landscape were thought out, pictured mentally, by reality designers. They were rendered in mental space like an architect's drawing of the house he proposes to build for you. Then this film or diagram was energized, expanded, infused with Light, commissioned and sent on its way. It was created in consciousness for consciousness, just the way any of you, any human, decides upon an action. It's enacted in the mind. This is mental or spiritual terraforming because this *Bardo* landscape for humans had to be generated; at one time, it did not exist. It had to be made real for you.

"People often talk about abolishing death, defeating death, killing death. This is where you'd have to do it. You would have to erase this programming grid. Certainly it could be done. The Supreme Being could do it in a millisecond. The trouble is it would leave you nowhere, like stepping off a cliff into an abyss. What would happen to consciousness after the biological life of its body ended?

"To use a different example, it would be like only being able to inhale, not exhale. The breath would have to stay inside you forever. Death is the needed exhale. This programming grid, this engineering film, this master Light temple map, scripts the complete respiration cycle, inhale, alive, exhale, death, and consciousness is the medium, the air that is ferried in and out of embodied life. I hope you can follow this. I am trying to use analogies that will illuminate this. Also, if you abolished death, you'd have to compensate by intensifying incarnate consciousness. You'd have to run the *Bardo* divestment show in sunlight hours."

Everything was on this *Bardo* slide. Everything we had seen and adjusted. The *Dhyani* Buddhas and their magnificent revelations about the *skandahs*. The circus acts of scary spirits dramatizing stages of consciousness and its liberation. The Egyptian playbook of the gateways, guardians, and personifications, the Tibetan script of the same processes but pictured differently, the Mayan script of *Xibalba* and its Kafkaesque lords, ambivalent, troubling, mercurial—all the cultural images projected forward like night landing lights at an airport, were encoded in this diagram that we were now brightening with the Elohim sword.

I suddenly understood how this would affect all living people. We already had the original programming grid for the *Bardo* in our psyche somewhere. The Underworld changes we had made and the Light infusion now underway would be immediately transferred to all copies of this *Bardo* film in alive humanity. It would have the effect of an instantaneous upgrade to the software programming.

"This is a heuristic algorithm," said a voice thundering from within the sword. It took me a moment to recognize it as Blaise. "The *Bardo* is a number grid, a mathematical formula, an algorithm that specifies all its actions and stages to produce an end result, the clarification and liberation of consciousness. The heuristic part is us, the Green Knight expedition, and any future expeditions. *We* are the self-learning component factored into the design of this algorithm, and later it will be other humans, then eventually more, and finally the whole lot.

"This *Bardo* script, this engineering diagram, originally conceived by a high god through a mental visualization process, is also written in numbers, as a code. I don't mean it crudely as to suggest humans are the product of a programming code, biological versions of computers. No. The computers themselves are crude analogies of this level of hyper-subtle programming and mathematical coding. Can you see the design necessity of this algorithm? We already have the precedent of the *skandah* grid, a generic, transpersonal cognitive mechanism by which consciousness construes, or generates, an external world filtered and validated through subjectively referenced qualities, the five *skandahs*.

"Why stop with that? The approach is viable. Why not have more programming grids for the other essential functions of incarnation and the activities of consciousness? The fact we are innately resonant with the Earth's Light grid in all its guises and phases points to the existence of a master programming grid for this *inside us*. Blaise once told me that in a subtle level of our genetic make-up we are already resonant with the Light grid design of the Earth and the use of geomantic practices that activate this linkage.

"That sounds like humans each have a copy of this *Bardo* Light grid programming matrix inside them, and though it remains latent for most people, it doesn't have to. This in turn reminds me of what I learned in my time with the Pleiadians. They are the master Light grid designers, creating nests for consciousness, including the bulk of the design work for Earth's Light patterns. The Pleiadian grid engineers have a full set of grid schematics in their minds, not just one grid which algorithmically specifies conditions in the *Bardo*, but the complete library of all their designs for planets and consciousness nests for souls.

"Can you see, or at least get a sense for, how this starts to reframe consciousness as a prime design and generative force, that all reality is projected *Bardo*-like? In that sense, the *Bardo* algorithm, the Underworld landscape, is a practice run for taking on this design function on a bigger scale, to appreciating it as a tool of consciousness and as a co-creative mandate indigenous to our own awareness. The question I am addressing with these speculations is this: How did the *Bardo* get here, become existent? We have a fair idea now of its contents and stages, but as a reality we are meant to enter, interact with, and exchange experiences with, how did it get here, gain traction in reality so we had to use it?

"It's the product of a heuristic algorithm that specifies its content and activities. That algorithm, that number matrix, spells out its life, actions, and purposes. You could call it a magic invocation spoken in number codes that generates a reality. It is invested with sufficient power of consciousness to reorganize the basic latent matrix of existence to match the pattern specified in this algorithm. *Copy this*, it commands, the quiescent, unformed *prima materia*.

"Do you follow my line of inquiry here? I'm trying to figure out how the *Bardo* got here, how it was created. It is, unarguably, a consciousness terrain. It is not a physical landscape. It is one made of Light, which is a densification of consciousness. That Light was instructed to behave and organize itself in a particular manner, to create stages, thresholds, dimensional gradients for a soul's experience to move through. How was it instructed? By a Light grid algorithm.

"To use an analogy, it is instructed through a programming matrix that spelled out all these details. This matrix first had to be thought out, pre-visualized, generated, coded, with all its details and sequences specified. The heuristic part comes in because this system was designed to be self-adapting; souls can flourish or fail in the *Bardo*, and it will adapt to them, adjust its manifestations to the soul's expectations, and to the experiences of all humans.

"By extension, there must be a corresponding Light grid algorithm that specifies the habitation of consciousness within a human body. This coding diagram must specify how consciousness will work with the *skandah* grid. But here is the cool part, the part that excites me, fires my imagination, pours on the accelerant. This hints at a heuristic algorithm that codes the human phylogeny itself, that spells out the human as consciousness code plus body code.

"This is important because it is the essence, the design core, of the Earth's Light grid, the algorithm that dictates the engineering schematics of an Earth human. I combine the terms because the Light grid specifies human and planet details which are virtually identical, only differing in the body form they occupy.

"All this may seem abstruse at first, but it's the meta-message the *Bardo* conveys. Everything in the *Bardo*, all its details, stages, and crazy spirits, hints at this. What also hints at this, quite broadly and unmistakably, is the fact that we are, according to Merlin, flushing the Light grid of the *Bardo* with sword Light.

"Don't you see, the fact we are doing this, the fact we *can* do this, points to the existence of the *Bardo* as a free-standing, created coding matrix for human consciousness. Even more rich is the fact that we do this with the same sword as the Elohim, the *Amesha Spentas*, and specifically, *Asha Vahishta*, used in the beginning when they used the power of *AL*, which this sword encapsulates, the correctness and absolute truth of original reality, which the sword imparts, to generate the human phylogenetic Light grid in the first place. We are coinciding with that original generative gesture. In fact, we are meant to. The Boss wants it.

"Our Green Knight expedition is part of the heuristic aspect of this coding. We're the deliberate, purposeful, invited agents of this heuristic aspect. It's a field test, a demonstration, of how the *Bardo* is self-learning, and the *Bardo* designers themselves are changing some of the basic coding specifications, most notably, cutting back on the horrid amnesiac aspect of the River Lethe aspect.

"I apologize if my analogies here are too materialistic, using computer-style language to suggest my points, but whatever analogy we use, you have to agree that consciousness has been designed and its *Bardo* movements choreographed, and that the phylogeny set-up is now undergoing a major programming upgrade.

"Something so insubstantial, as it seems to us occupying substantial physical bodies, meaning solid, full of bones and solidity, slowness, density, and gravity, something as ethereal as consciousness, is being shaped and redirected to perform in a certain new manner. I find it fascinating—in fact, it's more like an itch, a mental irritation, even a fever, to find out how that was done, what the mechanics of that choreography were, how the exact coding script reads."

Then Edward said, "If you were Isaac Asimov, you would explore how artificial intelligence, robotic consciousness, is coded then works backwards to humans to understand how human consciousness is scripted, coded, or, as you like to put it, choreographed. That was his syllogism regarding psychohistory, his theory of calculating the probability of mass events and large-scale sociological trends in the future by a kind of statistical, mathematical method, then using this information to nudge these mass events in desired directions by recognizing the crucial transition nodes and taking advantage of those moments.

"To achieve this, certain highly advanced robots studied human mental processes to better understand how the human brain formulates actions and plans, then incorporated this into the expanding psychohistory model. It was actually in service of their prime directive, to not harm humans, so they figured it best to anticipate all possible outcomes of actions to avoid any possible harm. Asimov's Foundation, both the series of seven books and the idea in those books, was a large institute in the galaxy that ran these psychohistory calculations and adjusted galactic events accordingly. Your heuristic algorithm for the human phylogeny and its Light grid seems to parallel Asimov's idea of psychohistory. Your Blue Room may have been the Foundation equivalent for geomancy, what you have been calling the Hierophancy, the place that directs the Light grid."

"Good comparison. Thanks, Edward,' said Blaise. "That may well be the next phase of Blue Room work, maybe why it was founded in the first place."

Merlin was nodding. I guess that meant he wanted us to discuss this. Now he gestured for us to resume our attention in the sword to infuse the *Bardo* more.

As the sword Light strengthened I saw it flushing through the *Bardo* grid. It was like a sunrise in which the sun not only breaches the horizon but seems to roll across it towards you, radically brightening the daytime, seemingly burning it up, consuming it in the maw of its terrific Light. We hadn't created this grid, but our contribution was refreshing it with illumination by the original Light.

I saw that originally, which means when the Earth's Light grid was installed, the designers created mental pictures of desired architectural forms and schematics of the desired processes in consciousness, the syllogisms of initiation, then energized them with Light, which is to say, with focused attention, as we were doing. Do this enough times or do it once with sufficient power and the place is real. The heuristic algorithm is the layer behind or before this outer mocked-up visualization. It is a mathematical infrastructure upon which you drape the created image, and when the algorithm is "turned on," it runs the visualization and automatically makes adjustments and updates.

I was taken with Blaise's ruminations about numbers, grids, and temples. I had never looked at Light temples that way before, as to the manner of their creation. It had been at first a big enough challenge even to see them with him. The after-death landscape was full of algorithms that scripted the necessary stages of the divestment of personality, the *skandahs*, and the processing of karma. Somebody—some very clever Somebody—had visualized all this, created it with mental pictures, and empowered those pictures to become this landscape. Now key details in that original grid algorithm had been changed, updated, or altogether retooled as a result of our expedition, and we were now refreshing its energy charge, like plugging in a weakened car battery to a fresh power source.

I realized we were not only infusing the *Bardo* grid with Light from where we stood, or presumed we stood, but we were now actually *inside* that landscape, in person (in whatever body that was), occupying different locations. I had mistakenly thought we were shining a bright flashlight on the terrain. No. We were fully inside it, just as the entire *Bardo* landscape was inside the sword.

I saw newly dead people entering the *Bardo*, watching the film reels of their just-finished lives, encountering the mental projections of their karma and the twists and knots they'd forced their psyches into while alive. I saw them meeting the *Dhyani* Buddhas, who rose up before them like utterly unexpected mountains. I saw these souls in various degrees of remembering their deep past, resisting it, embracing it, standing there in shock or ambivalence, their Higher Self coaching them gently to regard it as useful information pertinent to their destiny here. More souls seemed to be "getting it" than the impression we had when we started this expedition. Conditions were now more favorable to getting the *Bardo*. I imagined a popular line of teeshirts: "I got the *Bardo*!"

Merlin indicated he had something to say to us. He was looking at Blaise. "Your ruminations on self-adjusting and self-learning algorithms are relevant. The *Bardo* will now be acutely sensitive and responsive to any indications of an upturn in the facility by which souls within it understand the requirements and succeed in their work of processing their karma and dissolving their *skandahs*. Every indication put forward by these souls that they are finding the place easier, resisting it less, comprehending more of the necessities of its operations, will feed into the system; it will be like loosening the tightness of a rope knot.

"We believe this will gradually become additive, then exponential. Eventually, the *Bardo* will be a much easier landscape to negotiate. We even foresee the time when some souls might venture to say they rather liked the place, like you would say after a pleasurable vacation in some warm beach spot. I can almost hear these delightful quips of pleasure and commendation, like travel writers posting favorable reports about vacation possibilities for readers. People commenting, 'This place exceeded my expectations—five stars.' Or: 'You know, I think I'm going to miss this place; I never thought I'd be saying that!'"

In the weeks and months after our expedition I found myself, in moments of mental relaxation, revisiting the *Bardo* as if in real time though not being dead. It's the way your thoughts or mental imagery will return to a place of strong transmission, some geomantic node in a landscape new to you that created a strong, lasting impression. You go back to it; the mental attention you left there kept a place-marker open for you so in a sense you are always still there. It was like that with the *Bardo*. I checked with Edward and he reported similar feelings. No, I wasn't previsioning my own death. I didn't think I was anywhere near that.

The *Bardo*, through our expedition, had been revealed as a numinous landscape, a geomantic terrain, a visionary geography as the venerable Henri Corbin would say, a landscape which facilitates visions of your soul, its life, history, and prospects. Every time this happened I would return to myself with a new round of visionary recitals which I entered into my journal, fat now from all my travels. I heard from Pipaluk, and she said she was helping people she met visit this richly endowed world, acting as a travel guide, docent, and initiator. She said she was visiting the *Bardo* almost as often as she saw her many great-grandchildren; it had become a regular part of her life, a new domestic routine.

Philomena would drop in occasionally, materialize her form, play some Scriabin for me, ask about my writing and research, then wink off back to the higher planes. It's a strange marriage now, I suppose, but at least we keep in touch. She said Matthew was doing well, working on new recondite projects for the *Bardo*. Tommy was on a kind of sabbatical in some initiation school in the *Devachan*. And Blaise—he said he'd be seeing me fairly soon for a new round of projects. He didn't specify what they were, but knowing him, they would be mind-stretching adventures of some kind, solving a fresh round of mysteries.

About the Author

Richard Leviton is the author of 27 books on myth, consciousness, and the global geomantic landscape, notably *Theosophon 2033* (2015), *The Mertowney Mountain Interviews* (2014), *The Blaise Conjunction* (2013), *My Pal, Blaise* (2012), *Hierophantic Landscapes* (2011), *Walking in Albion* (2010), *Santa Fe Light* (2009), *Welcome to Your Designer Planet!* (2007), *The Galaxy on Earth, Looking for Arthur, The Emerald Modem, Signs on the Earth*, and *Encyclopedia of Earth Myths.*

He is the director/founder of the Blue Room Consortium, a cosmic mysteries think-tank based in Santa Fe, New Mexico. A trained and certified clairvoyant, Leviton teaches clairvoyant tools and development as well as their applications with geomantic protocols to engage with the planet—to "plug in." Since 1984, he has been interacting with and describing the Earth's Light body, and, through workshops, trainings, and geomantic field trips, facilitating people to have directed visionary encounters with the planet.

He may be contacted at: blaise@cybermesa.com or blaise@blueroomconsortium.com and through the website: www.blueroomconsortium.com

The Blue Room Consortium

The Blue Room Consortium, based in Santa Fe, New Mexico, and founded/directed by Richard Leviton, is a cosmic mysteries think-tank for Earth energies, mapping, and interaction. It's the authoritative information source for the Earth's visionary geography, providing an experiential guide to interacting with sacred sites and their Light temples and for understanding the Earth's geomantic plan and function. It teaches effective methods to beneficially interact with the planet. The Blue Room offers research, workshops, classes, field trips, tours, designer pilgrimages, geomantic maps, trainings, consultations, initiations, publications, and articles.

Clairvoyant Readings-Healings: Professional-quality clairvoyant readings (in 120-minute sessions conducted by telephone) that look at psychic conditions and the roots of problems or difficulties in making positive energy changes, then correct, adjust, or eliminate these factors so a person can take their next step.

Clairvoyant Tools and Development: Foundational acquisition of psychic tools and introduction to energies, psychic pictures, maintaining one's energy space, and more, in a structured one-on-one program of 12 two-hour classes (over the telephone).

Geomantic Immersions: Five-day field programs of active engagement, experience, and interpretation of geomantic features throughout the greater Santa Fe landscape through four different week-long formats, focusing on intensive introductory immersion and landscape zodiac work (an interactive terrestrial star pattern), given in a one-on-one format, meaning, one instructor to one participant.

Annual Geomantic Initiation Immersion Weeks: One week of intensive teaching, training, and field experience at each site for small group "boutique" workshops, given during the summer months, from April-September, to: Glastonbury, England; Avebury, England; Oaxaca, Mexico City, and Teotihuacan, Mexico; the Rondanes, Norway; and Chaco Canyon, New Mexico. These weeklong immersion intensives provide you with a comprehensive experience in the protocols of the Christed Initiation in the Buddha Body and field application of geomancy practices. One 7-day program is given per month, although the two England programs may be given together.

Christed Initiation in the Buddha Body (CIBB): A unique (i.e., nobody else teaches it) three-part training intensive in a one-to-one format featuring direct acquisition of the living Christ Light and presence within you.

The program is free of all dogmatic or religious content and is correlated with the Santa Fe geomantic landscape which also benefits from your initiation. The Christ Light is the pre-eminent tool for working with the Earth and its energies.

CIBB-1: A 6-day program in which you "access" the Christ Light.

CIBB-2: A 10-day program in which you "embody" the Christ Light.

CIBB-3: A 6-day program in which you "wield" the Christ Light.

The three components of the complete CIBB training can be done all at once or with gaps (of any length) between each segment.

Email: blaise@blueroomconsortium.com; blaise@cybermesa.com

Printed in the United States
By Bookmasters